PRAISE FOR THE BROTHER

"A fresh look at the atomic-bomb spies, Julius and Ethel Rosenberg, from the perspective of the man who stole the secrets and then gave up the Rosenbergs to the F.B.I.—David Greenglass. What makes the story especially poignant is that those whom Mr. Greenglass strapped into the electric chair were members of his own family—his sister and brother-in-law."

—*THE NEW YORK TIMES*

"A gripping account of the most famous espionage case in U.S. history . . . [an] excellent book, written with flair and alive with the agony of age."

—*THE WALL STREET JOURNAL*

"Could not have appeared at a timelier moment, if only to remind Americans that, in an excess of zeal, government agents and prosecutors can create a judicial process in which punishment exceeds the crime. . . . *The Brother* provides a fascinating narrative of growing up in East Side immigrant radical communities."

—*LOS ANGELES TIMES*

"[Roberts's] greatest investigatory contribution lies in finding Greenglass . . . and persuading him to talk."

—*CHICAGO TRIBUNE*

"Without equal in the vast literature about the Rosenbergs. Its uniqueness lies not in the fact that *The Brother* is the most current and comprehensive book about the Rosenbergs, or because Mr. Roberts successfully traced and dogged David Greenglass after his prison release and interviewed him at length. It is because his book stands by itself as an extraordinary literary achievement. He has given us a magnificently readable, intellectually rich work."

—*NEW YORK LAW JOURNAL*

"[A] terrific read . . . This story . . . will make your hair stand on end. Fourteen years in the making, this book reads like a spy novel, but every word is true."

—*LIZ SMITH*

"Offers fresh perspectives on the trial of the century . . . Roberts tenaciously tracked [David Greenglass] down. His remarkably engrossing *Brother* proves it was worth the effort."

—*NEW YORK POST*

"As told by . . . Sam Roberts, [the Rosenberg spy case] seems like a timeless Shakespearean tragedy. . . . Readers will receive no uplift from *The Brother*. What they will receive is a smart education about one of the most wrenching cases in American history."

—*ST. LOUIS POST-DISPATCH*

"A fascinating book . . . a sordid tale, as much about a family's conflicted loyalties as it is about espionage."

—*THE ATLANTA JOURNAL-CONSTITUTION*

THE BROTHER

THE UNTOLD STORY OF THE ROSENBERG CASE

WITH A NEW EPILOGUE

SAM ROBERTS

Simon & Schuster Paperbacks

New York   London   Toronto   Sydney   New Delhi

Simon & Schuster Paperbacks
A Division of Simon & Schuster, Inc.
1230 Avenue of the Americas
New York, NY 10020

First Simon & Schuster trade paperback edition September 2014

SIMON & SCHUSTER PAPERBACKS and colophon are registered trademarks
of Simon & Schuster, Inc.

For information about special discounts for bulk purchases, please contact
Simon & Schuster Special Sales at 1-866-506-1949 or business@simonandschuster.com.

The Simon & Schuster Speakers Bureau can bring authors to your live event.
For more information or to book an event, contact the Simon & Schuster Speakers
Bureau at 1-866-248-3049 or visit our website at www.simonspeakers.com.

Interior design by Akasha Archer
Cover design by Laurie Carkeet
Cover photograph courtesy of David Greenglass

Manufactured in the United States of America

1   3   5   7   9   10   8   6   4   2

The Library of Congress has cataloged the Random House edition as follows:

Roberts, Sam.
The brother: the untold story of the Rosenberg case / Sam Roberts.
p.   cm.
Includes bibliographical references and index.
1. Rosenberg, Julius, 1918–1953—Trials, litigation, etc. 2. Rosenberg, Ethel,
1915–1953—Trials, litigation, etc. 3. Trials (Espionage)—United States.
4. Greenglass, David, 1922– I. Title
KF224.R6 R63 2001   345.73'0231—dc21   00-054781

ISBN 978-1-4767-4738-5
ISBN 978-1-4767-4739-2 (ebook)

For Marie

Contents

Thirty-three years after he was arrested for conspiring to steal atomic secrets, I began my search for David Greenglass. He had changed his name and vanished. Once I found him, it took me thirteen years to finally persuade him to speak fully for the first time about why he enlisted as a Russian spy and later delivered his sister, Ethel Rosenberg, and her husband, Julius, to their deaths in Sing Sing's electric chair. Our more than fifty hours of uncensored conversations, fleshed out with other revelations about the investigation, trial, and execution of the Rosenbergs, form the backbone of *The Brother*.

David could not veto anything I wrote. He read it for the first time in this book. So did his wife and children, whom he never told about our collaboration.

THE
BROTHER

Did you ever read Five A.M.? *By that French writer, very famous French writer. In the fifties. He would wake at five in the morning, and that's the whole book. Thinking is the thing that keeps him from going back to sleep. All at five o'clock in the morning.*

I woke up. It was like clockwork. When I went to sleep I was like exhausted. I couldn't think at all. At five o'clock in the morning it began to go through my head. And through the head is like a thread which holds together all the various thoughts and what is the outcome of the whole thing. And it goes on and on.

So you have to tell the truth. You can't do anything else. There's no other way to go. You make the best deal you know how. And it didn't even occur to me, even in that, that anybody was dying.

—DAVID GREENGLASS

Chapter 1

≡≡≡

The Brother of Death

"I didn't cry. I didn't really kill them."

≡

David Greenglass never cried for his sister. He didn't cry when she was arrested, when she was convicted, or even when she was sentenced to the electric chair, so perhaps it wasn't out of character that he didn't cry on that hellish Friday in June 1953 when she died.

Of all the places David might have imagined himself at the age of thirty-one, having grown up on the Lower East Side of Manhattan and aspired to be an engineer, a maximum-security federal prison in the middle of Pennsylvania was just about the most improbable. Pointing fingers might have seemed tasteless on that of all days, but had David been groping for a scapegoat, his brother-in-law fit the bill.

"I was there because of Julius Rosenberg," he later said.

Well before that day, David had armed himself with an arsenal of alibis. That was his nature. When cornered, he instinctively cast about for a place to lay the blame and, after a perfunctory search, invariably found it elsewhere: a temptress, like his older sister, who seduced him with candy-coated ideology that clouded his ordinarily sober judgment; someone else's innocuous misstep that had tripped him up and sent him careering down a slippery slope; or a conspiracy by powerful people prejudiced against New Yorkers, communists, and Jews. A professional machinist fascinated by electricity, David insulated himself against the idea that the immutable laws governing causes and effects in physics also apply to the more ephemeral world of truth and consequences.

Which was why he so firmly believed that day that the events of the preceding ten years—events and their consequences that were to culminate that night in the first peacetime execution of American civilians for espionage—weren't his fault. In a funny way, David was right. As his mother reminded him, if he hadn't been color-blind, he would have been a Seabee, not an army draftee. Which meant he wouldn't have been granted that transfer, itself inexplicable, the day before his battalion was to be shipped overseas, wouldn't have been assigned to Los Alamos, and wouldn't have been recruited as an atomic spy.

And what had it all been for? The approval of the brother-in-law he now reviled? Blind loyalty to the Soviet Union, whose postwar belligerence had transformed even the Germans into victims and was sending David's own son diving under his elementary-school desk in futile air-raid drills? Still, no one could have imagined that David's role in the events of the previous ten years would generate a familial tragedy of epic dimensions, upend global politics, and shatter a generation. And for all his explanations and excuses, virtually nobody—David included—ever imagined that the death penalty would be imposed or carried out.

—

It was said that Sacco and Vanzetti united the American left, and the Rosenbergs irreparably divided it. There was little division over David, though. Xenophobic newspaper editorialists hailed him as a brilliant physicist, a courageous catalyst whose wrenching confession exposed a villainous spy ring that was plundering America's scientific secrets. His reputation for heroism, however, was short-lived. Closer examination soon revealed a pliant self-described patriot, neither brilliant nor courageous, who, floundering in quicksand of his own making, grasped at legal straws to save himself. After blurting out his incriminating confession within hours of his apprehension, he immediately threatened to repudiate it. He vowed to commit suicide if his wife, whom he alone had implicated, was prosecuted, too. His confession hadn't been cathartic, an FBI profile later concluded, "because the crime had not weighed on his conscience." Nor, apparently, did the death penalty later imposed on his sister, Ethel, and her husband, Julius. He finally joined in Ethel's appeal for presidential clemency only after being prodded, and even then he revealed as much about himself as about his emotional bond with his sister and brother-in-law. "If these two die," he wrote, "I shall live the rest of my life with a very dark shadow over my conscience."

Even then, he lied. There was no shadow. Because there was no conscience. Had there been, he would have been forced to confront a terrible truth, one that he managed to never contemplate: Perhaps everyone was right, after all—that while a jury had found his sister guilty of acting on her personal political convictions, and while a federal judge had sentenced her to death and a professional executioner had actually pulled the switch at Sing Sing, David himself had generated the lethal jolt when, wearing a weird smile on the witness stand, he delivered three days of testimony that was as flawed as it was fatal.

When David's public performance was finally over, he vanished from public view and lived out the rest of his life in pseudonymity. But the name David Greenglass survived, etched ineradicably in history's pantheon of contemptible characters, and became a noxious cultural touchstone. Dissecting the Rosenberg case, Rebecca West wrote that "few modern events have been as ugly as this involvement of brother and sister in an unnatural relationship which is the hostile twin of incest." In E. L. Doctorow's thinly fictionalized *Book of Daniel*, David was transformed into the drooling, senile Selig Mindish, a retired dentist of whom it was said, "The treachery of that man will haunt him for as long as he lives." And in the film *Crimes and Misdemeanors*, Woody Allen's character protested to Mia Farrow's that, despite all appearances, he still loves his oleaginous brother-in-law.

"I love him like a brother," Allen said dryly. "David Greenglass."

—

No one could say truthfully that David was indifferent to the fate of the Rosenbergs, but on the Friday of their deaths he feared more for his own life. He was worried that fellow inmates at the federal penitentiary in

Lewisburg, Pennsylvania, would make good on their muttered threats to murder him. David was an inviting target. His confession defined him as a traitor. But his remorseless testimony also condemned him as something else: "A rat," David said. Among Lewisburg's brotherhood of thieves, there was no question which was more reviled.

He was also worried about possible retaliation against his wife. If more than a week elapsed without mail from home, David panicked. "You have no idea how terrifying this long silence is to me," he wrote to his lawyer. "Maybe they killed her. Who knows?"

—

All that Friday, the drumbeat of radio bulletins drove the events of the previous ten years toward their crescendo and David to an elevated state of agitation. He was afraid, not tearful. He hadn't cried all day. He would not cry himself to sleep. At dinner, prison guards slipped him a potent sedative. By early evening, as an amber shaft of fleeing daylight swept across the ceiling of his cell, David was dead to the world. Sleep used to come naturally to him, in part because he was blessed with an unshakable faith in his own rectitude. Fueled by a wellspring of self-justification, his complacency demanded the most compelling motivation to overcome it. In other words, he had always been unwilling to get out of bed without a very good reason.

David Greenglass was the spy who wouldn't go out in the cold.

One reason he never graduated from the Young Communist League to full-fledged membership in the Communist Party was that it would have meant regularly rising before dawn on weekends to deliver *The Daily Worker* door-to-door in Lower East Side tenements. David even overslept on July 16, 1945, as many of his colleagues at the Los Alamos laboratory slipped away before sunup to witness the debut at Alamogordo of the atomic bomb—the bomb he was later charged with stealing for the Soviet Union. To immortalize the moment, Dr. J. Robert Oppenheimer, the laboratory director, reached into ancient Hindu scripture. He invoked the god Vishnu, who, to impress Prince Arjuna into unleashing a cruel but just war, delivered through the earthly figure of Krishna a litany of his most omnipotent incarnations. Oppenheimer quoted but one: "Now I am become Death, the destroyer of worlds." To justify his sleep, David reached for a more mundane rationale. "You have to understand," he shrugged, "I knew it went off."

Sleep, Virgil wrote of one of the two sentries guarding the vestibule of hell, is the brother of death.

—

All that unbearably muggy Friday, everyone in Ossining, New York—the grim village on the Hudson River north of New York City that was home to Sing Sing prison and that had inspired the idiom *up the river*—was anxiously awaiting word from Washington about the execution.

The matter of the Rosenbergs, whom the federal government accused of (among other things) having emboldened Joseph Stalin to instigate the Korean War, had festered far too long. By filing appeal after appeal, their lawyer, Manny Bloch, had succeeded in prolonging their lives for fully two years beyond the date on which Judge Irving R. Kaufman had originally scheduled their executions. Now it was the day *after* the third execution date set by Kaufman, and the Rosenbergs were still alive. The government's risky gamble—indicting Ethel, the mother of two young children, on flimsy evidence and sentencing her to death largely as leverage against Julius—had backfired. She hadn't flinched, and now American embassies worldwide were besieged. Even the pope had appealed for clemency. But the backlash had produced its own unintended consequences: Washington, holding the Rosenbergs hostage, worried that mercy would be misconstrued as weakness.

Just that week, Judge Kaufman had warned the Justice Department that with the Supreme Court adjourning for its summer recess, further legal wrangling might delay the executions until at least October. And by then, who knew what other obstacles would intrude, what new evidence would be uncovered or manufactured, or what further propaganda victories America's enemies at home and overseas would claim. The White House concurred. So, earlier that week, when Supreme Court Justice William O. Douglas had granted the Rosenbergs another reprieve, the government had already been galvanized to overturn it. Chief Justice Fred Vinson reconvened the Court in extraordinary session to hear arguments that the Espionage Act of 1917, under which the Rosenbergs had been convicted, had been superseded by the Atomic Energy Act of 1946 and that, therefore, the death sentences meted out by Judge Kaufman were invalid.

On Friday, precisely at noon, Vinson and the other eight justices emerged. Less than a minute elapsed before Douglas's stay was vacated. The executions were immediately rescheduled for 11:00 P.M.

—

At Sing Sing, executions were always conducted at that hour, though customarily on Thursdays. Prison officials granted few exceptions. Once, a condemned man begged for a one-day delay so he would not be put to death on his son's eleventh birthday. On another Thursday, Louis "Lepke" Buchalter, the notorious Brooklyn murderer, hinted he might confess and won a two-day respite until Saturday night. Sing Sing's Jewish chaplain then pleaded unsuccessfully for still another postponement, insisting that because of the Sabbath he wouldn't be able to leave his regular congregants in the Bronx until after sundown, which would give him insufficient time to comfort the condemned.

Now, appearing before Judge Kaufman on Friday afternoon, defense attorneys argued that executing the Rosenbergs at 11:00 P.M. that night, just after the start of the Jewish Sabbath—when Orthodox Jews refrain from unnecessary toil, even flicking on a light switch—would offend Jews everywhere. Everyone knew the Rosenbergs were Jewish; religion had been injected into the case from the start. It was, after all, no coincidence that the prosecutor was Jewish, that the trial judge was Jewish (he piously announced that he had prayed at his synagogue for guidance the night before he sentenced the Rosenbergs to death), and that the government had secretly enlisted the heads of major Jewish organizations to publicly rebut any charges of religious persecution. With the whole world watching, the government was not going to allow atomic espionage, which J. Edgar Hoover had proclaimed to be the crime of the century, to be marginalized as just another anti-Semitic vendetta.

Ordinarily, the sentencing judge decided in which week the death penalty would be imposed, but the day and hour were left to prison protocol. With so much at stake, though, Judge Kaufman telephoned the FBI at 3:05 P.M. to ask whether the hour of execution had been set yet. In fact, the executioner had already been summoned. And the warden had already instructed newsmen to report to the prison by 7:00 P.M. Revealingly, the judge suggested that they contact a rabbi to ascertain the exact hour of sundown. (According to Orthodox tradition, the Sabbath begins eighteen minutes before sunset Friday and ends the following evening.)

In court, Kaufman assured Bloch's associates that he shared their religious sensitivity and had already personally conveyed his reservations to the Justice Department. At 3:30 P.M., the defense lawyers left the courthouse believing that they had bought the Rosenbergs one more day of life.

The lawyers were wrong.

The Rosenbergs were not going to the chair on the Jewish Sabbath. Instead, they were rescheduled to die at 8 P.M. that night—three hours earlier than the customary time and minutes before the Sabbath was to begin. "They were to be killed more quickly than planned," the playwright Arthur Miller later said, "to avoid any shadow of bad taste."

—

From Sing Sing, Rabbi Irving Koslowe, the Jewish chaplain, called Judge Kaufman to plead for an extension until after the Sabbath. Invoking Talmudic law to hasten death would be an even greater affront to world Jewry, the rabbi argued. The judge explained that he had already been deluged with telegrams demanding that the execution be rescheduled from 11:00 P.M. "He said he consulted B'nai B'rith, and they said it would be a *shanda* [shame] for Jews to be executed on the Sabbath, so he set the time," Koslowe recalled. Kaufman added, "Rabbi, I want to get you home in time." Koslowe, unmoved by the judge's gesture, pressed. "I suggested Saturday night. I said, you prolong life a minute, the Sabbath is set aside. He said the president wanted them to be executed—that was his decision." Finally, Kaufman signaled that the conversation was over.

"Rabbi," the judge said, "you do your job. I'll do mine."

—

Except when they ate breakfast (oatmeal) and lunch (on Friday, fish), which this day was interrupted by the prison radio's broadcast of the bulletin from the Supreme Court, Ethel and Julius spent hours in the death house separated only by a wire-mesh screen. Ordinarily, visitors were allowed until 7:00 P.M. on the day of execution, but today events were too convulsive. Even when the execution had been scheduled for Thursday night at 11:00, however, the Rosenbergs had decided to spend what would have been their last day together. It was their fourteenth wedding anniversary.

Julius's brother and two sisters had paid their final visits earlier that week. So had Ethel's other brother, Bernie, her psychiatrist, Saul Miller, and the Rosenbergs' two sons, six-year-old Robby and ten-year-old Michael, who disturbed death-house decorum by wailing, "One more day to live. One more day to live." The FBI pronounced it "a very pleasant visit," presumably compared to the boys' first, nearly two years earlier, when Michael, quaking with rage, vowed revenge against his Uncle David.

—

On Friday, Ethel wrote her last good-byes to the boys. She also wrote the lawyer Manny Bloch, asking him to deliver a special message to Dr. Miller, telling him how much he helped her mature and trumpeting her belated emotional emancipation from her mother: "I want him to know that I feel he shares my triumph—for I have no fear and no regrets—only that the release from the trap was not completely effected and the qualities I possessed could not expand to their fullest capacities."

The condemned couple gathered the belongings that had personalized their six-by-eight-foot cells. Julius's filled three cartons and included a 1953 calendar, a complete listing of visits with Ethel and other family members, his insect collection, and a facsimile of the Declaration of Independence reprinted in *The New York Times* on July 4, 1951 (in February, he had renewed his *Times* subscription, but, prudently, only for three months). Julius asked for extra cigarettes, but with the execution and all the attendant rituals advanced three hours, there was no time, nor much inclination, for a proper last meal.

—

All that was missing was the executioner.

If one judge in New York or Washington could delay the execution simply by signing a piece of paper, so could one man at Sing Sing just by not showing up. That man was Joseph P. Francel. He was somewhere upstate, mundanely working his day job as an electrician.

Sing Sing's first executioner had dropped dead of a heart attack in the warden's office. The second had become a recluse. The third had shot himself to death in his cellar. The fourth had barely managed to escape when his house was firebombed. Francel was the fifth. And, at the age of fifty-seven, he, too, was fed up with nosy reporters, neighborhood gossips, and anonymous threats—not to mention other occupational hazards, such as the stench of urine, singed hair, and burning flesh and the indelible image of a human body bolting upright like a rag doll against the leather restraining straps. The job wasn't worth it. Not for the $150 a pop that New York State was still paying after all these years. As things turned out, this electrocution would be Joseph Francel's last.

At 4:22 P.M. Friday, the FBI's agent in Kingston, New York, reported that after searching for two hours, agents finally found Francel. It would take more than two hours to drive him the 105 miles from the Catskills hamlet of Cairo in a state-police radio car, but that would still leave well over an hour to test and prepare his instruments. In the fourteen years Francel had served as New York's executioner, the machinery of death had never malfunctioned sufficiently to spare someone's life. The legal system was another matter altogether.

—

In Washington, Manny Bloch tried to personally deliver a clemency request to President Eisenhower but was rebuffed at the White House gate. He left the plea, along with an incredibly obsequious letter to the president from Ethel. Overcoming what she characterized as her "innate shyness" and describing Eisenhower as "one whose name is one with glory," she invoked the successful appeal for mercy by Mrs. William Oatis on behalf of her husband, who had been condemned to death as a spy in Czechoslovakia. While ex-Nazis who murdered guiltless victims in Europe are "graciously receiving the benefits" of American mercy, Ethel wrote, "the great democratic United States is proposing the savage destruction of a small unoffending Jewish family." Her request was rejected unequivocally. "By immeasurably increasing the chances of atomic war," Eisenhower explained, "the Rosenbergs may have condemned to death tens of millions of innocent people all over the world."

A second platoon of lawyers was frantically pursuing a stay in New Haven, where the Court of Appeals for the Second Circuit was sitting. Two judges agreed to convene an appeals panel if the Rosenbergs' lawyers could persuade one more judge to join them. Shortly before 6:00 P.M., the pay phone rang at a gas station on the Post Road, where one of the lawyers was waiting. Judge Charles Clark was calling from his country club. Sorry, he apologized, he would not be the third man.

In Washington, another lawyer, Fyke Farmer, seeking yet another stay, desperately searched for Justice Hugo Black. Farmer pounded on the door of Black's home. Nobody answered.

In Dover Township, New Jersey, outside a white bungalow where the Rosenbergs' young sons were staying with a chicken salesman and his wife, Michael Rosenberg played catch until dark, then joined the adults inside, who were glued to the radio. He didn't tell the news to his brother, Robby, who, earlier in the day, was preoccupied with making a Father's Day card while Michael was riveted to the Yankees-Tigers game. (It was interrupted by a news bulletin: President Eisenhower had denied clemency.) Michael announced to waiting reporters: "You can quote me. The judges of the future will look back upon this case with great shame."

At 6:12, Julius's brother, David, arrived unannounced at Sing Sing, only to be escorted out thirteen minutes later. His arrival and unceremonious departure seemed peculiar because earlier in the week federal agents had mysteriously alerted FBI headquarters in Washington to expect his call. But David Rosenberg never called.

At 7:15 P.M., in Judge Kaufman's Lower Manhattan courtroom, still another lawyer, Daniel Marshall, meticulously challenged the Supreme Court's ruling. He pleaded with Kaufman to call Sing Sing and delay the execution until the arguments were completed. When Marshall concluded, it was 7:45 P.M. With twenty-eight minutes remaining until the Sabbath, Kaufman spoke four words: "Your petition is denied."

Near New York's Union Square, thousands had gathered for a candlelight vigil. At 8:00 P.M., a premature announcement that the Rosenbergs were dead triggered such hysteria that the police pulled the plug on the lone sound truck and aborted the rally.

—

The death house at Sing Sing is an impregnable prison within a prison. It was built in 1922, the year that David Greenglass was born.

A small army of state-police officers mans roadblocks and patrols the perimeter. Reporters and technicians lugging newsreel cameras and primitive television equipment perspire heavily in the day's last overheated breath.

Just before sunset, a young couple, Ted and Joan Hall, drive past the prison. They are on their way to a dinner party at the Westchester home of a colleague from the cancer hospital in Manhattan where Ted was hired as a research scientist after working at Los Alamos. A few months before, when it became clear to the Halls that the FBI suspected Ted was a Russian atomic spy but couldn't prove it, he had approached his Soviet handler with a chivalrous offer: "Perhaps I should give myself up and say, 'Don't pin it all on the Rosenbergs because I was more responsible than they were.'" His offer was rebuffed. The last movement of Mahler's Ninth Symphony is crackling from the car radio. The Halls silently drive on. "We were painfully aware that there, but for some inexplicable grace, went we," Joan Hall remembered. "And Ted would have been forced to claim innocence just as they did."

—

Inside Sing Sing, the warden instructs reporters and other official witnesses in death-chamber etiquette: talking, smoking, and unnecessary noise are not permitted. Above the door through which the condemned walk is a one-word command: *Silence.* The windowless chamber is painted white. It is brightly lit, but the sunset imposes a coppery glow through a skylight. Wooden pews face the electric chair, which is bolted to the concrete floor. It looks like an altar, flanked by an insulating rubber mat.

The chair was built to exacting specifications ("kiln dried red oak of first quality, free from knots, shakes and other imperfections, and to have a straight and uniform grain and to be of uniform color . . . to be finished smooth and clean, given two coats of the best grade furniture varnish"). Joseph Francel repeats a ritual he has performed a hundred times before. He tests the five leather straps to make sure that they are taut and secure. He submerges the electrodes for the head and leg in an enamel crock filled with five gallons of water. From an alcove, he sends the maximum 2,300 volts surging through the copper wire. This test is, by necessity, a short one. If the electrodes are left in the crock too long—more than a minute or two—the water will boil and permanently damage the amp meter.

The execution protocol is precise: an initial 2,000-volt shock for 3 seconds, dropping to 500 volts for 57 seconds, back to 2,000 volts, to 500 for another 57 seconds, and then to 2,000 for a final few seconds. Three jolts in all. The intermissions are to prevent the surge of electrical energy from cooking the flesh. As it is, body temperature reaches about 130 degrees, roughly the lukewarmness of rare roast beef. The temperature of the brain rises almost to the boiling point of water. Wisps of blue-gray smoke curl from the leather face mask. The mask is worn not as a convenience to the condemned but as a palliative for the witnesses. It prevents the eyes from popping out of the head.

———

The Rosenbergs will be the 567th and 568th prisoners put to death by electric chair in New York since 1890. Precisely a decade after Thomas Edison perfected the incandescent lightbulb, a state commission had proclaimed electricity "perhaps the most potent agent known for the destruction of human life." Why a consensus developed for an electric *chair*—rather than, say, a table—is conjectural. One enduring hypothesis is that a chair is the preferred venue of dentists, and among the early champions of electrocution was a Buffalo dental surgeon, Dr. Alfred P. Southwick. In any event, the electric chair was the quintessential capitalist tool. Its popular acceptance signaled the technological and commercial triumph of George Westinghouse's alternating-current supply system over Edison's direct current. Surreptitiously, Edison powered the first electric chair with Westinghouse generators, hoping to demonstrate conclusively their lethality. Alternating current ultimately prevailed, but both Westinghouse and Edison survived. William Kemmler didn't. After the Supreme Court ruled that electrocution was unusual but not cruel—that cruelty implies "something inhuman and barbarous, something more than the mere extinguishment of life"—Kemmler was electrocuted in 1890 for hacking his lover to death with an ax. Dr. Southwick pronounced the electric chair a success. "We live in a higher civilization from this day on," he said.

—

At a secret prison command post, the FBI maintains open phone lines to J. Edgar Hoover's office in Washington. Agents are armed with an elaborate protocol in case the Rosenbergs are finally persuaded to provide the "pertinent information" that would justify the bureau's recommendation of a last-minute reprieve. (Several other suspected members of the Rosenberg spy ring had already been placed under surveillance to prevent them from fleeing if word leaked that Julius or Ethel were cooperating.) An interview room is reserved where, Warden Wilfred Denno helpfully advised the bureau, "electric lights and power sources are available." Two stenographers are standing by. Specific questions had been drafted. They were unsurprising, except for one that was to be directed to Julius. It concerned the role of Ethel, whom Judge Kaufman had denounced as Julius's "full-fledged partner" in atomic espionage and whom President Eisenhower had publicly anointed as the spy ring's leader. The query was couched objectively. It wasn't phrased to provide a pro forma affirmation but, apparently, to solicit a frank answer. Which makes the question so disturbingly cynical. With only minutes to spare before the execution, the government wanted to know: "Was your wife cognizant of your activities?"

———

At 7:30, the Rosenbergs are returned to their separate holding cells on death row. Julius is thirty-five years old. This is his 767th day in the death house. It is Ethel's 801st. She is thirty-seven. There is no way to rehearse for this role, although this is not her first execution. In the 1930s, as an aspiring actress at the Clark House settlement around the corner from the Greenglasses' Lower East Side tenement on Sheriff Street, Ethel was cast in *The Valiant*. She played the younger sister of a condemned man who, seeking to spare his family pain and humiliation, tries to conceal his identity as he faces execution.

"It takes moral courage for a man to shut himself away from his family and his friends like that," the prison priest says.

"I've heard that repentance, Father, is the sick bed of the soul—and mine is very well and flourishing," the condemned man says. "I read a book once that said a milligram of musk will give out perfume for seven thousand years, and a milligram of radium will give out light for seventy thousand. Why shouldn't a soul—mine, for instance—live more than twenty-seven?" The condemned man assures the young girl that he is not her brother. Then, he stoically walks to his execution, delivering a giveaway line from Shakespeare's *Julius Caesar*: "Cowards die many times before their deaths; the valiant never taste of death but once."

In part because Rabbi Koslowe and prison officials have determined that Ethel is better prepared, Julius will taste death first.

"He was a little nervous," the rabbi said. "She was composed, stolid. There is no question in my mind that they were both determined to die."

Also, Julius's holding cell is closest to the death chamber, which means he won't have to pass Ethel's. As the last person scheduled to speak to the Rosenbergs, Rabbi Koslowe is charged by Attorney General Herbert Brownell with delivering the final entreaties. "Brownell said to me that if they gave a name through me to him, or names, a stay of execution would be determined," Koslowe later recalled.

Julius offers no names. He volunteers no other last words either.

The rabbi's last words to Julius are familiar. Leading the short procession, he intones the Twenty-third Psalm.

> *The Lord is my shepherd,*
> *I shall not want . . .*

Julius is wearing dark brown pants, a white T-shirt, and regulation prison slippers. He strikes the official witnesses as naked without his glasses and mustache. Once he is inside the death chamber, a single electrode is strapped to his leg. Another is affixed to his head like a skullcap.

At 8:04, Francel throws the switch. After three jolts, he cuts the power at 8:06:45. Julius's body is placed on a white metal cart and wheeled away.

———

Ethel's body will offer more resistance. Rabbi Koslowe appeals to her one last time to save herself. For her children's sake. "I came back and told her her husband was dead, did she have anything to say to me, a name to stay the execution," the rabbi recalled. "She said, 'No, I have no names to give. I'm innocent. I'm prepared to die.'" This time, the rabbi has chosen two more relevant biblical passages. Both are Psalms of David, the twenty-fifth (in which David repents his sins) and the thirty-first (in which David's whereabouts are betrayed).

> *O my God, in Thee have I trusted,*
> *let me not be ashamed;*
> *Let not mine enemies triumph over me. . . .*
> *They shall be ashamed that deal*
> *treacherously without cause.*

Ethel is wearing a dark green print dress and soft prison slippers like Julius's. Her hair is closely cropped.

> *Remember not the sins of my youth,*
> *nor my transgressions. . . .*

> *Consider how many are mine enemies,*
> *And the cruel hatred wherewith they hate me.*

What strikes the witnesses most is Ethel's composure. And her stature. Images in the newspapers and on the television screens make everyone look the same size, but Ethel is barely five feet tall.

> *For I have heard the whispering of many,*
> *Terror on every side;*
> *While they took counsel together against me,*
> *They devised to take away my life. . . .*
> *Let the wicked be ashamed, let them be put to silence*
> *in the nether-world.*
> *Let the lying lips be dumb,*
> *Which speak arrogantly against the righteous,*
> *With pride and contempt.*

Just as she is about to be seated, she extends her right hand to the two prison matrons who have been assigned to her. The older one grasps it. Ethel gently kisses her on the cheek. Eyes moisten, not only from emotion but from the lingering scent of the ammonia that the guards used to mop up after Julius.

> *Thou hidest them in the covert of Thy*
> *presence from the plottings of man;*
> *Thou concealest them in a pavilion from the*
> *strife of tongues.*

Racing the setting sun, Francel flips the switch at 8:11:30. Three two-thousand-volt jolts. Ethel's heart is still beating. Surprised, the prison doctors signal Francel. Two more massive jolts. The job is finished at 8:16.

The Sabbath began at 8:13.

—

Bob Considine of the International News Service is one of the pool reporters present. "They gave off different sounds, different grotesque mannerisms," Considine somberly briefs his colleagues. "When he entered the execution chamber, Julius Rosenberg didn't seem to have too much life left in him. She died a lot harder. And when she meets her maker, she'll have a lot of explaining to do."

—

Rabbi Koslowe received a police escort home to Mamaroneck to usher in the Sabbath. His son had turned eight that day. "He was sitting on the doorstep," the rabbi recalled. "I embraced him. But I wasn't prepared for a gay evening." Nor was he prepared for the oversize emotional baggage that the Rosenbergs had left behind. "Ethel disliked her brother intensely," Koslowe said. "She asked me to speak to their mother and tell her mother that her brother has 'decreed that I die.'" Two questions were to long bedevil Rabbi Koslowe. One, posed earlier that week by Michael and Robby on their final visit to Sing Sing, stripped the Rosenberg case, for once, of all its legal arcana, evidentiary complexities, and cold-war polemics. "The boys asked me if their parents loved them," Koslowe recalled. "I said yes. I'm a parent. I assume they did. But I was not prepared to answer that question." The rabbi wondered why, if Julius and Ethel's ambition was to raise their children in a better world, they would desert them. Perhaps the answer could be found in a Talmudic riddle he once posed to Ethel: If a man was washed overboard with his wife and child and could save only one, whom should he save? The wife, Ethel replied. "The wife is the tree, she will again bear fruit."

The other question that was to haunt the rabbi was one that for him struck at the heart of the prosecution's case. "I never understood why the judge had to equally involve them both," Koslowe said later. "All the government had on her was a letter she typed."

—

On the Lower East Side, Tessie Greenglass collapsed at the kitchen table on which David had been born. A doctor was called.

Ruth Greenglass, David's wife and partner in espionage, lived around the corner, but she wasn't home. She was being driven around Manhattan in an unmarked FBI car to shield her from prying reporters and protesters.

Julius's mother, seventy-one-year-old Sophie Rosenberg, was sedated in her Upper Manhattan apartment and was not immediately told that her son and daughter-in-law were dead.

At 8:45 P.M., after receiving confirmation from Sing Sing, Judge Kaufman left the federal courthouse for Connecticut to celebrate his wedding anniversary. A congratulatory telegram from J. Edgar Hoover was waiting. So was a contingent of federal guards, who had shadowed the Kaufman family for months. Hoover had warned the supervisor of the New York office, "Should anything happen to Judge Kaufman, the FBI could never live it down."

Julius's last request wasn't delivered until after he was dead. It almost wasn't delivered at all. Julius had conveyed it to Rabbi Koslowe on Friday, but in the chaos Koslowe forgot it until early Saturday morning. Despite the Sabbath, he phoned Sing Sing with an urgent message: "Julius Rosenberg had made a request that only his family or attorney Emanuel Bloch be allowed to claim both bodies—and not Ethel Rosenberg's family."

—

The funeral was held Sunday, the first day of summer, at I. J. Morris on Church Avenue in Brownsville, Brooklyn. It was humid and hot, 93.7 degrees, a record for June 21, until freakish thunderstorms dumped hail on selected neighborhoods in the metropolitan area, sparing Yankee Stadium in the Bronx, where a doubleheader with Detroit was uninterrupted, but striking nearby beaches, where three people escaping the heat were electrocuted.

Ten thousand spectators turned out for the Rosenberg funeral, my older sister and I among them. We had marked my sixth birthday the day before, but the celebration, around a rickety bridge table in our driveway, seemed oddly eclipsed by hushed conversations among the adults. The whispered names spoke so loudly for themselves. I knew that the Rosenbergs had two sons, one my age; that their mother, like mine, was named Ethel; and that she, like my sister, had a baby brother. The brother had told something about his sister that got the whole family in so much trouble that the parents had been sent away to a prison with a funny name. They would never come back. What happened that unbearably muggy Friday evening would define the legacy of the protagonists, of their children and their grandchildren, and of an unrelated six-year-old boy who two days later bore silent witness as a cortege bearing history silently, but indelibly, rolled by.

———

The Rosenbergs were buried in Wellwood Cemetery on Long Island, to the apparent surprise of cemetery officials, who complained that the plot had been bought under false pretenses, supposedly on behalf of two sisters killed in an automobile accident.

Tessie Greenglass didn't go. None of the Greenglasses did. "I don't attend political rallies," she told the FBI. Instead, Tessie instructed her son Bernie to write to his younger brother, David. She didn't want David to fret. And she wanted him to know that she hoped if he had to do it all over again, he would testify just as truthfully as he had at the trial. Five days later, Bernie's letter arrived at Lewisburg. He had written:

> It's been a long, long time since you heard directly from me, but at the present time I feel a few lines representing the views of the family, and mom in particular, will straighten out any doubts you may have.
>
> To begin with we feel you did the proper thing, whereas Eth and Julie did not. They not only did a disservice to the country but from a more personal viewpoint they put their children in a most horrible situation.
>
> Then too, they were willing to trade yours and your family's lives for their stinking principals, but only succeeded in forfeiting their own, by insisting that they were absolutely blameless, the victims of our government's frame-up—spearheaded by both you and Ruthie. Believe me Dave, I spent hours eating my heart out with Eth, but to no avail. According to her, Mom, Chuch, everyone connected with the case, and

your counsel all lied—and when I questioned her concerning some of the points of contention, she countered with the stock phrase, "Were you there" or "its a dirty lie." I got the impression that they wanted everything on their terms—and easygoing as I am, I did not relish the idea of being used, and that's exactly what they were doing, even as they did with you and Ruthie. Don't lose any sleep over them—for although I don't think they deserved what they got, nevertheless they were the masters of their fate and could have saved themselves, to say nothing of the heartaches they could have spared all their families and friends through the last 2½ years.

Despite Bernie's unqualified endorsement of David's behavior, David never slept quite so soundly again. Only a few days later, he wrote the federal director of prisons, requesting a transfer to Lewisburg's inmate-run farm to restore his shattered nerves. And for years, he awoke with a shudder around 5:00 A.M. *Thinking is the thing that keeps him from going back to sleep. . . . You have to tell the truth. You can't do anything else. There's no other way to go. You make the best deal you know how.* And to hell with everyone who thinks that they would have behaved any differently.

But then he would think back to when he was a little boy growing up on Sheriff Street and his sister read him Booth Tarkington novels and tutored him in French, and her boyfriend, the engineer, gave him his used college texts and other books, too. He would think about Ruth Leah Printz, the little girl around the corner whom he wanted to marry, and about all those immigrant families that struggled to escape the ghosts of the ghetto.

Sometimes they did escape the ghetto but not the ghosts. Even when she was a little girl, Ruth Printz, who would become David Greenglass's wife, was taunted unmercifully as a murderer. Even when he was a little boy, David Greenglass wanted to build a bomb.

Chapter 2

===

The House on Sheriff Street

"He said to me, 'Will you ever be a *mensch*?'"

≡

By the time David Greenglass left prison, Sheriff Street would be all but gone. Not just number 64, the five-story cold-water walk-up between Delancey and Rivington where he was born and raised, but four of the five blocks of Sheriff Street and everything that once flanked them, from Grand Street, where the Richard Hoe and Company printing-press factory towered over the tenements, to East Houston, abutting Hamilton Fish Park. Gone were the worn cobblestones, the fetid stalls where pushcart peddlers stabled their dusky horses, and the pungent Russian baths that used to stand just next door to number 64.

Even history would be obliterated. With all of the street signs removed, no one would ever ask how Sheriff Street got its name. They would never hear how Marinus Willett single-handedly prevented the Royal Irish Regiment from sailing away in 1775 with five cartloads of weapons—weapons that instead came to constitute the fledgling Continental Army's first arsenal in New York—and how, as a hero of the revolution, he fleshed out his résumé as mayor and sheriff. Sheriff Street was superimposed on what had once been farmland owned by the Willett family and by their neighbors, the Delanceys, Tories whose property was confiscated after the British were routed.

In the twenty years that David lived on Sheriff Street, he never heard of Marinus Willett. Instead, the protagonists of local lore included the Onion King, who lived across the street above a speakeasy and was reputed to have become a multimillionaire after buying up land dirt-cheap from desperate farmers in California; Mr. Bokunin, who regularly dissected other people's garbage as an urban-archaeology project; Mrs. Reisenfeld, who, without warning or apparent provocation, would laugh hysterically to herself; and Mrs. Freindel, whose chilling screams terrified passersby—especially her chief target, a little girl who lived around the corner.

All of them would be dead or gone by the time David was released from prison. Most of Sheriff Street itself was being bulldozed for a public-housing project. All that survived were the bittersweet memories of immigrant families who had struggled to fulfill Moses Rischin's definition of the ideal ghetto: one from which they could escape within a generation.

—

Barnet Greenglass, known as Barney or by his Hebrew name, Baruch or Borach, was born in Minsk. He arrived in New York in 1903, escaping a stepfather whom he detested so intensely that he had previously fled home to live in the factory where he worked. In 1909, Barnet and his wife, Beckie, had a son, Samuel Louis Greenglass. When Sam was two years old, Beckie died of kidney failure at age thirty-five.

Ten months later, Barnet married Theresa Feit, a twenty-four-year-old Austrian immigrant who lived around the corner on Willett Street. Theresa, the daughter of Hersh Feit and Ethel Vruber, was born in Galicia of Austrian and German heritage. Samuel, the stepson she inherited, was an only child for three more years until the birth in 1915 of Esther Ethel Greenglass. Bernard Abraham Greenglass was born in 1917. Five years later, after suffering four miscarriages, Tessie gave birth to David, her third and last child.

—

David was born on an unseasonably chilly March 2, 1922, delivered by a midwife in the Greenglasses' apartment on Sheriff Street. Barnet was in his mid-forties. Tessie was thirty-eight. She was elated. When recounting the story years later, she would remind David that he arrived just as she and her sister Regina, who was known as Tante Chucha, were baking challah for Sabbath dinner. "You interrupted me," Tessie invariably complained, reliving the moment in mock irritation.

Beyond the Greenglass family, the day of David's birth was largely forgettable. Congress was being warned again that shrinking the armed forces would endanger national security. Governor Harry L. Davis of Ohio vowed to abolish his state's death penalty. In Omaha, a "society woman" was electrocuted when she accidentally knocked an electric heater off a wicker hamper and into her bathtub. Locally, a woman, obligingly young and attractive, was found not far from the Rockefeller estate in Westchester County, nearly beheaded and with a cross carved into her face; a broken stiletto was discovered nearby in the snow. Police seized a cache of opium on Oliver Street, just a block from the house where Governor Alfred E. Smith had been born. A twenty-year-old woman, Dora Lefkowitz, tried to adopt the newborn baby boy she had abandoned two days before in a hallway on 105th Street—a hallway she chose, she explained, because it looked as if "nice people" lived there. For the second time in a week, Joseph Yatkowitz escaped from the Ward's Island insane asylum by paddling to Manhattan on a makeshift raft, only to be turned in by his father. The Unemployment Council convened what was billed as a mass rally; nine people showed up. And *The New York Times* was urging all Americans to contribute "every ounce of food and medicine or bit of clothing that they can spare" to President Warren G. Harding's Committee for Russian Relief.

—

According to family mythology, David was named for his great-grandfather, a farmer immortalized for stubbornly surviving to the age of 102, despite having been kicked in the head years before by a horse. ("And so," David said, "they figured the name is going to be good luck for me.") Unlike his siblings, David was not given a middle name.

The family name is also loosely documented. Glass could refer to an ancestor's profession—a glazier—or to anything transparent. The color green, according to genealogists, symbolized the tribe of Simon and was associated in Jewish mysticism with Raphael, the archangel who was a patron of the blind. During World War II, Bernie met a man in Vienna with the Germanic version of the name, Gruenglas. "He told me it means a man that made glass," David said. "And the glass, because of the imperfections, was green."

Decades later, the family name's origins prompted further speculation when a letter, found at the Albuquerque airport and attached to a *Time* magazine story about David's arrest, was forwarded to the FBI. Written in the margin was this cryptic comment: "The man's name was Greenglass. Evidently that's where you got this glass bottle." Federal agents traced the letter to an oilman in El Paso, who explained that he and his sister, whose name was Ethel, were speculating about how spies identify one another. He recalled reading that each received half of a broken bottle and confirmed their bona fides when they met by fitting the two broken parts together. Thus, Ethel's marginal notes about green glass.

—

The 1920 census counted about one thousand people living in each square block bordering Sheriff Street, an astronomical density, since most of them were crammed into low-rise tenements. Within the fifteen or so blocks bounded by Ridge, Rivington, Cannon, and Division streets, more than 16,500 people—constituting 3,500 families—occupied 363 dwellings. About 60 percent of them had been born abroad, the vast majority in Russia or Austria. Not even one in fifty residents was a child of American-born parents. Fully one fifth of the adults were illiterate. Barnet and Tessie each reported that their mother tongue was Yiddish. Tessie, according to the census form, also could not read or write English.*

The Lower East Side was a radical cauldron. In 1914, the district

---

* David later insisted that while his father was not so conversant in English, his mother was so fluent that she headed the mothers' club at a settlement house on Rivington Street. None of the scores of letters seized by the FBI years later was written by Tessie, though; several suggest that Ethel was writing on her mother's behalf. "She can just about sign her name," Ethel said.

had elected a socialist to Congress. Tessie (who was reputed to have once chained herself to a gate as a young suffragette) was nominally a democratic socialist—no dictatorship, thank you, by the Kaiser or by a czar or of the proletariat—but her politics were unsophisticated, which explains in part how she later wound up contributing to a door-to-door canvasser for the Nazis. He said he was representing the National Socialist Party, and to Tessie Greenglass that sounded close enough.

No godless communism either, for them. Of course, the boys were bar mitzvahed, but religious strictures were rigorously enforced only when Tessie's father was around. Then, Barnet, who usually derided religion as *Kinderspiel*—child's play—was importuned to attend Sabbath services across the street, unless it was summer and they were vacationing in the country, in which case he had to walk with his father-in-law several miles to the nearest *shul*. Tessie bought kosher meat but also bacon when her children wanted it. "My mother was very modern," David said. "Not when her father was alive, though."

But even David's grandfather, his Zayda, bent the rules. "I used to go to the bathroom with him," David recalled. "He'd turn the light on on the Sabbath. And I said, 'Bubbe says you're not allowed to turn the lights on on Saturday.' He said, 'In the toilets, there's no Saturdays.'" On Saturday afternoons, Zayda would fidget with his pipe, marking time until sundown to light up, and close one eye while David and his Uncle Shaya played chess. On *shabbos,* chess was indulged, but not pinochle. The distinction was Talmudic: Pinochle was played for money; it was gambling. Zayda had another rationale, which he kept to himself: He preferred to watch chess.

The Greenglasses lived on the ground floor of 64 Sheriff Street, behind Barnet's cluttered machine shop, which adjoined the only private toilet in the building. In the apartment itself, furniture and appliances were apportioned functionally and improvisationally. Directly behind the shop, where Tessie also stored the week's supply of clear, blue, and green glass seltzer bottles, was Barnet and Tessie's narrow, windowless bedroom. Then, the kitchen, dominated by a sauna-size bathtub that squatted on cast-iron legs and came with a versatile enamel cover. Tessie's kitchen boasted two stoves, one gas and one coal, but neither radiated sufficient heat. In winter, visitors sat with their feet in the oven to thaw out. The kitchen led to the dining room, formerly Sam's bedroom, where a fake fireplace and a real icebox flanked a large round table. A window looked out onto slum backyards with wooden outhouses, a family friend remembered, as well as "a tree that was trying to grow without ever succeeding." Tessie sometimes planted corn, which sprouted just high enough to be trampled by the Great Danes, German shepherds, or other oversize strays that Bernie regularly brought home.

—

In 1922, more than eighty people lived at 64 Sheriff Street, a traditional dumbbell-shaped tenement built in 1886. Many were couples with children who shared an apartment with assorted transient in-laws, siblings, nieces, nephews, and paying boarders. Even the furnace room was occupied—by Mike, an Irish-American First World War veteran, and Willy, a black man, both of whom, when they were feeling up to it, performed odd jobs for Barnet. Among the tenants in the 1920s were two tailors, Harry Zimmerman and Aaron Haber; Joseph Weiss, a peddler; Louis Marks, a garment presser; and Lustig Hersch, a truck driver. Two of Tessie's brothers, Abraham and Samuel Feit, both butchers, also lived in the building. Abe owned a farm in upstate Spring Glen, near Ellenville, which the Greenglasses visited during the summer. After witnessing his uncle butcher a calf there, David vowed never to eat meat again. His self-imposed ban lasted one week.

Greenglass relatives arrived, usually unheralded, with storybook adventures that were burnished by inevitable repetition. A deserter from the Kaiser's army introduced himself as Ben Babka, a cousin. Another cousin arrived from Germany in 1937 and superciliously announced that he was en route to Princeton to study theoretical physics with Einstein. Still another cousin, Julius Lewis, a muscular tailor, delighted the younger Greenglasses by recalling how he avoided German strafing in the First World War by hiding under a mule. He also left an impression by waking abruptly from vivid nightmares and thrusting his fist through the wall. Aunt Regina, a garment workers' union organizer, arrived after the war and remained for nearly four decades. David taught her English, and, while she welcomed his constructive criticism, she bridled whenever Tessie corrected her speech or, for that matter, when anything else stoked the embers of slights from childhood. "They were still arguing about things from the sandbox," David said.

———

David's sandbox was his father's machine shop. His favorite books weren't ethereal fairy tales; they were technical manuals. He attended P.S. 4, but most of what he remembers was learned from thumbing through machinery catalogs with his father or half-brother Sam and, later, imagining the future via Buck Rogers or from fanciful diagrams in *Popular Science*. "Sammy used to take me on his lap, and he would take the technical magazines and say, 'This is a capacitor, that's a coil, that's a transformer,'" David remembered. The place he most looked forward to visiting wasn't the circus or the zoo but the annual electrical manufacturers' trade show in midtown Manhattan.

David's favorite gadgets were electric. Turn a switch and something lights up. Cause and effect. Action and reaction. Electricity powers lathes and turrets, which, in skilled hands, could fabricate shapeless hunks of metal into tools and dies with which to manufacture even more intricate machines. His love of electricity inspired the black-light episode. After reading about the potential of a light source that would emit only ultraviolet rays, he helped himself to the black enamel his father kept to spiff up old sewing machines and dabbed it on an ordinary incandescent bulb. The result: a black bulb but no light. Quite a commotion ensued when his mother's cousin, Anna Babka, the mother of the young German army deserter, reached into a closet to turn on a light that somebody had mischievously painted black.

Anna Babka also bore the brunt of another experiment run amok. "I wanted to make a bomb," David recalled. He scoured Tessie's kitchen for bicarbonate of soda and vinegar. To make the bottled mixture even more volatile, he added an ample helping of sugar. Then, he capped it. Soon, *kaboom!* The bomb splattered crystallized sugar on Anna Babka's brand-new sealskin coat. "It never occurred to me that anything that would happen would be so devastating," he recalled dryly. "People got very upset with me."

Other kids treasured toys or athletic gear. David cherished machinery. David was so awed by a gleaming Ford Tri-Motor airplane on display at Grand Central Terminal that he struck a deal with his Tante Chucha: If he behaved at Uncle Izzy's wedding, she would take him for a ride on an airplane. He behaved; she delivered. At Glenn L. Curtiss Airport on Flushing Bay in Queens, they boarded a single-engine Bellanca for an unforgettable sightseeing tour of New York City. The plane had a special appeal for seven-year-old David: A Bellanca had been Charles Lindbergh's first choice of plane to pilot solo across the Atlantic.

David remembers sitting on Barnet's shoulders for Lindbergh's triumphal parade up Broadway in 1927, as well as the moment of silence at school four years later after another of his idols, Thomas Edison, died. Lindbergh and Edison were men who did things, men who made things. David also revered Albert Einstein, who conjured up abstruse theories that enabled other men to do things and make things. So what if nobody else could articulate those theories? Relativity, *shmelativity.* David remembered the explanation that his parents read in the *Forward,* paraphrasing Einstein himself.

Two men are sitting in the park—of course, it was told in Yiddish—and one says to the other, "Who is this man Einstein?"

"He wrote about relativity."

"Relativity? What is relativity?"

"Well, if you're in a room with a woman kissing her, an hour is like a minute. But if you should sit on a hot stove, a second is like a year."

"And from this he makes a living?"

—

"Are you comfortable?" Borscht Belt comics asked, and there was only one retort: "I make a living."

Barnet Greenglass made a living repairing machinery, mostly sewing machines for the garment industry. The shop generated enough income so that a modest surplus was turned over to a broker, who invested most of it in Cities Service, the oil refiner. When the market crashed in 1929, the stock became virtually worthless but eventually rebounded some. During the Depression, more people could afford to repair machinery than could afford to replace it. "We were not that poor," David said.

But Barnet's entrepreneurial reach far exceeded his grasp. "My father would buy equipment because he liked it," David said. Once Barnet paid eight hundred dollars for a sophisticated piece of machinery, certain he could resell it for four times as much. Except that the man he bought it from didn't own it. Tessie, who supplemented the family's income by collecting rents and arranging for repairs as superintendent of 64 Sheriff Street, was furious. "My father never signed checks ever again," David said.

—

For the most part, Tessie, not Barnet, was David's teacher. "My father taught me all kinds of stuff, but that was all mechanical," David recalled. And even in mechanics it wasn't Barnet whom David hoped to emulate but his mother's brother, Izzy, who worked alongside his father:

> My Uncle Izzy was somebody you'd want to be. He was a weight lifter, a skier, a machine gunner during the war in Germany. And he was a machinist and inventor. He wasn't tall. He was handsome. As a matter of fact, he looked a lot like a handsome Schwarzenegger. He used to tell me, in order to be a good machinist you had to be very very—you have to have patience. You should not do things in a rush, you should be careful what you do: *Measure three times, work once.* Do not assume anything. If somebody says this part is good, you check it before you do any work.
>
> Now, my father would take the same bushing and say, "Ah, ah, ah, push it on." Izzy would say, "Borach, did you measure it?" And Borach would say, "No, I didn't measure it, but look, it fit pretty good." So Izzy says, "Don't you think you should machine a new one and put it in?" And my father would say, "I'm the boss, I'm doing it my way."

Before Izzy quit to become foreman of another machine shop, he fashioned a bow and arrow for David from an umbrella spoke. "I promptly pulled the thing and hit him in the eye with it," David recalled. "He gave me a crack across the bottom and said, 'I make you a toy, you shoot me with it?' My father screamed like hell at me. And then he turned around and said, 'Izzy, who makes a thing like this for an idiot child?'"

Tessie was also the disciplinarian: "My mother used to say, 'You've got to be a little deaf, you've got to be a little blind. You have to let children do what they have to do. You have to hope that what you taught them, they'll learn.'" Tessie's coda was blunt, as David encapsulated it: "Honest, hard work and the ability to get a smack in the face and stand up again." The coda had a corollary that David invoked when throwing his weight around didn't work: "If you want people to be nice, say nice things."

"She knew that even if I was going to get punished in some way . . . I would tell her the truth," David said. "I would say a lie once in a while. . . . She would hit me with a broom. Not the stick, but the bristles. There was nobody really doing capital punishment, beating the hell out of me or anything. Nobody did that to any of us."

———

The Greenglasses weren't demonstrably affectionate. "I can't even remember my mother kissing me," David said. "Or my father. Never even hugged me." Still, David was Tessie's favorite. But her disproportionate doting fostered resentment among his brothers—"You also get beaten up for being the favorite," David said—and provoked even Barnet, the gentle junior partner, into a rare show of defiance. Nobody remembers how it began, but it culminated in an argument over David's hair. Tessie loved his long curls. Barnet, who was balding, didn't. One Friday afternoon, when David was four or five, his father announced that he was taking him for a haircut. "Don't you dare," David distinctly remembers his mother saying. Barnet took the dare. He ordered the barber not only to shear David's curls but to shave his head. "I came home, my mother begins to cry, and when I saw her crying, I began to cry," David recalled.

"And then my father felt very upset about the whole thing and he said, 'God, I'm sorry.'" For a while, David wore a hat; the cover-up didn't work. "People called me Knobby," he said.

David was also Ethel's favorite. She read boys' novels to him with a theatrical flair. She also tutored him in French. "He was my baby brother," she said later. "That is exactly how I treated him."

———

David was endowed with curiosity and, when a project engaged him, with industriousness. He precociously apprenticed himself to Sam Freund, an electrician, who was a friend of his father. He claims to have rewired an entire fifty-six-apartment building when he was only fifteen. After classes at Haaren High School, he took a seven-dollar-a-month part-time clerical job with the National Youth Administration. The summer he was seventeen, he assembled clutches. He briefly worked Saturday nights as a waiter at his Uncle Harry's ice-cream parlor in the Crown Heights section of Brooklyn, but he botched so many orders that he was reassigned behind the green marble counter as a soda jerk.

"You know your Davie and your Davie doesn't do anything that he can get away with in the line of work," he later confessed in a letter to Ruth. "When I was a teen-ager, I was supposed to meet my father and help him in the shop or someplace. What happened is, he would call my mother and say, 'He never showed up.' I went to the movies, I was talking to girls, whatever I did instead of coming and going where I was supposed to go. Then, because I didn't show up, he said to me, 'Will you ever be a *mensch*?'"

———

If there was a more impetuous child among the Greenglass boys, though, it was Bernie. "Bernie was somebody that would not take any guff," David recalled. "My brother beat up everybody." Bernie was invited along when Barnet, surrendering to Tessie's hectoring, was dispatched to collect overdue bills and loans. David recalled overhearing his father boasting to Tessie about one episode: "When the guy said, 'I don't want to pay you, I can't afford to pay you,' Bernie grabbed him by the throat and pushed him over to a window. It was a high loft. He said, 'Look, I'm going to throw you out the window if you don't pay my father when he asks you to be paid.' So the guy paid him." Bernie's exploits earned him the nickname "Loony," which hinted at the bravado that got him wounded twice as a tank commander in the Second World War and won him five Bronze Stars.

David was the youngest Greenglass sibling, but after he was born another young boy joined the household. The boy's sister used to be a part-time bookkeeper for Barnet; when their parents died and the nine children scattered, the youngest, Mendy, was invited to live with the Greenglasses.

Sam, the eldest brother, was a stepson, which, by his own reckoning, invariably set him apart. David was only ten when Sam married and moved away. He wasn't missed. His irascible reputation within the family was already established. Years later, David urged his wife, Ruth, to apply for a job at a company where, he wrote, the boss was well-regarded "in spite of his having Sam as a name."

—

Between 1922 and 1930, so many strivers graduated from the Lower East Side that, by one count, the area's Jewish population plunged by two thirds. All the Greenglasses got were good-byes. Many who were left behind bitterly matched their lot against what might have been. Or, worse still, against what already was, but for someone else. Tessie and Barnet never did escape Sheriff Street.

Another family that stayed behind was the Printzes. David and Ruth Leah Printz were childhood sweethearts. David later said that she "married into communism." It could also be said that she was born into it. Her birthday was, by most accounts, May Day, a birthday she shared with her father, Max, a Hungarian immigrant.* Her mother, Tillie Leiter, came from Austria. Ruth was the first of four children.

Ruth was born three blocks from Sheriff Street. Like David, she at-

---

* Records of her birth date differ. Some say May 1, 1923, which would have been about two months before her parents got married. Most say April 30, 1924, or May 1, 1924.

tended P.S. 4. As a young girl, she suffered from excruciating migraines and frequent nosebleeds. Even more intensely, she suffered from a memory that was to haunt her forever. She and a friend were playing catch. The ball rolled into the street. Her friend darted out between parked cars to retrieve it and was struck by a truck. "The mother used to curse Ruth all the time," David recalled. "She blamed her. She said, 'How come you survived and my daughter didn't?'"

———

When they met, David was fourteen, and Ruth was twelve. She worshiped this engaging teenager who could banter about science and politics and seemed destined to invent something or discover something or do something someday. David didn't have movie-star good looks, but he was cute, even cuddly, with hazel eyes, black hair that was on the curly side of wavy, and a mild-mannered good nature that proclaimed itself in his easy smile. David had dated other girls, but he was captivated by Ruth's moxie, as well as by the way she ran her comb through her light brown hair more often than necessary. "She was the smartest, the most cogently thinking," he recalled. She hung out at the Madison Settlement House, where she and several loyal girlfriends united—all for one and one for all—as a group they dubbed the AFO Club. At sixteen, she graduated from Seward Park High School, Ethel's alma mater, where Ruth had been a member of Arista, the national honor society, and assistant treasurer of the student body's general organization. In the *Almanac,* the Seward Park yearbook, the quotation under her name hailed her as "Elegant as simplicity."* Ruth graduated with a gold-seal diploma and was poised for college when her family persuaded her to take vocational courses instead.

"Her mother insisted that she learn how to type," David said.

---

* Probably borrowed from a poem by William Cowper, which continued: "and warm / As ecstasy."

Chapter 3

Ethel and Julius

"There's a fanaticism that runs through the Greenglass family."

═

A s Tessie and Barnet's oldest child and their only daughter, Ethel, born September 28, 1915, thrived in a world all her own. From Tessie's perspective, Tessie's sister Esther recalled, "Ethel was a snob, worrying over Italian arias and Russian peasants instead of her own family." To David, she "was a very fanatical lady. There's a fanaticism that runs through the Greenglass family. Fanatics can kill." The 1931 yearbook at Seward Park High School waffled about one of her classmates, Samuel Joel (Zero) Mostel, imagining him "a future Rembrandt or perhaps a comedian?"* The yearbook was unequivocal about Ethel's future—"Can she act? And how!"—and was eerily specific: In 1950, the yearbook predicted, she would be America's leading actress.

Ethel's face was angelic. She was diminutive if a bit dumpy and wore a back brace to correct a spinal curvature caused by scoliosis. Her increasingly challenging performances with the Alfred Corning Clark Neighborhood House troupe were generally acclaimed. She won the two-dollar second prize for singing at the Loews Delancey's amateur

---

* Mostel, who adopted Zero as his stage name, debuted on Broadway eleven years later.

night and competed on *Major Bowes' Amateur Hour* on national radio. At nineteen, she became the youngest member admitted to Hugh Ross's prestigious Schola Cantorum of New York and performed with the chorale at a concert directed by Arturo Toscanini himself at Carnegie Hall.

David attended more than a few of his sister's performances (although he was more likely to be found at the Odeon, which was known as the Rodeo because it featured so many Westerns). He cannot recall his mother going to a single one. Tessie did nothing to nurture her daughter's theatrical aspirations, which was why Ethel began skipping family dinners to sneak off to neighborhood cabarets, to perform or to socialize with other would-be bohemians, including an artist of whom she became enamored. "If Ethel had married that other guy," David later lamented, "everything would have been all right."

"Ethel was very secretive about her life," David recalled. "But my mother was a very shrewd lady. . . . She didn't get the whole story from her, and she knew she didn't get the whole story. My mother must have had times when Ethel didn't tell her the truth. See, my mother was a good interrogator and knew when I was lying to her and when I was telling the truth. She never said, 'Are you lying?' Neither did my father. They just knew."

—

Ethel wanted to attend college but went to work instead to help support her parents and younger brothers. Shortly after graduation from Seward Park, she answered a newspaper ad for unskilled workers at a paperbox factory on Bleecker Street. So many applicants showed up that the police used fire hoses to disperse the crowd. Ethel wasn't hired. She enrolled in a secretarial course and, after receiving a certificate attesting to her typing ability, found a clerical job in the garment center with the National New York Packing and Shipping Company.

During the Depression, getting a job was usually salvation. For Ethel, getting fired was an epiphany. A 1935 strike against National New York Packing by the Ladies Apparel Shipping Clerks Union was violent. It was personal. (The strike committee convened in her bedroom on Sheriff Street.) And it failed. Ethel was sacked. But she kept fighting. She appealed her dismissal to the newly created National Labor Relations Board, which, in one of its first opinions, ruled in 1936 that she had been fired in retaliation for her union participation and ordered her reinstated. While her case was pending, however, Ethel had indulged her two passions by performing at political events. She entertained on the picket line at Ohrbach's department store, where organized labor was hoping to gain a foothold, and at sit-ins at the city's Home Relief Bureau offices. Around Christmas 1936, when she was twenty-one and struck with stage fright, she sang "Ciribiribin," the Italian love song, at a benefit for the International Seamen's Union where a thoroughly smitten eighteen-year-old City College sophomore introduced himself as Julius Rosenberg.

—

Julius was born May 12, 1918, in East Harlem, the youngest child of Harry and Sophie Rosenberg, immigrants who fled the same Polish shtetl but met only in America. After Harry's dry-cleaning store failed, he returned to tailoring and sample making. The family moved to the Lower East Side, eventually to the Lavanburg Homes, a modern development on Goerck Street where Sophie had a brother-in-law who was the superintendent. The Rosenbergs had four other children before Julius: David was born in 1909, followed by Lena in 1912 and the twins, Ethel and Ida, in 1914. David won a scholarship to Columbia and later became a pharmacist. Ida, who was said to have suffered brain damage at birth, was institutionalized when Julius was a teenager.

The natural affinity between the baby boy of the family and his mother was cemented by a disproportionate number of medical emergencies. When Julius was three, he nearly died of measles. Later, he was struck by a taxicab, and Sophie carried him the half mile to Gouverneur Hospital herself. When he was ten, she delivered him to the emergency room again, this time with a burst appendix.

At about the same time as this last crisis, Julius discovered his first consuming passion. He began attending the Downtown Talmud Torah on East Houston Street, and unlike most of his friends, he insisted on remaining enrolled in Hebrew school after his bar mitzvah. A friend recalled playing stickball near the Lavanburg Homes one Saturday. The ball bounced right past Julius, but he refused to retrieve it on the Sabbath. The ball rolled down the block until it plunged through a sewer grate.

Sometime after Julius enrolled at Seward Park High School, his political conscience was pricked by a Delancey Street proselytizer exhorting a crowd on behalf of Tom Mooney, the imprisoned West Coast labor radical. Julius was so impressed that the next day he donated fifty cents (from the $1.10 he had earned selling candies on Sundays at a penny apiece) to the Mooney campaign. Further, Mooney's plight personified the difference between an abstract ethics lesson and a genuine moral crusade. Julius remembered that one of his religious-school teachers had invoked Isaiah to provide perspective on organized labor's demonstrations in Union Square against Ohrbach's department store: "Ohrbach is sitting in the temple now, but who wants his contributions? Let him pay his workers a living wage, then his contributions will be welcome." But when Julius challenged the rabbis to join him on the picket lines against Ohrbach and on behalf of the campaigns to free Mooney and the Scottsboro Boys, black men facing the death penalty in Alabama where they were accused of raping two white women, the chasm between preaching and practicing became apparent. The rabbis rebuffed him.

After failing the entrance exam for Cooper Union, Julius enrolled at City College's School of Technology, where a new passion, kindled on the streets and in the cellar social clubs of the Lower East Side, began to consume him.

———

As David, Ethel, and Bernie Greenglass got older, privacy was at a premium. The Greenglasses rented three additional rooms upstairs to accommodate their growing children. It was in his sister's front bedroom, which had a window and a secondhand piano, that David, then fourteen years old, first met Ethel's new boyfriend.

Julius arrived at the Greenglass household with impressive credentials. Even so, Sam Greenglass later revealed, Julius quickly found himself barred from 64 Sheriff Street because Tessie and Barnet disliked him intensely. Of all the things Julius could be accused of—and all the things he *would* be accused of—the one imperfection that bothered Barnet most seems inconsequential in retrospect: Julius apparently had lousy table manners. He spoke before he swallowed his food. Sometimes, he even appropriated Barnet's regular chair, oblivious to one of the few prerogatives that his future father-in-law was afforded. Further, Julius and his friend Milty Manes were known to amuse themselves by lustily regaling the children with this vulgar ditty: "A belch is but a gust of air coming from the heart. If it should take a downward course, it would be called a fart."

The Greenglasses' objection to Julius was largely cosmetic; Ethel's prospective in-laws raised a more pragmatic concern. The Rosenbergs wanted Julius to graduate from college before the couple got married so Ethel wouldn't have to support him. And yet, if not for Ethel, Julius might not have graduated at all. Though she enrolled in weekly lectures on acting and politics, she spent much of her time helping Julius with his homework. She typed his papers on a typewriter she bought for thirty dollars from a fellow thespian who, she recalled, "wanted very badly to get rid of it"—the same Remington portable on which a dozen years later she was accused of striking the keys, "blow by blow, against her own country in the interests of the Soviets." She also persuaded Julius to stay in school when he neglected his studies in order to fight fascism.

His inspiration for social protest was still largely an abstraction until one evening when Julius, working part-time as a soda jerk at the Hoffman Pharmacy in Harlem, witnessed injustice firsthand. A black man was struck by a bus. He was carried inside the store. While he waited nearly an hour for an ambulance, he bled to death.

At City College, which Julius attended with Joel Barr, Alfred Sarant, William Perl, Morton Sobell, and Max Elitcher—friends and potential recruits to espionage—Julius organized an affiliate of the Young Communist League, the Steinmetz Society, named for the German-born engineer whose outspoken socialism had been tolerated by General Electric (which manufactured, among its many other products, equipment for New York State's electric chair) because of his redeeming scientific contributions. Julius and his friends staged a raid on the *Bremen,* which was docked in New York, and ripped the Nazi standard from the flagship of the North German Lloyd line.

Julius was a man with a mission. Whatever else attracted Julius to Ethel, he was, as her psychiatrist later described him, "the antithesis of her brothers." Toward David, Julius was different, too. Whatever his motivation—buttering up the baby brother, cultivating a potential recruit, or, more likely, simply responding in kind to David's eager attentions—Julius embraced David without rivalry or resentment. David played the tyro, as he later put it, to Julius's professor. Julius gave David his used engineering texts and a slide rule, which David saved for years. ("I scratched out his name and put my name on," he said.) "The transfer of technical information, that kind of latched me on to him," David said, conjuring up a spy instead of a tutor.

Julius's classmate Marcus Pogarsky escorted David to a May Day parade and interspersed technical tutoring with simple interpretations of economic theory. Julius also gave David books and pamphlets expounding communism, the theory of social engineering that Julius patiently and passionately explicated (though, David later claimed, Ethel "had the influence about getting me in the communist web more than Julius, because I was already in it before I met him"). At first, David kept the technical texts and discarded the political tracts, until Tessie upbraided him one day for disrespecting the printed word—regardless of what those words conveyed. At Julius's suggestion, David read Thomas Paine's *Common Sense,* which left a big impression. So did eyewitness accounts of people who had seen the future themselves, particularly people of some social standing, like the man whose family owned a prosthesis store on Delancey Street and who told David he had visited the Soviet Union and "what a wonderful thing it was." A film also yielded a vivid image of the Soviet Union: "It was about the Russian Revolution, and I remember distinctly I was really shocked. This soldier is teaching this girl how to use a machine gun, and he grabs her breasts, and she hits him on the head. Believe me, it stuck in my mind."

—

Julius and Ethel were true believers. David truly didn't believe in much. At Haaren High School, the class struggle consisted of a single tumultuous boycott. David's recollection is that the protest was inspired by the quality of food served in the school cafeteria and not by the specter of fascism. And when he and his classmates were threatened with suspension, they capitulated quickly. His first formal political affiliation was with the Workers' Alliance, where he was lured largely by a handball league. He joined the neighborhood Young Communist League when he was sixteen, already indoctrinated by Ethel and Julius and receptive when a window dresser from the neighborhood issued this challenge: "If you believe in socialism, why don't you do something about it?" There, David found instant gratification. Sitting a few seats away at the very first meeting of the YCL's Club Malraux was a gorgeous redhead named Lillian, whom he had had a crush on in elementary school.

Communism's architecture also appealed to David. An earthquake-proof philosophical foundation supported a political structure that depended on the application of mechanical principles to economics. (David wasn't the first mechanic attracted to communism. Pierre Degeyter, a lathe operator, composed the haunting melody for the communist anthem, "The Internationale.") In 1939, his incontrovertible faith in his adopted party's durability survived its greatest test. For many Americans, the Soviets' nonaggression pact with Nazi Germany seemed less like pragmatic resilience than unprincipled reversal. It necessitated leaps of faith that defied gravity. Only one month before the pact was announced, Earl Browder, the American communist leader, declared that "there is as much chance of Russo-German agreement as of Earl Browder being elected president of the Chamber of Commerce." David, who was seventeen at the time, recalled his utter disbelief: "Let me tell you, that tried men's souls. But when you want to believe, you want to believe."

Once he hurdled that ideological chasm, any subsequent inconsistency was an inconsequential furrow.

—

Few recruits to any cause ever have the opportunity to test the true depth of their political commitment. When they do, the issues can be fundamental, such as war and peace, and the risks can be profound, such as losing a job or even a life. David measured his commitment to communism more prosaically: "It was not strong enough to go out and keep delivering papers on Sunday morning, that's for sure. I still remember one hallway I went into. It was deadly still. A dim light. It was a tenement house. And I was giving out *Daily Workers,* putting them on the doorstep of apartments. And I said, 'What the hell am I doing? This is ridiculous.'"

He attended YCL meetings only infrequently. He was delinquent in paying dues. He dropped out of the league altogether after a year or two. Although he believed that Marxism was the solution to most of the world's problems, he balked at the rigorous discipline demanded by card-carrying communism. As a result, he never joined the Communist Party.

Nor did he suit up for the Red Army. When the Soviets invaded Finland in 1939, ostensibly to support a puppet communist regime, "I said to Ruthie, 'I'm going to join,'" he recalled. "And she said, 'Are you out of your mind? You're out of your mind. You're not going to go if I have to handcuff you.' I was real gung-ho. I was serious as much as a seventeen-year-old can be, I guess. If Ruthie had not stopped me, I would have been in the Russian army fighting against the Nazis."

In hindsight, though, he said, "Julius was a guy that really lived communism. To me it was like a peripheral thing. I mean, I got ideas and so on, but I'm not a doer of things that are theoretical and political. There I was saying, 'Hands off Spain' and hands off this and that. But that's the last marching I ever did."

—

Julius lived communism so completely (and believed in keeping hands off Spain so literally) that he failed Spanish. He graduated from City College with a B.S. in electrical engineering one semester late, in February 1939—the same year that, according to the FBI, he joined the Communist Party. He finished seventy-ninth in a class of eighty-five. That

June, with Julius working part-time and attending an aeronautical engineering course, he and Ethel got married. Her brother Bernie was the best man. The couple's first home was Ethel's bedroom on Sheriff Street.

The following February, David graduated from Haaren High. His grades were fair. His conduct and character were described as good. (He had worked as a helper in the school's science office.) At commencement, the 250 Haaren seniors entered the auditorium to Felix Mendelssohn's "War March of the Priests." They sang Pietro Mascagni's "Still Is the Night," which ends with the plea, "O may Thy love and gentle grace on sinful mortals fall." In the *Quill and Hammer,* the yearbook editor, Leo von Gottfried, provided a frame of reference for his classmates' ambivalence about being thrust into a world at war when things at home were far from perfect: "We have all heard people complain about conditions in this country at the present. Surely, they do not stop to think of all that we have to be thankful for. Our country is still a democracy, and liberty continues to rule. Anyone with talent and the will to win, no matter what social or economic level he comes from, can attain success. The people rule in our fair land. The people, yes!"

Next to David's photograph, the very photograph that ten years later the FBI used to identify him ("All films reserved for future orders," a yearbook advertisement from the school photographer announced), he listed his goal as a career in engineering science. Many of the quotations accompanying other students' photographs appear to have been generic, but the yearbook editors seem to have taken special pains in David's case. They chose just the right aphorism to suggest a well-intended windbag. Of Davie Greenglass, the *Quill and Hammer* wrote:

> *Although he has a lot to say,*
> *We think he's grand, anyway*

Chapter 4

Drafted

"He was just bragging."

≡

Early in May 1940, with Julius still taking courses and awaiting the results of a civil-service exam in engineering, Ethel was hired as a clerk in the U.S. Census Bureau at $1,440 a year. The Rosenbergs spent the summer of 1940 in Washington. Julius affected a mustache so as to look more mature; while there is no indication that his appearance impressed anyone, by the end of the summer he was notified that he had been hired as a $2,000 a year junior engineer for the Army Signal Corps, inspecting electrical equipment that defense contractors were manufacturing for the government. Better still, the job was in New York.

Within a few months, though, a government background check belatedly uncovered two references in FBI files to Ethel.

Before they moved to Washington, while the Rosenbergs were sharing an apartment briefly with Marcus and Stella Pogarsky in the Williamsburg section of Brooklyn, a neighbor, identified as a Miss S. Liggetts, advised the bureau that Ethel had signed a nominating petition for Peter V. Cacchione, the Communist Party candidate for city council.*

---

* Cacchione lost on a technicality in 1939 but won two years later as the first avowed commu-

(A photocopy of the petition was consequently turned over to the FBI by the New York City Police Department's Red Squad.) The second entry in FBI files was dated May 25, 1940. An anonymous female tipster alerted the bureau that the Ethel Greenglass Rosenberg who had just received a job with the Census Bureau was "extremely communistic." What made that call even more intriguing, fully a decade before Ethel's brother David implicated her in a plot to steal the secrets of the atomic bomb, was that the informant, presumably to enhance her credibility, described herself as "a distant relative" of Ethel Rosenberg.

As a result, Julius's dream job as an engineer and his draft deferment were jeopardized. Twice, he was summoned by the Signal Corps to a loyalty hearing. "Even if she did sign a petition," Julius argued, "I don't see how that would affect me. After all, she is a different person and has rights." Acknowledging that "the relationship between a man and his wife is normally close," Julius persuaded the presiding officer that Ethel's decision to sign the petition must have been attributable to "carelessness on her part, or maybe she just lacked sales resistance." He disclaimed any personal interest in politics, much less in the Communist Party. He kept his job.

—

For some Depression-era Jews, anti-Semitism, which exposed the cruel hypocrisy of America's meritocracy, was what provoked them into radical causes. Even in New York, anti-Semitism was a fact of life. Julius had responded by taking a civil-service test and applying for a government job. David's response was less straightforward. He employed a pseudonym.

First, David had applied to Brooklyn Polytechnic Institute to study mechanical engineering. He listed Julius and Julius's best friend, Milton Manes, as references. He was admitted, but he goofed off so much—working part-time and socializing with Ruth—that he flunked all six

---

nist to hold elective public office in New York State, an election that sped the local repeal of proportional representation.

technical courses and was asked to withdraw. David worked briefly at the machine shop where Uncle Izzy was the foreman but was laid off. When he was eighteen, he applied to the Federal Telephone Company under the name David Greene—a surname inspired by the debonair British actor Richard Greene, who later played Robin Hood. On his employment application, he explained away his withdrawal from Brooklyn Polytech by claiming that he couldn't afford the tuition. He was hired as a toolmaker and machine-maintenance man in the Rectifier Division on the four-to-midnight shift.

Years later, after he was arrested, David was asked by a Jewish FBI agent whether anti-Semitism had driven him to communism: "And I started thinking. Well, I encountered anti-Semitism in school. I encountered Nazis in America. I got beaten up by people because I was Jewish and right on the Lower East Side. Three men, three Italian fascists, beat me up because I was in a parade against fascism. They didn't know I was a communist. They just beat me up because I was Jewish."

The job at Federal Telephone lasted just three months. David was told that he couldn't take off Yom Kippur, the Jewish day of atonement, as a holiday. But he was fired apparently for helping to organize the shop for the United Electrical, Radio, and Machine Workers of America, a communist-dominated union, although the company's pretext was that, instead of working, David spent hours in the men's room reading the newspaper. After an arbitration hearing, he was offered a lesser job at another plant but rejected it and prevailed upon his union to find him work elsewhere. That's how he was hired as a machinist at Peerless Laboratories on East Twenty-third Street and wound up in the army.

—

When the Rosenbergs returned from Washington, they lived briefly at Julius's parents' apartment before renting a furnished room near Tompkins Square Park. Ethel volunteered as a typist for the Federation of Architects, Engineers, Chemists, and Technicians, the union that Julius had joined in college, and for the East Side Defense Council. She also enrolled in dramatics and modern-dance classes at the Henry Street Settlement on a scholarship. Julius—who suffered from hay fever and boils and never felt comfortable being too far from his doctor, whom he periodically saw for injections—was traveling out of town for the Signal Corps more than he liked, but he was making a very respectable $3,600 a year. In the spring of 1942, he and Ethel found a three-room apartment for $45.75 a month, electricity included, at Knickerbocker Village, the thirteen-story, block-square complex located between the approaches to the Brooklyn and Manhattan bridges. From their eleventh-floor window, the Rosenbergs even had a river view. Knickerbocker Village was the first federally supported housing project. It boasted its own nursery school and playground, which recommended it as a fine place to raise a family. Ethel was nearly six months pregnant in November 1942, which is when David and Ruth got married.

—

It was Ruth's idea. "I don't believe I ever proposed marriage; it just was understood we were to be married," David recalled. "She may have said, 'Let's get married.'" (As she reminded David later, "I can be very persistent as you know dear.") Because David had not yet turned twenty-one, Tessie had to accompany the couple to the city clerk's office to sign the marriage license. The ceremony and reception were held on November 29 at Hennington Hall on East Second Street. Several hundred guests attended, including Bernie, who was stationed in Kentucky at the time but had slipped away without leave.

Until the wedding, David regularly gave his sixty-dollar-a-week salary from Peerless to his mother. She returned eight dollars to him for his expenses.

Ruth's parents were even poorer. Max Printz was making only twenty dollars a week as a fat trimmer in a slaughterhouse. Still, Ruth dreamed of college. To meet the entrance requirements, she enrolled in high-school courses in geometry, intermediate algebra, and chemistry and entered Brooklyn College in September 1942. But before the semester ended, she withdrew, citing, as David had, financial hardship. In Ruth's case, though, it was true. The Printzes still depended on their eldest child. Ruth had no choice but to get a job.

David and Ruth moved to a tiny apartment at 266 Stanton Street, which they furnished, in part, with surplus goods from Tessie and Barnet's empty nest around the corner on Sheriff Street.* When Ruth wanted to buy new furniture, David balked at the price. "Besides that," he said, "I happen to like the comfort of our bed. Pardon me, I should say Ethel's bed."

—

David wasn't happy at Peerless Labs. The work was tolerable, as were the hours. But the pay was not. He had started at fifty-three dollars for a sixty-hour week and some weeks made twice that. But now he was married. And he was restless. Bernie was already distinguishing himself overseas. Sam was working for the War Production Board in New Jersey. The Red Army's glorious defense of Stalingrad was turning the tide on the eastern front. American troops had just invaded North Africa. "I was beginning to chafe at the bit," David recalled.

He devised what seemed like a foolproof strategy for a raise. David had received an occupational deferment from military service a month before the wedding, so his boss at Peerless, which produced parts for aircraft and weapons, knew he couldn't be drafted. But why not create some leverage by threatening to enlist? He decided to sign up for the Seabees, the navy's construction division, where he figured that, at worst, he would begin with a machinist's rating, get free engineering training, and probably never see combat. At his navy physical, he was handed a chart with different-colored dots forming a mosaic. He couldn't distinguish one shape from the other. For the first time, he was diagnosed as suffering from dichromacy, a form of color blindness first described by John Dalton, the nineteenth-century English atomic scientist, and inherited recessively through the mother. David could barely recognize either green or red. The Seabees rejected him.

But by enlisting, he had jeopardized his deferment. His records were forwarded to the army (where the inability to decipher signal flags, for

---

* The Stanton Street tenement happened to be owned by Frank Wilentz, whose brother prosecuted the Lindbergh kidnapping case.

one thing, was less of an occupational hazard). On March 23, 1943, the army drafted him. The president of Peerless filed an appeal. David pleaded for a postponement until Passover ended at sundown on April 26. The draft board rejected both appeals. He was ordered to report to the Armed Forces Induction Center at the Grand Central Palace Hotel at 5:30 A.M. on April 5, 1943.

———

With acres of equipment requiring repair and modification, the army desperately needed machinists. A week after David was inducted and bused to Fort Dix for processing, he was transferred to the Army Ordnance Base at Aberdeen, Maryland, for basic training. At Aberdeen, he was given a copy of *The Ordnance Soldiers Guide*. It began with this inspirational message: "An American soldier can, if necessary, fight without food or shelter or medical care—but an army without weapons is lost." On the manual's first page, before the chapters on first aid or defense against booby traps, was a section entitled "Safeguarding Military Information."

David spent much of the summer of 1943 in Aberdeen, writing Ruth passionate love letters almost daily and visiting as often as he could get even a one-day pass. New York's Pennsylvania Station was an easy train ride and, for a soldier, a $4.50 round-trip commute. It was during one of those jaunts that David and Ruth joined Julius and Ethel at the movies. David doesn't remember which film was playing—it might have been *Mission to Moscow*. But he distinctly recalls his private conversation with Julius as the girls were gabbing while in line outside the Capitol Theater in Times Square:

> Julius says to me, "I tried to get into the Russian embassy." He actually went up to the Russian embassy. Can you imagine, the FBI probably taking pictures of it. They're taking pictures, and he goes knocking on their door, and he says, "Look, I want to be a spy for you." I mean, basically that's what he said. What chutzpah. What craziness. He was crazy. Fanatics are basically not rational. So he goes in, and they thought he was a plant, so they didn't let him do that. But finally he told them his

credentials. "Look, I got all these guys recruited into the Young Communist League. I've done this. I did that." And he mentioned all their names and said they're all engineers and they're going to go out in the field and so on.[*]

David also remembers Julius saying that he told the Russians that his brother-in-law had just been assigned to the army's Aberdeen Proving Ground, where new weapons were being designed, manufactured, and tested. He hadn't volunteered David's services, though. Nor did he ask David to provide information. Not this time. "He never said a word about that," David recalled. "He was just bragging."

---

[*] Alexander Feklisov, a Soviet agent, offered a different version of Julius's introduction into espionage. Whether or not Julius ever actually approached the consulate (and, indeed, the FBI regularly monitored it from a command post across the street at the Pierre Hotel), Feklisov said Julius "came to the attention" of Soviet intelligence in the spring of 1942 and was actually introduced to the KGB at a 1942 Labor Day rally—organized by the state Congress of Industrial Organizations on the Central Park mall—by an accountant named Bernard Schuster. A thirty-eight-year-old Warsaw-born New York University graduate, Schuster—code-named Echo—became Julius's Communist Party contact and the party's liaison with the Russian security services, as well as the party's New York State treasurer. On that sunny Sunday afternoon, as Nazi troops surged toward Stalingrad, the crowd of thirty-five thousand heard from, among others, Mayor Fiorello La Guardia, the singer Paul Robeson, and a Russian woman guerrilla fighter. Two months later, Semen Semenov, who preceded Feklisov as Julius's KGB contact, pronounced a judgment on Julius that was remarkably similar to the one Feklisov himself later issued on David. Julius, Semenov said, was "absolutely unripe in matters of working as an agent, our demands regarding the type of materials we acquire and elementary rules of *konspiratsia*."

Chapter 5

Mail Call

"Although I'd love to have you in my arms I am content without so long as there is a vital battle to be fought with a cruel, ruthless foe. Victory shall be ours and the future is socialism's."

=

David and Ruth wrote to each other almost every day, mash notes shot through with pet words and innuendo. Many of them concerned sex. David's second priority was food. Third on his agenda was politics, punctuated by his preachy, indomitable belief that wherever he was stationed—at Aberdeen, in California, in Mississippi, in Tennessee, and finally at Los Alamos—he could convert his fellow GIs to communism, and that together with their children he and Ruth would prosper in a utopian society free of squalor and injustice.

Most of Ruth's letters were embossed with kisses, smudgy red ones where her freshly rouged lips had caressed the paper. David's letters were peppered with platitudes about patriotism—some of them were even written on stationery imprinted with a miniature American flag. He boasted that not very many men in his company had managed to complete an uphill march with full field pack, "and I darling was among them exhausted but happy and confident in my superiority as a soldier of the great United States."

The Greenglasses' mistake wasn't so much what they wrote. After all, their sophomoric musings on life, love, and Lenin were composed in the miasma of lonely moments apart. None appears to have triggered any investigation or even so much as a single censored word. The Greenglasses' mistake, rather, was in saving these letters, which reveal sensibilities and confidences that they had never intended to share with anyone else. "You are the one person I tell my thoughts to that are of very real importance and that I would never tell anyone else," David wrote.

David's letters were affectionate but often lapsed into discussing pragmatic matters. "It really will be great seeing you in the flesh," he wrote Ruth just before she was to arrive for a visit. Then, he reported: "I cleaned the mold off the salami. The climate up here is swell for cheeses and Ritz crackers." And, casting aspersions against the Gulden name because it was Germanic, he instructed Ruth: "Send French's mustard." He described dinner with several soul mates, including a "very involved, abstract and theoretical" discussion with, among others, his bunk mate Hy Adler.

His earliest letters, written only a few months after he and Ruth had been married, made her blush. She started reading one in the relative privacy of her tenement's hallway; soon her face was beet red. "Every atom of my being yearns and cries for you," David wrote. He waxed romantic about biting her lips, her soft neck, her nipples—"It's like some entangling web of some spider but darling I'd come into your parlor any day of the week." Returning home on leave, David wrote, promised "hours of intimate love and unselfishness." (Home, as he further defined it, also "is a place where I can get a meal that I want when I want it.") In his mind's eye, he pictured Ruth running, "your breasts moving under your blouse." He asked whether she cut her fingernails—"at least I won't be scarred up again"—and added: "About my toe nails they are waiting for you to clip."

"Darling, I love you with all the goodness within me, and some of the badness," David wrote. "I want you more than life itself."

"I love you more than life itself," Ruth wrote.

Love is supposed to be blind, though not color-blind. "I'm longing to see your brown eyes," David wrote. To which Ruth replied, "They're blue."

—

Their love wasn't just physical, although David did worry about Ruth's weight. ("Are you reducing or are you still eating too much?" Still, he assured her: "You are definitely not buxom, you are just right.") Their love was also metaphysical, a natural affirmation of their unswerving devotion not only to each other but to a shared ideology—an ideology that they later repudiated as passionately as they originally embraced it.

"Dearest, I love you because we have such similar ideals and beliefs," David wrote. "These beliefs are the cement with which our physical and emotional affection is welded into what humanity calls love." He elaborated:

> Although we are materialists we base our materialism on humanity and humanity is love. It is the most powerful force in the world. It is causing us to win where we are outnumbered. The victory shall be ours. The freedom shall be greater because of our great feeling that only democratic and freedom-loving peoples can foster, Darling, and we who understand can bring understanding to others because we are in love and have our Marxist outlook.

David facilely reconciled his simultaneous advocacy of communism and preaching about patriotism, buoyantly optimistic that he would eventually enlighten the uninitiated. "I don't believe that the American people are hopeless after all," he said. "In the end it will be Europe and a large part of Asia that will turn Socialist and the American end of the world will of necessity follow in the same course. So, dear, we still look forward to a Socialist America and we shall have that world in our time."

David reassured Ruth, though, that the bond between them wasn't predicated on the proclamation of a socialist America: "Darling, I love you and no matter what happens in America politically." Lest Ruth ever doubt the depth of his affection, he added: "I love you with all the love of Marx and the humanity of Lenin."

———

David reminded Ruth not to divulge any details of his letters because loose lips could jeopardize the lives of Americans—including his brother, Bernie, who was now on the front lines in Europe with the First

Army's Thirteenth Tank Battalion. "We cannot allow the enemy to discover our secrets in ordnance or anything else," David wrote. "So mum is the word."

He asked Ruth to forward copies of *In Fact*, George Seldes's progressive newsletter, for a fellow GI who "says he will help me propagandize the company," but he added this cautionary note: "Cross your name and address out with black ink so that it is illegible." He asked Ruth for a subscription to the *New York Post*, though he really wanted the *Daily Worker*. Getting the party paper delivered, he acknowledged, "would just about put me in the guard house." Speaking of which, he wrote that "while on guard duty I met a comrade who has gotten into successive trouble after trouble. It seems that he stuck his neck out too much and he has been court-martialed and broken to a private and put in the guardhouse. He is very militant but he should have been more careful. The laugh is this: that the man assigned to guard him is another comrade! This one is more careful."

David defined *careful* loosely. When debating with other GIs, he made no secret of his political leanings.

> Darling, during lunch hour I had two discussions on political questions with some fellows. I used the utmost patience and care in the choice of words so that I could get my point across and still not be suspected of Communism. . . . I'll raise that flag yet so don't worry about the future. It's ours.

A few months later, he was even less circumspect:

> Of late I have been having the most wonderful discussions on our native-American fascists, and I have been convincing the fellows right along. I'll have my company raise the Red flag yet.

He modestly conceded that the philosophical foundation underlying his proselytizing deserved some credit:

> Boy I really got into a rip-roaring argument. Of course, when the dust of discussion settled I had convinced many of my listeners in at least

the morale [sic] right of our cause. You see, dear, it is not because I am so wonderful, but because our philosophy is so logical and correct that no argument can stand against it. I am sure that if we educated people to our point of view we would have a socialist America pretty quickly.

But reconciling the party's strategic and ideological gyrations periodically proved daunting. Ruth later explained that she and David consulted the Rosenbergs on party matters because they "had a greater understanding of communism" and "could settle any difficulties." The difficulties came in all sizes. After reading Budd Schulberg's *What Makes Sammy Run?*, David asked Ruth whether its publisher, Random House, was in fact "the Party press." The biggest intellectual challenge posed by communism, though, besides the Soviet nonaggression pact with Hitler, was Earl Browder's startling proposal to reconstitute the Communist Party in America as a vehicle for political education rather than for revolution.

Browder was an accommodationist who, inspired by the alliance of Roosevelt, Churchill, and Stalin at Teheran late in 1943, had concluded that America wouldn't be ripe for socialist upheaval after the war—an unorthodoxy that confounded lockstep loyalists, as David and Ruth's correspondence makes clear. After hearing Browder speak at Madison Square Garden, Ruth encapsulated his rationale this way: "When the war is over the people won't be ready to accept socialism and all its reforms and to offer it to them may alienate it more than ever." David expressed grave doubts to Ruth about revamping the party:

No matter what, I think it is a bad move. You see, dear, it is a symbol of strength and political understanding to me and to thousands of other former Y.C.L.'ers in the service. And its dissolution would seem to us as the taking away of support to our political beliefs. It would put us in the position of a thinking Socialist and not a doing one because of the lack of organization to carry out our program. . . . Find out from Ethel what she and Julie think about it. Ask her to get the literature.

David finally relented, bowing to the collective wisdom of clippings from *The Daily Worker* and *In Fact* and citations from the *New York Post* and from the books and Hollywood films—*Song of Russia,* for one, the movie starring Robert Taylor that *The New York Times*'s reviewer said demonstrated "a proper respect for the Russians' fight in the war"—that were following the Democratic Party line by glorifying the Soviet war effort. By June 1944, just before David expected to be shipped overseas, he wrote Ruth:

> Darling, I have been reading a lot of books on the Soviet Union. Dear, I can see how far-sighted and intelligent those leaders are. They are really geniuses, every one of them. I have been revising what I think and how I think politically. Having found out the truth about the Soviets, both good and bad, I have come to a stronger and more resolute faith and belief in the principles of Socialism and Communism. I believe that every time the Soviet Government used force they did so with pain in their hearts and the belief that what they were doing was to produce good for the greatest number.

Ruth has offered conflicting accounts of her political indoctrination—once even blaming Julius for recruiting her fully a year before she and David were married, although on another occasion she insisted that she met Julius only a few months before the wedding. Regardless, her indoctrination didn't end when David was drafted. She was so enraptured by a May Day rally that she enthused:

> Well sweetheart all I can say is that I am sorry I missed so many other May Days when I had the opportunity to march side by side with you. . . . Perhaps the voice of 75,000 working men and women that were brought together today, perhaps their voices demanding an early invasion of Europe will be heard and then my dear we will be together to build—under socialism—our future.

It was her birthday; David sent her gladiolus—pink, not red.

Ruth questioned communism's rejection of religion, she later said, but believed "in the principle of every individual having a square deal and every man having sufficient clothing and food." While David was in the army, she diligently sold memberships to a communist book club, absorbed the teachings of a coworker at the Brooklyn offices of the United Electrical, Radio, and Machine Workers of America (where she was a stenographer), attended rallies with Ethel and Julius, and finally joined the Club Lincoln of the Young Communist League at the invitation of a woman who recognized her as Ethel's sister-in-law and David's wife.

Ruth's continuing education wasn't confined to reading. One night, she and David's friend Normie Brown, a grocer whom he had known since junior high school, were returning from a double feature (*Pride of the Yankees* and *Background to Danger*—"Dutch treat, of course") in Brooklyn and passed through slums in Bedford-Stuyvesant that made the Lower East Side seem tolerable. "My blood boiled," Ruth wrote David (who empathized not just with black slum dwellers but with Ruth; it wasn't fair that she also had to endure Normie's persistent grousing when what he really needs, according to David's diagnosis, was "the sexual relationship of a girl"). Once, while delivering leaflets to the Sperry plant on Long Island, she marveled, "We have so much country, so much beauty for all to share it's unfair that some are so cheated." She fantasized that she and David would someday live in a village along the Long Island Rail Road, perhaps forty minutes from Times Square, to escape the degradation of the Lower East Side. "I don't want our children born in this neighborhood," she wrote.

Ruth later maintained that she was involved only spasmodically in the YCL. Actually, she briefly served as Club Lincoln's president. She attributed the promotion solely to the fact that her fellow club members were impressed that she was Ethel's sister-in-law. It was such a surprise, Ruth wrote David in August 1943, that a friend came to visit, "and he asked me if I was president of the 'club.' For a moment I didn't understand what he was talking about and then I told him I was." David was impressed with her political growth, to the point that he volunteered: "I notice that in these few short months you have developed politically to a point where I feel that you are a really capable comrade."

But even with support for communism near its peak—the party was now working for Roosevelt's reelection and for the war, too—Ruth

sometimes was thrust on the defensive. She recounted for David a ten-
dentious conversation about current events and "Moscow gold"—the
suspicion, later confirmed, that the party was being subsidized by the
Soviets—with two friends, Phyllis and Herbert Levinthal:

> It didn't take much time for me to notice that they were all anti-Soviet.
> They started shooting questions at me until I asked why I was being
> cross-examined. Phyllis piped up, "as president of the Y.C.L. you should
> know the answer." I have no idea how she found out about it but there
> was such scathing sarcasm in her voice that I picked up my head in
> surprise. Obviously they believe in Moscow gold. They think I have a
> private wire to get information daily from Joe Stalin himself.

To which David replied:

> Darling, you are right it is our twisted phsycollogy [sic] that is due in
> the greatest part to our "social structure," namely capitalism with its
> economic hold on everyone, teaching them to grasp what they can and
> giving them no real future to look to. Dearest, at present we are fighting
> a war to give people a chance at least. I hope that we can do away with
> the rotten structure as quickly as possible. . . . Dearest, you are no snob,
> what you say is true and there are only two ways to look at it. Either
> convert our friends or drop them. And I don't believe in giving up eas-
> ily, do you?

Neither did Ruth. She reiterated her faith in her mentor and in communism:

> Still, I hope that our children will be brought up in a socialist world and
> our money will be useless, I look forward to that day when necessities
> and luxuries are to be had by all and sundry just so long as he justifies
> living by working.

Faith alone was insufficient. Ruth was replaced as president of Club
Lincoln after, at most, a few months. She lamented that she hadn't paid

more attention to David, so that she could better practice what he had preached.

> And now I must admit that on a great many of those occasions I didn't listen to what you were saying. I was just thrilled by you and your voice sounded like music from a harp. . . . Now, even though you would believe otherwise, even at this time I'm not up to your level when it comes to political understanding and the ability to analyze a new situation.

Subsequently, Ruth wrote that she arrived for a meeting of the club just as the remaining members were voting to dissolve it:

> It was a flop. There was no interest, no cooperation, nothing. The place was dirty . . . four months behind in rent, two in electricity. . . . Meanwhile, the county has chosen certain choice people (yes dear, I'm one of them) to start an S.O.S.—Sweethearts of the Service club down here on the east side. It would be an all-girls' club, of course, and I think that that type of thing will have great appeal to our neighborhood.

By this time, it appeared that David was to be stationed in California indefinitely, and Ruth, in her first foray as a camp follower, was determined to find a job and perhaps start a family there. David had been too lazy to join the Communist Party. Ruth was too conscientious. On Lincoln's birthday, she wrote David that she was resisting a friend's entreaties:

> It seems that the Party is having a recruiting drive and I've been "invited" to join. . . . I told Libie that I'd join, but not until I got back from California. However, she said it was important that I join now because there was a drive going on, but I didn't feel that way. When I join, I want to become active—not just to enroll, pay dues and then leave and send my dues in. I don't want to be that kind of a member.

Chapter 6

===

The Replacement

"The sergeant treated me like I had killed someone."

=

David's trove of letters chronicle not only his ideological odyssey but an uneven army career defined by occasional disputes with superiors over minor disciplinary infractions. All those rules were anathema to him.

But as Ruth reminded David, arguing with his superiors wouldn't get him anywhere either as a proselytizer or as a private: "Remember what Julie told you," she wrote. "As a Communist it's up to you to set an example to the other soldiers and you can't do that if an officer bears a grudge against you."

After two months at Aberdeen, where he attended basic machine school and ordnance school, David was transferred to the South Gate General Motors plant near Los Angeles. Then, after a few weeks in the mountains at Big Pines Camp, he joined the 305th Ordnance Regiment, 3113d Ordnance Base Machine Shop at Santa Anita Race Track. He was housed in a former stable that not long before had been used for Japanese-American internees. From there, he was sent to Fort Ord, the giant installation near San Francisco, where his job was to inspect equipment being shipped overseas, and then to Pomona Ordnance Base at the Los Angeles County Fairgrounds, where he spent about three months overhauling tank motors.

David found small arms more fulfilling. He and other machinists customized weapons for officers, working at night and making twenty-five or thirty dollars per freelance job. They installed sights on hunting rifles and pieced together guns from discarded parts or sometimes from brand-new ones that were generously declared surplus. The only caveat was that they be devoid of serial numbers.

Pomona also was where David was volunteered to pick up the company's food ration at the base commissary. The company cook, a German Jew from Milwaukee, referred to his kitchen as "starvation alley" and advised David: "'First, get everything they give you. When they turn their back, take another side of beef.' I said, 'What's gonna happen?' He said, 'The sergeant will say put it back.' I said, 'What else could happen?' He said, 'Ah, if he's real nasty he could write you up; you could get court-martialed.' He said, 'On the other hand, you could get not much food to eat here.'" The incentive outweighed the risks, but David quickly realized that he could be scapegoated. After they were caught, "I called the master sergeant a schmuck," David recalled unapologetically.

> He was from Pennsylvania, so he knew the word. He says, I'm putting you in the automobile pool, on the truck pool. . . . There was this fucking guy who was from someplace down south. A Jewish brogue is what he said I had. He said, You fucking Jews, you Jew boys, he says, you are unbelievable. You think you can get the niggers on us, and stuff like that. So I said to him, I'll tell you something, you get what you deserve. He said, I'm gonna get a gun and shoot guys like you. So I went back to the master sergeant and said to him, Look, I apologize. Let me go back. He says, Why? I told him. So he let me go back.

During a barracks inspection in California, some dirt was discovered under David's bunk. Stung by the rebuke, he wrote home: "The sergeant treated me like I had killed someone."

The number of stripes on a person's sleeve impressed David less than the number of points in his IQ. "While at Dix I met four comrades and boy were they tops in their respective lines," he wrote. "One of them had 150 IQ out of a possible 153. We made quite a group." David proudly reported that he had tested at 120 himself and scored even better in mechanical aptitude. "I got one of the highest marks—133 out of 150," he wrote, which meant "I have genius rating or superior superior mechanical aptitude as is said in the army." What's more, he wrote, "these marks were made without hardly a try."

———

In California, he quickly found common ground with those fellow soldiers (and their girlfriends or wives) who fit into one or more categories: New Yorkers, leftists, and ethnic Jews, though not necessarily religious ones. After attending Jewish High Holy Days services in 1943, he was invited to the home of a refugee dermatologist and his family. He reassured Ruth: "Don't worry. They are not religious people and they are definitely radical from what I see they have in their library and how they talk about world affairs." David also chronicled in detail a bout of drunkenness with another GI and his girlfriend. He was abstaining on a day trip to Salinas until the others complained that David was "a wet rag, a sourpuss and that I was keeping them from enjoying themselves." He succumbed and got stinking drunk.

———

With David gone and Julius often away, too, Ethel and Ruth grew closer. "Your Ruthie," Ethel reported, "is one grand gal and she commands universal respect." Ethel also reported that they saw *Destination Tokyo* on a girls' night out. Ethel wrote: "She . . . manages to ingratiate herself with everyone—even your nutty brother Sam."

"Tell Ethel that I received a letter from her (if she can call it that)," David groused to Ruth. Michael had been sitting on Ethel's lap as she wrote, which might have accounted for sentences that trailed off at a twenty-degree angle and sometimes wended their way around the page. "It was quite a job deciphering her handwriting," David complained. "I really have a lot of trouble reading her mail." Ethel's theme was consistent: Tessie and Barnet were worried enough about Bernie, so much so that Barnet wasn't even told that Bernie, wounded once, was back in action. Barnet was driving Tessie crazy. Ethel berated David for giving his parents something else to worry about. She called him a "lazy son of a gun" for not writing even once a week, then denounced him as "thoughtless and neglectful" after failing to write for three weeks. "I finally asked Ruthie whether or not you were in some kind of jam or weren't feeling well," Ethel wrote. "She assured me that nothing was wrong, but that makes it doubly hard to understand your long silence."

Ethel would threaten the ultimate sanction: no letters, no cookies. And when he finally did write, Ethel replied, "You know, you really are a character, telling Mom to 'put more raisins in them next time.' Boy what a little pig."

Ethel wasn't much better about corresponding with David, although she did double duty as her parents' designated scribe. The few letters that survive avoid any mention of politics, which suggests that either Ethel was being more discreet than David in her correspondence or that Communist Party infighting and even the fate of Soviet Russia weren't high on her agenda.

The bond between Ethel and Ruth was cemented by Michael Rosenberg. Ruth attended his *bris*. Julius didn't; he was in Florida on assignment for the Signal Corps that day. Raised in a permissive household, Michael regularly called adults—including his parents—by their first names. But for a long time, Aunt Ruthie was known only by the stuffed animal that she brought him one day as a gift. Whenever Michael saw her, he shouted, "Horse!" Ruth bragged about Michael at the office, where her coworkers teased her about when she and David were going to start their own family. She wrote that a colleague piped up: "Dave will be home very soon—it will be over in a year and a half." Ruth wrote David: "Do we want to wait that long?"

The answer was no. Nearly a year after David was drafted, Ruth decided to join him in California. She found a job there at the Joshua Hendy Iron Works, not as a sweat-stained Rosie the Riveter but as a clerk. It wasn't paradise, but at least it was two months of conjugal living until David was transferred again. After returning from California in May 1944, though, Ruth informed David that they would have to wait to start their own family after all. "You are not a poppa," she wrote.

That same month, David and his company boarded a train in California that he figured would deliver them directly to an embarkation port from which they would be shipped overseas. Instead, the unit was transferred to the Mississippi Ordnance Plant (MOP). Ruth immediately tackled the visitation logistics. She determined that David could make it home from Mississippi on leave: forty-six hours and seventy-five dollars via Pullman. A few weeks later, he was granted a two-week leave, presumably his last opportunity to go home as the 613th Ordnance Base Armament Maintenance Battalion was finally being ordered overseas.

—

David left Mississippi on D day. Julius and Ethel took the Greenglasses to a Spanish restaurant on West Fifty-second Street in New York for a bon voyage dinner. David didn't expect to die or even to see combat. As he had written Ruth earlier: "My company was an ordnance company so what the hell, we're not going overseas to kill or get killed." At least he would be more directly involved in the war effort. But when David returned to Mississippi, he was shocked to discover that the battalion was going overseas without him. It was to leave July 6, stopping first at Fort McClellan, in Alabama. That same day, David, unsure of what was happening, tried nevertheless to reassure Ruth, this time about the fact that he was *not* going overseas:

> Dear, don't worry about the fact that I was taken out of my old outfit. It was a matter of politics. The First Sergeant didn't like me and, besides that, some of my politics must have reached his ears. This theory was upheld by the fact that another fellow from my former battalion, of like political opinion, was also chosen for this outfit. So you can see, dear, one of the higher-ups got rid of me.

On June 30, 1944, special orders transferred David from an armored-vehicle maintenance unit to Company B, First Battalion, Fourteenth Training Group. No reason was recorded. On July 6, 1944, another set of special orders arrived at MOP. Six soldiers, each identified by name, were ordered to report to the Special Engineer Detachment, Manhattan

District, in Oak Ridge, Tennessee. On July 14, Captain Thomas C. Spain, the classification and assignment officer of MOP, replied that one of the six soldiers was away without leave. Spain asked permission to substitute David Greenglass. On July 26, David was transferred to Oak Ridge.

———

Oak Ridge was fifty-nine thousand mostly muddy acres of red limestone, isolated in an armpit of the Appalachian foothills. This was Site X, where the government had built an entire new town and mammoth factories to refine uranium 238 into uranium 235 in order to be able to build a secret weapon. At Oak Ridge, David's impressions echoed Lincoln Steffens's of Soviet communism: Here was a government-owned-and-operated company town. It could use some lessons in tolerance but—in the South, no less—the town fathers had even recruited blacks to help out. David ecstatically wrote Ruth:

> Dear, I am watching the future here and it works. Of course, there is a lot to be done yet in the way of tolerance but on the whole everything here is rosy. It's just like the things we are fighting for. We are copying wholesale from that great scholar Karl with a k. Dearest, I am glad to be part of the wonderful future. . . . You can feel in the atmosphere a kinship brought about by the system the people live under.

After Army Intelligence delivered what David later described as a "security pep talk," he became marginally more circumspect. On July 29, he wrote Ruth:

> Dear, I am working on a classified project so you will just know about my camp life but not my work. In fact, none of my friends or relatives have to know where I am stationed. That is, of course, the ones I write to and they won't be told any more than that I am stationed here. The rest shouldn't even know that.

David dribbled out enough details, however, that Ruth was able to write, "It looks as if you'll really be working now and you need no longer feel badly about not doing your part for the war." It was also the first time that he mentioned the *Manhattan Project,* which prompted Ruth to ask:

Tell me dear does the "Manhattan" in your address mean that all the men there are from this district originally, or that they're scheduled to come here, or is it just there for the lack of a better address. Do you know yet what you'll be doing? Dear why all the secrecy this time, it excites me. I want to know what's what.

Ruth pressed further:

Darling, from what you say I have an idea of where you are. I guess you're not far from Knoxville and the T.V.A. Project. But I can't pry you with questions. . . . Julie was in the house and he told me what you must be working on. Sweets, I can't discuss with you (and certainly no one else either) but when I see you I'll tell you what I think it is and you needn't commit yourself.

David didn't commit himself, even though he wouldn't see Ruth again for nearly four months, until after Thanksgiving. After just a week at Oak Ridge, he was transferred again. In a letter composed August 4 on a westbound train from Tennessee and postmarked Kansas City, David cautioned against further speculation and announced that henceforth he would have to be more guarded in what he wrote:

Dear, I have been very reticent in my writing about what I am doing or what I am going to do because it is a classified top secrecy project and as such I can't say anything. In fact, I am not even supposed to say this much. Darling, in this type of work at my place of residence there is censorship of mail going out and all off the post calls. So dear, you know what I didn't want you to say anything on the telephone. That is why I write C. now, dear, instead of Comrade. . . .

Your husband, lover and Comrade, Dave.

P.S. . . . Not a word to anybody about anything except maybe Julie.

Chapter 7

Los Alamos

Did you ever say to Julius, Hey how did I get to Los Alamos? Did you
have anything to do with it? Was that just coincidence?

"I said it to him once. You know what he said to me? 'I don't know.'"

Was that believable?

"I think he was full of shit. What do you think, it's the first time he lied
to me?"

When else did he lie to you?

"Well, when he said to me: 'Don't worry. Everything'll be fine.'"

═

Two questions would forever dog the army about David's assignment
to Los Alamos. The first was, How did he get there? David later
suspected that his transfer from the maintenance battalion couldn't possibly have been coincidental, that some superior officer with communist connections must have slipped him past higher-ups to penetrate
America's most secret military installation. No evidence supports this
assumption.

The second question was, How did David get his security clearance?
That's easier to answer: He lied.

When he was asked to list "all clubs, societies, unions, associations,
religious affiliations or any type of organizations with which you have in
any way whatever been connected in the past," David "admitted," as the

FBI later described it, only to being a member of the United Electrical, Radio, and Machine Workers of America. He coyly omitted the Young Communist League. "Nobody ever asked if I was a communist," he said.

David didn't want any slipups. He wrote Ruth that he had listed his Uncle Izzy and three former bosses at Peerless as work references and instructed them on how to respond: "Dear, I wish you would speak to them and Izzy and let them know that I am in the Army and that I am not getting a different job. You see they are to be my references on my ability. I think they will know me as Greenglass but let them know that I am Greene. You may tell them all you know so that they will get it straight." Peerless replied to the army in a form letter that David had been employed as a turret lathe machinist and "could be reemployed by that company" should he someday reapply. Army intelligence interviewed five supervisors and coworkers. In another form letter, Brooklyn Polytechnic Institute reported that it had no record concerning David's activities or character.

The individual character references gathered by the FBI were unanimous. David's friend Normie Brown replied that he had known David for twelve years "and that his reputation for honesty and integrity was good," and volunteered that David was "mentally alert, resourceful and a true friend." Morris (Moishe) Baum, a clothier, wrote that David was "loyal, honest and a swell fellow to know." And Bea Gottesman, a neighbor from Rivington Street for ten years, said David's "reputation for honesty and integrity was good and that he had always shown initiative and was reliable and a good, sincere friend."

On September 8, 1944, an Army Corps of Engineers intelligence officer in New York reported that a personnel investigation of David Greenglass had been "completed with favorable results. All evidence indicates subject to be loyal, honest and discreet. If professionally qualified, he is recommended for employment as planned." On September 12, Major Peer de Silva, the area intelligence officer for the Corps of Engineers, advised the Technical Area at Los Alamos that David had been granted a provisional clearance to perform classified work. A week later, a memo to the district intelligence officer for the Corps of Engineers advised that David Greenglass had been granted a full security clearance.

"We tried to be extremely careful in the selection of personnel that went there," Colonel John Lansdale, Jr., a Harvard Law School graduate who had been in charge of military intelligence for the project, said later, "although as the pressure of time, as time went on and the pressure of speed became greater, these things tended to be—the care of the selection of personnel tended to be relaxed somewhat."

—

David arrived in New Mexico on August 6, 1944. That same month, at the Glenn L. Martin plant in Omaha, the air force began modifying seventeen B-29s to accommodate atomic payloads. General Leslie R. Groves, the head of the Manhattan Engineer District, figured the first bombs would be ready by mid-spring.

On the train from Tennessee, David had written Ruth that he was headed for someplace called Lamz—actually Lamy, which was the stop for Santa Fe on the railroad's main line between Chicago and Los Angeles. By shuttling passengers a half hour by bus or special train or station wagon from Lamy into Santa Fe proper, transcontinental trains could avoid climbing two thousand feet through the Glorieta Pass. Spanish explorers named the blood-red range, which frames the Rockies, the Sangre de Cristo—the blood of Christ.

The entire population of Lamy, which was several hundred on a busy day, could easily have squeezed into one New York City subway train. The tallest structure was a wooden tower, which supplied water to parched steam locomotives. The railroad station was a beige stucco Spanish mission–style building, across the street from a sprawling restaurant, which, according to local lore, had briefly held Billy the Kid while a posse, having just recaptured him, refreshed itself.

By comparison, Santa Fe was downright cosmopolitan. Some of its streets were still unpaved, but that was part of the charm that attracted tourists, even during wartime. They stayed at La Fonda, the largest hotel. They ate at the Plaza Café. They danced at the Pasatiempo. The Indian School on Cerillos Road was on few tourist itineraries. The camp on West Alameda that housed Japanese-American civilians and captured soldiers was off-limits altogether. It was not unusual for people to arrive in Santa Fe from Lamy, report to Dorothy McKibbin's cramped office at 109 East Palace Avenue, board what had once been a shiny new school bus or a station wagon driven by a soldier, and disappear into the hills to the northwest.

"When I visited Santa Fe a few months before the first test of the bomb," John Gunther, the globe-girdling author later wrote,

> the town was well aware that something strange was going on, but nobody knew what. But I heard—even then—about mysterious explosions in the nearby hills, about an inner cadre of officers who were never permitted to leave their quarters even for matters of life and death, about the incessant road traffic up the mountains under cover of night, about workers who went into those desolate hills by the thousand, and for months were not seen again.

—

Everyone in Santa Fe knew there was a secret installation on the 7,200-foot-high mesa where, until February 1943, a rugged ranch school boasting the highest tuition in the United States ($2,400 per year) had imposed its own brand of conformity on, as Gore Vidal later described it, "allegedly disturbed, allegedly rich" teenage boys—among them Gore Vidal. The school was founded in 1917 and was called Los Alamos—the poplars—after the trees that were abundant in the canyon that bordered the mesa to the south. They were making something secret up on the Pajarito Plateau, or the Hill, as Santa Feans called it. But very few people knew exactly what. "Windshield wipers for submarines," was the locals' standard rejoinder to out-of-towners. Speculation was fueled by the influx of men in suits, some of them with their families and some with unfamiliar accents. And if many of them seemed out of place in rural New Mexico, where people of Spanish and American Indian descent outnumbered non-Hispanic whites, New Mexico must have seemed equally foreign to the newcomers, who arrived bewildered but awestruck by the stunning terrain and by the kaleidoscope sky.

Los Alamos's fifty-four thousand acres—nearly four times the area of Manhattan—were nestled against the Jemez Mountains on the caldera of a dead volcano that, in its prehistoric heyday, had lobbed molten bombs as far as Kansas. Volcanic ash hardened into tuff, which the Rio Grande and its tributaries had sculpted into flat-topped mesas, from the Spanish for *table*. Flanking the mesas were barren canyons and desert dotted with piñons and junipers. Pottery shards, obsidian arrowheads, and archaeological ruins are all that remain of the first known inhabitants of Los Alamos, the Anasazi Indians, who disappeared mysteriously several centuries ago.

What common denominator could be used to make this rugged landscape familiar to people used to living on verdant campuses or in medieval cities? An orientation packet suggested they imagine "a mixture of mountain country such as you have met in other parts of the Rockies, and the adobe-housed, picturesque southwest desert that you have seen in Western movies."

—

Los Alamos met most of the original security specifications for the project. It was more than two hundred miles from any international boundary. It was isolated, to protect the installation from intruders and to safeguard the nearest neighbors from accidental detonations. Whether an atomic bomb would work at all, or whether it would touch off a chain reaction that would ignite the atmosphere and incinerate the planet, was the stuff of cold-sweat nightmares—and also of a good deal of friendly wagering among the project's physicists. Everybody agreed, though, that radiation wasn't good for you. At Los Alamos, two accidents dealt horrible reminders that radiation can kill.*

—

Sentries on horseback patrolled the perimeter. But children whose par-

---

* On August 21, 1945, Harry Daghlian was working alone in his laboratory arranging twelve-pound bricks of uranium. He accidentally created a low-grade critical assembly, burning his hands as he tried desperately to separate the bricks. He succeeded, but not before they delivered a fatal dose of radiation. Daghlian died twenty-four days later. By 1946, two lab employees had died from exposure to radiation; during the same period, six were killed in automobile accidents.

ents worked at Los Alamos (and who typically left the doors to their homes unlocked) periodically punched holes in the fence to retrieve toys and pets. "All through the war," the physicist Joseph O. Hirschfelder remembered, "the security guards left a little hole in the fence so that the Indians could climb through and come to the moving pictures (admission 12 cents), and also do their shopping in the PX."

The only secrets stolen from Los Alamos were carried out one of the two main gates. So was a turret lathe, which a machinist from one of the shops in the Technical Area arranged to sell to a stranger he had met at the bar of La Fonda in Santa Fe. The machinist unbolted the turret lathe from the floor, disassembled it, used a portable crane to maneuver it into a borrowed army truck, covered it with a tarp, and drove through the gates. He was arrested when the prospective buyer turned out to be an undercover army agent.

Inside the post, security warnings were plastered everywhere. A memo urged: "If any persons seem to you unduly curious, and above all, if they seem to be gathering information without appearing curious, report this matter to us at once. We shall not embarrass you nor any innocent person." The memo cautioned that machinists and other support staff "have signed the Espionage Act and clearance forms have been sent in for them, but we have no assurance beyond our own personal judgment that they are reliable and loyal." Finally, the memo warned: "We are extremely eager not to let the nature of the personnel and the researches become known locally, since once that is known it would not be too hard to guess what our real job is, and we would be exposed to all the hazards of espionage and sabotage which this would invite." One eye-catching poster featured a drawing of a woman emerging from the shower, her private parts covered only by a skimpy but deftly draped towel. "Don't Reveal Secret Information," the caption said. Another proclaimed: "If you question it—report it!" One poster even unambiguously defined questionable behavior: "Espionage = spying. Subversive = advocating revolution. Sedition = promoting disloyalty."

At Oak Ridge, David had signed a six-point memorandum on safeguarding information that concluded: "I certify that I have read and understand the above order and will comply throughout and that I am aware of the penalties provided for the violations thereof." At Los Alamos, every employee was also given a security lecture by army intelligence. The message was twofold: All information concerning the project was classified; disseminating that information was punishable under the Espionage Act. The Tech Area's security handbook didn't say explicitly to whom the information should not be disseminated. It referred only to the enemy.

Most Los Alamosans took the warnings seriously. Some took them as a challenge that pitted scientific ingenuity against military intransigence. The physicist Richard P. Feynman was engaged in a perpetual cat-and-mouse game in which the mouse usually won:

> One day I discovered that the workmen who lived further out and wanted to come in were too lazy to go around through the gate, and so they had cut themselves a hole in the fence. So I went out the gate, went over to the hole and came in, went out again, and so on, until the sergeant at the gate begins to wonder what's happening. How come this guy is always going out and never coming in? And, of course, his natural reaction was to call the lieutenant and try to put me in jail for doing this. I explained that there was a hole.

A second wire-mesh fence, nine and a half feet high, topped with two strands of barbed wire, and equipped with automatic alarms and sophisticated sensors, surrounded the Technical Area, which was bathed with 1,500-watt floodlights at night. High-level employees who were allowed or required to take trips away from Los Alamos were accompanied by armed military police. Fingerprints were checked with the FBI, but some scientists who had fled the Nazis were wary, and one even refused to comply. "I had no doubt that if the Germans won the war they would swiftly begin rounding up everyone in the Manhattan Project for execution," said Eugene Wigner. "And the roundup would go easier with fingerprints."

A system of code numbers for everything from driver's licenses to gasoline-ration coupons was instituted to conceal the presence of certain key personnel whose identities might suggest the nature or the scientific agenda of the project. That arrangement posed countless personal inconveniences and one overarching conflict: Project employees were required to pay income taxes, but the U.S. residents couldn't vote in the 1944 presidential election unless they had retained their registration in other states and obtained absentee ballots.

Mail was routinely censored. Certain words were verboten: *uranium, fission,* or even *physicist.* Richard Feynman was instructed to inform his wife, who was living in Albuquerque, not to complain in writing about censorship. So he wrote, "I have been instructed to inform you not to mention censorship in your letters." His letter was swiftly returned by the censors. Finally, his wife sent him an advertisement that read: "Send your boyfriend a letter on a jigsaw puzzle. We sell you the blank, you write the letter on it, take it all apart, put it in a little sack, and mail it." Her letter was accompanied by a plea from the censor: "We do not have time to play games. Please instruct your wife to confine herself to ordinary letters."

The chief security challenge, according to an official history of Los Alamos, was to reconcile two goals: "Everyone working on the project should have access to whatever information is required for doing his job competently and expeditiously. This creates the problem of preventing the dissemination of information thus obtained, and gained from others through association."

A caste system was codified by different-colored photo-ID badges. For two weeks, one researcher substituted his dog's picture for his own but was admitted to the Tech Area anyway. When a young woman was reprimanded by a guard for clipping her badge to the back pocket of her blue jeans, she replied tartly: "Why? You never look at my face." During most of the time David was assigned to Los Alamos, laborers and others allowed the least access to sensitive areas wore blue. Scientists and others with total access wore white badges. David's badge granted intermediate access. It was red.

———

David was never charged with, nor did he ever acknowledge, gaining illegal access to classified documents. But it might not have presented much of a challenge had he tried. A few months before he arrived at Los Alamos, the laboratory director, J. Robert Oppenheimer, complained that during nightly inspections of offices and laboratories as many as thirty classified documents a week were being fished from desktops and other unsecured areas. And even though some documents had been placed in safes and secure filing cabinets as required, those safes and cabinets were frequently left unlocked. Three weeks after David arrived, Oppenheimer received a memo describing security in one of the machine shops as deplorable. "The machinists know entirely too much about types of work, scheduling, end uses of parts that they are building, etc.," the memo warned, blaming the lapses on "the fact that low shop efficiency forced the scientists of the Ordnance Division into entirely too much contact with individual machinists."

"Actually," said Bernice Brode, whose husband, Robert, headed the group that designed the fusing and firing mechanism for the bomb, "anyone who had wanted to could have given away secrets." Only a few tried, which is all the more remarkable considering that so many of the scientists could have been suspects. "Think of the paradox," Laura Fermi, wife of the physicist Enrico Fermi, later wrote. "No other country but the United States would have entrusted foreigners, some of them from enemy countries, with work in the most secret project, that involved the national defense." Of the two Los Alamos alumni who would be prosecuted for atomic espionage, one was a foreigner: Klaus Fuchs, a refugee from Germany. The other one, David Greenglass, was an American soldier.

———

John Manley, an American physicist, later said of Klaus Fuchs: "He worked very hard for us, for this country. His trouble was that he worked very hard for the Russians, too." Fuchs was a communist. But the British, who knew this, never told the Americans, and U.S. Army Intelligence never investigated him independently for fear of insulting the British. Nor, General Groves later suspected, had the British thoroughly conducted their own investigation. "I have always felt," he later wrote, "that the basic reason for this was the attitude then prevalent in all British officialdom that for an Englishman treason was impossible, and that when a foreigner was granted citizenship he automatically became fully endowed with the qualities of a native-born Englishman."

Groves had a different attitude about Americans. He recognized that many of his prospective recruits had been students and teachers on university campuses during the Depression, when, as he wrote, "there was more than the usual amount of sympathy for communist and similar doctrines." Groves drew individual distinctions, though, usually on the basis of how closely a suspect had toed the party line. "To remove him would create only a greater hazard, particularly if he thought our suspicion of him unjustified," Groves explained, adding parenthetically: "I remembered that Benedict Arnold's treason had been sparked by his feeling that he had been treated unfairly."

Even someone who falsely denied ever having been arrested might be retained, "depending on his attitude when questioned, the seriousness of his arrest record, the quality of his work, his absentee record, and the need for men of his particular ability." The government drew the line, though, at anyone convicted of rape, arson, and other serious crimes that constituted presumptive evidence of a weak moral fiber. Moreover, anyone convicted of those offenses might be vulnerable to blackmail.

—

At Los Alamos, as Richard Rhodes wrote in his definitive book about the bomb, America was racing an imaginary clock.

On December 6, 1941, on the eve of the Japanese attack on Pearl Harbor, American scientists had convened in Washington to advance the atomic-bomb program from research into actual development. But in Germany, several elements conspired to irrevocably shift industrial resources from a theoretically feasible atom bomb that might destroy a whole city—more efficiently, though not necessarily inflicting greater devastation, than the subsequent Allied carpet bombing—to increasingly promising guided missiles that might finally force Britain to submit. The scientific solution to building a superbomb was already in hand, the Nobel laureate Werner Heisenberg declared, but the technical prerequisites would take two to four years for production to begin.

The German weapons project was confined to treading water, albeit "heavy water"—a compound in which water's oxygen was replaced with painful slowness by deuterium in order to be able to moderate a fission reaction—at an existing plant in Vemork, Norway. On February 27, 1943, Norwegian commandos dispatched from Britain sabotaged the installation. About one year later, after an Allied air raid destroyed the site's power plant, the Nazis prepared to transplant the operation to Germany, including the cache of heavy water, which was transported in thirty-nine drums labeled POTASH-LYE. On February 20, 1944, an Allied saboteur's time bomb pierced the hull of the ferryboat *Hydro* and sent the drums of heavy water tumbling to the bottom of Norway's Lake Tinnsj.

General Groves was charged not only with inventing a bomb but with monitoring—and disabling—the Nazis' efforts to invent one first. In the vanguard of the Allied invasion, a Manhattan Project counterintelligence force swept through the Black Forest and captured Otto Hahn, who with Fritz Strassman had first split the uranium atom in 1938, and Heisenberg himself. Samuel Goudsmit, a University of Michigan physicist and the scientific director of the mission, later recalled, "Sometimes we wondered if our government had not spent more money on our intelligence mission than the Germans had spent on their whole project."

———

The Russians began building their bomb in 1939. Soviet scientists suspected that fission research was already being conducted in Germany—then putatively an ally. By 1940, they also suspected a research program was under way in the United States. One by one, the names of leading American scientists had been vanishing from the most prestigious technical journals. "[I] remember [G. N.] Flerov's paper on the spontaneous fission rate of uranium-238 in 1940," the Canadian physicist J. Carson Mark later recalled. "He reported his work in the *Physical Review* and didn't get a rise out of any American physicist. . . . He then said, 'Gee, the Americans didn't comment on this. That's the kind of thing they would have gotten very excited about six months ago. They must be working on something secret.'"

"Secrecy," Richard Rhodes wrote, "itself gave the secret away."

Chapter 8

===================

The Go-Between

"We are going to Santa Fe or Albuquerque in a week or two so that we can watch the Indian silversmiths at work and steal some of their secrets."

===

David couldn't have arrived at Los Alamos at a more propitious moment. The Manhattan Project needed machinists. The Soviet Union needed another spy.

At about the time that David surfaced as a potential source—no matter how minor—at the prime target of Soviet espionage, the NKGB's most promising prospect suddenly had gone incommunicado.* The Soviet courier Harry Gold had lost contact with Klaus Fuchs. Ironically, the communications gap proved to be temporary and fortuitous: Fuchs was being transferred to Los Alamos and would arrive there a week after David did. (And Ted Hall, a young graduate student at the University of Chicago on leave from Los Alamos, was still a few months away from

---

* The Soviet state security services went by numerous names after the Bolshevik revolution, including but not limited to the Cheka, the GPU, the OGPU, the NKVD, the NKGB, the MGB, and the KGB; NKGB is used here for uniformity.

volunteering vital scientific information to a Soviet journalist who doubled as an espionage agent.) Suddenly the Soviets were presented with another opportunity in the person of David.

Two opportunities, actually.

A few months earlier, Julius had been asked casually by his Soviet contact, Alexander Feklisov, to suggest a safe house that could be used by agents to duplicate secret documents and for other covert operations. The matter might have been discussed over the summer, perhaps when the Rosenbergs vacationed with Ruth at Budd Lake, New Jersey. In September, with David away from home indefinitely, Julius suggested the Greenglasses' apartment.

Feklisov delivered Julius's suggestion to his superior, Leonid Kvasnikov. At about the same time, Feklisov later recalled, Julius reported David's vague description of his whereabouts: a secret installation in New Mexico perched on a six-thousand-foot-high plateau. Soviet agents in New York, including Kvasnikov and Anatoly Yakovlev, recognized the site. In fact, the Soviets had already given the installation a code name that reflected their assessment of the American commitment and of the project's potential. They called it Enormous.

Fate had intervened, and Julius was beside himself, Feklisov recalled:

> By mid-1944 Libi [a diminutive of Julius's code name, Liberal] had been well into his assumed role of an omnipotent recruiter. Blessed with friends who shared his views and attitudes he developed an idea that all his friends were our potential recruits. And the Greenglasses seemed a perfect target! Idealistic Libi had no doubts in his beloved wife's younger brother. And David's newlywed wife Ruth might have won his favor with her demonstrated left-wing enthusiasm and activism in a Young Communists' cell.

Julius trusted David. He believed in him so completely that in 1944 when Feklisov fretted that a twenty-two-year-old college dropout was too immature to be entrusted with keeping secrets, much less stealing them, Julius replied: "Why? How can you doubt. He is a one hundred percent reliable guy devoted to our cause and would never fail us—and he is our relative. I will give my right hand to be chopped if he lets us down." Feklisov also said Julius trusted Ruth equally.

Years later, Feklisov divorced himself altogether from the decision to recruit David. He said he had questioned David's youth and immaturity, the fact that he "had not yet seen life, had no practical experience." Feklisov insisted that "from the very beginning, I had no great enthusiasm—to say the least—in involving David Greenglass," though his colleagues did. Yakovlev, said Feklisov, had been "unable to hide his excitement."

"To me the figure of a 21 year old mechanic seemed so irrelevant that I did not give any great importance to Libi's initial suggestion," Feklisov said. "But . . . Kvasnikov saw David's young age . . . as an asset: with time and training he could be developed into a valuable source."

The safe-house suggestion was shelved. Instead, Soviet agents in New York sought permission to recruit Ruth as an intermediary who could enlist David and then, without arousing suspicion, move to New Mexico to serve as his courier. On September 21, 1944, the station chief in New York cabled Lieutenant General Pavel M. Fitin, the NKGB intelligence-service director in Moscow, to relay Julius's offer and to recommend "the wife of his wife's brother." The cable characterized her as an "intelligent and clever girl" and David as "a mechanical engineer . . . now working at the Enormous plant in Santa Fe, New Mexico," and as a member of the Communist Party.

On October 3, 1944, the NKGB's Moscow Center granted the New York station's request to recruit Ruth and David. Moscow recommended Harry Gold as their contact and assigned them noms de guerre. Ruth was given the code name Osa, which is Russian for *wasp*. David was called Shmel (bumblebee), and later Kalibr.* In both English and Russian, *caliber* can mean either the diameter of a bullet or a person's degree of worth.

———

* Bizarrely, this also was the onetime code name of the American journalist Walter Lippmann.

Julius had recruited Ruth as a go-between. The bureaucrats in Moscow had granted their approval. But nobody had told—or even asked—David.

From Los Alamos, David's letters still gushed with thinly veiled encomiums to communism. In retrospect, two of those missives seem decidedly cryptic, but there may be less there than meets the eye. One, dated October 23, 1944, stated: "I went to speak to that person I told you about. Well, the outcome of that was that I should see him Thursday or Friday and he would let me know then. I have every confidence dear so don't worry." David later suggested that the conversation probably concerned a promotion or a leave, not espionage. A second letter, dated November 4, 1944, concluded: "My darling, I most certainly will be glad to be part of the community project that Julius and his friends have in mind. Count me in dear or should I say it has my vote. If it has yours, count us in."

David's letters were also resonant with patriotism. After attending a screening of *Dragon Seed,* Pearl Buck's wrenching tale of a Chinese family and nation torn asunder by the Japanese invasion, he wrote: "I felt such intense anger and dissatisfaction with everything. I wanted to be over there fighting, killing Japanese fascist vermin." The letters also hinted at a larcenous streak. David wrote that he and a barracksmate were "going to Santa Fe or Albuquerque in a week or two so that we can watch the Indian silversmiths at work and steal some of their secrets."

With their second wedding anniversary approaching, David and Ruth had been separated longer than at any time since they had gotten married. David cobbled together a few days' leave and summoned Ruth to Albuquerque. Lamenting that he had missed another pro-Soviet rally at Madison Square Garden, he wrote: "The two of us together at such a meeting is like building the future." That political future, he suggested, would unfold with the 1948 presidential election. By then, he wrote, presumably referring to their progeny, "we should have made our contributions to the world, at least one such contribution." On October 31, 1944, Ruth wrote:

David dearest I'm very excited about going to see you. I think of little else. . . . Time was when people said it's wonderful to have a husband—

that's been altered slightly to it's wonderful to see your husband. . . . The next four weeks are going to seem like a lifetime.

Two weeks later, Ruth wrote David that she had traipsed around with the Rosenbergs all day and joined them for dinner, "and I needn't say that I thoroughly enjoyed myself." Responding, in part, to Feklisov's wariness about the dependability of the Greenglasses, Julius provided his own account of that evening. In Julius's version, Ruth was depicted as a much more willing accomplice than she later portrayed herself to be. In a stilted third-person account forwarded to Moscow by Feklisov, Julius described a conversation that in some respects was strikingly similar to Ruth's version:

First of all, Julius inquired of Ruth how she felt about the Soviet Union and how deep in general her communist convictions went, whereupon she replied without hesitation that to her, socialism was the sole hope of the world and the Soviet Union commanded her deepest admiration.

Julius then wanted to know whether she would be willing to help the Soviet Union. She replied very simply and sincerely that it would be a privilege; when Ethel mentioned David, she assured us that her judgment was also David's understanding.

Julius then explained his connections with certain people interested in supplying the Soviet Union with urgently needed technical information it could not obtain through the regular channels and impressed upon her the tremendous importance of the project in which David is now at work. Therefore, she was to ask him the following kinds of questions:

1. How many people were now employed there?
2. What part of the project was already in operation, if any; were they encountering any difficulties and why; how were they resolving their problems?
3. How much of an area did the present set-up cover?
4. How many buildings were there and their layout; were they going to build any more?
5. How well guarded was the place?

Julius then instructed her that under no circumstances should they discuss any of these things inside a room or indeed anywhere except out-of-doors and under no circumstances to make any notes of any kind. She was simply to commit to memory as much as possible. Ethel here interposed to stress the need for the utmost care and caution in informing David of the work in which Julius was engaged and that, for his own safety, all other political discussion and activity on his part should be subdued.

At this point, we asked Ruth to repeat our instructions which she did satisfactorily.

Four days after this dinner, New York cabled the NKGB's Moscow Center that Ruth had agreed to cooperate.

———

After dinner with Ruth, Ethel finally caught up on her correspondence with David. In earlier letters, David had boasted about his growing success at poker. But his boasts were soon belied by frequent appeals for more money—another ten dollars here, another twenty there. In those appeals and in David's reluctance to write, Tessie Greenglass may have seen a painful parallel between her husband's own financial failures and her youngest son's refusal to grow up. Finally, she exploded. Which is why Ethel, playing the uncharacteristic role of peacemaker, wrote to her brother that November 23: "Dear Davey, Mom herewith apologizes for her slur on your character. It will never happen again, she assures you."

Three of David's letters to Ethel had gone unanswered. She was preoccupied with Michael as usual, and her chronic back pain, coupled with low blood pressure, made her tire so easily that she had hired a housekeeper. Julius was busier than ever, too, working overtime for the Signal Corps and, according to Soviet cables, frustrated by his inability to carry out even the elementary photography required to duplicate secret documents. Ethel wrote David that doing justice to Michael's latest exploits would require a letter in itself, and that meanwhile "an earful" from Ruth would have to suffice. "When you are in on furlough in January we hope, we hope, we hope, you'll get information as to his doings and development at first hand." Ethel added that Tessie was sending cookies to satisfy David's "insatiable appetite." (A cake she sent was inedible; a rat got to it first.) Julius sent his love. And, almost as an afterthought, Ethel wrote: "Incidentally, we all wish you a very happy anniversary. May all future ones be celebrated in a home of your own choosing."

Ethel's letter didn't mention the dinner with Ruth (unless her references to Michael were really encrypted instructions). And if there were any messages hidden in the letter at all, they got to Los Alamos late. The air-mail letter was returned to Ethel for insufficient postage.

———

David pronounced himself "giddy with delight" anticipating Ruth's trip but reminded her: "The room will cost four dollars per day, so come prepared." She did: Julius provided her with $150 for expenses. That would more than cover the difference between riding in coach to New Mexico ($98 round-trip) and riding in Pullman ($170), as David wanted her to do. She wrote David that she would try to get a reservation from Chicago on the Santa Fe's El Capitan streamliner (the only Santa Fe train that would not accept corpses), which left at 5:45 P.M. and arrived in Albuquerque at 3 P.M. the following afternoon. No train could be swift enough, though.

"I wish," Ruth wrote, "I could sprout wings and go to you."

Chapter 9

Route 66

"Tell him, I'll do it."

≡

Thanksgiving leftovers were only just being recycled, but in the spirit of Christmas shopping Levine's department store in Albuquerque was already pushing rayon panties at two for a dollar. The first flurries were drifting in New Mexico's afternoon sky. But because of the war, few holiday lights were splayed across the Central Avenue storefronts. About the only glimmer of Christmas color visible was at the few intersections where traffic lights glowed alternately red and green, defining the short stretch of Route 66.

The *Albuquerque Journal* and *Herald* were still publishing daily ledgers of local boys killed overseas. But with American troops now poised at the Rhine, American planes bombing Japan, and with Roosevelt reelected, the transplanted retirees, the TB patients who had come for the cure, the soldiers and their families in the surrounding army camps, and the nisei farmers whose forebears had emigrated from Japan generations ago but whose vegetables were being boycotted by local merchants were praying that this might be the last Christmas before peace on earth returned and a brave new world would dawn.

—

Ruth left New York on Friday, November 24, the day after Thanksgiving, just to be sure that what with erratic wartime schedules and military priorities, she wouldn't miss a day with David. She spent Saturday in Chicago, jockeying for a connection to Albuquerque and biding time in between. She bought a hat at Marshall Field's, then ducked into a movie theater and cried through *Since You Went Away*.

Every seat on every westbound Santa Fe Railroad train from Chicago was accounted for. Ruth even called the airport; the few scheduled flights were full, too. She returned to the railroad ticket window and waited. As the line inched forward, she could overhear the same ritual duet performed by would-be passengers and the ticket clerk before each disappointed prospective purchaser slinked away or stomped off. Ruth got lucky. With forty minutes left before the El Capitan was scheduled to depart, a last-minute cancellation freed up one seat. "I was never so relieved in all my life," Ruth wrote.

Nearly twenty-four hours later, at 4 P.M. Sunday, she arrived at the Santa Fe depot on Silver Avenue in Albuquerque and immediately checked into the Franciscan, the oversize faux-adobe hotel that she had wired from Chicago to advance her reservation. She unpacked in her tiny room near the elevator, then went for a stroll down Central Avenue, past Cook Sporting Goods, dominated by a sign in the shape of a rifle—but the size of a howitzer—pointing skyward and past the Charles of Manhattan Beauty Shop. She saw her second movie in two days—this time, *Hail the Conquering Hero*. By Sunday evening, she had personalized the pleasant but anonymous room by placing David's photograph on the sturdy wooden desk, where she sat down at 9:30 P.M. to write him one more letter before his scheduled arrival there on Wednesday. As she was leaving New York, five of David's daily letters had arrived in a bunch, and, rather than waste time on trivialities once they were finally together, Ruth figured she would dispose of as many of his questions as possible in advance. "I definitely did not get fat in spite of your dream (now I can be sure dreams are phony) but you'll see for yourself," she wrote. She said she brought along David's sweater and scarf, obviously alerted to the vagaries of New Mexico weather. (The year before, it had snowed as late as May 9, and one storm, a more seasonable one, had dumped several feet of snow on Los Alamos overnight.) Ruth also reassured David that even if she was jeopardizing her job to visit him, it was worth it: "David darling please don't be a worrier. You're always telling me that then you turn right around and do the same thing. What does it matter if I lose my job. I've been wanting to quit for a hell of a long time . . . after all dear I'm not really a war worker."

Her five-page letter was embossed with the familiar red lips—at least half a dozen pairs of them puckered up in a variety of suggestive positions and pressed to the paper. The letter ended with three postscripts:

"You are my reason for being.

"Come quick, I miss you so.

"See you Wednesday—do something to make Father Time hurry, he's awfully slow just now."

All five pages were on Franciscan stationery, which featured a rendering of the 142-room building on the top and its credo on the bottom: "The Most Unique Hotel in the World." Just beneath that slogan, Ruth scribbled an addendum: "What does it matter without you?"

———

Father Time took Monday and Tuesday off. Ruth went window-shopping and caught up on the news: Stalin signaled the start of a new propaganda war by denouncing Japan as an "aggressive nation," though Russia was still abiding by its neutrality pact with the Japanese; an investigation was winding up into whether any commanders should be court-martialed for negligence at Pearl Harbor; a cabinet committee was completing a lengthy report that documented Nazi atrocities; and Colonel Elliott Roosevelt, the president's second son, was preparing to marry the actress Faye Emerson on the rim of the Grand Canyon. Except for the ubiquitous Indian souvenirs and a limitless variety of items crafted from turquoise and silver, the advertisements didn't seem to promise much that Ruth couldn't buy for less in New York. The New Mexico Book Store was offering a brand-new release, though: the new illustrated Modern Library version of Dostoyevsky's *Crime and Punishment*.

———

David arrived in Albuquerque on Wednesday morning, dusty and rumpled after the nearly three-hour ride from Los Alamos in a borrowed car. First, he stopped at Maisel's Indian Trading Post on West Central and bought Ruth a twenty-dollar turquoise-and-silver ring for their anniversary. Because Ruth's letter hadn't arrived in Los Alamos by the time he had left, David trudged from one hotel to another until he found her at the Franciscan. The elevator next to Ruth's room whirred and rattled all night, but it didn't disturb David and Ruth one bit. David was twenty-two, and Ruth was twenty. As he later explained, "I was a soldier on leave!" The mission from Julius was also the thing furthest from Ruth's mind.

———

On the afternoon of Saturday, December 2, 1944, when most of their fellow hotel guests were huddled in the lobby listening to the Army-Navy game on KGGM, David and Ruth Greenglass went for a short walk. It was to rupture their lives and transform history. Arm in arm—David in his khaki dress uniform and Ruth in a gold-colored skirt and matching jacket—they strolled down Central Avenue, past the stores and holiday shoppers, past the zoo and the baseball diamond at Tingley Park and its ersatz white-sand beach flanking a freshwater lagoon. Workmen were tacking up the bunting for Monday's war-bond rally, which, as the *Albuquerque Journal* reported, would thrill schoolchildren with a simulated battle complete with "pretty pink clouds from a smoke bomb" and a demonstration of real flamethrowers that produced twenty-foot-high sheets of fire. David and Ruth meandered toward the sluggish, brown rivulet that, in season, had been the mighty Rio Grande. They talked about their families and about election night a few weeks earlier, when David had been riveted to the radio into the early morning. With Roosevelt elected to a fourth term, he wrote Ruth, who still wasn't old enough to vote, "Now we can look to the future without fear of seeing a new war there. But we must always be vigilant. The price of democracy is ceaseless vigil." (David added rhetorically: "Did Sammy vote for Dewey? I'll never be able to understand his stupid viewpoint.") With only one day left in their extended anniversary weekend, politics provided Ruth with the perfect segue. As David recalled, Ruth got right to the point.

"I have a message from Julius," Ruth began.

He tells me you're working on a supersecret thing. And he would like this information to be transmitted to his friends. He said the Russians were our allies. We should really help them. And the bomb that's being made will be a tremendous help to them. It's not fair that the United States should keep it a secret. They're allies. They're fighting on the same side. He said, "If all the nations had the information, then one nation couldn't use the bomb as a threat against another."

"It's your choice," Ruth said. "I'm not really happy with it."
Her husband really was.
"Tell him," David said, "I'll do it."
"Well," Ruth replied, "if you want to."

—

Ruth may not have been the zealous spy that Julius depicted. But nor was she, in fact, as reluctant a coconspirator as she has subsequently presented herself. If she really was reluctant, even frightened by the prospect of taking foreign policy into her own hands, why did she? One reason, perhaps, was that she was unsure how her husband would respond. Would an indolent young man who had refused to join the Communist Party because he was unwilling to get up early really be amenable to stealing the blueprints for the atomic bomb? Would a college dropout whose words always outstripped his actions eagerly pitch in to transmit those plans to America's most incongruous wartime ally, the Russians? Maybe David would reject Julius's invitation. Then, Ruth could have the best of both worlds: She would have redeemed her obligation to Ethel and Julius to deliver the message; and she would have fulfilled her own hopes that David would dissuade himself. Then again, maybe she protested too much. Conspiracy was a legalism that even many lawyers didn't understand, but apparently it never occurred to Ruth that merely delivering the message to David was illegal—or even patently improper.

—

The sun was setting behind the purple cones of extinct volcanoes as the Greenglasses returned to the Franciscan that evening. For dinner, Ruth changed into a dress with a sweetheart neckline—David's favorite. Afterward, he rattled off the answers to Ruth's questions. "She asked me to tell her about the general layout of the Los Alamos atomic project, the buildings, number of people, and stuff like that; also scientists that worked there, and that was the first information I gave her." He provided the names of Harold C. Urey and Robert Oppenheimer and of "Nicholas Baker," whose real name, David had learned, was Niels Bohr, the Danish theoretical physicist who had fled the Nazis the year before. Knowledge of Bohr's very presence in New Mexico might suggest to Soviet scientists which course of atomic research the Americans were pursuing. Then David instructed Ruth to repeat what he had told her and to memorize it.

David and Ruth walked the few blocks to the KiMo, which proclaimed itself "America's Foremost Indian Theatre," to see *Tall in the Saddle,* the John Wayne film, featuring Ella Raines and Gabby Hayes, about a laconic, woman-hating cowboy who is framed for a crime he didn't commit. The Western was coupled with a newsreel. Also, there was a trailer for the KiMo's next offering, *The Conspirators,* a spy melodrama with Hedy Lamarr and Paul Henreid that one reviewer mocked as "a travesty on international intrigue."

—

On Monday morning, David slipped out of the Franciscan before dawn. It was snowing. He climbed into a borrowed car and drove off with new determination—to Algodones, where the two-lane highway veers northeast toward Santa Fe, then to Pojoaque and left on Route 4, past abandoned pueblos and arid plateaus honeycombed with caves and covered by rabbit brush and Apache plume, over the wooden suspension bridge spanning the Rio Grande at Otowi, and past Wait's Tea Room. The last twelve miles were the most rugged: sequential hairpin turns on a narrow, washboard road, lined with sentrylike boulders, that rose, winding, two thousand feet from the canyon to the crescent-shaped Los Alamos plateau.

David slowed at the gate, where a large sign warned visitors to stop and show their badges. He continued for three more miles, parked at the barracks, changed hurriedly into fatigues, and briskly walked the nearly two miles to the second barbed-wire perimeter that defined the Technical Area. It was too late for breakfast, but he grabbed a copy of the Los Alamos *Bulletin* to make sure there was nothing else he had missed. For one thing, he found that he had returned to camp in time to catch *Above Suspicion* that night, starring Joan Crawford and Fred MacMurray. David went directly to Theta Shop, where he and other machinists were embodying abstract formulas as the precise metal components of the world's first atomic bomb.

—

As David was beginning his first day as a spy, army censors were processing a letter from Ethel—this one addressed to David and Ruth in New Mexico. Dated December 6, Ethel's letter reported, without elaborating, that "we received your telegrams and your letter." She mentioned nothing about Ruth's mission but posed three seemingly innocuous questions: "Have you received the package of cookies we sent you?" And, "How are things working out with you. Are you spending the time enjoyably? I guess so."

Ruth was getting ready to leave the Franciscan for the Santa Fe depot and to buy a coach seat on the California Limited. It was 3 P.M. Monday, and she had already checked out of her room, to avoid extra charges. While seated in the hotel lobby surrounded by luggage, Ruth had begun a letter to David by apologizing for her sloppy handwriting—the chair's arms were too narrow to make much of a desktop. Then she reflected on the joyous few days they had just shared: "I should be used to it by now but every time we say good-bye it's just as hard," Ruth wrote. "Can't help it dear, we were meant to be together for always." She still hadn't gotten a train reservation, but was determined to leave that night. "Darling when I've been somewhere with you I just can't get myself to stay on without you."

By midmorning, it was snowing, just as David had predicted—"it seems to me you're almost always right. I've got a lot to learn to even catch up with you"—and Ruth worried that he might catch cold. "Good health is ultra-important to being a good father (soon, I hope)," she reminded him. Ruth also promised to restock his larder at Los Alamos with "nasherei" so that he and his friends wouldn't have to resort to "fish and such stuff" in the mess hall. She promised to write from Chicago, perhaps even sooner: "Life has been good to us dearest except for the interval you've been in the Army, and although that did break things up, we've been kind of lucky and we have a whole lifetime before us to continue making memories."

Taking her cue from David's code, she signed the letter, "Your wife, C, and sweetheart."

—

Ruth's trip from New Mexico early that December was worse than the one going out. The train that left Albuquerque Monday evening was stranded with a burned-out cylinder in Newton, Kansas. She finally got to New York on Thursday night. She wrote David: "You see, sweets, I got home (I don't really think of any place as home unless I am with you. It is our house until you come home and then it takes on a new air and is truly home.) at about 9:30 P.M. and was a little *fa-tumult*, saying hello to everyone and so on."

That weekend, Julius dropped by the Greenglasses' apartment on Stanton Street. As usual, he came alone.

"He was almost always alone," Ruth said later. "He asked me if I had spoken to David, and what he had to say, and then I told him that David consented to do this and I wrote down the things he had told me as best as I could remember." Julius, Ruth recalled, "said he would see David when he came home on furlough, whenever that would be."

David was beginning to wonder when it would be, too. On December 4, the day that Ruth left for New York, David got some perturbing news. The furlough he was expecting, his first in nearly six months, had evidently been postponed. "I am damned angry," David wrote Ruth, "and if they think I won't do anything about it they're crazy."

Chapter 10

I Spy

"I visualize things—that's what I do for a living."

═

David Greenglass cozied up to his first espionage contact because their commanding officer banned pinups from the barracks. The arbitrary order was a challenge to any red-blooded GI, and Ben Bederson and Bill Spindel, two of David's barracksmates who unwittingly became his sources for scientific secrets, responded in kind. Spindel pinned up a life-size photograph of Franklin D. Roosevelt, from one of Bederson's copies of P.M., the left-wing tabloid. And lest anyone order this pinup removed, Spindel affixed a caption in large block letters: COMMANDER-IN-CHIEF.

David and Bederson had bunks within whispering distance of each other, but the pinup episode was David's first insight into Bederson's politics. He was tall, blond, from the Bronx, and twenty-three years old. As a child, he had lived in Russia for six months while his father opened a huge cafeteria in a Moscow factory. He played in an International Workers Order drum-and-bugle corps but had been disappointed in the Young Communist League because it "seemed primarily interested in distributing leaflets and did not seem to be accomplishing anything of a constructive nature re social problems."

The previous spring, Bederson and a private, Irving Schmolka, got themselves into a jam with the army after they politely, but pointedly, posed a question to the Surgeon General of the United States. In a letter from Los Alamos, they inquired "whether or not you are carrying out one of Hitler's (and Fascism's) Doctrines in segregating the blood plasma of Negroes and whites?" Within a week, they received a disarmingly candid reply from Major F. N. Schwartz of the Medical Administration Corps. While there was no scientific basis to separate blood plasma, he wrote, many whites would object to having Negro blood injected into their veins. Schwartz acknowledged that the objection might indeed be the result of prejudice and ignorance. Bederson and Schmolka thanked him for "a very interesting answer, and the frank explanation" and added: "Since it is so unusual, we ask your permission to make it available for public consumption by releasing it to the Press." The government wouldn't bite. Instead, Schmolka was transferred.[*]

This, coupled with the fact that Bederson began soliciting contributions for the Roosevelt campaign and that his family lived in a union-sponsored cooperative apartment in the Bronx, catapulted him onto David's list of potential sources for classified information and made him one of the eighteen or nineteen he targeted as possible fellow spies.

—

David was a member of the Special Engineer Detachment, a ragtag mix of technicians, graduate students, and junior scientists who had already been in the armed forces or for whom the War Department had been unable to request deferments without betraying the Manhattan Project's supersecret status. More than one in four had a college or graduate-school degree, usually in engineering, chemistry, physics, or mathematics. Many of them had never undergone basic training. Many were big-city boys and alumni of Depression-era university campuses where, as General Groves had acknowledged, "there was more than the usual amount of sympathy for communist and similar doctrines." That David

---

[*] With few exceptions, soldiers assigned to Los Alamos weren't transferred to other installations or to combat, for security reasons.

was later described as the fulcrum of the sympathizers' shockingly public political plotting was largely a consequence of the fact that he, more than any of the others, not only acted out his radical fantasies but eventually got caught.

In one stanza to a ballad called "Los Alamos Blues," an anonymous member of the Special Engineer Detachment wrote:

> We're on a secret mission
> And secret work we do
> Where we're not to tell folks what we know.
> But I don't know, do you?

In fact, a foreman, Hugh Holland, said, Los Alamos employees came and went practically at will and talked freely among themselves, assuming each had been cleared and could be trusted. It was, Holland explained, "common knowledge among workers" that the equipment they were using to engineer and design prototypes was being used "to make tests on a bomb."

The Special Engineer Detachment barracks at Los Alamos were less akin to a furtive communist cell, though, than to a rowdy college dormitory. "No, I'm not in Albuquerque," David reassured Ruth, despite the return address on the letterhead. "It's just that I'm writing on Benny's pilfered stationery." Then he proceeded to the important news: "Tonight instead of eating Army food, we that is Hy, Ben and myself had ourselves a meal of sardines, anchovies, Toll House cookies and (bah) milk." Political bull sessions had their place, of course, but the chief source of oral gratification in the barracks was food. And while David sometimes admitted to saving some special goodie just for himself, the salamis and homemade cakes that Tessie Greenglass shipped from Sheriff Street endowed him with a magnetism that his personality and his politics did not always provide.

The scientists and technicians who bunked there played craps in the latrine. They transformed a corridor into a bowling alley, substituting beer bottles for wooden pins. Their mascot was a grungy mutt that answered to Dusty. Bathroom humor inevitably intruded in lofty debates about socialist dogma, genocide—by the Nazis, by the Russians, by the Allies in firebombing German cities, and, potentially, by the Americans in Japan—and the peacetime potential of nuclear power, especially because one of the barrackmates was a chemist whose sole job was to test human feces for traces of radioactivity.

Outsiders greeted most of the carryings-on with disdain—"They were all filthy in their personal habits," one soldier said of David and some of his friends—rather than with outright suspicion. "We were," Ben Bederson admitted later, "the sloppiest guys in the army."

Members of the Special Engineer Detachment lived up to the division's name. They were special, surely, by the standards imposed on ordinary GIs. And as time went on, their detachment from the customary strictures of military discipline became almost complete. They weren't slackers. They often worked late at night in the shops and laboratories—well beyond their official shifts. But not always on official business. A War Department circular warned that government property was reserved solely for actual work in progress and that "a contrary application for the advantage, comfort, convenience or pleasure of any person is strictly prohibited." That warning was routinely flouted. David and his fellow machinists fabricated radios, phonographs, and other jury-rigged devices.

In August 1944, the month that David arrived, Major T. O. Palmer, the new commanding officer of the SED, mercifully ended the morning bugle call and calisthenics.

"We weren't disciplined at all," David said. "Los Alamos was the least army place I've ever been in my life."

Bernice Brode recalled an early, formal military review on the baseball field in front of Fuller Lodge, an oversize log cabin left over from the Los Alamos school:

All of us came with our children to see the show. The MP's, the post soldiers, the Women's Army Corps and even the doctors made a fine upright showing as they marched across the field, but the newly-arrived SED boys were terrible. They couldn't keep in step. Their lines were crooked. They didn't stand properly. They waved at friends and grinned. The situation was not helped by the fact that they received the loudest applause from the bleachers. The visiting brass let it be known that they were displeased, and one general even called them a disgrace to the Army.

Once, she wrote, a drill sergeant became so frustrated that he allowed a member of the SED to substitute for him momentarily:

He shouted orders in imitation of the sergeant's voice: "Thumbs up, thumbs down. Thumbs wiggle-waggle." Even the sergeant broke down and dismissed them. . . . The drill stopped and the inspection let go so they could sleep in the morning.

Discipline wasn't much better on the firing line. (David had already earned his marksman's medal anyway.) Phyllis Fisher, a social worker whose husband, Leon, was a physicist, never forgot that what ordinarily might have been solely a military matter generated a larger constituency.

They seemed to be shooting at random in every direction but at the targets. Children were picking up spent shells all over the grounds surrounding the range. Concerned moms protested at the town council and to the military command, but with no success. It looked as though the rifle range was there to stay until one fortuitous, glorious day when a fire burned it completely to the ground. It was never rebuilt.

The blaze was blamed on a GI who had accidentally dropped his lit cigarette into an oil pit that had been dug beneath the targets to capture those few spent slugs that actually landed in their vicinity. Without conventional bullets whizzing by indiscriminately, the community with the goal of producing a weapon of unprecedented mass destruction suddenly felt much safer from friendly fire.

———

During his brief exposure to Oak Ridge, David had likened the degree to which government provided for everyone there to that of a socialist paradise. He never made the same claim about Los Alamos, where, compared to the regular army, the SED was a privileged group. But its members were still relegated to second-class status behind civilian scientists and their families. The disparities, according to the official army history, "severely strained the morale of many junior scientists and technicians." Spouses of the more senior civilian scientists were allowed to work at Los Alamos and even to live there in apartments that, while primitive, were better than barracks (although the squat furnaces, fired by New Mexican soft coal, generated so much heat that walls were sometimes too hot to touch and coated Los Alamos with a fine layer of soot). Housing was assigned strictly according to the number of family members, and rent was calculated as a percentage of salary. Yet among the most privileged Los Alamosans some saw and feared the egalitarianism that David had found so fetching at Oak Ridge, seeing in it dogmatic Marxism. The army was running Los Alamos "on a socialist basis," Laura Fermi complained. It was, she said, "the closest I have seen in America to a communistic type of living on a somewhat large scale."

—

A Manhattan Project alumnus once said that for scientists Los Alamos had the same allure that Hollywood had for starlets. Real-life spying, on the other hand, proved to be more tedious than what Hollywood portrayed. David did not rifle desks to ferret out atomic secrets. He didn't have to. "Guys were all around me," he said. "I just listened. Stuff was in the shop; I didn't miss it. I visualize things—that's what I do for a living. I just stored it in my head."

He devoted only so much energy to distinguishing one high-exposure lens curve from another, though. Or to espionage altogether. He already had a full-time job at Los Alamos, and by all accounts he performed it conscientiously. "You know, Le Carré gets to everybody—they think that a guy who's a spy, it's on his mind all the time," David said. "I had other things to do. In my case, I would spy at the opportune moment, and that's it."

By questioning Ben Bederson, David said, he learned details about the trigger mechanism and the capacitors, which produce the sparks that detonate the conventional explosives arranged around the plutonium heart of the atomic bomb. Bederson later told the FBI he couldn't recall ever telling David anything about the bomb, "but that it is probable he did do this, as he undoubtedly would have told Greenglass what the items were that he was working on had Greenglass inquired."

From Manny Schwartz, a Canadian-born mathematician from Chicago, David ascertained what he later described as the exact amount of plutonium necessary to produce a critical mass. "Manny Schwartz told me that a B-29 had to be refitted for the bomb, but the exploding material was only about the size of a baseball," David said. Schwartz was five years older than David and lived with his wife in a Los Alamos apartment. He was a math whiz who virtually disappeared into the world of numbers for hours or days at a time until the solution to some particularly vexing equation presented itself. David and he sometimes met for coffee or went hiking. They had dinner at the Schwartzes' apartment with other buddies. And from time to time, someone made a passing reference to an unfamiliar technical term or to the latest rumor that another refugee scientist had arrived, and David's curiosity would kick in.

Charles Critchfield, a physicist, later said that David might even have gotten himself invited to some of the weekly scientific colloquiums, recalling that he "kept bugging us, saying he was as important to the project as anyone else." A committee of scientists rejected his request but was overruled, Critchfield said, by Robert Oppenheimer himself. "He was enough of a nuisance around here," Critchfield said. David recalled being invited by James Tuck, a tall, skinny British scientist, but after two or three sessions it dawned on him that going to the movies was more fun. Nevertheless, he and Tuck talked often about some of Tuck's esoteric inventions. "He would say, 'You're driving me to insanity,'" David recalled, "because I would ask questions."

———

David insisted that he never personally recruited anyone to be a spy. "What am I, stupid?" he asked rhetorically. "I mean, come on, I was living precariously already."

Bill Spindel recalled otherwise. "Leaning toward communism as opposed to Hitler and fascism was not unusual," he said.

> People who were left-wingers, especially, shooting their mouths off, were not automatically suspected of being a spy. But the fact that he was shooting his mouth off proves he was stupid. He made no bones about it—that his brother-in-law was a communist and he was proud of that. He tried to recruit other Jews from New York to help out "our loyal Russian allies." He tried to give me this pitch once. I said, "What are you, crazy? That's being a spy. No one elected you to make international policy for the nation."

Another barracksmate, Benson Zweig, said that David's political rants—he repeatedly praised organized labor and commended the Russians for their wartime accomplishments—were inescapable. Still another soldier, with whom David played poker, remembered David's unstinting admiration for the Soviet Union and his unceasing advocacy for an Allied second front against the Nazis in Europe. A fellow machinist said that, upon reflection, he remembered David as "an argumentative person [who] belittled religion and desired to argue with the boys who attended church." This soldier dismissed David's complaints generally as "GI gripes" but also volunteered that David seemed overly interested in the fate of an employee who was transferred from Los Alamos after it had been discovered that he had belonged to a Communist front organization. In retrospect, the fellow machinist said, perhaps he should have detected the hints David dropped in his economic prescriptions, such as when he boasted that after the war he would pay all his employees premium union wages and even allow them to share in the profits.

Thomas A. Fineberg, a member of the Army Corps of Engineers, later said that he had recognized David as "somewhat to the left" because he favored higher wages, strikes, and more equality in general. But another barrackmate recalled that Fineberg himself bragged that while he shared a lot of ideas with the communists, he had originated those ideas. Fineberg and Greenglass, the soldier later told the FBI, both regularly read *The New Republic* and boisterously called the most salient articles to the other's attention. The soldier also said that he had heard that when Fineberg was traveling by train in the South, he demanded to be allowed to sit in a railway car reserved for black GIs.

Hugh Holland, David's immediate supervisor, was struck that David took the "side of communism one hundred percent" and was "definitely pro-Russian" and "liberal minded and a loudmouth." Holland also said, though, that David "was well-informed, intelligent, and always had statistics to support arguments." David, Holland said, once complained to fellow employees that Army Intelligence ordered him to cancel his subscription to *P.M.* or *The Daily Worker*. John P. Fitzpatrick, the master sergeant of X Division, recalled David as a "loud talker and possessing a rather argumentative disposition."

Still, few of David's coworkers ever put two and two together—his proselytizing on behalf of a largely communist agenda and what Holland later called his insatiable curiosity "regarding all phases of the development in Los Alamos"—to conclude that David Greenglass was systematically milking them for information on behalf of a foreign government. Any suspicions his colleagues might have harbored were allayed because, apparently, they considered David too stupid and too outspoken to be a spy.

Ben Bederson later described himself as having been sympathetic toward Russia and neutral toward communism. In contrast, he said, he knew David "to be either a member of the Communist Party or a communist sympathizer" who "invariably adopt[ed] the communist line." "He never made any secret of his politics," Bederson said later. "Many people who were much less close to communism got into a lot more trouble with security." Bederson also described Ruth Greenglass, whom he met in Albuquerque, as "much more outspoken concerning her communist sympathies" and probably "the driving force behind the communist sympathies of David Greenglass." Years later, when he was being considered for another government position, Bederson, according to the FBI, said he "realizes now that he should have reported David Greenglass to the authorities for his, Greenglass', advocacy of communism, but explained that he did not do so as 'about 40 people, including group leaders, already knew about Greenglass' pro-communist arguments.'"

Among those people was another member of the SED who, on the basis of a friend's assessment that David was loudmouthed, disturbing, not well-liked, and an advocate of socialism, expressed surprise soon after David's arrest that "he had not been apprehended before he was."

"He was," Bederson said, "a jerk."

———

David was once almost reassigned and not merely to another barracks. Politics does not appear to have been behind the proposed transfer, however, nor competence. It was sheer force of personality: David's. Wendell E. Marshman, the assistant leader of X Division, said later that while neither he nor John Fitzpatrick ever had a reason to question David's loyalty, they considered him obnoxious and unable to get along with his fellow employees. Fitzpatrick requested that David be transferred, Marshman said. Instead of being transferred, he was promoted.

———

For all the army's success in recruiting American and foreign scientists, the Manhattan Project was being jeopardized by a shortage of civilian and military machinists. At Los Alamos, machinists were already working a fifty-four-hour week when an interoffice memo to Oppenheimer warned that some shops were weeks or months behind schedule. The memo blamed the shortage on bureaucratic black holes and on Army Intelligence: "We have no way of locating machinists who would be willing to come here, and it takes so long to clear them through G-2 and the War Manpower Commission after they have been located and persuaded to come that we are apt to lose them." Another memo recalled that because of incompetent recruiters, fully half of one complement of twelve mechanics had been found to be unqualified. (Among the questions on which candidates were graded: "When doing precision work, how much metal should be removed by using a straight-fluted reamer?" and "How many set screws are there in a lathe dog?")

Despite the flood of disparaging evaluations unleashed later by David's arrest, his technical proficiency impressed more than one accomplished scientist and engineer at Los Alamos. David, said Hugh

Holland, "was one of the better machinists." Holland, less than two years David's senior, was foreman for nearly a year, until February 1946. He recommended David as his successor. Holland cited David's "seniority, his technical knowledge of machinery and his good workmanship." David got the job.

—

The new Theta Shop, where David was assigned, was housed in a 4,800-square-foot, one-story, L-shaped building in the heart of the Technical Area. The shop and its ten or so machinists moved there from the second story of a nearby building after it was determined that a trace of radiation was seeping from the shop beneath them. The Theta building included a wood workshop, an experimental engineering shop equipped with drill presses, a grinder, and a milling machine, and an administration office. The office contained a safe, which was supposed to be accessible to shop employees only when they received specific permission. Stored inside were documents, precious metals, blueprints, and materials and components for testing, "a lot of which was classified material," Wendell Marshman recalled, though "not always designated as such."

In the argot of Los Alamos, X Division's job was the "Study of Symmetry of Collapse and Future Methods for Its Improvement." That meant surrounding a lot of tubular pipes and spherical objects with explosives and blowing them up. Then, taking pictures with X rays and high-speed cameras—fifteen thousand frames per second—to find just the right way to trigger the explosion so that the detonation waves strike the sphere on its entire surface simultaneously.

A gun design—firing one piece of fissionable material at another— was the detonating device of choice for a bomb with a U-235 core. A plutonium core, though much more efficient, would require a faster trigger. Seth Neddermeyer, a thirty-six-year-old physicist from Cal Tech, suggested another method that would sustain a chain reaction. The physicist Robert Serber had hinted at that method in a crude sketch—no less crude, really, than the ones David later produced for the FBI. It looked like a wheel with four spokes. His instructions advised: "If explosive material were distributed around the ring and fired the pieces would be blown inward to form a sphere." During the winter of 1944, John von Neumann provided the theoretical foundation for the implosion lens, which is what David and the other technicians in Theta Shop spent months calibrating and machining. Richard Rhodes described it:

> The implosion lens system von Neumann designed was made up of truncated pyramidal blocks about the size of car batteries. The assembled lenses formed a sphere with their smaller ends pointing inward. Each lens consisted of two different explosive materials fitted together—a thick, fast-burning outer layer and a shaped slow-burning solid inclusion that extended to the surface of the face of the block that pointed toward the bomb core. The fast-burning outer layer functioned for the detonation wave as air around an optical lens functions for light. The slower-burning shaped inclusion functioned as a magnifying glass, directing and reshaping the wave.

Theta Shop's job was to make the molds in which the explosive lenses were cast, to engineer other parts from scientists' rough sketches, and to maintain equipment at nearby testing sites. Just as in David's earliest scientific experiments with black lights and bombs, trial and error, rather than established science, prevailed at the test site. The canyons, which not long ago had echoed with the sound of a bell summoning schoolboys to dinner, now reverberated with jarring shock waves and barely muffled booms of one prototype or another for a bomb with the potency of twenty thousand tons of TNT.

David was one of the machinists assigned to fabricate the precision molds for high-explosive lenses.* The two-dimensional test molds were

---

* Prodded by British scientists, Winston Churchill had personally cabled President Roosevelt to complain that the Americans were overlooking the potential of dynamite lenses. Churchill had also complained that his scientists were being shunned by the Manhattan Project; Roosevelt agreed to invite a British delegation, which proved to include, among others, Klaus Fuchs. As a sop to the British, the explosives expert George Kistiakowsky finally agreed to consider using dynamite for the bulbous implosion bomb that was dubbed Fat Man, after Churchill.

made by outlining the shape of a lens on an eight-by-twelve-inch steel plate. Then the plate was sectioned off into two separate parts for slow and fast explosives (a little like the compartmentalized metal trays in the mess, except less elaborate). Two-dimensional lens molds were easier to make, but they produced detonation waves that were only cylindrically convergent. Lenses made from three-dimensional molds produced the kind of spherically convergent waves required to crush the plutonium ball at the core of an atomic bomb.

More than fifty thousand machining operations were performed on more than twenty thousand castings (several times that number were discarded because of imperfections) before the bomb itself was tested in 1945. Without an accident. Except for a leak.

—

On December 16, 1944, Leonid Kvasnikov outlined for General Pavel Fitin of NKGB headquarters in Moscow the information Ruth had brought from David, including the presence at Los Alamos of Robert Oppenheimer and also of George Kistiakowsky—the latter already mentioned, according to the cable, by another Soviet source at Los Alamos, Theodore Hall. Also, Kvasnikov reported, David had concluded independently that atomic weaponry should not be developed secretly and that when Ruth broached the subject he had agreed immediately.

—

Julius was Jewish, and moreover real communists don't believe in Christmas. But on December 24, 1944, he left home early to deliver a present to Alexander Feklisov. He changed buses and subway trains several times before entering an Automat near Times Square. Feklisov had presents, too, from Gimbels: a watch with a stainless-steel band for Julius ("I remember the visceral revulsion that Libby had for gold"), a

---

Kistiakowsky culled the list of X Division personnel, he remembered, and "singled out individuals who hadn't contributed anything, constituted a group out of them, and so dynamite didn't delay the project in the slightest." David wasn't among them.

chestnut-colored crocodile handbag for Ethel, and a stuffed teddy bear for Michael. Julius surprised Feklisov with a gift-wrapped box draped in a copy of that morning's *New York Times*. The box was so cumbersome that the typically circumspect Feklisov abandoned security and austerity. He waited for two women chatting at a nearby table to leave. Then, instead of wending his way home on public transportation, he hailed a taxi directly uptown to the Soviet consulate. Feklisov unwrapped the box, ripped away the paper and cotton-wool padding, and extracted an oblong metal object. He recognized it immediately. It was a proximity fuse: an antiaircraft device calibrated to detonate explosives that don't strike their target but come close enough to inflict severe damage. The fuse was fully assembled. The box contained spare parts, to boot.

Thanks to Julius, the Soviets were already mass-producing a proximity fuse, using drawings that he had provided earlier. But no one had asked him to steal an actual fuse. No one thought it was possible—or worth the risk. Initially, Moscow chided Julius's handlers and demanded an accounting. Julius readily provided one. As Feklisov recollected, Julius, while working as the Signal Corps' acting resident inspector-in-charge at Emerson Radio and Phonograph on Eighth Avenue, spotted a defective fuse, rejected it, and placed it aside, but separate from the faulty parts that were to be destroyed. Over the next three months, he methodically replaced the broken components with working ones.

Smuggling the fuse out of the inventory room presented a bigger challenge. David later testified that Julius claimed to have carried the fuse out in his briefcase. According to Feklisov, Julius devised a more elaborate scheme. He waited until a few days before Christmas, for his turn to accompany the truck driver who routinely removed defective parts from the plant. He stowed the fuse in a box that was indistinguishable from the other cargo and placed it in the back of the truck. Documents were verified at the gate; the truck rumbled onto the streets of Lower Manhattan. As the truck proceeded downtown, Julius asked a favor: Would the driver stop for a moment so Julius could buy some last-minute ingredients for Christmas dinner? The driver graciously agreed. Julius purchased the items, packed them in a cardboard carton, and placed them in the back of the truck. Just one more favor:

Would the driver mind very much looping past Knickerbocker Village so Julius wouldn't have to lug the purchases home later? Again, the driver agreed. When the truck stopped on Monroe Street, Julius removed both boxes. Feklisov quoted Julius: "I have long dreamed of taking the initiative, of doing something if not heroic but brave to please you and myself. Millions of soldiers and officers of the Red Army are daily facing infinitely greater risks than I did!" Feklisov said later that he was deeply moved. He admonished Julius but thought to himself: "One who does not take the risk does not triumph."

—

By mid-December, David had managed to get his furlough reinstated (or, as the NKGB described it, he "got the vacations he had the right to"). It was scheduled to begin the weekend after Christmas.

On Sunday, December 31, 1944, Secretary of War Henry Stimson conferred with President Roosevelt. The subjects were Russia, the secret S-1 atomic-bomb project, and the shape of the postwar world. Stimson recorded the meeting in his diary: "I told him of my thoughts as to the future of S-1 in connection with Russia," he wrote. "That I knew they were spying on our work but that they had not yet gotten any real knowledge of it. . . . I said I had no illusions as to the possibility of keeping permanently such a secret but that I did not think it was yet time to share it with Russia."

The next day, David Greenglass arrived in New York from New Mexico.

Chapter 11

===

Espionage 101

"The simplest things are the cleverest."

==

On January 1, 1945, the day that David Greenglass returned home to New York, nearly one thousand German fighter planes pummeled Allied airfields in northern France. Off the Philippines, Japanese kamikaze pilots were reconnoitering American naval vessels on the eve of a ten-day battle that was to damage or sink fifty-three American ships. At twelve minutes after midnight on New Year's Day, a German V-1 flying bomb exploded in Antwerp, killing dozens of civilians. But the winds of war were blowing against the aggressors. In the Pacific, more than sixty thousand American troops were preparing to land on Luzon. On their western front, German troops were being repulsed in the Ardennes and Alsace. Six million Russian soldiers were massed on the eastern front.

But the forced glow with which the new year had begun the night before was already giving way to the stark realities of a nation still at war. For every ubiquitous war-bond poster that featured smiling refugees proclaiming that had their parents not emigrated they would now be starving in Poland or buried in Russia, there were also reminders that the streets of New York weren't paved with gold and that even supposing equality of opportunity, the fruits of democracy, capitalism, and human nature were distributed unequally. Huge signs in the communal changing rooms at Klein's department store on Union Square warned in English, Italian, and Yiddish: "Do not disgrace your family. The punishment for stealing is jail."

The Greenglasses' Stanton Street apartment had no telephone. So instead of waiting for an invitation, Julius just showed up. David and Ruth weren't ready to receive company—they were still in bed—but they welcomed him anyway. As they recalled it, Julius dispensed with the platitudes inherent in any homecoming. He congratulated David on agreeing to the proposition conveyed in Albuquerque four weeks earlier by Ruth. Then, David and Julius engaged in what Ruth described as a technical discussion. Before requesting a progress report from David, Julius volunteered his own version of how to build an atomic bomb. His analysis was rudimentary—which explained why the Soviets might have wanted to debrief David themselves. But it was detailed enough for David to recognize that the bomb Julius was struggling to describe wasn't the one that David was working on. Instead, it was the gun-triggered uranium device, a model that was already being rendered obsolete as Los Alamos scientists transformed their implosion theory into a workable weapon.

Julius might have been momentarily embarrassed, but his embarrassment was subsumed by the prospect that his young brother-in-law, a recruit whose utility and maturity Alexander Feklisov had challenged, was after only a month undercover delivering intelligence that was previously unknown to the Russians. Julius, according to David, suggested that David transcribe everything that he could recollect about Los Alamos. Then Julius posed an irresistible proposition: Would Ruth be interested in moving within weekend-commuting distance of David? "I said I would be very happy to be near David, and he said, 'You are going to go there,'" Ruth recalled. "Well, we spoke about whether I was going to work there or not and he said that I would probably be able to find a job, but not to worry about the money."

That evening, David committed to paper the names of scientists, details of technical processes, and physical layouts that he had learned since the previous August and all that he had memorized during the month since Ruth had recruited him as a Soviet spy. David also sketched a lens mold. To the uninitiated, it bore a striking resemblance to a four-leaf clover except that it was hollow in the center. David said Julius returned to the Greenglasses' apartment the next morning to collect David's notes and to invite the Greenglasses to dinner that night.

When the Greenglasses got to the Rosenbergs' apartment, another guest had preceded them. Ruth had met the woman before. David hadn't, but he recognized her name once they were introduced. She was Ann Sidorovich, and David knew her husband, Mike. The Sidoroviches had also lived in Knickerbocker Village before buying a house in Chappaqua in northern Westchester County. Julius and Mike had been high-school classmates and had both worked for a fledgling aeronautical company before Julius joined the Signal Corps. Unlike David, who had briefly romanticized about enlisting in the Red Army, Mike had actually joined the Abraham Lincoln Brigade and fought for the Loyalists in Spain.

Ann left after only a half hour. David and Ruth later said she had been visiting the Rosenbergs that evening so the three of them could get acquainted for a later rendezvous. Julius, they said, explained that after Ruth moved to New Mexico, Ann would probably be the conduit for the atomic secrets Ruth received from David. In all probability, Ruth would meet Ann in a Denver movie theater. There, in the dark, they would exchange pocketbooks. "I asked if her husband knew about what she was doing," Ruth recalled, "and Julius said no, he didn't know, that he would not approve that Ann was in it."

But suppose Ann couldn't come? How would Ruth recognize a substitute courier? While David remained in the living room, listening to music and leafing through books, Ruth joined Julius and Ethel in the kitchen. She later recalled: "Julius took the side of a Jell-O box and cut it in an odd fashion and he gave me one half and he said, 'This half will be brought to you by another party and he will bear the greetings from me and you will know that I have sent him,'" Ruth said, sounding downright biblical. Ruth emerged from the kitchen holding the side of the box that was imprinted with the cooking instructions. David was clued in that Ruth wasn't trading recipes with the Rosenbergs but that this was Espionage 101.

"Julius had the other part to it," David said, "and when he came in with it, I said, 'Oh, that is very clever,' because I noticed how it fit, and he said, 'The simplest things are the cleverest.'" Ruth put one of the two pieces of the box in her wallet and then placed her wallet in her purse.

———

David's leave that January was also chronicled by the NKGB, presumably with Julius playing the narrator.

New York reported to Moscow that production at Los Alamos had fallen behind schedule. According to David, a visiting army colonel complained, "If we work so slowly in the future, the Germans and Russians may be the first to use the bombs while we don't have them"—more fodder for Moscow's paranoia. David handed over generalities: a list of scientists whom he considered progressive and pro-Soviet; an explanation of his work producing devices to measure the power of explosives in various lenses; the existence of four nearby proving grounds where the lenses were tested. "As it seems to us," the NKGB concluded, "Kalibr himself doesn't know all the details of the project." But he was unquestionably in a position to learn more. And he came equipped with a courier. Ruth planned on remaining in Albuquerque six or seven months, and then, if all went well and she was pregnant, returning to New York to give birth. "We suppose that Wasp's staying in Albuquerque will let us study better the procedure of work and people of the camp," the NKGB concluded, "and in case of Kalibr having valuable data she may come to Tyre to inform us."

———

On January 18, 1945, David left New York to return to New Mexico. Ruth went job hunting.

"After you left last night," she wrote David, "I felt sort of queer and empty inside." Two weeks later, she reported that she had interviewed for a job as an addressograph operator at a magazine that, apparently, didn't look kindly on Jews or union members. "I'm glad I didn't take it though because it meant perjuring myself," she wrote. "The employment application asked for union affiliations, which meant that I had to lie about my reference. Then they asked about church affiliation and so on." Later that day, Ruth was offered a job and accepted on the spot. She began working the next day for the American Jewish Congress, waiting for Julius to deliver on his invitation to move to New Mexico.

That same week, Julius, again unexpectedly, dropped by the Greenglasses' apartment. Ruth's younger sister was living with her while David was away, and the three of them bantered briefly in the kitchen. "After a few minutes, he asked my sister Dorothy to take a book and go into the bathroom," Ruth later testified. "He said he had something private to discuss with me." Dorothy, who was sixteen at the time, elaborated: "Julie asked me to go, to leave the room, take a book and leave the room. I said all right, I would go into the bedroom. He said no, he wanted me to go into the bathroom and close the door, and I did."

Ruth remembered Julius's agenda vividly: how she would make contact with Ann Sidorovich or another Soviet courier. Instead of in Denver, the rendezvous would take place in front of a Safeway market in downtown Albuquerque on the last Saturday in April or the first Saturday in May.

On February 24, Ruth wrote David that she had compiled a list "of all the hundred or so items that I have to take care of before I leave." She and David would be living together again for the first time in more than a year. And, best of all, she was pregnant.

—

Julius's job with the Signal Corps had kept him out of combat. Suddenly, he was worried that it was going to land him in jail.

Government agents had managed to infiltrate the Communist Party just about as successfully as party members and sympathizers had insinuated themselves into the U.S. government. If they had just switched places, it would have saved everyone a lot of trouble. Sometime in 1944, the FBI sent Army Intelligence a photostatic copy of a Communist Party membership card, dated December 12, 1939, in the name of Julius Rosenberg. There was no proof that the card belonged to the Signal Corps' Julius Rosenberg, though—the same Julius Rosenberg who in 1941 had acknowledged that his wife had signed a Communist Party petition but only to accommodate a stranger who was collecting signatures.* Later in 1944, the FBI forwarded a second card to Army Intelligence, this one reporting Julius Rosenberg's transfer to another communist club. The card identified the new club. Also, it gave the cardholder's address.

In early February 1945, Julius gratefully returned to work to catch up on inspections that had been interrupted by an elevator operators' strike. But on February 9, the Signal Corps suspended him. On March 26, he was fired. The New York station of the NKGB immediately notified Moscow, which instructed Leonid Kvasnikov:

> The latest events with [Julius Rosenberg], his having been fired, are highly serious and demand on our part, first, a correct assessment of what happened, and second, a decision about [Rosenberg's] role in the future. Deciding the latter, we should proceed from the fact that, in him, we have a man devoted to us, whom we can trust completely, a man who by his practical activities for several years has shown how strong is his desire to help our country. Besides, in [Rosenberg] we have a capable agent who knows how to work with people and has solid experience in recruiting new agents.

Moscow concluded incorrectly that Julius was fired not merely because he had lied about having joined the Communist Party years earlier but because American counterintelligence agents suspected him of spying. The NKGB suggested that Julius confine his campaign for reinstatement to a routine union grievance and not mount a legal appeal that

---

* Julius's detachment seems to be evidenced in an incident that was relayed to the FBI years later. Jack Kirtz, a former classmate of Julius's also employed by the Signal Corps, said that in 1943 reports reached the army that a considerable amount of defective radar equipment was being approved at the Jefferson Travis Company, a Manhattan manufacturer where Julius was the resident inspector. Kirtz said he confronted Julius, who admitted that "this had been going on for some months" and that he "was not too aware of the defective nature of the equipment." According to Kirtz, Julius said that he had been summoned by an official of the company who said, "You are a family man and can use some money" and offered Julius a bribe to approve the equipment. Julius insisted that he refused the offer but told Kirtz that he hadn't reported it to the FBI "because he was a family man and did not want to get into any trouble."

would only attract greater scrutiny. But Julius knew his rights. When National New York Packing fired Ethel because of her labor-union organizing, she turned to the National Labor Relations Board for redress. Now, Julius did what any self-respecting American citizen would have done: He contacted his congressman.

Samuel Dickstein was six years old when he immigrated to the United States from Lithuania with his parents in 1887. His father became the cantor of an Orthodox *shul* on Norfolk Street. Dickstein became a fixture in Democratic politics, representing the Lower East Side since 1917 on the city's Board of Aldermen, in the State Assembly, and, since 1923, in the House of Representatives. A passionate antifascist, he was instrumental as early as 1934 in creating a special congressional committee to investigate Nazi subversion in the United States. In 1938, that panel entered the lexicon of American witch-hunting as the Dies Committee, and it later evolved into the House Committee on Un-American Activities. By the time Dickstein left Congress at the end of 1945, the committee was his greatest legacy. Not even Julius Rosenberg knew that Samuel Dickstein had been on the NKGB's payroll.

Dickstein came to the attention of Soviet intelligence in 1937. An NKGB report described him then as an extortionist who supplemented his congressional salary by selling American citizenship to immigrants. That same year, according to the NKGB's records, Dickstein visited the Soviet ambassador in Washington. Professing sympathy for the Soviet Union, Dickstein was quoted as offering to sell intelligence linking German and Russian fascists. They settled on a relationship that lasted for nearly two years, at times netting Dickstein $1,250 a month as a retainer and up to $1,000 for each pro-Soviet speech (in 1938, he publicly denounced the Dies Committee for focusing excessively on communists), until the NKGB concluded that it had been more than justified in the doubts expressed in his original code name: "Crook."

Julius went to Washington on a Saturday morning in April only to be informed that the congressman was in New York for the weekend. He returned home by train that same evening, disheartened but less a victim of an anonymous and omnipotent system than of his own naïveté.

—

To the Russians, Julius's loyalty was never an issue, only his zeal and audacity. Within two weeks of the Signal Corps' decision to suspend him, Moscow ordered the NKGB station in New York to release Julius from his responsibilities as a group handler. Sensitive to his physical and emotional state, Moscow added this personal aside: "Before ceasing direct connection with Rosenberg, it is necessary to explain to him the need to halt personal contact and to instruct him about the need to be careful, to look around himself." Four months later, after Julius had been hired back by Emerson Radio as a civilian, the New York station advised Moscow that he "is slightly pained and suffers from the fact that he is left without people but fully understands the correctness of our plan to compartmentalize his group. The main thing he can't reconcile himself to is his relative inactivity. At every meeting, he asks us to allow him to bring materials out of the plant and thus benefit us."

—

Ruth Greenglass arrived at the Santa Fe Railroad depot in Albuquerque on March 3. It was a Saturday, so David was there to meet her. This time, it wasn't necessary to cram lovemaking and sight-seeing into one long weekend. Ruth wasn't just visiting; she had given up the couple's Stanton Street apartment and was transplanting herself to New Mexico. She roomed at the El Fidel for five days, switched briefly to another hotel, encamped temporarily in an apartment rented by a GI who was on furlough in the east (the GI's wife "was seeing things under her bed," David recalled. "She'd think there were German spies next door to her. I said to my wife once, 'She doesn't think about Soviet spies at all.'"), and then moved in with Bill Spindel's wife, Sarah. After a few weeks, Ruth was hired by the Department of Agriculture's Soil Conservation Service. Soon, she took a better job as a clerk handling gasoline-rationing coupons for the federal Office of Price Administration. A colleague steered her to a $30.50-a-month apartment one block off Central Avenue and not far from the Spindels.

Ruth rented apartment 4 in a singularly unattractive two-story house at 209 North High Street, near Copper. The gray cement-block finish was punctuated by oversize pink windowsills. A large screened-in porch provided a sweeping vista to the corner of North High and Central, where a baleful neon sign beckoned customers to the Criswell Car Company's lot of secondhand cars. In 1945 Albuquerque had only about half again the number of inhabitants as sleepy Santa Fe. North High Street was almost out of town. From the second-floor windows, Ruth could look toward the Sandia Mountains and glimpse wild horses grazing in the piñon-peppered foothills. The pride of the neighborhood was that a famous opera singer who had fled Germany during the First World War used to live in the house next door.

The Greenglasses' apartment was at the top of the stairs in the rear. The bedroom was thirteen feet square. The kitchenette was tinier (though a neighbor recalled that "the couple ate extremely well, that Ruth always prepared huge meals on the weekends that David came home"). The shared bathroom was across the hall. The only telephone belonged to the landlord, downstairs. As much as Ruth complained about not being in New York, nobody remembers her ever phoning home or making a single long-distance call.

The house was owned by W. B. Freeman and his wife, Margaret. Her father, Pete Scherer, whom everybody called Pappy, lived there, too. Like virtually everyone in Albuquerque, the Freemans had moved there from somewhere else—in their case, only the year before, from Evanston, Wyoming, where they had owned Freeman's Cabins and Auto Courts. A postcard described Freeman's as "known from coast to coast." Their house on High Street was to become even better known.

And it would become known to the NKGB through Tessie Greenglass's unwitting complicity. "Ruth will give us her Albuquerque address in a letter to her mother-in-law," Soviet agents in New York assured Moscow.

—

In his ideal world, whether communist or capitalist, David never would have gotten a car. But now that Ruth was living in Albuquerque, thumbing rides was unreliable and unpredictable. By 1945, the army had relaxed its regulations against outside travel by GIs stationed at Los

Alamos, and David routinely bent those rules even further by leaving on weekends without making his departure a matter of official record. The practice was commonplace. David described it as "sneaking out." Once, he recalled, when he was hitchhiking from just inside the guard post at the East Gate of Los Alamos, a sedan rolled to a stop. A soldier was driving, but a mustached man in civilian clothes who shared the backseat with a uniformed officer offered David a ride to Santa Fe. Of course, he accepted. Convenience was his chief motivation, but it was coupled with curiosity. As David settled into the front passenger seat, the man in mufti behind him introduced himself as General Groves. They chitchatted briefly, then rode in silence until the car skidded to a stop with a flat. While the driver changed the tire, the general and his entourage engaged in what to David seemed like a ritual that they must have performed whenever their travel through isolated patches of New Mexico was interrupted: The general gripped his revolver; the officer tossed a tin can across the road; the general fired in rapid succession. He rarely missed. "It was very impressive," David recalled. He was so unself-conscious about espionage that it struck him only much later that this tale was the stuff of spy novels: The head of the entire Manhattan Project had, unknowingly, given a lift to a Soviet secret agent.

The chances of regularly finding a ride—much less with General Groves—were too remote, though. So David, Bill Spindel, and another GI, a redheaded draftsman named Aaron Baumgarten, invested two hundred dollars apiece in what even at that time could be classified as a vintage Dodge.

Keeping your car in good condition, an advertisement for Fred's Texaco in Albuquerque reminded motorists, "is keeping a trust with your country." When the car broke down one day in the desert, David lost whatever trust he had earned with his colleagues. As David tells the story, he ingeniously bailed everyone out by wielding just the right tool.

Bill Spindel tells a very different story.

When we got the car, I suggested the first day that we hadn't checked whether we had a spare tire or a lug wrench. I mentioned this at noon Saturday. David said, "I'll take care of it." I also mentioned we should measure the lug to make sure we had the right size wrench. He knew better—he could just tell by looking. At five o'clock, when he came out, I asked him if he had measured. He said yes. Well, in the desert about fifteen miles from Los Alamos, a tire blew. I said, "It's lucky that we checked there was a spare." Indeed, there was a hydraulic jack. There was a paper bag with a handle and two sockets. One was too small. The other was too big. "Oh," David said, "I forgot to tell you. The shop didn't have the size we wanted, so I got one smaller." I was so furious I took the twelve-inch handle of the wrench and chased him around the car.

The three owners were stranded on a deserted stretch of what passed for a highway. It was getting dark and cold. They were tired and hungry. And two of them were furious. They were building an atomic bomb but couldn't fix a flat. Even David later admitted that his ingenious solution hadn't been an unqualified success. "We heard this rattling, and we didn't know what it was," he said, "but we found out when we got to Albuquerque that the nuts had come off and were caught in the hubcap."

Three weeks later, the incompatible partners sold the car for $450. Then, Spindel and Ben Bederson asked to be transferred to another barrack. Recalling their move, a fellow GI later said of Bederson: "It became apparent that Mr. Greenglass was not possessed of the same intelligence as was William Spindel and himself." [*]

—

Ruth was soon bedridden because of complications from her pregnancy. She became so ill that she temporarily abandoned the apartment on North High Street and moved back with Sarah Spindel for companionship. On April 18, 1945, she suffered a miscarriage. As a result, she was too sick to keep the rendezvous at the Safeway store that had been arranged for the last Saturday of April or the first Saturday of May.

"I wrote Ethel a letter telling her that I had had a miscarriage and

---

[*] Spindel later told the FBI, "I almost saved the country a large amount of money by killing David Greenglass."

was confined to bed," Ruth recalled. "Ethel said that she was sympathetic about my illness and that a member of the family would come out to visit me the last weeks in May, the third and fourth Saturdays."

———

At one-thirty on the afternoon of Saturday, May 19, armed with the Jell-O box top in her wallet, Ruth stationed herself at the Safeway store. The box top had made only one other appearance since January. When Ruth first moved to New Mexico, David was afraid she had forgotten it; he wanted to see it again just to make sure.

Ruth waited for an hour. Nobody made contact. The following Saturday, May 26, Ruth repeated the routine, except that this time David was in town, and, incredibly, she brought him along for company. They waited again for an hour, but no one, familiar face or not, approached them. Had she mistaken the instructions? Maybe she had inadvertently broken the rules by bringing David. Maybe this was all some stupid joke. Maybe, as she was beginning to suspect, Julius was just a jerk.

———

By early June, melting snow from Colorado roared through the gorges of New Mexico as the Rio Grande redeemed its name, gloriously defining Albuquerque's western and southern perimeters as it flowed to the Gulf of Mexico. Old Town Plaza had been magically transformed for the annual Fiesta of San Felipe de Neri. For the first time in four years, there were reasons, beyond ritual, to celebrate. The war in Europe was over. Hitler was presumed dead. In a message to Congress, President Truman proclaimed America "at the peak of its military strength" and warned Tokyo, without hinting specifically at the superweapon being assembled at Los Alamos, that Japan's war machine and its cities were targeted for even greater devastation than the Allies inflicted from the air on Germany. Truman tempered his threat with a sobering warning for the American public to expect ferocious defense by the Japanese. John Gunther, the journalist, was at this time nearly halfway through his itinerary of all forty-eight states as he researched *Inside U.S.A.*, when he was asked in Santa Fe about the prospects for communism. He dismissed it as an impossibility in the United States but opined that "this is a revolutionary age and it is clear that Russia represents more than we do what the masses want in Europe."

All that week, Ruth fully expected to receive a letter with new instructions to meet someone, sometime, somewhere. None came. So when David returned to Albuquerque on June 2, neither he nor Ruth intended to park themselves in front of Safeway for a third futile stakeout. That night, they went to the movies. *Salome, Where She Danced* with Yvonne De Carlo was playing; so was a new Abbott and Costello feature and another episode of *The Thin Man*, along with *Target Tokyo*, a film on the firestorm unleashed by B-29s. The Greenglasses returned to North High Street late. Since the afternoon, the temperature had dropped by about half, into the forties. Pappy Scherer was already asleep. So were the Freemans. Which is why David and Ruth didn't learn until Sunday morning that a visitor—the first one in the two months Ruth had been living there—had dropped by unexpectedly on Saturday evening. He returned, though, the next morning, just as David and Ruth were finishing breakfast. Responding to a knock, David, half dressed, opened the door to find a stocky, moonfaced man wearing a suit and an expression of barely concealed surprise.

Chapter 12

Moscow Gold

"Harry and I had an affinity."

═══

The Soviet contact whose real name was Semen Semenov had warned Harry Gold that he could not engage in espionage indefinitely. "He said I had already been in it too long—because not only was it too much of an ordeal, but inevitably a slip would occur, possibly not even one of my own making, and then exposure would follow."

When he went to New Mexico that June, Harry Gold knew he was making a gigantic mistake. He never should have been ordered to visit David Greenglass. Because of their brief encounter at the door to apartment 4 at 209 North High Street just after breakfast on June 3, 1945, David would spend more time growing old with Harry Gold than with either of his own children.

———

Harry Gold had an aversion to the truth. It was true that Harry had been born in Bern, Switzerland, in 1910 and that he came to America with his family when he was four. Because of spelling discrepancies on their immigration papers, the family was almost barred from entering the United States. At Ellis Island, the name was officially changed from Golodnitsky. That marked the beginning of a lifetime of lies. Harry often prattled on about his children, volunteering to David and even to total strangers that he was married to a redhead and that they had twins named Davey and Essie. He would also tell close associates that he had a brother who had been killed by enemy fire in the Pacific, but that, too, was no more truthful than many of the other stories that Harry would tell about himself.

He had been imbued with socialism early on—Eugene V. Debs and Norman Thomas were boyhood heroes—and he was impressed that in the Soviet Union anti-Semitism was specifically against the law. He remembered anti-Semitic slights he had suffered in South Philadelphia as a child and at work, though he also recalled how fairly he was treated by the Jesuits at Xavier University in Cincinnati (from which he graduated summa cum laude). He lived with his father, a cabinetmaker for RCA, his mother, who sometimes innocently accompanied him on his rounds as a courier, and his brother, Joseph, in Philadelphia. By profession, he was a chemist. What Harry did not tell anyone—his parents, his brother, or even the woman he hoped to marry—was that since 1935 he had been a secret Soviet agent.

He was recruited to espionage by a friend who asked him to obtain from his employer, Penn Sugar, the formula for processing vitamin D concentrate from fish oil so that it could be mass-produced in Russia to compensate for endemic dietary deficiencies. Harry was struck by the Soviet veneration for American industrial know-how and by how dead set the Russians were against technical innovation. The Russians wanted purloined plans only for proven processes and formulas and actually rejected proffered information on potentially improved, but largely untested, versions.*

Like David, Harry invested in war bonds and considered himself a patriotic American, was rejected when he wanted to join the military after Pearl Harbor, and felt a repugnance for communist-style dis-

---

* This bias even proved true with the atomic bomb. Soviet scientists might have developed a better version and even sooner but for Moscow's insistence on duplicating the American model.

cipline. Harry didn't much like the communist practice of separating parents from their children—he and David both believed in what were later called family values—or the bohemian theories of free love that he saw embraced, though not necessarily practiced, by acquaintances during endless Saturday evenings of self-indulgent bloviating in Greenwich Village. Harry objected most strenuously, though, to the Soviet notion of group calisthenics. The group part of it robbed people of individuality. The calisthenics part was no great shakes either. He preferred vigorous rooting for the Athletics or for the University of Pennsylvania football team.

"Harry and I," David said years later, "had an affinity."

———

Harry knew his latest NKGB contact only as John, one of those monosyllabic all-American pseudonyms that the Russians typically adopted as a respite from names that seemed to average a tongue-twisting dozen syllables. (Semenov, John's predecessor and a Jewish graduate of MIT who officially worked for Amtorg, the Soviet trade agency, was called Sam.) John was younger and taller than Harry and, like many of the men whom Harry would later describe, much more handsome. John's face and brown eyes were framed by a shy, boyish grin and by a lock of dark hair that insistently drooped across his forehead. As often as several times a week, Harry met his Soviet contacts in New York, on remote subway platforms or in darkened movie theaters (including one painfully obvious house in Times Square that showed only Russian-language films). More than once, though, they broke the rules by retreating to the Ferris Wheel Bar in the basement of the Henry Hudson Hotel on West Fifty-seventh Street, where they ordered double Canadian Clubs. In a euphoric haze, they would toast a benign future in which they could both live normal family lives. During one boozy encounter, John let slip that he ached to be reunited with his wife and children, who had temporarily returned to Russia—including a daughter named Victoria because she was born on that victorious day that the Germans surrendered at Stalingrad. That slip later enabled the FBI to identify John as Anatoly Antonovich Yakovlev, a clerk at the Consulate

General of the USSR in New York, and finally by his real name, Anatoly Yatskov.

Harry's meeting with John in Volks Grill at Forty-second Street and Third Avenue, in the shadow of the El, on the last Saturday in May was all business. Harry already knew his mission: to reestablish contact with Klaus Fuchs. They had lost touch in 1944 after Fuchs, a member of the British delegation of atomic scientists, was reassigned from a laboratory on Church Street in Lower Manhattan. Harry caught up with him months later at Fuchs's sister's house in Cambridge, Massachusetts, and learned that he had been transferred to Los Alamos. Harry arranged to contact Fuchs in Santa Fe on the first Saturday in June.

Harry had no qualms about that assignment. He had put in so much overtime at Penn Sugar that he had plenty of vacation days to devote to missions away from Philadelphia. Fuchs was familiar. No secret greeting would be required as it had been the first time, early in 1944, when they made contact on a Lower Manhattan street corner.* Fuchs was a genius, a word, Harry later emphasized, "I always use with caution" and one that he bestowed on no other principal in his unhappy history.

A few days before Fuchs's penultimate meeting with Harry at the Castillo Street bridge in Santa Fe, John and Harry met at Volks, a folksy, fifty-year-old German restaurant ("not a place for the Van-Astorbilts," one guidebook advised coyly) popular for its seasonal game and home-made pigs' knuckles. John handed him a slip of onionskin. It said, "Greenglass—209 North High Street" and included a typed four-word secret greeting. John advised Harry to memorize the message, then destroy it. John also gave him a jagged piece of cardboard cut from a packaged food carton and an envelope containing five hundred dollars. "Yakovlev told me that the man Greenglass, whom I would meet in Albuquerque, would have the matching piece of cardboard," Harry later

---

* The contact was to ask directions to Chinatown, to which Fuchs would respond, "I think Chinatown is closed at 5 P.M." Harry carried gloves (three of them) and a book with a green cover, while Fuchs, tall and thin with oversize horn-rims and stiffly repressed Continental manners, gripped a tennis ball, which might have struck some passersby as odd, since it was winter. They then dined at Manny Wolf's steak house on Third Avenue.

testified. "Yakovlev told me that just in case the man Greenglass should not be present when I called in Albuquerque, that his wife would have the information and that she would turn it over to me."

Harry had never doubted the professionalism of his handlers. This time, though, he feared they were leaving themselves—and their courier—vulnerable to a potentially fatal mistake. After ten years of spying for the Soviet Union, Harry figured he had learned to distinguish which rules were inviolable. It was one thing for him to buy time to complete college by placating a Soviet contact with profiles of mythical recruits. Or to indulge in friendly drinks with John or Sam. But it was quite another to assign the same courier to make contact with two agents operating independently, to make Harry the nexus of two distinct espionage operations. That all but guaranteed that some day, if somebody slipped up, the story that dribbled out would not end with Klaus Fuchs and Harry Gold. John might just as well have ordered him to deliver an engraved invitation to J. Edgar Hoover to go to Albuquerque and arrest Harry Gold.

—

Volks was beginning to fill up with Saturday-evening regulars. Harry and John had already moved once, from the bar to a more secluded banquette in the rear of the restaurant. They argued. Finally, John cut Harry off: There was no choice. The mission was vital. Another courier, a woman, was originally given the assignment, but her trip had had to be postponed. She was no longer available. Harry Gold was. He never forgot John's next words: "That is an order."

—

Harry zigzagged furtively from Phoenix to El Paso and finally to Santa Fe. To avoid having to ask strangers for directions, he stopped at a museum, where he helped himself to an adobe-colored street map. The Castillo Street bridge wasn't much of a bridge, but the Santa Fe River wasn't much of a river. He arrived there precisely at 4:00 P.M. Fuchs was waiting in a borrowed car. He handed Harry an envelope. Their meeting lasted twenty minutes. Fuchs passed on one other important piece of information: The Americans were planning to test an atomic bomb in the New Mexico desert in July.

There was no circuitous way from Santa Fe to Albuquerque, just a bus. Harry boarded it late that afternoon and arrived at the depot two hours later. He was hot. And he was exhausted. The altitude extracted a physical toll, too. Harry was only thirty-five, but his double life was inflicting a palpable penalty. (Years later, he blamed his chronic exhaustion in part for the moral lapses that freed him to rationalize each step down a slippery slope of secret revelations, from vitamin D to the A-bomb.) Harry, still troubled by the prospect of making a new contact, waited until twilight. Then he proceeded to the address on North High Street, where Pappy Scherer told him that the Greenglasses had gone out for the evening but would probably be at home early the next morning. (Harry later remembered Pappy only as a tall, white-haired man with a slight stoop.) Harry returned downtown. The hotels were booked. The only bed he could find was in the hallway of a rooming house, where he slept fitfully, jarred by the sirens of police cars corraling wayward GIs.

Sunday morning, Harry checked into the air-conditioned Hilton on North Second and Copper. He then returned to North High Street, arriving about eight-thirty. He climbed a steep staircase to the second floor and knocked on the apartment door. The door was opened "by a young man of about twenty-three with dark hair," Harry recalled. "He was smiling. I said, 'Mr. Greenglass?' He answered in the affirmative." David was still wearing pajama tops over his khaki army pants. He didn't seem to be expecting anyone. "I was shocked," Harry said later. "I was expecting a civilian."

Exactly what Harry Gold said next would be debated for years. He would say that he identified himself as "Dave," and the next sentence that Harry and David and the FBI ultimately agreed upon—"I come from Julius"—seems to be what logic dictated that he would have said, had he been speaking logically. David was as surprised as Harry was. If the Greenglasses were still expecting anyone familiar, it was Ann Sidorovich. And if a man was coming instead, David might have expected Ann's husband, Mike. David asked for identification. Harry handed him a small piece of cardboard.

David later said that he then retrieved the matching piece from the wallet in Ruth's handbag; he also recollected subsequently that "Ruth gave it to me from somewhere." He and Harry didn't spend more than a moment trying to fit the two pieces together precisely because, as Harry later said, "you could see at a glance that they were the same thing."

It's unclear whether David had ever drafted any notes or diagrams for Ruth's fruitless stakeouts at the Safeway in May, but he told Harry he would need until mid-afternoon to prepare a written report. As Ruth retreated into the tiny kitchen—"I didn't like the situation well enough to be friendly," she later said—David offered Harry a slice of kosher salami. Harry wasn't hungry.

David was exhilarated. This, after all, was his first contact with a professional spy. There were lots more Americans at Los Alamos, David gushed, who considered the Russians a benevolent ally and who would be willing to share any of the scientific secrets that had been entrusted to them.

Harry had hated this special mission from the start, and now here he was exposing himself as a spy to a harebrained amateur who was openly recruiting prospective Russian spies at the U.S. government's most secret military installation. He denounced David's cavalierism as "extremely hazardous" and "foolhardy." Harry left after fifteen minutes with two indelible impressions: his surprise at discovering that David was a GI; and that every week David received a small salami and a loaf of pumpernickel from New York. Harry promised to return around 3:00 P.M.

By that time, David had filled a letter-size envelope with the schematic drawings of a high-explosive lens mold and its use in implosion experiments, explanatory notes, and a list of potential recruits that he had committed to sheets of white, eight-by-ten, ruled paper.

Harry handed David an envelope. "I felt and realized there was money in it, and I put it in my pocket," David recalled. He didn't know how much money—the sealed envelope contained twenty-five circulated twenty-dollar bills—but, David remembered, "it had a nice solid feel."

In 1945, five hundred dollars was worth about five thousand of today's dollars. It was what Ruth would make working for six months for the Office of Price Administration; it was enough to pay the rent on the North High Street apartment for sixteen months.

"Will it be enough?" Harry asked.

"Well," David guessed, "it will be plenty for the present."

"You need it," David remembered Harry saying, apparently referring to the medical costs of Ruth's miscarriage. David was disappointed, though. "I felt there should've been more," he said, "but somebody gives me money, I take it."

Harry detected David's discontent. "Well, I will see what I can do about getting some more money for you," he offered. At the same time, though, he was reminded about his conversation the day before on the Castillo Street bridge. Yakovlev had instructed him to delicately offer Klaus Fuchs $1,500. Fuchs, Harry said later, "turned the proposition down cold."

The encounter between Harry Gold and the Greenglasses that afternoon lasted fewer than ten minutes. David said he might be in New York on a furlough around Christmas and that if Harry had to reach him he could contact his brother-in-law. David claims to have given him the telephone number. Harry said that he intended to return to Albuquerque in early fall and might see David again then. They waited for Ruth to finish getting dressed (David was already in uniform), then left the apartment together. They walked a few blocks down a back street to the USO, where the Greenglasses peeled off. Traffic was stopped for a religious procession. After it passed, Harry continued to the Santa Fe Railroad station, relieved to be leaving Albuquerque. David and Ruth lingered only briefly at the USO. "As soon as he had gone down the street," David recalled, "my wife and myself looked around, and we came out again and back to the apartment and counted the money."

—

Monday morning, David left for Los Alamos. Ruth went to the Albuquerque Trust and Savings Bank, where she opened a joint account. She deposited $400, bought a $50 war bond for $37.50, and put the remaining $62.50 aside for household expenses. Overnight, the mission to which she had reluctantly agreed the previous November had been recast in a wholly different light. A story in the *Albuquerque Journal* later that week must have given her another jolt. A U.S. Navy officer from New York, two State Department employees, and three other New Yorkers, including the editor of *Amerasia* magazine, were accused of conspiring to possess or transmit defense secrets. The events of the weekend had also instilled in Ruth a deeper appreciation of the meaning of "Moscow gold," the epithet (and, given Harry's involvement, a homonym) that she had invoked the year before when she had recounted for David a grilling she had received from some anti-Soviet acquaintances. "Obviously they believe in Moscow gold," Ruth wrote at that time. "They think I have a private wire to get information daily from Joe Stalin himself."

Neither David nor Ruth ever contemplated returning the money they got from Harry, but Ruth testified years later that the transaction immediately troubled her. "I think I realized it most clearly after Gold left and then again after the bomb had been dropped on Hiroshima," she said. "I was under the impression at first that Julius said it was for scientific purposes we were sharing the information, but when my husband got the five hundred dollars, I realized it was just C.O.D.: He gave the information and he got paid."

—

At 10:00 P.M. on Tuesday, June 5, Harry Gold delivered two manila envelopes to Yakovlev on a deserted stretch of Metropolitan Avenue in Brooklyn. Inside one, labeled "Doctor," was the information from Fuchs. David's was in the other envelope, which Harry had labeled simply "Other." Two weeks later, Harry met Yakovlev again—this time in Queens, at the Main Street terminus of the Flushing subway line. "Yakovlev told me that the information which I had given him some two weeks previous had been sent immediately to the Soviet Union," Harry recalled. "He said that the information which I had received from Greenglass was extremely excellent and very valuable." But on June 26, the New York station reported to Moscow that the information David gave Harry—whose code name was Arno or Goose—was "lowly qualified," which "we suppose it is due to an insufficient qualification of Kalibr, on the one hand, and to suddenness of Arno's arrival to him, when he had no prepared materials, on the other."

Chapter 13

Little Boy and Fat Man

"You gotta understand something.
I knew it went off."

≡

As utilitarian and uninspiring as Los Alamos was, Alamogordo, 160 miles southeast of Albuquerque, was even more remote, primitive, and grim. Amenities were all but nonexistent. Even staples were scarce because supplies were shipped by labyrinthine routes to protect the secrecy of the site and to prevent anyone from associating it with atomic research, much less with Los Alamos. Most of the two hundred or so personnel stationed there by the summer of 1945 were restricted to the base full-time. Which is why, in the weeks before the test, David wasn't flattered when he was invited to join a select crew of scientists and technicians at Alamogordo. He later said that Ben Bederson—who was subsequently assigned to Tinian, where the Hiroshima and Nagasaki bombs were assembled before the 1,500-mile flight to Japan—was chosen because "he was basically a physicist who knew a lot about electronics." And frankly, David said, "the electronics on this bomb was not that complicated. I could have done it. An electrician from the street, if you gave him a circuit drive diagram, could have done it."

—

Early on the morning of July 16, 1945, the official witnesses waited for hours in dugouts, slit trenches, and control bunkers. Most shivered in the dark, some incongruously smeared with suntan lotion, following the physicist Edward Teller's recommendation, to protect against radioactive glare. Their eyes were riveted on the barren stretch of desert grimly dubbed the Jornada del Muerto, the Journey of Death, to memorialize the fate of stranded Spanish caravans.

A surprising number of unofficial witnesses waited that morning, too. Los Alamos had been abuzz with rumors, and so many of David's colleagues had disappeared on official business over the weekend or suddenly decided to go camping near Los Alamos or in the Sandia Mountains east of Albuquerque Sunday night (some positioned themselves strategically for unobstructed views to the south; others drove to the north with their families in case things went awry) that there was no doubt something momentous was in store.

In a memo to Secretary of War Stimson, General Groves recounted the tense prelude of thunderstorms and lightning strikes that delayed the test for ninety minutes and nearly postponed it altogether. "As I lay there in the final seconds," Groves later wrote, "I thought only of what I would do if the countdown got to zero and nothing happened."

But something did happen, something that finally doomed the wistfulness of those scientists who feared success—before the test, one of them said facetiously, "Aren't we lucky to be here where nothing we do can possibly hurt anybody?"—as much as failure. Just before dawn, a giant fireball exploded into an amorphous mass of dust and gaseous iron, soaring a mile a minute and transforming itself into the paradigmatic mushroom cloud, which nuzzled the substratosphere. The blast left a 1,200-foot-wide crater in the desert, fusing the sand into what came to be known as trinitite—nuggets of unmistakably green glass.

Shock waves destroyed a forty-ton steel tower a half mile from ground zero and broke at least one window 125 miles away. General Groves was not uncomfortable with superlatives, but even he was stunned. He had been hired to head the Manhattan Project on the strength of the reputation he earned building the world's biggest office fortress—a building distinguished in part by the fact it was designed to include twice as many toilets as necessary, to comply with Virginia segregation laws—for the Army Corps of Engineers. The event at Alamogordo overawed even that mammoth edifice: "I no longer consider the Pentagon a safe shelter from such a bomb," Groves concluded.

—

Scores of eyewitnesses within hundreds of miles struggled to describe what they had seen or heard the morning a man-made sun dawned half an hour before the real one.

Klaus Fuchs recalled that as the shape of the gaseous orange cloud over the desert rapidly morphed from a misshapen brain to a mutant mushroom, he and his fellow physicists regarded what they had wrought with a religious reverence. The only word Fuchs could think of was *awe*.

The sky over Alamogordo exploded with such intensity that nearly two hundred miles from ground zero, a woman watching from Sawyer's Hill, behind Los Alamos, vividly recalled "the blinding light like no other light one had ever seen. The trees illuminated, leaping out. The mountains flashing into life. Later, the long slow rumble." Legend has it that even a blind woman miles away supposedly saw a sudden flash. David Greenglass didn't. Neither the blinding light nor the long rumble woke him. Years later, he awoke by five-thirty regularly, but at the time he could sleep without having to worry very much about his work, about his wife, about children, or even about the world war. If the experiment near Alamogordo didn't ignite the Earth's atmosphere and destroy the planet altogether or turn out to be a dud, then the war would finally be over, within weeks or maybe months at the most.

—

It was one thing to decide against subjecting oneself to the harsh New Mexican desert day after day in July. It was quite another, though, to deliberately sleep through the first test of the atomic bomb. Especially if you were a spy.

And not just any bomb. This wasn't Little Boy, the uranium weapon triggered by the surefire gun detonator, which was to be dropped on Hiroshima. Fat Man—the implosion bomb being tested at Alamogordo—was much more theoretical, from its plutonium core to its high-explosive lens configuration. It would have been embarrassing at best, and a horrific breach of secrecy at worst, to have had it land intact, undetonated, on a Japanese target. Fat Man was the bomb David had worked on for nearly a year, for which he had machined lens after lens, about which he had surreptitiously and illegally gleaned details from unsuspecting sources. But if it meant getting up two or three hours early, forget about it.

David never felt guilty about having slept through the test. Either the bomb was going to work or it wasn't. David was cocky enough from what he remembered from high-school chemistry and from his rudimentary understanding of physics to figure that, at worst, the bomb would just fizzle, leaving the scientists who had placed their careers, their lives, and their souls on the line bitterly disappointed but alive. It wasn't as if David wouldn't find out. The word would get around. Something this big, the culmination of two years of work by thousands of soldiers and civilians in three secret cities, couldn't be hidden indefinitely. Probably even by the time he awoke, people would be talking. He was right.

"You gotta understand something," he said later. "I knew it went off."

—

A *New York Times* reporter—William Laurence, who had been invited as a War Department historian—witnessed the explosion from twenty miles away that morning, but no story appeared in the next day's newspaper, not even the cover story invented by the army. Instead, a prepared statement attributed to William O. Eareckson, commanding officer of the Alamogordo Army Air Base, and released at 11:00 A.M. was dutifully reported elsewhere by the wire services:

> Several inquiries have been received concerning a heavy explosion which occurred on the Alamogordo Air Base reservation this morning. A remotely located ammunition magazine containing a considerable amount of high explosives and pyrotechnics exploded. There was no loss of life or injury to anyone, and the property damage outside of the explosive magazine itself was negligible. Weather conditions

affecting the content of gas shells exploded by the blast may make it desirable for the Army to evacuate temporarily a few civilians from their homes.

General Groves himself had insisted on the last sentence as a precaution: Shifting winds suggested that the army might have to hustle some isolated ranchers out of harm's way if radioactive fallout began blowing in their direction. Joseph O. Hirschfelder and other scientists monitoring the largely untested fallout later detected an alarming array of telltale evidence, from skin tumors in cows that grazed perilously close to ground zero to the surprise of Eastman Kodak technicians who discovered that wheat harvested in Illinois was inexplicably too radioactive to be used as packaging material for the company's photographic film.*

Another contingency cover story was never published or released, although the very fact that it was even prepared reflected the disquiet hanging over the desert that morning. William Laurence wrote an unsigned, hold-for-orders story reporting that Oppenheimer and other prominent scientists had been killed in an accident at Oppenheimer's New Mexico ranch. Laurence also prepared lengthy obituaries on Oppenheimer and the other scientists—as well as on himself.

Within hours of the blast, the *Alamogordo News* suggested that the explosion—accident or not—was the product of "some experimentation." Like many newspapers, *The Santa Fe New Mexican* printed a two-paragraph Associated Press dispatch. (It appeared beneath a story on the theft of a portable radio from a local homeowner.) The AP story, which was based on the army's official release, was sufficiently vague for average readers but contained enough hints to prompt at least one congratulatory telegram to General Groves from scientists at the Hanford plutonium plant in Washington, who were suspicious of the cover story

---

* The following week, *The Santa Fe New Mexican* published a simple atomic primer that included the following question and answer:

Q. *Does the atomic bomb on exploding have deadly emanations in its wake?*
A. *The War Department says no.*

because they doubted that high explosives and gas shells would have been stored together.

The explosion at Alamogordo reverberated halfway around the world. Its timing was intended to strengthen President Truman's hand as the opening round of the cold war was being waged with the Soviet Union at the summit of Allied leaders in Potsdam. For months, Truman and Winston Churchill had hoped that a Soviet declaration of war against Japan might, by itself, induce the Japanese to surrender. In February, Stalin had promised to open a second front against the Japanese no later than three months after the war ended in Europe. But with the Soviet Union already exerting hegemony in Poland and staking ambitious territorial and political claims to the Balkans, Austria, Turkey, and the Mediterranean, it seemed that the price of Russian participation in a Far Eastern campaign might grossly exceed the bounds of Anglo-American gratitude. "Once in there," Secretary of State James Byrnes confided, "it would not be easy to get them out."

When the Potsdam summit ended, the president presumed that the secret of Alamogordo was intact. Truman later recalled that on July 24 "I casually mentioned to Stalin that we had a new weapon of unusual destructive force. The Russian Premier showed no special interest. All he said was that he was glad to hear it and hoped we would make 'good use of it against the Japanese.'"

About two weeks later, in Hiroshima, Japan, unidentified aircraft were sighted heading toward the city. An air-defense alert was sounded immediately. But there appeared to be too few planes to constitute a threat. The all clear was given. Moments later, the United States dropped the uranium bomb, Little Boy.

The Santa Fe New Mexican was available that afternoon at the Los Alamos post exchange. On page one, the larger headline announced:

ATOMIC BOMBS DROP ON JAPAN

Another headline, smaller, but above the first one, was predictably provincial:

LOS ALAMOS SECRET DISCLOSED BY TRUMAN

Flanking a story from Washington that the government was ending the rationing of tomato juice were several sidebars about the bomb. President Truman declared that "the force from which the sun draws its power has been loosed against those who brought war to the Far East."

Another story began: "Santa Fe learned officially today of a city of 6,000 in its own front yard. The reverberating announcement of the Los Alamos bomb, with 2,000 times the power of the great Grand-Slammers dropped on Germany, also lifted the secret of the community on the Pajarito Plateau, whose presence Santa Fe has ignored, except in whispers, for more than two years."

The August 6 paper carried two other noteworthy items. Inside, the headline over a map warned ominously that Soviet Russia was now the "greatest land power in world history." And the final two paragraphs of the lead story from Washington quoted President Truman:

" 'It has never been the habit of the scientists of this country or the policy of this government to withhold from the world scientific knowledge,' Mr. Truman said. 'Normally therefore everything about the work with atomic energy would be made public.' That will have to wait, however, he said, until the war emergency is over."

One vital secret was made public prematurely the very next day, but hardly anybody noticed.

Months later, Admiral William S. (Deke) Parsons would draft a memo to the new director of Los Alamos on the secrecy of the implosion trigger. His memo helps explain why one word—a word transmitted to the Soviets by David Greenglass and elaborated upon by Klaus Fuchs and Theodore Hall, a word that, in retrospect, seemed so deceptively simple—later provoked so much controversy. Parsons's memo was itself immediately classified as secret.

"It may seem that implosion is such an obvious method of assembly that it would naturally occur to any group of intelligent individuals faced with the problem of designing a bomb," Parsons wrote. "This might be the case, but it certainly was not so at Los Alamos during the

May–October 1943 period." Parsons went on to say that the concept probably would have been shelved by the end of 1943 had it not been for Seth Neddermeyer's obstinacy, the collective brilliance of the brains behind the project, and a lot of luck despite repeated failures. Instead of declassifying the details of implosion, Parsons recommended that a few more facts be released about the already obsolete gun-assembly method used in the uranium bomb dropped on Hiroshima and mentioned in the biography of the bomb prepared for the government by Professor Henry De Wolf Smyth of Princeton, the authorized and selective history of the Manhattan Project. Under those circumstances, Parsons concluded:

> I rate the chances as very good that if we collectively kept our mouths shut about bulbous bombs, shaped charges, high explosive assembly, lenses, equations of state of materials at several times normal density, and implosion itself; and perhaps released a little more than Smyth said about the gun, a competitor seeking to assemble U-235 would not ever arrive at implosion assembly. If he ran into our difficulty in the case of plutonium, my guess is that he would be sufficiently stumped to lose a great deal of time while investigating the problem and attempting to obtain our solution by espionage or an international horse trade.

Fully five years later, officials of the Atomic Energy Commission spent months squabbling with the U.S. Attorney's office in New York over whether the word *implosion* could even be mentioned, much less defined, during the Rosenberg trial. And when the word was finally revealed in the testimony, it seemed so novel, so counterintuitive, that *The New York Times* published a separate article just to define it.

It was as if no one had read *The Santa Fe New Mexican* the day after Hiroshima and two days before the bombing of Nagasaki.

There, on the August 7, 1945, front page, was a surprisingly full explanation of how to make an atomic bomb. The writer, William McNulty, chattily reported that the night before, with so many Los Alamosans celebrating, his assignment was to produce a concise primer on how to smash an atom. "Lots of people walking around and saying, 'I still don't get it,' were no help whatever." Which is why, as journalists have tended to do when in search of a source, McNulty retreated to La Cantina, a popular bar, and had a real, imagined, or cleverly disguised conversation with a source he described only as "a know-it-all so-and-so from way back."

Tucked in the middle of McNulty's story was a definition of *implosion*: "You take an explosion. As you remember from your first-year Latin—the 'ex' means exploding out. Okay, that's your ordinary explosion of matter. TNT being transformed into rubble and debris. Next we got to think of the opposite of explosion, which would be 'plosion' with an IN." But since *inplosion* sounds awkward, the story explained, a somewhat more felicitous *im* was substituted and the word became *implosion*.

That front-page story should have triggered alarm bells because it wasn't about the Hiroshima version of the bomb. It described an experimental implosion bomb, the type that had been tested three weeks before at Alamogordo but that was not dropped on Nagasaki for two more days.

—

The two bombs together killed between one hundred thousand and two hundred thousand people instantly. The final death toll was immeasurably higher. There isn't much question that the bomb shortened the war in the Pacific. By how much and at what price is debatable.* Should the Japanese have been invited to witness the Alamogordo test before the bomb was dropped on Hiroshima? Was the Nagasaki bomb necessary, too? Recent scholarship suggests that Japanese rulers had conceded privately by then that the war was lost but still planned to ferociously defend the Home Islands in order to improve the terms of surrender.

On August 8, the Soviet Union declared war on Japan.

---

* Whether that development actually lengthened the war in Europe, though, is difficult to calculate. "By taking all of these scientists and engineers off conventional military research on guns and rockets," Joseph O. Hirschfelder, who was a group leader in the ordnance and theoretical divisions at Los Alamos, said later, "it probably took an extra six months before the peace with Germany was achieved."

On August 14, a thousand Japanese soldiers stormed the Imperial Palace, seeking to prevent the emperor from reading his proclamation of surrender. But the proclamation had already been recorded for broadcast and the next day, August 15, following the playing of the Japanese national anthem, the people of Japan heard their emperor's voice, most of them for the first time. He was accepting the Allied provisions for peace, he said, because the enemy "has begun to employ a new and most cruel bomb, the power of which to do damage is indeed incalculable, taking the toll of many innocent lives."

On September 2, Japan formally surrendered. The Second World War was over.

—

Byron Price, the Federal Director of Censorship, hailed the atomic bomb as the best-kept secret of the war.* The FBI announced that it, too, had helped to safeguard that secret. The bureau said it had reviewed the fingerprints of 269,303 prospective Manhattan Project employees (an astonishing 31,223, more than one in nine, had criminal records that warranted further investigation) and had conducted a background check on each person employed by the project. Eight Nazi saboteurs were prevented from destroying Tennessee Valley Authority generating plants that supplied power to Oak Ridge. Five other Nazi spies assigned to ferret out atomic secrets were turned into double agents who fed doctored data to Berlin and who also kept the FBI abreast of which questions German scientists wanted answered.

After the bombs were dropped on Japan, David received a form let-

---

* In mid-1943, not long after the Los Alamos laboratory opened, Price's office issued a directive that was intended to guard against even clues gleaned by omission. Mention of imaginary elements was proscribed in order to divert attention from uranium alone:

> You are asked not to publish or broadcast any information whatever regarding war experiments involving: Production or utilization of atom smashing, atomic energy, atomic fission, atomic splitting, or any of their equivalents. The use for military purposes of radium or radioactive materials, heavy water, high voltage discharges, equipment, cyclotrons. The following elements or any of their compounds: polonium, uranium, ytterbium, hafnium, protactinium, radium, renium, thorium, deuterium.

ter from Lieutenant Colonel Stanley L. Stewart of the Army Corps of Engineers. "The security restrictions on our part of the work have been more rigid than on any other portion of the entire Manhattan Project," Colonel Stewart wrote. And they would remain rigid. "Loose talk and speculation, particularly by individuals now or formerly connected with the project, jeopardize the future of the nation and must be controlled."

Within just a few days of Japan's surrender, the army granted David home leave. On September 10, 1945, the day that David and Ruth arrived in New York, Henry Hathaway's *The House on 92nd Street* was released in Hollywood by Twentieth Century–Fox. It was billed as a film noir that melded authentic footage of G-men in action—including J. Edgar Hoover, at his desk, looking vigilant—with understated performances by Lloyd Nolan and a workmanlike cast of lesser-known actors. From the opening credits, there was never any doubt that the good guys would win. But after production of the film was finished, America finally clinched the victory at Hiroshima and Nagasaki. Screenwriters inserted this epilogue, delivered in appropriately stentorian tones:

Process 97—the atomic bomb—America's top secret, remains a secret.

Not one single act of enemy-directed sabotage ... was perpetrated within the United States.

Nor was one major war secret stolen.

Chapter 14

Diamonds

"I said, 'Let's not do it. They'll get mad at us,
and they'll put us in jail.'"

===

Tuckered out from the long train ride home to New York, David and Ruth went directly to his parents' house on Sheriff Street. They were still asleep when Julius rousted them late the next morning. "He got me out of bed, and we went into another room so my wife could dress," David recalled. Julius demanded details about the project that Hiroshima had transformed from a coveted but merely hypothetical secret into a superweapon that had surpassed every military expectation. "He said to me that he wanted to know what I had for him," David said. "I told him, 'I think I have a pretty good description of the atom bomb.'" Julius, according to David's testimony, handed him two hundred dollars and asked him to write up the description and deliver it to the Rosenbergs' Knickerbocker Village apartment that afternoon.

The previous spring, in Albuquerque, Ruth had played the willing accomplice, even though the war in Europe had been over for weeks, and the Soviets' nemesis had been vanquished. And while she later described the five hundred dollars delivered by Harry Gold as dashing whatever idealism she still harbored, she deposited most of the money in her savings account the very next day. This time, though, Ruth said, she was even more reluctant. "The bomb had already been dropped on Hiroshima," she said, "and I realized exactly what it was, and I didn't feel that the information should be passed on."

"My wife didn't want to give the rest of the information to Julius, but I overruled her on that," David said. After brunch, David completed a drawing of the bomb and filled a dozen loose-leaf pages with explanatory notes—including an explanation of how to suspend the plutonium core to increase the explosive yield—and still another list of potential espionage recruits. At about 3:00 P.M., David and Ruth borrowed Ruth's father's car and drove the half mile to Knickerbocker Village.

About the only thing everybody agreed on later was that the Greenglasses did, indeed, go to the Rosenbergs' apartment that afternoon. Was Michael there, too? Was the housekeeper home? Did David and Ruth stay for dinner? Did Julius have David's handwritten notes typed up and then incinerate the originals in a frying pan? The eyewitness accounts were to be contradictory. No physical evidence from the scene was ever produced. The judgment on exactly what transpired in the apartment and during the rest of David's leave would be rendered by a jury and by history.

—

The night before David's leave ended, he borrowed Max Printz's 1935 Oldsmobile again. As he recalled, first he drove downtown to Knickerbocker Village to get Julius. Then, they headed up First Avenue, past the hulking Tudor City apartment complex, and parked partway down the block from what he remembered as a dingy bar and grill a few steps below sidewalk level.* Julius entered the bar, where, Alexander Feklisov later said, he introduced Julius to another man, apparently Anatoly Yakovlev, whom Julius escorted to the car and introduced to David only by a first name. Yakovlev slipped into the backseat, and he and David cruised up First Avenue, under the Queensboro Bridge,

---

* Feklisov recalled that it was on Third Avenue, under the El. He also placed the drive-by interview in January 1945, not September.

and over to York Avenue. David wasn't in the most talkative mood. It was late, nearly 11:30, and he and Ruth were supposed to catch a train the next day. David drove cautiously, with one eye darting to the rearview mirror, trying to catch a better glimpse of his passenger. It was too dark. Also, the brim of the man's hat was pulled down over his forehead and cast a shadow across his face. "He kept asking me questions about this lens mold, and in driving in a New York street, trying to watch the road, and at the same time expounding on a scientific subject," David recalled, he wasn't contributing many insights. "Each time I turned around to emphasize a point, he would put his hand to my face and say, 'Keep your eyes on the road.'" From his questions, the man seemed to know a good deal about explosives—not much more or less, as it turned out, than David did. "I was being very busy with my driving, I didn't pay too much attention to what he was saying, but the things he wanted to know, I had no direct knowledge of, and I couldn't give a positive answer."

Following his passenger's directions, after about twenty minutes David returned to the bar, dropped him off, and drove home.

Yakovlev, Alexander Feklisov said, remembered David as "a man who smiled."

The fragmentary paper trail that survives in the NKGB archives suggests that Yakovlev didn't leave empty-handed. Later that September, he reported to Moscow that David had been "assigned to gather detailed characteristics on people he considered suitable for drawing into our work" and was given "the task of gathering samples of materials" used in the bomb. According to Yakovlev, while David was on leave in New York that September he delivered to Russian agents a cartridge for the new exploding-wire detonator that had just been invented at Los Alamos by Luis Alvarez and machined in the Theta Shop.*

---

* Three months later, on December 27, 1945, a memo from Vsevolod Nikolayevich Merkulov of the NKGB to Lavrenti Beria, the head of the NKVD, the state security service, described in detail an electric detonator for the atomic bomb and was accompanied by a diagram "obtained through our agents." During all of his subsequent interviews, David never revealed the existence of the detonator to the FBI.

"Why did I bring it home? Maybe they asked me for it," David said. "Who the hell knows?"

How? Had he simply slipped the device into his pocket and walked out the door?

"I have a tendency to do that," David replied.

—

It was also during his September leave, David recalls, that Julius first broached the suggestion that David remain at Los Alamos indefinitely, as a civilian. Not only would it benefit David's career, but, as Alexander Feklisov's farsighted colleagues in Soviet intelligence originally suggested, by the time he fully matured he would have burrowed sufficiently into the core of Los Alamos or of some other secret installation that he could be activated as a full-fledged Soviet mole.

But Germany and Japan had surrendered, so the original justification for helping the Russians—the presence of a common enemy—no longer obtained. And even if a superseding argument was now being advanced—the postwar balance-of-power rationalization—David had other priorities. He preferred to return to New York and start a family. "Julius said that he wanted me to stay there so I could continue to give information," David recalled. "I said, I would like to leave the place. I would like to come home."

—

Ruth also hated New Mexico. As much as she had longed to escape the Lower East Side, she never felt at home in Albuquerque. She was bored. She was lonely. She had few friends. After work, she would get together with her neighbor across the hall, Rosalea Terrell, a retired telephone operator. Terrell remembered Ruth saying once that "she had lived in big apartment houses all of her life, had never seen vegetables or farm produce being grown, and even said she would like to quit office work and get some sort of a job on a farm while living in that area." But Ruth's colleagues at the Office of Price Administration complained later that her New York chauvinism had rapidly asserted itself. She even belittled the Rio Grande and said New York had rivers "you could not see across."

Ruth, said Margaret Freeman, her landlady, "was always bragging about the nice apartment they had in New York."

Still, Terrell remembered Ruth as "a very nice considerate person." In contrast, she recalled, David had not been very well liked "because he was rather loud or noisy, slammed doors going in and out of the house and his apartment, and made a lot of noise going up or down the stairs no matter what time of day or night it was." There is no evidence that David purposely stomped around to deflect suspicion, on the theory that any man who was seen so rarely—he insisted that he was simply catching up on sleep—had better make himself heard lest his neighbors conclude that he had something to hide. Thanks to Ruth, he perpetrated the impression that he was discreet. Terrell later said David "had been very secretive concerning his assignment at Los Alamos"—so secretive that, she was led to believe, even his wife didn't know what he did at Los Alamos. When the news broke that the bomb had been developed at Los Alamos, Terrell said, Ruth told her "that David had never even mentioned to her that his assignment involved anything of that nature."

———

By September 1945, after thirty months of frenzied construction and research, Los Alamos was in limbo. The city that had sprouted on an arid mesa had suddenly put itself out of business.

"We were busy, busy, busy," David recalled. "Then it stopped being busy after the bomb was dropped."

On October 1, 1945, Oppenheimer proposed an interim mission for Los Alamos: to build and stockpile more atomic bombs as a negotiating chit for international arms control. "To weaken the nation's bargaining power during the Administration's attempt to bring about international cooperation would be suicidal," Oppenheimer said. His anointed successor as director of Los Alamos, Norris Bradbury, suggested that about fifteen bombs be built in the three years or so before weapons production would no longer be necessary.

Two weeks later, on the morning of October 16, all of the denizens of the Los Alamos lab gathered for the first time. This was not so much a celebration as a closure ceremony. The day might come, Oppenheimer said, when "mankind will curse the names of Los Alamos and Hiroshima."

After other sobering and self-congratulatory speeches, members of the Special Engineer Detachment were issued shoulder patches with a special insignia—a horseshoe-shaped cluster of leaves—drawn from standard military heraldry. Its shape immediately evoked a toilet seat, which suggested a commendation won not for feats of skill or endurance but by default, as a result of their isolation. Ben Bederson mused that the isolated SEDs were actually being cited for having the lowest incidence of venereal disease in the army.

—

David didn't ski, but during his ample time off during the winter of 1945–46, he helped build a ski lift out of spare pulleys, ropes, motors, and other parts. He also finally found a use for the special skills he had first used to singe Anna Babka's fur coat on Sheriff Street. He helped clear a slope of trees and stumps by blowing them up. "We had a lot of surplus plastic explosive, the demolition explosive," George Kistiakowsky recalled, "and if one builds a half necklace around the tree, then the explosion cuts it as if you had a chain saw—and it's faster. A little noisier, though." The winter recreation project was so successful that Admiral William S. Parsons was moved to deliver this sweeping appraisal of Los Alamos: "Isn't it wonderful," he said, "to see five thousand people intent on a single purpose: skiing."

—

David also threw himself into an even more ingenious experiment involving explosives. This one was a secret, just between David and Henry Linschitz, and they fully intended to keep it that way. Linschitz, who was raised in the Washington Heights section of Manhattan, had been doing graduate work in chemistry at Duke University until he quit to join Kistiakowsky at the Explosives Research Laboratory near Pittsburgh and later at Los Alamos. He met David at Theta Shop. "We were kids," Linschitz recalled. "By unfortunate coincidence, Greenglass wound up machining some of the lens molds for high explosives and found himself in this particularly strategic position. He wasn't subtle. He wasn't discreet. He was not a Fuchs, a master of spying and intrigue. He was just a clod." Still, David impressed Linschitz as a pretty good machinist and a man who wouldn't mind bending the rules, possibly to make a buck. When Linschitz decided to test his high-concept hypothesis and needed someone who knew how to blow things up, he enlisted David.

"He says," David remembered, "'Let's make diamonds.'"

On the face of it, the hypothesis seemed plausible: The carbon residue of dead plants and animals was transformed into gem-quality diamonds by relentless pressure from the Earth's mantle over millions of years; implosion could achieve the same result in a split second. As if they were alchemists, David and Linschitz placed a handful of lampblack inside a hollowed-out copper sphere and surrounded it with crude replicas of the A-bombs' explosive lenses. Then, they adjourned to a nearby canyon, took cover behind a berm, and detonated their gadget.

As the smoke cleared, Linschitz and Greenglass sliced open the sphere expectantly. They could detect tiny flecks that seemed to glisten when they caught the light. After several tries, they gave up. Producing an artificial geode instead of industrial-grade diamonds—much less diamonds of gem quality—wasn't good enough. And perfecting the process wasn't worth the risk, which in David Greenglass's case might seem strikingly inconsistent. "I said, I'll help you as much as I can. But he says, 'You know what this is costing Uncle Sam? Ten grand a shot!' I said, 'Let's not do it. They'll get mad at us, and they'll put us in jail for doing this kind of experiment.' And he said, 'They'll never find out.'"

Why would David nonchalantly risk the death penalty for committing espionage on behalf of a foreign government but worry about getting caught for conducting unauthorized but largely harmless experiments? David was baffled by this comparison. Imagine, he said, equating covert intelligence gathering with in-your-face misappropriation of government property in broad daylight, and on a weekend no less, when it couldn't be disguised as official business.

"Come on, that's a big difference," David replied. "I mean, you're not doing anything under the table, you're actually making an explosion at the site. And probably on a day off."

Perhaps after one freelance experiment too many, the U.S. Engineers Office issued Circular No. 228. It was a warning to all personnel at the laboratory, which owed its very existence to making bigger and more destructive explosive devices than had ever been devised. Circular No. 228 was unequivocal: "Use of fireworks or pyrotechnics for amusement is prohibited on the project." Only one exception was granted. "There is no objection," the circular said, "to the use of cap pistols by children."

Chapter 15

Blackmail

"Why should I be on the bottom end?"

≡

David was discharged from the army on February 28, 1946. It was the same date that, had the atomic bomb been a dud, American military strategists had been planning to invade Honshu, the principal Japanese island. David shipped home a duffel bag of clothes and souvenirs from Los Alamos and an Indian rug he bought from the Freemans and drove to the separation center at Fort Bliss, Texas. He was mustered out with the army's American Theater, Good Conduct, and Victory citations but without a job or a place to live.

Nearly seven hundred thousand men and women were demobilized that month, the latest wave among the more than six million who, since the war ended, had been returned to a civilian life starkly different from the one they had left. David's train home from El Paso passed not far from Fulton, Missouri, where, on March 5, Winston Churchill proclaimed that "an iron curtain" had descended on the ancient states of central and eastern Europe. The world was warily adjusting to an unpredictable and conflicted peace. In a speech drafted for Bernard Baruch that same month, Herbert Bayard Swope dubbed the conflict a "cold war"—a phrase that seemed so forbidding that Baruch deleted it from his appeal to the United Nations for nuclear cooperation, only to invoke it the following year without fear that it would become self-fulfilling and too late for it to be prophetic.

The atomic bomb, which rendered world war obsolete, also defined the peace. On March 1, 1946, Harold C. Urey, the Nobel Prize–winning physicist, warned that there was no practical defense against atomic weapons. Any suggestion to the contrary, he said, was just a ploy to vest the military with control over nuclear power. In London, the Sun Life Assurance Society apparently agreed; that same day, it announced that no new insurance policies would pay claims for deaths resulting from atomic bombs. Urey also maintained that the publicly released Smyth Report contained "most of the information that spies could possibly collect."

—

However humble, home had seemed a safe haven for Americans before the war. Suddenly, it was within reach of the rest of the world. The rosiest vision that Ambassador W. Averell Harriman could muster on his return from Russia was that war with the Soviet Union was not inevitable. For nearly four years, Russia had been America's ally against a common threat. But for more than twenty years prior to that, Russia and what it represented *was* the threat. "It is a fact that the Russian ideology is completely different from ours," Harriman said in a radio interview on the eve of Churchill's speech. "But if we both adopt the attitude of live and let live, as to internal affairs, and if we both respect the right of all people to choose their own way of life, this barrier needn't be insurmountable."

Instead, one new provocation after another pushed the level of mistrust, and with it the barrier between the two nations, higher and higher. The State Department vigorously protested the Red Army's refusal to relinquish the wartime foothold it had gained in Iran. The U.S. Navy complained to Moscow that Russians had fired at American planes near Manchuria.

—

When they returned from New Mexico in March 1946, the Greenglasses seemed to have pretty much outgrown their communist pretensions. Ruth attended a few communist political meetings in Chappaqua but no longer flirted with joining the Communist Party. David had voted for Roosevelt by absentee ballot from Los Alamos in 1944 (Ruth wasn't old enough to vote); now, both enrolled in the American Labor Party.

The 1946 congressional elections did not bode well for the Democrats, much less for the ALP. For the first time since Herbert Hoover was president, the Republican Party regained control over the House of Representatives. A nation that had fought its way out of the Depression largely by mobilizing for war was now adjusting to the economic vagaries of peace. At home, that adjustment depended on GI benefits and other government subsidies to integrate returning veterans, as well as on entrepreneurs like William Levitt, who began mass-producing a community of homes on Long Island.

Abroad, there was no mistaking the enemy. At home, though, Americans were still ambivalent about rendering judgment retroactively. Even as late as 1949, amid the tumultuous House Un-American Activities Committee hearings and the tempestuous trial of Communist Party leaders in the very courtroom where the Rosenbergs were later tried, the Truman administration's Loyalty Review Board cleared one suspected Communist, William Remington. The board concluded that the government's wartime attitude toward Russia, in 1942 at least, "was such that giving the Russians information with respect to the progress of our war effort wouldn't necessarily spell disloyalty." But to Americans who insisted that the Communist Party was too small to pose a serious threat to American democracy—and that the threat of abridging civil liberties and political freedoms was more dangerous—J. Edgar Hoover supplied an allegedly mathematical justification: "In 1917 when the Communists overthrew the Russian Government," he said, "there was one Communist for every 2,277 persons in Russia. In the United States today there is one Communist for every 1,814 persons in the country."

———

It was too soon to say that the party was over. But the very same week that the State Department and the navy lodged their protests against the Soviet Union, there was Earl Browder, the pragmatic former chief advocate of a live-and-let-live strategy in America, complaining that he had been slandered and spied upon by former colleagues before losing his job as general secretary of the Communist Party and then being ousted from the party altogether. He had been so vilified by his fellow communists that he found himself left with only one alternative: to become a paid economic adviser to big business. *The New York Times* captured his plight in this headline: BROWDER SAYS COMMUNISTS FRAMED HIM, FORCING HIM TO GET A CAPITALISTIC JOB. That Browder was also being subsidized as the American representative of the Soviet Union's state-owned publishing house, though, prompted conspiracists to suggest that he was being kept on political life-support, in case the Communist Party expediently needed his brand of accommodationism again. To which Browder replied: "You give the Party credit for too much subtlety."

A poll commissioned in 1946 by the National Association of Teachers of Speech cataloged the ten worst-sounding words in the English language. The words offered a window on what America found offensive: *cacophony, crunch, flatulent, gripe, jazz, phlegmatic, plump, plutocrat, sap,* and *treachery.* If the list hadn't been alphabetical, *treachery* probably would have come first. And on a list of postwar synonyms for *treachery, communism* might have been number one.

A few months later, *Look* magazine devoted five full pages to a self-help guide to what was fast becoming an American obsession: "How to Spot a Communist." This was no reactionary screed but a methodically rational analysis. It frankly discounted any possibility that the democratic system was seriously threatened by violent revolution or even by systematic communist political victories. Still, communism was deemed a menace to American life because it could penetrate legitimate organizations—"particularly the muddled labor and liberal groups"—and because the American Communist Party unswervingly espoused the swerving Soviet agenda. The article was a field guide to whether your neighbor, your union leader, or the liberal organization to which you contributed were covertly communist. An accompanying cartoon helpfully explained how to guard against communist infiltration. (The communist characters looked just like loyal Americans except, of course, they wore black suits; the good guys wore white.) The article's catalog of identifying characteristics included: denouncing the war waged by Britain as "imperialistic" until Germany invaded the Soviet Union; routinely dismissing all critics, regardless of their politics, as fascists; regularly receiving favorable publicity in communist publications; viewing every controversy through the prism of a class struggle; and imposing a double standard that magnifies complaints about the United States and minimizes criticism of Russia.

The article included a psychological primer that drew heavily on the work of Dr. David Abrahamsen, a Norwegian psychiatrist.

Communists are aggressive, frustrated, deprived, weak personalities who intensely hate their immediate surroundings—"the people we frequently call maladjusted." Abrahamsen identified them further as dupes who "were unable to find psychic security in their personal lives, or were unable to obtain affection from their fathers or mothers" and weren't able to "develop adult feelings." Their betrayal, he found, "may have deep psychological roots, particularly in their relationship to their mothers. Betraying the mother country is, in a psychological sense, betraying the mother."

—

David's first stop in New York was his mother's house at 64 Sheriff Street. This was to be the last time he returned there to live. Ruth, who had come home a few days earlier from Albuquerque, was three months pregnant. They needed their own apartment. David said that Julius offered them an apartment near Greenwich Village rent free or at nominal cost, but they decided against it because they were already too beholden and, as David later insisted, "I did not wish to have any further participation in Soviet espionage."* For the short term, Ethel invited them to stay in the Rosenbergs' three-room Knickerbocker Village apartment

---

* Julius was said to have had access to two apartments. One was on Avenue B. The other was on Morton Street. David said later that Ruth wouldn't have liked the Morton Street apartment, where, for a time, Julius's friend Joel Barr encamped, because it was on the top floor of a six-story walk-up.

while they took Michael to the Rivercrest Inn in the Hudson Valley for ten days to recover from a tonsillectomy.

Housing was scarce in New York. Classified ads for Apartment Wanted—"Desperate returning veteran, wife, need place to go," read one—overwhelmingly outnumbered the offerings listed under Apartment for Rent. Ex-GIs who had groused about jerry-built army installations were applying eagerly for emergency housing in converted barracks at the former Coast Guard station at Manhattan Beach in Brooklyn and at the former army terminal at Fox Hills on Staten Island. David invoked his veteran's preference to bypass the postwar waiting list for a telephone, but finding someplace to install it was tougher.

It took two months. David and Ruth finally rented an apartment at 265 Rivington Street, a shabby tenement above Red's Grocery and an electrician's shop, right around the corner from Sheriff Street, and down the block from Ruth's father's dry-goods store and from where her parents lived.

—

Most of the Greenglasses still assembled for dinner on Friday nights or Sunday afternoons in Tessie's dining room on Sheriff Street, although Ethel and Julius no longer attended regularly. This was just fine with Sam, who, after a vitriolic row about politics, had stormed out of Michael's birthing party in 1943, vowing never to speak to the Rosenbergs again. David saw less and less of his sister, too. Ethel was consumed by caring for Michael; and within a year, she gave birth to a second son. Tessie's matriarchy was unraveling. "You know what 'grow away' means?" David said. "Grow away? After the war, you grow away from siblings. Believe me, you do. There's no way you can help yourself."

Julius had also grown away from his father. They had quarreled frequently over religion and politics. His dismissal from the Signal Corps, as a direct result of his politics, sealed the estrangement. But during the summer of 1946, Harry Rosenberg had to be hospitalized, and everyone pitched in. David gave blood. During the last week of July, Julius camped by his father's bedside. On August 1, Harry Rosenberg died.

LOWER EAST SIDE, NEW YORK CITY

1. Tessie and Barnet Greenglass, 64 Sheriff St.
2. The Printzes, 256 Rivington St.
3. David and Ruth Greenglass, 265 Rivington St.
4. Alfred Corning Clark House, 285 Rivington St.
5. David and Ruth Greenglass, 266 Stanton St.
6. Ethel and Julius Rosenberg, Knickerbocker Village, 10 Monroe St.
7. G & R Engineering, 300 E. Second St.
8. Pitt Machine Products, 370 E. Houston St.
9. Gouverneur Hospital

Five days later, at the Jewish Maternity Hospital in Manhattan, Ruth Greenglass gave birth to a son, Steven Lawrence.

———

From their eleventh-floor apartment at the end of a long hall in Knickerbocker Village, the Rosenbergs could envision a future, not just by looking out the window but by eavesdropping on the Red-diaper-baby games Michael Rosenberg played and on the balladic progressive exhortations that spun from the family's phonograph.* The future was harder to imagine from the Greenglasses' walk-up on Rivington. They were consumed by the present. Ideology might be the means to a better end some day, but the surefire vehicle to self-improvement today was a good job.

During David's leave the previous September, he and Julius had vaguely discussed the possibility of some joint business venture. Julius was still working for Emerson Radio then but figured, correctly, that with wartime contracts evaporating he would be let go. Sure enough, at twenty-seven he was jobless. Most of his fellow engineering graduates of City College were working for major companies or for the government, or else they were earning advanced degrees. Julius was a political pariah and a security risk. Moreover, he had done nothing to distinguish himself as an engineer.

By default, he decided to start his own business. First, he enlisted Bernie Greenglass, who lived a few blocks away on Cannon Street and who hadn't found steady work since he had been discharged from the army. David recalled: "Julius must have thought—I can just picture his psychology—'This is a perfect cover-up, a patriotic war veteran in business with me.'" Julius also recruited a venture capitalist, Isidore Goldstein, who was an accountant and fellow tenant at Knickerbocker Village. Each invested $1,500 to establish a government-surplus hardware business, which they named United Purchasers and Distributors.

---

* Michael remembers a labor versus capitalist version of cowboys and Indians. Also, crawling on all fours, making believe he was a bridge, while Julius pretended the blocks he rolled across Michael's back were American and Russian convoys. When a German "convoy" arrived, Michael would stand up. "Hey," Julius would say. "Shake hands, bridge. You killed the fascists."

Unfortunately, the luckless partners purchased more screws, wrenches, nuts, bolts, and other hardware than they were able to distribute. For the several months that their venture floundered, they encamped in Barnet's machine shop on Sheriff Street and at another temporary home, the T & S Sewing Machine Company. T & S was owned by a former partner of Uncle Izzy, who introduced his nephews as decorated war veterans (a superfluous identification in David's case since he was still in uniform). Julius introduced himself as their brother-in-law and as a former government employee.

David's former bosses at Peerless Labs, the last place he had worked before the war, had offered to take him back at sixty-five dollars a week—"terrific money then," he said. But the invitation to join Bernie and Julius in a business—their own business, and one that would thrive on a stream of orders referred by his father and Uncle Izzy—seemed irresistible. On April 18, 1946, David formally joined the newly constituted G & R Engineering. The R stood for Rosenberg, the G for Goldstein and for Greenglass. "All power to the proletariat" was a noble slogan for the masses, but David's personal credo was "Where's mine?" As he later recalled: "In my mind, I said, this whole method of capitalism is for the birds. But I'm not a revolutionary—'Let's shoot this guy and take over.' That's nonsense. But I said, 'Why should I be on the bottom end? I'll be one of the people who own the shops.' I said, 'I might as well go into business. Why should I work for some other guy for sixty-five dollars a week?'"

—

G & R Engineering was capitalized with a two-thousand-dollar loan from Uncle Izzy and nearly five thousand that Bernie had borrowed from relatives earlier to invest in another company, Radar Fabrics, which never materialized. The partners opened a modest shop at 200 East Second Street in a storefront stocked with machinery purchased from the War Assets Administration. The shop was David's domain. Julius was the designated rainmaker, tapping his connections—old Signal Corps buddies, friends from City College, and even contacts at Amtorg, the Soviet international-trading agency.

Whatever else he was, Julius Rosenberg was not a great engineer. He was a worse businessman. He did land at least one major job from a former classmate—producing a radar aerial and parts for winding machines for as much as eight hundred dollars a month. Among Julius's other contacts was Philip Saloff, an electrical engineer who had been an organizer for the Federation of Architects, Engineers, Chemists, and Technicians and by then had become the purchasing agent for a Stamford, Connecticut, company that manufactured recording disks and tapes. Julius tried to persuade Saloff to hire G & R—once to weld a copper belt and another time to supply reels for recording tape. But after visiting the shop, Saloff pronounced the place too poorly equipped.

Julius wasn't above overstating the capacity of the shop, though, or the credentials of his partners. One City College classmate, Stephen Javna, later remembered how far Julius had reached in persuading him to give G & R a subcontract to manufacture caps and cores for solenoid pumps, which control the pitch of airplane propellers. Julius introduced Javna to David, who, Julius announced grandiloquently, had "worked with Oppenheimer during the war." Javna was impressed enough to commission G & R to fabricate parts for the pumps he was supplying to the Curtiss-Wright Propeller Division. The original contract was for three thousand dollars. By the time the order was filled, Julius had managed to more than triple the price, to ten thousand dollars. Still, G & R barely made a profit. Because the shop lacked the proper equipment, much of the work had to be subcontracted to a company in the Bronx, until Javna canceled the contract, blaming what he later described as "unsatisfactory work."

Julius introduced David as "a smart technical man" to another prospective customer, also an old friend from the Federation of Architects, Engineers, Chemists, and Technicians. Instead of being impressed, the friend remembered being appalled: "He could at least have wiped the dirt off his hands and come up and given me a decent handshake. He was sulking, . . . and Julie tried to pass it off with a 'Don't mind him, he's like that sometimes.'"

At times, David said, Julius would take on jobs just to keep G & R busy, even if it meant running in the red. David recalled that Julius allowed him to make some sewing-machine parts for a neighborhood inventor, Oscar Stetner, even though they would lose money on the order and Stetner was an outspoken anticommunist (who, the FBI later noted, "spent all of his money trying to perfect a sewing machine, but was unsuccessful in this, inasmuch as he died about 1948"). Another contract, for plate knives for sewing machines, lost money, too. The company refused to pay until it could sell the sewing machines, and G & R was unwilling to press for payment since the salesman was not only head of the dealers' association and a Republican district captain but was believed to be a gangster's good friend. G & R was also paid three hundred dollars to make dies for a machine that would punch holes in plastic handles for a luggage company. The partners didn't own the proper die-making device. They bought one for more than three hundred dollars.

Figuring that what they really needed was an infusion of capital for more equipment, Julius and the Greenglasses enlisted another investor—David Schein, a matzo manufacturer—and in 1947 reopened at 370 East Houston Street under a new name, Pitt Machine Products. The location presented only one drawback: Some of their machines shook so violently that the floor of the makeshift synagogue upstairs vibrated. The shop was shuttered on the Sabbath.

Buoyed by Schein's investment, the partners bought out Goldstein and spent about eight thousand dollars more on government surplus machinery. Invoking a veterans' guarantee provision, they applied for a $4,500 loan from the Reconstruction Finance Administration. As the government unloaded war matériel and private industry retooled for civilian manufacturing, plenty of equipment was for sale cheap. But bargains could be illusory. Attending his first auction, in the basement of a factory on the West Side, David spotted a mammoth automatic turret lathe. It was sophisticated enough to impress any prospective client—and his partners. David guessed that a new turret lathe would retail for upward of twenty thousand dollars. For some reason, though, bidding was light. For the incredible price of sixty-seven dollars, David managed to walk away with a turret lathe. Well, almost. The machine had originally been installed in the basement as the building was going up. To dismantle it would require breaking down a concrete wall and would cost thousands of dollars. "I never realized that they were not responsible for taking it out of there, I was," David recalled. He walked away not only without the turret lathe, but without his sixty-seven dollars.[*]

———

There was nothing wrong with starting off as small businessmen. Plenty of respectable entrepreneurs begin that way. But each of the joint ventures organized by Julius and the Greenglass brothers was destined to stay small—to shrink, even. And the more Pitt shrank, the larger it loomed as a wedge that would irrevocably divide the Greenglasses and the Rosenbergs.

None of the principals ever went hungry. But from 1946 through 1948, G & R Engineering and Pitt Machine Products subsisted largely on the patronage of the partners' family and friends.[†]

A sampling of expenditures included the $310 that David withdrew to make a down payment on furniture for his apartment and two hundred dollars to Tessie for Barnet's help on the Javna contract. One category of expenses appeared only irregularly: salaries. When business was good, David's salary might be as high as fifty-five dollars a week. But those weeks were rare. In 1947, David reported his total income at $2,250, an average of less than forty-five dollars a week. Pitt at one time employed as many as twenty machinists. Within two years, David was the foreman of a machine shop with no employees. By October 1948, only he, Bernie, and Julius were left. Working full-time mostly to pay off the shop's considerable debts, David never received any salary from Pitt again, and he and Ruth lived off their dwindling savings. The

---

[*] Barnet's business ineptitude may have been genetic. When David was still in the army, he confided to Ruth that his own shortcomings seemed awfully familiar. "After the war is over I shall never bother with the handling of money and all such things dealing with our personal savings and decisions concerning business," he wrote. "I have so much confidence in my wife and too little confidence in my own business activity. When I do my inventing, you my sweet will handle the business end of it."

[†] David said later that he was unaware of any money the Russians might have pumped into the two companies, nor did the FBI ever find evidence of any.

Rosenbergs hardly lived extravagantly either, but, David said later, Julius "claimed that he obtained money for living expenses from his friends."

David obtained money the hard way. He borrowed. He borrowed from the business. He borrowed from the bank (three hundred dollars from National City Bank in 1947 and the same amount two years later). But David's chief banker was Julius Rosenberg. None of Julius's anonymous benefactors was ever identified, though he hinted at one. Early in 1949, Ruth had cut her leg in an accident, and the doctor's bills were putting another crimp in the Greenglasses' bare-bones budget. David begged Julius for a loan, but according to David, Julius said he was short of funds and would have to contact a friend* who had worked as a two-hundred-dollar-a-day consultant on the Aswan Dam in Egypt. That dam-consultant story would be repeated ad nauseam for decades, presumably as further evidence of an inexhaustible hoard of Moscow gold. Only it wasn't strictly true. There may have been a consultant, and the amount of two hundred dollars may have been mentioned. But Ruth later recalled calculating at the time that the consultant friend was making about ten thousand dollars a year, which would have meant a still handsome but not as princely two hundred a *week*.

During the summer of 1948, David's cousin Julius Lewis gave him two hundred dollars so Ruth could rent a room in a boardinghouse in the Catskills for the season. When David visited her there, she recalled, he said that Julius had just given him eight hundred dollars. He deposited most of it in their bank account but gave Ruth sixty, which she distinctly remembered because on the way to the movies in Monticello she bought herself a pair of copper earrings and still had plenty left to throw Steven a bigger second birthday party than the one she had planned. David also urged Bernie to borrow from Julius. "I knew he had access to money that I didn't have access to," David said.

The Greenglass brothers borrowed from Julius even to bury their father. The winter before, Barnet had fallen on the icy sidewalk in front of a hardware store at Sheriff and Rivington Streets and broken his hip.

---

* Later identified as William Perl, who, like Alfred Sarant, Joel Barr, and Morton Sobell, was Julius's City College classmate.

He was incapacitated for months. (The Greenglasses sued.) In March 1949, Barnet died. Julius paid David and Bernie's share of the cemetery plot and the other funeral costs.

By then, David and Julius had implicitly established what David described as "a different relationship" about money. It might also be called blackmail. "I believe he made these loans to me without expecting repayment," David said, "because of the knowledge I had of his Soviet espionage activities."

Chapter 16

Venona

"They made a very huge mistake; it was a violation of every spying technique in the world."

=

American counterintelligence agents got two lucky breaks that enabled them to grasp the scope of wartime Soviet infiltration. In September 1945, Igor Gouzenko, a military-intelligence code clerk at the Soviet embassy in Ottawa, defected with hundreds of classified documents. Just about the same time, Elizabeth Bentley, a disillusioned NKGB courier, turned herself in to the FBI. Both revealed that the Russians had penetrated the Manhattan Project.

After committing a clumsy mistake in the embassy's cipher room that summer, Gouzenko had been ordered back to Russia. Instead, he slipped out one evening with a cache of secret cables and walked into a looking-glass world of Canadian diplomacy. He was dismissed as a crank by officials who were shocked at the possibility that the Soviets were spying on Canada and fearful that granting sanctuary to Gouzenko might offend Moscow. After a day of trying to defect, he was finally taken into protective custody just as his former comrades were breaking down his apartment door.

Bentley, a Vassar graduate and Communist Party member, was

studying for her master's degree in Italian at Columbia in 1938 when she was hired by the Italian Library of Information. Appalled to learn that the library was a fascist propaganda front, she volunteered as a Soviet informer. She fell in love with one of her contacts, Jacob Golos, the Russian-born founder of a Soviet-sponsored tourist agency. Through Golos, she met Abraham Brothman, a chemical engineer who became one of Harry Gold's sources.

Bentley titillated the FBI by hinting at another connection as well. On a summer evening in 1942, Bentley said, she and Golos were driving to dinner on the Lower East Side "when he stopped the car near Knickerbocker Village and got out to meet a tall, thin, bespectacled man on the street." Golos identified the man as an engineer. "He did not elaborate on the activities of this person and his associates nor did he ever identify any of them except that this one man to whom he gave my telephone number was referred to as Julius," Bentley said. "However, I do not believe this was his true name."

Bentley offered no corroboration. As a result, her revelations produced more in the way of firings than prosecutions. FBI Supervisor Robert J. Lamphere later lamented that the bureau had failed to aggressively follow up Bentley's leads. "For example," Lamphere said,

> a cursory investigation of Abe Brothman turned up a business partner, Jules Korchein, whom the FBI thought for a time might be "Julius." But when agents discovered that Korchein didn't live in Knickerbocker Village and didn't precisely match the description Bentley provided, the investigation was dropped. Had a list of Knickerbocker Village tenants been properly pursued, the name of Julius Rosenberg would have turned up, a man with the name of Julius who did fit Bentley's description.

—

Bentley's defection posed a genuine threat to Soviet intelligence and perhaps to Julius Rosenberg himself. His Soviet contact, Alexander Feklisov, arranged to brief Julius in mid-December 1945—a liaison that assumes special significance because an NKGB report of the encounter

is the only Soviet-era record released so far that suggests any direct involvement by Ethel Rosenberg in an espionage conspiracy.*

On the afternoon of December 15, 1945, Feklisov visited his pregnant wife in a Brooklyn maternity hospital, then ducked into a Turkish
bath to dodge possible surveillance. At 11:00 P.M., he entered a store
down the block from the Rosenbergs' apartment in Knickerbocker Village. Among the customers was Ethel Rosenberg—her presence was the
signal that Feklisov's rendezvous with Julius could proceed safely. After
buying bread and two bottles of milk, as if he were returning home to
his apartment in the neighborhood, Feklisov followed Ethel home five
minutes later. The NKGB account does not mention Ethel again. In the
kitchen of the Rosenbergs' apartment, Feklisov bombarded Julius with
questions. Obviously, Julius knew Jacob Golos—he was one of Julius's
contacts until Golos's death in 1943, when Julius was reassigned to
Semenov and Feklisov. Did Julius know any of Golos's friends? Only
one, Julius was quoted as replying, Bernard Schuster, the Communist
Party official with whom Julius had been meeting monthly. Any women
friends? None, Julius replied. Then he remembered one: Whenever Julius needed to see Golos urgently, he called Golos's secretary from a
telephone booth.

But why all the questions? Feklisov finally got to the point: "I let
Rosenberg know that Golos's secretary (I didn't name her) had betrayed
us and that in this connection we worried very much about him." Feklisov said he instructed Julius that if the FBI interrogated him, he must
deny belonging to the Communist Party, since he had already done so
twice to the Signal Corps, and it would be "illogical" for him to admit it
now. He must burn all his notes and cease all contact with Soviet agents
until the third Sunday in March 1946, when he should appear at the
Colony Theater on Second Avenue and East Seventy-ninth Street for a
cloak-and-dagger encounter worthy of the movies. Julius was to carry

---

* Feklisov later wrote: "It is certain Ethel shared the convictions of Julius and recognized without doubt his collaboration with Soviet spies. However, she had never participated in these
clandestine activities." In his memoirs, Feklisov went even further: "The fact is, I never did
meet Ethel," he wrote.

a copy of the *New York Post*. His contact would be holding a copy of *Reader's Digest* in his left hand and would ask: "Aren't you waiting for Al?" To which Julius would reply, "No, I'm waiting for Helen." The contact would then respond: "I am Helen's brother. She asked me to tell you something."

The NKGB imposed an intelligence-gathering lockdown in the United States for nearly two years. Julius largely ignored it.

With the defections still very much on his mind, on October 10, 1946, Anatoly Yakovlev booked passage on the SS *America* from New York to Le Havre. Officially, he was the Soviet vice-consul in Manhattan. He was being transferred to a comparable post in Paris. Yakovlev was scheduled to sail November 14. He was detained, not by U.S. government agents but by agents provocateurs among the proletariat: a maritime workers' strike. He was invited by the carrier to reconfirm his reservation for December. (Printed at the bottom of the company's stationery was the exhortation: "Keep America Strong on the Seas. Travel and Ship in American Ships.")

The day before he departed, Yakovlev shared a farewell toast with Harry Gold. Their encounter began routinely, which meant that Harry discreetly didn't ask where Yakovlev had been or what he had been doing since they last met, eleven months before. To square past accounts, Yakovlev gave Harry several hundred dollars in cash.

In the interest of closure, Harry informed Yakovlev of what he later described as "an error I had made in procedure and which could possibly preclude my doing any further work for the Soviets." Given how vehemently opposed Harry had been to compromising his connection with Klaus Fuchs by contacting David Greenglass in June 1945 (even David concluded: "They made a very huge mistake; it was a violation of every spying technique in the world"), it is impossible to imagine what Harry was thinking in March 1946: Having been laid off by Penn Sugar, he had injected himself into the nexus of yet another spy ring by going to work for one of his former sources, Abraham Brothman. Worse, he revealed that "Frank Kessler," the name Brothman had known him by, was an alias. If the Soviets had been ruthlessly efficient, they would have eliminated Harry Gold. Instead, Yakovlev turned beet red. He threw down enough cash to cover the cost of their drinks three times over and, without saying good-bye, left the bar, muttering: "You shouldn't have done it. You don't know what harm you have done!" Gold never saw Yakovlev again.

The next day, Yakovlev left the United States and his espionage apparatus that had been penetrated by informers, some of whom were known to the Russians years before they were exposed to the American public.

Bentley's defection wasn't revealed publicly until 1948, when she testified before the House Committee on Un-American Activities as the "blonde spy queen" and the "red spy queen"—a prized catch in the government's vigilance against subversion. Hardly anyone noticed at the time when she disclosed that, during the war, a Soviet sympathizer in the White House had learned that American cryptographers were poised to break a Russian secret code. For nearly three decades, the National Security Agency later reported, "this fragmentary anecdote remained virtually all that the public would hear about one of the cold war's greatest intelligence coups." It was called Jade, Bride, and Drug before it was finally code-named Venona.

—

The NKGB typically shipped bulky documents by diplomatic pouch; shorter and more urgent messages were encrypted and then sent by commercial radiogram. Since just before the war, the army's Signals Security Agency had been collecting copies of cables and radiograms sent by Russian nationals to the Soviet Union. Unread copies of those messages had piled up by the thousands because the key to Soviet codes eluded American military intelligence. Then, late in 1942, intercepted cables between Tokyo and Japanese military attachés in Berlin and Helsinki suggested that cryptographers in Finland were succeeding where the Americans had failed and were sharing their progress with Japan. Spurred by that breakthrough and concerned that Russia and Germany might again negotiate a separate peace, the Signals Security Agency began a special program in February 1943 to break the Soviet code.

"The simplest things are often the most clever," David Greenglass had quoted Julius Rosenberg as saying about the jagged Jell-O box recognition device—a corollary, perhaps, of Einstein's prescription that "things should be made as simple as possible, but not any simpler." In this vein, the Soviet code was diabolically simple. First, the text of a message was translated into numbers derived from a codebook, with each word or common phrase corresponding to a four-digit numeric code group. Then, to obscure the code groups, the message was enciphered. Digits were transcribed from pads printed with sixty five-digit numbers on each page. Copies of those pads were shipped periodically by diplomatic pouch to Soviet code clerks overseas. Each page of each pad was numbered so the same pages would be available to the sender and the recipient. And each page was to be used only once, which meant that without the specific page in hand it would be all but impossible to decipher the message.

But late in 1943, Lieutenant Richard Hallock of the Signals Security Agency astutely stumbled upon an opening: He noticed that some of the pages from the one-time pads appeared to be duplicates. Cecil James Phillips of the National Security Agency later concluded that early in 1942, with Moscow under siege by the Nazis, the NKGB's cryptographic center had printed duplicate copies of thousands of pages. By late 1945, Meredith Gardner and his code breakers stationed at Arlington Hall, a former girls' school in Virginia, had figured out the Russians' formula for encoding English letters. Soon, they began deciphering specific messages.

As intelligence officials suspected, these weren't just secret diplomatic or trade messages. One cable, dispatched from New York to Moscow on December 2, 1944, revealed the names of seventeen scientists purportedly working on "the problem of atomic energy." Here was evidence, however disjointed, of infiltration of the highest levels of the American government.

On August 30, 1946, Gardner distributed six copies of a top-secret eleven-page report on "cover names in diplomatic traffic" that, he acknowledged, in its present state "tends to arouse curiosity more than it does to satisfy it." Gardner categorized names derived from animals, plants, and mythology, names of places and institutions, and Christian names of Russian and non-Russian origin. On page 9, he listed a separate category, miscellaneous, that began with this entry:

LIB?? (Lieb?) or possibly LIBERAL: was ARTENKO until Sept. 1944. Occurs 6 times, 22 October–20 December 1944. Message of 27 November speaks of his wife ETHEL, 29 years old married (?) 5 years, ". . . husband's work and the role of METR(O) and NIL."

Chapter 17

===

Liberal

"He had nobody to confide in who
had been involved in this."

=

Alexander Feklisov never forgot his earliest encounters with Julius Rosenberg. "Without thinking of conspiracy," Feklisov recalled, "he would be going to our meetings as to a feast." Even decades later, Feklisov shuddered at the memory of one of their first rendezvous. It was a warm autumn evening. Feklisov spotted Julius approaching jauntily, a slight, mustached man "without his jacket, his shirt over his trousers, a cigar in his mouth and having noticed me in the crowd is waving to me, 'Good evening, Comrade.' " Julius, Feklisov concluded, "loved intelligence work with its romantic aura elevating him above the monotony of every day life." David described his brother-in-law more bluntly. Julius, David said, "loved being a spy."

By mid-1945, though, Feklisov suspected that Julius was being followed. His suspicion appears to have been unwarranted; Julius wasn't even on the government's radar screen. Elizabeth Bentley was still months away from referring to him, and the encoded radiogram that mentioned his code name was just an enigmatic jumble in a stash of unread messages. As the FBI's Robert Lamphere later lamented, the only federal agents who expressed even the remotest interest in Julius between 1945 and 1950 were the Internal Revenue Service bureaucrats who routinely processed his meager tax returns.

—

David sometimes ran errands for Julius, who apparently had few qualms about confiding in him. "You must understand," David said later, "that he had nobody to confide in who had been involved in this. . . . I was near at hand and right under his feet every day." He recalled only one occasion in five years when Julius was obsessively secretive. It started with a telephone call to the machine shop. "After Julius hung up, he told me that he had to go out to meet the caller, who was waiting on the corner," David said. "I started to go out with Julius, being curious. . . . Julius, however, did not want me to go, saying, 'I do not want you to see this man so stay in the shop.' Julius did not return to work that day."

In contrast, David recalled Julius once opening a desk drawer at the machine shop and showing off a Leica camera in a brown leather case that he said he had bought at Willoughby's. He said he "sometimes fastens the camera to a drop-leaf table in his home." David also remembered standing by the milling machine when Julius divulged to him and Bernie that research scientists had overcome the theoretical obstacles to an atomic-powered airplane.

David was familiar with Julius's friend Joel Barr, who occasionally worked at the machine shop on what David remembers only as "an electronics apparatus of some kind" for himself. In 1947, Barr delivered a metal toolbox with photographic equipment, developing pans, clamp-on floodlights, and books on photography and announced that Julius said he could store his equipment in the basement. Barr was sometimes met there by his girlfriend, Vivian Glassman, who was "exceedingly friendly" with Ethel and Julius, David recalled, and regularly baby-sat the Rosenberg children on Wednesday afternoons when Ethel vanished to conduct what David described as "her mysterious business." The family learned later that her business had nothing to do with national security but with Ethel's own. Wrestling with her roles as a daughter and as a mother, she was engaged in a petit bourgeois exercise: She was seeing a psychiatrist.

David also remembers Julius's asking him to run a mysterious errand, though it may be another case of less than met the eye. But the episode may be significant for an entirely different reason altogether: It lends context to a seemingly cryptic phrase that has been embraced— by David Greenglass and Alexander Feklisov among many others—as incontrovertible proof that David eagerly accepted Julius's invitation to spy for the Soviet Union. David included the phrase in the letter he wrote Ruth from Los Alamos on November 4, 1944: "My darling, I most certainly will be glad to be part of the community project that Julius and his friends have in mind. Count me in dear or should I say it has my vote. If it has yours, count us in."

The errand was to deliver an envelope containing one thousand dollars to Russell McNutt, whom David had first met in 1946 when McNutt, who had worked at Oak Ridge, was negotiating to become G & R's South American contact in a machinery-export business. Julius had known McNutt for years. (Thus it seemed odd that he did not deliver the envelope himself.) They had met through Russell's brother, Waldo, whom the Rosenbergs had befriended when they spent their summer vacation in 1941 on his farm on the Connecticut River in Haddam. According to the FBI, the McNutts were communist sympathizers, perhaps even card-carrying party members. Russell McNutt was also a capitalist, the principal in a proposed real-estate development in northern Westchester County. For years, his family owned a hilly forty-acre tract adjoining the Taconic State Parkway near Yorktown Heights. He intended to clear the land and construct a community of homes, perhaps as a commune for like-minded people as well as for profit. Among the other would-be capitalists he recruited as investors was Julius Rosenberg. David later estimated that Julius invested as much as five thousand dollars in the project, including the one thousand that he may have borrowed from Tante Chucha and which, at Julius's behest, David was asked to deliver to Russell McNutt at his firm, Industrial Planners and Designers, on Columbus Circle in Manhattan.

The possibility that Julius was flush enough to invest in a real-estate development before his business went belly-up isn't far-fetched. Nor is the notion that living in a monolithic community of like-minded individuals would have appealed to him.

Years later, after the November 4 letter to Ruth was released by the FBI, Alexander Feklisov said that the correspondence represented "the best proof of David's enthusiasm in suggesting his assistance in providing information to the Soviet Union." David later said that he, too, assumed the references to Julius's friends were to fellow communists and that the community project was some future espionage enterprise. Maybe they were. But read in context, and as a reply to an earlier letter from Ruth, the community project may have been just that: a community project. Her letter refers to Julius's hopes of investing in a housing development in Westchester after the war and estimates that the homes will cost about two thousand dollars each. In a subsequent letter, Ruth repeated that "Julie said that he was counting on us for one of the families in this community of homes to be built after the war."*

———

Except for the two brief encounters with Harry Gold and the twenty-minute ride with Yakovlev in 1945, everything the NKGB knew about David Greenglass and everything that he knew about the NKGB came through one individual: Julius Rosenberg. That might help explain Alexander Feklisov's assessment of the Greenglasses early in 1947, just after he left New York for Britain to handle Klaus Fuchs. Feklisov had no firsthand knowledge and was undoubtedly extrapolating from Julius's inflated opinion of his own powers of persuasion or from his puppylike desire to please. Feklisov pronounced the Greenglasses "young, intelligent, capable, and politically developed people, strongly believing in the cause of communism and wishing to do their best to help our country as much as possible. They are undoubtedly devoted to us."

By 1947, evidence of that devotion is hard to come by, except in NKGB files, which, while convincingly specific, were largely regurgitations of accounts from Julius and may prove to be as tainted with un-

---

* Among the papers found in Julius's apartment after he was arrested was a manila envelope with blueprints of the housing development in Yorktown Heights. On one plot, the word *SOLD!* was written in pen.

corroborated allegations as many FBI files are. Julius may have been exaggerating, to increase his own value to the Soviets. NKGB agents also may have overstated their own roles. And even today, David may be lying (to support his generally consistent alibi that his spying was limited to wartime, when the Soviet Union was ostensibly an ally of the United States).

Presumably through Julius, the Soviets had suggested that David get a college degree, preferably at someplace like the University of Chicago, where he could reestablish contact with Manny Schwartz and other young scientists he had met at Los Alamos (and to whom the Soviets, expectantly, had already assigned code names). David recalls stubbornly rejecting the Russians' insistent career counseling, via Julius: He should return to Los Alamos to take a civilian job; he should parlay his Manhattan Project experience into a subsidized college education; he should apply to the new national laboratory opening at Brookhaven on eastern Long Island. (Julius later reversed himself on that last recommendation, David recalled, because he became concerned that the application would prompt another background investigation.) David offered no shortage of excuses: Ruth was pregnant; her pregnancy was precarious; the baby was due just one month before the fall 1946 semester was to begin.

As a result, Feklisov envisioned the Greenglasses serving as couriers or as group handlers. Moscow concurred. "Although he has the possibility of returning to work at an extremely important institution on 'Enormoz,' Camp 2," an NKGB message to New York said, "because of his limited education [Greenglass] will not be able to obtain a position in which he could become an independent source of information in which we are interested." The NKGB also reported that in early 1949 David was finally persuaded to apply to the University of Chicago (where the Russians would pay his expenses plus a stipend of $125 a month) but was rejected because there were no vacancies. David later insisted that he had never applied to the University of Chicago, much less been rejected. Further, no evidence suggests that the Greenglasses assumed either role, as couriers or as handlers of a group of agents.

Until the very end, NKGB reports, usually quoting Julius, suggest that David never wavered fundamentally. The reports seem believable, largely because they specify so many dates, names, and places that Julius or anyone else who might have fed them to Moscow risked almost certain exposure if any detail proved false. But the specifics also seem to be contradicted by David's deteriorating relationship with Julius and his disillusionment with Soviet communism.

—

Increasingly, Americans whose political philosophy had been shaped in the thirties on college campuses or unemployment lines or by anti-Semitic slights from Gentile employment agencies were challenged to justify Moscow's excesses. Its ends seemed less consistent with the idealistic goals of global communism than with the particularly Russian legacy of czarism and imperialism. Stalin refused to relinquish the territory conquered in the Second World War. He installed puppet governments in Eastern Europe. He banished Marshal Tito, who had dared to create his own personal brand of communism in Yugoslavia. He brooked no dissent from the Communist Party in America. And he stoked bloody insurgencies in Greece, China, and Indochina, as well as political subversion that threatened freely elected democratic governments in France and Italy. Stalin, by personifying the inconsistency between ideal communism and its embodiment, became the perfect foil: Die-hard communists could still sympathize with the plight of the proletariat and complain about income inequality and racial segregation in America but divorce themselves from Stalinism.

What finally drove David from communism, he said, was Stalin's bullying in Berlin. In June 1948, the Russians severed all road and rail connections between the western sectors of the city and western Germany. The Soviets claimed the blockade was retaliation for the other occupying powers' decision to create a capitalist West Germany. Their blockade was also a gamble that the United States would not unleash its nuclear monopoly to defend Berlin. What America, Britain, and France launched instead was an airlift. With, as it later turned out, the complicity of Soviet air-traffic controllers, the airlift eventually delivered eight thousand tons of supplies a day to the besieged city.

The blockade didn't convert David to capitalism, just away from communism.

> My attitude is, if you have an idealistic feeling that communism is a great system, how can you follow all the other stuff? On the one hand, this is what they're doing for the benefit of mankind. On the other hand, you go to the gulag. You can't justify it. If the means is crappy, the end has gotta be crappy even if it started out good. That's a fact. History teaches you that time and time again. If you have a system that's no good and you can't get rid of it by peaceful means, to overthrow it and get a million people killed and then institute a system that's even worse—you've gotta be an idiot.

—

David later maintained that the blockade of Berlin also turned him against Julius. It was the first time that David expressed the depth of his disillusionment.

"Julius was a charming con man," David said.

> It didn't occur to me right away, but in 1948 I could see that everything was a facade. He was the essence of the—what is it—the commissar. He was no joke. He would cajole you to do what he wanted, but he was the kind of guy that would say, "Take him out and shoot him."...
>
> It took quite a great amount of courage for me to stand up and talk that way to him, because I had, for years, not in any way disagreed with him, and all my disagreements I kept to myself, because I felt that he could be vicious in a tirade. That unleashed the wellsprings. He turned me every way but loose. He tongue-lashed me so badly that I didn't know whether he made a mat to step on out of me. I felt, well, I had better keep my opinions to myself, because I felt that if I gave him the idea that I was completely unreliable, that there would be some type of repercussion that I would not particularly desire.

—

By 1948, David and Ruth abandoned the American Labor Party and enrolled as Democrats.

———

David's business acuity evolved even more slowly than his political sophistication. His evolution in both domains was circumscribed by his ambivalence toward Julius. He could challenge his brother-in-law's bedrock political principles once, then bite his lip and vote however he pleased. But business was more personal. Dissolving the partnership would amount to public affirmation that another dream had failed.

Even before the paychecks stopped coming altogether in 1948, David considered quitting Pitt Machine Products. He and Ruth had discussed it to death. So had Bernie and his wife, Gladys. They hesitated, though. One reason was family loyalty. Another was a wisp of wishful thinking that a lucrative contract from one of Julius's friends might yet revive Pitt or at least maneuver it within striking distance of solvency. No such contract ever came.

Instead, in 1948, David registered for the night session at Pratt Institute in Brooklyn but dropped out because Julius complained that he wasn't adequately supervising the machine shop and Pitt had had to hire another foreman to replace him. In 1949, David finally reached the inevitable conclusion that the partners—two of them, anyway—had been deluding themselves. He filed a job application with the Capital Employment Agency, blaming "no business" as his reason for leaving Pitt. He listed three references. Julius Rosenberg was the first.

David was hired at seventy-six dollars a week by Arma Engineering, a small factory in the giant Bush Terminal industrial complex on the South Brooklyn waterfront. His shift was 4:45 P.M. to 1:15 A.M., with a half hour for "lunch." Arma was working on a number of contracts from the navy, some of them classified, including research and development of radar and of a gyroscope to improve the accuracy of weapons. No background investigation of David appears to have been conducted. By September 19, 1949, though, he apparently felt that he could, in good conscience, sign an antisabotage oath that said he "did not then and would not later advocate or hold membership in any organization or group that advocated the overthrow of the Government."

NKGB messages between New York and Moscow as late as 1950 suggest otherwise.* But, crediting David's growing disillusionment with both Julius and communism, the messages strain credulity. Again, though, they are so detailed that, if fabricated, they had to have been the work of a pathological liar who wasn't afraid of getting caught. And David himself would later tell congressional investigators that Julius urged him to steal secrets from Arma. NKGB agents in New York wrote Moscow on January 13, 1950, that David was assembling a radar stabilizer for tanks, which, they went on to explain, "must keep the gun constantly directed at the target regardless of vibrations of the tank itself while moving during the battle." A message from New York said that David had volunteered to take a camera into the Arma plant to photograph the device. Moscow, rejecting David's offer as too dangerous, suggested he provide sketches from memory instead.

---

* And Arma was targeted by Soviet agents at least once before, as far back as 1931.

Chapter 18

The Bomb

"It never occurred to me to say anything like 'I helped them do it.' What the hell, I mean it was something in my past."

≡

Washington was deeply skeptical about Russia's scientific and industrial prowess, but Soviet treachery worried America more. In 1947, the Air Force was ordered to develop a system for detecting foreign atomic tests. One early system, code-named Project Mogul, depended on acoustic devices carried aloft by balloons. When the instruments were tested high above the New Mexico desert, they didn't detect any foreign nuclear explosions, but the balloons themselves were detected by people on the ground—producing a durable legacy of UFO sightings. By 1949, the navy had launched Operation Rain Barrel, which measured radioactivity in rainwater collected in 2,500-square-foot aluminum pans on the roof of the Naval Research Laboratory in Washington, D.C., and other sites. Specially equipped Air Force reconnaissance planes based in Alaska also had begun to regularly monitor the atmosphere.

On September 3, 1949, one of those converted B-29s cruising off Siberia's Kamchatka Peninsula sniffed unusually high levels of radioactivity. In the months that the monitoring program had been operating, 111 alerts had been logged at the yellow-brick building on G Street in

Washington that housed the AFOAT-1 Data Analysis Center, a futur-
istic, windowless conference room secured by a steel door and dominated by a seven-foot globe. Each report was investigated, and each
was later attributed to natural causes. This 112th alert was recorded on
Labor Day weekend. Clattering Teletype keys suddenly intruded on
the holiday torpor, triggering a technological dragnet. Alerted by the
Air Force, other scientists were able to chart a huge radioactive cloud
drifting east. The cloud eventually split up over Canada, with one mass
blowing toward Britain and the other moving south, later lingering over
Washington, D.C., long enough to contaminate the Naval Research Laboratory rainwater. Government scientists attributed the cloud to a Soviet nuclear device detonated less than a week earlier, somewhere on the
barren steppes of Kazakhstan, three thousand miles west of where the
B-29 had first intercepted radioactive dust.

The scientists were right. After the German invasion in June 1941,
radar and mine detection had taken precedence. But atomic bombs had
rebounded onto the Soviet research agenda in 1943 when a government
advisory committee recommended that research be resumed under the
direction of a forty-year-old physicist, Igor Kurchatov. Early on August
29, 1949, in the desert about one hundred miles south of Semipalatinsk,
the Soviets tested an atomic weapon that bore a striking resemblance
to the Fat Man plutonium implosion bomb that the United States had
dropped on Nagasaki. Lavrenti Beria, who headed the NKVD and also
had overall responsibility for the atomic program, called Moscow, where
it was 5:00 A.M. He demanded that Stalin be awakened.

"What do you want? Why are you calling?" the Soviet leader reportedly demanded.

"Everything went right," a relieved Beria replied.

"I know already," Stalin said, and hung up.

—

On September 23, President Truman disclosed that the Soviet Union had
successfully tested an atomic weapon. The test had to be considered a scientific and a military breakthrough, even if, as most Americans assumed,
it was largely the result of thievery rather than of technological parity.

It was also a political wake-up call. Washington could no longer claim a nuclear monopoly. The Democratic administration, on whose watch Russian agents had absconded with America's most closely guarded secrets, could no longer justify constraints on defense spending.

Within months, the Central Intelligence Agency completed a sobering assessment of Moscow's nuclear potential. "The continental U.S. will be for the first time liable to devastating attack," the CIA concluded. By 1953, Russia would likely have one hundred plutonium bombs comparable to the one dropped on Nagasaki. By 1955, the Russians would have twice as many. "Preliminary and highly tentative U.S. estimates indicate that an atomic attack of approximately 200 bombs delivered on prescribed targets might prove decisive in knocking the U.S. out of a war." The inevitability of war was tempered by a practical assessment that Moscow would rather achieve domination by indigenous revolution. In contrast, State Department analysts concluded that America's atomic monopoly and economic superiority had deterred Moscow from a military strike, but that "Soviet development of an atomic weapon may have decisively changed this situation, particularly if surprise employment of the weapon could sharply reduce retaliatory action or make it impossible." By April 1950, the National Security Agency was painting an even bleaker picture. Communist success in China "provides a springboard for a further incursion in this troubled area," the NSA concluded, presciently pinpointing the policy change that was to emerge starkly only two months later in Korea. That the Soviets now possessed atomic weapons, the NSA said, puts a premium not only on a surprise attack against the United States but on "piecemeal aggression against others, counting on our unwillingness to engage in atomic war unless we are directly attacked."

Washington faced a peculiar public-relations challenge: how to prepare patriotic Americans for the possibility of an atomic attack without transforming them into fatalists eschewing the backyard bomb-shelter fad or into better-red-than-dead pacifists. In 1950, the government released a study by Arnold Kramish and other scientists to catalyze a constructive civil defense. "It is hoped," the authors wrote, "that as a result, although it may not be feasible completely to allay fear, it will at least

be possible to avoid panic." Among other things, they recommended
that anyone seeing a sudden flash of light should drop to the ground in
a fetal position for ten seconds, after which "the immediate danger is
then over, and it is permissible to stand up and look around to see what
action appears advisable."

In retrospect, lots of advice about how to survive a nuclear holocaust seems pretty loopy. "What is your town doing about parking?" one
guide asked. "Congested streets are one of the worst hazards you will
have to deal with in an A-bombing." Dr. Ralph E. Lapp, in a book titled
Must We Hide? suggested that America's industrial spine would be less
vulnerable if urban planners created "rod cities" as long as fifty miles but
only one mile wide.

Richard Gerstell, a consultant to the Office of Civil Defense, peppered
his paperback guide, *How to Survive an Atomic Bomb,* with relentlessly
cheerful asides. Yes, many Japanese bore burn scars from the atomic
bombs dropped at Hiroshima and Nagasaki, but "*not one* of those scars
has turned into cancer yet—in the five years that have passed." In the
same vein, the book pointed out that "some Japanese men and women
could not have children for a while after the bombings, but almost all
of them have since returned to normal and produced healthy children.
(Even when these Japanese could not have children, they were still able
to have sexual relations. There's a difference.)"

What to do while you're lying flat on your stomach in the basement
waiting for the all clear? "Lots of people have little tricks to help steady
their nerves at a time like that—like reciting jingles or rhymes or the
multiplication table," Gerstell advised. Anyway, he figured, "one atomic
bomb dropped on New York City would probably kill at most 1 in 100
people there" (a proportion that, if not quite acceptable, seemed less
alarming than if readers had done the math and arrived at the raw total:
seventy thousand people). His thesis in a nutshell: "The atomic bomb is
a terrible weapon BUT not as terrible as most of us believe."

Any doubts as to how terrible were thoroughly obliterated by Ches-
ley Bonestell's illustration on the cover of *Collier's.* His terrifying oil
painting might have been mistaken for a picture of Mount Vesuvius
transplanted to Lower Manhattan, but the headline was a dead give-

away: HIROSHIMA, U.S.A.: CAN ANYTHING BE DONE ABOUT IT? Ground zero for the hypothetical attack was where defense officials calculated an enemy bomb would do the most damage: the Lower East Side.

———

On the Lower East Side, David took the news about the Soviet bomb in stride. "It never occurred to me to say anything like 'I helped them do it,'" he recalled. "What the hell, I mean it was something in my past."

———

In the frenzied interval between the actual Soviet test and the White House announcement, American intelligence had sniffed something else in the air. In mid-September, cryptographers at Arlington Hall finally deciphered a crucial 1944 Soviet radiogram from New York to Moscow. The message revealed that one of the members of the British scientific mission to the Manhattan Project was a Soviet agent. The message also encapsulated a classified scientific paper on the experimental gaseous-diffusion process for refining uranium. "When I read the KGB message," Robert Lamphere, the FBI liaison to Arlington Hall later recalled, "it became immediately obvious to me that the Russians had indeed stolen crucial research from us and had undoubtedly used it to build their bomb." Lamphere immediately requisitioned the gaseous-diffusion report from the Atomic Energy Commission, and the FBI determined that it had been written by Klaus Fuchs. A search of FBI files turned up two more incriminating references to Fuchs. One was a German document captured after the war that identified Fuchs as a communist who was subject to arrest by the Gestapo. Fuchs's name was also listed in an address book confiscated from a Soviet military-intelligence agent who had been arrested in Canada in the Gouzenko investigation. Everything the FBI knew about Fuchs fit comfortably into the profile sketched by the Soviet radiogram. "Thus," Lamphere later wrote, "by the time of President Truman's announcement, we had a prime suspect for the KGB spy who had stolen A-bomb secrets and given them to the Russians."

———

Earlier that summer, Harry Gold was working with atomic energy again, this time for America, using radioactive isotopes to conduct heart research at Philadelphia General Hospital. Gold hadn't heard from the NKGB since his aborted farewell toast with Anatoly Yakovlev in 1946. On July 18, 1949, however, Harry received a coded letter from the NKGB requesting a meeting one week later. He failed to appear, insisting later that he had forgotten his three-year-old instructions about when and where to meet. On September 10, an NKGB agent visited him at home. Nothing Harry told the agent was reassuring: Two years earlier, he said, a federal grand jury investigating Soviet subversion had asked him about his relationships with Abraham Brothman and Jacob Golos. Harry said that he testified that the relationships were purely professional—he and Brothman met Golos as chemists seeking jobs. The NKGB wasn't assuaged. Too many loose threads were dangling for the FBI not to notice. After the meeting, the New York station informed Moscow that while Harry remained devoted, "it is difficult to foresee how he will behave at an interrogation if the FBI undertakes further inquiry of the case." Moscow responded decisively: Get ready to smuggle Gold out of the United States. On October 24, he was told to prepare to flee. Harry was reluctant. He insisted that the FBI was no longer investigating him, and that if he disappeared, his brother, Joseph, would probably be fired from his navy job, as a security risk; there would be no one to support their father. The NKGB assured Harry that his family would be provided for. Only then did he agree to explore possible escape plans, among them joining a Quaker medical commission leaving soon for China.

—

Klaus Fuchs was worried about his elderly father, too. In October 1949, Klaus dutifully informed the security officer at the Harwell atomic research center in Britain that Emil Fuchs had been offered a professorship at the University of Leipzig, in East Germany. His disclosure, consistent, perhaps, with his Quaker forthrightness, may have been a preemptive way of advising the British government that he might be vulnerable to pressure from the Eastern Bloc. But by then, British intelligence was already attuned to the FBI's suspicions about Fuchs. In December 1949, William Skardon, an MI5 agent, conducted the first in a series of interviews designed to win Fuchs's trust. The NKGB's Moscow Center, drawing on details from its moles, described what happened next: "Fuchs admitted his membership of the Communist Party in the past, but completely denied being a spy. Skardon played on Fuchs's loyalty to his English friends and colleagues and appealed to his feelings of gratitude towards Britain, which had given him shelter and provided him with his life's work. These tactics evidently worked and called forth in Fuchs a psychological conflict."

———

Holidays usually meant having to spend more money on food and gifts, and money was never a gratifying subject of conversation in the Greenglass household. Ruth had been nagging David for months, since he quit the family business, about redeeming his twenty-five shares of outstanding stock in Pitt Machine Products. Finally, before going to work at Arma one afternoon, David visited the Pitt machine shop and confronted Julius. According to David, Julius explained that he was already trying to borrow five thousand dollars from a cousin to buy out David Schein's shares. Then, he would deal with David's. Meanwhile, Julius urged, just sign over the stock, have the certificate notarized, and deliver it to him. David, mistrustful, had to think fast. He lied. He told Julius that the stock certificate wasn't readily accessible, that it was locked up in a safe-deposit box—otherwise he would gladly hand it over without immediately getting cash in return.

If David hadn't found Julius that day, Julius would have found David. He, too, had a message. David remembers the words vividly: "You're hot. You will have to begin thinking about going away to Paris." David was stunned. He had a new job, a wife who was pregnant again, and the expectation of finally collecting a few thousand dollars from a star-crossed business venture so he could repay his debts and move to the suburbs. Now, he was being told matter-of-factly that he should be poised to skulk away through Paris to some godforsaken country in Eastern Europe and then to Russia or else risk imprisonment by remaining in the United States.

David was growing more and more agitated. Julius suggested they adjourn to a luncheonette on Avenue C. They slipped into a booth and ordered coffee. When the waitress was out of earshot, Julius elaborated: "Something is happening which will cause you to leave the United States," David remembered him saying. David and Ruth should apply to the State Department for passports and to the French consulate for visas. He should state that their purpose in traveling to France was to dispose of property there. They were to take a ship from New York to Cherbourg or Le Havre.

When David returned home, he delivered Julius's message about the stock. Ruth wasn't pleased. They agreed that Julius could not be trusted. Ruth was already upset enough, David recalled later, that he didn't tell her what else Julius said. David couldn't get it out of his mind, though. On New Year's Eve, he and Ruth attended a party at the apartment of their friend Jack Schleider on Forsythe Street. With his friends, David swapped stories, celebrated, and counted down the seconds until 1950—all the time wondering whether he would ever spend another New Year's Eve with them again.

———

The second half of the American century opened to generally good reviews. War had finally subsided in the Middle East. France had just granted domestic sovereignty to Vietnam, although nationalist-front guerrillas led by Ho Chi Minh were challenging the new government. China had finally fallen to the communists, but a nationalist garrison had managed to escape to Formosa, where Chiang Kai-shek pledged to resist "as long as the Soviet aggressor occupies one inch of our territory." Near Manhattan's Foley Square, the jury in the spy trial of Judith Coplon, a former Justice Department official, was digesting conflicting explanations for several furtive rendezvous between Coplon and the Soviet engineer Valentin Gubitchev. (The prosecution insisted that their peculiar meanderings proved they were spies; the defense countered that they were merely having an affair.) At the Astor Hotel, representatives of fifty-eight national organizations, including the Improved Order of Red Men, were convening an "All-American Conference" to form a united front against communism.

In Washington, Representative Richard M. Nixon, Republican of California, joined other congressmen in lambasting Secretary of State Dean Acheson for his continued support of Alger Hiss, the former State Department official soon to be convicted of perjury for denying that he had been a member of the Communist Party. Nixon accused the Justice Department of planning to undermine the prosecution of Hiss by leveling perjury charges against his chief accuser, Whittaker Chambers. (Nixon said he knew this on "unimpeachable authority.") Reminded that President Truman had dismissed the House Committee on Un-American Activities' investigation of Hiss as a "red herring," Representative W. Kingsland Macy, Republican of New York, complained that by summoning up that of all similes, the president "unwittingly used the prestige of his high office on behalf of one of his country's enemies."* At Iowa State College, Eleanor Roosevelt had this to say about testimony that led to Hiss's conviction: "One thing troubles me. If you had been disloyal and your conscience troubled you, the only way you could go scot free would be to accuse someone else of the things you were accused of."

Mid-century was a time to reflect. *The New York Times* wistfully recalled that in 1850, Congress produced a compromise intended to avert a war between North and South. "The division of 1950," an editorial noted, "is deeper and cuts through not one country but the world. And in this greater and darker crisis there are no hopeful signs of a Compromise of 1950." Lamenting a deep national sense of instability, the paper concluded, "Perhaps we will have to get used to the thought that we are in for a long period of uncertainty. Worry is one of the penalties of living in an age of decision. The rewards are also present. Living can never have been more interesting than it is today. The humblest of us can never have had a greater opportunity to affect the course of history."

---

* The original meaning of the phrase had nothing to do with communism at all but described a herring cured with saltpeter and dragged across a trail to distract tracking dogs.

—

On Friday, January 27, 1950, thirty-eight-year-old Klaus Fuchs nervously got off a train at Paddington Station in London. He was met by William Skardon of Scotland Yard. It was a bleak winter day, but they walked the few blocks to the War Office, where Fuchs dictated his confession.

—

In New York that week, the temperature broke a January record—just above seventy degrees. At Rockefeller Center, the skating rink was closed. Early Friday morning, the telephone rang in the Greenglasses' apartment on Rivington Street. The caller said his name was Lawrence Spillane. He identified himself as a special agent of the FBI.

Chapter 19

Shmel

**"I know when to be nervous and
when not to be nervous."**

The first time the FBI called on them, the Greenglasses were in Albuquerque, in 1945, and while the couple had good reason to be nervous, the inquiry turned out to be routine. The agent who visited the house on North High Street merely wanted to confirm that the woman who rented the second-floor rear apartment frequented by a young man in uniform was in fact who Ruth and David said she was: the wife of a GI stationed at Los Alamos, not a recruiter for a foreign-intelligence service or a courier for enemy spies.[*]

By 1950, Ruth was unaware of any burning reason to be alarmed. Los Alamos and all that it evoked was, as David dismissively put it, "something in my past."

---

[*] Ruth had already had one solo run-in with the FBI. She was alone in the apartment one night when an agent conducting a routine security check telephoned to confirm her identity as the wife of a Los Alamos employee. Ruth refused to talk to him. "I don't know who you are," she said. When the agent showed up in person and identified himself, David recalled, "She gave him hell: 'What are you coming to my door at ten at night?'" Undaunted, the agent returned to the apartment one weekend. This time, he was armed with David's photograph, to verify that the man who Ruth claimed was her husband was, indeed, David Greenglass.

When Agent Spillane phoned, David feigned nonchalance. The FBI man asked to meet with the Greenglasses that afternoon at their apartment. David explained that he had to leave for work by 4:00 P.M. Perhaps an appointment could be scheduled for some other day. Spillane said he didn't want to wait. Anyway, he explained, this was not a complicated matter—it wouldn't take long.

David agreed to meet at two. He assured Ruth there was nothing to worry about. He quickly got dressed, stomped down the steps, and proceeded at an unusually brisk gait to Pitt Machine Products to find Julius. Luckily, Julius hadn't gone to lunch yet. He was calm. His message was soothing. Don't panic. Yes, you're hot, but not *that* hot. Not yet, anyway.

Promptly at 2:00 P.M., Agent Spillane knocked on the Greenglasses' door. David introduced him to Ruth and pointed out Steven, who was three and a half and between naps. Spillane was ushered into the kitchen, where David and Ruth joined him at the table. They waited for Spillane to get to the point. When he did, they were surprised.

At the request of the Atomic Energy Commission, the FBI had, for several months, been investigating the theft of uranium from Los Alamos during the war.[*] The theft was of wholesale proportions: hundreds of the hollow, golf-ball-sized uranium-238 hemispheres that had been sliced and diced in weapons research could not be accounted for. Apparently, however, they had been removed one by one. Confronted by the FBI, former Los Alamos workers were sheepishly fessing up to having taken the hemispheres home as souvenirs—they made nifty ashtrays.[†]

---

[*] The original target of Spillane's investigation was Dr. Ralph E. Lapp, a Manhattan Project scientist who had gone on to the University of Chicago. Lapp was attached to the Research and Development Division of the army's general staff, when, in 1949, he predicted that it would be fruitless and prohibitively expensive to convert American cities into underground strongholds. He maintained that "guided missiles may do much to seek out and explode atom bombs before they reach their objectives, but it is difficult to conceive of this process being perfected to the point where it will guarantee that no bombs will get through the defense." Lapp's conclusion about a missile defense shield was unusually candid—maybe too candid: "If one coldly analyzes the use to which these bombs can be put in time of war and one considers that other nations will have the same type of weapons, then it is apparent that our military position is actually weakened."

[†] Even before Spillane reported the results of his interviews, J. Edgar Hoover was questioning

David informed Spillane that, yes, he remembered seeing a uranium hemisphere and maybe even held one, but he certainly never took any and, truth be told, never entered the so-called tube-alloy shop where they were machined.

He had, of course, lied.

David had visited the shop at Los Alamos, and more than once. He knew that other workers had taken uranium souvenirs. He had taken at least one himself. He sent it home after the war in a sock. In fact, at the very moment that Agent Spillane was interviewing David, the uranium souvenir was very slowly decaying in a closet not fifteen feet from Steven Greenglass's crib.

Of all the potential crimes that the FBI might be knocking on his door to investigate, David never would have guessed this one. With all he might have to hide—the stolen detonator cap that he had given to Julius, a Lucite disk (part of the detonator) that he also had taken home from Los Alamos—the only thing that Spillane appeared to be interested in was a useless lump of uranium. What have you got to hide if nobody's looking for it? Why not confess, retrieve the uranium from the closet, insist that you meant no harm, wish Agent Spillane a pleasant weekend, and send him on his way?

But suppose that the government actually intended to bring criminal charges against these souvenir hunters? What if this whole line of questioning was just a ruse, a clever strategy to lower his defenses and then to ensnare him in some real or imagined sinister plot? David figured he couldn't afford to tell the truth.

"When he left, I said to Ruth, 'You know, I think I better throw that away,'" David recalled. "She said, 'What?' And I showed it to her."

The hemisphere was emitting infinitesimal amounts of gamma rays, too little even to register on the film badges that Los Alamos machinists

---

whether the considerable effort recovering souvenir ashtrays was justified. "It is not considered that the security importance of the uranium metal involved is sufficient to warrant further steps to recover additional pieces of the metal, unless there is evidence indicating that the pieces of uranium metal involved are component parts of weapons, facsimiles thereof, or are measured in kilogram amounts," the Atomic Energy Commission wrote Hoover.

wore (although the film was far more sensitive to heavy doses than to the cumulative effect of low doses). As a teenager, Steven Greenglass became ill. David never figured it had anything to do with the hemisphere, but something had gone terribly wrong, perhaps on the one day, shortly after Japan surrendered, when the gates atop the mesa at Los Alamos were proudly thrown open to servicemen's wives and other invited guests. When she visited that day, Ruth was pregnant with Steven.

—

Late on Saturday, the day after Spillane's surprise visit, David walked the six short blocks along Rivington to East River Park. With the studied nonchalance of a boy skipping rocks across a stream, David lobbed two pieces of U.S. military property into the swift current: an army-issue sock and the uranium hemisphere that he had secreted inside it. The East River is barely twenty feet deep at that point, and since it is not really a river at all but a churning tidal basin, it is possible that the uranium is now buried under a layer of silt not far from where David threw it.

"It's probably at the bottom of the East River this moment killing fish," David said.

On Sunday, David slept late. It wasn't until almost lunchtime that he returned to the machine shop to brief Julius on Spillane's agenda. Julius was relieved. Spillane's narrow focus might have been a diversion, but nothing else about the interview suggested anything Machiavellian. Indeed, subsequent FBI memos describe the interview as taking place "prior to our knowledge of his involvement in Soviet espionage." Then again, the probability of an FBI agent suddenly showing up at a Los Alamos veteran's tenement doorstep claiming to be looking for an inconsequential amount of uranium four years after it was supposedly stolen might, to an outsider, seem far-fetched. Except for one thing: David was guilty. And Julius knew it.

—

David acknowledges having told Julius earlier about the uranium souvenir. He told his brother, Bernie, too. He insists he never gave the sample to Julius or to anyone else and that it was still in his apartment on the Friday afternoon when Spillane called.

Again, NKGB files tell a different story.

Anatoly Yakovlev reported to Moscow as early as September 1945 that one of David's jobs at Los Alamos was—as he put it, using the Russian code word for the bomb and U.S. Army code for uranium— "gathering samples of materials used in the balloon, such as tube alloy." In July 1948, the NKGB in New York learned, presumably through Julius, of a small piece of plutonium that David kept in a lead box before disposing of it in the East River.* The NKGB also reported that he had kept a sample of U-238, which the New York station said it sent to Moscow on December 18, 1948.

—

On Friday, February 3, 1950—exactly one week after Spillane visited the Greenglasses—London newspapers revealed that Klaus Fuchs had been arrested on a tip from American counterintelligence and charged with spying for the Soviet Union. William Laurence wrote in *The New York Times* that Fuchs had, by himself, advanced Soviet nuclear-weapons development by at least three years and by as many as ten.

David was on his lunch hour at 9:00 P.M. and had just started reading the paper when a colleague at Arma pointed to the front-page story. " 'I see they caught one of our boys,' he said, and I said, 'What are you talking about? Why do you say one of our boys?' He was pretty open about it. He said, 'Well, he's a communist, and I'm a communist.' " That he assumed David was, too, suggests that David hadn't entirely abandoned or hidden his sympathies.

---

* The two versions are difficult to reconcile. David indignantly debunks the possibility that he pilfered any plutonium: "Never in a million years. Plutonium is poison. I would have been dead years ago," he said. But he acknowledged helping himself to a uranium hemisphere and telling Julius about it after the war, although it's unclear why he would have waited until 1948 to boast about his souvenir. David insists that he took only one hemisphere. If, in fact, he had taken two, that could account for the NKGB's otherwise mysteriously specific reference.

—

The next morning, David was awakened by Julius's insistent knocking on the door of his apartment. As David recalls it, Julius invited him to come for a walk. "This guy Fuchs is the man who was contacted in this country by 'Dave,'" David recalled Julius saying, referring to the code name that Harry Gold had given when he had contacted the Greenglasses in New Mexico in June 1945. "Now, you will have to leave." Why me? David asked. Why not "Dave"? Ethel had raised the same question, Julius replied.

David insisted lamely that he hadn't been nervous when Spillane had visited. "I knew they were just fishing, you understand?" he said. "I knew it." David made no such pretense of cockiness after Julius's visit. "Then I knew I was under a threat," David recalled. "I know when to be nervous and when not to be nervous. When Julius came, then I began to get nervous."

—

David and Julius walked up Sheriff Street to Hamilton Fish Park. David said that before he went anywhere he would need money to pay his debts. Julius changed the subject. The Russians, he explained mysteriously, "try to work six months ahead of the FBI," which seemed to mean that if Fuchs began confessing to British intelligence in mid-January, American agents would be closing in on "Dave"—and on David Greenglass—by early summer.

Except that American counterintelligence agents weren't even looking for anyone named Dave or David.

In the confession that Fuchs dictated on January 27, he acknowledged that "I shall have to help as far as my conscience allows me in stopping other people who are still doing what I have done." Conscience aside, Fuchs added: "There is nobody I know by name who is concerned with collecting information for the Russian authorities. There are people whom I know by sight whom I trusted with my life and who trusted me with theirs and I do not know that I shall be able to do anything that might in the end give them away."

But Fuchs's confession wasn't all that David had to fear.

The FBI wasn't relying only on Fuchs. Meredith Gardner and his cryptographers were methodically deconstructing their cache of Soviet cables, and slowly fragments were emerging that appeared to fit a pattern. An American translation of the cable used the Russian code names: Osa for Ruth, Kalibr for David, Liberal for Julius, and Tyre for New York.* From November 1944: "Osa has agreed to cooperate with us in drawing in Shmel (henceforth Kalibr) with a view to Enormous. On summons from Kalibr she is leaving on 22 November for the Camp 2 area. Kalibr will have a week's leave. Before Osa's departure Liberal will carry out two briefing meetings." And in mid-December 1944:

Osa has returned from a trip to see Kalibr. Kalibr expressed his readiness to help in throwing light on the work being carried on at Camp-2 and stated that he had already given thought to this question earlier. Kalibr said that the authorities of the Camp were openly taking all precautionary measures to prevent information about Enormous falling into Russian hands. This is causing serious discontent among the progressive (workers) . . . the middle of January Kalibr will be in Tyre. Liberal referring to his ignorance of the problem expresses the wish that our man should meet Kalibr and interrogate him personally. He asserts that Kalibr would be very glad of such a meeting. Do you consider such a meeting advisable? If not, I shall be obliged to draw up a questionnaire and pass it to Liberal. Report whether you have any questions of priority interest to us.†

By now, the code breakers knew that Camp 2 was Los Alamos. Tyre was New York. And Enormous obviously meant the atomic bomb. But

---

* Some names had historical connotations. Others were mythological. Some were whimsical. New York was Tyre, for the ancient Phoenician trading center in what is now Lebanon (it was famous for its lavish clothing; after two thousand or so years, it was destroyed by Moslems in 1291).

† Not until 1976 was American intelligence able to decode another December 1944 message to Moscow, this one prudently suggesting that Julius handle David and Ruth rather than assign them to Harry Gold, code-named Arno: "We consider it risky to concentrate all the contacts relating to Enormous on Arno alone."

who was Osa? More important, who was Kalibr, the Los Alamos worker originally known as Shmel?

On Tuesday, February 7, 1950, FBI headquarters in Washington dispatched an urgent Teletype, sent over Hoover's name, to the Albuquerque bureau:

```
IMMEDIATELY CHECK RECORDS LOS ALAMOS, FOR INDIVID-
UAL EMPLOYED IN 44 AND 45 BY NAME SHMEL. POSSIBLY
PHONETIC. SHMEL SCHEDULED TO MAKE TRIP TO NEW YORK
CITY MIDDLE JANUARY, 45 FROM LOS ALAMOS. POSSIBLE
SHMEL SCIENTIST, BUT THIS NOT KNOWN DEFINITELY. HE
WAS BEING RECRUITED BY MGB.*
```

—

In Albuquerque, the Teletype was turned over to Agent J. Jerome Maxwell. His job was twofold: first, to identify Shmel; then, to find him. Except for the urgency, the assignment seemed fairly straightforward. After all, how many people could share the name Shmel (assuming that Shmel was not a pseudonym)? And at a secret installation like Los Alamos, where every arrival and departure was supposed to be logged methodically, how hard could it be to confirm whether an individual was away during a specific period of time or not? But more than five years had elapsed. Thousands of GIs had been mustered out of the military. Thousands of civilians had gone on to graduate schools and to other government jobs. The army had kept one set of records, the University of California, which administered the laboratory, another set. Jurisdiction over the lab had since been transferred to the new Atomic Energy Commission. Records of individual leaves were notoriously sketchy.

---

* The message is significant for another reason. Declassified in 1999 in response to my request, it offers further evidence that Venona played a vital and contemporaneous role in American counterintelligence. The message, and others that were recently declassified, doesn't come close to completely fleshing out the FBI's case history—thousands of pages of documents are still secret—but it does help connect the bureau's investigation into Soviet espionage with the ongoing effort to decipher the NKGB cables.

Some reflected only the total number of days during any given month that an employee was away, rather than the specific dates.

A follow-up message to Albuquerque airmailed two weeks later from Washington relied heavily on the Venona decryptions (with some minor discrepancies, reflecting cruder code breaking and translations, later reconciled) and supplied additional hints. That memorandum added more details:

On November 14, 1944, it was reported that Osa (Wasp) had agreed to collaborate with the K.G.B. in recruiting Schmel (Shmel), who was to be designated by the cover name of Kalibr (Caliber). He was to be used in connection with the infiltration of atomic energy developments in the United States. According to a telephone call to Kalibr, she was leaving for Los Alamos on November 22, 1944. Kalibr was to have a week's leave.

On December 16, 1944, it was reported that Osa had returned from her trip to see Kalibr. She had reported that Kalibr had expressed a readiness to work for the K.G.B. in connection with the Los Alamos project, and he had advised that he previously had considered the matter. Kalibr further stated that the Los Alamos authorities openly took all kinds of precautions to prevent information on atomic energy research from reaching Soviet hands.

The memo also reported that Kalibr had revealed that Oppenheimer and Kistiakowsky were working at Los Alamos.

Within a few weeks, the FBI was closing in on a suspect. Agents in Albuquerque identified him as Luis Walter Alvarez. Alvarez had come to Los Alamos by way of the Radiation Laboratory at Berkeley and MIT. He was a codiscoverer of the East-West Effect in cosmic rays and was also instrumental in developing radar systems that proved vital both to Allied air defenses and to strategic-bombing missions. Alvarez shared another distinction: Flying nearly five miles over the New Mexico desert in a B-29 as the first atomic bomb was detonated, he was one of those who coined the fungal metaphor that was to be incorporated into the iconography of the cold war. At first, he said, the fireball resembled "a parachute which was being blown up by a large electric fan." Within seconds, as the cap of smoke and dust soared higher, a narrower stem became visible, which, he said, gave the cloud "very much the appearance of a large mushroom."

Alvarez wasn't a perfect fit for Shmel, but close. He was a scientist, which meant he would have had access to secret information. He had worked at Los Alamos from April 1944 through September 1945, which encompassed the period in question. He was away intermittently during that period, though apparently not in New York.

The investigation turned up two other tantalizing tidbits. One was a November 15, 1944, Teletype from Los Alamos to the U.S. Engineers Office at Berkeley asking for "some evidence of indiscretions committed by Alvarez" before a determination could be made on whether he had violated army censorship. The Teletype didn't elaborate, but the agents concluded that the coincidence "might be extremely important in the event this was a telephone call," since the decrypted cable reported that Osa had gotten "a telephone call to Kalibr" (although a later version of that cable was translated as saying that she was going to New Mexico "on summons from Kalibr"). Further investigation found that the censorship violation didn't involve a phone call, merely that Alvarez had blabbed about his work to relatives in Minnesota, who told their neighbors, who happened to be related to a scientist at Berkeley.

The other, more incriminating evidence against Alvarez was uncovered in California, where he had been born in 1911. The agents reported: "Referenced letter from San Francisco reflects that the middle name of Alvarez on his birth certificate is Shmel." The agents reported further:

> His mother's name is shown as Harriet S. Alvarez. Since Alvarez is a Spanish name and as he was born in San Francisco, California, it would not be unusual for his mother's maiden name to be listed as his middle name. If Shmel is his mother's maiden name, it would not be unusual for him to be called by that name, in view of his apparent Spanish ancestry, especially if it were not desired that his true identity be known to others.

By March 6, 1950, the FBI had concluded that Alvarez appeared to be an "excellent suspect."

———

But too many other potential suspects were turning up, many almost as suspicious. Agents identified no fewer than one hundred workers or their spouses who had been absent from Los Alamos in early January 1945, plus others who had been away at the end of November 1944. So many of those workers had, at one time or another, joined a leftist organization or expressed sympathy for a leftist cause or were on one's mailing list or were related to someone who was born in Russia or had once marched against fascism that the pool of potential suspects overwhelmingly outnumbered the membership of any Communist Party cell to which Julius Rosenberg had ever belonged.

Other scientists were suspected because they had "most frequently been described as being among the group of 'progressives' or 'liberals' at Los Alamos." One scientist was reported by his cousin's ex-wife to have attended a party in New York where his relatives "discussed Russia, the Communist Party, and political and world affairs." (Her former husband, she said, was "not a member of the Communist Party because of his professional status as a veterinarian.") The mother of the cousin's ex-wife said that when her son, the brother of the cousin's ex-wife, announced that Paul Robeson, Jr., had been forced to withdraw from Cornell University after a white woman was discovered in his room, the scientist was supposed to have remarked: "That couldn't happen in Russia."

Suspicion fell on an individual much more quickly than it would ever be lifted. Agents delving into the archives of vital records in Sacramento unearthed Luis Alvarez's birth certificate, only to find that his middle name was illegible. Still, they concluded that it "was most probably spelled Schmoll"—despite the fact that the same document conclusively established that his mother's maiden name wasn't Schmoll or Shmel or Schmel or anything else remotely "un-American" but Harriet Skidmore Smyth.

Edward Teller, the Hungarian-born physicist, first emerged as what agents in Albuquerque originally called "a most logical suspect" and then upgraded to "excellent suspect" and, finally, "principal suspect." During the war, Teller had run the Hydrodynamics of Implosion Division at Los Alamos under Hans Bethe. After the war, he was promoted to associate director for weapon development and emerged as the leading advocate for research into a thermonuclear bomb. Teller had been suspiciously close to Klaus Fuchs. While Richard Feynman, by then at Cornell, all but boasted to the FBI that he had been Fuchs's best friend at Los Alamos, Teller was described by agents as a "close associate" who had not only known Fuchs at Los Alamos but entertained him at his home in 1947 and had "considerable contact" with him in England as recently as the summer of 1949. It was Teller who had recommended Theodore Alvin Hall—"identified as a Soviet espionage agent while at Los Alamos"—for graduate school at the University of Chicago after the war, Teller who made frequent trips from Los Alamos and "could have furnished information to the Russians on a regular basis," and Teller who, the agents noted, had been "outspoken against furnishing atomic energy information to Russia, which appears strange in view of the fact that his parents and other relatives are in Hungary under Communist domination."*

———

At the same time that Edward Teller's travels were being scrutinized, agents learned that David's barracksmate, Bill Spindel, had been on furlough from mid-October 1944 through early November. There was no evidence he had taken a trip home to Brooklyn at that time. Nor was there any record of him having a leave later in November. But investigators surmised that he might have visited his wife then, since, as agents noted, "it was customary for service men to make trips to Albuquerque on week ends to see their wives at that time." And he was described

---

* It was also Teller who, four years later, was to testify against J. Robert Oppenheimer at a loyalty hearing convened by the Atomic Energy Commission; Oppenheimer was stripped of his security clearance, which meant he was no longer allowed to read some of the scientific papers that he himself had written.

as very closely associated with four colleagues and probably associated with three others, "all of whom have Russian backgrounds and some Communist connections." Agents learned that in January 1945, Spindel had been belatedly granted his diploma by Brooklyn College—a diploma that entitled him to the highest security clearance. A further check of the records found, however, that several months elapsed before the diploma was engraved and that Spindel didn't personally claim it until the following June.

Finally, even Hoover seemed to have lost patience. "The leads should be designed to develop information concerning the individuals' leave in November, 1944, and travel in January, 1945," he ordered the Albuquerque office. "The setting out of leads to develop Communist or subversive activity on the part of a suspect is of no immediate value pending the determination of the foregoing."

———

By the end of March, six weeks after Hoover's original urgent message, the FBI still hadn't identified anyone who had been assigned to Los Alamos during the war, who had been granted a week's leave in late November 1944, and who also had gone to New York City in January 1945.

On March 31, with his investigation into the missing uranium still incomplete but already superseded by more pressing events, Agent Spillane filed his report with the New York bureau. It contained nothing incriminating about David Greenglass, nothing that would have triggered alarms demanding further investigation—especially in light of the Atomic Energy Commission's complacency about the case. Less than three weeks later, though, David's name surfaced in the search for Shmel.

Frustrated, the FBI had recast its net. Agents focused on the intersection of two other criteria suggested in the Soviet cables: individuals who had been absent from the installation in January 1945 and who also had listed their permanent residence as New York City. On April 18, 1950, an urgent Teletype from Albuquerque reported that six members of the Special Engineer Detachment fit that description. They were listed alphabetically. The second name on the list was that of a David

Greenglass of 266 Stanton Street, New York City. He was also reported to have been on furlough from December 30, 1944, to January 20, 1945. The Teletype noted that Greenglass, along with others on the list, had an additional notable characteristic: at least one parent had been born in Russia. The six had something else in common, too, something that once again stymied the FBI. Manhattan Engineer District files at Los Alamos, the Teletype reported, "contained no derogatory information concerning any of these individuals."

Albuquerque asked the New York bureau to search its files.

Chapter 20

═══════════

What Did You Do in the War?

"If we had steam heat this wouldn't have happened."

═══

Had they known to do so, the FBI agents in Albuquerque could have asked the agents in New York to listen to the radio. They might have heard David Greenglass being interviewed on WOR about, among other things, what he did during the war.

It was mid-February 1950, a few days after Senator Joseph McCarthy's infamous "I have here in my hand" speech.* What happened, in retrospect, was just a prequel to the more indelible drama that unfolded a few months later, belying the literary allusion that there are no second acts in American lives and the later media-driven redefinition of celebrity that allots ordinary people their fifteen minutes of fame. At the time, though, it seemed to David as if nothing—not even the atomic bomb—could eclipse the mortal calamity that had suddenly befallen his family.

—

---

* McCarthy, addressing a Lincoln Day audience in Wheeling, West Virginia, claimed to have a list of 205 Communist party members who were still working for the government even after their names were identified to Secretary of State Dean Acheson.

Valentine's Day was cold, wet, and windy. A dozen New Yorkers died in accidents on ice-coated highways or from heart attacks after shoveling heavy slush off sidewalks and driveways. Uncertainty and potential hardship loomed in much of America that winter because 370,000 rogue members of John L. Lewis's United Mine Workers were defying a federal court mandate and their own union's back-to-work order. In New York, where the public had, for months, been urged to conserve water (a helpful hint printed just below a story on Klaus Fuchs that day said users of washing machines should wait until they had accumulated a full nine-pound load), the legislature empowered Governor Thomas Dewey to ration coal because the supply in some parts of the state was down to three days' worth. Water the Greenglasses couldn't live without. About coal they couldn't care less. Their apartment wasn't heated by coal. Actually, it wasn't heated at all. The only artificial sources of heat in the apartment were the kitchen stove and a small gas heater that David had installed in the bedroom that winter after Ruth had become pregnant again.

Valentine's Day was a Tuesday. David had worked the night before, and as he climbed the tenement steps shortly after midnight his face still stung from the icy rain. He had already read the evening papers during his break at Arma, so he headed straight to bed. With the outside temperature hovering around freezing, he left the bedroom heater on.

The next morning, Ruth woke up first, which was not unusual, even when David hadn't worked the night before. She made Steven breakfast, puttered around the apartment for a while, then, about 11:00 A.M., returned to the bedroom to wake her husband. As she leaned over the bed to gently shake him, the bottom of her flannel nightgown brushed against the gas heater. The contact was brief but just long enough for the flame to ignite the flannel. David was awakened by her screams.

He bolted up to find Ruth engulfed in flames. He beat the flames with his bare hands. Then, he yanked the covers off the bed and wrapped them tightly around Ruth. That smothered the fire, but the charred nightgown stuck to her body. Her skin was blistered nearly from head to toe. And God knows what had happened to the six-month-old fetus in her womb. David rushed Ruth to Gouverneur Hospital, where she was diagnosed with first-, second-, and third-degree burns and shock. David was treated himself for second-degree burns on both hands.

Ruth desperately needed blood. Her blood type was O-negative, which meant she could receive blood exclusively from others with the same type, or only about one in twenty people. Gouverneur and the American Red Cross jointly issued an appeal for donors, which is how lurid accounts of Ruth's accident were published in the *New York Post* and how David wound up on WOR with, as he remembered it, Gabriel Heatter.

———

Heatter was a connoisseur of the human-interest story (his daughter Maida later did the same for desserts).* While he lionized Russian soldiers as America's allies during the Second World War, he also regularly distinguished between them and their government. Because the communists "had friends in many important groups in this country," Heatter later recalled, his anti-Soviet commentaries triggered what he described as the most critical period of his career. It was during the war, too, that he first auditioned what would become his celebrated on-air signature. Week after week, the war news seemed to get worse. Finally, when the United States sank a Japanese destroyer, Heatter proclaimed: "There's good news tonight." From that day on, he tried to inject some glimmer of hope into every broadcast.

Harvesting good news from the interview with David Greenglass must have been challenging. Ruth's immediate survival, and the baby's, depended on transfusions of blood that the hospital didn't have. David's hands were heavily bandaged, and as he leaned into the microphone he quivered from the pain. His story was painful, too, and bitter: how even before Steven was born the Greenglasses began prospecting for an apartment with central heating, how they couldn't find one that

---

* She popularized "FBI Chocolate Layer Cake," which her mother served one night when J. Edgar Hoover came to dinner; Hoover jokingly threatened an investigation if he didn't get the recipe.

they could afford, how they wore their overcoats inside on cold days, and how they had applied for public housing and had been rejected. "For seven years," he said (as if four years, the actual time, wasn't long enough), "I have been searching for a steam-heated apartment. If we had steam heat this wouldn't have happened. I went to the city authority, but they said they couldn't help me as long as I had an apartment."

In the entire preceding year, the Greenglasses had made only two long-distance calls from their apartment. Both were in May 1949 to Levitt and Sons, the builders whose mass-produced 750-square-foot Cape Cod–style houses on a former Long Island potato field became emblematic of suburbia. The houses sold for about seven thousand dollars, or sixty-five dollars a month, which in the first half of 1949, when David was earning no salary at all, was more than the Greenglasses could afford.

—

As David later recalled the interview, Heatter, who had been born on the Lower East Side, asked David about growing up there. He asked where David had gone to school. He asked how David met Ruth. He asked about where David had worked. Finally, he asked what David had done during the war. David hesitated. Suddenly, he was no longer the inconsolable victim, the devoted husband and father agonizing over a disfiguring accident. Heatter's question transformed David into a potential fugitive, a hunted man with a hidden past who within the previous two weeks had been visited by a federal agent claiming to be investigating the theft of uranium and warned by his brother-in-law that he would have to flee the country because the FBI was closing in. David recovered quickly enough to mumble something about having worked at a classified installation out west. Before he was asked to elaborate, the radio interview was over.

Chapter 21

"Red Hot"

"What I did was in order to placate Julius."

=

Just after Klaus Fuchs's arrest was made public in February, the New York NKGB station reported to Moscow that "in late January, agents of American counterintelligence" had interviewed David Greenglass at his place of work (untrue) and then at his apartment "under the pretext of investigating uranium thefts from Los Alamos in the past." In this case, pretext was a revealing word. The NKGB knew full well that David had stolen uranium from Los Alamos. But given the context of the Fuchs case and the NKGB's suspicions that Harry Gold had defected, Soviet agents couldn't believe that that was all the FBI was after. The good news—presumably relayed by Julius—was that David hadn't confessed to the theft of uranium, much less to atomic secrets. Still, after assigning new code names ("Zinger" for David, "Ida" for Ruth, and "King" for Julius—but, again, none for Ethel), Moscow expressed its anxiety in this prescient memo (in which "the competitors" referred to American agents) to the New York NKGB station in April 1950:

> In the case of [David] and [Ruth], the competitors have not only a clear and for them unquestionable association with our work but the fact of their having passed to us secret materials on the atomic bomb. On

these grounds, the competitors will exert strong pressure on [David] and [Ruth], threatening and using other measures right up to their arrest, and in the end will force them to testify with all the consequences proceeding from this for King, his group, and all of our work in the country.

An NKGB operative named August responded later that month. His report to Moscow seemed to suggest that he was as worried about prying reporters as about the FBI:

[Julius] informed me that currently [David's] departure . . . is difficult for family reasons. First, his wife is due to bear a child in a month. Second, about two and a half months ago, [Ruth] was passing by a gas cooker [sic] and her dress accidentally caught fire. [Ruth] was heavily burned and spent about 10 weeks in a hospital, returning home only a week ago. In the hospital, she was given nearly 40 blood transfusions, so serious was her condition. Since her blood type turned out to be very rare, [David] made a speech on the radio with an appeal to donate blood to save her. The campaign to help [Ruth] was also backed by the Red Cross. . . . Some time ago, I saw a story in the Post about this accident; however, not then knowing [David's] exact name, I didn't pay attention to it. [Julius] also told me that this story had been described in the Post. Thus, [Julius] thinks that [David] will be unable to leave the country in the near future. Undoubtedly, this case drew public attention to [David], and we don't rule out that sometime an idle reporter might come to their apartment for an interview.

The agent reported that he had asked Rosenberg to assure his brother-in-law that the NKGB would assume the costs of caring for unspecified family members whom David and Ruth would leave behind in America and would completely underwrite their departure for France as tourists and also their resettlement, probably in Czechoslovakia, en route to Russia.

"After I said this," August advised Moscow, "Julius remarked: 'If he goes there, make a good Communist out of him.' I asked Julius immediately whether he considered David a bad Communist. He answered that recently David had hardly read any party publications, and, naturally, his education must be supplemented."

Neither Julius nor August sounded altogether persuaded. That alone should have spurred the Russians to evacuate the Greenglasses. But then, as August had foreseen, another complication arose. On May 23, the New York station notified Moscow: "About 10 days ago, Ruth gave birth to a girl, and . . . is still not sufficiently recovered from the illness she had, . . . and, naturally, she can't undertake a trip now."* David and Julius agreed, according to the NKGB correspondence, not to attempt anything for at least several months. Probably not until the fall.

Harry Gold's arrest changed all that.

———

Klaus Fuchs was safely imprisoned—he was sentenced in March to fourteen years—but what about his American courier? Who, and where, was his contact "Goose"?

From Venona, the FBI knew that the courier had connections to Abe Brothman (whose closest association with weapons research was a machine he developed for filling aerosol insecticide bombs) and that he had considered opening a laboratory in 1944 or 1945. (Investigators checking New York City Fire Department records were dismayed to discover that the Bureau of Combustibles had issued seventy-five thousand permits in 1945 alone.) The FBI also was thwarted by Fuchs's status as a British citizen. Within twenty-four hours of Fuchs's arrest, Special Agent Lish Whitson of the FBI arrived in London. But American investigators were rebuffed because, as Sir Percy Stillitoe, the director general of MI5, apologized, the British courts might dismiss the case and even sentence his intelligence officers to jail for revealing details of Fuchs's confession. After another month had elapsed, the FBI complained that "the delaying tactics on the part of the British had seriously impaired the Bureau's efforts to identify the American contacts of Fuchs and had otherwise hindered the investigation." American agents were unable to

---

* Barbara Helene Greenglass was born on May 16.

interview Fuchs at the Wormwood Scrubs Prison until May 20—nearly four months after his arrest. Fuchs agreed to the interview, with a caveat: "I am not prepared to answer questions of a purely personal nature concerning my friends," he told MI5. "Otherwise, I am prepared to give all the help I can."

Fuchs did, at least, characterize his American contact, although how he distinguished that characterization from "purely personal" details isn't clear. Fuchs told Special Agent Lamphere and Assistant FBI Director H. H. Clegg that his contact may have been Jewish, may have lived in Philadelphia, and was probably a chemist or engineer. Eventually, the FBI displayed 279 photographs to Fuchs. He did not identify Harry Gold until after Gold confessed.

—

The Soviets, however, assumed that Klaus Fuchs had been betrayed by Harry Gold. If so, they wondered, was Gold already in custody in January? Or was the FBI hoping to enlist him as bait for unsuspecting Soviet agents? Could the NKGB afford to find out? A meeting with Gold had been prearranged for Sunday, February 5, which turned out to be two days after Fuchs's arrest was reported. Rather than risk exposing Gold's regular contact, another agent unknown to Gold but armed with his photograph was assigned. Moscow then rescinded the order and flatly forbade anyone from showing up at the rendezvous. That cable didn't arrive in time; the agent saw Gold waiting as scheduled on a Queens street corner. Gold later identified the operative to the FBI but never publicly.

Gold kept two regularly scheduled appointments on the street corner near Jackson Heights, "even though both were fruitless—no one came." At 10:00 A.M. on the first Sunday of the month, Harry was to appear at a newsstand under the Ninetieth Street–Elmhurst Avenue station of the Flushing elevated subway line. His contact, very possibly someone he had never met before, was supposed to stand across the street. He described the encounter this way: "Now, if there was no business to be transacted between the two of us, we were merely to stay on our respective corners, facing each other. The recognition signals were to be as follows: I was to be smoking a pipe with a curved stem and a large bowl. I have such a pipe. The other man was to be smoking a cigar. If a contact was to be consummated, the other man would ask, 'Can you direct me to the Horace Harding Hospital?' I was to answer, 'Yes, I am going that way, come along with me.'"

Gold was getting anxious. He had kept the first of the two Sunday-morning appointments, he later wrote, "when I became worried over what the Russian knew, which had made him hint that I might have to leave this country." By the second meeting, Harry was frantic. The timing couldn't have been more filled with foreboding—the very Sunday following the announcement of the arrest of Fuchs. "I went there in utter panic," Harry wrote. As he paced on the corner under the El and puffed nonchalantly on his curved-stem pipe, he noticed that he was being eye-balled by a man standing across the street. The man had a mustache and was wearing glasses. He had on a brown hat and a light brown overcoat. He was unfamiliar, but he was smoking the obligatory cigar. Each re-garded the other warily. Finally, the other man relinquished his corner and passed Gold by. "In passing me," he recalled, "he peered somewhat closely at my face."

"It was at this second rendezvous," Gold later wrote, "that I was scru-tinized by a man whom I was later to recognize, from his newspaper photograph, as Julius Rosenberg."*

———

On May 15, 1950, a secret government memo summarized several months of remarkable progress by the Venona cryptographers. The FBI document credited Venona with information that "enabled our identifi-cation" of Judith Coplon as a Soviet agent and reported that "our inves-tigation of Fuchs was initiated on information" from Venona, too. "We

---

* Gold said later that he observed Julius at the Federal House of Detention twice in August 1950, and "I am now positive he is the man who passed me" at the February rendezvous, and "I make this identification without any qualification whatsoever." The government wasn't so sure; Gold would be called as a witness for the prosecution in the Rosenberg trial but was never asked to testify about this encounter.

are currently attempting to identify Fuchs' American espionage contact, 'Goose,' who not only apparently operated Fuchs while Fuchs was in the United States," but possibly Abe Brothman, too. The FBI memo also reported progress in identifying a former Manhattan Engineer District employee whose cover names were Shmel and Kalibr:

> He was to be contacted near Los Alamos in the latter part of November, 1944, by one Osa. It was later reported that he had been contacted and was willing to assist the MGB. It was also reported that he arrived in New York City on leave in early January, 1945. We originally thought he might be Luis W. Alvarez, a prominent physician now employed at the Radiation Laboratory in Berkeley, California, but upon the receipt of the information from the source that the individual had arrived in New York City in early January, 1945, we determined that Alvarez was not there at that time. We are conducting an intensive investigation to develop this individual's identity, hampered by the fact that certain leave records at Los Alamos have been destroyed. We are also, through investigation, attempting to identify Osa.

Inexorably, the investigations into the identity of Shmel or Kalibr and the earlier inquiry into missing uranium began to converge around David Greenglass. The man who brought all of the elements together was Harry Gold.

Five years—almost to the day—after Harry found the Castillo Street bridge on his map of Santa Fe, the FBI used the very same map to find Goose. Defying everything he should have been taught in spy school, Harry had squirreled away the map in a sectional bookcase in his room in his parents' house in Philadelphia. It remained there until an FBI agent whom Harry had insouciantly allowed to search his room reached for Harry's worn copy of Walker, Lewis, and McAdams's *Principles of Chemical Engineering* and found the map behind it.[*]

"So, you were never west of the Mississippi," the FBI agent said.

---

[*] Harry later said that he had intended to sanitize the room but instead went to visit a dog that had undergone an experimental gastrectomy.

"How about this, Harry?" To which, Harry later recalled, he was about to reply with a hastily contrived story about his abiding interest in the Southwest and in the books of J. Frank Dobie (he did have one book by Dobie on the very same shelf) and to explain that he had written to the museum and requested the map. Instead, he sank into a chair, asked the agents to give him just a moment to collect himself, and then confessed: "Yes, I am the man to whom Klaus Fuchs gave the information on atomic energy."

———

As Harry was being driven to downtown Philadelphia by federal agents to be debriefed on the fifth floor of the Widener Building, he had already formulated a strategy that was rooted in the ethos of South Philadelphia, where he had been raised. Everyone on Philip Street knew that too many cops were brutal, had gotten their jobs by paying off politicians, and were on the take. "I could never read, even in later years, of a man turning state's evidence to save his own hide without experiencing a shudder of revulsion," Harry recalled. Therefore, he resolved to "confess fully to having been a Soviet agent for 11 years, but would only disclose the activities where they involved Klaus Fuchs and myself—the others I would cover up."

That proved to be even easier than expected when it came to recounting the events of June 1945. "The David Greenglass incident," Harry said later, "I had actually completely forgotten about." In his account, Harry recalled: "Until some time after my arrest, all memory of this incident had fled from me (probably this was because Yakovlev had subsequently—and with intent to mislead—told me that the information received was of no value). And I had forgotten the man's name completely."

The FBI brought Harry's brother, Joseph, downtown because Harry wanted to confess to him face-to-face. Harry's father and brother offered to mortgage their home to hire a lawyer. By then, though, he figured he no longer needed a lawyer; he asked to meet with the federal judge who had arraigned him the day before, James McGranery, and requested counsel who would facilitate his full confession. The judge arranged for a Philadelphia lawyer, John D. M. Hamilton, the former chairman of the Republican National Committee. On Friday, May 26, Harry was joined in the judge's chambers by his court-appointed lawyers and an FBI agent. "I amazingly found myself irresistibly revealing more and more of the true facts," he said. As one FBI agent put it, "Every time you squeeze him, there is some juice left."

If Harry had been more thick-skinned though, the government would have been bereft of a prosecutable case, barring the unlikely cooperation of Klaus Fuchs. "Fuchs would be an essential witness," the Justice Department concluded, "in view of the lack of corroborating evidence and the lack of other witnesses who could appear against Gold."

—

On Wednesday, May 24, 1950, the day after Ruth returned home from the hospital where she had given birth to a baby girl, Julius Rosenberg delivered the New York *Herald Tribune* to the Greenglasses' door. The main headline announced buoyantly that General Motors and the United Auto Workers had struck a five-year agreement that might finally bring labor peace to the automobile industry. Just underneath that, also on the upper right corner of the front page, was a second headline:

U.S. ARRESTS GO-BETWEEN
FOR SOVIETS IN FUCHS CASE

The story identified the go-between as a Swiss-born chemist from Philadelphia named Harry Gold. The name didn't ring a bell with the Greenglasses. The photograph did. The story didn't mention Albuquerque, but it said that the criminal complaint, filed by the federal government in U.S. District Court in Brooklyn, referred to an encounter between Gold and Fuchs in Santa Fe in 1945. Furthermore, Gold and an otherwise unidentified "John Doe" were said to have committed espionage "against the peace and dignity of the United States."

—

For decades, Washington endured bruising cold-war propaganda and even let some suspected spies escape prosecution in order to avoid compromising its Venona intelligence coup. Had they been made public or introduced as evidence, decoded Soviet cables might have gone a long way toward persuading some people that the Rosenbergs were guilty of more than belonging to the Communist Party (though not necessarily of stealing atomic secrets) and that the highest levels of the Communist Party in the United States were aware of and even involved in Soviet espionage. By helping to distinguish real threats from hyperbole, disclosure of the decoded cables might even have restrained or at least undermined the excesses of McCarthyism. But the top priority of policy makers in Washington was to protect the secrecy of the Venona Project at all costs, so as to keep from the Soviets the unsettling fact that some of their most confidential cables had been penetrated by American intelligence. Not even President Truman was told of Venona's successes. The American public was not to learn of its existence for decades.

If Washington had pursued and revealed its full arsenal of evidence, prosecutors might have constructed convincing cases that apportioned blame more fairly and produced sustainable guilty verdicts that would not only be upheld on appeal but accepted in the court of public opinion with fewer scabrous recriminations. Most American Communist Party leaders might have been fully exposed as handmaidens of Moscow. In contrast, most rank-and-file communists might have been dismissed, rather than persecuted, as blind but largely well-intentioned defenders of a lost cause.

Venona, former Senator Daniel Patrick Moynihan wrote, might have "informed the legitimately patriotic American left that there was, indeed, a problem that the Federal Bureau of Investigation, for example, was legitimately trying to address. But this did not happen. Ignorant armies clashed by night."

The irony is that Stalin knew, perhaps as early as 1948. And the United States knew that Stalin knew when an American cipher clerk was identified as a Soviet mole in 1950. "And so," Moynihan later wrote, "into the house of mirrors."

—

To this day, Feklisov and others believe that Fuchs was betrayed by Harry Gold. But as long ago as spring 1950, Moscow had acquired a British intelligence memo that described the genesis of Klaus Fuchs's confession. The memo didn't even mention Harry Gold. Instead, it recounted that in late August 1949, the FBI had forwarded to British intelligence information that "during the war, there had been a leak to the Russians relating to the work of a British Atomic Energy Mission in the United States. Research into British files of that period, combined with the Federal Bureau of Investigation's research and investigation in the United States, showed that Dr. Emil Julius Klaus Fuchs fit such facts as were known." Within two months, the NKGB had gotten hold of a much more detailed version of the events leading to Fuchs's arrest. By then, the Soviets had concluded that Gold was not, after all, the FBI's source of the original evidence against Fuchs. Instead, on May 29, 1950, the NKGB informed Stalin that the source was squarely in the Kremlin's backyard: The Americans had broken the Soviet wartime code.

Five days after Gold's photograph appeared on the front page of the *Herald Tribune,* the NKGB briefed the Kremlin, with this revelation from its moles in Britain:

> The American deciphering service worked for a long time on one of the telegrams from the New York station, referring to 1944–1945 when Fuchs was in the U.S. Having failed to decipher this telegram completely in late 1949, the Americans passed it to British counterintelligence, which managed to decipher it to the end and to find out that Fuchs was an agent of Soviet intelligence, passing us important data about the work of the American and English atomic centers where he worked. . . .
>
> The verification showed that, in the war years, there had been an extensive telegraph-ciphered correspondence on matters of intelligence work by Fuchs between our station in New York and Moscow. Short excerpts of materials on the atomic bomb, received from him, had been passed, and in one of the telegrams his family name and detailed data about him were even mentioned.

> Our specialists admit the possibility of the English deciphering our telegram, processed by a used table of reciphering gamuts.

In other words, Soviet cryptographers had screwed up by reusing a one-time code book. Seeking to reassure the Kremlin that the NKGB was on the ball, the report reaffirmed that all Soviet operatives known to Fuchs or to Gold had already been spirited out of Britain and the United States. Also, the NKGB reported that "measures to bring out of the U.S. four agents previously connected with Gold, facing a threat of exposure in case of the latter's confession, were also taken." Those four agents were not identified—not even by code name. But from the events that followed it appears that those agents included David and Julius.

———

Literally overnight, the proposed plan to evacuate the Greenglasses was amended and accelerated. The suggested tourist itinerary through France and Czechoslovakia was scrapped, perhaps because the Greenglasses would have had to apply for passports, and David's service with the Manhattan Project might trigger an investigation.

On May 24, the same day that Julius delivered the newspaper with Harry Gold's photograph to David, the New York station sought and received Moscow's permission to expedite the Greenglasses' departure through Mexico. To remain much longer would "inevitably lead to their arrest." They would have to go by mid-June at the outside, and in order to do so, Moscow advised, they might have to flee without their full complement of family members. In David's case, that might mean just taking Ruth and their infant daughter. It might even mean that Julius and David would have to escape by themselves. "If I get word that it is too hot, we will just take off and leave the children," David quoted Julius as warning. "I couldn't be that ruthless," David said.

This time, the Soviets were serious, warning that the entire espionage apparatus in the United States would be jeopardized if the two couples were captured. Simultaneously, they were preparing against the growing likelihood that—because of blundering, indecision, and the possibility that Julius wouldn't abandon his ailing sister-in-law—their escape plan might never be fully carried out. Moscow warned the New York station that Julius and David and their wives "must be told that counterintelligence may use blackmail, invent various stories about the fate of those who left and those who remained, referring to their alleged confessions. Therefore, they shouldn't believe in these stories but stand firmly on their positions." On May 25, Moscow told New York to give the two couples ten thousand dollars and to instruct them to have photographs taken of each family member so that passports could be fabricated in Mexico. That same day, Moscow also enlisted its agents in Mexico City and Stockholm to investigate the availability of direct passenger-ship service between Mexico and Sweden, to advise which travel documents would be required, and to find a secure place in Mexico where two families with children could be stashed meanwhile. Should neither of its charges be able to make it to Mexico, Soviet intelligence was exploring other contingencies. Moscow also instructed the New York station to suggest to Julius that, if he and his brother-in-law were unable to flee the country immediately, they temporarily go underground.

Suddenly, the months of improbable musings on what-if hypotheses were mutating into horrible realities. Or, perhaps, into opportunities. On May 25, Julius delivered one thousand dollars in cash to the Greenglasses. (They used it to pay down an installment loan on furniture, a bank loan, a debt to a neighbor, and a typewriter.) He promised four thousand more. (By one account, six thousand more.) Julius did not bring that day's *Herald Tribune,* the one with the headline that cried out:

KEY RED ATOM SPY RING HUNTED HERE, GOT GOLD'S SECRETS

Julius also invited David to join him outside for another walk.

A few weeks earlier, David had finally relented and turned over the notarized certificate of Pitt Machine Products stock to Julius (this occurred on May Day, which is not customarily celebrated with capitalistic transactions). All David received in return was a promise that he would be paid just as soon as Julius settled the business's outstanding debts. (Ruth had bought a book of promissory notes and filled them out for Julius to sign; he refused, saying his word was sufficient.) But David was now insisting that he had no intention of leaving without settling his debts. Years of working for Julius, David estimated, had left him with three thousand dollars in unpaid bills. Finally, he was in a position not so much to profit from his brother-in-law's predicament or to get even as to collect what he deserved:

"What I did was in order to placate Julius," David said.

The Russians wanted to make sure we were leaving. He had told them that I'm under his thumb, right? Well, we both agreed we didn't want to go to Russia. We both agreed on that. They said, well, you're going to Czechoslovakia. So I said, It's too close to Russia, I didn't want to go to Russia. I didn't think it was a worker's paradise anymore, so what the hell was I going to go there for? I listened to his conversation because if I didn't listen to the conversation he wouldn't have given me the five thousand dollars, which would allow me to do something else. . . . I just wanted to disappear for a while. I wasn't going to be able to work. I needed some money. At that time, five thousand dollars would take care of you for a whole year and maybe even longer.

Ruth later described what happened when Julius delivered the four thousand dollars on June 2. "At that time," she said, "David and I had already discussed it and decided not to tell Julius that we weren't going to leave because David felt that if he knew of our intentions, some physical harm might come to us, that it would be best to let him believe we were going." Before Julius took David for a walk, Ruth recalled, Julius "was very melodramatic, discussed everything in whispers, he was under the impression there were ears all over the house."

—

Max Miller usually didn't work weekends. On Sunday, May 28, though, he was in his photo shop at 130 Clinton Street when the four Greenglasses arrived to have their photographs taken. It was Barbara's first outing, so even though it was almost summer she was swaddled in a blanket. Miller photographed David and Ruth individually and the family as a group. David sat behind Ruth, sporting an open-collar long-sleeve shirt, his hands awkwardly on his thighs. Ruth wore a short-sleeve print dress. Her brow was creased. Barbara sat on Ruth's lap. Steven, dressed in a plaid shirt and shorts, hugged her right hip. Ruth wrapped one arm around each to keep them from squirming. The baby's eyes were shut, but Steven looked as if he was about to bolt. He was just tall enough to hide his father's chin, but not his lips, which were pursed in the closest approximation of any in the picture to a pleasant, if slightly vacuous, expression. Nearly a year later, after Miller's recollection was refreshed by the FBI, he recalled only how David and Ruth had had a hard time getting Steven to smile.

David returned to Miller's shop later that day to pick up the developed pictures. On May 30, Memorial Day, Julius came by the Greenglasses' apartment to get the photographs.

By then, the FBI was only a few days away from having David's photograph, too.

Drawing on details in Harry Gold's confession, the FBI had dubbed David "Unknown American No. Five." One of the other four was Alfred Dean Slack, whom Gold had contacted in upstate New York, but it turned out that each of the other three was a "figment of his imagination" to cover his tracks, as the FBI explained in abandoning its search for those mythical suspects.

But Harry Gold over time unleashed a torrent of clues that helped the FBI piece together a profile of Unknown American No. Five. By Thursday, June 1, during a conference in Judge McGranery's chambers, Harry revealed to Agent Scott Miller the names of Alfred Slack and Thomas Black—two suspects already known to the bureau—and mentioned a "noncommissioned soldier who resided in Albuquerque, New Mexico, in 1945 and was attached to Santa Fe." By that evening, Harry remembered that he had been shocked after he got to Albuquerque to discover the man was a GI—a corporal or a sergeant; that he was a mechanic or an electrician or a draftsman or a physicist's helper; that Harry had given the man an envelope containing five hundred dollars in cash (the soldier expected the money, he said); and that his wife had joined him in New Mexico only a few months before. Harry could picture the couple, too. The man wasn't more than twenty-five years old and appeared youthful and tanned. His general appearance was "very engaging." He was about five foot seven, 170 pounds, with dark curly hair, light or brown eyes, a snub nose, regular teeth, and a mouth that Harry described as "somewhat broad." He remembered them as Jewish and apparently natives of New York (though with a Bronx or Brooklyn accent)—perhaps because only moments after he crossed the threshold of their apartment, he was offered something to eat.

Harry could also visualize the couple's second-floor apartment and the house itself but not the number or even the street name. He imagined the walk from the Hilton: up the street, on the same side as the hotel, past the Santa Fe Railroad tracks for maybe five blocks, or maybe eight. Then he turned left. The street was shaded; it was June, so he remembered the shade.

FBI agents in Philadelphia asked their Albuquerque counterparts to forward all available street maps of the city and photographs of the streets that Harry remembered. "All investigation in this case must be in a highly discreet manner," the Philadelphia bureau specified, although J. Edgar Hoover was already being advised that one agent had made an educated guess as to the suspect's identity: "Special Agent Scott Miller suggested that Theodore Hall, subject of an espionage case, might be identical with this individual."

The maps and photographs were forwarded as requested. But Harry's description proved to be so vivid that the very next afternoon, on Friday, June 2, agents in Albuquerque reported breathlessly that they had tentatively identified the house and who had lived there five years previously.

The unknown American had a name.

At 5:47 P.M. Mountain Standard Time—five years almost to the day that Harry Gold first called on the Greenglasses—the following telegram was sent by the Albuquerque bureau to New York, Washington, and to the army records center in Kansas City:

RE PHILA. TEL TO ALBUQUERQUE THIS DATE. IN-
VESTIGATION IN AREA SUGGESTED BY TEL REFLECTS
HOUSE LOCATED AT TWO NAUGHT NINE NORTH HIGH,
SITUATED GEOGRAPHICALLY TO SOMEWHAT RESEMBLE
PREMISES DESCRIBED BY GOLD AS SITE OF CONTACT
WITH UNSUB. LANDLORD ADVISES THAT THIS TWO-
STORY HOUSE IN NINETEEN FORTYFIVE CONSISTED
OF SEVERAL APARTMENTS, ONE OF WHICH OCCUPIED
BY LANDLORD AND WIFE AND ANOTHER OCCUPIED BY
INDIVIDUAL IDENTIFIED DAVID GREENGLASS.

Within fewer than twenty-four hours, and without the benefit of computers, the FBI determined the suspect's army serial number, the span of his service at Los Alamos, the unit to which he was assigned, his work history from 1940 until he was drafted in 1943, his date of birth, his parents' names and their nationalities, his hometown and permanent address, his wife's name, and her former employer.

David Greenglass was not unknown to the Albuquerque bureau of the FBI. Just five weeks before, pursuing the leads developed by Venona, Agent J. Jerome Maxwell had turned in his report on furloughs by personnel at Los Alamos. Page thirty of that report "discloses a David Greenglass," the Albuquerque bureau's June 2 teletype revealed. "Similarity between names and physical descriptions noted," the Teletype continued, with famously bureaucratic understatement. In the New York bureau, the full significance of the similarity was greeted with exuberance. The same David Greenglass who matched some of the characteristics of the mysterious Shmel now also seemed to fit the profile supplied by Harry Gold. On June 2, Special Agent in Charge Edward Scheidt wrote this memo in New York:

At 4:30 P.M. today Mr. Carl Hennrich of the Bureau advised that in all probability the unidentified soldier from whom GOLD said he got espionage information is DAVID GREENGLASS, Army Serial No. 32 88 24 73.

Mr. Hennrich said that GREENGLASS is a "red hot" subject at the moment.

David didn't go to work on Friday, June 2. As he remembers it, on Sunday, June 4, Julius dropped by the Rivington Street apartment. It was to be his last stroke of good timing: The FBI was preparing to begin full-time surveillance of the Greenglasses the next day. Julius delivered an inch-thick package tied with heavy twine and sealed with tape. He placed it on the mantel in the bedroom.

Julius being family, David figured he would wait until later to count the contents. Which is not to say the package was far from his mind as Julius invited him for another walk around the block to test whether he had memorized the specifics of his itinerary and the passwords that would smooth his escape to Mexico and from there to Europe.

At Delancey and Columbia, David spotted Diana and Herman Einsohn on the opposite side of the street. It would have been both impolite and foolish to pass them by: He had lent them forty dollars to pay their rent the month before. David crossed the street, heartily greeted the Einsohns, collected a check for forty dollars made out to Ruth, and crossed back to rejoin Julius.

As soon as David returned home, he went straight for the package on the mantel. It was wrapped tightly in what appeared to be a torn brown-paper bag. He peeked at the inch-thick stash. There were twenties on top, tens underneath: the promised four thousand dollars. That was as much as David made in a year, after taxes, and more than enough to pay for a new house in Levittown. ("No man who owns his own house and lot can be a communist," William Levitt once said.) He stashed the package in the chimney flue and secured it with industrial tape. A few days later, he called his brother-in-law, Ruth's sister Dorothy's husband, Louis Abel. "Bernie, I figured, he was too ambiguous, he couldn't be on my side," David later recalled. "My mother couldn't be on my side either. But Louis could. He was the other side of the family, related to us through blood."

Even the trusting Abel was curious about how David, who always seemed to need money, had suddenly come into a small fortune. David replied that if he had his druthers, he would get rid of the money altogether, flush it down the toilet. Abel didn't want to embarrass David, so he didn't press him. He posed only one question.

"I asked David if it was stolen," Abel recalled later, "and he said no."

Monday, June 5

David got up early. Then he did something more extraordinary: He showed up at the Arma plant in Brooklyn hours before his scheduled shift. He asked the day supervisor for a six-week leave of absence to take care of his wife. With four thousand dollars in cash stashed away, he could easily afford six weeks off. He even could have quit. But he was being responsible, thinking about job security.

Operating from a truck and an unmarked car stationed down the block, four FBI agents began their stakeout of 265 Rivington at 11:00 that morning. Several times over the next few days, they worried that David had become "surveillance conscious." In fact, David had spotted what he believed was a suspicious van. He invited Ruth to the roof to see for herself. A sign on the van said it belonged to the Acme Construction Company, 1400 First Avenue, Manhattan. When the Greenglasses checked the telephone directory, there was no such listing. "The neighborhood in which Greenglass lived made a discreet physical surveillance next to impossible," the FBI acknowledged.

Shortly before 1:00 P.M., an unidentified man in a 1950 dark green Kaiser picked up the Greenglasses and drove them to Gouverneur Hospital, apparently to check on Ruth's recovery. At about 2:00 P.M., they emerged from the hospital and walked home. Later, they visited Ruth's parents across the street and David's mother around the corner. The FBI was filming and photographing them along the way.

David did not go to work that afternoon. He was awaiting word on his requested leave. The FBI had been there, though, interviewing the personnel manager and collecting employment records, a copy of David's fingerprints, and a photograph. Agents also found David's high-school-yearbook photos.

Tuesday, June 6

David and Ruth went shopping. At 5:55 P.M., David greeted an un-identified man outside the house. They hailed a taxicab, which took the three of them to Beth Israel Hospital. At 7:45 P.M., all three shared a taxi home.

In New York, FBI agents conducting a credit check inspected the Greenglasses' charge-account application at Macy's. David reported earning $107 a week at Arma. He said his weekly salary at Pitt had been $110 but didn't point out that he rarely collected it.

Julius Rosenberg was said to be recovering from strep throat, which had kept him out of the office for more than a week, so it was no surprise to Charlie Bozsik, who had succeeded David as the Pitt Machine Products foreman, when Julius didn't show up at work. According to records reviewed later by the FBI, Julius was apparently well enough to close the Rosenbergs' checking account. He also redeemed $770.75 worth of U.S. savings bonds. Julius authorized Pitt's lawyer, Solomon H. Bauch, to empower Bernie Greenglass to sign company checks. Bauch said later that Julius told him that the Rosenbergs were "contemplating a trip."

Imagine if they had taken that trip. They were not suspects. They were not being followed. They would not know until the next day that the Greenglasses were under surveillance. Exactly why Julius and Ethel never fled—regardless of whether they were genuinely guilty or just legitimately frightened by America's escalating frenzy of anticommunism—may never be known for sure. Perhaps it was Moscow's bumbling lack of urgency.* Alexander Feklisov later suggested another motivation, a profoundly personal one, that constrained the Rosenbergs. David never doubted Julius's loyalty, nor Ethel's. Neither did Feklisov. Julius was so shaken by Ruth's accident and concerned about her pregnancy, Feklisov said, that he simply "couldn't abandon

---

* Although later that month, Moscow managed to deliver Morris and Lona Cohen, two vital members of the NKGB's "volunteer" network, out of the United States for other assignments. (The Cohens later retired in the Soviet Union, where they were said to have resented the disproportionate publicity received by the Rosenbergs.)

his sister-in-law." Feklisov added: "We will see later on in which way Ruth rewarded his solicitude."

Wednesday, June 7

At 2:45 P.M., the Greenglasses took Steven and his three-week-old sister to a playground at Sheriff and Broome Streets, in the shadow of the Williamsburg Bridge. At 4:35 P.M., David and Steven walked to a carnival at Delancey and Columbia. On the way home, they stopped at 64 Sheriff Street.

The FBI's surveillance logs describe June 7 as another day of "no pertinent activity." Soviet intelligence suggests otherwise. Sometime that afternoon, according to an NKGB report, Julius Rosenberg was approaching the Greenglasses' tenement when he noticed a car across the street. There were other vehicles parked on Rivington Street, but this was the only one directly opposite number 265. It was also the only one with three men inside, all staring at the building's front door. Julius later reported, according to the NKGB, that he naturally assumed the men were FBI agents. Why Julius would have brazenly gone inside regardless of his suspicions is anybody's guess, as is why he assumed that that was less risky than calling David on the telephone (there has never been any evidence that the phone was tapped) or communicating through an intermediary.

Once inside, David passed Julius a note warning that strangers had been watching the building all day. Still, David and Julius felt confident enough to carry on a conversation. According to the NKGB memo, Julius warned David to remain at home and await further instructions. Immediate escape was no longer practical. His departure for Mexico "would depend now on the presence of surveillance," the NKGB memo said.

Suddenly, for the first time, Julius broached a painful subject: the danger of arrest. Whatever happens, Julius urged, don't reveal any of your operational activities. Both the NKGB's account and David's own recollection agree on one point: Under no circumstances, David said, would he ever become an informer. As David later recounted it, Julius asked: "'What are you going to do now?' I said, 'I am not going to do anything. I am going to sit—I am going to stay right here.'"

Then Julius left.

David Greenglass never spoke to Julius Rosenberg again.

Thursday, June 8

David and Ruth didn't stay right at home. They visited her parents' apartment across the street. Afterward, they shopped in the neighborhood.

In Brooklyn, Harry Gold and two confederates known by the aliases John and Sam were charged by a federal grand jury with conspiring with Dr. Klaus Fuchs to transmit atomic secrets to the Soviet Union.

In Albuquerque, investigators inspecting the records of the Albuquerque Trust and Savings Bank discovered that the Greenglasses opened an account there on June 4, 1945. Their first deposit was four hundred dollars in cash, lending weight to Harry Gold's recollection that he gave them five hundred dollars the day before. (During the nine months that the account was active, they made only four other deposits: one for fifty-five dollars and the rest for five dollars each.)

In Manhattan, Julius Rosenberg arrived for a meeting with his Soviet contact. Julius was agitated and suggested they walk. When they were two blocks away, he revealed that David was being watched constantly. The contact ordered Julius not to visit David again. Instead, in a tacit acknowledgment that American counterintelligence was closing in, the contact proposed that Ethel go to the Greenglasses' apartment and retrieve three thousand of the four thousand dollars that Julius had given David the previous weekend. If FBI agents searched the apartment, so much loose cash could be incriminating. No evidence suggests that Ethel was actually enlisted to reclaim the money, although the NKGB account suggests that she would have been amenable to the mission.

Anyway, David had already given the package to Louis Abel, who had secreted it inside a hassock. A few days later, Ruth dropped by and asked Abel for one hundred dollars so she could buy a dress and a gift for a friend's wedding.

In Washington, a Senate subcommittee disclosed the gist of secret testimony given two months earlier by J. Edgar Hoover. Seeking a bigger budget to hunt atomic spies, Hoover warned that fifty-four thousand Communist Party members and another half-million sympathizers had gone underground to foil the FBI and would be harder to uncover than Nazi agents because many were not aliens. "There is less likelihood for a native-born citizen to attract suspicion than there is for an alien," Hoover said, "because he blends into the very background which he would destroy."

Friday, June 9

David and Ruth stayed home. David phoned Arma to ask about his leave. It was denied. He promised to report to work again on Monday night, June 12, and told his supervisor that he would send Ruth away to recuperate by herself.

In Philadelphia, Harry Gold failed to identify photographs of David from 1940 and surveillance photos taken within the past few days. Agents said Gold was being "cautious and hesitant" because he had only met the GI briefly, and, given "that the nature of the charge is so grave," he was reluctant to identify the suspect from a photograph. He described David as "naïve," only a "novice" as a spy.

In New York, agents seeking a mid-1940s photograph of David approached only one former employer, Federal Telephone. The others weren't contacted "in view of indicated acquaintanceship with family."

In an urgent Teletype to Hoover, Edward Scheidt concluded that Gold had been "milked dry" about the Greenglasses. Echoing a conclusion reached by his subordinates four days earlier, Scheidt recommended that David and Ruth be interviewed immediately. He offered no fewer than five reasons: Greenglass was cleared to do classified work at Arma; all other avenues of investigation had been exhausted, "and there are no substantial leads outstanding"; Greenglass might be less cooperative if Gold gets a substantial sentence; "it does not appear likely that an unproductive interview at this time would in any way interfere

with further investigation"; and, finally, if Greenglass agreed to cooperate, he could be taken to Philadelphia to "confront Gold for further
identification" before Gold was transferred to some distant penitentiary.
Scheidt's message concluded:

```
AS THIS CASE PRESENTLY STANDS AND EVEN CONSIDERING
MOST PROFITABLE OUTCOME OF OUTSTANDING LEADS, THE
CASE IS NOT STRONG LEGALLY FROM A POINT OF PROOF
OF ESPIONAGE OR CONSPIRACY BECAUSE OF LACK OF COR-
ROBORATION. IT IS BELIEVED THE BEST POSSIBILITY OF
STRENGTHENING THE CASE IS A SUCCESSFUL INTERVIEW
WITH GREENGLASS AND WIFE TO OBTAIN CORROBORATING
FACTS WHICH CAN BE PROVED BY INVESTIGATION.
```

Saturday, June 10

At 10:30 A.M. David went for a haircut around the corner on Columbia Street. At 11:10, David left the barbershop, stopped briefly at his
mother's house, then met Ruth at the playground at Sheriff and Broome.
About an hour later, David, accompanied by another man (and presumably by Ruth, too), left pushing a baby carriage. They stopped at
her parents' house. Then, accompanied by the man and an unidentified woman, they hiked the quarter mile to 619–23 East Fifth Street.
They remained there until 2:45 P.M., then went window-shopping. The
Greenglasses returned home at 5:00 P.M.

Sunday, June 11

The last day before David was due back at work was anything but routine. At 11:15 A.M., he boarded a crosstown bus on Delancey Street and
got off at Essex Street, where he bought a ticket at the Short Line Bus
depot. A half hour later, he boarded a number 183 bus to the Dixie
Hotel bus terminal on West Forty-third Street, across from the *New*

York Times building. At 12:30 P.M., David boarded a number 188 bus. FBI agents followed in an unmarked car.

For more than three hours, they tailed the bus north and west, grunting into low gear to negotiate the Shawangunk Mountains. David got off in Ellenville, at the Shamrock Hotel. He placed a long-distance telephone call, then waited for nearly an hour until a 1937 Chevy sedan pulled up. David got in. With FBI agents in tow, the driver left Ellenville by Cape Road and jounced for ten miles past Merriman Dam and Beaver Dam, and finally, shortly after 5:00 P.M., up a hundred-foot-long driveway to a semicircle of five bungalows. No evasive driving techniques were noted.

Leo Brooks's Farm and Bungalow Colony, three miles from Grahamsville, was sandwiched between a farm owned by Mrs. Brooks's cousin and the Beaverdam Club, a private fishing and hunting club whose membership, the FBI learned, was "allegedly restricted" to Gentiles. To this day, David can't say for certain whether Brooks's Farm, which he found through an ad at the very bottom of a page of classifieds in the *New York Post* that Friday, was to be, as he had implied to his boss at Arma, simply a summer retreat where he was sending Ruth to recuperate or a remote mountain hideaway where he intended to go on the lam until all this spy business blew over.*

The trip to Brooks took six hours on three buses and a car. After all of eighteen minutes, David got back into the Chevy for the return ride to Ellenville. He caught the 6:00 P.M. Short Line bus and arrived home a few minutes before midnight.

Monday, June 12

At 12:50 P.M., the Greenglasses left Barbara with Ruth's parents. David, Ruth, and Steven took a taxi to Gouverneur Hospital, where doctors

---

* The ad promised modern four-room units with new refrigerators, a children's playground and wading pool, and spring water.

examined Ruth's burns. They left Gouverneur at 1:55 and took the bus to go shopping. As he had said he would, David returned to Arma. He left for work at 3:40 and returned home at 2:10 A.M.

FBI agents reported that after being watched and followed for a full week, David Greenglass had become "surveillance conscious."

In the Catskills, Agents Vincent Loughlin and Louis Hurley retraced David's route of the day before. They determined that the 1937 Chevy was registered to Leo Brooks. As they were reconnoitering, Mrs. Brooks bolted from the bungalow colony and flagged them down. She was hysterical. A large snake had made itself at home in the grass near her house. The agents later reported, without elaborating, that they had "disposed of the snake." (David, demonstrating his sense of humor, later said, "I put it there.") Mrs. Brooks was grateful, though getting her to cooperate probably would not have presented a challenge under any circumstances. "It is apparent," the agents reported later, "that Mrs. Brooks is very talkative and very emotional, but friendly." She and her husband lived in one of the five bungalows. They had already rented three others for the season, which customarily lasts through the Jewish holidays in September. The fifth had just been rented. The wife of a man who had inspected the premises the day before telephoned that morning to say they would take the bungalow for the season at $350.

Tuesday, June 13

An ambulance from Gouverneur stopped in front of 265 Rivington. At 11:45 A.M., David accompanied Ruth to the hospital. Her burns had become infected. David stayed for a half hour, then returned home. After lunch, he briefly visited Ruth's parents across the street. At 3:42 P.M., David and an unidentified man walked to Columbia and East Houston streets, where they got into an old Chevy and drove to Arma.

In Albuquerque, FBI agents found the Manhattan Project daily reports, which were supposed to list anyone away from Los Alamos on assignment or leave. David's name did not appear on any of the reports from June 1 through June 7, which suggested that he was there then.

Wednesday, June 14

At 11:25 A.M., David visited the Printzes' store. Twenty minutes later, he went by bus to the bank to deposit the rest of the thousand dollars that Julius had given him three weeks before. Next, he walked to Gouverneur Hospital to visit Ruth for the better part of an hour before leaving for Arma.

While David was taking the subway to work, the rest of his life was being decided in Washington. At 4:07 P.M., the New York office received a Teletype from headquarters authorizing an interview with David Greenglass.

Thursday, June 15

In Washington, Attorney General J. Howard McGrath announced the arrest of Alfred Dean Slack, a forty-four-year-old Syracuse chemist, for espionage. The announcement said that Slack admitted to providing Harry Gold with classified information from the Holston Ordnance Works at Kingsport, Tennessee, in 1943 and 1944.

At 12:11 P.M. on Thursday, June 15, New York sent the following Teletype to FBI headquarters in Washington. Marked urgent, it said, in part:

```
DAVID  GREENGLASS  WILL  BE  INTERVIEWED  ONE
THIRTY  PM  JUNE  FIFTEEN  AT  HIS  HOME  AT  WHICH
TIME  HE  WILL  BE  INTERVIEWED  ALONG  LINES  HE  WAS
PREVIOUSLY  INTERVIEWED  AS  REPORTED  IN  REPORT
OF  SA  LAWRENCE  W.  SPILLANE,  MARCH  THIRTYFIRST
LAST  .  .  .  UPON  CONCLUSION  OF  SUCH  INTERVIEW
A  REQUEST  WILL  BE  MADE  FOR  A  VOLUNTARY  WAIVER
OF  SEARCH  OF  GREENGLASS  APARTMENT  AND  HIS  SAFE
DEPOSIT  BOX.  SUBSEQUENT  TO  PROPOSED  SEARCH
DAVID  GREENGLASS  WILL  BE  INTERVIEWED  SPECIFI-
CALLY  RE  GOLD  AND  HIS  CONTACT  WITH  GOLD.
```

It was chilly for June. And just damp enough to force the Dodgers and Giants to cancel their afternoon home games.

David emerged from the apartment at noon. He visited Ruth at Gouverneur for forty minutes. He left Gouverneur at 1:00 P.M. On the way home, David stopped at the Printzes' store to brief Ruth's parents on her recuperation: The doctors expected her to be discharged from the hospital as soon as Friday.

At 1:35 P.M., he said good-bye to the Printzes. At least four sets of eyes were watching him. He stomped up the stairs at 265 Rivington. The baby hadn't been fed yet, so David began mixing her formula and warming the bottle. He was still in the kitchen when someone knocked on the door. Not the hesitant *tap-tap-tap* of a neighbor, but the insistent *rap-rap* of a man who is accustomed to doors opening, one way or another.

Chapter 22

==========

The First Confession

**"The only contrition was I'm sorry
my wife and kids were involved."**

=

The interview with David Greenglass, slated for 1:30 p.m., started sixteen minutes late. FBI agents John Lewis and Leo Frutkin began by recycling the familiar questions about missing uranium that Agent Spillane had posed at the same kitchen table in January. This time, though, David knew that the hemispheres on the agents' agenda were global, not golf-ball-sized. The give-and-take proceeded with a certain inevitability. The agents, stolid, square-jawed men with dark suits and fedoras, were polite. David was confused, he said later. "I just finished the mathematics required for the whole week worth of [baby] formula, right? Got that part of the picture? Here comes a knock on the door, and the guy comes in, and now I know that the chickens came home to roost. I was outwardly very calm. But I was very much upset.

"This thing was five years ago," he continued. "Maybe I'm sorry I did it, maybe I'm not, but I thought it had all gone away, and now I got this fucking FBI at my door."

—

Lewis and Frutkin had no arrest warrant. They didn't even have a search warrant. Legally, they had virtually nothing to go on except Harry Gold's vague recollection of a GI whom he couldn't positively identify from photographs, who lived in a boardinghouse that had since been remodeled, who may have mentioned a father-in-law in New York whose name may have been Philip, whose wife deposited four hundred dollars one day after Gold said he gave the couple five hundred, and who had been absent from Los Alamos on two or more occasions when—according to sources that could not be compromised much less confirmed in court—a mole in the Manhattan Project was passing atomic secrets to Soviet agents in New York and Albuquerque. Simply insufficient evidence, the FBI concluded, to warrant the prosecution of David Greenglass.

Without David Greenglass.

"Without his confession, I doubt that there would have been a case," James Kilsheimer, an assistant federal prosecutor, said. "Harry Gold could have testified against him, but whether that would've been sufficient to warrant the death penalty for David, I doubt it. Would there have been a case without David Greenglass? No."

Eleven minutes after Lewis and Frutkin arrived, they persuaded David to sign a consent form authorizing them to search the four-room apartment and "to take from my residence any letters, papers, materials or other property which they may desire." Frutkin made the first find. Gingerly picking through the drawers of the night table, he discovered a membership card from the International Workers Order. David explained that he and Ruth had joined the group in order to qualify for cheap medical insurance, but he had quit to protect his job at Arma once Attorney General Tom Clark listed the IWO as a subversive organization. Frutkin also found a cache of two dozen photographs, including the elusive images that the FBI had been seeking for weeks of David and Ruth in Albuquerque in 1945. There was no point in waiting to complete the search. At 2:26 P.M., Frutkin delivered the photos to Agent William Norton, stationed downstairs. They were immediately dispatched to Philadelphia to be shown to Harry

Gold. "Identification by Gold will, of course, make the interview of Greenglass on a much sounder basis," the New York office advised. Meanwhile, he "is being interviewed along general lines until the photographs have been displayed to Gold."

Frutkin returned to the apartment, joined by Agent John Harrington. Lewis made the next discovery. On a shelf over a closet in the room next to the kitchen, he found a footlocker. David not only insisted that it hadn't been opened in years but asked if Frutkin, in searching the bedroom, happened to have stumbled across the key. Funny thing was, Frutkin had found a key in the night table. David inserted it in the rusted keyhole; it wouldn't turn. Instead, he used a screwdriver to jimmy the latch. It was jammed, not locked. Inside, the agents found a trove of handwritten letters that David and Ruth had exchanged during the war, socked away, and probably forgotten. Never betraying their heightened expectations, Lewis and Frutkin flipped through the letters. None explicitly referred to espionage or to stealing atomic secrets, but their existence was so tantalizing that, without waiting to see what else turned up, Norton delivered the entire footlocker to the New York FBI office in Foley Square.

David was asked if he and Ruth owned a safe-deposit box. Yes, he replied, at the Manufacturers Safe Deposit Company on Grand Street. He authorized the agents to search it. This time he found the key, but it was already 3:15 P.M.: The bank had closed. David assured the agents that they weren't missing much, though. His war bonds had all been cashed, he said, and most of the important papers were at home anyway because he had recently submitted them to the New York City Housing Authority when he applied for a government-subsidized apartment. (He was deemed ineligible, he said, because his salary exceeded the income ceiling.)

While agents downtown scrutinized the letters and other personal effects, Lewis and Frutkin scoured the apartment. David accompanied them. He responded when they asked him to identify a particular item, but he didn't volunteer anything—in part, because he couldn't really remember which papers and other artifacts had accumulated over five years that investigators might find valuable.* The agents took samples from the Smith-Corona noiseless portable typewriter that David said he and Ruth had bought earlier in the year. They also found a copy of a War Department memo dated August 7, 1945, the day after the first use of an atomic bomb in warfare. The memo, addressed to workers at Los Alamos, praised their "high devotion to patriotic duty." It concluded: "Each of you has done his own job and kept his own secret."

David's secret wasn't exactly the one that the War Department wanted kept. He kept the memo, though.

———

If a case was to be made against the Greenglasses on the basis of physical evidence, the photographs and letters would have to do. And they did. As Raymond Whearty, a Justice Department supervisor, informed Irving Saypol, the federal prosecutor, the following morning, "photographs of Greenglass and his wife were the only things of any prosecutive value which were obtained." Moreover, agents reviewing the inventory of items seized during their thorough search of Harry Gold's house in Philadelphia had "failed to reflect any material that had any bearing upon David Greenglass."

Shortly after 5:00 P.M., about three hours after David had authorized Lewis and Frutkin to conduct a search, they invited him downtown to continue their conversation—just a suggestion that they would all be

---

* They found some college chemistry textbooks that Julius Rosenberg had given to David years before. The agents' inventory included Ruth's Albuquerque Public Library card, her union card from Local 1 of the United Office and Professional Workers of America, a bill for IWO dues for March, April, and May 1949; Ruth's address book (which, among other entries, included a furrier on West Thirtieth Street and a phone number for Marion at 799 Broadway identified only as "county," and which was Young Communist League headquarters); a second address book that apparently belonged to David (among the listings were Ben Bederson in the Bronx, Thomas A. Fineberg in Chicago, Hugh R. Holland on East Eighteenth Street, Henry Linschitz in Washington Heights, New York University, and William Spindel); an army document marked "restricted," which announced David's promotion in April 1945; form letters from Colonel K. V. Nichols of the Army Corps of Engineers and from Undersecretary of War Robert P. Patterson thanking Manhattan Project workers for their service; and a Lucite disk that David described as "some part of the atomic bomb, but wasn't certain which part."

more comfortable there tying up some loose ends without the children (Tessie or Dorothy Printz was already baby-sitting) or other distractions. He agreed. The FBI couldn't have been more accommodating. To spare David embarrassment, Harrington left the apartment first, joined Norton in the bureau car, and drove to the intersection two and a half blocks east. They turned right and waited near the corner. At 5:25 P.M., Lewis and Frutkin left the tenement with David. They strolled casually in the light drizzle—about as casually as FBI agents accompanying a suspected spy could—to the car. David was ushered into the backseat and driven downtown. He never returned to 265 Rivington Street.

—

In 1950, the FBI's New York office occupied the upper floors of Cass Gilbert's neoclassical U.S. District Court House in Foley Square. Lewis and Frutkin escorted David to Conference Room U on the twenty-ninth floor, where they were joined a few minutes later by Norton and Harrington. The agents were still awaiting word from Harry Gold in Philadelphia. David described his family but was a little vague on some details (his half-brother, Sam, was "about" forty years old; Bernard was a machinist and assistant manager "of an unknown company"). David's most revealing answers were to two questions posed around 7:00 P.M.: Was he hungry, and, if so, what would he like for dinner?

While David was gulping down two hamburgers, ordered from an Italian deli behind the courthouse, and a cup of coffee, Colonel Wilfred A. Steiner of the U.S. Air Force was at the Astor Hotel conjuring up a horrifying vision of how New York would fare after a nuclear attack. Addressing the economic-mobilization course of the Industrial College of the Armed Forces, Steiner enumerated the medical supplies required to provide ideal care to a severe burn victim (an example with which David, had he been in the audience, would have been painfully familiar): forty-two tanks of oxygen, 2.7 miles of gauze, and forty pints of whole blood. Steiner estimated that an atomic attack would inflict severe burns on as many as one hundred thousand New Yorkers. "Where," he asked, "would New York get four million pints of blood?" Medical reserve officers in the audience gasped. Now that he had captured their attention, Steiner veered to a more practical alternative. He concluded his speech by delivering a vigorous plea to make the Communist Party illegal.

—

David was just finishing dinner at 9:07 P.M. when Special Agent Arthur Cornelius, Jr., called from Philadelphia. Harry Gold had identified the 1945 photograph of David and Ruth standing on the porch of 209 North High Street. On the back of the photo, Gold wrote: "This was the man I contacted in Albuquerque, New Mexico in June 1945 on instructions from my Soviet espionage superior John."

For the first time in the more than seven hours that David had been in the company of federal agents, the tenor of the conversation shifted perceptibly. David was asked to recall a visit to Albuquerque from a Soviet courier in June 1945. When he hesitated, he was confronted with the fact that his photograph had been positively identified by Harry Gold.

What could he say?

Here he was, twenty-eight years old, married, a father of two with a steady job. For the second time in his life, he was being thrust into a role where he mattered more than anyone. The agents did not relate what else, if anything, Gold had said transpired, except that Greenglass might have mentioned Ben Bederson's name as a potential recruit for espionage. Nor did they mention Gold's account that he had given David money. They didn't have to. According to Lewis and Frutkin, "Greenglass immediately, by inference, indicated that he was the guilty person."

For weeks, he had been anticipating this moment, but he had never scripted a response. He had never stopped to think through how much he would admit or whom he might incriminate. He had mulled over the implications of fleeing the country and flatly decided against it. But he had never really considered the consequences of admitting his guilt. He had never considered consequences, period, because he had never really considered himself guilty.

At 9:25 P.M., David Greenglass confessed.

—

From that moment, the game changed. It was no longer cat and mouse. Now and forever, it would be cat and rat. David explained that he had been expecting the agents ever since he had seen Gold's photograph in the newspaper. He insisted that only his love for his wife and children had prevented him from either committing suicide or escaping "into the hinterlands of the United States where he could never have been found." Paris, Mexico, Czechoslovakia, or Moscow were never serious options. It was Leo Brooks's Farm and Bungalow Colony in the Catskills or bust.

He admitted that he had met a man in Albuquerque in June 1945, furnished him information, and received five hundred dollars in return. Not for the money, though—for the cause. He had worked on the atom bomb and his wife, a communist, had recruited him to give information to "our allies."

He was not remorseful. "The only contrition was I'm sorry my wife and kids were involved," he said later.

David spewed out more details, then changed them. "If you would ask me, did I deliberately lie to them? At first I did," he acknowledged later. He told Lewis and Frutkin that he hadn't known he was working on an atomic bomb until Ruth told him; then, he said he had learned about the bomb earlier from colleagues. ("Greenglass," the FBI said, "stated that he feels that it is his duty to protect his wife and his family to the best of his ability under the circumstances.") First, he claimed he didn't know who had enlisted Ruth to recruit him as a spy; then he said it was Julius. ("Greenglass," the FBI noted, "said that he had admitted this lie because he felt that investigation might well reveal the true facts. It should also be noted that at the time Greenglass claimed that he had no personal contact with Rosenberg concerning espionage activities.") He recalled giving Harry Gold a sketch of a high-explosive lens mold "or something of that type of thing" and produced a rough replica of the drawing for Lewis and Frutkin. He acknowledged that he had told Gold that Oppenheimer and Kistiakowsky were working at Los Alamos and also about "a world-famous scientist" working under an assumed name, whom he later identified as Niels Bohr.

A government stenographer was summoned.

—

At 11:54 P.M., the stenographer, Frances Devlin, started transcribing her notes. She delivered three typed pages one hour later. David remarked that the stenographer was "an awful slow typist." His statement said, in part:

On or about November 29, 1944, my wife, Ruth, arrived in New Mexico from New York City and told me that Julius Rosenberg, my brother-in-law, had asked if I would give information on the Atom Bomb and stated as a reason for that that we are at war with Germany and Japan and that they are the enemy and that Soviet Russia was fighting the enemy and was entitled to the information. On that basis, I agreed to give whatever information came to me in the course of my employment at Los Alamos, New Mexico, at the Los Alamos Atom Bomb Project. This message, which my wife conveyed to me, was not her own idea but was an idea given to her by Julius Rosenberg.

About February, 1945, my wife moved to Albuquerque, New Mexico, from New York City. Three or four months later she had a miscarriage. Approximately a month after that time, a man came to the place where Ruth was living, 209 North High Street, Albuquerque, New Mexico. I did not know this man's name at the time but recently recognized his pictures in various newspapers as being Harry Gold. He had with him a torn or cut piece of paper card which fitted a torn piece of paper card furnished me as a means of identifying this man. I cannot recall at this time whether this torn piece of card was given to me by my wife, Ruth, at the time she moved to Albuquerque, New Mexico, from New York about February, 1945, or whether I received it from Julius Rosenberg while I was in New York City on furlough between about December 20, 1944 and January 20, 1945. Gold gave me an envelope containing $500. Gold said to me that I was living in a poor place at the time he gave me the $500. I furnished him with information concerning the Los Alamos Project, although I did not do it for the promise of money. . . . I felt it was gross negligence on the part of the United States not to give Russia the information about the Atom Bomb because she was an ally.

My wife was not in the room at the time I received the money from

Gold and at the time I gave him information about the Los Alamos Atom Bomb Project. I gave Gold the information without expecting money for it.

David signed the statement at 1:06 A.M. Lewis and Frutkin witnessed it. Devlin remembered the time because as David signed the statement he was laughing. "I expect to have my day in court, at which time I will plead innocent, repudiate this statement, and claim I never saw you guys," he said. Then, at 1:10 A.M., David wrote on the back of Gold's photograph: "This is the picture of the man who was the recipient of my information at Alb."

———

Even before David signed the confession, Washington directed the New York office to place Julius Rosenberg under surveillance first thing in the morning. The FBI had already discovered a brief file on Rosenberg, "showing that the Army had trouble with him because of his Communist leanings." The New York office's William Whelan was worried, though. Knickerbocker Village was a massive apartment complex with numerous exits.* Agents didn't even know what Rosenberg looked like; they would have difficulty spotting him.

Washington was more worried. David said he would have fled had it not been for his wife and infant daughter. Rosenberg had a wife and children, also, but maybe once it became public that Greenglass had been apprehended, Rosenberg, too, would be tempted to run. New York was ordered to contact Rosenberg at home at 8:00 A.M. and to "question him concerning his knowledge of Greenglass, and if appropriate, work into questioning him on his own activities." The New York office was also directed to detain David overnight.

Since they had first encountered David nearly twelve hours earlier, Lewis and Frutkin reported, he had "exhibited a friendly attitude toward all of the F.B.I. personnel and seemed to be in good spirits." By the time

———

* Today, signs outside warn that the premises are under electronic surveillance.

he confessed, they said, he was "in a rather light mood." Frutkin played a special role in cultivating David. He was the good cop. He was also one of the few Jewish FBI agents. David recalled later: "He said, 'What was there about America that made you feel that you had to be a communist?' I said to him, 'I had no idea about betraying the United States. All I had in mind was helping a guy that was at war fighting the Nazis.'"

Frutkin suggested that since David could not be brought before a federal magistrate until morning, he might as well bed down at the New York office. David didn't have to be persuaded. He replied that he would rather not go home. He didn't want to attract publicity.

At 1:32 A.M., June 16, Lewis and Frutkin placed David Greenglass under arrest. He was allowed one telephone call before being led to the nurse's office on the sixth floor where he would spend the rest of the night under guard. David phoned his other brother-in-law, Louis Abel, to say he wouldn't be home that night. He asked Abel to engage a lawyer—suggesting O. John Rogge—and to tell Ruth that he had given the FBI a statement.

Tell her, he said, not to worry.

Chapter 23

The Formula

"All you need is one guy to get caught.
One guy that's not smart."

David awoke at eight. He was so disoriented that he peered at a birthmark on his arm, a mark that, by definition, had been there all his life, and mistook it for a needle prick. "I looked at it," he recalled, and said, "Well, Jesus, did you guys give me some truth serum?"

Leo Frutkin had dozed overnight on an adjoining cot in the nurse's office. Two other agents, Robert Royal and Harold Good, had been stationed just outside the door all night. Agents Frutkin and Lewis treated David to breakfast at a coffee shop around the corner, then walked him to a barbershop for a shave and haircut. He was in the chair when a *Daily News* headline grabbed him: Another Red spy linked to Harry Gold had been arrested. David was startled but only momentarily. The story was about Alfred Dean Slack. David told the agents he had never seen Slack before or even heard his name.

By the time they returned to the courthouse at 10:00 A.M., Julius Rosenberg was there as well.

Julius had been at Foley Square for more than an hour. Armed with buttered rolls and containers of coffee, Agents Norton and Harrington had walked over early in the morning to Knickerbocker Village in order to surprise him before news spread that David was in custody. Julius was surprised. He was shirtless.

———

Once David started talking, he couldn't stop.

"They were all nice guys," David remembered. "They're nice people. They're not out to beat up or anything, nothing like that. They didn't act like I robbed a bank. They know that they can talk and get anything they want, just by talking and by offering you something, like not arresting your wife. That's the way they do it."

Interviewed again by Lewis and Frutkin for an hour after breakfast, David began embellishing his earlier statement. He recounted his only liaison with a real live Russian. David couldn't identify him. Lewis and Frutkin showed him a selection of photographs of suspected Russian agents, including Anatoly Yakovlev and Semen Semenov. David shuffled them for a while and finally concluded that Semenov came closest. He was hazy about when the meeting took place but was more inclined to believe that it was September 1945, rather than the previous January, because the Russian had asked him to amplify on the notes he had given Gold. David dictated a second statement to Frutkin, then signed it:

> I recall that when I was on furlough from the Los Alamos Atom Bomb Project, my brother-in-law, Julius Rosenberg, in New York City, asked to see me one night. I had a previous appointment of a social nature to see some personal friends and cut the appointment short in order to meet my brother-in-law, Julius Rosenberg. I borrowed a 1935 Oldsmobile and drove to the vicinity of about First Avenue, somewhere above East 42nd Street, but below East 59th Street probably. I parked the car at the curb, on a north bound street facing north. Julius Rosenberg walked over to the car and told me to wait. Then he walked away and came back with a man and introduced him to me by a first name which I do not recall. Then the man got into the car and I drove around while the man asked me questions about a high-explosive lens which was being experimented with at [the] Los Alamos Atom Bomb Project. I tried to describe the lens to the man while I was driving. When the man left the

car about fifteen minutes later, I went home. Julius, after introducing the man to me, had left. This furlough was either the one before I met Harry Gold [in] the summer of 1945 or after that time.

Other details dribbled out. David was asked whether Gold had identified himself by name at either of their two brief meetings. David didn't think so, then suggested that Harry might have used the name Dave, but finally rejected that possibility.

—

Legally, there was no debate about what to do with David: draw up a complaint against him in Albuquerque, the jurisdiction in which the transaction between Harry and David had occurred, and arraign him in New York. "We must move promptly, so as not [to] be charged with holding Greenglass illegally," Hoover scrawled on one early-morning memo. On a second one, he was even more emphatic: "I want prompt arraignment."

But what to do about the other two suspects named in David's confession, Ruth Greenglass and Julius Rosenberg? That was the subject of a 10:00 A.M. meeting in Washington convened by Assistant Attorney General James McInerney. Justice Department officials were informed that Julius had voluntarily accompanied agents to the courthouse and was being questioned at that very moment. Ruth was still hospitalized and had not yet been interviewed. The Justice Department's Ray Whearty recommended that the New York office immediately contact her doctor for permission to do so. If she could physically tolerate an interview, she should be questioned at once. McInerney and the other Justice Department representatives concluded that on the basis of David's statements alone, "process should not be issued at this time" against Ruth Greenglass and Julius Rosenberg.

—

While federal law-enforcement officials were conferring in Washington, O. John Rogge called the FBI's New York office at 10:25 A.M. to formally give notice that he was representing David Greenglass. He asked what charges were being lodged against his client and was told that the specifics were still being considered by the department. Within a half hour, Rogge's partner, Herbert J. Fabricant, arrived at the courthouse and was shown to conference room B. Lewis and Frutkin's interview with David ended.

Fabricant's began. The agents said that Fabricant could see David alone, although they would prefer that one of them was present. David preferred otherwise, so they departed. They shut the window but left the door ajar.

"I joked with these guys; I know what they are and who they are," David told his lawyer. Fabricant was flabbergasted at David's hubris. After fingering his wife as an intermediary and attributing the original plot to his brother-in-law, how could he possibly have concluded that he had outwitted the FBI? "He told me that he had made a number of confusing statements purposely in order to confound the F.B.I. and to draw attention from his wife who is in the hospital," Fabricant noted. As for the spy plot itself, Fabricant recalled, "His wife apparently originally told him that his brother-in-law, Julius Rosenberg, had suggested this (and so I fail to see how his mind operated in connection with keeping his wife out of the picture . . .). I asked him if he was going to cooperate with the government. He said 'Hell, no.' I asked him whether he recognized that he made it very difficult for anyone to help him. He said he did."

David later told his lawyers that he "definitely placed my wife out of the room at the time of Gold's visit"; that he originally told the FBI "I didn't know who sent Gold to me"; and that, while he reproduced a pencil sketch of the lens-mold experiment for the agents, "I can honestly say the information I gave Gold may be not at all what I said in the statement."

Amazingly, David also asked Fabricant to get in touch with Julius, who was being interrogated simultaneously in the same building. Why contact the brother-in-law whom he had just implicated? "I wanted Julius to put up money. For bail, everything, bail, lawyer, the whole works," David explained later. "I was there because of Julius Rosenberg." David doubted that his own half-brother, Sam, would help, though. "He is a terrible reactionary," David said.

After thirty-five minutes, Fabricant concluded: "Greenglass appeared articulate, at ease, and in good shape physically. He did appear in complete control of his faculties."

—

In Albuquerque, Agent J. Jerome Maxwell filed a complaint with U.S. Commissioner Owen J. Mowrey at 9:36 A.M., Mountain time. It accused Greenglass, Gold, Yakovlev, and unnamed others of conspiring to deliver and attempting to deliver to the Soviet Union "documents, writings, sketches, notes and information relating to the National Defense of the United States, to wit, documents, writings, sketches, notes and information relating to atomic energy and nuclear fission." According to the complaint, the conspiracy began on or about January 1, 1945, "the United States then and there being at war."

Mowrey signed the arrest warrant one minute later.

—

At 12:55 P.M., the U.S. Attorney's office in New York notified Agent Lewis that a warrant had been issued in Albuquerque. Arraignment was promptly scheduled for 1:20.

Wearing light blue pants, a white shirt, and a khaki windbreaker, David joked with an FBI agent as he waited in the tiny ground-floor hearing room for the arraignment to begin. If anyone had any doubts that David was a trophy defendant, the federal prosecutor erased them at once. "He worked on the bomb itself," U.S. Attorney Irving Saypol announced. He sought bail of one hundred thousand dollars, prompting Rogge to complain, "We've lost our heads in this country. Fear and hysteria are wiping out another provision of the Constitution." Rogge suggested that five thousand dollars would be more appropriate but added, "I do not know whether this defendant can even raise that much." Saypol replied that the only hysterics in evidence were being generated by Rogge, at which point the federal magistrate, Edward W. McDonald, interjected: "The only thing that makes us all a little hysterical is the seriousness of the charge." He granted the government's request and fixed bail at one hundred thousand dollars.

During the entire arraignment, David uttered thirteen words. They are a frosted window into his state of mind. Either he was ingeniously laying the foundation for an insanity defense or he was utterly bewildered. Rogge was describing his client's roots in the community, as evidence that he should be released on bail.

"You do have two children, don't you?"

"Yes," David replied. "I have to go home and make the formula for my baby."

—

Flanked by U.S. marshals, David was escorted to the detention center on West Street. He was stripped of his shoelaces and belt to thwart a possible suicide attempt. "As they closed the door, I lay down and I said, 'Jesus, when the hell do I see my daughter again?'" he recalled.

> I lean back and look up. I hear a commotion outside. A real commotion. I turn around, I see four burly guards and they're beating the hell out of an inmate. And then they open up the door, and they throw him right next door to me. I feel untouched by this, you understand. Like, it's not my problem. On the other hand, I said, "Boy, that poor guy got the hell beaten out of him." You know, I said, "Well, this is going to be some stay."

—

At Gouverneur Hospital, the swelling in Ruth's left leg had subsided, and she was due to be released later that afternoon. She was feeling better, too, until Louis Abel arrived and reported that David had been arrested. He also relayed David's message not to worry.

Her next visitor was the FBI.

At 1:30 P.M., with a doctor's permission, agents began interviewing her. She confirmed the barest outlines of what the FBI already knew. She had visited Albuquerque in November 1944 to celebrate her second wedding anniversary. She moved there the following March to be closer to her husband. The only visitors to her apartment during the year she lived there were a few fellow employees and the wives of other GIs. Nobody by the name of Harry Gold (or Frank Kessler or Frank Martin, two of his aliases). No one who looked like Harry Gold. She saw Gold for the first time when his photograph appeared in the newspapers after he was arrested.

The agents confronted her with Gold's confession. Then, they delivered their coup de grâce: Not only had Gold himself admitted visiting the Greenglasses in 1945, but her own husband had independently confirmed Gold's visit, too.

Ruth was dumbstruck. Who knew what to believe? Louis Abel had mentioned that David had given the FBI a statement, but how much had he even remembered from five years ago, much less confirmed or denied? Ruth refused to answer any further questions. Max Printz arrived at the hospital to retrieve his daughter, and the interview was over.

The FBI debated what to do next. Ruth could be brought by ambulance to the courthouse to confer with David. Washington vetoed that alternative for appearances' sake. "It would appear rather ridiculous," the FBI's Alan Belmont said, "to have her carried into the Marshal's Office on a stretcher."

———

All this time, agents were still interviewing Julius.

He confessed to nothing—and never would. But he, alone among the family members questioned on that Friday, mentioned the name of Ethel Rosenberg. Julius casually included her in his accounting of the Signal Corps' explanations for his dismissal: The first was that he belonged to the Federation of Architects, Engineers, Chemists, and Technicians, which was a communist union, so therefore he must be a communist; second, he had lived in Brooklyn with Marcus Pogarsky, a member of the Communist Party who held party gatherings in his home and whose tenancy at 111 South Third Street coincided with the regular appearance of *The Daily Worker* under apartment doors; and third, Ethel Rosenberg had signed some petition to place a Communist Party candidate on the ballot for municipal elections. And, oh yes, the fourth reason: The government claimed to have evidence that Julius himself belonged to the Communist Party.

Julius said he remembered during the war his brother-in-law David mentioning something about working on a secret project, but Julius said he hadn't even heard of the atomic bomb until after it was dropped, much less discussed the technicalities of it beforehand or deduced David's involvement. In late summer 1944, he heard that David was working for army ordnance in New Mexico; that fall, Ruth told him that David was working on a secret project at Los Alamos; only after Hiroshima, Julius told the FBI, had "he assumed that since David was working on a secret project in New Mexico, David must have been working on the Atom Bomb."

Julius remembered that David had visited New York on furloughs and that Ruth had visited David in New Mexico and eventually moved there, but he was vague about the dates. On one furlough, he recalled, David was wearing an Eisenhower jacket, so it must have been early spring. When the agents pointed out that since David was stationed in New Mexico he probably was outfitted with a summer uniform, Julius corrected himself and said it might have been very early spring. (If the furlough was from New Mexico, it had to have been either January or September.) Julius remembered seeing David then but only socially and mostly at the homes of David's or Ruth's parents. Harrington asked whether Julius had spent any time alone with David. No, he replied. Then, as the FBI put it, he "admitted" seeing David alone just once, but only at a neighborhood pool hall called Sammy's. David, he said, was "very fond of shooting pool."

The questions became more accusatory. Had he asked Ruth to sound out David about turning over confidential information to the Soviets? Had he arranged for a Soviet courier to contact David in New Mexico? By what means would the courier identify himself? Had he introduced David to a Soviet agent who questioned him about explosive lenses while David drove around Manhattan's East Side? Julius indignantly denied everything. He couldn't have pried secrets from David about his work at Los Alamos because he lacked the technical expertise to pose such questions. Moreover, Julius explained, this whole entire plot was implausible from the start for one fundamental reason: He did not, he insisted, even know any Russians.

Exasperated, Julius demanded to know—as Ruth had—whether David himself had leveled these accusations, and if so, he wished to hear them directly. What, Julius was asked, if his accuser agreed to confront him? Even if David marched in and made these charges eyeball to eyeball, Julius replied, he would unequivocally deny them.

Six hours had passed, and the agents were getting nowhere. "Three times during the day I thought [Julius] was at a point where he would disclose," Agent William Norton recalled. "Then, he'd take a deep breath and start all over." Sometime during the six hours of interviews, Julius received one phone call, from Ethel, although there is no record of what they discussed. The agents asked Julius for permission to search his apartment. He declined.* He also refused to answer any more questions until he talked to his lawyer. At Julius's request, Norton dialed the office of Victor Rabinowitz, the lawyer whom Julius had contacted about his Signal Corps case. Rabinowitz wasn't in, but another lawyer in the office took the call.

"Are you under arrest?" the lawyer asked Julius.

"I don't know," Julius replied. "He says, 'Ask the FBI if you are under arrest.' And I asked Mr. Norton, 'Am I under arrest?'

"He says, 'No.'"

Julius made an appointment for 5:00 P.M. at Rabinowitz's office on Beaver Street. He promptly but politely bade the FBI agents good-bye. On his way out of the courthouse, a copy of the *New York Post* caught his eye. An ex-GI from New York had been arrested and charged with giving atomic secrets to the Soviet Union. Julius might have been struck with the same thought that entered David's mind after the arrests of Klaus Fuchs and Harry Gold. "All you need is one guy to get caught," David said. "One guy that's not smart."

---

* According to a jailhouse informer, Julius was concerned that the FBI would find his Leica camera and seven thousand dollars in cash hidden in a phonograph in the bedroom.

—

"It seemed too ridiculous to believe," said David's cousin Florence Dubner, who remembered him as pleasant enough, if a bit simple. "Little David a Russian spy!"

Tessie Greenglass told newsmen who thronged the vestibule of 64 Sheriff Street that, as far as she knew, her "baby" had been "pushing an army wheelbarrow" in New Mexico. "This I can tell you," she said. "You have a child under your arms until a certain age and then you can't butt in." Asked if she had any other children, Tessie identified David's two brothers. She said David also had a sister but refused to give her name.

"You have the wrong fellow," Tillie Printz, Ruth's mother, announced. "David is a very honest fellow. It's a big mistake."

Joe Schall, an electrical contractor and neighbor at 265 Rivington, was incredulous. "He never gave me any communistic talk," Schall said. "I'm sure he didn't do whatever he did out of being a communist or for any unpatriotic reason."

But many of the people interviewed were not defiant. They were defensive in the face of questions often framed as accusations. How could you not have suspected him? Hadn't you read all those warnings on how to spot a communist? And, by implication, perhaps you overlooked the obvious giveaways because you were a tad too sympathetic to the Soviets yourself.

Hannah Schoenberg, another neighbor, said she and her husband, Morris, who was in the photography business, used to baby-sit Steven Greenglass, but that the families had become estranged "because the Greenglasses had the habit of borrowing food items and never returning them" and "were difficult people to be sociable with since they had no outside interests and always only talked about how smart their child was." She said she suspected all along that the Greenglasses were communists because they regularly read *P.M.* and because Ruth once told her about a friend who had pressure on her brain and said that "Russia was the only place where an operation to relieve this pressure could be successfully performed."

The Freemans, the couple who owned the house on North High Street in Albuquerque, described Ruth as "the smart one in that family."

"We did interview Mrs. Greenglass when she rented the apartment because that is always our practice," W. B. Freeman recalled later. "We don't allow any drunkenness or rowdiness in our apartments. Of course, if I'd known what they were doing to steal atomic secrets I certainly would have turned them in."

Chapter 24

Mr. Cooperation

"These people were ruthless."

≡

Sunday, June 18, 1950, was Father's Day. At 4:00 p.m., Oetje John Rogge and another associate, Robert Goldman, visited the Greenglasses' apartment, where an emergency family conclave had been convened. Ruth was home but still bedridden. Sam and Bernie came by. So did Louis Abel and Uncle Izzy Feit.

For all the shock and uncertainty, the agenda was uncomplicated: Which friends and relatives could be solicited to raise bail? Who was going to pay the lawyers and how much? What were the implications of adjudicating the case in New Mexico instead of New York? Legally, what avenues were available to David?

The question of bail was disposed of quickly. There were few sources to tap. Ruth and the lawyers compiled a list of seven names: Abe Feit, the butcher; his son-in-law; Sam Greenglass; a cousin; and three friends of the family. Nobody ever put up a dime. David had distant relatives with considerable resources who also refused to contribute. According to David, "They didn't want to get involved because they were involved in other things."

Paying the lawyers didn't loom as an immediate problem, what with the packet of cash that David had given Louis Abel. It also yielded one great irony: The Russian government thus paid for David Greenglass's legal defense.

The topic of New Mexico handed Ruth her first opportunity to vent after days of herculean self-control. First, she warned that the state would be "a very bad place to try the case since the citizens did not like the GI's because of the big boom and then the big slack, because of anti-Semitism and because the local citizens all felt bitter about the wives of the GI's taking jobs there."

Then, prodded by Rogge (rhymes with "foggy") and Goldman, Ruth provided some insights into David's personality, some of them unflattering. Goldman's notes of the meeting may have focused on the negatives, though, since those were the character flaws that defense lawyers would have to guard against. Ruth said David "had had a 'tendency to hysteria.' At other times he would become delirious and once when he had the grippe he ran nude through the hallway, shrieking of 'elephants' and 'lead pants.' She had known him since she was 10 years old. She said he would say things were so even if they were not. He talked of suicide as if he were a character in the movies but she didn't think he would do it." (David later confirmed one episode of delirium but insisted that it had happened when he was a child.)

Finally, Ruth launched into a tirade against FBI agents, placing the accusations against David in the perspective of a six-month investigation. She delivered what was, at best, an incomplete version of Agent Spillane's interview earlier in the year about the missing uranium. Ruth insisted that she "would not have allowed her husband to bring anything home after Hiroshima had disclosed what the project was. She intended to raise a family and did not want that kind of material around." That incident, coupled with the recent weeks of nonstop surveillance, suggested to her that the Greenglasses were "the object of persecution." Over the weekend, she reported, neighbors offered to circulate a petition on David's behalf. The *Jewish Daily Forward*, which she described as "very excited by the anti-Semitic issue," offered to provide a lawyer. But David had already chosen Rogge. (It wasn't immediately clear whether he was representing David or the Greenglasses together, although Ruth said later, "Anyone who represents my husband represents me; we are a unit.")

Rogge had spent most of the meeting listening. Then he proceeded to outline three alternatives, according to Goldman's notes: "If Dave was innocent he should talk; that if not it would be advisable not to talk but to let the Government prove its case. The third course was that of cooperation." Cooperation—helping the government prove its case against someone else as opposed to merely talking about his own involvement— was discussed at length, Goldman wrote, followed by "a long discussion about JR." That long discussion must have been a real eye-opener for the other relatives in the room.

Julius had gotten them into this. It was up to Rogge to get them out.

—

"It is not too much to say that Mr. Rogge broke the Rosenberg case," Roy Cohn, another former federal prosecutor, later wrote. "Which is the very definition of irony."

Rogge was a former assistant attorney general, appointed under the New Deal and fired in 1947 by Attorney General Tom Clark for publicly linking Alf Landon, Wendell Willkie, Tom Dewey, and John L. Lewis with Nazi efforts to defeat FDR. In 1948, he ran for the U.S. Senate on a ticket headed by Henry Wallace. He was a registered agent for Marshal Tito of Yugoslavia but couldn't swallow Stalinism. The FBI looked at Rogge and saw only Red. Whatever his motivation in enlisting his clients to cooperate with the government, the FBI never completely trusted him, and at least one official suspected he was merely "attempting to get back on the right bandwagon." Hoover once warned an associate to "be most circumspect in any conversation with Rogge." Hoover signaled his mistrust even more subtly, advising his secretary that in replying to Rogge to use regular FBI stationery and not the director's personal letterhead.

Years later, Rogge wrote a book called *Why Men Confess: From the Inquisition to Brainwashing.* Amazingly, Rogge never mentioned his most famous client, David Greenglass, perhaps because Rogge was more intent on analyzing the fundamental moral, religious, and philosophical foundation that motivated confessions rather than cynical self-interest.* David didn't confess to bare his soul but to spare himself and his wife.

In his book, Rogge identified factors that appeared to leave American GIs vulnerable to Chinese communists: guilt and sin, rebellion, "paucity both in the number of their human relationships and the amount of affection involved in them," and a need for punishment (a category in which Rogge surprisingly lumped the Rosenbergs, who, in fact, had stubbornly chosen not to confess). "The communists and the ex-communists among us have shown a great need for punishment."

Nevertheless, "ours is the accusatorial as opposed to the inquisitorial system," Rogge wrote. "I did not press for confessions" as assistant attorney general, he continued. "Since I have been in private practice I have sought to have confessions which my clients have given invalidated." Why didn't he pursue that legal strategy in the very beginning of the Greenglass case? The FBI and federal prosecutors had their suspicions.

—

On Tuesday, June 20, Irving Saypol reported to Ray Whearty that Rogge would be dropping by, that he had already complained that he hadn't had a vacation in three years, and that he wanted to take the entire summer off—first to attend a music festival and then to visit his mother-in-law in Minnesota. To which Saypol sniffed: "Apparently, he is not much concerned about his client's welfare."

---

* Delving first into Hindu philosophy, Rogge probed what he called the "primeval well-springs" of confession:

> According to Manu one who confessed was freed from guilt as a snake from his slough. James told the early Christians that by mutual confession and prayer they would be healed. John told them they would be cleaned from all unrighteousness. Publilius Syrus (c. 42 B.C.) wrote: "Confession of our faults is the next thing to innocence." Even Goethe regarded a confession favorably and credited it with absolution: "I went on with the poetical confession I had begun, that, with this self-tormenting penance, I might attain an inner absolution." The most poignant evaluation came from Oscar Wilde in *De Profundis*. "A man's very highest moment is, I have no doubt, when he kneels in the dust and beats his breast, and tells all the sins of his life."

The next day, immediately after Rogge left the prosecutor's office, Saypol briefed Whearty about Rogge's offer to cooperate. The government was playing hard to get.

"He says he wants to discuss possibilities in the light of cooperation," Saypol reported. "I didn't press at this stage. I said that was something I had to consider. You know of any cooperation his client can offer?"

"No, he talked to the FBI," Whearty replied. "He didn't say anything. He skirted very carefully around the edges of everything that might hurt. If he wants to cooperate and talk freely, you know the usual terms, we make no commitments but, if he is cooperative, we will call it to the court's attention. That's it."

Rogge also arranged to confer with one of Hoover's lieutenants, Mickey Ladd, in Washington the following Monday afternoon, June 26. Rogge was beginning negotiations about his client's fate with two distinct handicaps: David had not yet agreed to cooperate beyond his initial confession; and he might have already perjured himself. Robert Goldman cautioned that "if the course we follow is 'cooperation' then we should be sure that no issue is made of the *possibility* that, before we came into the case, the client may have made misleading or false statements in his statement after arrest."

Ladd reported that Rogge appeared to be laying the groundwork to divert the FBI from Ruth Greenglass to someone else:

Mr. Rogge stated he was considering the desirability of having his client, David Greenglass, cooperate fully with the Bureau; that he thought it might be beneficial to Greenglass. He stated he has criticized the government on numerous occasions in the past because he feels the government has no right to investigate associations and thoughts of an individual, but that a matter of this kind, involving espionage, is in his opinion entirely different.

He stated he did not know whether Mrs. Greenglass was involved in this matter; that he doubted that she was a Communist, but that he felt his client might be able to furnish some helpful information concerning another subject, namely his own brother-in-law.

Within twenty-four hours, two developments on opposite sides of the world boded ill for the Rosenbergs.

In Philadelphia, Harry Gold refreshed his recollection about the name of the uncle or in-law whom David had suggested he contact in New York in December 1945. It was, he now maintained, Julius, not Philip. "It should be noted," the Philadelphia office reported, "that this Julius is probably identical with Julius Rosenberg." (When FBI agents showed Gold a list of fourteen surnames, however, "he passed by the name Rosenberg stating that it meant nothing to him.")

And at 4:00 A.M. on June 25, 1950, thousands of Russian-trained North Korean troops supported by Russian-built tanks burst across the Thirty-eighth Parallel and invaded South Korea. On June 27, President Truman authorized American military forces to repel the invasion.

—

From the beginning, Ruth favored helping the government. As Rogge put it, she said she wanted to cooperate "by all means." Rogge said he had told her that while he could make no promises, he had represented Willie Bioff, the labor racketeer who had metamorphosed into a witness for the prosecution and "succeeded in obtaining leniency." Rogge had finally broached the subject of cooperation with David, too. When FBI agents visited him in his office on lower Broadway in the first week of July, Rogge announced that "now he has the authority of his client to offer his cooperation." While the Justice Department mulled over his offer, he said, "he does not want the matter discussed with Rosenberg."

Edward Scheidt of the New York bureau wired Washington:

Rogge feels that Greenglass has not made complete divulgence of his activities. From the family relationship of Ruth Greenglass, the subject, and Julius Rosenberg, his brother-in-law, there are doubtless other items that might be disclosed and Rogge feels he will obtain these items in subsequent consultations with his client. As one item, Rogge specified, "they" wanted Greenglass to stay on at Los Alamos and he refused. Rogge said he desires his client to cooperate with the Government because in so doing the identity of a more important individual or individuals might be ascertained.

Rogge offered a tantalizing detail: Harry Gold wasn't supposed to have been Greenglass's contact in New Mexico. If only Harry would reveal the source of the torn box top he used as a recognition device, who knew where the trail might lead? (By then, unknown to Rogge, Gold already had done so; he said it was Yakovlev.)

"He offered this item as evidence of good faith to cooperate," Scheidt reported, although, he added, "Rogge said there is only one other person that Greenglass could implicate and that is his brother-in-law." Nonetheless, Scheidt concluded: "We believe valuable info could be obtained from David and Ruth."

The next day, the Justice Department expressed concerns about where the investigation was going. The answer was, nowhere without a cooperative witness. McInerney advised Hoover: "No testimony of David Greenglass against his wife would be binding against her nor would her testimony be binding against him even if either were willing and competent to testify against the other."

—

In New Mexico, U.S. Attorney Everett Grantham convened a special grand jury for July 6 to indict David, but two potential impediments loomed. The first was a temporary accounting problem: The U.S. marshal's office in Newark had run out of money a few days before the end of its fiscal year and couldn't afford to serve a subpoena on Wendell Marshman, one of David's former supervisors at Los Alamos, or pay for his transportation to New Mexico to testify. The second problem went to the heart of the continuing investigation: the possibility of a runaway grand jury that might upset plea negotiations by indicting everyone in sight. Washington had warned the Albuquerque FBI office on July 3 that indicting Gold in New Mexico might interfere with his cooperation in other cases. A Teletype from Mickey Ladd continued:

```
DEPARTMENT HAS STATED CASE AGAINST RUTH GREEN-
GLASS AND JULIUS ROSENBERG INSUFFICIENT FOR
PROSECUTIVE ACTION AT THIS TIME. FOR YOUR CONFI-
DENTIAL INFORMATION, O. JOHN ROGGE, GREENGLASS'
```

ATTORNEY, HAS BEEN IN TOUCH WITH DEPARTMENT RE
COOPERATION ON PART OF HIS CLIENT. NO AGREEMENT
EFFECTED TO DATE IN THIS REGARD BY DEPARTMENT.
IN EVENT ROGGE DECIDES TO HAVE GREENGLASS AND
HIS WIFE FURNISH ADDITIONAL INFO PROSECUTION
OF ROSENBERG MAY BE POSSIBLE.

The Justice Department also cautioned Grantham that "the evidence was not too good" against Ruth, and her indictment "might possibly interfere with the investigation."

On July 6, David—and only David—was indicted by the federal grand jury in Santa Fe. The indictment largely echoed the original complaint. Drawn from the affidavits of FBI agents, it specified four overt acts alleged to have been committed in New Mexico in June 1945.

———

The Greenglasses were beginning to close ranks, increasingly convinced that David and Ruth were, in fact, guilty but had been ensnared by David's scheming sister and brother-in-law. The only way to extricate David and Ruth was to let Julius fend for himself. No one imagined then where that strategy would ultimately lead. William Reuben, who in a series of articles for *The Guardian* later denounced the entire case against the Rosenbergs as a government hoax, said as much: "I don't think that the first compromise Ruth and David Greenglass made with the authorities ever led them to imagine what the final step would be." So did Miriam Moskowitz, who was Ethel's jailmate briefly after being convicted with Abe Brothman for conspiracy to obstruct justice in a related case. "In his eyes, there was no choice," Moskowitz said of David. "He had a new baby. His wife had been ill. They had him over a barrel."*

———

* Imagine the NKGB's predicament. Was David cooperating or wasn't he? In the month after he was taken into custody, neither Ruth nor Julius nor anyone else was arrested. On July 13, the same day that the New York *Journal-American* reported that Saypol and Rogge had been seen "practically arm in arm," Moscow asked New York whether the NKGB should offer a new lawyer to the Greenglasses, since Rogge appeared to be an FBI plant. The Soviets reconsidered,

Still, the stumbling block for the prosecution, Saypol said, had been "the brother-in-law who had sent his wife on two occasions to the Greenglass home, beseeching the wife to prevail on the husband not to talk." Meanwhile, the FBI was worried that the Department of Justice was squandering Rogge's offer of cooperation. "If the record is clear that the price of the information is too high, we are on safe grounds, perhaps," the FBI's William Whelan advised Washington. "However, if this matter has not been given full and appropriate consideration, Rogge may be in position to embarrass the Department and the F.B.I."

Whelan also suggested that Justice "consider postponing the sentencing of Gold until after Greenglass had been milked dry."

———

On July 13, Rogge and Goldman met with David and Ruth in the U.S. Attorney's office on the fourth floor at Foley Square. They were joined by the prosecutor. In his notes of the meeting, Saypol said he made no commitments "in respect to prosecution of others or refraining from prosecution, including particularly Mrs. Greenglass." Ruth asked about the maximum penalty. Saypol replied that the statute called for capital punishment. He also made a pitch for keeping the high-profile case within his jurisdiction. Saypol said David could plead guilty in New York or risk going to trial in New Mexico where, he pointed out, "I would have no more to say in the case."

David began talking again the following day; separately, Ruth made herself available to be interviewed, too. She and David shared many recollections though there were several relatively minor inconsistencies. David thought he first learned of Ann Sidorovich's prospective role as a courier only after Ruth moved to Albuquerque; Ruth said it was discussed the previous January in Julius's apartment. David said Julius gave him money from time to time between 1946 and 1948, but "Ruth ap-

———

though, figuring that Ruth might assume the new lawyer was a plant—ironically, not of the NKGB but of the FBI.

parently does not know this." David said Julius called him to arrange a meeting with the Russian agent, but the Greenglasses had no telephone at the time.

—

After conducting a cursory check on July 14, the FBI reported that Julius was "following a normal pattern of activity." As a result, amazingly, agents said "they do not contemplate spot checking Rosenberg over the weekend for the reason that they could not do so without unnecessarily alarming Rosenberg."

—

On Saturday, July 15, Ruth visited Tessie to discuss the legal strategy recommended by Rogge. Ethel stopped by Sheriff Street that afternoon, congenial as could be under the circumstances. The circumstances didn't make for much conviviality, though. Thanks to Ethel and her husband, Tessie's favorite son was in jail. Ruth was still free, but only because the government was using her as leverage on David, just as it would do with Ethel on Julius. So when Ethel greeted her mother and sister-in-law with some admiring words about Ruth's two-month-old daughter, Tessie did not indulge in idle chitchat.

"If you don't talk," she would tell Ethel, "you're gonna burn with your husband."

Ruth remembered an awkward visit by Ethel to 64 Sheriff Street in mid-July. Ethel came bearing a pie and gifts for Steven, then invited Ruth for a walk around the block to suggest a legal strategy for David. Ruth recalled:

> She said her counsel advised her to see me personally and get assurances from [me] that David would not talk. She said it would only be a matter of a couple of years, and in the long run we would be better off; that Julius had been picked up by the F.B.I. for questioning. He said he was innocent and that he had been released; that she had no doubt that he would probably be picked up again. He would continue to say he

was innocent. That if David said he was innocent and Julius said he was innocent, it would strengthen their position; everybody would stand a better chance, and she said do you think it is a dirty shame for David to take the blame and sit for two?

Their relationship finally reached the breaking point when Ethel visited Ruth on Rivington Street and offered to baby-sit Steven and Barbara for a few days so Ruth could recuperate from weeks of coping with anxiety and unwelcome notoriety. Ruth not only rejected the offer but accused Ethel of a capital crime. David later seconded her conclusion:

"They tried to kidnap my kids. Ethel came to the house and said to Ruthie, 'Why don't you go away for the weekend? We'll take care of the kids.'

"And she said, 'No way.' She said, 'No way.'

"'Well, what are you worried about?'

"'Because you'd hold them hostage.'"

David said he was so sure of this because of something Julius had said earlier that year:

We were once sitting on a bench and I said, "Look, you know, I can't understand why I have to leave the country when you can send the guy I met in Albuquerque." Julius said, "Well, it doesn't matter. Stalin says that it doesn't matter. In a war you can lose divisions so long as you win."

I said, "Oh, I see, my life and my wife's life, my children's lives, are not that important."

"Well, nobody's important compared to the whole overall idea."

I would bet my life on it. That if my wife had given them the kids, that would be the Damocles sword hanging over my head. These people were ruthless.

On Monday, July 17, with a plea deal still not fully negotiated, David and Ruth provided the FBI with separate sworn statements. David's filled seven single-spaced typed pages. He dribbled out more details on the incidents he had already described and also provided new information. He told of his second furlough, in September 1945, when he gave

Julius an unsealed envelope "containing information I had been able to gather concerning the atomic bomb, as well as a couple of sketches of the molds which make up the atom bomb" (he did not remember whether Julius read this or what he did with it); of conversations after the war in which Julius said "he has been extensively engaged in Soviet espionage" and had contacts with scientists and engineers in Cleveland and upstate New York, one of whom was a two-hundred-dollar-a-day consultant on a dam project in Egypt; of Julius delivering microfilm to Russian couriers in New York movie theaters and sometimes photographing documents himself with a Leica camera in one of two apartments he maintained in lower Manhattan. There was more: David said that Julius knew of government research into a sky platform that could permanently stay in space and of research into atomic-powered airplanes and that when Julius had worked for the Signal Corps he had stolen a highly secret proximity fuse from Emerson Radio.

"Periodically, since I was discharged from the army," David continued,

I have borrowed sums of money from Julius Rosenberg in different amounts up to $200 each which probably totals about $1,000. On each occasion, Rosenberg would tell me that he would have to borrow the money from someone else to let me have it. I regarded each of these as loans but because of my knowledge of Rosenberg's Soviet espionage activities, I believe that Rosenberg regarded them as blackmail.

In the same vein, David related Julius's instructions on fleeing the country but added:

My wife and I decided not to leave the country but wanted to give Rosenberg the impression that we intended to leave. We decided to go to the mountains in upstate New York and stay there until Rosenberg left the country as he indicated he would do. We planned to return to New York City after we learned of Rosenberg's departure. I assume that Rosenberg has not departed from the United States because he is under surveillance by the Federal Bureau of Investigation.

The same day, Ruth dictated a statement to Agents Harrington and Norton. Recounting her meeting with the Rosenbergs before she visited David in November 1944, she elaborated on Ethel's role. According to Ruth's account, Julius said Ruth might have noticed that Ethel had stopped going to party meetings or functions that had a "Red" tinge to them and had stopped buying *The Daily Worker*. That was because after two years of trying to connect with the right group, he had gotten involved with the "Russian underground."* Julius told Ruth that David was working on a bomb "more dangerous than any weapon that had ever been used." Ruth was reluctant to ask her husband to "make scientific information available to the Russians," but Ethel, "who was present during the conversation, told me that I should at least ask" David if he would be willing to do so. David was shocked at first and said no. The next day, he agreed. Ruth also recounted a conversation with David about a meeting of between twenty and thirty minutes with a Russian in New York: "David said that Julius Rosenberg introduced David to this unknown man saying 'This is Dave.'" She also elaborated on the recognition signal (recalling that Julius gave one half to David and said he would give the other half to their dinner guest that night, whose name was Ann) and on the visit from Gold. "We opened the envelope which this man had given David and discovered that it contained $500," Ruth said. "The taking of the money made David and me feel worse because it was now apparent that we were not just passing information but rather that we were being paid for it." Nearly five years later, Ruth recalled, Julius delivered the *Herald Tribune* with Gold's photograph and "told us that we had to leave the United States because sometime between June 12 and June 16 something would happen to us." Julius said he would get passports and a doctor's letter saying we had been inoculated against smallpox. He gave the Greenglasses one thousand dollars (she deposited half in a checking account and used the rest "to pay some debts

---

* If Ruth's recollection was correct, it seems odd but not impossible that Julius would have broached his public estrangement from the party with Ruth for the first time in November 1944—more than two years after he had, according to Alexander Feklisov and other sources, insinuated himself into Soviet intelligence.

and household expenses"), returned with another four thousand, and "promised us an additional $2,000 which we never received from him.

"Julius Rosenberg told us that he thought it was a golden opportunity for us to go to the Soviet Union," Ruth said, adding this disclaimer: She and David never intended to leave the United States "because this is our country and we want to stay here and live here and raise our children. I would like to point out that we accepted the money from Julius Rosenberg because David said that if Julius suspected that we would not leave the United States that some physical harm might come to us or our children."*

—

At some point, agents escorted Ruth to the room where the FBI fingerprinted and photographed criminal suspects. She was asked to pose for a mug shot. This was unusual. She hadn't been indicted, she wasn't under arrest, nor did prosecutors expect to lodge charges against her. Just a formality, the agents explained. They simply needed a current photo to show to witnesses and suspects as the investigation unfolded and as they corroborated her confession. But the impression that endures from this image is unmistakable: intimidation.

—

Every development in the case was immediately relayed to Washington. At 4:55 P.M. on July 17, Alan Belmont phoned Whelan to say that a two-hour conference between the FBI and the Justice Department had just concluded with a decision to authorize a complaint against Julius Rosenberg.

---

* As detailed as it was, Ruth's sworn statement could only accommodate some of what she had told investigators during her interrogation. She had also described Joel Barr's girlfriend Vivian Glassman in great detail, recalled that Julius told her that he tried to recruit Marcus Pogarsky "to furnish information to the Russians" and was disappointed when he refused, and remembered that Ethel had injured her back when she was one and a half years old and had to lie on a bed board and that Julius suffered from boils, colds, and the flu. "Most of the Rosenberg family have low resistance," she reported.

And *only* against Julius Rosenberg.

"On Ruth Greenglass, the Department is not authorizing at this time," Whelan noted. Not as long as David was cooperating.

The Justice Department didn't authorize an indictment against Ethel Rosenberg either, not without corroboration from David.

"The Department has advised that they do not believe there is sufficient evidence developed to charge Ethel Rosenberg," Whelan reported in a damning appraisal of the prosecution's case. "So far it appears there would be just one witness against Ethel to show her complicity, which witness would be Ruth, since so far it appears the only thing David knows about Ethel's involvement is what he has learned from Ruth or the involvement that David knows about, Ruth does not know about and is separate and distinct from the activities which Ruth knew about."

The Justice Department concluded that there was not even sufficient evidence to search the Rosenbergs' apartment. Therefore, Whelan advised his agents to wait until Julius returned home so that once an arrest warrant was issued "we can arrest him at the apartment and search his apartment incidental to the arrest."

After the Greenglasses' statements had been typed and signed, Agent Norton filed a formal complaint against Julius Rosenberg before Judge John F. X. McGohey at 6:45 P.M. One hour later, Norton and Harrington, joined by five other agents, arrested Julius in the Knickerbocker Village apartment. Five additional agents waited outside, then entered to conduct a search.

Robby was already asleep. Michael was listening to an episode of *The Lone Ranger* on the radio. As he remembered it, the hero was being framed by bandits armed with the Ranger's signature silver bullets. Just as the fraud was being exposed by a good guy who scraped the bandits' bullets and revealed them to be merely silver-colored, FBI agents switched off the radio. Michael switched it on again. They dueled until Michael—distracted momentarily by Ethel's sudden demand, "I want a lawyer!"—finally surrendered. "And daddy was gone," Michael remembered.

"Ethel, his wife, made a typical Communist remonstrance, demanding a warrant and the right to call an attorney," according to the FBI's version of the arrest. "She was told to keep quiet and get in the other room with the children, which she did. Inasmuch as the children were making a considerable fuss and Ethel refused to talk at all," the FBI reported, it was decided that the search would be more productive if it were conducted unimpeded. Ethel was asked whether there was someplace else she would be more comfortable. At her direction, two agents drove Ethel and the children to Tessie Greenglass's house on Sheriff Street.

Trying to be friendly, Michael told one of the agents that he always listened to him on the radio show called *This Is Your FBI*. When Michael reported his father's arrest to Elizabeth Phillips, the therapist he had been seeing weekly, he announced: "Well, the good guys got the bad guy."*

———

Julius Rosenberg refused to cooperate. Once it became obvious that Julius had no intention of talking, Belmont instructed Whelan to "consider every possible means to bring pressure on Rosenberg to make him talk, including consideration of additional charges being filed against Rosenberg at Albuquerque and a careful study of the involvement of Ethel Rosenberg in order that charges can be placed against her if possible."

Yet Julius and Ethel and David and Ruth seemed largely oblivious to that possibility. A few days after his arrest, Julius weighed in with a suggestion that didn't betray an inkling that Ethel might be prosecuted. "You realize that you will be an important witness in my case," he wrote Ethel, "so take an active role."

Julius also reported that he was adjusting to the prison routine, playing Ping-Pong in the recreation room and handball on the caged-in roof. But the detention center on West Street wasn't big enough for both Julius and David. Within a day or two, after they nearly encountered

---

* A neighbor interviewed by the FBI complained that the Rosenbergs played music at all hours and were unbearably noisy, but "they appeared to adore one another, and were so good to their children that the children were completely spoiled and would eventually suffer because they would not be able to withstand any adversity."

each other on the handball court, David was transferred to the eleventh floor of the Tombs, the ziggurated city jail that derived its uninviting name from an Egyptian-revival predecessor that once had stood across Centre Street. Saypol arranged the transfer, he said, "because it is desirable to take [David] away and keep him separated from Rosenberg."

"It was like going from the Arctic zone in the wintertime to Puerto Rico," David recalled. Prisoners lived in a dormitory and could fraternize freely. There were cooking facilities and a separate visiting room. Ruth could deliver chocolate bars and salami. The other inmates had a name for the eleventh floor. They called it the "singing quarters."

—

The only way for the government to guarantee that David would keep singing was to dangle Ruth in legal limbo. On August 10, the FBI formally asked the Immigration and Naturalization Service to place Ruth's name on the Departure Control Program's lookout list. And Saypol was still warning Rogge and his partners that "it might wind up with Mrs. Greenglass indicted." During a subsequent interview that month with one of Saypol's assistants, Myles Lane, Ruth elaborated for the first time on Ethel's role before Ruth went to Albuquerque. The more she remembered, the more she incriminated Ethel:

"Did she tell you to use your influence upon your husband?"

"She could hardly have said that," Ruth replied, "because I was against it."

"Did she ask you to use your influence upon your husband?"

"No, she said she felt it would be something he would want to know."

"Did she say she thought it ought to be done?"

"She implied as much."

"Did she actually say that?"

"She wouldn't feel he would want to do it and that I should tell him about it if she was against it."

—

Ethel was summoned twice before the same grand jury that indicted Julius. The evidence was flimsy, even hearsay. On August 7, she invoked the Fifth Amendment. On August 11, she was summoned again. This time, if she refused to answer questions, the government would charge her with conspiracy. She refused. Before she reached the bottom of the courthouse steps, she was arrested. She posed for her FBI mug shot in the white gloves and powder-blue dress with white polka dots that she had worn to court. And she called Michael at the apartment. "You can't come home?" he recalled asking. "She told me no. She remembered a scream and that scream gave her nightmares for the rest of her life."

The FBI also corralled Julius's former classmates. One, Max Elitcher, was mentioned in a 1944 NKGB cable that was decoded in 1948, prompting FBI agents then to follow him from Washington to New York, where he visited another fellow classmate, Morton Sobell. The agents concluded that Elitcher realized he was being followed, so they peeled off. According to Elitcher, he and Sobell that evening delivered a roll of film to Julius Rosenberg.

This time, the agents had Rosenberg in custody but couldn't find Sobell. He hadn't been at work at Reeves Instruments in Manhattan since June 16—the day David's arrest was announced—and hadn't been seen at all by his neighbors in Flushing or by his one-armed housekeeper since June 22. When the FBI interviewed Elitcher on July 20, he recalled a visit from Julius Rosenberg during the summer of 1944. The next day, Elitcher volunteered that Sobell had been an intermediary in recruiting him to espionage. By mid-August, federal agents had found Sobell, his wife, and their infant son in Mexico; they drove him hundreds of miles to the border and arrested him.* At the arraignment, Irving Saypol said Sobell had dealings with Julius Rosenberg in the conspiracy to supply Russia with atomic secrets. That was accurate according to the legal definition of *conspiracy* but grossly overstated Sobell's role. He had

---

* At the FBI's request, the CIA had staked out a statue of Columbus in Mexico City that David described in his confession as a way station on his escape route. He was to send a letter to the Soviet ambassador there and show up three days later at the "plaza de something or other" holding his middle finger in a guidebook. A man would approach. Pretending to be from Oklahoma, David would say, "That is a magnificent statue." To which the man would reply, "Oh, there are much more beautiful statues in Paris."

nothing to do with supplying atomic secrets to Russia, and the prosecution later admitted as much. But Saypol reported that if Sobell was included in a superseding indictment "containing an overall conspiracy charge to commit espionage, not only with respect to nuclear fission and the atom bomb, but one which would also include other matters affecting national defense, the chances of convicting Sobell would be materially strengthened."[*]

———

When superseding indictments charging Julius and Ethel were handed up August 21, David and Ruth were not among the defendants. Still, Ruth reported to Robert Goldman that David was apprehensive because some of his cellmates at the Tombs had primed him with horror stories about his pending imprisonment. Goldman was reassuring: "I told her that we were happy to say that few of our clients went to jail but those who did had never had such a complaint." Ruth also was pleased to hear that Rogge claimed a close relationship with another New Deal appointee, James V. Bennett, the U.S. Director of Prisons. "This impressed her," Goldman reported, "because she feels that Dave may not get a suspended sentence and is worried about the kind of treatment he will get."

———

Rogge was apparently still on vacation on August 23 when the Rosenbergs were arraigned. That morning, Julius's lawyer, Emanuel Bloch, surmised correctly that because David was named merely as a coconspirator in the New York indictment, he must be cooperating with the government. Ruth, too. But more than two months after David's arrest, prosecuting Ruth hadn't been ruled out. "There was no indication that Ruth is to be indicted and neither Herb not I wanted to raise the point," Goldman wrote later that day. "I had the inference that they were not

---

[*] On Sobell's telephone pad, the FBI found a number for Arma, the Brooklyn company where David worked. The only connection appeared to have been that Arma and Reeves Instruments had occasional business dealings.

planning to indict her but I could be wrong and I didn't even want to ask the question."

The answer did not necessarily revolve solely around legal vicissitudes, so, apparently with Rogge's blessing, Ruth embarked on a public-relations campaign to distinguish the gullible Greenglasses from the bewitching Rosenbergs. She agreed to meet with Louis Schaeffer of the *Jewish Daily Forward,* which had no sympathy for the Communist Party but was always vigilant against anti-Semitism. After interviewing Ruth at home and over lunch at Lüchow's, the popular German restaurant on East Fourteenth Street, Schaeffer reported backhandedly that for a Jewish girl, "aside from the misfortune into which she was drawn, we have no reason to be ashamed of her." Her father had worked as a coal miner in Scranton, then at a slaughterhouse in New Jersey. As a teenager, David appealed to her "because of his earnestness, quietness and mild character." Together, they had a daughter and a "talkative boy of four who wants to be a cowboy." Ruth dutifully visited David at the Tombs twice a week.

Schaeffer's articles are illuminating primarily because they offered the first insights into how the Greenglasses' transformed themselves into victims. Schaeffer described Julius as "the intellectual of the family," though to Ruth he was more like a Fagin whose gang of thieves trafficked in government secrets and who, in return, received some psychic and monetary reward. "Ruth throws all the blame for her husband's acts on Julius Rosenberg and his wife Ethel," Schaeffer wrote.* For David and Ruth, Schaeffer said, the epiphany (not his word) came in June 1945 when they received the money from Harry Gold: "The pair looked at each other and for the first time there ran through their minds the thought that something was not right. But it was too late."

---

* The articles were already being published when Schaeffer informed Ruth of a conversation he had had with Manny Bloch and his father, Alexander Bloch. Because of Manny Bloch's political notoriety, he hinted that he would defer to his father as lead counsel for the Rosenberg defense. Ruth asked whether the father would follow the strategy already signaled by the son. "If Alexander Bloch does that," Schaeffer quoted Ruth as saying, "he is leading them to the slaughter."

Why didn't they confess to the FBI immediately? "That is the trag-edy," Ruth lamented. "That is what troubled us. David realized that he took a false step in giving Gold information, but you must bear in mind that David's sister and her husband, Julius Rosenberg, were involved. In general it is very difficult to be a stool-pigeon, particularly for a Jew. And when it concerns your own family the problem is even more difficult."

Ruth recalled that Julius wanted the Greenglasses to remain at Los Alamos, that he was angry when they decided to return home, "and that was the beginning of our unfriendliness, particularly between me and my sister-in-law." According to Schaeffer, everyone who knew them agreed that Ethel "is the dominant person." As Ruth recalled, her sister-in-law "did not buy from a butcher or grocer unless he were an open sympathizer toward Soviet Russia. She considered everyone who was against communism her personal enemy."

In contrast, Ruth was said to navigate by enlightened self-interest. "David did not want to confess," Schaeffer reported, "but young Ruth, with her strong character, made David look the truth in the face that they were drawn into the net through David's sister Ethel and her hus-band Julius Rosenberg." Schaeffer reported that Ruth was embittered but at peace with that truth. She recalled her emotional state when David was arrested. "It was the first night in the past four years, since Mr. Gold's visit to my husband in Los Alamos, that I slept well," Ruth told Schaeffer. "I can say the same thing about David."

———

The wheels of commerce kept pace with the wheels of justice. On July 20, three days after Julius's arrest, Dun & Bradstreet warned its subscrib-ers not to extend credit to Pitt Machine Products. After reviewing Pitt's books with the foreman, Ethel wrote Julius that "it is imperative to sell the shop." They did.

Ruth also had designs on the business. With David and Julius both in jail and Pitt on the block, she asked Rogge's firm to sue her brother-in-law for the Greenglasses' share of the proceeds from the sale. Bernie Greenglass said he believed that Julius's failed capitalist venture was sold for as much as ten thousand dollars to a New Jersey man, also named

Rosenberg, who manufactured whipping-cream machines. (Its most popular product was the distinctly nonproletarian Aristocratic Whipper.) Manny Bloch indicated that the business had been liquidated for only half that amount, though even so David and Ruth might still have been entitled to between one and two thousand dollars. Rogge's partner suggested the possibility of attaching the Rosenbergs' bank account, claiming "the proceeds of what we would allege to be a fraud in that Rosenberg never had any intention at the time he made the agreement with the Greenglasses to pay them any money." But in researching the legal precedents, Robert Goldman found that the Greenglasses would have to prove that Julius intended all along to defraud them.* No suit was filed.

Shortly after Labor Day, Ruth applied for welfare.

She submitted an application to the New York City Welfare Department's Division of Veterans Administration at the unlikely address, for a welfare office, of 500 Park Avenue. Ruth itemized $3,530 in personal debts (all of which could have been paid off months earlier with the $3,900 that she had turned over to Rogge and which was not listed as income). Her list included $1,800 to David's Aunt Chucha, $650 to Bernie, $500 to Sam, and $30 for the balance still due on a typewriter. The Greenglasses' assets consisted of a $50 balance at Public National Bank and a $500 life-insurance policy. Ruth said she had also applied for help from the Prison Association and had been granted all of $10. She reported on the application that her brother-in-law Sam was unwilling to assist them financially, that David's sister and her husband were in jail, and that the rest of the relatives, including David's brother Bernie, were unable to help.

On October 23, Ruth's application for assistance was denied. The reason cited was her failure, for 1949 and from June 1950 to the present, "to explain adequate and reasonable management" of her resources.

---

* Also, suing might substantiate Manny Bloch's defense that the Greenglasses were motivated by revenge. "Do we help Bloch's theory of the case if we now start a civil suit and ask for a receiver?" Goldman wrote.

—

In September, the FBI interviewed Sam Greenglass. The following month, agents talked to Bernie.

On the day of his interview, Sam visited Ethel at the Women's House of Detention. Sam said he begged her to cooperate for her children's sake, but she insisted she had no information to give. "She has absolutely no concern for her children," he said.

Sam told the FBI that David had initially resisted efforts by Julius and Ethel to convert him to communism but had been largely won over after Julius bought him a chemistry set. (David remembers chemistry books, not actual chemicals or apparatus.) Sam recalled a vow he made in 1943 never to see the Rosenbergs again but volunteered that even though they hadn't spoken in seven years he believed that Julius "was entirely capable of this sort of thing." Sam said he had no inkling that his half brother was involved until the previous May, right after Harry Gold's arrest, when David said, without elaborating, that he was in serious trouble.

Sam also allowed that the death penalty would be too good for Julius and Ethel.

Tessie Greenglass was equally empathetic. According to Sam, when Tessie had visited her daughter recently, she suggested that Ethel divorce Julius and cooperate with the government. Ethel ordered Tessie never to visit again. Referring to David, Ethel was quoted as telling Tessie: "You are helping him and you are killing me."

A week later, Sam wrote Ethel that he had visited Tessie, who was caring for the Rosenberg boys. Michael had proclaimed his mother's innocence. "How can you have the bitter thought on your conscience to let this child down in such a horrible way," Sam wrote. "How can mom keep those two children—They are wearing her away very quickly—I must say you have done and are still doing a very wonderful job—There is not much more disgrace you could bring to your family—but now your great problem seems to be—to get rid of them—one at a time."

Bernie, who now lived in New Jersey and worked for a fabric company in the Garment Center, had little to offer the FBI. He was still grieving because his wife, Gladys, had died the month before from Parkinson's disease. Yes, Bernie said, of course he knew Ethel and Julius were sympathetic to communism, but neither ever told him flatly that they had joined the Communist Party. Unlike Sam, Bernie found something nice to say about Julius, describing him as pretty conscientious about their business, calling the shop every day, even when he was incapacitated for weeks at a time with hay fever. In late May or early June, Bernie recalled, Julius had complained of lung trouble and had said he would be going on vacation for a few weeks.

Bernie was also interviewed by Manny Bloch, who wanted to know whether rifts in the business had reverberated among the Greenglass relatives. Bernie's reply was unvarnished. "Julie always had to be the boss," he said. "In fact, Julie has to be King Tut or nothing and so there were many little arguments between Dave and Julie."

There was no rift between Ruth and Ethel, Bernie insisted. Between Ruth and Julie? "Yes, because of the business," Bernie replied.

———

Prosecutors reconciling relatively minor inconsistencies in the recollections of David and Ruth also had Harry Gold's version to contend with. Harry, who had pleaded guilty on July 20 in Philadelphia to conspiring with Klaus Fuchs to commit espionage, had given investigators a slightly different account of the June 1945 meeting in Albuquerque. He said, for example, that David told him that "had I not brought the $500 along with me that it would have been impossible for Mrs. Greenglass to continue to stay in Albuquerque any longer." Harry still equivocated about whether the name *Julius* had ever come up. Recalling a conversation with Ruth, Harry said during an interrogation by Myles Lane, "I believe she stated to me that she had recalled a Julius, and I understood that Julius was a relative of hers."

Lane responded, "Can't you state definitely whether she actually said or didn't?"

Harry needed no further prompting. "The word 'believe' was an unfortunate slip," he continued. "What I intended to say was I recall very definitely this morning meeting that Mrs. Greenglass told me she had seen and spoken with a Julius in New York, just prior to her coming to Albuquerque in April 1945."

—

In a continuing effort to synchronize their conflicting accounts, David and Harry were interviewed together at the Tombs the day after Christmas "for their concerted effort in recalling the incident." David still thought Harry had introduced himself as Dave. Harry recalled using the name Kessler. But he remembered that the Greenglasses commented that the name was the same or similar to David's or to another relative's and "therefore, Gold now believes that Greenglass's recollection is correct and that he did use the name of 'Dave.'"

Gold still recalled delivering "greetings from Ben." David discounted that version. He said the name *Ben* wouldn't have meant anything to him, whereas greetings from, say, Julius would obviously have struck a responsive chord. "Gold's spontaneous comment to this was possibly Greenglass was right," the FBI reported, adding, though: "Gold, however, is not at all clear on this point."

By that point, one thing was clear: The government was not going out of its way much to reward cooperation. Pleading guilty and declining to bargain for leniency, Harry Gold had been sentenced to the maximum prison term, thirty years.*

—

By billing the atomic spy case as the crime of the century, as J. Edgar Hoover had, the government upped the ante for everybody, informers included. FBI files are riddled with messages from ordinary Americans who volunteered their unsubstantiated suspicions in the interest of national security. Most had nothing to gain. Some did, though, whether it was settling an old score, self-aggrandizement, or ingratiating themselves with the government. In jail, there was no shortage of inmates willing to trade information for future favors.

At the federal detention center on West Street, at least two prisoners claimed to enjoy the confidence of Julius Rosenberg. One was Mario

---

* Attorney General McGrath had recommended twenty-five years. After Harry expressed remorse, Judge McGranery sentenced him to thirty. McGranery later succeeded McGrath.

Gilbert Russo, who was awaiting deportation to the Dominican Republic. He told the FBI that Julius had tried to enlist him in a bizarre plot to spirit a dozen of Julius's accomplices out of the country through Miami Beach. According to Russo, the plot revolved around a clandestine rendezvous near the telephone booths in a hotel lobby. It was to be sealed with what might, at first, have seemed to be an unlikely recognition signal—"Hopalong Cassidy is a tough hombre"—although it couldn't be discounted completely because Julius did, after all, read a lot of cowboy stories to his sons. (The FBI took Russo seriously enough to contemplate monitoring him after he was deported and letting him ensnare the unsuspecting accomplices, although that plan was apparently discarded as impractical.) In contrast to this tale, Russo's accounts of conversations with Julius appeared to conform to actual events. Russo reported that Julius's brother, David Rosenberg, enclosed photos of Michael and Robby in a letter to Julius in which he described the boys as "constantly crying and asking for him and their mother." According to the FBI, "Rosenberg told Russo that he got his brother-in-law involved in the atomic bomb case by asking him to get documents for him from the Los Alamos project. Rosenberg said that one of his supervisors asked him to get info on the atomic bomb at any cost. Rosenberg sold his brother-in-law on the idea of getting the information and then he 'ratted on me.'"

Russo passed along another piece of information, which didn't fit as neatly with the government's view of the evidence or with its emerging legal strategy. Russo said he was told by Julius that his "wife was only slightly involved, though she knew about Rosenberg's activities."

The FBI's second source at West Street was Jerome Tartakow, who established a fruitful relationship as an informer not long after Julius's arrest. He maintained that relationship after he was released by insinuating himself into the Rosenberg defense and even the Rosenberg family. The whole body of what Tartakow delivered to the FBI offers so much detail, so many insights that few people other than Julius would have been privy to, and even a few conclusions that contradicted the government's own assessment of the evidence, that it would be foolhardy to discount it altogether. But why would a supposedly accomplished Russian spy spill his guts to a total stranger?

On January 18, 1951, Tartakow told the FBI that the Rosenbergs and their lawyers were hoping to head off any more visits to Ethel from Tessie. Tartakow also delivered a more intriguing—and damning—morsel. He quoted Julius as explaining that "all of the wives of men who perform work for the Russians are checked" and that his own wife "had done many things on her own with relation to Soviet espionage."

What things? The FBI wanted details, but Tartakow couldn't provide any. The government turned again to the Greenglasses.

Chapter 25

A Lever

"Hi, Arnold, how are you?"

═══

On February 2, 1951, federal marshals delivered David from the Tombs to a conference room in the thirty-two-story U.S. Court House, a tower that rises majestically from a colonnaded base and is crowned with a gilded pyramid. An audience was already assembled to witness his technical confession. In the history of American nuclear-weapons research, it was the most distinguished group of scientists ever convened to be briefed by a lowly machinist.

After months of relying on secondhand synopses of debriefings by the FBI, government scientists were determined to find out for themselves just how much a vocational-high-school graduate who had flunked out of college in his first term, who had never taken a single course in nuclear physics or in higher mathematics, and whose job, as a supervisor described it, was "to produce parts from drawings—he made no contribution to design of products," could have possibly found out about or figured out the atomic bomb when he was a twenty-three-year-old army sergeant at Los Alamos.

This was no mere academic exercise. It was integral to an elaborate, high-stakes legal and psychological gamble.

—

Among the biggest secrets of the bomb was that it worked. The government gave that secret away in 1945 when it detonated over Japan the only two weapons in its atomic arsenal. To make the case that Soviet spies conspired to steal other atomic secrets, prosecutors had to prove that those secrets were vital to national defense. And to demonstrate that the secrets were worth protecting, they might have to be revealed.

Convicting the defendants was just the first step. The government's chief goal was to wring a confession from Julius Rosenberg, the putative ringleader of an espionage operation that had been pilfering American military and industrial secrets for years. The identities of a dozen or so other members of the ring were known to the government but couldn't be disclosed in court without publicly compromising the secret that President Truman didn't know but Joseph Stalin did: The United States had broken the Soviet wartime code. Therefore, the other members of the ring could not be indicted, much less convicted unless Julius corroborated the government's case. "Rosenberg's only concern," a jailhouse informer told the FBI, "is that his wife Ethel might break down" if he got the death penalty. Julius was an ideologue, but he might just break to save his wife, the mother of their two children, if she, too, were threatened with decades of imprisonment or even execution. Maybe, after all was done and said, the Rosenbergs would prove as compliant as the Greenglasses.

Theoretically, that strategy seemed sound.* But with the trial of the Rosenbergs only two weeks away, the government still faced two daunting challenges: Prosecutors lacked sufficient evidence to convict Ethel Rosenberg, much less to warrant the electric chair or even a stiff prison sentence; and they hadn't persuaded the custodians of America's atomic secrets to grant them free rein in proving that the level of secrecy breached by Julius Rosenberg justified the death penalty. For months, a

---

* Under current rules for federal prosecutors, however, "the death penalty may not be sought, and no attorney for the Government may threaten to seek it, for the purpose of obtaining a more desirable negotiating position."

philosophical and bureaucratic tug-of-war raged between prosecutors and the Atomic Energy Commission over how much to compromise security to smash a spy ring that might still be operating inside the nation's atomic installations.

"Imagine how dopey that was?" Roy Cohn, an assistant prosecutor, later recalled. "Here the whole case was predicated on the fact that the Rosenbergs and their co-conspirators had delivered the sketch to the Soviet Union six years earlier. So who would we be keeping it from?"

But the staff of the Atomic Energy Commission still considered David's sketches of high-explosive lens molds, his work on implosion experiments, and his detailed description of the bomb itself so sensitive that they could not be declassified without unacceptable risk.

That's what today's briefing was all about.

———

David shuffled into the conference room shackled. His audience included Myles Lane, the assistant prosecutor; Dr. James G. Beckerley, the AEC's director of classification; Arnold Kramish of the Division of Intelligence; Dr. Frederic de Hoffman from the Los Alamos lab; William D. Denson of the AEC's Legal Division; and C. A. Rolander, Jr., of the Division of Security. Before they were introduced, David surveyed his anonymous inquisitors, then suddenly beamed as he spotted a familiar face.

"Hi, Arnold, how are you?" David said, looking unself-consciously at Kramish.

"Hey, nice to see you here, David," Kramish replied, equally affably.

The rest of the room was stunned. Lane's jaw dropped. But David recognized Kramish from Los Alamos, where he had been an army corporal designing dummy bomb drops and perfecting the detonators for the Nagasaki bomb. Actually, Kramish was surprised, too. The black-and-white newspaper photographs published eight months before when David had been arrested didn't do him justice. They depicted a man grown five years older and thirty pounds heavier from home cooking. Absent the shackles and the extra pounds, though, David was still that "moonfaced, happy little guy," who, as Kramish later observed, had "no intellectual depth whatsoever."

David did, however, have a pretty good memory.

In what amounted to a rehearsal for the trial, David was asked whether he had attended any scientific colloquiums at Los Alamos (no, he replied); what documents were available to him (none, only a few shop drawings); whether he knew the components of the high explosives that were being shaped into lenses (he knew them by name—Composition B, for instance—but not their ingredients); what code names he remembered ("tube alloy"—the government's secret name for uranium—and, on prompting, "49"); and how much he had learned about what was going on at other Manhattan Project sites (he knew that "Pasco"—the Hanford installation—made plutonium).

The AEC scientists were especially interested in David's familiarity with Walter Koski's research. The Soviets had been, too. While David made molds for Koski's experiments, he said, typically the pattern had been drawn by someone else directly on two-inch-square aluminum stock. But he volunteered that he had overheard or deduced much more during his eighteen months at Los Alamos and that most of what he learned he had forwarded faithfully to Moscow. He submitted a revised sketch after he learned that a hollow metal tube was used in the implosion experiments. He described levitation—which gave the imploding shell time to acquire momentum before it struck the solid core and which was still considered top secret. From the fact that a B-29 had to be rebuilt, he surmised the rough size of the bomb and the cradle in which it would rest, and he guessed that a barometric fusing device would detonate the bomb at a prescribed altitude as it parachuted toward the ground.

David didn't know everything, of course. James Beckerley and Arnold Kramish concluded that "(1) he is not technically competent beyond his abilities as a machine shop man (e.g., he did not seem to be aware of published information on atomic energy); (2) he may be readily confused by a competent technical cross examination." He was apparently unaware that the beryllium sphere contained polonium. He referred to a barium plastic shield (he had seen one in Sygma Building), though the bomb core was actually shielded not by barium but by boron. Also, Kramish reported in a memo to the files, "Greenglass at this time seems completely unaware that each detonator contains two spark wires, each set off independently to assure firing of the detonator at the proper moment. Hence, there is some confusion in his testimony in correlating the number of condensers, detonators, and molds. The number 36 for the molds is, however, correct." (Kramish, as it turned out, was confused, too, a reminder that even an expert's opinion, much less a novice's, can be nitpicked. "I made a small error in evaluating his confession," Kramish acknowledged. "There were thirty-two.")

The government scientists attributed David's technical errors "to lack of understanding or forgetfulness," adding: "It was the opinion of the interviewers that Greenglass was making a conscious effort to reconstruct the circumstances of the disclosure." Furthermore, they said, "Greenglass has not fabricated any substantial part of his story since no inconsistency could be detected." Some of his information was derived from "judicious guesses from information randomly gathered." Nonetheless, the breadth of what David had been able to see, hear, and surmise, Kramish said later, "was somewhat shocking to us at the time."

After David had been interviewed for six hours, the commission's director of security concluded: "His proposed testimony, unless restricted by the AEC, will reveal considerable weapons information which is now classified as 'restricted data.'" However, since "Fuchs provided the Russians with considerably more weapon information than supplied by Greenglass," and since Fuchs and Greenglass spied successfully before getting caught, "it appears reasonable to assume that the Russians already have the information which Greenglass would disclose at trial." Moreover, the technical information that David delivered to Soviet agents was of a "rather general and vague nature."

Perhaps the commission was being too proprietary. But the guardians of America's atomic secrets still seemed to fear that classified information could be compromised by allowing David to testify unfettered. (The previous July, Rolander had said he was "mildly concerned" that the language of the original indictment itself had, in effect, declassified the principle of the lens mold.) Above all, the AEC was adamant about not making David's sketches public.

Commission officials also feared that related testimony would further compromise national security. "For Greenglass's testimony to stand up," Roger M. Anders, the Department of Energy's official historian, later wrote,

> experts familiar with the design of atomic weapons would have to attest to the general, if not the specific, accuracy of his story. And should a technical expert reveal in his testimony one detail of the atomic bomb other than what had been specifically declassified by the commission, he could provide Russia with other secrets of bomb design. Added to what Greenglass and Fuchs had already given to the Russians, such disclosure could be a serious blow to America's superior technological position in the nuclear arms race.*

The prosecution wanted to assume that all the information had already been passed to the Russians. But suppose it hadn't been? Suppose some or all of it had gotten garbled in transmission? Suppose, on the witness stand, David blurted out some theory or fact or scientific term that he had forgotten to tell the Russians about originally? How many people actually shared these concerns isn't certain, but they were so pervasive, and patriotism seen as so precarious at that point, that the Rosenberg defense itself bought into the perception, thus transforming that perception into a cruel reality.

———

On February 7, Assistant Attorney General James McInerney reported that he had consulted with the judge to whom the trial had just been

---

* On May 19, 1950, the AEC had furnished the FBI with the conclusion that Fuchs had provided the Russians with "very important information concerning weapons, and with regard to the Trinity (plutonium implosion) type weapon it was concluded that the essentials of the bomb in adequate detail were turned over either while Fuchs was at Los Alamos or later." On June 15, a hand-delivered memo from J. Edgar Hoover to the State Department provided more from the Fuchs debriefings: "Fuchs said that he would estimate that the information furnished by him speeded up by several years the production of an atom bomb by Russia because it permitted their scientists to work primarily on the development of fissionable material in view of the fact that the method of detonation was available to them.

assigned, Irving R. Kaufman, about the death penalty. The judge "is pre-pared to impose it if the evidence warrants," McInerney said.

The next day, Myles Lane outlined the government's case to a special executive session of Congress's Joint Committee on Atomic Energy. The trial was scheduled to start in only one week, although given the enor-mous pool of potential jurors being assembled and the fact that Saypol had just finished prosecuting another communist, William Remington, Lane figured it would be postponed. Again, the prosecution's goal was to impress upon the committee that capital punishment demanded a higher threshold of evidence. Arguing that the death penalty for Julius was "im-portant, very important," Lane repeated David's account of Julius's other exploits, including the theft of one of the first successful proximity fuses and of information about something Lane described as an "air platform":

> I never heard of it, and I thought that was something out of Jules Verne, but I understand it was actually a project which the Government con-templated where they were going to fly rockets 3,000 or 4,000 miles in the air, have them remain stationary for a time—it may never have worked out, but they had the theory that when the Earth rotated on its axis, the things would be activated and float down and hit certain spots.
>
> I cite that to show you the limit to which these people have gone. Rosenberg seems to be the key to the whole picture. He is the corner-stone. We feel that if we can really break him, that he will open the gates and give us information which will lead to a lot of other individuals.

Lane couched his argument clinically: "The only thing that will break this man Rosenberg is the prospect of a death penalty or getting the chair, plus that if we can convict his wife, too, and give her a stiff sentence of 25 or 30 years, that combination may serve to make this fellow disgorge and give us the information on those other individuals. I can't guarantee that."

"He is pretty tough, isn't he?" asked the committee chairman, Sena-tor Brien McMahon.

"It is about the only thing you can use as a lever on these people," Lane replied.

"Mr. Lane, what kind of a fellow is Rosenberg, a tough egg?" McMahon asked.

"Rosenberg, I would say he is a tough sort of an individual," Lane replied. "He knows his way around, he refuses to give us any statement after he was arrested, he gave a brief statement to the F.B.I. prior to the time of his arrest. He is a graduate of City College. I don't think from a scientific angle he knows as much as Greenglass does, but as you know, he is Greenglass's brother-in-law.

"Rosenberg's wife is Greenglass's sister. So you have that angle, too, of a brother who is testifying against a sister where the death penalty is involved in the case."

"Is Greenglass ready to tell everything?" Congressman William Sterling Cole asked.

"Apparently."

"Even that which would involve his sister?" Cole asked, addressing the core question.

"Yes, but he is a little reluctant," Lane replied. "That is the one point where he is reluctant, but he doesn't tell us too much about that, but Greenglass's wife will also testify. The only thing we have against Mrs. Greenglass is the conference they attended where they made arrangements for this box top and for the information to be passed on. The case is not too strong against Mrs. Rosenberg. But for the purpose of acting as a deterrent, I think it is very important that she be convicted, too, and given a stiff sentence."

"Who is defense counsel?" Senator John Bricker asked.

Gordon Dean, the Atomic Energy Commission chairman, jumped right in. "Defense counsel is a professional commie, isn't he?" Dean said.

"As I understand it," Congressman Charles Elston interjected, "you were apprehensive that counsel for the defendants might ask some questions which would bring out new or additional information."

"I expressed that fear," Dean replied.

"If that were true, it would mean that counsel already has the information."

"Yes."

"Since counsel has some communist ties or at least is suspected of it, they already have the information. So you would only be bringing out what counsel already knows and which they probably would transmit to foreign agents if they are communists."

"All of the evidence is that the information Greenglass would give from the stand in all probability got to the Russians through Fuchs, through Gold, through Rosenberg," Dean replied, "plus the fact that the analysis of the Russian explosion itself indicates that they had a bomb of this type shot off by the implosion principle. . . ."

Later in the briefing, Dean candidly restated the government's strategy toward Julius: "If there is any way of breaking him by having the shadow of a death penalty over him, we want to do it. He is a tough man and may not break, but his wife is in this too, and faces a 25 or 30 year sentence, and I think he might talk, and if he did, he would certainly open up an awful lot."*

Lane acknowledged that "it is not too difficult to get a conviction in some conspiracy cases," but that the death penalty imposed a higher burden. "I seriously doubt from [my] own experience," Lane said, "that any judge would impose a death penalty merely because a man testified there was an agreement and they passed out information respecting the number of people that were working there or the names of scientists who were working there."

Wouldn't this procedure become self-defeating, one committee member asked—releasing the top-secret information that was stolen in order to get a conviction to prevent people from stealing top-secret information? Yes, Senator McMahon said, but defendants are entitled to challenge all of the evidence against them.

"Who says that?" Congressman Cole asked.

---

* The prosecution wasn't plotting strategy in the dark. One source, which the government itself considered of "unknown reliability," provided some of the foundation for that strategy. He told the FBI that Julius was worried that any sentence "would be a severe blow" to Ethel and that she "might break down" if Julius was sentenced to death. The informer offered another insight that would later color the government's view of Julius's resolve: He flatly rejected the possibility of being traded to the Soviets for an American spy and prohibited his lawyers from doing anything else that would "compromise their position."

"The Constitution says so," McMahon replied.

Gordon Dean restated Lane's predicament: "Mr. Lane feels that if you don't prove in this case that he [Julius] transmitted something very vital as of 1945, as distinguished from simply the population figures of Los Alamos and the names of some scientists there, you certainly couldn't impose a death penalty on the man."

And certainly not on the woman.

Chapter 26

Talking the Talk

*"Your memory gets very strange,
even after five years."*

≡

The other woman—Ruth Greenglass—was doing everything she could to cooperate with the government. She tattled to the FBI about Tessie Greenglass's further estrangement from Ethel. She reported on a prospective witness, who would be out of town over Lincoln's birthday and might stay away for a few weeks, which suggested that she was not going to testify for the Rosenberg defense. A few days later, Ruth recalled the gist of perhaps the only potentially incriminating letter that Ethel had mailed to New Mexico: Ruth was to have expected a visit from a family member on either of the last two Saturdays in May 1945. Since no family member had ever visited her in Albuquerque before and because there was no reason for Ethel to have referred cryptically to a genuine relative, Ruth had interpreted the seemingly innocuous reference to mean that the bearer of the partial Jell-O box top would materialize on one of those days. The FBI again searched the trunkload of letters seized from the Greenglasses' apartment but could not find that one.

As the trial approached, Ruth was being pressed by the prosecutors to elaborate on every detail of her account. She even remembered something that she had told Rogge months earlier but which *he* had forgotten to tell the FBI: that at Julius's request the Greenglasses had posed for passport photos the previous May. The photographer, Max Miller on Clinton Street, probably could corroborate their order.*

Each recollection helped flesh out the government's case. "Anything that could button it down, we wanted," James Kilsheimer, an assistant prosecutor, said later. Still, all of them taken together didn't warrant a sentence of twenty-five to thirty years' imprisonment, much less the death penalty, against Ethel Rosenberg.

Even at this late date, the evidence against Ethel was largely tangential. It would leave the jury a generous degree of latitude and the opportunity to grant her the benefit of the doubt in weighing the seriousness of the overt acts attributed to her. Certain assumptions were indisputable: Ethel was a dutiful wife. She was ideologically, emotionally, and romantically inclined to fully support her husband's commitment to the Soviet Union. She was his partner. But was she a spy? Was she legally guilty of conspiracy just because she might have urged Ruth to pose a question to David? Or because she happened to have a box of Jell-O in her kitchen? Or because she had mailed a letter mentioning a family member, which a jury was supposed to interpret, beyond a reasonable doubt, as meaning a Russian espionage courier?

The government had no source but the Greenglasses. Morton Sobell wasn't saying anything and never would. Max Elitcher didn't know anything. The only witnesses who could implicate Ethel were her brother and sister-in-law, and they had now been milked dry.

But then, Roy Cohn recalled, "John Rogge told me one day that David was holding back on Ethel, that if I talked to him again I might get the true story."

Whatever Rogge could do to ingratiate his clients with the government would, naturally, benefit them. All Ruth said later was that Rogge "asked me to tell the truth." Whatever deal—implied or inferred—that Rogge believed he had with Washington must have been contingent on

---

* She appeared to have held back nothing, even supplying the bureau with a romantic photo of the Rosenbergs taken in Central Park a few summers before.

David revealing all he knew. By February 1951, Rogge had to have understood that what the prosecutors needed most was whatever David and Ruth knew about Ethel. Cohn recalled:

> Obviously this didn't mean that all I had to do was walk in and David Greenglass would bring up his sister. It meant I could use leverage I hadn't thought would work before. That is, I could tell David that we knew he was protecting Ethel, and that unless he told us what HE knew about her activities we could not guarantee that Ruth, his wife, would be safe from prosecution. Until then, she had been an unindicted co-conspirator. It was the only deal we thought we could make, because David was not about to give us Julius without that arrangement. But the understanding had been that he would tell all. Now he was holding back about Ethel. So he had reneged on the deal. Such was my message to him, and he responded with alacrity. Whatever Rogge had said to him—and Rogge never told me, nor did I ask—convinced David Greenglass, and his wife (whom Rogge also represented), to finally tell us the real story about his sister.

David wasn't shy about saying there were some things he didn't remember. When he was asked early on about the money Ruth said she got from Julius to go to Albuquerque, he assured prosecutors that he didn't have a great deal to offer. "Whenever it comes to money I get a blank spell," David said. He also wasn't above tailoring his responses to place himself in the best possible light. For example, he told prosecutors he was a Truman supporter in 1948 when, in fact, he had voted for Henry Wallace. Since Truman had been elected and was still president, David figured it wouldn't hurt him to be with the winner. (It's arguable whether he would have been as convincing had Dewey won.) "You tell them a thing like that, it makes you not on the other side," he later explained.

David assumed he had bamboozled the system. But by then the government knew its chief witness inside and out. Agents had been debriefing him for eight months and had taken his measure. An FBI report completed just after the trial characterized him as having "a friendly, easy going, self assured manner," as being "extremely garrulous and expound[ing] at length on inconsequential matters," and as being "sometimes impatient and sarcastic." The analysis concluded that David "appears both courageous and honest," is "loyal to his family and friends and is generous to the point of improvidence." He enjoys jokes and "takes pleasure in attempting to startle others by his unexpected knowledge of facts and situations." David "dresses in a sloppy manner and in rather poor taste, possibly because of color blindness," doesn't like to shave regularly, has his hair cut infrequently, smokes moderately, doesn't drink much, but is "extremely fond of food and tends towards obesity." At the same time, he "is inclined to avoid physical exercise." The agents determined that David enjoyed "tampering with gadgets, and attempting to improve them," and they pronounced him to be of "above average intelligence and is better informed than his scholastic achievements would seem to indicate."

Politically, he was described as "a Communist at heart" who followed the party's activities through its publications until about 1948. Psychologically, the FBI believed that David hadn't derived "any personal feeling of relief by his confession because his crime had not weighed on his conscience." David had pleaded guilty to conspiracy in October and then to a superseding indictment on February 2.

But when it came to Ethel's role, David didn't have much left to contribute. He had no reason to implicate her, nor any desire to do so, nor, as far as he understood, any grounds. In his July 17, 1950, statement, he recalled that he delivered sketches and notes to Julius in September 1945 on a Manhattan street—not at the Rosenbergs' apartment. Two weeks later, when Myles Lane was questioning Ruth, Lane suggested that perhaps *she* had typed David's notes before giving them to Harry Gold. The prosecution was aware that, according to an informer, Julius regularly typed documents himself at a Morton Street apartment—placing rubber caps on the typewriter's feet and letting the water in the sink run to mask the sound. Even after Ethel was indicted, when, presumably, the prosecution already had the evidence it needed, Lane asked David for the umpteenth time whether his sister was even present during any of his conspiratorial conversations with Julius.

"Never," David replied.

"Did Ethel talk to you about it?"

"Never spoke about it to me, and that's a fact. Aside from trying to protect my sister, believe me that's a fact."

In retrospect, with the trial about to begin, perhaps the prosecutors' persistent harping on Ethel—where was she, what was she doing, what did she say—should have been a giveaway. But no one was so transparent as to declare that the government's strategy depended on the Greenglasses incriminating Ethel. Nobody said, crassly, We need you to conjure up some recollection that would justify our threatening the electric chair for Julius and Ethel Rosenberg.

Once Ruth had recovered from that first bedside interview by the FBI, she had been unambiguously in the government's corner. She was so sure that Julius had cheated her husband that she was ready to sue him while he was in jail. She was so terrified by the Rosenbergs' fanaticism that she refused to entrust her children to Ethel's care. Ruth shared none of David's ambivalence about his sister. And just ten days before the trial, something happened to alter Ruth's story—a change in attitude, perhaps, or a provocative question that jogged her memory. Whatever it was, her answer sealed Ethel Rosenberg's fate.

———

On February 19, Ruth remembered receiving in Albuquerque, in May 1945, a letter from Ethel. This was the letter in which Ethel wrote that "a member of the family would come out to visit." Ruth described the letter as "instructing her to be available for an espionage contact." On February 23, the day after George Washington's birthday, Ruth Greenglass was interrogated again at the U.S. Courthouse. Present were Agent Harrington of the FBI and James Kilsheimer, one of Saypol's assistants. The full transcript has never been found in government archives, but much of what Ruth revealed during the interview she later repeated on the witness stand.

According to a synopsis of that interview, Ruth first talked about her dinner with Ethel and Julius in November 1944, then about David's furlough in January 1945, the courier's visit that spring, and finally the September episode at the Rosenbergs' apartment in Knickerbocker Village:

Ethel said that she believed that David would want to furnish such info and that she wanted David to furnish info. . . . Ruth said that she mentioned to Julius that David had a very poor handwriting and that it would be difficult for Julius to read it. Julius replied that that was O.K. because he would have his wife, Ethel type it for him. . . . She mentioned to Ethel that she looked rather tired and Ethel replied that she had been up late the night before typing the material that David had given to Julius and typing other material that Julius had received. She told Ruth that she always typed Julius' material that he received and occasionally had to stay up late at night to do this. Ethel told Ruth that Julius was fully engrossed in the work he was doing and all he talked about was his work. She stated that he was away from home many times and stayed out late at night and that this was O.K. with her because she was satisfied with what Julius was doing. She [Ruth] said that she received a letter back from Ethel about May 7 in which Ethel advised her that someone from her family would come out to see them about the last part of May. Ruth said that this was the letter that gave her the instructions to make the contact in front of the Safeway store.

She said that she told David that to do any further work for Rosenberg in this regard would make him a traitor. . . . She said that Julius took the info into the bathroom and read it and that when he came out he called Ethel and told her she had to type this info immediately. She said Ethel then sat down at the typewriter which she had placed on a bridge table in the living room and proceeded to type the information which David had given to Julius. She said that at times Ethel was unable to decipher David's handwriting and David would look over her shoulder and tell her what he had written. She said that at other times Ethel would read a sentence aloud and comment that it was not correct grammatically and that she and Ethel assisted by Julius would correct the sentence grammatically. . . . Julius gave David $200 and told him to have a good time on his furlough. . . . She said that Julius and Ethel were elated with the info that David had turned over.

The government, unsurprisingly, was even more elated with what Ruth had turned over. Immediately after the interrogation, a lengthy synopsis was classified as urgent and sent by Teletype directly to J. Edgar Hoover. Ruth was questioned again the following day, a Saturday. Court wasn't in session; on the upper floors of the U.S. Courthouse, only skeleton staffs manned the offices of the U.S. Attorney and the FBI. The only sound was the occasional echo of shoes on the marble floors.

David was brought to the U.S. Courthouse two days later, on Monday, February 26. Saypol and Roy Cohn were in Mexico, mopping up the murky details of Morton Sobell's arrest. James Kilsheimer, Ruth's recent interrogator, interviewed David. Again, no verbatim transcript has been found in government files. During a protracted session, David volunteered little and largely just responded to the prosecutor's prompts. But he did corroborate Ruth's revised account. That evening, in an urgent Teletype to Washington, the New York bureau informed Hoover that David had "furnished in substance the same info as related by Ruth Greenglass." Finally, more than eight months after his arrest and only eight days before the trial was to begin, prosecutors had found their smoking gun.

Supporters of the Rosenbergs later argued that as the trial approached the government must have subjected the Greenglasses to immense pressure. They claimed that the prosecutors, inspired by the use of a typewriter as evidence in the Alger Hiss perjury case, invented another typewriter and imagined Ethel Rosenberg's fingers on the keys. It's impossible to prove that the story was "invented." But, unbeknownst to the Rosenberg defense, the Greenglasses had told a very different version to investigators months earlier and, presumably, in their still-secret testimony to the grand jury.

David was trained as a draftsman; his handwriting was surprisingly neat. Much more decipherable, in fact, than Ethel's. Still, "when David gave Julius the handwritten notes," Ruth testified, "I said that I hoped that Julius would be able to read it because David's handwriting was very difficult to understand. He said not to worry, that Ethel would type it. She was quite used to his handwriting."*

---

* Alexander Feklisov said later that David's handwritten notes that Julius passed along in January 1945 and David's notes that Harry Gold delivered to Yakovlev in June 1945 were perfectly

"Without the typing it would have been a weaker case, a much more difficult case," James Kilsheimer said later. "Would she have gotten the death penalty? Probably not." Would Ethel have even been convicted, much less executed, on the basis of Ruth's testimony alone? "Maybe so," Kilsheimer replied tentatively. But there was no question that the case against her rested on David's willingness to testify—testimony Ruth would corroborate—that Ethel had typed his handwritten account of highly classified scientific secrets so that her husband could deliver them to the Soviets. The smoking gun was Ethel's Remington typewriter. "That was the key to the whole thing," Kilsheimer said.

Robert Royal, one of the FBI agents assigned to the case, would describe David as sincere. "Once he became a Christian, he went all the way," Royal said, speaking metaphorically. He was less generous about Ruth's motives. "A sister-in-law has all kinds of reasons," Royal said.

"Ruth was in the same predicament as Ethel was," Agent William Norton said later. "David, in effect, put himself in the position of sacrificing his life for hers. They had him dead to right, and he knew it. You don't have to be a space cadet to figure that. You have to look at the whole picture: It was either them or us. They were trying to protect themselves."

At first, James Kilsheimer recalled, David "was protecting himself and his wife; for a while, he was protecting Ethel somewhat. David was a nice schmo. He was not the brightest guy in the world and not the dumbest guy. He was just an ordinary guy. He wasn't stupid. He wasn't naïve. He figured he had been caught.

"Recollection is a funny thing," Kilsheimer said. "It takes time to re-create in your own mind what happened six or seven years ago."

"Your memory gets very strange, even after five years," said David.

---

legible. Feklisov did say, though, that the handwriting was "crabbed" and childlike and that one sketch, whatever its scientific value, looked to him like a watermelon rind.

Chapter 27

Trial and Error

**"She told me that she didn't think
it was a good idea."**

≡

The Rosenberg trial began on Tuesday, March 6, 1951, in room 107 of the U.S. Courthouse. The trial opened in what Meyer Berger of *The New York Times* wrote was a "deceptive silence." At precisely 10:30 A.M. ("I am quite a fussbudget about being prompt," Judge Kaufman warned on the second day), Martin Schaefer, the court clerk, solemnly called the case: "The United States of America versus Julius Rosenberg, Ethel Rosenberg, and Morton Sobell." The original grand-jury charges, filed the previous August, had been superseded, first in October and then in January, by more detailed indictments that also named David Greenglass and Anatoly Yakovlev and that had grown to include twelve overt acts. But by the time the trial began, the number of defendants had been reduced to three again. Yakovlev, no longer in the United States, was beyond the jurisdiction of the court.

One reason for the apparent silence was that the acoustics were so poor in room 107 that sounds identifiable as words as they left the mouths of lawyers, witnesses, and the judge often dissipated into indistinguishable muffles. Justice is supposed to be blind, not deaf, but more than a few times during the trial, words, phrases, and entire sentences had to be repeated.

The courtroom was dimly lit. High chandeliers delivered a pale yellow light to the chestnut-paneled chamber. The light was particularly punishing to men, most of whom were rendered cadaverous. Women wearing makeup at least looked alive. On the first day, Ethel Rosenberg contributed the only dab of color; she wore a white blouse with a scarlet bodice. She sat between her codefendants, with Julius on her left and Morton Sobell on her right. She was invariably described as petite and placid, Julius as pale and fidgety.

The pride of prosecutorial young lions was formidable: Irving Saypol, his chief assistant Myles Lane, and his other assistants Roy Cohn, John M. Foley, James Kilsheimer, and James Branigan, Jr. The defense team was more eclectic: Emanuel Bloch representing Julius Rosenberg; his father, Alexander, for Ethel; Harold Phillips, a real-estate lawyer, and Edward Kuntz for Sobell.

For all the egos and agendas involved in the case, this was indisputably Judge Kaufman's trial. He lobbied vigorously for it. He got it. And he would never be rid of it. "My burning desire at this time is to be a credit to you, the President, and my country," he had written Attorney General McGrath late in 1949, after he had been appointed to the federal bench by President Truman at the age of thirty-nine—the youngest judge in the Southern District of New York. "I shall approach my task with deep humility, for to judge man is almost a divine prerogative."

Irving Kaufman was only five foot four. He was forty-one years old and so prickly and imperious that Julius Rosenberg characterized him as "a cross between a rabbinical student and an army sergeant."

One of five children of a humidor maker, Kaufman graduated from Fordham Law School when he was only twenty, a year before he was even eligible for admission to the bar. His mastery of the required religious curriculum at the Jesuit university in the Bronx earned him the sobriquet "Pope Kaufman." He was later dubbed "the Boy Judge." Early in his judicial career, he was sometimes confused in public with Judge Samuel H. Kaufman, who presided over the first perjury trial of Alger Hiss. The confusion was not to last very long.

When it came to communists, he was known as a hanging judge. In November 1950, he sentenced Abe Brothman to seven years imprisonment and Miriam Moskowitz to two years for obstructing justice by influencing Harry Gold's grand-jury testimony in 1947. Complaining that the law did not allow stiffer penalties, he said at sentencing: "I have no sympathy or mercy for the defendants; none whatsoever."

—

Court administrators had prudently assembled a pool of more than three hundred persons, a record number, from which to choose twelve jurors and four alternates. The first day and a half was spent culling them. Some complained that their employers couldn't spare them the six weeks that the trial was expected to take. (The government alone said it was prepared to call more than one hundred witnesses.) Some were excused because they said they opposed the death penalty, others because as veterans of the Second World War they maintained that they could not be unprejudiced in judging defendants accused of betraying their country during wartime. Was anyone biased against the principles of atomic warfare or nuclear weapons? the judge asked. (None said yes.) Did they harbor extreme political views? The judge recited a catalog of presumably biased publications, submitted by lawyers for both sides, which ranged from *The American Legion Magazine* to *The Daily Worker;* an employee of Time-Life who said he shared most of his employer's views on international affairs was challenged by the defense; a reader of the *National Guardian* was challenged by the government. Were they familiar with anyone associated with the prosecution or the defense or were they connected in any way with law enforcement? So many veniremen asked to be released that an exasperated Judge Kaufman declared skeptically: "I hope all these statements are being made in good faith and not in an effort to avoid what might seem to the jurors an unpleasant task."

—

The eleven men and one woman who finally constituted the jury were sworn in just before 1:00 P.M. Wednesday. They were a decidedly middle-class bunch, sharing three traits: None had asked to be excused; none was opposed to capital punishment; and none—unlike the judge, the chief prosecutors, the most damning witnesses, and all three defendants—was Jewish.

That the jury included no coreligionists of the Rosenbergs was to become another blot on the trial. The fact is, though, that a number of Jewish veniremen excused themselves from serving. Also, while nearly one in three residents of New York City at the time was Jewish, the Southern District of New York encompassed a wide swath of the Hudson Valley and only two of the city's boroughs, Manhattan and the Bronx. Moreover, it is debatable whether the presence of one or more Jews on the jury would have made any difference. Prosecutors said later they were seeking to exclude only two groups categorically: unpredictable oddballs and also housewives (less because housewives might sympathize with a mother than because their own maternal responsibilities might intrude if deliberations ran late or if the jury was sequestered overnight). Defense lawyers wanted iconoclasts—defined to include women and blacks—anyone who wouldn't bend to prevailing sentiment. But the defense, too, was uncertain whether a Jewish juror would necessarily be more severe or more sympathetic.

The jury foreman, Vincent Lebonitte, was a thirty-year-old assistant sales manager at Macy's in White Plains. Like Judge Kaufman, he had graduated from Fordham, where he had majored in psychology. He was an army veteran whose last posting had been as a military policeman in Germany. Years later, Lebonitte told Ted Morgan of *Esquire* that when he was assigned the number-one seat in the three-tiered jury box, he didn't feel up to it. But he said: "I thought, if I beg off somebody else might be anxious to get a spot like this. I knew it had to do with a conspiracy to commit espionage. Suppose one of their cohorts was in the spot? Would they chicken out? I forced myself to stay."

The other jurors included five Bronx residents—a housewife, a bus-company bookkeeper, an accountant, an oil-company auditor, and a restaurateur—a caterer for the Seminole Tennis Club in Forest Hills, Queens; and a Manhattanite, the lone black, who worked for Consolidated Edison. The rest were from Westchester County: a bank examiner,

Ethel Greenglass Rosenberg and David Greenglass outside their childhood home on Sheriff Street. This photograph was probably taken during World War II when David was in New York on leave or shortly after he was discharged in 1946. It is the only known picture of just the two of them together.

Growing Up

The house on Sheriff Street: no. 64, on the Lower East Side of Manhattan, where David was born, the Greenglasses were raised, and Tessie was the superintendent. In this 1930s view, Barnet's sewing-machine repair shop is to the left of the entrance. The entire block was obliterated in the late 1950s to make way for subsidized high-rise housing. (New York City Department of Records and Information Services)

Put up yer dukes: Young David,
striking his most aggressive pose.

Favorite son: David
with his mother.

GREENGLASS, E.
Can she act? And how.

GREENGLASS, DAVID
Davie
64 Sheriff Street, Manhattan
Science Office Helper
*Although he has a lot to say,
We think he's grand, anyway*
Engineering Science

Ethel's and David's high-school
yearbook photos.

Her brother's keeper: Ethel (standing, right)
and David (middle, left) with cousins. The
Greenglasses vacationed in upstate New York at
an uncle's farm.

Couples

Julius and Ethel Rosenberg: After he and Ethel were married in 1939, Julius grew a mustache so that he would look more mature when he applied for a government job. (National Archives)

David and Ruth Greenglass: This photo seems to have been taken outside the house in Albuquerque where Ruth lived while David was at Los Alamos. (National Archives)

Men at Work

In the army, David, too, affected a mustache, perhaps to emulate Julius.

The brothers Greenglass: David, Bernie (a war hero, who served in Africa and Italy), and Sam (a jeweler and watchmaker who worked for the War Production Board in New Jersey).

David with his tools: This photograph was probably taken inside the Manhattan machine shop in which David, Bernie, and Julius were partners.

Nuclear Family

David and Ruth, their son, Steven, and their two-week-old daughter, Barbara. This is one of the photographs that the Greenglasses had taken at Max Miller's studio in 1950. The government said that these were for forged passports Julius Rosenberg would provide so that the family could flee, via Mexico, to Eastern Europe. The Greenglasses maintained that they never intended to leave the United States and were merely placating Julius. (National Archives)

The party's over: The only known photograph of the Rosenbergs and the Greenglasses together, probably in the late 1940s. David blacked out the faces of the other guests at this unidentified affair.

The First Confession

News accounts of David's arrest on June 16, 1950, drew a curious crowd to the Greenglasses' tenement at 265 Rivington Street, around the corner from Sheriff Street and just up the block from where Ruth's parents lived. The building had been under surveillance by the FBI for nearly two weeks, although agents complained that it was difficult for them to remain incognito in the neighborhood. (Library of Congress–Bettman/Corbis)

Once he began cooperating with prosecutors, David was lodged in the so-called singing quarters of the Tombs. He was frequently taken to the U.S. Courthouse for questioning, as in this photograph from July 1950. (Associated Press)

A mother's lament: Tessie Greenglass, interviewed by newsmen after David's arrest. This photograph seems to have been taken in David and Ruth's apartment, where Tessie was baby-sitting Steven and Barbara. (Associated Press)

The Other Shoe

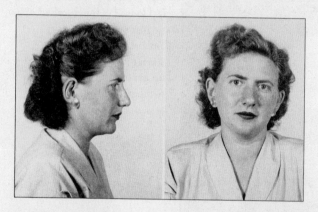

Because she and David cooperated, Ruth was never arrested. Instead, she was named by the federal grand jury as an unindicted coconspirator in espionage. These photographs were said to have been taken only so that other witnesses and suspects in the case could identify her, but they give every appearance of being mug shots and must have further intimidated her. (National Archives)

The Rosenberg defense argued that Ethel was "a housewife, basically a housewife and nothing more." This photograph, taken before she was arrested, shows her being exactly that. (Bettmann/Corbis)

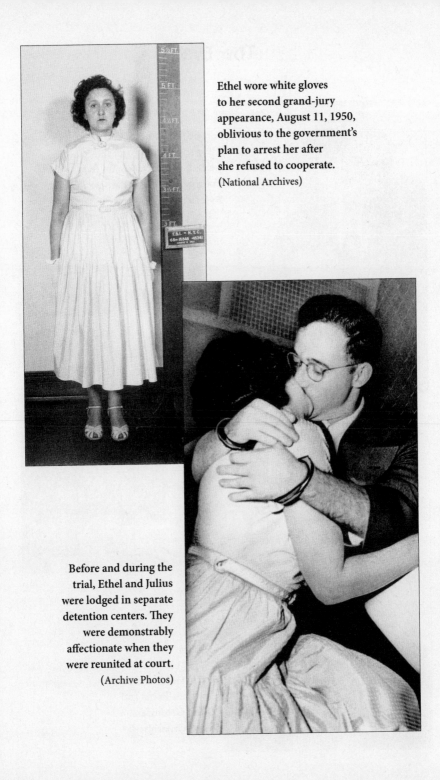

Ethel wore white gloves to her second grand-jury appearance, August 11, 1950, oblivious to the government's plan to arrest her after she refused to cooperate. (National Archives)

Before and during the trial, Ethel and Julius were lodged in separate detention centers. They were demonstrably affectionate when they were reunited at court. (Archive Photos)

The Trial

For the prosecution, U.S. Attorney Irving Saypol (seated) with his assistant Roy Cohn behind him. (The New York Times)

The boy judge, Irving R. Kaufman, presiding. (Associated Press)

Harry Gold, the courier for Klaus Fuchs and David Greenglass. (National Archives)

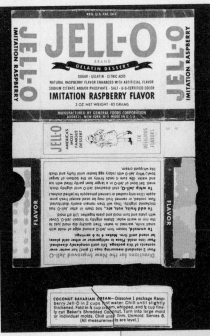

Government Exhibit 33: not the real Jell-O box that David Greenglass and Harry Gold used to identify themselves to each other, but the courtroom prop. On the witness stand, David demonstrated how Julius had cut the panel (at bottom). (National Archives)

Government Exhibit 8: a sketch of the atomic bomb, drawn by David on the eve of the trial. He said it was a replica of the one he drew for Julius in September 1945. The Rosenberg defense committed a fatal error by asking that the sketch be impounded—suggesting that it was a secret still worth protecting. (National Archives)

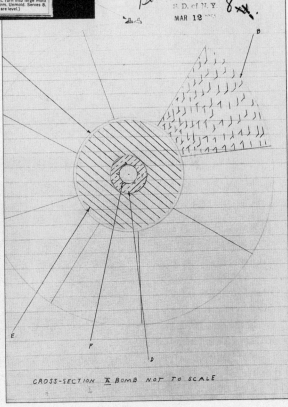

The Sentence

Manny Bloch, the Rosenbergs' lawyer and friend, shepherded Robby Rosenberg, age five (left), and Michael Rosenberg, nine, on a winter visit to their doomed parents at Sing Sing. This photograph was taken on February 14, 1953, after President Eisenhower had denied clemency. Four months later, the Rosenbergs were executed. (Associated Press)

Robby and Michael were adopted by Abel and Ann Meeropol and grew up largely out of the limelight. They revealed themselves as Rosenbergs in the mid-1970s and published a joint memoir, *We Are Your Sons*. They now live in Massachusetts. (Arthur Grace)

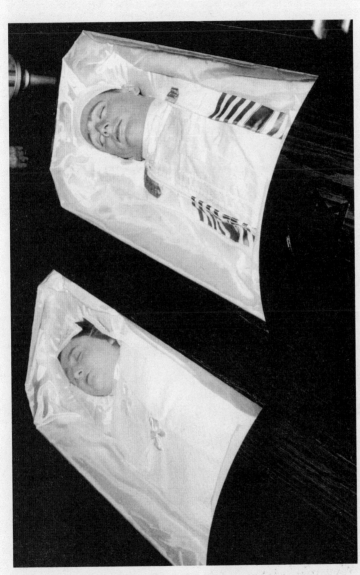

On Saturday, June 20, 1953, the night after the execution, mourners were permitted to pay their last respects to the Rosenbergs. Julius had been given a skullcap. A silk scarf covered the bare spot on Ethel's head where an electrode had been attached in the death house. The Rosenbergs were buried on Long Island the next day. (Archive Photos)

The last good-bye: David, heeding the warning on the taxicab window, watched his left hand as he departed the Federal House of Detention in Lower Manhattan on November 16, 1960. Reporters pursued but lost him. "All I want," he said, "is to be forgotten." He now lives under an assumed name. (Associated Press)

the secretary of the State Board of Commissioners of Pilots, a soft-drink-company bookkeeper, and a rotogravure-company estimator.

The judge admonished the jurors not to read anything in newspapers or magazines or to listen to anything on radio or to watch anything on television that referred directly to the case. That left them considerable latitude, though, to keep up with an expanding menu of provocative stories appearing about other crimes and the cold war. At home, the House Committee on Un-American Activities released a compilation of 624 groups and 204 publications that had been declared subversive by one government agency or another. Washington was treated to the unlikely spectacle of Senator McCarthy testifying that Earl Browder, the former Communist Party secretary general now charged with contempt of Congress, had demonstrated "complete cooperation" with a Senate subcommittee investigating communist infiltration of the State Department. In its weekly update, the Defense Department placed the total number of American casualties of the Korean War at 52,448, including 7,857 killed but not counting several thousand more who had been felled by disease and frostbite. In the last week alone, the number of battle casualties had increased by more than 1,700. Everyone was concerned about civil defense. Small wonder then that the five racetracks in and around New York announced that they would open their doors as welfare centers in case of enemy attack. (The six hundred pari-mutuel windows would serve as booths where the injured and homeless could register.)

—

Next, Kaufman disposed of various defense motions. With the preliminaries done with, it was Saypol's turn to present the government's case.

Saypol was forty-seven, the son of Russian immigrants whose name had been changed at Ellis Island from Sapolsky. He had been born on Chrystie Street on the Lower East Side and raised in East Harlem. His father was a building contractor. Young Irving's career goal was related, but he got to fulfill it only vicariously: He wanted to be an electrical engineer. After graduating from Brooklyn Law School, he had been named assistant chief U.S. Attorney in 1945, and, after successfully prosecuting

Alger Hiss, Judith Coplon, William Remington, and the eleven Communist Party officials indicted under the Smith Act, he was later lionized by *Time* magazine as "the nation's Number One legal hunter of top Communists."

"While some of my assistants assisted in preparation for trial and I let four of them examine some of the witnesses, I took the lead," Saypol said later. "I was the only prosecutor in the Rosenberg case." He was a stickler who never missed an opportunity to seize on someone else's vulnerability, no matter how trivial. Early in the case, when a top Justice Department official complained that a news release from Washington revealed too much, Saypol concurred. "I agree with you," he said, "and it also had split infinitives."

Saypol was five foot eleven and an imposing figure, with a square jaw, which spoke to his rigid disposition, and steady blue eyes. Saypol was also, according to Roy Cohn, "one of the easiest men in the world to dislike."

Saypol assured the judge that his opening statement would take all of twelve minutes. Delivering his remarks in soft but measured tones, he then took twice as long. He meticulously defined a conspiracy:

> When any one of the persons who have entered into this agreement and understanding to violate the laws of the United States does any overt act, that is, any physical act, to help along the conspiracy, to further its objectives, to carry it into practical operation, when any one of the persons having entered into this agreement does any such act, then all those other persons who had entered into this agreement and understanding with him become guilty of the crime of conspiracy. Therefore, in this case, proof of only one such overt act by any of the conspirators would be sufficient to complete the conspiracy. That is obvious, because common sense tells us that when a number of people enter into a widespread agreement and conspiracy, such as we have here, each one cannot do all of the dirty work himself.
>
> In this case you will hear proof, not only of a single act in furtherance of the conspiracy by one of the conspirators, but the evidence here will show many acts by each and every one of the defendants and of the

conspirators, all of such acts performed in furtherance of this conspiracy to commit espionage for the benefit of the Soviet Union.

The evidence will show that the loyalty and the allegiance of the Rosenbergs and Sobell were not to our country, but that it was to Communism, Communism in this country and Communism throughout the world.

Manny Bloch interjected, as he was to do repeatedly. "If the Court pleases," Bloch said, "I object to these remarks as irrelevant to the charge before the Court and jury and I ask the Court to instruct the District Attorney to desist from making any remarks about communism, because communism is not on trial here. These defendants are charged with espionage."

Echoing Bloch, Kaufman reiterated: "The charge here is espionage. It is not that the defendants are members of the Communist Party or that they had any interest in communism." (He interrupted Saypol a few moments later to correct himself: "I want to correct that. The charge is conspiracy to commit espionage.") "However, if the Government intends to establish that they did have an interest in communism, for the purpose of establishing a motive for what they were doing, I will, in due course, when that question arises, rule on that point."

Saypol apologized to the jury for Bloch's interruption. For all his meticulousness in outlining the legal grounds to prove conspiracy, Saypol vaulted an ethical divide by equating conspiracy with treason—a charge that was not lodged and that demanded a higher burden of proof.

"The evidence will show their loyalty to and worship of the Soviet Union, and by their rank disloyalty to our country these defendants joined with their co-conspirators in a deliberate, carefully planned conspiracy to deliver to the Soviet Union the information and the weapons which the Soviet Union could use to destroy us," Saypol declared.

The evidence will reveal to you how the Rosenbergs persuaded David Greenglass, Mrs. Rosenberg's own brother, to play the treacherous role of a modern Benedict Arnold, while wearing the uniform of the United States Army.

We will prove that the Rosenbergs devised and put into operation, with the aid of Soviet nationals and Soviet agents in this country, an elaborate scheme which enabled them to steal through David Greenglass this one weapon that might well hold the key to the survival of this nation and means the peace of the world, the atomic bomb.

The evidence will show how at the behest of the Rosenbergs, Greenglass stole and turned over to them and to their co-conspirator Harry Gold, at secret rendezvous, sketches and descriptions of secrets concerning atomic energy and sketches of the very bomb itself.

The defendants barely reacted, except to shift their feet slightly under the table. When Saypol finished, the defense immediately invoked his reference to communism as grounds for a mistrial. Kaufman denied the motion. But he reminded the jury, "The charge in this case, again, I tell you, is conspiracy to commit espionage, in that matters vital to the national defense were transmitted to Russia for the purpose of giving Russia an advantage."*

Manny Bloch, who had made his reputation as a civil-rights lawyer, gave, as promised, a brief opening statement. It consisted largely of an appeal to the jury not to be swayed by "bias or prejudice or hysteria," adding: "All we ask of you is a fair shake in the American way." Bloch acknowledged that the Rosenbergs were charged with "a very grave crime." But, he cautioned, establishing what was to become a parallel track of the trial, the government had to prove not that the defendants "believed in one ism or another ism, but that they conspired to commit espionage."

Manny Bloch, who was not yet fifty, was followed by his father, seventy-year-old Alexander Bloch, whose specialty in commercial law

---

* And, again, the judge stood corrected, after Phillips reminded him that "no where in the indictment is it stated that information actually was transmitted. The indictment charges that a plan was laid to transmit information." Later still, Kaufman elaborated further as to why the law didn't distinguish between friends and foes: "So that there be no misunderstanding whatsoever as this case unfolds before you, I want you to bear in mind that the law makes no distinction between transmitting or intending to transmit any information to a country whether friendly or unfriendly because as the United States Supreme Court said in a case which is rather important on this subject, unhappily the status of a foreign government may change."

was the buying and selling of bakeries. This was his first criminal case. Painting a most sympathetic portrait of Ethel, the elder Bloch said:

> You are not to condemn her because her brother is a self-confessed traitor, or her sister-in-law is mentioned in the indictment and who, I understand, has not been arrested and will tell you she was guilty as charged in the indictment.
>
> She was a housewife, basically a housewife and nothing more. She was dragged into this case through the machinations of her own brother and her own sister-in-law, who in order to transfer and lighten their burden of responsibility, accused her of being a co-conspirator.

Sobell's lawyers insisted that their client was innocent of espionage conspiracy and reminded the jury that the burden of proof was on the government.

—

On Thursday, the government called its first witness. He was not a household name and never became one. He was Max Elitcher, a tall, lean electrical engineer who had met Morton Sobell at Stuyvesant High School and had been a classmate of both Sobell and Julius Rosenberg at City College. Elitcher was the thirty-two-year-old father of two infants; his backyard abutted Sobell's in Flushing, and after the war they worked together at Reeves Instruments.

Shortly before the trial, prosecutors posed a question to Elitcher that they probably wished they had asked sooner: What would he say if the defense asked why he left the Communist Party?

"I'll tell them the truth," Elitcher replied. "I still am a member of the Communist Party."

Saypol was stunned. To him, membership in the party was tantamount to treason. That was also the underlying thrust of the prosecution. What would it say about the government's credibility if its first witness was an unrepentant communist? Luckily for the prosecution, O. John Rogge represented Elitcher, too. Prosecutors summoned him to the courthouse to confer with his client. After a few moments, Rogge emerged smiling. "Max," he announced, "has just left the Communist Party."

Once on the stand, Elitcher testified about efforts by Rosenberg and Sobell to recruit him to the Communist Party and to espionage, when he worked for the Bureau of Naval Ordnance in Washington during the war and later as a colleague of Sobell at Reeves Instruments.

When asked about Communist Party membership, Elitcher mentioned the Young Communist League. Responding to defense objections, the judge struck any references to the league and advised Saypol: "Get to the Communist Party."

Later, Roy Cohn interjected that in philosophy they were one and the same. "I don't think we can establish that the Young Communist League at meetings told members to go out and steal classified information. I certainly think we can establish that the Young Communist League and the Communist Party both were progressive organizations which believed in Soviet Russia as a model and a guide."

Saypol agreed: "That is the God that they direct themselves to, both of them."

When Saypol tried to elicit from Elitcher the names or initials of people he met at Communist Party meetings in Washington, Harold Phillips objected. The initials *J.S.*, he maintained, might be taken for those of Joseph Stalin. "Well, if the initials are 'J.S.' you will stipulate that it wasn't Joseph Stalin. Proceed," Kaufman remarked dryly. Laughter rippled through the courtroom.

Under cross-examination, Elitcher explained why he had confessed when he had been interviewed by the FBI the previous July:

> I hadn't approached the FBI in advance, because I felt that there were implications to even my bringing up the subject. However, when they came to me, I, after a short talk, I freely told them of the story, and since I felt that there might be no reason to hide it, as they might know about it anyway, however, I felt that the only course I could take was to tell the complete story, which I did.

It was arguable whether Elitcher told the complete story when he confessed or when he testified. What he told, though, constituted vir-

TRIAL AND ERROR • 313

tually the only evidence against Morton Sobell. None of it touched on atomic espionage. Elitcher testified in detail about meetings with Rosenberg and Sobell in Washington and in New York—meetings at which, he said, they sought unsuccessfully to recruit him as a spy. But the defense scored several rhetorical points: Elitcher never gave Sobell or Rosenberg any of the documents or secrets they were alleged to have been seeking; although he had been fired by Reeves two weeks before the trial, he had bought a new car since then (suggesting that the government was subsidizing him); and he had regularly seen a psychiatrist twice a week (implying, perhaps, that he was mentally unbalanced).*

Perhaps because Elitcher's credibility was suspect, Sobell declined to testify in his own defense. He left it to his lawyers to rebut the testimony of Mexican and American authorities that he had fled to Mexico immediately after David's arrest and had hidden there behind several aliases—behavior consistent with that of a man who was frightened, guilty, or both. Elitcher was excused by mid-afternoon Friday, which meant that the main event of what was billed as the trial of the century was to begin before court adjourned for the weekend.

—

Irving Saypol later said that "a well-turned case is just like a stage play, really." But in the professional theater, even protagonists sometimes forget their lines and improvise, which can prove especially daunting to the actor on the receiving end of a suddenly spontaneous colloquy, particularly when he happens to be an understudy. Which is what happened to Roy Cohn when he began questioning David Greenglass.

Cohn had just celebrated his twenty-fourth birthday, though even at that age his piercing blue eyes were already shielded by heavy lids. Like Kaufman, Cohn was a prodigy. He had breezed through college and law school (Columbia in both cases) by the age of twenty. Cohn was not only precocious, he was brash, and he made a career out of knowing

---

* Elitcher testified that after he underwent therapy, "our married life did adjust itself, and I will say right now that it couldn't be much happier as married life goes."

which buttons to press and which levers to pull. The son of a Democratic machine–made State Supreme Court justice, he was admitted to the bar and hired by the U.S. Attorney's office on the same day, and in 1950 he got himself promoted to be Saypol's confidential assistant—a glaring misnomer, since he strategically leaked stories to his claque of journalists and because the first priority on his agenda was invariably to assist himself. Cohn was not so much a great lawyer as a savvy practitioner of situational immorality. He defined his life by an axiom he invoked years later after delivering "Fat Tony" Salerno, a Mafia leader, to an acquittal on tax-evasion charges. Salerno might have been "technically guilty," Cohn acknowledged, but "truth is hardly ever an absolute. There are so many elements."

Cohn was recruited to examine David Greenglass at the trial only after Saypol had soured on Myles Lane for sharing too much about the prosecution's vulnerabilities with politicians and bureaucrats in Washington. Saypol had a second reason for replacing Lane. The prosecution's original strategy, as Lane envisioned it, was to overwhelm the defense with a vast chorus of corroborators and collaborators who, while some might be hostile, would verify enough details to constitute an irrefutable case. Cohn favored a simpler approach, unencumbered by balky witnesses and uncharted detours, that emerged as the more appealing alternative after prosecutors scored two breakthroughs on the eve of the trial: First, when Ruth and David said they remembered that Ethel had typed David's notes; second, when the FBI reported the day before the trial was to open that "after considerable reflection" Harry Gold was finally "quite certain" that he had delivered "greetings from Julius" in June 1945.

Until the last minute, there was confusion over the breadth of David's technical testimony, and the sudden switch of prosecutors made the Atomic Energy Commission scientists even more anxious. The night before David was to testify, Cohn had him delivered from the Tombs to the U.S. Courthouse for still another rehearsal. The next day, David still forgot to follow the script. Repeatedly, he also had to be asked by Kaufman or by Cohn to raise his voice. But spectators were spellbound. During the brief pauses between questions, the courtroom was silent.

David may have been a "self-confessed traitor," as Alexander Bloch characterized him, and "a modern Benedict Arnold," as Saypol described him, but Cohn introduced him to the jury as an ordinary guy—not some feral rodent clawing his way out of a trap but a pliable, if pathetic, human being resorting to what anyone in his position would do to survive. Where did he live? How old was he? Where were his parents? Who were his other siblings? To whom was he married? Did he and his wife have any children? Which schools did he attend? What did he do during the war? It didn't take long for David to tell his first lie.

"Now, would you tell us at this point when it was that you learned for the first time that the Manhattan Project District was the district of the United States Army concerned with the construction of the atomic bomb?" Cohn asked.

"When my wife came to visit me in November 1944 she told me that Julius had told her—"

Manny Bloch interrupted. "I object," he said, "to any conversation between the witness's wife and himself outside the presence of the defendant Julius Rosenberg."

"She is named as a co-conspirator," Kaufman replied.

"I respectfully except," Bloch said.

"Objection overruled."

"Will you tell us again?" Cohn resumed. "I think you said the time was November 1944?"

"Right."

"What did your wife tell you?"

"She told me that Julius had said that I was working on the atomic bomb."

"And that was the first you knew of it?"

"That was the first I knew of it."

Cohn introduced a photocopy of the security regulations David had received when he had arrived at Los Alamos. He led David through an explanation of the different-colored security badges and the identity of some of the scientists who worked there, including Dr. Walter Koski.

"I believe Dr. Koski is here in court," Cohn said. Koski rose from his seat opposite the jury box. Yes, David said, he recognized Koski. He managed to glance toward Koski and then back to Cohn without ever meeting Ethel's insistent gaze.

Cohn abruptly shifted his line of questioning. "I think you have told us, Mr. Greenglass," Cohn said, "that your sister, Ethel, was a number of years older than you are. Is that correct?"

"Six or seven, something like that," David replied. And yes, he had gotten to know Julius Rosenberg before he and Ethel married when David was seventeen.

"Now, did you have any discussion with Ethel and Julius concerning the relative merits of our form of government and that of the Soviet Union?"

This time, Alexander Bloch objected to the question "as incompetent, irrelevant and immaterial, not pertinent to the issues raised by the indictment and the plea."

"And," Manny Bloch added, "upon the further ground that this will obviously lead to matters which may only tend to confuse the jury and inject inflammatory matter which will make it difficult or almost impossible for the jury to confine themselves to the real issues in the case."

"Your Honor," Cohn continued, "of course, the views of the defendants on the relative merits of this country and the Soviet Union are extremely relevant when the charge is conspiracy to commit espionage, in that material would be transferred to the Soviet Union to be used to the advantage of the Soviet Union."

After a prolonged exchange, Kaufman overruled the objections.

David replied that he had had numerous discussions, several times a week, with Ethel starting in 1935 and with Julius two years later and continuing until 1945 or 1946. Cohn asked whether the conversations continued pretty much within the framework of a freshman comparative-government course.

"Well, roughly they did," David replied. "The conversations on the merits of socialism over capitalism, I think, in the beginning were more vehement."

"Mr. Greenglass, please," Manny Bloch broke in, "it is difficult to hear you."

"In the beginning they were more vehement."

"Well now," Bloch said, apparently sorry that David spoke up, "I object to that."

"Yes," Kaufman said, "I will sustain that."

"Talking about socialism over capitalism," Cohn continued, "did they specifically talk about socialism as it existed in the Soviet Union and capitalism as it existed here?"

"They did."

"Which did they like better? Did they tell you?"

Again, Bloch objected to the question, this time as leading and suggestive.

"I will sustain the objection on that ground, which they liked better," Kaufman replied. "But you tell us whether or not on any occasion they told you that they preferred one over another."

"They preferred socialism to capitalism."

"Which type of socialism?" the judge asked.

"Russian socialism."

Cohn turned to the Greenglasses' November 1944 wedding anniversary in Albuquerque. David recalled that toward the end of that extended weekend, he and Ruth went for a walk on Route 66 toward the Rio Grande. Cohn positioned himself by the jury-box rail. After each answer, he stared at the jurors for effect. They were transfixed as David implicated his sister in the espionage plot. Ethel was transfixed, too. She turned deathly pale; at one point, she pressed her fingers tightly against her eyeballs and let her head droop to her chest as David testified:

My wife said that while she was still in New York, Julius Rosenberg invited her to dinner at their house at 10 Monroe Street. She came to dinner and later on there was a conversation between the three present, my wife, my sister and my brother-in-law. It went something like this: Ethel started the conversation by stating to Ruth that she must have noticed that she, Ethel, was no longer involved in Communist Party activities . . . that they don't buy the *Daily Worker* anymore or attend meetings, club meetings. And the reason for this is that Julius has finally gotten to a point where he is doing what he wanted to do all along, which was that he was giving information to the Soviet Union. And

then he went on to tell Ruth that I was working on the atomic bomb
project at Los Alamos, and that they would want me to give information to the Russians. My wife objected to this, but Ethel said—[*]

Manny Bloch objected to the characterization.

"Is this what your wife told you?" Kaufman asked.

"Mr. Greenglass is relating what his wife said to him," Cohn replied.
"I assume that he is doing his best to recall the words that were spoken."

"If she used the word 'object' of course I will withdraw my objection," Bloch said.

"Did you wife use the word 'object'?" the judge asked.

She told me that she didn't think it was a good idea . . . and that she
didn't want to tell me about it. . . . But they told her that I would want
to know about it and I would want to help, and that at least—the least
she could do was tell me about it. So that was the conversation. At first
she asked me what I thought about that. At first I was frightened and
worried about it and I told her. . . . I told my wife that I wouldn't do it.
And she had also told me that in the conversation, Julius and Ethel had
told her that Russia was an ally and as such deserved this information
and that she wasn't getting the information that was coming to her. So
later on that night, after this conversation, I thought about it and the
following morning I told my wife that I would give the information.

She asked me to tell her about the general layout of the Los Alamos
atomic project, the buildings, number of people and stuff like that; also
scientists that worked there, and that was the first information I gave
her.

---

[*] According to Ruth's original account to the FBI, it was Julius, not Ethel, who started this conversation. And David's version of how he learned that the Manhattan Project was developing
an atomic bomb was repeatedly revised (first, he blurted out to the FBI that he had learned
it from Ruth; the next day, he protected her by insisting that he had known about it from
colleagues for months; and finally, he returned to the first version to buff his brother-in-law's
credentials as an omniscient spymaster).

Cohn turned next to the January 1945 furlough. According to the script, David was supposed to testify about the list of scientists he had handed Julius and other general information, leaving it to Koski (the next witness) to field Cohn's questions and thus the potential cross-examination about sensitive scientific matters. Instead, David recalled Julius's request that he "write up anything that I knew about the atomic bomb."

"Anything else?" Cohn asked, trying to lead his witness.

David paused, nervously interlocking his fingers. "He gave me a description of the atom bomb," David replied, referring to the gun-trigger detonator. He also recalled that the next morning, he provided Julius with sketches of the lens molds and descriptions of how they worked, as well as another list of scientists assigned to the Manhattan Project.

Cohn suggested that since the prosecution was about to begin a new phase of questioning, this would be a good time to stop for the day. It was a half hour shy of 4:30 P.M., Kaufman's appointed quitting time, so he apologized to the jury: "Well, it sort of goes against the grain of my Scotch soul, but it looks like we have got to adjourn early today."

After court adjourned and a few minutes before he was to confer with government scientists again, Saypol telephoned Ray Whearty at the Justice Department in Washington. Saypol complained vehemently about the Atomic Energy Commission's demand to micromanage the case by reviewing a transcript of Greenglass's rehearsal. Whearty expressed surprise that the commission's concerns hadn't already been fully resolved, but Saypol reminded him, "You know from practical experience you never can forecast" what a witness will say, and "you have got to prove this matter was vital in national defense."

This reminded Whearty that Saypol had requested a copy of the minutes of Myles Lane's closed-door appearance in February before the Joint Committee on Atomic Energy. The minutes were classified, which made Saypol's next suggestion so extraordinary. He asked Whearty to mail the minutes to New York.

"We can't send it in the mail," Whearty said.

"It can't?"

"No."

"I will send somebody up tomorrow," Whearty said. "If you want that thing, I will make it a point to get somebody up there with it."

"Tomorrow or Sunday," Saypol said. "It will be good if I can run through it before Monday." He asked again: "You are afraid to send it registered mail?"

"Yes, sir."

Chapter 28

The Gamble

**"My wife had remarked to Ethel
that she looked tired."**

≡

The trial resumed on Monday, but testimony was delayed by two developments involving Max Elitcher. First, the prosecution turned over transcripts of Elitcher's statements to the FBI and of his grand-jury minutes to the defense to assuage concerns about discrepancies. Kaufman told lawyers to review the transcripts over lunch, then delivered a lecture on the work ethic: "You don't eat for an hour. I don't. I eat for 10 minutes. I have a sandwich and coffee. You can arrange to have a sandwich and coffee brought in for you today, but we must move this trial along, and I am not going to have a delay by these so-called side-issues." Second, Saypol revealed that, on Saturday, Elitcher had received an anonymous letter at home. "Watch out for the time bomb," the letter warned.

—

After he retook the stand, David testified that Julius "said he wanted a list of people who seemed sympathetic with communism and would help furnish information to the Russians." In January 1945, "Julius came to the house and received this information," David testified, "and my wife, in passing, remarks that the handwriting would be bad and would need interpretation and Julius said there was nothing to worry about as Ethel would type it up, retype the information."

The next day, or perhaps two days later, the Greenglasses went to dinner at the Rosenbergs' apartment. That's where they met Ann Sidorovich. The five of them bantered before dinner, then Ann left. David continued the narrative:

> It was at this point that Julius said that this is the woman who he thinks would come out to see us . . . at Albuquerque to receive information from myself.
>
> They wanted us to meet this Ann Sidorovich, so that we would know what she looked like; and that brought up a point, what if she does not come? . . . So Julius said to my wife, "well, I will give you something so that you will be able to identify the person that does come." . . . Rosenberg and my wife and Ethel went into the kitchen and I was in the living room; and then a little while later, after they had been there about five minutes or so, they came out and my wife had in her hand a Jell-O box side. . . . And it had been cut, and Julius had the other part to it, and when he came in with it, I said, "Oh, that is very clever" because I noticed how it fit, and he said, "The simplest things are the cleverest."

At which point, with customary flourish, Cohn produced the prop that was to become emblematic of the Rosenberg trial: a Jell-O box. "Your Honor," Cohn began,

> at this point I would like—this will be quite important—to have the witness, as best he remembers it, take this Jell-O box and cut the correct side into two parts, just as he remembers it was cut on that night, in January of 1945, and I would like to ask him to indicate to the Court and jury which side he kept and which side Rosenberg kept. . . . Will you take Government's Exhibit 4 for identification and this pair of scissors, and address yourself to the appropriate side and cut it into two pieces. Cut it into two pieces resembling the two pieces you saw that night in Rosenberg's apartment?

No precise accounting exists of how many boxes were mutilated in rehearsing this moment. Just as Cohn had intended, the courtroom was riveted on the witness as David performed legal origami. He accepted the scissors and separated the side panel of the carton by making one cut vertically and then a second cut diagonally. David held up one of the two pieces. "This is the side I had," he said.

"Where did you last see this other side on that night?" Roy Cohn asked.

"In Julius's hand," David replied.

—

Starting with David's testimony, the Rosenberg jury heard more details about Jell-O than about the atomic bomb.[*]

Bloch's cross-examination of David's Jell-O revelations was withering. David admitted that the box he cut in court was, of course, not identical to the one that had come from the Rosenbergs' kitchen. Well, Bloch asked, how did they differ?

"They made a darker colored box at the time. It seemed to me much darker than this, than the way it is now."

"Any other difference?"

"I didn't read the Jell-O box then and I haven't read this one now."

"How," Bloch demanded, "can you answer or how did you answer intelligently my question before when I asked you whether or not this box was substantially similar to the one that was used at the Rosenberg house?"

"It said Jell-O on both boxes," David replied.

---

[*] A food product congealed with gelatin was patented in 1845 by Peter Cooper, the industrialist who founded the Cooper Union for the Advancement of Science (to which Julius Rosenberg applied but wasn't accepted). The commercial, fruit-flavored version was invented in 1897. Because it originated with animal hooves, questions persisted about whether it could be kosher, but the manufacturers persuaded generations of rabbis that it could pass muster under Jewish dietary laws because it had been reprocessed beyond recognition. During the war, sugar shortages put a crimp in the supply, and shortages of everything else boosted demand. Jell-O could be combined with almost any ingredient to stretch a meal.

Originally, Jell-O was manufactured in strawberry, raspberry, orange, and lemon flavors. For his courtroom demonstration, Roy Cohn chose raspberry.

"Is it imitation raspberry?" Bloch inquired.

"Is that material?" Judge Kaufman asked.

"It might be," Bloch replied.

"Or, is it facetious?"

"No, no," Bloch assured the court. "It might be."

"This was imitation raspberry flavor," David confirmed.

"What was the one you say was used in Rosenberg's house?"

"I really don't know," David replied.

Bloch was unrelenting. Next, he traced the provenance of the two pieces of Jell-O box. He wanted to know when David next saw the piece that Ruth had placed in her wallet. And when he last saw either piece. And he challenged David to describe a single word that appeared on Ruth's piece of the box. David couldn't. Then, Manny Bloch dropped what he intended to be a bombshell, though neither the jury nor the judge, much less the witness, had the slightest idea what he was hinting at.

"Did you ever hear of the words 'coconut Bavarian cream'?" Bloch demanded.

"Did I ever hear of the words? I have heard them around, sure."

"Did you ever hear of the words 'coconut Bavarian cream' or do those words mean anything to you, with reference to the Jell-O box which you say was cut up in the Rosenberg house?"

"Doesn't mean anything to me," David replied.

It didn't mean anything to anyone else either. And suppose the words had meant something to David? What would that have proved? How would that have shaken the prosecution's case? Manny Bloch was grasping for anything that might render the whole Jell-O episode as a courtroom contrivance. To demonstrate the dogleg cut that David said Julius had made in the Jell-O box, David snipped the top panel of the box, opposite the drawing of the little girl who proclaimed Jell-O "America's Favorite Dessert." Only when the two pieces were fitted close together was it clear that imprinted on the panel was a recipe for coconut Bavarian cream.[*]

———

Prompted by Cohn on redirect examination, David delivered his audience back to the dinner at the Rosenbergs' apartment in January 1945.

"Now, was there any further conversation between you and your wife and the Rosenbergs on that evening?"

"Well, the Rosenbergs told my wife that she wouldn't have to worry about money because it would be taken care of—I mean, she would be able to get out there and live out there, if she wasn't able to work the money would be forthcoming."

"Was that in your presence?" Kaufman asked.

"In my presence."

"Both of them said that?"

"Julius, and Ethel backed it up. Earlier in the evening, during these conversations, my wife had remarked to Ethel that she had looked kind of tired and she said she was tired because she—"

"Who said this?" Cohn interjected.

"My wife had remarked to Ethel that she looked tired."

"Ethel looked tired?"

"And Ethel remarked that she was tired between the child and staying up late at night, keeping—typing over notes that Julius had brought her—this was on espionage."

Manny Bloch, apoplectically, objected. "I move to strike out the last," he said.

"Did she say that?" Kaufman inquired.

"She said 'in this work.' She also stated that she didn't mind it so long as Julius was doing what he wanted to do."

———

* Dissolve one package raspberry Jell-O in two cups water. Chill until slightly thickened. Fold in ¾ cup cream, whipped, and ¾ cup finely cut Baker's Shredded Coconut. Turn into a large mold or individual molds. Chill until firm. Unmold. Serves eight.

David recounted the events of 1945 more or less chronologically (placing his drive with the Russian in January, though, rather than September), including Ruth's move to Albuquerque in late winter and Gold's visit in June.

"Did you have any discussion with Gold about the money?" Cohn asked.

"Yes, I did. He said, 'Will it be enough?' And I said, 'Well, it will be plenty for the present.' And he said, 'You need it,' and we went into a side discussion about the fact that my wife had a miscarriage earlier in the spring, and he said, 'Well, I will see what I can do about getting some more money for you.'"

—

To impress the jurors—and to intimidate the defense—Saypol stacked the prosecution table with scientific experts whose very presence suggested to the jury that the stakes must be extraordinary.

Cohn introduced a sketch of the lens mold that David said he delivered to Julius. It was not the original sketch—presumably, that one had been microfilmed and spirited off to Moscow in 1945—but one that David had drawn the day before. David also explained the schematic view of a lens-mold experiment that he drew for Harry Gold. Cohn interrupted with another flourish: David was temporarily excused; Dr. Walter Koski took his place on the stand. Koski was enlisted to walk the jury through the Manhattan Project and to translate David's imprecise technical testimony into a coherent and authoritative explanation of high-explosive lenses. He, rather than David, would thus field any technical questions. Responding to Saypol, Koski explained, "A glass lens essentially focuses light. An explosive lens focuses a detonation wave or a high pressure force coming in."

After Koski confirmed that he remembered David from Theta Shop, Saypol directed Koski's attention to two of David's sketches and asked: "Is that a reasonably accurate portrayal of a sketch of a type of lens mold or lens that you required in the course of your experimental work at the time?"

"It is," Koski replied.

"Would you recognize it as a reasonably accurate replica of the one you submitted to the Theta machine shop?"

"Yes."

Saypol asked whether the experiments were unique.

"To the best of my knowledge and all of my colleagues who were involved in this field," Koski replied, "there was no information in text books or technical journals on this particular subject."

"In other words, you were engaged in a new and original field?"

"Correct."

"And up to that point and continuing right up until this trial has the information relating to the lens mold and the lens and the experimentation to which you have testified continued to be secret information?"

"It still is."

Manny Bloch asked the judge for a few moments to digest Koski's testimony. "Since I am not a scientist," he said, "I don't want to query about matters which might appear asinine." He began by discrediting David.

"Mr. Greenglass was a plain, ordinary machinist, was he not?" Bloch asked. Saypol objected; Kaufman permitted the characterization.

"Correct," Koski replied.

Repeatedly, Bloch belittled David's sketches as unsophisticated and so lacking in details and dimensions as to be useless.

"This is a rough sketch," Koski replied, "and, of course, is not quantitative, but it does illustrate the important principle involved."

"Now, weren't the dimensions of these lens molds very vital or at least very important with respect to their utility in terms of success in your experiments?" Bloch asked.

"The physical over-all dimensions that you mention are not important," Koski replied. "It is the relative dimensions that are."

"Now the relative dimensions are not disclosed, are they, by these exhibits?"

"They are not," Koski conceded.

Saypol interjected. "The important factor from the experimental point of view is the design, is it not?" he asked.

"Correct," Koski replied.

"That was original, novel at the time, was it not?"

"It was."

"Can you tell us, Doctor, whether a scientific expert in the field you were engaged in could glean enough information from the exhibits in evidence so as to learn the nature and the object of the experiment that was involved in the sketches in evidence?"

"From these sketches and from Mr. Greenglass's descriptions," Koski replied, "this gives one sufficient information, one who is familiar with the field, to indicate what the principle and the idea is here."

—

After lunch, David Greenglass returned to the stand. Cohn jogged David's memory about a conversation with the Rosenbergs after dinner at their apartment in January 1945:

"Well, at this point Mr. and Mrs. Rosenberg told me they were very happy to have me come in with them on this espionage work and that now that I was in it there would be no worry about any money they gave to me, it was not a loan, it was money given to me because I was in this work and that it was not a loan."

"Did they say anything about the source of that money?" Cohn queried.

"They said that it came from the Russians who wanted me to have it."

Cohn turned to David's last furlough, in September 1945. When did he next see Julius Rosenberg? David clasped his hands in his lap. He began smiling.[*]

"He came up to the apartment and he got me out of bed and we went into another room so my wife could dress," David said.

"Did you have a conversation in that other room?"

"I believe we did."

"What did he say to you?"

---

* He explained later that he was oblivious to his expression, but that it couldn't have been a smile. Rather, it must have been merely a neurotic reaction to a "horrible" moment, not a gleeful or vindictive taunt.

"He said to me that he wanted to know what I had for him."

"Did you tell him what you had for him?"

"Yes. I told him, 'I think I have a pretty good description of the atom bomb.'"

"The atom bomb, itself?"

"That's right."

David testified that Julius gave him two hundred dollars more and asked him to write up the description of the bomb. Ruth balked, but David said he overruled her, almost valiantly: "I have gone this far and I will do the rest of it, too." Cohn submitted another sketch, this one identified as a replica of a cross section of the bomb that he gave Julius that evening.

"By the way," Cohn asked, "who was present when you handed the written material including this sketch over to Rosenberg?"

"My wife, my sister, Julius and myself," David replied.

"By your sister, you mean Mrs. Rosenberg?"

"That is right."

At this moment, Bloch interrupted. He asked the court to impound David's sketch. The prosecution was stunned.

"That is a rather strange request coming from the defendants," Saypol said.

"Not a strange request coming from me at the present," Manny Bloch replied. "Let me say by way of explanation, Mr. Saypol, that despite the fact that the Atomic Energy Commission may have declassified this, I was not at all sure in my own mind, and I am talking privately, whether or not even at this late date, this information may not be used to the advantage of a foreign power."

"I had assumed I was on the horns of a dilemma," Saypol replied, still startled by Bloch's maneuver. The prosecutor reviewed the debate within the government about how far to go in sacrificing secrecy, summing up that "the primary obligation in the administration of justice was that the defendants were entitled to be apprised of the nature of the case against them." Saypol neglected to reveal, though, that the government's primary goal in disclosing secrets was to justify the death penalty.

Bloch had rolled the dice. How could his clients' patriotism be questioned when they, too, would not selfishly risk national security just to further their own defense? But Bloch blundered. By accepting the prosecution's unchallenged claims of secrecy and national security, he validated them. If the drawings and the details were so trivial, as the defense had implied, why impound them? And if they needed to be protected at this late date, they must have been worth stealing in 1945. Gloria Agrin, a junior member of the defense team, explained later that the Rosenberg lawyers took the government's word. "Was this rough half-assed sketch of Greenglass's of any use to a foreign power? We had no way of knowing," she said. "Bloch wanted to show the court we are just as patriotic as the others. He was trying to avoid the death sentence by lifting the stigma of treason. It was a courtroom decision, made on the spur of the moment."

Morton Sobell's lawyer Harold Phillips immediately divorced himself from Bloch's gamble. Phillips was unwilling to stipulate the confidentiality of the drawings or their pertinence to national defense. "I do not feel that an attorney for a defendant in a criminal case should make concessions which will serve the People from the necessity of proving things, which in the course of the proof we may be able to refute," Phillips said at the bench. But in open court, Bloch declared again that "in the interests of national security, any testimony that this witness may give of a descriptive nature concerning the last Government exhibit might reveal matters which should not be revealed to the public."

"Therefore," Judge Kaufman prodded.

"And, therefore," Bloch continued, "I felt that his testimony on this aspect should be revealed solely to the Court, to the jury and to the counsel and not to the public generally."

In response, Kaufman declared a short recess and ordered the courtroom cleared. But on returning to the bench, he advised counsel that reporters were "rather agitated" that they were barred along with the public. Saypol didn't object to the press witnessing the interrogation of Greenglass, but Bloch did—compounding his initial blunder. Kaufman overruled him. As a result, Bloch's willingness to stipulate the secrecy of the exhibits was doubly ironic: Everyone would benefit from the arrangement except for the defendants. A court clerk summoned the reporters, who returned to their front-row seats. Kaufman explained: "My personal feeling in the matter is that all of this testimony that is anticipated has probably fallen into the hands of those from whom we are trying to keep the information." He couldn't be certain, though, he said, so "we are going to trust to your good taste and your good judgment on the matter of publishing portions of this testimony."

"The Solomonic decision by Irving Kaufman was out of the Marx Brothers," Roy Cohn later recalled. "The spectators were ordered to leave the courtroom, but the press was allowed to remain!"

—

Following the judge's cue, the press refrained from reporting details of David's technical testimony and from reproducing Government Exhibit 8, which was identified as a cross section of the atomic bomb. Roy Cohn's interrogation of Greenglass went unreported by the press and was deleted from the official transcript.

"Tell us," Cohn said, "how you described the cross-section of the atomic bomb."

"I have 'a,' which points to two detonators, each mold," David replied.

Each high explosive lens, there were 36 of them, that I have pointed to as "b" had two detonators on them, that is, two detonators connected to capacitors which were charged by suitable apparatus and was set to go off by a switch that would [go] through all 72 condensers at once. There were two detonators on each lens so in case of failure of one, the other would go off. And beneath the high explosive lens there was "c," I have marked, a beryllium plastic sphere, which is a shield for the h.e., the high explosive. Then I have "e," which is the plutonium itself, which is a fissionable material. That is also a sphere. Inside that sphere is a "d," is beryllium. Inside the beryllium there are conical shaped holes marked "f.". . . Now, the beryllium shield protects the high explosive from the radiation of the plutonium. This is to prevent the h.e. from deteriorating and not go off until it is set off. At the time of the discharge of the condensers the high explosive lens implode, giving a concentric implosion to the plutonium sphere on the inside. This in turn does the same to the beryllium, and the beryllium is the neutron source which ejects neutrons into the plutonium, which is now at a super or hyper-critical stage because of the high pressure heat, and nuclear fission takes place.

Just to make sure that the jury understood the import of all that jargon, Cohn asked David: "That completes the description of the atomic bomb as you furnished it to defendant Rosenberg in September 1945?"

"That is right, that does."

—

Kaufman impounded the official court reporter's untranscribed stenographic notes and Exhibit 8 itself.

With David's technical testimony, authenticated by Koski, Cohn had firmly established the victim of the conspiracy: America's nuclear-weapons monopoly and, with it, the safety of every American man, woman, and child. Now, he was poised to introduce what he later declared was the smoking gun.

When the FBI had interrogated the Greenglasses about Ethel Rosenberg a few weeks earlier, David had merely corroborated Ruth's recollection. Now, on the witness stand, he was cast more prominently, as his sister's chief accuser.

"Now," Cohn continued, "will you tell us what happened, Mr. Greenglass, after you handed this sketch and the descriptive material concerning the atomic bomb to Rosenberg? What did he do, and what did the others there do?"

"Well, he stepped into another room and he read it and he came out and said, 'This is very good. We ought to have this typed up immediately.' And my wife said, 'We will probably have to correct the grammar involved,' because I was more interested in writing down the technical phrases of it than I was in correcting the grammar. So they pulled—they had a bridge table and they brought it into the livingroom, plus a typewriter."

"What kind of typewriter?"

"A portable."

"Then what?"

"And they set that up and each sentence was read over and typed down in correct grammatical fashion."

"Who did the typing, Mr. Greenglass?"

"Ethel did the typing and Ruth and Julius and Ethel did the correction of the grammar. While this was going on, sometimes there would be stretches where you could do—there wasn't too much changing to be made, and at this time Julius told me that he had stolen the proximity fuse when he was working at Emerson Radio."

Bloch objected. Kaufman cut him off: "This is not limited to atomic information. This charges a general conspiracy to give information to the U.S.S.R. Objection overruled."

"I except, and I ask for a mistrial on the basis of your ruling," Bloch said.

"Overruled."

"By the way," Cohn continued, "you turned—I think you have told us on several occasions that you turned over this sketch and descriptive material to Rosenberg, is that right?"

"I said that before."

"And that it was typed by Mrs. Rosenberg?"

"That's right."

"Do you know what happened to the original notes after the typing was completed?"

"The original notes were taken and burnt in the frying pan and then flushed down the drain."

"Who did that?"

"Julius did that."

"Pardon me?"

"Julius did."

Prompted by Cohn, David wove together separate examples of Julius's suspicious behavior—his friend Joel Barr's departure for Europe, his familiarity with the sky-platform project, his rendezvous with Russian agents. Asked whether the Rosenbergs had received any rewards from the Russians, David said Julius told him he had gotten a watch as a gift and that Ethel had received a watch, too ("I don't recall when that was, but I do recall that my wife told me about it"), and a console table.

"Did you ever see that table?"

"I did."

"At their home?"

"I did."

If the Rosenbergs got watches as gifts, they must have done something to deserve them.* If the Russians bought the Rosenbergs something as mundane as a console table, it must have had some secret, sinister purpose, like espionage.

Again, David lied.

—

On Tuesday, David Greenglass resumed the stand for the third day.† Inexplicably, he was smiling again. He recounted his conversations with Julius after Klaus Fuchs's arrest became known in February 1950:

"Rosenberg said to me that I would have to leave the country; think it over and we will make plans to go. Well, I told him that I would need money to pay my debts back so I would be able to leave with a clear head, and Rosenberg said that he didn't think it was necessary to worry about it. But I insisted on it, so he said he would get the money for me from the Russians. He then went on to say—I protested further—"

"I move to strike out the word 'protested,'" Manny Bloch said.

"Tell us what you said," the judge advised David.

"I said, 'I wouldn't be able to'—'I didn't think it was wise to go right to the consulate here and ask for a passport,' and he said, 'Oh, they let other people out who are more important than you are,' and I said, 'Is

---

* David claims never to have gotten any gifts himself, except, of course, for thousands of dollars in cash. He also says he was appointed as a major in the Russian intelligence service (Julius was a colonel, he said), though the chief perquisite that came with the title was free rides on the Moscow subway.

† This time he had competition. Upstairs in the same courthouse, a bashful Frank Costello was testifying before Senator Estes Kefauver's nationally televised hearings into organized crime. At the request of Costello's lawyers, the television camera was trained on the witness only from the necktie down. His sweaty fingers performed a minuet that was as expressive as anyone's face could be. *The New York Times* anointed him "TV's First Headless Star."

that so?' And he said, 'Yes, well they let Barr out, Joel Barr, and he was a member of our espionage ring.'"

—

Manny Bloch began his cross-examination with a single goal in mind: He had to prove that whatever else David was, he was also a vengeful liar. Compounding Bloch's other handicaps, he was suffering from a bad cold. But he succeeded on his first try.

"Did you just testify that you didn't see your brother-in-law, Julius Rosenberg, from the time that you told him that you were going to stay here and you weren't going to leave the country, until you appeared here in court?"

"I did."

"Was that the truth?"

"Well, I had seen him."

"Was it the truth?"

"That was not the truth."

"You did see him, didn't you, between that period?"

"I did."

"Where did you see him?" the judge interjected.

"I saw him in jail," said David.

"Did you talk to him?"

"No."

"You mean you just saw him; you looked at him and you saw him?"

"They brought us into a room together, the authorities at West Street, and told us to stay apart and I didn't say anything to him and he said nothing to me."

Bloch drew David back to the Greenglasses' wedding anniversary in Albuquerque in November 1944.

"From the time that you told your wife that you were not interested and that you wouldn't do this work, to the following morning when you told her you would, did you consult with anybody?" Bloch asked.

"I consulted with memories and voices in my mind."

"Physically, did you consult with anybody?"

"No."

"Did you see the Rosenbergs during that period?"

"No."

"Did you talk to the Rosenbergs by telephone during that period?"

"No."

"How old were you at this time?"

"Twenty-two."

"And when you finally said to your wife the following morning after she invited you to engage in spying you did this and said this and then disclosed information of your own free will; isn't that correct?"

"That is correct."

"You knew at that time, did you not, that you were engaging in the commission of a very serious crime?"

"I did."

"Did it occur to you on November 29, 1944, or November 30, 1944—and I don't want to quibble about the date—at any rate, did it occur to you at the time that you finally said to your wife 'I will do this' and then transmitted to her certain information, that there was a possible penalty of death for espionage?"

"Yes."

"You knew that?"

"I did."

"When you said to your wife, 'Yes, I will do it,' is that correct?"

"That is correct."

"Are you aware that you are smiling?"

"Not very."

"And you knew when you said to your wife, 'yes, I am going to give you the information,' that took place somewhere in the latter part of November 1944, that you were violating the oath that you took here in New York City at the time of your induction—did you know that?"

"I did."

"Did it enter your mind?"

"Violation of that oath did not enter my mind."

"Did you believe you were doing an honorable or dishonorable thing?"

"I didn't even think of it that way."

"How did you think of it?" Kaufman asked.

"I thought of it from what I had—on the basis of the philosophy I believed in. I felt it was the right thing to do at that time."

"And," Manny Bloch asked, "did you continue to think that what you were doing after November 29, 1944, and up to and including the time that you got out of the Army, that you were doing the right thing?"

"I was having my doubts."

"When did you begin to have doubts?"

"Almost as soon as I started to do it."

The judge interjected again. "Now you saw Mr. Rosenberg in January 1950, I am sorry—1945. Did you say anything to him about your doubts on the propriety of what you were doing?"

"No, I did not say anything to him because, as I said, when I first started to do it was one of the motivating factors for doing it. I had a kind of hero-worship there and I did not want my hero to fail, and I was doing the wrong thing by him. That is exactly why I did not stop the thing after I had the doubts."

"You say you had a hero-worship?" Bloch asked.

"That is right."

"Who was your hero?"

"Julius Rosenberg."

"Did you have any doubts when you, as you testified, got a thousand dollars from Mr. Rosenberg in June 1950?"

"I felt that I was giving nothing for this thousand dollars; I had plenty of headaches and I felt the thousand dollars was not coming out of Julius Rosenberg's pocket, it was coming out of the Russians' pocket and it didn't bother me one bit to take it, or the $4,000 either."

"Did you consider that the services that you rendered to the United States during your Army career warranted an honorable discharge?"

"I did my work as a soldier and produced what I had to produce and there was no argument about my work, and since the information went to a supposed ally at the time, I had no qualms or doubts that I deserved the honorable discharge."

"And you felt at that time you were entitled to an honorable discharge, is that right?"

"That is right."

"Do you feel that way now?" Kaufman asked.

"No, I don't."

"When did you change your mind as to whether or not you were entitled to an honorable discharge?"

"I never thought about it until this moment."

—

Bloch probed David's relationship with his siblings (for some reason, when Bloch asked whether Sam had the same mother and father as David, he replied, "As far as I know") and his love for his wife.

"You love her very dearly, don't you?"

"I do."

"Do you love her more than you love yourself?"

"Oh, I think—" Kaufman interrupted.

"I do," David replied.

"I am satisfied with the answer," Bloch said.

"I dare say," Kaufman continued, "that would be a difficult question for any of us to answer, Do we love somebody more than we love ourselves?"

"I could retort, but I am refraining," Bloch answered. "We are dealing with a peculiar kind of witness."

"I object to that," Saypol said.

"I move that be stricken," Cohn chimed in.

"Yes, that will be stricken," Kaufman said. "I suppose all the government witnesses are peculiar in the eyes of the defense."

"Yes," Cohn said, "and vice versa."

—

Bloch returned to David's relationship with his sister.

"Do you bear any affection for your sister Ethel?" he asked.

"I do."

"You realize, do you not, that Ethel is being tried here on a charge of conspiracy to commit espionage?"

"I do."

"And you realize the grave implications of that charge?"

"I do."

"And you realize the possible death penalty, in the event that Ethel is convicted by this jury, do you not?"

"I do."

"And you bear affection for her?"

"I do."

"This moment?"

"At this moment."

"And yesterday?"

"And yesterday."

"And the day before yesterday?"

"Well now," Kaufman asked, "how far are you going to go?"

Before Bloch could answer, David replied: "As far back as I ever met her and knew her."

—

Bloch asked about Agent Spillane's visit to the Greenglasses' apartment on Rivington Street early in 1950. David's response had a glaring omission:

> "One man called me up on the phone and he said he would like to see me. He came to my house; he sat down at my table; I offered him a cup of coffee and we spoke—he did not say to me that he suspected me of espionage or anything else—he just spoke to me about whether I had known anybody at Los Alamos, and that was the gist of the whole conversation. He walked out of the house maybe an hour later, and that is all there was to it."
>
> **"Did he ask you any questions, either directly or indirectly, with respect to your knowledge of any illegal activity that occurred at Los Alamos while you were there?"**
>
> "I don't recall exactly what the whole conversation was about. It made very little effect on me, because it didn't—I mean, it didn't seem like anything. He discussed with me—when he came into the house it was very difficult to find out what he wanted. He didn't come out and

say that he wanted some information. He just talked around the point. I didn't get what he really wanted to find out."

"Were you frightened at the time that F.B.I. man came down to see you in February [*sic*] 1950?"

"Well, I wasn't exactly calm."

"You didn't tell that F.B.I. man at that time, that you had engaged in any illegal activity at Los Alamos, did you?"

"I didn't tell him, but I was pretty well on the verge to tell him."

Bloch jumped to June 1950, when the FBI visited the Rivington Street apartment a second time, and asked:

"Now, when they searched your apartment, did you realize that you were a suspect?"

"I would have to be awful dumb not to."

"Did you conscientiously withhold any facts that night?"

"No, I did not conscientiously withhold those facts."

—

After lunch that day, Saypol reported to the judge that Tessie Greenglass had called to complain that "some of the relatives have made it impossible" for her to see Ethel. Alexander Bloch dismissed Tessie's complaint as a misunderstanding. "I will use my good offices and tell her to come here," Saypol said. "Aside from that I don't want any part of it."

—

Resuming his cross-examination, Manny Bloch plumbed David's memory and state of mind at the time he confessed. Why, for instance, had he originally mentioned that in June 1945 Gold gave him money but didn't specify how much? Had he forgotten the five hundred dollars?

"Before June 15, 1950 and during the intervening period from June 1945—that is about five years—did you at any time know precisely how much Gold gave you in the early part of June 1945?"

"At certain times a man's mind is funny. Sometimes I will remember it and sometimes I won't later on. There was no reason to recall it in that period."

"It wasn't your intention at that time to give every minute detail?"

"Not intention, but I couldn't remember every minute detail that had occurred. It is beyond human ability to do so."

Bloch asked about David's phone call to Louis Abel on the night he confessed:

"Now, I am asking you whether or not, when you called up your brother-in-law to get a lawyer, you had in your mind that the lawyer should represent your wife?"

"To represent me."

"Only you?"

"When I say that, I don't know who else was involved, in the sense that I don't know what the Government was going to do. They were just talking to me."

"You involved your wife that night, did you not?"

"Well, I don't know sufficiently enough about the law to realize that I did involve my wife."

"Didn't you tell the F.B.I. that night that your wife came out to Albuquerque?"

"That is absolutely true."

"And made an invitation to you to commit espionage; you told [them] that, did you not?"

"That's right."

"You also told them, did you not, that she had accompanied you to Rosenberg's house in September 1945; you told them that, did you not?"

"That's right."

"You also told them that your wife had received from you the money that Gold had given to you in June 1945; you told them that, did you not?"

"I did."

"Did you tell the F.B.I. about your wife's participation in the Jell-O box incident?"

"I did. But let me point out, as a lawyer—as I wasn't a lawyer, I didn't know it was an overt act or anything else. How was I to know that? I just told them the story as it happened. That was all I was interested in getting out."

"You were interested in getting out," Bloch repeated.

"I said, all I was interested in was getting out the story. Don't misconstrue my words."

David recalled that at the arraignment the next morning he had been oblivious to the proceedings:

"I didn't pay much attention to what the complaint said and you can—I—I don't even believe I heard the words in the complaint."

"You didn't hear the words?"

"No."

"Were you excited at the time?"

"No, I was just dull."

"Were you dull because you didn't sleep very much the previous evening?"

"It could be one of the contributing factors."

"How about now; do you feel sharp?"

"Sharp enough."

"Do you believe that by giving testimony in this case that you will be helped in terms of the severity of the sentence to be imposed upon you by the Court?"

"I don't believe that I in testifying will help myself to that great an extent."

"When you say 'to that great extent,' would you like to clarify that for the jury?"

"To any great extent."

"Would you say to any extent?"

"To any extent."

"All right. Do you believe that by testifying here in this trial that you will help your wife?"

"I don't know what the Government has in mind with my wife and I can't answer for them."

By then—and since the original indictment in July and in light of all of the subsequent superseding charges—David knew that Ruth had not and presumably would not be charged as a defendant; she had been named only as an unindicted coconspirator.

Next, Bloch tested David's scientific knowledge. David answered easily.

"Do you know what an isotope is?" Bloch asked.

"An isotope is an element having the same atomic structure, but having a different atomic weight."

Then, Bloch tried to suggest that David wasn't in a position to learn the secret to the bomb, much less to steal it.

"Now, the job that you did was only a part, however, of the matter, or the material that was to be constructed in connection with an overall blueprint; isn't that so?"

"Sometimes, yes. Sometimes it was something by itself."

"And when it was something by itself, wasn't it just the construction of some little metal bar or some other appliance?"

"A lot of little appliances go into making something bigger."

Bloch had David describe his modus operandi as a spy:

I would usually have access to other points in the project and also I was friendly with a number of people in various parts of the project and whenever a conversation would take place or something I didn't know about I would listen very avidly and question the speakers as to clarify what they had said. I would do this surreptitiously. . . . I was in the room when I heard discussions about implosion effect experiments, implosion effect of lenses, while some scientists were discussing it in the office of the building I was in. The curve looked the same to me, maybe a little flatter or a little more tapered but I couldn't tell which curve was—I mean it would be very difficult to tell which one was the improvement over the other.

"Now, I believe on your direct examination you told us, in substance, that you snooped around to get information; isn't that right?" Bloch asked.

David nodded.

"Don't shake your head," Judge Kaufman admonished. "You had better answer."

"Oh, yes, yes," David said.

Bloch then asked for two examples of information that David had elicited while engaging in or eavesdropping on conversations:

"I came into a room; there was a piece of material on the table; I picked it up and I said, 'It is an interesting piece of material and it is interestingly machined.' The man I spoke to and another man [who] was there said, 'Oh, that is neutron source,' and explained how it was used, in a conversation.

"Another instance. A man came in to me with a sketch—with a piece of material; said 'machine it up so that I would have square corners, so I could lay out a lens, come over and pick it up.' I would go over to his place; he was a mathematician, a scientist, he had laid it out, and I would say, 'What is the idea?' He would tell me the idea."

"Tricky like, eh?"

"Nothing tricky about it."

—

Wednesday was David's fourth day on the witness stand. Bloch delved into his business relationship with his brother-in-law:

"Now, weren't there repeated quarrels between you and Julius when Julius accused you of trying to be a boss and not working on machines?"

"There were quarrels of every type and every kind. I mean there were arguments over personality, there was arguments over money, there was arguments over the way the shop was run. It was quarrels, just business quarrels—"

"Well, whether you call them—"

"Just a moment," the judge interjected. "He wasn't finished."

"We remained as good friends in spite of the quarrels."

"Did you ever come to blows with Julius?"

"No, I didn't."

"Do you remember an incident when you were sitting in the corner candy store at Houston [Street] and Avenue D when your brother Bernie had to separate the both of you?"

"It slipped my mind."

"What slipped your mind?"

"I mean I didn't remember it."

"Do you remember it now?"

"I do."

"You do. Did you hit Julius?"

"I—I don't recall if I actually hit him."

"Subsequent to that," Kaufman asked, "had you patched things up?"

"Certainly," David replied. "We were very friendly after that."

David tried to put his relationship with Julius in some perspective. Yes, there were arguments, in particular the ongoing contention about getting Julius to sign a promissory note in return for David's stock in the business. "I mean we had some heated words about it, but we still weren't at each other's throats about it," David said.

———

At 12:10 P.M., the prosecution called Ruth Greenglass. She was the government's fourth witness, a self-possessed brunette whose hair was swept back in a large bun. It rested securely on the nape of her neck, just touching the high collar of her severe black dress. *The New York Times*, taking extraordinary liberties, described her as buxom. Ruth was a motormouth in ordinary conversation. Today, she was in high gear, practically sputtering out her responses, as if she had waited a long time for this moment or couldn't wait for it to be over.

"Madam, could you sit back," the judge asked.

"Yes, I am sorry."

"And just speak a little slower, please."

James Kilsheimer, Saypol's twenty-nine-year-old assistant, guided Ruth through her personal introduction to the jury, then turned abruptly to November 1944 and the conversation in the Rosenbergs' apartment before she left for Albuquerque. She testified in vivid detail, recalling her surprise that Julius knew what David was working on at Los Alamos:

I asked him how he knew, because I had received an affidavit from the War Department telling me . . . that my mail to David would be censored and his to me, because he was working on a top secret project.

And he said—I wanted to know how he knew what David was doing. He said that his friends had told him that David was working on the atomic bomb, and he went on to tell me that the atomic bomb was the most destructive weapon used so far, that it had dangerous radiation effects, that the United States and Britain were working on this project jointly and that he felt that the information should be shared with Russia, who was our ally at the time, because if all nations had the information then one nation couldn't use the bomb as a threat against another. He said that he wanted me to tell my husband David that he should give information to Julius to be passed on to the Russians. At first I objected to this. I didn't think it was right. I said that the people who are in charge of the work on the bomb were in a better position to know whether the information should be shared or not. Ethel Rosenberg said that I should at least tell it to David, that she felt that this was right for David, that he would want it, that I should give him the message and let him decide for himself, and by the—Julius and Ethel persuaded me to give my husband the message and they told me the information—

"I move to strike it out," Manny Bloch said.

"All right," Kaufman concurred. "Strike out the word 'persuaded.' As a result of this conversation you decided to give your husband—"

I decided to give my husband the message, and Julius Rosenberg told me the things that he wanted me to ask my husband, the information that he wanted me to bring back. He wanted a physical description of the project at Los Alamos, the approximate number of people employed, the names of some of the scientists who were working there— something about whether the place was camouflaged, what the security measures were and the relative distance of the project to Albuquerque and Santa Fe. Oh—and he told me—I am sorry—he told me also to tell David to be very circumspect not to indulge in any political conversations and to be very careful not to take any papers or sketches or blueprints, not to be obvious in seeking information, to relate to me only what he retained in his memory. . . . My husband did not give me an immediate answer; at first, he, too, refused, and the following day he told me that he would consent to do this.

Then, Ruth recalled a discussion with Ethel at the Rosenbergs' apartment in January 1945. After dinner, David and Julius discussed how to detonate an atomic bomb. Ruth engaged her sister-in-law in a separate conversation:

Well, Ethel said that she was tired, and I asked her what she had been doing. She said she had been typing; and I asked her if she had found David's notes hard to distinguish. She said no, she was used to his handwriting. Then she said that Julius, too, was tired; that he was very busy; he ran around a good deal; that all his time and his energies were used in this thing; that was the most important thing to him; that he was away a good deal and spent time with his friends; that he had to make a good impression; that it sometimes cost him as much as $50 to $75 an evening to entertain his friends. And then we spoke further, I said that I expected to be very lonely in Albuquerque, and Ethel said that I would make friends; that after a while I would probably meet other people there from New York.

Ruth also recalled that Julius joined in the conversation after she expressed concern about whether or not she would find work in New Mexico: "I said that I was worried, I had just lost my job and I didn't know how I was going to manage to live until David should find a place for me to live in Albuquerque; and Julius said not to worry about that, that he would take care of my expenses; the money was no object; the important thing was for me to go to Albuquerque to live."

When Kilsheimer asked Ruth whether Julius considered the money a loan, Ruth replied: "No—yes, he did. He said that from then on we had a different understanding; any money that he gave us was a gift; he was not lending it to us; there was no question of returning it." Nor, Ruth said, did Julius ever ask to be repaid for the $150 he had given her before she had gone to Albuquerque in November. Then, Judge Kaufman inquired as to whether Ruth ever asked Julius directly where the money was coming from.

"Yes, later on I did."
    "What did he tell you?"
    "From his friends."
    "Did he tell you who the friends were?"
    "Well, in another conversation he did."
    "Who did he say they were?"
    "The Russians."

Kilsheimer directed Ruth to David's September 1945 leave in New York. Ruth testified that the morning after they arrived from New Mexico, Julius woke them up and asked for whatever information David had immediately:

"And what occurred after Rosenberg left your house?"
    "I did not want him to give the information to Julius. The bomb had already been dropped on Hiroshima and I realized exactly what it was and I didn't feel that the information should be passed on. However, David said that he was going to give it to him again, and before he wrote out the information we went down to eat first."

"Now what occurred in the Rosenbergs' apartment on that afternoon in September of 1945?"

"David gave Julius the written information. Julius said he was very pleased to get it and he went into another room to read it over, and after he wrote it he said this had to be gotten out immediately and he wanted to type it right away."

"After he wrote it?" Kaufman asked.

"After he read it, I am sorry. And Ethel got out a typewriter and sat down to work on the notes."

"On what type of a typewriter was it?" Kaufman continued. "I mean, was it a standard model or a portable model or what?"

"It was a portable—I believe it was a Remington."

"And where was the typewriter placed?"

"On the bridge table."

"All right. Now what occurred after the typewriter was placed on the bridge table?"

"Well, Ethel was typing the notes and David was helping her when she couldn't make out his handwriting and explained the technical terms and spelled them out for her, and Julius and I helped her with the phraseology when it got a little too lengthy, wordy."

Kilsheimer asked Ruth about Julius's assurances in 1950 that fleeing the United States would not be calamitous or particularly disruptive:

"I said, 'We can't go anywhere. We have a 10-day old infant'; and Julius said, 'Your baby won't die. Babies are born on the ocean and on trains every day.' He said, 'My doctor said if you take enough canned milk and boil the water, the baby will be all right.'"

"Did Julius Rosenberg tell you where you should go?"

"Yes."

"Where did he tell you that you should go to?"

"To the Soviet Union."

"Was anything else said concerning arrangements for leaving?"

"Yes. He gave my husband a thousand dollars. He said, 'Buy everything you need. Don't be too obvious in your spending. You have a month to spend it in, and I will bring you more.' He said, 'Leave all your household effects. Just take your clothing and what you need for the children and leave.'"

—

Alexander Bloch began his cross-examination of Ruth by trying, as Manny Bloch had with David, to pinpoint when the Greenglasses realized they had done something wrong. Alexander Bloch took Ruth back to early 1950, trying to amplify David's account of Agent Spillane's visit. Ruth stymied Bloch, wriggling out of every rhetorical dead end.

"Were you frightened by the call of that F.B.I. man?"
"Yes."
"You were frightened because you knew you had committed a crime?"
"No."
"Did you then realize that you had committed a crime?"
"No."
"Do you realize today that you had committed a crime?"
"I don't know what is legally a crime. I don't think I am in a position to say."
"Do you think that acting as a spy against the interests of the United States is a crime?"
"I think it is wrong."
"It is wrong?"
"Yes."
"When did you first realize that it was wrong?"
"I have always known it was wrong."
"Why were you frightened?"
"I think everyone is apprehensive when the F.B.I. interviews them."

Ruth said she didn't recall that the Greenglasses considered confessing to espionage when Agent Spillane came calling at their apartment.

"I don't recall that."

"You have no recollection of that?"

"No."

"You have a pretty good memory haven't you?"

"In some things."

Bloch asked Ruth about her state of mind at the time Julius urged the Greenglasses to flee, as well as at the time they noticed they were under surveillance. He asked whether David and Ruth discussed what they would do if either was arrested. Ruth replied that she didn't think the FBI was really after either one of them.

"I thought the F.B.I. was leading to somebody other than my husband," Ruth said, "that they wanted somebody much more important than he."

"So you were talking about your husband leading to somebody else?"

"Well, we weren't going around and leading the F.B.I. to anybody else. I thought that they wanted someone with whom my husband had been involved who was more important than he, who had been involved more deeply than he."

"So you thought your husband would go scot free because he could lead to someone else?"

"I didn't think so but I didn't want my husband ever to be arrested."

"Did you think that your husband would never be arrested?"

"I hoped he wouldn't."

"And the same hope was applicable to you?"

"Yes."

"Did you at any time for years prior to June 1950 worry about this thing that you had done and the thing that your husband had done?"

"Yes."

"Were you afraid of punishment?"

"I was afraid of the story coming out."

"Well, did you ever talk it over with your husband and tell your husband, 'In the event of your being arrested or my being arrested, we are going to go to the District Attorney and tell him certain things which will lead to somebody else'?"

"I told my husband in 1946 that I wanted to go to the F.B.I. with the story. However, there had been nothing happening, everything was very peaceful and we thought perhaps it would die down and the thing would never come to light, so we did nothing about it."

"And you were at peace and calm about it?"

"I was not calm."

"Well, what was the cause of the absence of calm on your part?"

"It's not easy to live with something that you know is wrong."

"Well, when you say you know it's wrong, was it wrong in your opinion morally?"

"I felt that we had taken something into our hands that we were not equipped to handle with, we were tampering with things that were beyond our knowledge and understanding, yes."

"Did your husband ever tell you that the thing he was doing and the thing you were doing, that is, spying, was a crime?"

"We didn't discuss it from that standpoint."

"Never discussed it at all?"

"Oh, we discussed it but not that way."

"In what way did you discuss it?"

"Well, I had felt that it was wrong; I didn't think that he should have done it to begin with but my husband felt he wanted to and as his wife I went along with him."

"Do you remember the payment of $500 that you received?"

"I do."

"Where was that turned over to you?"

"In Albuquerque, New Mexico."

"And you knew that that $500 was paid to your husband by Gold?"

"From Julius."

"And you knew that that was compensation for spy work?"

"That was the first time I knew it."

"That is the first time you knew that your husband was being paid?"

"No, I was under the impression at first that Julius said it was for scientific purposes we were sharing the information, but when my husband got the $500, I realized it was just C.O.D.; he gave the information and he got paid."

"Well," Kaufman asked, "would your position in the matter be stated accurately if I stated that you believed you would be punished but hoped you wouldn't be?"

"Yes. He is my husband. I didn't want to see him punished."

"How about yourself?" Alexander Bloch asked.

"Does anyone want to punish himself?"

"I didn't hear that."

"Does anyone want to punish himself?"

"You were very anxious to escape punishment here, were you not?"

"Yes."

—

On Thursday, Alexander Bloch began probing more deeply the deteriorating relationship between the Greenglasses and the Rosenbergs. After Steven was born in 1946, Ruth said, she visited Julius and Ethel "very infrequently." What about that console table, the one that Julius supposedly had modified for spy photography? Hadn't Ruth just testified for the prosecution that she had seen the table in the Rosenbergs' apartment in 1949? *

"I say either in 1948 or 1949," she replied.

"Now," Bloch asked, "didn't something happen in the beginning of 1949 and the end of 1949 that created hostility between you and the Rosenbergs?"

"No, there was no hostility."

The same could not be said about the repartee between Ruth and Alexander Bloch. Finally, she acknowledged that while there hadn't been arguments over the management of the machine shop, there had been discussions about it:

---

* On July 15, 1950, Ruth told the FBI that, after the war, Julius had offered the Greenglasses an apartment on Avenue B in which there was a drop-leaf table outfitted with clamps that Julius used "to do photographic work in his espionage activity." Agents Norton and Harrington, who went twice to the Knickerbocker Village apartment, first to question Julius and later to arrest him, did not recall ever seeing a drop-leaf or console table there. An August 5, 1950, report by Agents Frutkin and Lewis, based on four interviews with David, does not mention any console table in his statements, although the agents said that David recalled that Julius had a drop-leaf table in his apartment that was equipped to hold a Leica camera.

"Well, over a period of time Ethel Rosenberg had been complaining that David and Bernie were not paying attention to the shop, that Julius was doing all the work, working hard, David and Bernie weren't keeping the proper hours, and they were wasting their time in talking where Julius was coming in there in the morning hours, that they were coming in at 10 or 10:30, and he was sick a great deal of time and he was tired of the whole business.

"I said I didn't think my husband was being paid commensurate with the work done."

"And did you also complain to members of the family that your husband was losing his investment in that business?"

"I don't think I did."

"Well, was he losing his investment in that business?"

"We lost everything in that business."

"Well, aren't you a bit angry at either Mr. or Mrs. Rosenberg because they did not pay you what you think you were entitled to?"

"I don't think I am angry. I just can't understand their actions because there was a debt due."

"You are not angry?"

"No, I am not angry. I just can't understand people who do not pay their debts, Mr. Bloch."

"And you resent it?"

"I don't think I resented it. I couldn't understand why [I] wasn't being paid for what was rightfully mine."

"And you do not resent it now either?"

"Would I get anything with resentment?"

"Well, I am asking you whether you resent it now?"

"No."

Pressed by Manny Bloch, Ruth recalled a family conference at Sheriff Street, just before the Greenglass brothers went into business with Julius Rosenberg. Tessie was there, too.

"Did you tell Julius Rosenberg that you thought your husband wasn't getting enough salary?" Bloch asked.

"I can't answer that just that way, Mr. Bloch. Julius Rosenberg told me in 1947 that he didn't care whether the business was a success or not, and I was very enraged. I said that David and Bernie had put all their earnings into that business. To them it meant something; they were earning a living, and he said he didn't care because he could get $10,000 or $15,000 as a front for any business for his activities."

"Isn't it a fact that one of the complaints that was made by Julius Rosenberg against your husband was that he, Julius Rosenberg, was working too hard and that your husband was loafing on the job?"

"That is an untruth."

"Whether it is an untruth or not, did he make that complaint?"

"He complained about a great many things."

"I am asking you, Mrs. Greenglass, whether he complained specifically about this?"

"I want to say this: when they went into this thing my husband was the one who was going to teach other employees under the GI Bill of Rights, under the work and training program—he was going to teach them the work and train them to be machinists. Julius's job was to solicit business. He could hardly say that my husband was loafing. Julius was not working on machines. Only on occasions; he wasn't steadily at the machines in 1946 and 1947."

"Julius wasn't?"

"No."

"Julius wasn't a machinist?"

"But he claimed to be a big engineer."

"As a matter of fact, Julius was the one who went out and tried to get business?"

"So he couldn't say that my husband was loafing. If he got the business David produced it."

"Maybe you misunderstand me. I am not trying to say that your husband may not have had a justifiable grievance. All we are trying to find out is whether Julius Rosenberg complained that your husband was loafing, that is all."

"I didn't say my husband had a grievance. I said Julius complained. He complained about so many things."

"And amongst the other things that he complained of was the fact that your husband David would disappear from the business during the day and go home and help you with the household duties, isn't that correct?"

"That is ridiculous. He came home for lunch."

Judge Kaufman interjected: "Now you are missing the point. He is asking you whether Rosenberg ever said that; not whether it is true, but whether Rosenberg ever said that."

"Yes, he said it."

Manny Bloch completed his cross-examination of Ruth, then conferred briefly with his father.

"My dad points out just one question which he thinks I overlooked. Were you told by Julius Rosenberg on May 24, 1950, that he couldn't give you any money on the claim that your husband made against him for the disposition of the stock, because he had given [David] Schein $1,000 and he didn't have any more cash at hand?"

"No, my husband didn't ask for payment on his stock. Julius Rosenberg said that he would bring my husband $6,000 more. That was not coming from the business, Mr. Bloch."

"Who was it coming from?" Kaufman asked.

"From the Russians," Ruth replied, "for us to leave the country."

—

The prosecution summoned Ruth's sister, Dorothy Abel, and her husband, Louis, to flesh out details of the Greenglasses' testimony. Then Myles Lane, Saypol's forty-two-year-old chief assistant, called Harry Gold.

Prompted by Lane, Gold recounted his instructions from Anatoly Yakovlev before meeting the Greenglasses in New Mexico. He described his two brief encounters with David and Ruth at the Albuquerque apartment. Regardless of whether he delivered "greetings from Julius" to the Greenglasses, as he testified, or from anyone else, he acknowledged that he had never met the Rosenbergs. But his testimony about the Jell-O box established a seamless link between Julius and Yakovlev. Despite abundant evidence suggesting that Harry was endowed with an agile imagination, the defense declined to cross-examine him.

The judge adjourned the trial so Saypol could attend his son's wedding Monday afternoon. On Tuesday, the trial entered its third week with a cameo appearance by Elizabeth Bentley, the celebrated Red Spy Queen. She testified that among her sources was a telephone contact who identified himself only as "Julius" and who lived in Knickerbocker Village.

On Wednesday afternoon, March 21, the government rested its case.

Chapter 29

≡≡≡

The Defense

"Julie, I am in a terrible jam."

≡

Manny Bloch called Julius Rosenberg for the defense.

Julius seemed largely at ease, with his legs crossed and his hands clasped. He wore an unassuming gray suit and white shirt, which accentuated his gaudy silver-and-maroon tie. Bloch elicited the requisite professional and personal history from Julius, spending what seemed like a disproportionate amount of time on the furnishings in the Rosenbergs' apartment. Then, Bloch invited Julius to refute, point by point, the Greenglasses' testimony.

No, he never gave Ruth Greenglass even one single penny. He never received secret information from her. He never saw sketches of lens molds or anything resembling lens molds until the government introduced them as evidence. Time and again, Julius unwaveringly dismissed Bloch's wordy regurgitation of each and every Greenglass accusation with the same three unadorned words.

"Did you know in the middle of November 1944 where Dave Greenglass was stationed?"

"I did not."

"Did you know in the middle of November 1944 that there was such a project known as the Los Alamos Project?"

"I did not."

"Located in New Mexico?"

"I did not."

The questions became more complex. Julius's answers required more elaboration. Judge Kaufman, who had insisted that communism was not on trial, kept pressing Julius to define his political philosophy, or, as Kaufman put it, "the respective preferences of economic systems between Russia and the United States." Julius explained that he was not an expert on comparative economics, and, while he owed his allegiance to the United States,

> I felt that the Soviet government has improved the lot of the underdog there, has made a lot of progress in eliminating illiteracy, has done a lot of reconstruction work and built up a lot of resources, and at the same time I felt that they contributed a major share in destroying the Hitler beast who killed six million of my co-religionists, and I feel emotional about that thing. . . . My personal opinions are that the people of every country should decide by themselves what kind of government they want. If the English want a king, it is their business. If the Russians want communism, it is their business.

Kaufman wouldn't relent: "Well, did you ever belong to any group that discussed the system of Russia?"

"Well, Your Honor, if you are referring to political groups—is that what you are referring to?"

"Any group."

"Well, Your Honor, I feel at this time that I refuse to answer a question that might tend to incriminate me."

—

Julius and Ethel had received conflicting advice from their lawyers but decided jointly to invoke their Fifth Amendment right against self-incrimination when they were asked about their affiliation with the Communist Party or any of its subsidiaries. It was a calculated risk, and they miscalculated. No matter what the judge said, no confessed communist could plausibly expect to receive the benefit of the doubt. To be sure, denying membership in the party might subject them to perjury charges, which, at the time, might have seemed like a more immediate threat than the death penalty. But no matter what the Constitution said, the jury would assume that the Rosenbergs' refusal to testify freely must mean they had something to hide. Ethel's claim of constitutional privilege during her grand-jury testimony also was held against her. Gloria Agrin, who assisted in the defense, explained later: "They were communists but they were afraid that if they admitted it they would be questioned about their communist connections, and be asked to implicate others, and be cited for contempt of court."

Manny Bloch rescued Julius from Kaufman's colloquy on theoretical politics and returned to the Rosenbergs' dinner at their apartment with David and Ruth in January 1945. Julius resumed his three-word mantra:

"Did you ever have any transaction with the Greenglasses in which a Jell-O box was involved?"

"I did not."

"Did you know anything about the atom bomb at that time?"

"I did not."

"Did you discuss politics with them that night?"

"Well, as every intelligent American did in those times, we discussed the war."

Saypol interrupted. He asked that the answer be stricken as unresponsive. Bloch consented, until Saypol added gratuitously, "I don't want this man set up as a standard for intelligent Americans," to which Bloch objected. Kaufman was Solomonic. "Disregard Mr. Saypol's statement," the judge ruled, "and strike from the record 'intelligent Americans.'"

Next, Bloch asked Julius to recount his meeting with Ruth before she moved to Albuquerque. Julius's stilted account contradicted Ruth's but allowed for enough leeway to square with the version delivered by Dorothy Abel:

> When I entered the apartment she whispered in my ear, "I would like to talk to you alone. Tell the kid to go into the bathroom." . . . Ruthie told me something to this effect: "Julius, I am terribly worried. David has an idea to make some money and take some things from the Army"; and I told her, "Warn David not to do anything foolish. He will only get himself in trouble. I have read some accounts in the newspapers about some GI's doing foolish things and taking parts and gasoline from the Army, and their getting themselves in trouble," and I told her, "Don't tell—make sure to tell him that he doesn't do anything of the sort."

Bloch asked Julius whether he had ever seen a copy of David's sketch of a cross section of the atomic bomb, but the court clerk reminded Bloch that the sketch had been impounded at the defense's request. As a result, the man accused of delivering the original sketch to the Russians five years earlier wasn't allowed to inspect a replica during his own trial. In any case, Julius said, he never received any such sketch from David, nor did Ethel ever type David's handwritten description of the bomb. Again, the judge interjected:

> **"Is your wife a typist?"**
> "Yes, she is."
> **"Do you have a typewriter at home?"**
> "That is right."
> **"What sort of typing did your wife do at the house in 1944, if any?"**
> "I don't recall her doing the typing at the house at all."
> **"How about 1945?"**
> "1945, too."

Ethel typed only, Julius explained, if he needed a letter for business or for a job or for his union or the East Side civil-defense council, to which she belonged.

Manny Bloch resumed his examination.

"Did you ever take any material that was ever transmitted to you by Dave or Ruth Greenglass and turn it over to the Russians or anybody else?"

"No, I did not."

The judge requested a clarification. "Did you know any Russians at that time?" he asked. "By Russians, I mean people who were Russian citizens."

"You mean citizens of Russia?"

"That is correct."

"No, I didn't."

"Didn't know any at all?"

"None at all."

Bloch extracted only one admission from his client. Showing Julius the brown-paper wrapper that had allegedly contained the four thousand dollars, he asked:

"Now there is Scotch tape there. Did you ever put any Scotch tape on a wrapper like that?"

"No," Julius replied, "but I have used Scotch tape."

He denied urging David to enroll in MIT or any other college in that league. It would defy logic, he said: "It was very unlikely that I could suggest it because he probably couldn't get into those places. He didn't have the qualifications."

What about the "sky platform" project? Julius dismissed that, too, with a plausible denial:

"I don't remember the specific incident but at that time in the *Popular Science* magazines and in the newspapers there was some talk about the Germans had done some work on some kind of suspended lens in the sky to concentrate the rays of the sun at the earth, and that is what I believe was the discussion we might have had at that time. Greenglass used to read the *Popular Mechanics* and the *Popular Science* and he always talked about things like that at the shop."

"Did you ever say at that time that you got the information from one of your boys?"

"I did not."

Prompted by Bloch, Julius delivered a glib and self-assured spin on the financial conflicts with his brother-in-law and their deteriorating personal relationship.

"Well, about the middle of May, I can't tell the exact date, David came to my shop one morning. He came into my office. I was sitting in my office, and he said, 'Come on outside, I want to talk to you.' I said, 'Look, Dave, I got to conduct my business. Let us talk here.' He said, 'No, it is important. Let us go outside.' Well, I walked outside of the shop with him."

"Tell us about the conversation you had," Bloch asked.

Dave said to me as follows: "Julie, you got to get me $2,000. I need it at once." I said, "Look, Dave, you know the arrangements I made with you. I obligated myself to Dave Schein. I gave him a down payment of $1,000. I have no cash left. You can't get blood out of a stone. I just don't have the money. What do you want it for?" He said, "I need the money. Don't ask me questions." I said, "Dave, you are getting very excited. What is the matter with you?"

According to Julius, David said that the least Julius could do was ask his doctor to certify that David had received a smallpox vaccination and to ask what other shots were needed to enter Mexico. The judge interjected:

"Now, up to that time you had been having some heated arguments, as you call it, heated arguments with David, and I take it you were not particularly friendly with him then, were you?"

"Well, I would say this: that I was not antagonistic to him. He was my wife's brother."

"But you were not friendly. That friendship had been strained."

"Yes, there was strain."

"Can you think of any reason why on this occasion he would come to you and confess to you and ask you to help him out instead of going to somebody else?"

"I have no idea why he came to me."

"You didn't attempt to ascertain from any other source or have anybody else like your wife talk to her brother to find out what was wrong?"

"Well, that night when I came home I told my wife about the incident and my wife told me, 'What is the matter? Is Ruthie nagging Dave again for money?' I said, 'No, it doesn't seem to be that. He must be in some trouble. I don't know what it is.' And I recall at that time in my mind the incident—the instant he told me what happened to him in February [sic] when the F.B.I. had come around to visit him and question him about some uranium, I thought maybe it had something to do with that or had something to do with a conversation Ruthie had with me many years back."

After still another furtive conversation with David, Julius said he confided in Ethel: "Your brother is in some trouble; he is acting peculiar and strange and I don't know what to do about it; and you know that he has had it in for me and our relations haven't been the best."

A few days later, Julius recalled, David summoned him urgently to the Greenglasses' apartment. David was shirtless. He looked haggard. Something must be very wrong, Julius assumed, because David said, "We will go downstairs without having any breakfast."

"Julie, I am in a terrible jam," David said, according to Julius. He needed a few thousand dollars in cash. "Well, Julie, I just got to have that money and if you don't get me that money you are going to be sorry."

"I said, 'Look here, Dave, what are you trying to do, threaten me or blackmail me?'"

David was "puffing and I saw a wild look in his eyes," Julius testified. He suggested that David go home and take a cold shower. "I was afraid that he might do me bodily harm," Julius said. Still, he explained, Ethel prevailed upon him to drop by the Greenglasses' apartment again:

Well, I didn't have a chance to go over the next day—it must have been a day or two after, I dropped in on the Greenglasses and they just got up that morning and I remember sitting down at the kitchen table and

Ruthie said, "Hello," to me and I looked at the baby—I went into the bedroom and looked at the baby, and I noticed everybody was cool to me and I didn't want to bring the subject up in Ruthie's presence—I did not even know if she was aware of Davey's trouble, I did not want to aggravate her. I saw that Davey was calmer at this point and wasn't going to do anything rash so I picked myself up after a few minutes and left the apartment.

That is the last time that I saw Dave Greenglass.[*]

"And you can't think of any reason whatsoever," Judge Kaufman asked, "can you, why Dave Greenglass would, of all people he knew, his brother, all the other members of his family, single you out, as he did apparently and as you say he did, and say that you would be sorry unless you gave him the money?"

"Well, he knew that I owed—he had an idea that I owed him money from the business, and I guess that is what he figured[:] he wanted to get the money from me."

———

Outside the courthouse, the lunch break was interrupted by a commotion as Alger Hiss surrendered to begin serving his five-year sentence for perjury. He was herded into a U.S. marshal's van and shackled to a mail thief.

After lunch, Bloch asked Julius to reconstruct his first brush with the FBI, after agents knocked on his door the previous June 16.

"I went into the bathroom with my wife and asked her, 'Do you think I ought to talk to these gentlemen?'" Julius testified. "She said, 'You know, if Davey is in some sort of trouble, if you can help my brother, talk to them.'"

Julius said he was cooperative until the agents announced that David had implicated him in espionage.

"So I said, 'That couldn't be so.' So, I said, 'Where is David Green-

---

[*] Presumably, Julius meant this was the last time he conversed with David.

glass?' I didn't know where he was because I knew he was taken in custody. They wouldn't tell me. I said, 'Will you bring him here and let him tell me that to my face?' And they said, 'What if we bring him here, what will you do?' 'I will call him a liar to his face because that is not so.'"

———

With only one hour left until court was to adjourn for Good Friday, Saypol began his cross-examination with a bang, literally. Julius had denied collecting money for the Joint Anti-Fascist Refugee Committee, but Saypol produced one of the committee's collection cans, which had been seized in the Rosenbergs' apartment.* He set it down on the jury-box rail with a convincing thud. Julius insisted repeatedly that he was a patriotic American. Responding to persistent questioning from Saypol and Kaufman about dual loyalty to the Communist Party, he again invoked his constitutional right against self-incrimination.

———

After court, Louis Schaeffer of the *Jewish Daily Forward* informed Saypol that Tessie Greenglass was "aroused" by Julius's misstatements on the stand and demanded an opportunity to refute them. Saypol arranged to interview Tessie on Saturday morning, March 24. Whatever she told Saypol, he decided against calling her as a witness for the prosecution.

———

On Monday, Saypol resumed his cross-examination. Why, he demanded, would Julius go into business after the war with a man who, according to Julius, had "larcenous ideas" about stealing from the army?

"David Greenglass talked about a lot of things," Julius replied. "He used to boast about things. I don't know if he really did a thing like that, or just talked about it."

---

* The can, emblazoned with the appeal to "Save a Spanish Republican Child," also bore a New York City Welfare Department seal authorizing solicitations.

"Did you tell the agents about that when they interviewed you on June 16?" Saypol inquired.

"They didn't ask me about that."

"Did you think you should have volunteered it to them?"

"Well," Julius replied pointedly, "when a member of the family is in trouble, Mr. Saypol, you are not interested in sinking him."

"Were you trying to protect him at that time?" Kaufman asked.

"Well, I didn't know what he was accused of, Your Honor. I had a suspicion he was accused of stealing some uranium at that time."

"Well, in connection with that, were you interested in protecting him?"

"I wasn't interested in doing him any harm at that particular point."

"Were you interested in protecting him, I asked you."

"Well, I felt that when a man is in trouble, the one thing his family should do is stick by the man, regardless of the trouble he is in."

Resuming his jousting, Saypol hurled daggers at Julius's politics and challenged his earlier claims that the Soviets had progressed under communism. What were his sources? How did he know the Soviet government has improved the lot of the underdog? What newspapers did he read that in?

"Various newspapers."

"You mean, *The Daily Worker*?"

"On occasion; *The New York Times*."

"Any others?"

"Yes."

"What others?"

"The *Herald Tribune,* the *World Telegram.*"

"*The Wall Street Journal,* perhaps?" Saypol baited.

"No, I don't read *The Wall Street Journal.*"

Saypol again delved into Julius's relationship with David. Their familial bond had deteriorated by 1948, when David enrolled in night school at Pratt and neglected the machine shop, Julius testified: "We had arguments continuously on the business." Saypol opened the door for Julius to deliver a stinging slap at Ruth.

"Now when you told Ruthie about it, what did she say?"

She said I was taking advantage of him; I was trying to make him a menial. I was trying to treat him like a worker and not a partner. As a matter of fact, we had so many arguments concerning his technical ability that at one point in the business I had to hire a foreman over him, and he told me in many words after that, "How do you think I felt, Julie, when I had to work for my own worker?" I told him, "Well, if you keep on producing rejects and losing money in the business and you don't know how to handle the men, we will never make a living."

By the way, Mr. Saypol, all these heated discussions about the stock and the resignation were mainly prompted by his wife. She was the one who kept agitating for these discussions.

Saypol acidly belittled Julius's account of his May 1950 conversation with David in Hamilton Fish Park, when he said that David had demanded two thousand dollars and had asked if Julius could obtain a smallpox-vaccination certificate. Saypol's cross-examination exposed a daredevil leap of logic that was to prove fatal.

"What did you think, he had smallpox?"

"No, I didn't think so."

"What could he do with $2,000 assuming he had smallpox. Did he tell you?"

"No, he didn't tell me."

Saypol then plowed through what appeared to be a potentially major paradox in Julius's testimony, that David's threats against him amounted to blackmail.

"What did he say he would do if you didn't give it to him? You said he said you would be sorry."

"Yes," Julius replied. "I consider it blackmail when someone says that."

"Did he say what he would do to you?"

"No, he didn't."

"Did he say he would go to the authorities and tell them you were in a conspiracy with him to steal the atomic bomb secret?"

"No."

"Do you think that was what he had in mind?"

"How could I know what he had in mind?"

"What do you mean by blackmail then?"

"Maybe he threatened to punch me in the nose or something like that," Julius replied lamely.

Kaufman asked whether Julius reported David's threats to the agents who questioned him in June 1950.

"I did not, sir."

"What was the reason for not telling them that?"

"The way I was brought up," Julius replied gamely. "I don't inform on my wife's brother, and whatever he did, I didn't know about and that is for him to decide, for him to answer."

—

The defense called Ethel Rosenberg. She testified only briefly before court adjourned for the day, but it was long enough to leave an impression. Her diminutiveness had already been much remarked upon, as well as her apparent placidity and stoicism. She wore a black skirt and, perhaps defiantly, a pink blouse, and she performed to stereotype: bloodless, not a warm, cuddly mom whom no juror would dream of executing. The most expression she displayed was to wrinkle her brow and knot her fingers frequently, as David did. Like Julius, she repeatedly cloaked herself in the Fifth Amendment in response to questions about communism.

On Tuesday morning, Alexander Bloch elicited from Ethel a conversation she had in July 1950 with Ruth, who had just visited David in jail. They picked the Greenglasses' daughter, Barbara, up at Ruth's parents' house, placed her in the carriage, and were walking around the block. This was the conversation in which, Ruth said, Ethel had beseeched her, in effect, to let David take the fall and not to cooperate with the prosecutors and the FBI. Ethel's version was altogether different:

I said, "Look, Ruth, I would like to know something: Are you and Davey really mixed up in this horrible mess?" First, she hesitated. So I said to her, in order to encourage it, in order to encourage her, "You know how I feel towards Davey. You know how I always felt towards him and how I have always felt toward you, although I must say that you people haven't always reciprocated, especially in the last year. However, that is besides the point. I want you to know that even if you did do this, and Davey, my attitude towards you and my feelings toward you won't change. I will stand by and help in any way that I possibly can. But I am his sister and I do have a right to know."

At that she flared up and she said, "What are you asking such silly questions for? He is not guilty and of course I am not guilty and we have hired a lawyer and we are going to fight this case because we are not guilty. Did you think we were?"

And I said, "Look, I really didn't know what to think any more. There have been reports in the newspapers about confessions and much as I believe, always believed in Davey, I really began to wonder. I had to hear it from your own lips."

And she said, "Well, now you have heard it and it is the truth. Neither of us is guilty."

Time and again, the judge played prosecutor, eagerly plugging strategic gaps in the government's case. He had reminded the jury more than once that communism wasn't on trial, but he pounced on conflicting loyalties as a possible motive.

"Well, what were your own views about the subject matter of the United States having any weapon that Russia didn't have at that time? That is, in 1944 and 1945?"

"I don't recall having any views at all about it."

"Your mind was a blank on the subject?"

"Absolutely."

Alexander Bloch asked about Ethel's relationship with her baby brother.

"Did you love him?"

"Yes, I loved him very much."

"Did he sort of look up to you?" the judge asked.

"Yes."

"And your husband. Before the arguments that were discussed here in court?"

"He liked us both. He liked my husband."

"Sort of hero worship?"

"Oh," Ethel scoffed, "by no stretch of the imagination could you say that was hero worship."

Like Julius, Ethel testified that she had never participated in espionage, never typed information concerning the atomic bomb, never even knew a single Russian personally. She also corroborated Julius's account of his concerns about David's desperation:

"I said to my husband, 'Well, doesn't he know the kind of financial situation we are in? Didn't you tell him you can't give him money like that?' And then I remember saying something to the effect that 'If Ruthie doesn't stop nagging him for money, she is liable to give him another psychological heart attack like he had in the winter.'"

———

Saypol's cross-examination was unforgiving. He sought to ensnare Ethel with her own words, reading from the transcript question after question that she had refused to answer before the grand jury and suggesting that if she wasn't guilty she should not be afraid of incriminating herself. He was completely unmoved by Ethel's exculpatory trial testimony, couching every question as damning, regardless of her answer.

"A little while ago you said you did everything to help Davey, do you remember that?" Saypol asked, insinuating for just a moment that he was exploring a sister's loyalty to her baby brother.

"Yes," Ethel replied noncommittally.

"Did you help him join the Communist Party?"

———

Ethel recalled that before she was arrested the previous August, she had visited the Federal Detention Center on West Street, where Julius told her that he had encountered David during their rooftop recreation time.

David was hostile and, according to Julius, told officials: "If he comes anywhere near me I will knock his head off."

"You profess a love for your brother, don't you?" Saypol asked.

"You mean I once had a love for my brother."

"You mean that that has changed?"

"I would be pretty unnatural," Ethel replied, "if it hadn't changed."

—

The Rosenberg defense rested.

The government called three rebuttal witnesses. One was Evelyn Cox, who had been the Rosenbergs' housekeeper in 1944 and 1945. She remembered the console table and testified that Ethel said "a friend of her husband gave it to him as a gift."

Another was Ben Schneider, a professional photographer. Even after the trial began, agents were still pursuing loose ends, including Ruth's recollection that the Greenglasses had posed for passport photos—maybe the Rosenbergs had, too. The FBI didn't find Schneider until the day before he took the stand. Agents showed him photographs of the Rosenbergs. He recognized Julius but not Ethel, although he recalled that the man in the photograph was accompanied by a woman and two small children. At Saypol's request, according to an FBI memo, Schneider was brought surreptitiously into the courtroom. Julius was testifying at that moment; Schneider positively identified him to federal agents. Later, when Ethel was sparring with Saypol, Schneider was returned to the courtroom. He identified her, too. He was shown snapshots of the children but said only that they "looked familiar."

Late on Tuesday, Schneider testified that he remembered the Rosenbergs' visit to his shop a year earlier because he had few other customers that Saturday. Manny Bloch challenged Schneider's recollection, suggesting that perhaps business was better than he remembered.

"Now there are some Saturdays when you do a rather rushing business?" Bloch asked.

"Not a rushing business," Schneider replied.

"Well, a good business?"

"Did you say 'a Russian business,'" Saypol interjected, "or 'rushing business'?"

Schneider said he remembered the Rosenbergs because their two sons were "unruly, sort of," and "I was afraid they would spoil or mess something up and told them to go out and come back in about 20 minutes to a half hour." Julius returned to the shop alone, picked up the photos, and paid Schneider nine dollars.

"And is that the last time you saw him before today?" Saypol asked.

"That's right," Schneider replied.[*]

—

Court began an hour early on Wednesday, March 28, for closing arguments. This was the fifteenth day of a trial that had been expected to last six weeks. The prosecution had produced only twenty-two witnesses of the more than one hundred it had placed on standby, the Rosenberg defense just four (Ethel, Julius, and representatives of Macy's and the *Herald Tribune*).

To the end, Manny Bloch never deviated from his original strategy: to discredit the Greenglasses as self-serving liars; to portray the Rosenbergs as scapegoats who, whatever their political leanings, remained red-blooded American patriots; and, obsequiously and cynically, to appeal to the hubris of a judge who was hard-boiled but wanted to be perceived as fair. The first words of Bloch's summation were to haunt him:

It is usual when you come into a house to say good evening, and it has sprung up in court that there are certain social amenities, certain preliminaries, certain graces that one goes through before one gets into the facts of a case, and I would like to say to the Court on behalf of all defense counsel that we feel that you have treated us with the utmost courtesy, that you have extended to us the privileges that we expect as lawyers, and despite any disagreements we may have had with the

---

[*] The government's third rebuttal witness was Rogge's secretary. She testified that Louis Abel delivered $3,900 in cash to Rogge's office on June 16, 1950.

Court on questions of law, we feel that the trial has been conducted and we hope we have contributed our share, with the dignity and that decorum that befits an American trial.

Echoing his brief opening argument, Bloch declared that the case wasn't about communism or about tensions between the United States and the Soviet Union but about evidence. He reminded the jurors that they were New Yorkers—"We are a pretty sophisticated people. People can't put things over on us very easily"—and described them as lucky:

> You have been fortunate because you have seen unfolded before you one of the most moving dramas that any human being could concoct. You have seen a brother testify against his sister, in a case where her life might be at stake. You have seen issues dealing with the atomic bomb, the most terrible and destructive weapon yet invented by man. This case is packed with drama. Playwrights and movie script writers could do a lot with a case like this. You have been fortunate. You had a front seat.

Exhibit by exhibit, Bloch ridiculed the physical evidence: the jagged Jell-O box; the collection can ("They got him with the goods, with a tin can"); the nominating petition Ethel signed for Peter V. Cacchione. ("Nobody ever accused Peter V. Cacchione of doing anything wrong or illegal while he was a Councilman.")

Fundamentally, Bloch declared, "this is a case of the Greenglasses against the Rosenbergs."

> You know, before I summed up, I wanted to go to a dictionary and I wanted to find a word that could describe a Dave Greenglass. I couldn't find it, because I don't think that there is a word in the English vocabulary or in the dictionary of any civilization which can describe a character like Dave Greenglass.
>
> But one thing I think you do know, that any man who will testify against his own blood and flesh, his own sister, is repulsive, is revolting, who violates every code that any civilization has ever lived by. He is the lowest of the lowest animals that I have ever seen.

I wonder whether in anything that you have read or in anything that you have experienced you have ever come across a man who comes around to bury his own sister and smiles. . . . Is that the kind of a man that you would believe in your own life or would you punch him in the nose and throw him out and have nothing to do with him because he is a low rebel?

And he was arrogant; he was arrogant. He felt he had the Government of the United States behind him. He had a right to be arrogant; he had a right to be arrogant, because I want to say right now that the Greenglasses put it all over the F.B.I. and put it all over Mr. Saypol's staff, and I submit that they are smarter than the whole bunch.

If this is such a terrible crime, and I tell you gentlemen it is a serious crime, a most serious crime, don't you think that the Greenglasses put it over the Government when Ruth Greenglass wasn't even indicted?

Ruth Greenglass got out. She walked out and put her sister-in-law in.

Bloch found David's one redeeming trait, then fashioned it into a weapon:

Maybe I was a little too harsh on Dave Greenglass, because if the human race could produce a Dave Greenglass I am afraid we would all get terribly pessimistic about the future, but there is always something good in every human being, some trait of warmth, of love. Dave Greenglass loved his wife. He loved her more than he loved himself. . . . And, ladies and gentlemen, this explains why Dave Greenglass was willing to bury his sister and his brother-in-law to save his wife.

What about the money from the Russians? They paid off a few household debts and put $500 in the bank as a deposit on a bungalow. David didn't feel any qualms about stealing the money. So, not only are the Greenglasses self-confessed spies but they were mercenary spies. They spied for money. . . . They would do anything for money. They would murder people for money. They are trying to murder people for money.

Now I tell you what the plot of the Greenglasses was here. Twofold. Greenglass figured that if he could put the finger on somebody, he would lessen his own punishment; and he had to put the finger on somebody who was here in the United States, and he had to put the finger on somebody who was a clay pigeon; and that man sitting there is a clay pigeon because he was fired from the Government service, because it was alleged that he was a member of the Communist Party; and he was a guy who was very open and expressed his views about the United States and the Soviet Union, which may have been all right when the Soviet Union and the United States were allies, but today is anathema.

And so Greenglass—and entre nous, I submit that it wasn't Dave Greenglass; I think this part was hatched primarily by Mrs. Ruth Greenglass. I think you can ascertain people; I think she is the smarter of the two—and this is the perfect target, this terrible spy, this big racketeer.

What kind of a man was this? Is this a [Frank] Costello? Is this your concept of a racketeer? Is this your concept of a pay-off man, a man who lived in a Knickerbocker Village apartment at $45 a month . . . whose wife did scrubbing and cleaning and who had two kids, and who had a terrible struggle?

"Now, look at that terrible spy," Bloch said, pointing to Ethel. "Look at that terrible spy and compare her to Ruthie Greenglass, who came here all dolled up, arrogant, smart, cute, eager-beaver, like a phonograph record. . . . Maybe some of you are more acute in sizing up women than others, but if Ruth Greenglass is not the embodiment of evil, I would like to know what person is?"

Bloch praised Julius for trying, "like a schnook," to help a family member in trouble. "Even if he knew that Davey was guilty of the most terrible crime, he would never have squealed on him," Bloch argued, echoing Julius's testimony as well as David's own assessment of his brother-in-law's coda.* A three-month case had petered out in just three weeks. Where were the witnesses that the government had promised? Weighing all of the evidence, the jurors "can come to no other conclu-

---

* Who knows what the Rosenbergs would have done in similar straits? David thought he did. "Julius didn't squeal," David said later. "Ethel wouldn't have named me either."

sion than these defendants are innocent and you are going to show to the world that in America a man can get a fair trial."

—

Edward Kuntz summed up for Morton Sobell, who sat through the trial intrigued by the testimony but largely a spectator. Kuntz reminded the jury that Sobell was not named in even one of the overt acts in the indictment, never worked on the atomic bomb, did not have access to nuclear secrets, and was not accused of stealing any.

After lunch, Saypol began his closing argument with the same pedantic definition of *conspiracy* he had summoned up when he had opened his case. But he methodically stripped away the layers of legal arcana, theatrically building to a stem-winding finale:

> I have said that there is much about this that we have not disclosed or that we do not know, but there is one part of the scheme that we do know about. You know about it because it was disclosed right before you. We know that these conspirators stole the most important scientific secrets ever known to mankind from this country and delivered them to the Soviet Union. We know that Julius Rosenberg and Ethel Rosenberg infected Ruth and David Greenglass with the poison of communist ideology. We know that Julius Rosenberg and Ethel Rosenberg were engaged in a continuing campaign to enlist recruits for the Soviet cause through the Communist Party. And we know that in 1944 Julius and Ethel Rosenberg carried their campaign one step further and persuaded David Greenglass to steal atomic bomb secrets for the Rosenbergs to be turned over to the Soviet Union.

Making few apologies for David and Ruth, Saypol rebutted the defense's rationale point-blank:

> There is no condonation for the activities of the Greenglasses in 1944 and 1945. David Greenglass is a confessed member of the Rosenberg espionage ring. You heard his testimony and you observed him. You heard him confess his guilt. You heard him describe in detail his par-

ticipation in this conspiracy. By his own plea of guilty, by his own voluntary act, without weaving a web of lies in an attempt to deceive you, he has made himself liable to the death penalty, too. The spurious defense that Greenglass or the Greenglasses, in order to satisfy a business grudge, a business dispute against the Rosenbergs has concocted a story about espionage . . . is as much of a concoction as the story of the defendants that Greenglass went to his worst enemy, Julius Rosenberg, for help when he wanted to flee the country.

Greenglass's relations toward his older sister, Ethel, and her husband Julius were such that he was willing prey to their communistic propaganda. He committed this crime because they persuaded him to do it.

The issue in this case, we are all agreed, transcends any family consideration; but clearly the breach of family loyalty is that of an older sister and brother-in-law dragging an American soldier into the sordid business of betraying his country for the benefit of the Soviet Union. The difference between the Greenglasses and the Rosenbergs? The Greenglasses have told the truth. They have tried to make amends for the hurt which has been done to our nation and to the world. The Rosenbergs, on the other hand, have magnified their sins by lying.

On David's September furlough, Rosenberg got from him the cross-section sketch of the atom bomb itself and a 12-page description of this vital weapon. This description of the atom bomb, destined for delivery to the Soviet Union, was typed up by the defendant Ethel Rosenberg that afternoon at her apartment at 10 Monroe Street. Just so had she on countless other occasions sat at that typewriter and struck the keys, blow by blow, against her own country in the interests of the Soviets.

The defendants before you are parties to an agreement to spy and steal from their own country, to serve the interests of a foreign power which today seeks to wipe us off the face of the earth. It would use the produce of these defendants, the information received through them, from these traitors, to destroy Americans and the people of the United Nations.

These three defendants stand before you in the face of overwhelming proof of this terrible disloyalty, proof which transcends any emotional consideration which must eliminate any consideration of sympathy. No defendants ever stood before the bar of American justice less deserving of sympathy than these three.

———

After a brief recess, Judge Kaufman delivered his charge to the jury. It took him more than an hour to define the boundaries of the indictment and the latitude for deliberations. The judge reviewed the legal contours of conspiracy: The government needed to prove only one of the overt acts, but any of those acts committed to further the conspiracy need not be criminal in itself. The indictment referred to a "foreign nation," not an enemy. Therefore, it made no difference whether the Soviet Union was an ally when the conspiracy occurred. Proof of Communist Party membership may be relevant only to the question of intent. Finally, Kaufman cautioned: "You cannot allow a consideration of the punishment which may be inflicted upon the defendants to influence your verdict in any way; the desire to avoid the performance of an unpleasant task cannot influence your verdict."

At 4:53 P.M., the jury retired. The first item on the agenda was dinner. The jurors were led to an Italian restaurant behind the courthouse. Shortly after 6:00 P.M., they returned to a room just in back of the jury box. The room was bare except for an oblong table and twelve chairs.

The foreman, Vincent Lebonitte, solicited first impressions. Several jurors volunteered their most indelible memories of the testimony. Few involved giving the defendants the benefit of the doubt. Sobell's Mexican itinerary, his use of aliases, and his refusal to testify in his own behalf didn't augur well for a not-guilty verdict. Nor did the Rosenbergs' decision to invoke the Fifth Amendment. And despite Kaufman's repeated admonitions, communism *was* on trial. "Although it was never proved in court, I felt they were members of the Communist Party," said one of the jurors, Howard Becker, a bank auditor. "That doesn't necessarily mean they were spies. But after all, the communists were out to overthrow the government."

Other calculated risks by the defense had backfired, too. Chief among them was Manny Bloch's request to impound David's descriptions of the atomic bomb. Bloch burnished his clients' patriotism at the expense of their credibility: If what David had stolen was so inconsequential, what was the point of impounding it? Several other defense claims raised more questions than they answered. One attempt, in particular, to deflect David's accusations resonated like a thunderclap: Jurors were stupefied by Julius's testimony that he had interpreted the threats that had accompanied David's demands for money as blackmail. Which secrets in Julius's past could be held hostage? What did David have on him? What did Julius have to hide?

At 6:40, the jurors requested a copy of the indictment and the witness list. At 8:10, one juror asked to hear Ruth's damning testimony of Julius's first approach to her in the Rosenbergs' apartment in November 1944. The court reporter read Ruth's testimony aloud. At 9:42, the jurors resumed deliberations. And all the while, as they listened to the staccato patter of the stenographer's tape, as they visualized the demeanor of the defendants, as they examined the exhibits and perused the crude drawings that could have passed for pictures of almost anything—all that time, they were preoccupied by a singular challenge: taking the measure of a man who had testified against his own sister.

"Here was a brother sending his sister to the gallows to save his own skin," Lebonitte said. But the same instincts that Bloch had assailed as so repulsive, so self-serving, struck the jury very differently. David's testimony wasn't evidence of his evilness, it was a proof of his sincerity. "Why would a boy go to this great length to testify against his sister and brother-in-law and build up such a preponderance of evidence against them, knowing it might mean their lives?" said Harold Axley, the Bronx restaurateur. "I could not visualize this happening. I still can't. I felt that he could not have been lying about doing in his own sister." James Gibbons, the bus-company bookkeeper and Transport Workers Union member, agreed: "The most terrible and unforgivable thing in the whole case for me was a brother testifying against his sister. I couldn't understand it then and I don't understand it now. Jealousy's just not enough— you just do not testify against a relative unless there is something in it."

At Lebonitte's direction, the jurors periodically wrote *guilty* or *not guilty* on small slips of paper and passed their verdicts to the foreman. From the beginning, only one or two voted for acquittal, and Lebonitte said later that their uncertainty was never a question of innocence or guilt but of clemency. One juror, Lebonitte recalled, "was squeamish about the possibility of a woman being put to death. He was under the impression that it was almost a foregone conclusion that she would suffer the loss of her life. He also brought out the mother angle. It was not a dissent on the evidence. It was a dissent for sentimental reasons. The idea that a mother with two children could be put to death was revolting to him."

Some jurors reasoned that the death penalty was only a remote possibility anyway. Others suggested that if anyone should have had qualms about punishment it was the Rosenbergs for having subjected their children to this ordeal. But James Gibbons was adamantly opposed to executing Ethel Rosenberg: "I believed they were guilty then, and I believe it now, but there were two children, and I had two of my own."

At 10:55, Vincent Lebonitte sent a note to the judge: "One of the jurors has some doubt in his mind as to whether he can recommend leniency for one of the defendants. He is interested in knowing your mind on the matter." Kaufman summoned the jury and reread the portion of his original charge about punishment. If the jury wanted to make a recommendation, it could, he said. However, he cautioned, "it is my prerogative to follow or disregard any recommendation that you may make on the matter of punishment."

At 12:22 A.M., the jury announced that it was deadlocked. Lebonitte attributed the stalemate to a "still existent dissident vote amongst us." Exchanging notes with the jury, the judge asked whether a verdict had been reached on any of the three defendants. "We have reached our verdict on two of the defendants," the foreman replied, "and we prefer to reserve rendering our verdict on all these defendants until we have complete unanimity." This provoked courtroom speculation: Had the jury already decided on Ethel Rosenberg and Morton Sobell but not on Julius? Had the Rosenbergs both been convicted while one juror remained unpersuaded by the tangential evidence against Sobell? Was it all about Ethel and the less compelling evidence against her or about rank sentimentality?

After nearly seven hours of deliberations, the jury reached one unanimous decision: to retire for the night. Marshals canvassed Manhattan hotels to find one with twelve single rooms on the same floor. They booked the Knickerbocker on West Forty-fifth Street off Times Square, where the jurors arrived after 2:00 A.M.

—

Five hours later, marshals roused the jurors for breakfast at Schrafft's. Deliberations resumed shortly before 10:00 A.M. It is a bedrock truism of legal lore that all juries enjoy fulfilling their judicial obligations before the weekend begins. But this was not one of those hopelessly stalemated let's-get-it-over-with-so-we-can-go-home negotiations. The jurors had virtually decided the night before. All except for one.

By Thursday morning, James Gibbons was still undecided. But with his fellow jurors assuring him that the sentence should not be on his conscience—the verdict would be unanimous and anonymous, and he would never be held solely accountable—he appeared to be wavering. "I had the feeling that he had convinced himself about it all alone in bed," Howard Becker remembered. Vincent Lebonitte volunteered a different version: "I changed his slant on it. I told him, 'Look, possibly this woman that you want to save will someday be part of a conspiracy to transmit secret information to a foreign power that would result in your own doom and the destruction of your wife and your children.' That changed his way of thinking."

Gibbons offered his own unsatisfying recollection: "I felt like Pontius Pilate washing his hands."

At 11:01, after seven hours and forty-two minutes of deliberations, the twelve jurors entered the courtroom. Vincent Lebonitte delivered the verdicts, one by one: The jury found each of the three defendants guilty as charged. The Rosenbergs appeared to be unmoved. Sobell was stunned.

—

Manny Bloch, Irving Saypol, and Judge Kaufman congratulated one another. (The judge, ambiguously, thanked the defense lawyers for "demeaning themselves as attorneys should.") "My own opinion," Kaufman concluded, "is that your verdict is a correct verdict.

I must say that as an individual I cannot be happy because it is a sad day for America. The thought that citizens of our country would lend themselves to the destruction of their own country by the most destructive weapon known to man is so shocking that I can't find words to describe this loathsome offense.

The case itself has implications so wide in their ramifications that they involve the very question of whether or when the devastation of atomic war may fall upon this world.

Julius Rosenberg and Morton Sobell were led away in handcuffs. Ethel, unfettered, was returned to the Women's House of Detention in Greenwich Village.

The judge scheduled sentencing for the following Thursday. The jury made no recommendation for leniency.

—

David Greenglass wasn't surprised by the verdict. He was apoplectic. Not because his sister and brother-in-law were convicted of capital crimes and might receive the death penalty on April 5, but because he was scheduled to be sentenced the very same day.

"He has a natural feeling about being part of the same deal with his sister and brother-in-law," John Rogge's partner, Herb Fabricant, informed Saypol. The prosecutor seemed uncomprehending.

"Over the fact he was in it?"

"And he testified against them and all that sort of thing. I think it is a perfectly understandable psychological thing," Fabricant explained. He acknowledged that while David's primary motivation might be his psychological aversion to being sentenced on the same day as the Rosenbergs, he also had a practical stake. "On the other hand," Fabricant said, "I am sure he feels he may get some kind of better treatment, too."

Saypol still couldn't grasp why David was so concerned.

"I am sure the judge wouldn't give him capital punishment," Saypol said.

Chapter 30

Death by Electrocution

"Have you anything that you want to say?"

"Nothing."

≡

The verdict touched off rounds of self-congratulation. "Again, I say a great tribute is due to the F.B.I. and Mr. Hoover for the splendid job that they have done in this case," Kaufman declared. J. Edgar Hoover congratulated Saypol: "This case is truly a sterling example of our democratic processes in action and a distinctive achievement to be enrolled in the annals of our American courts' history."

Saypol relented and agreed to postpone David's sentencing one day, which freed him on April 5 to give his undivided attention to the Rosenbergs and Sobell. "In terms of human life," he declared at their sentencing, "these defendants have affected the lives, and perhaps the freedom, of whole generations of mankind." The statute provided for only two alternatives: death or up to thirty years in prison. Saypol was baffled by why Congress hadn't provided for a longer maximum prison sentence. Given the alternatives, he concluded: "Leniency would be merely an invitation to increased activity by those dedicated to the concept that compassion is decadent and mercy an indication of weakness."

Bloch also professed to be in a bind. His clients still insisted on their innocence. "And they have informed me," he said prophetically, "no matter what, they will always maintain their innocence." That eliminated penitence as a ground for mitigation. Instead, Bloch urged Kaufman to judge the Rosenbergs in the context of 1944 and 1945 when great statesmen—he mentioned Winston Churchill and FDR— remarked "that the Soviet Union was to be helped, was to be trusted, and was to be taken as a full-fledged ally." Clearly straining, Bloch invoked an unfortunate phrase—*hero worship,* which David had used to describe his devotion to Julius—in laying the foundation for another misguided argument: that the atomic bomb had been magnified beyond the bounds of reality and that "it is not the horrible thing that is represented to the Court." Quoting scientists for the first time, he suggested that Russia would have gotten the bomb anyway and concluded: "Let's not believe, as seems to be current in American thinking, that our entire security depends upon the atom bomb, a thought expressed by Mr. Saypol when he said that our boys are dying in Korea because of the Rosenbergs."

On cue, just as Judge Kaufman started speaking, the bell of St. Andrew's Roman Catholic Church tolled noon. "Because of the seriousness of this case and the lack of precedence, I have refrained from asking the Government for a recommendation," Kaufman said. "The responsibility is so great that I believe that the Court alone should assume this responsibility."

He wasn't, however, telling the truth. The judge neglected to say that he had repeatedly sought guidance from the government.

"The day before sentence he asked for my views," Saypol acknowledged later. "I gave them and he inquired regarding the views of the Department of Justice. I had not solicited any. He asked me to seek these." Saypol flew to Washington that afternoon to meet with Peyton Ford, the deputy attorney general, and James McInerney, an assistant attorney general, who also volunteered Hoover's view. Virtually everyone favored the death penalty for Julius, but then opinion split. "There were differences all around among them," Saypol said, "but capital punishment for one or both was in, not out." That night, Saypol returned to New York, where he encountered Kaufman at a banquet. "In the presence of the judge," Saypol recalled, he phoned Peyton Ford for final word on whether officials in Washington had reconciled their views. They had not, he told the judge. "I was then asked by the judge to refrain from making any recommendation for punishment the next day in the course of my closing statement at sentence," Saypol said.

Roy Cohn had reported to the FBI earlier that week that Kaufman had also discussed the sentencing with Circuit Court Judge Jerome Frank, who recommended against the death penalty. Frank suggested that Kaufman also consult with Judge Edward Weinfeld, who was reported to have favored the death penalty. Cohn said he himself recommended capital punishment but thought that sentencing Ethel to thirty years might yet encourage her to inform. Cohn said he told Kaufman: "She's worse than Julius. She's the older one, she's the one with the brains, she recruited her younger brother into the Young Communist League and into the spy ring, she's the one who typed the atomic-bomb documents, she engineered this whole thing, she was the mastermind of this conspiracy." In condemning her, Cohn cited only one corroborated overt act by Ethel, though—the one that, on the eve of the trial, Ruth remembered and David confirmed: "She's the one who typed the atomic-bomb documents."

Hoover, who favored death for Julius and Morton Sobell, preferred thirty years imprisonment for Ethel ("the mother of two small children . . . presumed to be acting under the influence of her husband. The evidence at the trial showed her participation as consisting of assisting in the activation of David Greenglass as an espionage agent and the typing of data furnished by Greenglass"). Hoover proposed that David get fifteen years. ("He was a very important witness for the prosecution and furnished information to the special agents of the Bureau which led to the securing of corroborative information of great value at the trial.") Cohn reported that Kaufman intended to sentence David to thirty years, though Cohn, too, recommended fifteen. To which Kaufman was quoted as saying that whatever the government recommended, he intended to add another five years.

—

Julius Rosenberg, who was to turn thirty-three on May 12, swayed slowly on the balls of his feet. Ethel, who was thirty-five, stood at his right, betraying little reaction until the judge described her as a "full-fledged partner" in espionage. Then, the knuckles of her right hand whitened as she gripped the chair in front of her. After taking sole responsibility for his decision, Judge Kaufman contrasted the Rosenbergs with Nathan Hale, whose bronze figure in City Hall Park, a few blocks away, was a grim reminder both of courage and of its consequences:

> I consider your crime worse than murder. . . . I believe your conduct in putting into the hands of the Russians the A-bomb years before our best scientists predicted Russia would perfect the bomb has already caused, in my opinion, the communist aggression in Korea, with the resultant casualties exceeding 50,000 and who knows but that millions more of innocent people may pay the price of your treason. Indeed, by your betrayal you undoubtedly have altered the course of history to the disadvantage of our country. No one can say that we do not live in a constant state of tension. We have evidence of your treachery all around us every day—for the civilian defense activities throughout the nation are aimed at preparing us for an atom bomb attack.
>
> I have deliberated for hours, days and nights. I have carefully weighed the evidence. Every nerve, every fiber of my body has been taxed. . . . I have searched the records—I have searched my conscience—to find some reason for mercy—for it is only human to be merciful and it is natural to try to spare lives. I am convinced, however, that I would violate the solemn and sacred trust that the people of this land have placed in my hands were I to show leniency to the defendants Rosenberg. . . . You are hereby sentenced to the punishment of death, and it is ordered upon some day within the week beginning with Monday, May 21, you shall be executed according to law.

The execution was only seven weeks away.

—

Turning to Sobell, the judge reiterated what was obvious to anyone who had sat through the trial: The evidence did not suggest atomic espionage on his part. Therefore, Kaufman declared, "I cannot be moved by hysteria or motivated by a desire to do the popular thing." He sentenced Sobell, who was thirty-four, to the maximum thirty years' imprisonment.

—

Lodged in separate detention cells in the courthouse basement immediately after sentencing, the Rosenbergs serenaded each other (she, "One Fine Day" from *Madama Butterfly* and "Good Night Irene"; he, "The Battle Hymn of the Republic").

—

On Wall Street, the stock market scored its widest gains of the year. Rumors of peace in Korea had been depressing prices; the gains were attributed to ominous statements by President Truman and House Speaker Sam Rayburn raising the specter of another world war.

—

Outside 64 Sheriff Street, reporters awaited reaction from Tessie Greenglass. She sobbed when informed of her daughter's sentence.

—

Kaufman agreed to postpone David's sentencing, but not for a full week, as Rogge had requested. Just for one day.

"I don't think that any long statement should be made, because no one knows better than I do the part that Mr. Greenglass played in this case," Kaufman said. "I know it required a great deal of courage. The jury believed it. I believed it. I thought he was telling a credible story. It is a most unusual situation."

"It is the toughest I have ever been in, Judge," Rogge replied.

"A brother testifying against his sister," Kaufman continued. "I suppose that he did a lot of soul-searching and came to the conclusion that what he was doing is bigger than his relationship with his sister."

—

At 2:00 P.M., Friday, April 6, the clerk announced the sentencing of David Greenglass. Ruth Greenglass was seated in the front row of the courtroom, just behind the rail. David Greenglass stood at the defense table, on the spot where his sister had received the death penalty the day before. He wore a double-breasted brown suit, white shirt, and a brown-and-white tie. His hands were clasped behind his back.

Saypol spoke first. He recalled that even after David had confessed, the next day, at his arraignment, he had still protested his innocence.

"Through Ruth Greenglass, his wife," Saypol said,

> came the subsequent recantation of those protestations, their cooperation and the disclosure of the facts by both of them. They were told before that their conduct in these disclosures in no way implied any commitment to them regarding the prosecution of either. The effect of their behavior as is now evident to all is reflected by the verdict. It was my duty to decide who should be considered for indictment by the grand jury. I am morally satisfied in my decision.
>
> As forceful as your Honor has been in the case of the other defendants, you should now be inclined toward a demonstration of the broad tolerance of the Court in the presence of penitence, contriteness, remorse and belated truth. I recommend that the defendant be imprisoned for a term of 15 years.

Despite Kaufman's reminder the day before that a long statement on David's behalf was unnecessary, Rogge delivered a thirty-six-minute plea for mercy. He warned that fifteen years was a sentence severe enough to discourage other miscreants from turning state's evidence. "Any sentence in excess of five years . . . defeats any good purpose that a sentence in this case could have," he said. He recommended a year and a day.

"David's fuzzy thinking occurred at a time when Russia was a wartime ally, and many other people among us were engaged in fuzzy thinking about the Soviet Union at that time," Rogge said. "As a matter of fact, it continued for most of us until 1948."

"Well, let's get one thing clear," Kaufman interrupted. "Russia didn't come to our aid in this war. We came to Russia's aid."

Rogge credited David's description of his potential escape plans to Mexico with helping the government to apprehend Sobell; with finding

Evelyn Cox, the Rosenbergs' maid; and also with locating Dr. George Bernhardt, Julius's physician, who had testified to Julius's request about smallpox vaccinations.

Even Axis Sally and Tokyo Rose got less than fifteen years, Rogge said. As he continued, he left no good deed by David unmentioned: "You have here an individual who is wholly without malice, if your Honor please. I mean you have someone—I know that he not only gave blood during the second World War, but I see he has an emblem on his coat today that he gave blood recently. . . . He should be praised not punished."

David faced the floor. This time, he was not smiling.

"Have you anything that you want to say?" Kaufman asked him.

"Nothing," he replied.

In contrast to his avowals the day before, Kaufman did not deliver a peroration on a jurist's lonely introspection about crime and punishment. Nor did he volunteer that the incontrovertible message in Saypol's sentencing statement was, as James Kilsheimer told him, "But for Greenglass there would have been no case against either of the Rosenbergs and probably none against Sobell either." Demonstrating all the sternness he could muster, the judge lavished praise on David for telling the whole truth and nothing but the truth:

> The fact that I am about to show you some consideration does not mean that I condone your acts or that I minimize them in any respect. They were loathsome; they were contemptible. I must, however, recognize the help given by you in apprehending and bringing to justice the arch criminals in this nefarious scheme, Julius Rosenberg and his wife, Ethel Rosenberg. You have at least not added to your sins by committing the additional crime of perjury. . . . By your assistance in this case you have helped us strike a death blow to the trafficking in our military secrets, to the advantage of a foreign nation.
>
> You like so many other foolish men and women believed that Soviet Russia was Utopia. You learned that when you enlisted in what you believed was a cause of the liberation of men you were in effect enlisting in the Russian Foreign Legion.
>
> However, David Greenglass, you found your way back before the

curtain fell on your life. You repented and you brought to justice those who enlisted you in this case.

Justice does not seek vengeance. Justice seeks justice, but you deserve punishment, punishment which balances the gravity of your offense as against your aid. I want you to know that I have given deep consideration to your case with full recognition of the aid which you have given the Government, fully cognizant of the gravity of this offense.

It is the judgment of this Court that I shall follow the recommendation of the Government and sentence you to 15 years in prison.

Ruth Greenglass shuddered; she nearly toppled from her seat. Her head dropped to the wooden rail, which she grasped with her right hand to steady herself. Fifteen years. Fifteen years from that day David would have wasted one third of his life in prison. She and David would have been separated for nearly two thirds of their marriage. By 1966, Steven would be twenty; Barbara would be sixteen. Ruth had never expected this.

Exactly what Rogge and the Greenglasses had expected was never stated publicly. From the beginning, their strategy had been not to antagonize the government at any cost. As shocked as they were by the sentence, there were no sufficient grounds to reverse course—not when their fate remained in the hands of the prosecution and of prison and parole officials. But FBI and Parole Board files suggest that the Greenglasses were genuinely stunned by what they saw as Kaufman's severity. Those records imply that Rogge and McInerney had discussed David's punishment in detail and that, as a result, Rogge had led the Greenglasses to believe that he had negotiated a three-year sentence at worst. In fact, Rogge later told the Parole Board that McInerney "told him that if Greenglass 'told the whole story' he should be given a suspended sentence." *

---

* There is no record that McInerney acknowledged any such deal or that he was in a position to deliver on it. McInerney did say, then, though, that he was immediately writing a letter recommending David for parole when he became eligible (to which Hoover commented: "We will be no party to any 'deals' or recommendations entered into by McInerney").

After announcing the sentences, Kaufman discreetly made it known that his decisions had taken an enormous toll. The judge "plainly showed his burden of responsibility," *The New York Times* reported the next day, adding authoritatively that "in the last week he had a bit more than 10 hours' sleep" and that "several times he went to his synagogue seeking spiritual guidance." Just how much divine inspiration Kaufman actually sought or received is a matter of conjecture. "So far as I know, the closest he got to prayer was the phone booth next to the Park Avenue Synagogue," Cohn said, which is where, he claimed, Kaufman called him from to solicit advice.

Among the many congratulatory notes the judge collected was one from Attorney General McGrath. "I know it took tremendous courage to pronounce that historic sentence," McGrath wrote. Kaufman responded: "The sentence was the only one which I could in good conscience impose in this case."

The severity of the sentences surprised many people, among them Vincent Lebonitte. "I would have accepted the life sentence, 30 years, 25 years," he said. He added, however: "I felt good that this was strictly a Jewish show. It was Jew against Jew. It wasn't the Christians hanging the Jews. . . . The Jews hated the Rosenbergs for the disgrace they had brought upon their race."

Chapter 31

Sing Sing

"My troubles...are all due to the ignorance and low intellectual level of some of the inmates."

=

Sentenced to death and eventually delivered to Sing Sing, Ethel and Julius Rosenberg emerged as international icons, highly prized props in a globally choreographed propaganda campaign that generated broad sympathy, from Picasso to the pope. The death sentences were postponed pending appeals. The propaganda proved more enduringly valuable to the Soviet Union than had whatever fleeting atomic secrets Julius had handed off from David Greenglass.

Nearly the only people who still seemed to care what happened to David were his mother and his wife.

The impressions forged by the trial endured for decades, creating a mythology in which the Rosenbergs—guilty or not—were martyrs to cold-war paranoia and repression and David Greenglass was a reviled footnote, rebuffed even by history in his quest to be forgotten. Monuments rose to the Rosenbergs—one still is tended lovingly in Cuba; visitors still leave small stones, in accordance with Jewish custom, at the granite tombstone engraved with their names in a Long Island cemetery. Michael and Robby Rosenberg embraced the surname of their adopted parents, but they proudly resurfaced a quarter century ago as Julius and Ethel's flesh-and-blood legacy.

Overnight, *Greenglass,* too, had become a household name. Even before David was sentenced, Ruth had considered changing her last name and her children's. She temporarily used her maiden name, Printz, or an anglicized version, Prince. Within a year or so, though, a partner at Lazard Frères, the investment-banking firm, reported to the FBI that Ruth had worked there as a stenographer and had recently been let go in part because of numerous absences but also because a number of her colleagues recognized her from news photographs. Louis Abel, David's brother-in-law, was fired around the time of the trial. David's brother Bernie, too, lost more than one job because of the family's notoriety.

Greenglass never earned its own listing in the dictionary, like *Cain* or *Judas* or *quisling* or *Benedict Arnold.* But Julius Rosenberg, for one, declared not long after the trial, "History records that David Greenglass stands without parallel and ahead of even Judas Iscariot in infamy." Julius branded his brother-in-law a "trapped self-confessed spy, who bore false witness against two innocent people and was responsible for his Sister, his own flesh and blood being sentenced to the electric chair. This act alone will have him go down in history as the most infamous informer."[*]

David was indisputably a rat, an epithet that originated in British politics to describe converts to King George I and that spawned a family of variants, including *squealer.* Another synonym, *stool pigeon,* derives from the nineteenth-century hunters' practice of capturing, blinding, and binding a pigeon to a stool or post to lure others. *Canary* was another avian variant, inspired by its ability to sing. Whatever the meta-

---

[*] Woody Allen invokes the family name not only in *Crimes and Misdemeanors* but also in *Annie Hall:* "I always felt my schoolmates were idiots, Melvyn Greenglass, you know, fat little face."

No one, however, likened David to David Kaczynski, a social worker who turned in his older brother, Theodore, as the Unabomber in 1995, battled to spare him the death penalty, and refused a million-dollar reward.

Nor has David been compared to Barbara Walker, who informed the FBI in 1984 of her suspicion that her husband, John, was a Russian spy. She did not realize that her tip would also implicate their son.

phor, the traits it conveyed were distinctly human: to inform and to betray.

The Ten Commandments warn against bearing false witness. And three times a day, observant Jews recite their blessings along with a curse against squealers, whether they are bearing false witness or not. *L'mal sheenim al t'hee tikvah:* May informers (or heretics, betrayers) find no hope. Liars were assigned to the eighth circle of hell. Traitors were consigned to spend eternity in the ninth, one step from Lucifer. In Sidney Kingsley's seminal play *Dead End,* the villain was indisputably Spit, the Snitch. In a treatise on treachery, Robert D. King, a professor of Jewish studies at the University of Texas, challenged E. M. Forster's assertion that he hoped he would have the guts to betray his country rather than his friend. "Forster's is a false dichotomy," King wrote. "You cannot betray your country without at the same time betraying at least some of your friends."

———

As the jury had just taken the measure of the main prosecution witness, now the experts weighed in. Not long after Judge Kaufman imposed sentence, Congress's Joint Committee on Atomic Energy explored the motivations of David Greenglass and the three other known betrayers of the Allies' atomic program: Klaus Fuchs; Alan Nunn May, a British scientist; and Bruno Pontecorvo, an Italian working for the Canadians. Of the four, David was the only American and also the only one who smiled when testifying. "He seemed to enjoy discussing his own insight into weapons data," the committee said. What common motivations drove these four men?

"It is evident," the committee concluded, "that a lack of moral standards, combined with an overweening and childlike arrogance—all induced by exposure to Communist recruiting techniques during early manhood—characterizes the atom spy." All four "had been pulled into a Communist apparatus which systematically destroyed their sense of moral values and substituted the facile capacity for rationalization found in the code of totalitarian dictatorship. Just as adherents of such a code sometimes tend to be arrogant and humorless, so there may also have been a powerful element of ego gratification in the actions of the atomic spies." The committee quoted from *Science and Common Sense* by James Conant, the president of Harvard, on what makes scientists tick. Because they are blindly disciplined in their work, Conant wrote, "one would not be surprised, therefore, if as regards matters beyond their professional competence, laboratory workers were a little less impartial and self-restrained than other men."*

A profile of David prepared for the FBI immediately after the trial concluded that his confession had been cathartic:

> It appears that he was pleased to have the course of events relieve him of the problem of making this difficult decision. After his confession, Greenglass appeared to derive considerable satisfaction from the attention and publicity he received in the preparation for the trial of the conspirators against whom he testified. He appears to be satisfied with his 15 year sentence.

—

David was transferred to Lewisburg federal penitentiary on July 6. The Bureau of Prisons did its own evaluation when David entered federal custody and also conducted perfunctory annual reviews. David's suggest that as the product of a happy home, he managed to emerge from a neo-Dickensian economic plight with modest potential. "A congenial relationship has always existed in the family, which was a closely-knit union," the evaluation said. "He is indicated as the only delinquent in the family," the profiled continued.† During his early development, David "had few opportunities and only the bare necessities of life." Nonetheless, his mother described him as "a calm child with a very happy disposition who liked to read and experiment a great deal" and managed

---

* A fellow physicist once said of Fuchs: "I have never before known a person who possesses such a marvelous ability to think in abstract terms who is at the same time so helpless when it comes [time] to either observe or evaluate reality."

† Another in the series of reports stated, though, that he had three brothers—either a mistake or a reference to Mendy—"who have not been in any difficulties, and one sister, who has been in similar criminal activities."

to register a 127 IQ. On the California Occupational Interest Inventory, David did best in mechanical aptitude (with a score of 90) and worst in business (he scored only 1). His second-best score—40—was in the category called *manipulative*. David denied "neurotic traits as a child." A battery of tests and interviews revealed a history of behavior that, under the circumstances, doesn't seem deviant. He was characterized by "a moderate disregard for social convention, marked suspiciousness and, under stress, tendencies to react immaturely, to internalize difficulties by mild psychosomatic complaints and to experience moderate shifts in mood and behavior. The subject is moderately defensive and gives some evidence of trying to appear in a socially acceptable light."

Psychiatrists described David as "a slightly tense, slightly apprehensive individual" who "attempts to place himself in the best possible light, and to minimize the seriousness of his activities." The doctors reported to prison authorities no evidence of "psychotic manifestations or disabling mental order" and said that David denied "homosexual activities." All the testing was encapsulated in a nine-word diagnosis: "Superior intelligence. Inadequate Personality with some emotionally immature traits." The prescription was even milder: further counseling from the prison rabbi.

The authorities said David "appears desirous of making a good institutional adjustment, although he is fearful that he may be the victim of an assault by other inmates." There is no evidence that he was physically attacked, but he was abused verbally by convicts who were contemptuous of his treachery toward his sister. "Let me say here that none of my troubles come from any official sources," David wrote Rogge. "They are all due to the ignorance and low intellectual level of some of the inmates." Ruth complained to the FBI about "intolerable" conditions at Lewisburg—"fellow prisoners refused to talk to him, spit in his food, and make life generally miserable"; further, "in order to make his isolation complete, the prisoners have allegedly forbidden Harry Gold to speak to him, and the latter has complied." In fact, the specialists monitoring David concluded that he was "thoroughly frightened" by the prison's pressure groups and refused to leave his cell except within sight of a guard. "He will undoubtedly become something of a problem while in this institution," they concluded, "but will not of his own volition, do anything to foment those problems."

———

On November 22, 1951, David complained to Rogge that he hadn't heard from Ruth since her last visit, on October 31. "I am quite perturbed," he wrote. "I find myself thinking exclusively of what could have occurred." Five days later, Rogge wrote to say that he had just spoken to Ruth; he assured David that he needn't fret. "You must remember Dave that she has her hands full with taking care of a job and the children," Rogge wrote. "There may very well be times when she cannot possibly find time to write."

In any event, Ruth was worried, too. When she left after one routine visit to Lewisburg, she was terrified that she would never see David again. Rumors were rife that if Ethel was executed, David would be killed, too. As the prison chaplain drove Ruth to the Lewisburg train station, he confided a similar warning: Some of the inmates who had taken part in a recent murder considered it a dry run for their execution of David Greenglass.

———

Ethel was transferred to Sing Sing on April 11, 1951, from the Women's House of Detention in Manhattan, where the warden reported that Ethel "dreaded each day because it brought her that [much] closer to her punishment" and that she "would rather kill herself than face the electric chair." City officials appealed plaintively to their federal counterparts: "In view of the fact that she is a Federal prisoner and not a State or City prisoner, it would cause embarrassment to the Department of Correction if she did commit suicide." The transfer isolated her further for five weeks, until Julius finally joined her there on May 16. After that, they were allowed to visit once a week, a wire-mesh grill separating them.* Between visits, they communicated prolifically by letter.

After a few months at Sing Sing, Julius seemed just as dyspeptic about

———

* For the ensuing two years, they would spend more time together than David and Ruth.

Irving Saypol's elevation to the State Supreme Court and about the National League standings as about the prospects of his appeal. "Gloom of glooms the dead Dodgers lost the pennant and now I'm rooting for the Giants to lick the Yankees," Julius wrote. "When will the N.Y. Yankees become part of modern American baseball and lift the discriminating ban on Negro baseball stars."

Meanwhile, Ethel railed against her family's complicity with prosecutors as "the sting of a certain group of poisonous snakes of my sorry acquaintance." But she also rhapsodized about the flora at "Ossining Manor"* and eagerly anticipated twice-a-month visits from Dr. Saul Miller, her psychiatrist, and from Julius's siblings, as well as letters from Michael and Robby.

—

When Ethel had been arrested, Michael and Robby—then seven and three—had been taken to their grandmother Tessie's apartment. The boys were too much for Tessie to handle, so the house on Sheriff Street became only the first stop on a odyssey that shunted them to Julius's mother in Upper Manhattan and to the homes of family friends, with time spent at more than one orphanage.†

Robby believed Tessie had another agenda in moving them along. "She was using the threat of putting us in an orphanage to coerce my mother. And while I can't say for certain that the Government was putting her up to it, I believe that to be the case," he later wrote.

> She didn't have the heart to say, "I'm doing this because your mother's not listening to what I say." She had to make up a story. . . . She said this

---

* One hundred and twenty years earlier, Alexis de Tocqueville visited Sing Sing and also waxed poetic about the vista: "I must except the view of the Bay of Naples, out of deference to the opinion of the civilized world, but with that exception, the world has not such scenery."

† After Bernie's wife, Gladys, died, their daughter, Sharon, was parked at Sheriff Street, too, but only briefly before being sent to a foster home herself. The Rosenberg boys were also sent to their Aunt Ethel, Julius's sister, but her husband, whose family survived the Holocaust, didn't want to invite more trouble by taking them in.

is a cold-water flat and the toilet freezes in the wintertime, and it's not a safe place for children to live. So I remember going into the bathroom and peering down into the toilet to try to find some ice and of course there was no ice, it wasn't yet winter anyway.

After the Jewish Welfare Board took custody of Michael and Robby, Judge Kaufman informed the FBI that an acquaintance connected with the board described both children as "in a very maladjusted state of mind." Michael "particularly seemed to have developed a complex and allegedly stated that he was going to devote his life to avenging his parents." The judge, who had three sons of his own, said he was "wondering whether he ought to send for the boys and talk with them." He never did.

Before Michael and Robby visited their parents at Sing Sing, Ethel and Julius were consumed with how to handle their questions about why their father was, as he put it, "sans mustache" and, inevitably, about the physics of the electric chair.*

Julius pronounced the boys' subsequent visit "just perfect." But his elaboration belied any possibility that the hourlong discussion focused on how the world was a better place with the harnessing of electricity. Michael asked about how people die, and whether there was an electric chair at Sing Sing. Julius assured him that his parents were innocent and could avail themselves of many avenues of appeal, but Michael was "terribly upset." As Julius wrote, Michael then addressed a prison guard who was monitoring their conversation. "You'd better watch me," the

---

* Ethel meticulously drafted a monologue that first addressed the rift between the Greenglasses and the Rosenbergs. She described her brother and sister-in-law as "sick, unhappy people" who dealt with their own dilemma by "lying about us." Ethel urged her children not to torment themselves with problems that were really the Greenglasses' responsibility, notwithstanding the fact that, as she wrote, "you wish that you could kill those who are responsible for the crime that has been committed against us." She added, comfortingly, "it's perfectly natural to feel that way."

Then, Ethel addressed an even more delicate question. The children were to visit their mother and father separately. In case Michael neglected to interrogate her first about the mechanics of the death penalty, that "lovely job" would fall to Julius. She described it as painless, like "a highly magnified electric shock that anybody might sustain."

boy said, "for I don't want my mother and father to die, for if they do, I'll kill Dave."

In her letters and court documents, Ethel echoed Michael's vitriol. David, she wrote, was motivated, in part, by "his animal desire to preserve himself and his wife, the mother of his children," who "knowingly appropriated the venal fruits of her husband's criminality." In contrast, she wrote, "the modesty of our standard of living, bordering often on poverty, discredits David's depiction of my husband as the pivot and pay-off man of a widespread criminal combination, fed by a seemingly limitless supply of 'Moscow gold.'" Her appeal reached biblical and operatic proportions:

> How firm is a verdict predicated upon the testimony of "accomplices," trading their Judas-words for a few years of their miserable lives?
>
> We have never been able to comprehend that civilized and compassionate consciences could accept a smiling "Cain" like David Greenglass—or the "serpent," Ruth, his wife—who would slay, not only his sister, but his sister's husband, and orphan two small children of his own blood.
>
> Ruth goes free, as all the world now knows; David's freedom, too, is not so far off, that he will not have many years to life, a life—if we should die—that, perhaps, only a David Greenglass could suffer to live.

Ethel also wrote Julius's sister Lena: "And you don't know how I abhor the fact that they were people who belonged to me that did your brother and all those dear to him such a horrible wrong . . ." Julius wrote Ethel that he was struggling through Carleton Coon's *A Reader in General Anthropology,* which he had borrowed from the prison library, for answers "about the vermin that bore false witness against us," Julius wrote. "So far, I find that the primates and primitive men are too humane to display any traces of similar degradation."

—

Tessie's overtures to Ethel were never welcome. When Tessie visited Sing Sing in January 1953, Ethel proclaimed herself stupefied by her mother's "bold-faced immorality" in suggesting that Ethel embrace David's version of the events regardless of their veracity. "I protested, shocked as could be," Ethel wrote Manny Bloch. Ethel asked whether her mother was urging her to commit perjury. To which Tessie, according to Ethel, "shrugged her shoulders indifferently and maintained doggedly, 'You wouldn't be here!'"

Ethel urged Tessie to appeal to David instead and offered to pay her way to Lewisburg. "Whatever unfounded fear of reprisal" was motivating him, Ethel wrote, her life was in jeopardy, not his, and if she was willing to maintain her innocence in the face of his lie, why couldn't David "be man enough to own up at long last, to this lie, and help save my life, instead of letting it be forfeited to save his face!"

On March 14, 1953, Tessie and Bernie visited Ethel, and accounts of this meeting reached the government from, among others, Ruth Greenglass. (Tessie and Bernie had asked her not to brief the FBI about the visit because they feared some official retaliation against Ethel, but Ruth had her own agenda.) Ruth, the bureau noted, "believes that Ethel will try desperately to involve herself, (Ruth), if she should ever talk." According to Ruth, Ethel had branded her mother a witch and accused her of "being with the enemy" because she had accompanied Ruth to visit David at Lewisburg. Tessie had urged Ethel to think of Michael and Robby. According to Ruth, "Ethel brushed off this remark with, 'Don't mention the children. Children are born every day in the week.'"*

Ruth also reported that Tessie had gone to see Manny Bloch and "accused him of not trying to free her daughter and that his main job was to make sure that they never talked, and the best way to secure this end was to have them electrocuted." To which Bloch replied chivalrously that if Tessie were not a woman "he would really tell her what he thought of her." Tessie was subsequently confined to bed with high blood pressure.†

---

* The assumption was that the party, presumably, would take care of the kids. Or, as an FBI informant reported, relating a 1951 comment of Julius's, "He is satisfied that his children will be placed in a progressive foster home and will be well taken care of."

† Tessie Greenglass wrote to President Truman and then to President Eisenhower, pleading

In the nearly two years since his sister had been sentenced to death, the key government witness hadn't lifted a finger or said a word in her defense. He might never have intervened at all, except for the suggestion of a stranger. Predictably, the genesis of David's appeal for clemency on his sister's behalf originated outside the Greenglass family. On February 16, 1953, David Liberson of the *Jewish Daily Forward* wrote Rogge:

> I feel that you probably share the sentiments of myself and many others: that the Rosenbergs, guilty as hell of that abominable crime, should not pay with their lives in accordance with American standards of justice but that they are trapped by the iron curtain which they themselves have wrung down and certain acts of the courts which, while perfectly legal and fair might have been different under other circumstances. . . .
>
> According to testimony and what you yourself have stated to me, David Greenglass had told everything truthfully. He has done so with the fond hope that while he is helping his country he is by no means sending to their deaths his sister and brother-in-law. Since he is a fairly sensitive person, it is clear that he cannot and can never have peace of mind if he feels that he has not done everything in the direction of

---

for executive clemency. Her letters were forwarded by Rogge, who was placed in the unusual posture of appealing for mercy for the victim of his own clients' testimony. Tessie made two points, with which, Rogge wrote, he concurred:

> She wishes to suggest, in the first place, that permitting the death penalty to be carried out will be a mistake tactically, for it will play into the hands of the Communists. It is her view that Communist leaders look forward almost desperately to the death of the Rosenbergs and the sealing of their lips forever. The Communists will then proceed to martyr the Rosenbergs and our Government will never be able to hear from them the balance of the espionage story. On the other hand, if the death sentence is commuted to 30 years, the Rosenbergs, alive, may some day reveal the facts as well as prevent the propaganda.

> She also wishes to suggest that if the trial judge had not been both young as well as a coreligionist of the defendants, and therefore anxious to demonstrate to the world that his people did not condone the actions of the Rosenbergs, he would never have imposed the death sentence originally. An older judge who tempered justice with mercy would not have imposed so severe a penalty.

commuting the death sentence of the Rosenbergs. Should he not, therefore, make a plain, sincere and unequivocal statement that no matter what the difference of degree of guilt between himself and the Rosenbergs, it is certainly not enough to warrant a prison term in one case and death for the others? Should he not inferentially declare that such a sentence—death for his sister and brother-in-law—is terribly unfair not only to the Rosenbergs but, also, to him since it puts upon him an intolerable burden?

Liberson concluded by saying that if he were David Greenglass, he would be looking for every opportunity to do something. He wasn't David Greenglass, though. Until Ruth showed Liberson's letter to David at Lewisburg in mid-March 1953, it hadn't occurred to him to get involved, either to save his sister's life or to salve his conscience. Finally, in a letter addressed to Rogge and forwarded to President Eisenhower on March 20, David delivered what his lawyer described as an "eloquent" plea for leniency. David wrote, in part:

It has been quite some time since I've written you last. A lot has happened since then and I felt that I must break my silence and let you know where I stand on certain occurrences. I don't know whether it will help, but I would like you to present my views to the agency or agencies that can possibly commute my brother-in-law's and sister's terribly harsh sentence.

When I was first arrested I felt that I had to perform some act of contrition for the wrong I had done my country, my family, and myself. The way to do this was to tell the truth trusting this nation of ours to be just yet merciful. In my case I have little reason to find fault with that line of thought. I little realized that it would be otherwise for my sister and her husband.

Guilty they are, but the sentence is still one that puts a stain on the record of these United States. I know that if these people would tell their story they would be given a chance for life, but if they do not they will die. Now how could those deaths be of help to the country? As a deterrent? Never. How can you deter a fanatical communist? On the contrary, they will be used as a motive for a new propaganda drive by the Soviet Government, charging the U.S. with "brutality." Then there is the very real harm that the knowledge these people have will die with them and this great underground web of espionage will continue to operate without fear of detection.

Living in jail is such that even the strongest is willing to talk to reduce his time. There you have the chance to gain this knowledge that would otherwise be done. The other way is a blind alley.

I would be less than human if I did not state that if these two die, I shall live the rest of my life with a very dark shadow on my conscience. If you've ever hurt someone you have loved, even inadvertently, then you know how I feel. Here I had to take the choice of hurting someone dear to me and I took it deliberately. I could not believe that this would be the outcome. May God in his mercy change that awful sentence. Amen.

David ended his letter with a personal aside to Rogge, expressing hope that it would do some good. Then, he added: "I hope that you will handle this with the utmost discretion, my wife, my children, and my mother can do without the publicity."

Chapter 32

Relativity

"I told them how to make it. And if someone put a gun
to my head, I could make one now if I had to."

=

Behind the welter of arcane legal arguments, the Rosenbergs' appeals were framed as two fundamental questions: Could a twenty-two-year-old who had graduated only from a vocational high school, who had been kicked out of college for failing every course, whose knowledge of nuclear energy had been gleaned largely from the pages of *Popular Science,* and whose official duties at Los Alamos were limited to making molds in which conventional explosives were poured—and who later admitted that he couldn't distinguish one lens shape from the other as far as which worked better—fathom the innermost mechanisms of an atomic bomb, ferreting out arcane details, absorbing them, remembering them, and then conveying them to others months later? And, even if so, how valuable were those details to the Soviets?

The most durable weapon that the Rosenbergs and their defenders could wield was inside David's head. Ethel belittled her brother as "a simple machinist, an incompetent, and otherwise, a scientific illiterate"—arguments that the defense had largely abdicated during the trial.

Defending her husband's mental acuity, Ruth Greenglass combed her files and found the letter that Julius wrote on August 18, 1949, giving his highest job recommendation to the man he was now denouncing as a technological Neanderthal. "This man," Julius wrote as president of Pitt Machine Products, "has worked very efficiently doing experimental engineering, working out design details, and putting them into production." Ruth volunteered to the FBI that the letter probably had been typed by Ethel Rosenberg.

But Henry Linschitz, a scientist who had befriended David at Los Alamos, later dismissed David's bomb sketch as "correct in its most vague and general aspects" but otherwise "garbled, ambiguous and highly incomplete." Physicist Philip Morrison didn't equivocate. He ridiculed David's drawings as "a caricature" of the bomb. "A man like Greenglass, who had no technical training of consequence, and no opportunity to transmit written or numerical data, samples, or accurate drawings, could not possibly transmit information which might be of value for its technical content," Morrison wrote in seeking clemency for the Rosenbergs. "Indeed in the trial record, Greenglass tells a story of his automobile ride with a Soviet inquirer who asks him questions which do touch upon the sort of information that might really prove useful technically. Yet by his own account he could answer not one of these technical questions."

Many of David's detractors were enlisted by Manny Bloch and other defenders of the Rosenbergs. The scientists' arguments were typically twofold: Give David Greenglass the benefit of the doubt; still, there was no way he could have grasped enough nuclear physics to ask the right questions, much less to understand and then lucidly convey the correct technical answers. And even if he had been intellectually capable of stealing the secret to the atomic bomb, there was, in fact, no "secret" to steal. As Manny Bloch later put it, "In other countries, and particularly in the Soviet Union, they knew both the theory of all of the processes as well as the reduction of those theories to practice and that the only secret . . . was that it could work."

In soliciting scientific support, Bloch typically attached a copy of the expurgated trial transcript and posed nine questions, the gist of which was whether someone of David's background could have produced the sketches unaided in 1945 and reproduced them solely from memory five years later. Generally, those who submitted affidavits were unambiguous: Perhaps it was conceivable that in 1945 David sketched simple pieces of equipment that he himself had constructed, but it was far-fetched to maintain that five or six years later anyone could produce those sketches in detail without some help. While maintaining that the drawings introduced at the trial were amateurish, Bloch and the scientists he enlisted insisted that even those crude schematics were far beyond David's ken—at best, he must have been coached. "Even though you could teach a parrot to repeat certain words," Bloch argued, "there are certain things that you can't teach a parrot and you can't teach a man of Greenglass's education, as these experts say, how to draw a sketch of a cross-section of the atomic bomb, which set forth the function of each of its parts and the interrelation of these parts in order to produce a working mechanism."

Thomas Reeve Kaiser, a British physicist, insisted that even in 1945 David could not have produced the sketches. "It is possible that any person working in or visiting a scientific laboratory could reproduce sketches and written material describing his impressions of the apparatus and experiments," Kaiser wrote. "Having had the experience of reading newspaper articles dealing with scientific work, written by non-scientific reporters after a visit to a laboratory, I am emphatic in saying that such material could only be accurate and of any value if the person concerned was scientifically trained in the appropriate field of science."

Some of the scientists did dispute Bloch's premise that only someone with a doctorate in nuclear physics could have grasped the principle of the atomic bomb. Not surprisingly, those conditional responses were omitted from the defense briefs that Bloch filed with the court.[*]

"Without prejudging your client's case," Norbert Wiener, a mathematics professor at MIT advised, "I may say that the line of defense suggested by your questions seems to me extremely weak. I would hesitate

---

[*] The author found them later in Bloch's files, made available by Marshall Perlin, the lawyer who handled Sobell's appeals and who represented the Rosenbergs' sons.

to make any close association between a person's formal education and his ability to perform."

E. U. Condon, a former Los Alamos physicist, wrote from Corning, New York, that he doubted that David could in a freehand drawing provide with precision much of value to the Russians. But Condon cautioned that if Bloch's "idea is that Greenglass is not competent to have done the things he says he did which undermines his credibility if it does not actually indicate perjury," then "I am afraid that I could not give answers in support of such a position, for my feeling is that he probably could have done all that he claims to have done. . . . My feeling is that the evidence indicates some degree of guilt," he wrote, "but that in view of Greenglass' general incompetence and that the same material and much more was actually given away through other channels, and that the Rosenbergs' role seems to have been merely that of minor links in a transmission chain, that the death sentence for the Rosenbergs is completely unjustifiable."

Harlow Shapley of Harvard College Observatory agreed about the sentences, adding, though: "I assume that the Rosenbergs are at least guilty of indiscretions that our hindsight now sees as treason."

From Cornell, Hans Bethe—whom David had included on his roster of possible espionage recruits—replied with perhaps the most incriminating letter of all.

Bloch had asked, "Could a person of Greenglass's background and experience have produced drawing solely from memory in 1944 and 1945 sketches of the lens molds he allegedly turned over to Rosenberg (and Gold)?"

"Yes," Bethe replied. "In order to make such drawings, a person must have a good memory, preferably a visual one, and must have had close contact with the making of lens molds. Apparently Mr. Greenglass worked on these molds for a considerable period of time and must therefore have been very familiar with their shape. His memory probably was further improved by his desire to remember."

In 1950 and 1951, could Greenglass have produced replicas of the sketches drawing solely from memory and without any outside aid or assistance and coaching?

"Yes. His close and prolonged association with the manufacture of these molds would make it possible for him to remember. Moreover, the transmission of this information to the Rosenbergs must have been a major event in his life and made it difficult for him to forget."

Could Bethe, a trained scientist, drawing solely from memory, produce such a sketch today?

"Yes. If I had worked on a problem like this, I could."

In 1945, drawing solely from memory and without any help, could Greenglass have produced a schematic drawing of an experiment on implosion effects utilizing high explosive lenses, plus appropriate descriptive material?

"Yes. This is entirely possible if he worked on this subject. It is not certain, of course, whether his description was accurate. But, if this description came into the hands of a trained Russian scientist, it is likely that it could have been deciphered even if it was not accurate."

Could Greenglass have produced in 1950 or 1951 replicas of that schematic drawing, which he allegedly turned over to Gold in 1945, drawn solely from memory?

"Yes."

Could a person of Greenglass's background and experience have produced in 1945 a sketch of a cross section of the Nagasaki type of atom bomb together with twelve pages of matter explaining the functions of such a bomb and its component parts solely from memory?

Yes. In this case, the accuracy of his sketches and description would be more doubtful than in Question 4, but again could be of great help to a trained Russian scientist who might have obtained sketches and description. Moreover, it seems important to consider Greenglass's intent. His testimony shows that he had the intent of conveying to the Russians, through the Rosenbergs, as much of the design of the bomb as he could learn about, and as accurately as he could describe it.

In 1951, could Greenglass have produced a replica of that sketch?
"Yes."

Bloch did not submit the responses of Wiener, Condon, Shapley, and Bethe, among others, in his brief to the appeals court. The scientists' testimonials that he did submit were unpersuasive to judges whose own children were dabbling in what seemed to their parents like rocket sciences: "I have seen little sketches drawn by little children or little boys of the so-called space ships, seven or eight years old," Judge Sylvester J. Ryan told Bloch. "I am saying I have seen them in my own household, sketches of space ships which have amazed me, all properly labeled and designed."

One other expert opinion generated by the Rosenbergs' defenders never saw the light of day. The more that William Reuben, a journalist for the leftist *National Guardian,* studied the evidence and the record, the more he became convinced that if there was a secret to the atomic bomb David Greenglass wasn't capable of prying that secret loose. Like Bloch, Reuben solicited testimonials from scientists whom he considered sympathetic. Among them was Albert Einstein.

Einstein was, indeed, sympathetic. But, since David's drawings were never revealed in open court and remained under seal, Einstein, like most of the scientists rallied by the defense, had never analyzed the complete testimony or the exhibits. Moreover, Einstein himself had been deemed too great a security risk to be invited to Los Alamos, so he had no firsthand experience to draw upon.

Einstein's handwritten reply, in German, was translated and transcribed by his secretary. "Dear Mr. Reuben," he wrote in a one-paragraph letter dated March 29, 1952,

After careful study of the material which you kindly presented to me, I have come to the conclusion that it is impossible for me to issue a statement concerning the Greenglass testimony such as suggested by you. This is out of the question if for no other reason because the testimony itself is not accessible. But if even the testimony would be made accessible, I would hardly feel sufficiently sure about it to be able to say that a person like Greenglass could not have prepared it on his own, without outside help.

—

For years, critics of the government's case have tried to have it both ways: Not only was David too dumb to grasp the principles of implosion, but whatever scientific crumbs he managed to sweep off the machine-shop floor were so rudimentary that they would have been useless to Soviet scientists.* Edmund Palmieri of the Federal District Court, in rejecting an appeal by Morton Sobell, addressed the paradox. Palmieri noted that Sobell first claimed David Greenglass committed perjury because it was improbable or inconceivable that he could have drawn the exhibits, but Greenglass was faulted subsequently because the drawing failed to measure up to a scientific standard of perfection. Palmieri wrote:

> [This] view might be relevant had Greenglass testified that he had purloined at Los Alamos and turned over to the Rosenbergs a set of blueprints, working drawings, dimensional plans and written specifications for the production of plutonium and the bomb, and that Exhibit 8 and the 12 page description purported to convey that information. But this was neither Greenglass's testimony nor his role in the conspiracy. His role was to get classified information—to get what he could. . . . Were there a complete consensus of all the learned atomic scientists in the world that his description was deficient, it would not draw in issue the truthfulness of his version of what he then transmitted to the Rosenbergs.

The authorities could not justify putting two people to death, though, for passing worthless pseudoscientific babble and cartoonish illustrations to a foreign power. Instead, the government insisted that, through David Greenglass, the Rosenbergs had given away America's most vital military secret "years before our best scientists predicted Russia would perfect the bomb." As a result, the argument went, they perpetuated—if

---

* Marshall Perlin, the lawyer for Sobell and the Rosenbergs' sons, stated: "The best you can say is that there was a meaningless transmission of information which technically might have been sufficient as a matter of law for conviction." When David's impounded sketch was finally made public in 1966, Perlin said: "The theory had been ever since the trial that Greenglass, a machinist with a high-school education, could not have drawn it. Now our contention is that anyone could have drawn it because it doesn't represent the bomb or contain secrets."

not provoked—the cold war and precipitated the Korean War. What's striking, in retrospect, is not just how many people in the government promoted this theory but how many believed it.

How valuable David's drawings and documentation were to the Soviets' nascent nuclear program is difficult to assess because of the profusion of politics and the paucity of available science. Each answer is freighted with other baggage: The FBI claimed to have solved the crime of the century; the NKGB to have saved the Soviet Union by penetrating America's most secret installation;* American intelligence officials insisted that security was tight enough to prevent a major leak (except in the case of Fuchs, for whom the British had vouched, and Theodore Hall); Russian scientists boasted they were well on their way to building a bomb without any outside help (and that they were actually delayed by the stolen secrets, which they used to replicate the successful Fat Man model instead of testing a more advanced version of their own); American scientists agreed that while the Russians didn't really need outside know-how, they were probably helped some by hindsight about the Manhattan Project's mistakes and successes.

Henry Linschitz recalled that fully two years elapsed between the first implosion experiments in the United States and the final achievement of a lens implosion. "It is not possible in any technologically useful way to condense the results of a $2 billion development effort into a diagram, drawn by a high school graduate on a single sheet of paper," Linschitz said. "The information given by Greenglass evidently tells nothing of the prodigious and many-faceted effort, which also would have to be repeated in toto by the Russians."

Harold C. Urey agreed: "The value of the Greenglass sketch and statement, if they were transmitted to the Soviet scientists and engi-

---

* On February 28, 1945, the NKGB submitted to Lavrenti Beria a comprehensive report on nuclear weaponry, including implosion research, based chiefly on intelligence from Hall and Greenglass. More details on implosion reached Russian scientists from Fuchs, but not until April 6. Notes delivered by David Greenglass in September 1945 included two potentially valuable pieces of information, according to Richard Rhodes: an experiment designed to reduce the amount of plutonium needed to make a bomb and another to increase the efficiency of the explosion.

neers, would be of very minor importance." But not valueless. Linschitz said that the government's Exhibit 8, the sketch of a lens cross section, "is correct in its most vague and general aspects, that explosive 'lenses' were used to achieve implosion of a core containing plutonium and beryllium components, the overall system being arranged in an essentially spherically symmetrical configuration." Echoing Hans Bethe's assessment that the drawings and documentation "could be of great help to a trained Russian scientist," Linschitz continued:

> After this analysis, what information can one say these drawings finally convey? Essentially, we are left with the then classified words or concepts, "lens" and "implosion," together with a general impression of spherically disposed components and convergent detonations. Does this constitute a "substantially accurate representation of the principle" of the bomb? In my opinion, no. Nevertheless, it is clear that such a judgment must be a highly subjective one indeed. A diagram that may obviously represent a "principle" to a research expert who has devoted years of hard work and worry to the problem, and who cannot help but correct and fill in the gaps subconsciously with his own knowledge, may be totally useless to a technician who has actually to construct the device. We undoubtedly have such a situation in Exhibit 8.

Philip Morrison, who called David's sketch "barren of any meaningful or correct quantitative information," nevertheless defined David's role in the context of technology and of the paranoia that permeated the Russian security services: "His evidence makes plain that Fuchs is not in fact a double agent, or a man purposely misinformed, telling a false or exaggerated story to mislead his Soviet contacts. For the Los Alamos laboratory is working on implosion lenses, as a simple machinist, a stranger to Fuchs, now independently says. This is valuable information, worth getting, as any intelligence service will readily testify."

Lieutenant Colonel John A. Derry, an electrical engineer who had testified as one of two expert witnesses for the Rosenberg prosecution, was asked recently to reassess the value of David's drawings and documentation. Derry had been Groves's liaison with Los Alamos. During and after the trial, Derry's credentials were questioned repeatedly by the Rosenbergs' defenders: He was an engineer, not a physicist, and his role was largely administrative, not scientific. But his testimony was considered so sensitive that when he took the witness stand Judge Kaufman again cleared the courtroom of spectators. Saypol asked him whether David's description of the bomb, coupled with his sketch, "demonstrate substantially and with substantial accuracy the principle involved in the operation of the 1945 atomic bomb."

"It does," Derry replied.

"Can a scientist, and can you, perceive what the actual construction of the bomb was?"

"You can."

"To a substantial degree?"

"You can."

A half century later, Derry was asked whether, in retrospect, the sketch and the description were of any value.

"Oh, it would help, sure. The Soviets were looking for anything," he said.

How much would it have helped?

"It's insignificant, except this: It's corroboration," he said.

But by definition the very fact that virtually every bit of information attributed to David was corroborative means that Fuchs and Hall had already given it to the Soviets.

"I didn't know that at the time," Derry said.*

---

* Another Manhattan Project alumnus with impeccable credentials as a scientist was asked to reflect on the Rosenberg case. "I'm embarrassed," Dr. Edward Teller said. He paused a moment, then added tentatively: "I remember the name. They passed information in 1945. They were executed." So far, so good. In hindsight, was the information they passed of any scientific value? Teller said he could only guess (in fact, he said he preferred not to be quoted at all, since it was only a guess). "My guess is that the Soviets got enough from Fuchs," he said, "and additional details from Rosenberg might have been confirmation but weren't essential."

—

Whatever the government believed in the early 1950s, a consensus has emerged since then. Responding to Manny Bloch's appeal for expert witnesses to discount David's drawings, Harlow Shapley of Harvard wrote: "I have often thought that the publication of the [1946] Smyth report, ordered by General Groves and his colleagues, gave many times as much information to the Russians about atomic energy researches as has been given by Fuchs and the others mentioned in your letter."[*] In March 1954, nine months after the Rosenbergs were executed, Dr. James Beckerley, the AFC's director of classification, was quoted as saying:

> The atom bomb and the hydrogen bomb were not stolen from us by spies. Espionage played a minor role in the attainment of successful weapons by the Soviets. Atom bombs are not matters that can be stolen and transmitted in the form of information. The Swiss watchmaker, for example, does not export all his secrets when he exports a watch.

That same spring, no less an expert than General Groves himself discounted the efficacy of the information the Rosenbergs were accused of forwarding from David Greenglass. Testifying during the Atomic Energy Commission hearings into Robert Oppenheimer's security status, Groves was asked whether Fuchs was the sole source of leaks about Los Alamos. Groves replied:

> No. I think the data that went out in the case of the Rosenbergs was of minor value. I would never say that publicly. Again, that is something, while it is not secret, I think should be kept very quiet because irrespective of the value of that in the overall picture, the Rosenbergs deserved to hang and I would not like to say anything that would make people say General Groves thinks that they didn't do much damage after all.

---

[*] Richard Rhodes wrote that the Smyth Report "supplied the Soviet Union with information on atomic bomb development nearly equivalent to all the information it had acquired laboriously during the war through espionage."

David Teeple, the assistant to the commission's chairman, dismissed the general's admission as "another example of Groves' talking too much." Groves's statement was deleted from the official hearing transcript.

—

The report of Congress's Joint Committee on Atomic Energy in April 1951 estimated that the combined activities of the four spies had advanced the Soviet atomic-energy program by at least eighteen months, meaning that "if war should come, Russia's ability to mount an atomic offensive against the West will be greatly increased by reason of these four men." Placing David's contribution in perspective, the report said:

> The bomb sketches and explanations that Greenglass—as a virtual layman—could prepare must have counted for little compared with the quantitative data and the authoritative scientific commentary upon atomic weapons that Fuchs transmitted.
>
> Greenglass's value to Russia in generally corroborating Fuchs's statements and perhaps in supplying miscellaneous information which Fuchs omitted is not to be discounted. It is even possible moreover, that Greenglass—in the narrow but important field of his own work upon high explosive lens molds—was able to convey practical data and know-how beyond Fuchs's understanding. Yet, everything considered, Greenglass appears to have been the least effective of the four spies, ranking behind Alan Nunn May in this regard. Had there been no Klaus Fuchs, Greenglass would take on far greater importance. Needless to say, this evaluation does not detract one iota from the horror of this man's crimes nor lessen his legal and moral guilt.

It does, however, raise legal and moral questions about the overheated oratory surrounding the decision to execute the Rosenbergs, Ethel especially. Whatever else Julius Rosenberg delivered to the Russians, they would have built the atomic bomb without him. True, the Soviet bomb resembled Fat Man down to the bolts. David might, by a few weeks at most, have been the first to cue Soviet scientists about implosion, but he mostly validated other, more detailed intelligence. "I told them how to make it," David would boast later. "And if someone put a gun to my head, I could make one now if I had to." George Kistiakowsky, who was chief of the Explosives Division at Los Alamos, demurred. With Stalin hell-bent on developing a bomb and with Fuchs transmitting highly detailed technical information, Kistiakowsky said later, "The very crude sketches of Greenglass could not have been of great importance. Maybe of no importance whatsoever."

The nation that General Groves had dismissed in 1945 as too backward industrially to ever make an atomic bomb—"Why," he said, "those people can't even make a Jeep"—built and successfully tested a nuclear weapon that was no more 100 percent Russian than the American bomb had been 100 percent American. But if David Greenglass hadn't been substituted at the last minute for an AWOL soldier in Mississippi and instead sat out the rest of the war machining tank parts in an ordnance depot in Fontainebleau, would it have made one iota of difference to the success of the Soviet nuclear-weapons program?

"As it turned out, probably none," Hans Bethe said.

"Were they any farther because of David Greenglass's information? Not one iota," Arnold Kramish, the former AEC scientist, concluded fifty years later. "It pales in comparison to what Fuchs and Ted Hall gave, but we didn't know it at that time. It would have had no effect whatsoever. I used to think it would have, but not now."

Chapter 33

Blindman's Buff

**"I want to be able to work at some manual labor
in the fields so that I can sleep at night again."**

Even in the face of death, the Rosenbergs sustained themselves with
something that David Greenglass lacked. "We have the courage," Julius wrote, without irony, "because of our convictions."

Despite their convictions, Ethel and Julius didn't die when they were
supposed to. Not in the week of May 21, 1951, when their executions
were originally scheduled by Judge Kaufman, nor on the several subsequent dates set after it appeared that all avenues of appeal had been
exhausted. In late December 1952, the judge agreed to meet with Julius's
family. The courthouse was festooned with Christmas decorations, but
the spirit in the judge's nineteenth-floor chambers wasn't celebratory.
Leonard Sand, Kaufman's law clerk at the time and later a federal judge
himself, recalled the moment: "I think he said in essence that the Rosenbergs were the masters of their fate. It ended with the mother bursting
into tears and shouting at the judge."

By 1950s standards, when, ordinarily, executions followed convictions
by months, the pace of judicial review seemed nothing short of leisurely.

Judge Kaufman himself was often volunteering, at the slightest provocation, that his stewardship of the case was subject to an unprecedented number of reviews—surely more than he believed were warranted. But this wasn't just any execution. It was the first in peacetime for espionage and the first of a woman by the federal government since the Civil War.*

After the Supreme Court declined to review the case, Kaufman rescheduled the execution for the week of January 12, 1953. But it was delayed again by further appeals, sparing President Truman a decision. On February 16, President Eisenhower denied clemency.†

———

The entire Rosenberg defense depended on challenging David's credibility, and he had provided enough ammunition with which to impugn his testimony. As the Rosenbergs' son Michael later wrote:

[It] is not that the theft of uranium indicates criminal activity on the

---

* The government figured to mute the outcry by demonstrating that the Soviets and their puppets in Eastern Europe were worse. At Roy Cohn's request, the FBI contacted a researcher at Columbia who was just completing a book on the communist purge trials. However, while some Soviet women had been sentenced to Siberia and others had disappeared, none, the researcher concluded, had been tried and sentenced to death. This, the researcher reported, "was not startling as very few women were involved."

† Of the Greenglasses, Herbert Brownell, the attorney general, advised Eisenhower: "They were, it is true, co-conspirators with the Rosenbergs, but a reading of the record indicates that their testimony was credible and was sufficiently supported by circumstantial evidence. At any rate, the jury believed them, and there is no reason why you should not."

Another security lapse was likely still bothering Eisenhower at this time. In January 1953, John Archibald Wheeler, a Princeton physicist and Manhattan Project alumnus, was traveling by train to Washington. Violating security regulations, he took with him classified excerpts of a report that analyzed the value of lithium 6 for thermonuclear weaponry, including the amount that would be needed and the means of manufacturing it. The secret report also explored how much of that information might already have been given to the Soviets by Klaus Fuchs. As the train arrived in Washington, Wheeler gathered his belongings, checked the lavatory, enlisted the porter, and questioned several other passengers, but the secret report had vanished. Wheeler's car was nudged onto a siding, and federal agents scoured it. They searched the tracks from Trenton to Washington. The report was never found. Eisenhower was furious. He summoned the AEC members and delivered an unvarnished lecture on the risks posed by security violations, and he demanded that Wheeler be officially reprimanded. The Rosenbergs' application for executive clemency reached the president's desk a few weeks later.

part of David Greenglass which would frighten him into confessing to espionage because he was really guilty of this theft. The significance is that it is an example of perjury at the trial—a trial at which credibility was the most important issue. . . . If the jury had been informed of these Greenglass perjuries, they might not have been so willing to believe the charges against our parents.[*]

After the war, David had boasted about the stolen uranium to Julius and Bernie and now, with two lives hanging in the balance, Ethel was pressing Bernie to publicly confirm the theft.[†] Informers at Sing Sing may have garbled the story, but their version suggested that David had stolen more than uranium during the war. Those sources—presumably guards or fellow inmates—quoted Julius as telling Ethel that it was important for Bernie (whom Julius disparaged as a "weak sister") to get an affidavit from David affirming "that the tools, which he obtained, had not been bought by his wife, but had been stolen by him from the Army, and that David Greenglass told Bernie that there was some uranium among the tools."

Even at this late stage, a legal victory for the Rosenbergs might make the Greenglasses vulnerable to further prosecution. To guard against that possibility, Ruth sabotaged the Rosenberg defense by divulging its strat-

---

[*] Rereading David's testimony was "very revealing as to his personality; arrogance & cocksure attitude," Julius wrote, adding perceptively that in recounting the fateful walk with Ruth on Route 66 in November 1944 "[David first] felt it was [the] right thing to do then he remembers Rogge's instructions & must show equivocation[,] that he was led." Whatever Julius lacked in grammar and punctuation, he compensated for with passion. But another letter, this one from Julius to Manny Bloch, would have raised questions about Julius's own believability. He suggested that he might have fudged in sworn testimony, although it would strain credulity to imply that there was any moral equivalency between his defenses against self-incrimination and the embellishments that David volunteered or willingly embraced. Still, Julius admitted that, contrary to his trial testimony, he might well have discussed with David the merits of one form of government over the other, but he added: "Since when are permissible expressions of belief such as statements made in private conversations showing a preference for forms of government and economic organization of society admissible as material evidence in criminal prosecutions for high crimes?"

[†] Julius obviously knew about the stolen uranium before the trial, but his lawyers might have figured that he could have implicated himself by raising the issue.

egy to the government. She alerted the FBI that the Rosenbergs intended to prove that David had, indeed, stolen uranium from Los Alamos, had lied about it, and was therefore vulnerable to manipulation when federal agents came calling in 1950. Ruth promised the FBI that she would talk to Bernie and "would see to it that he made no such affidavit."

But the Rosenbergs enlisted a higher authority, Sing Sing's Jewish chaplain, Rabbi Koslowe. Bernie Greenglass and David Rosenberg visited Koslowe at his home in Mamaroneck. The rabbi asked Bernie directly whether David Greenglass had ever told him about the stolen uranium. Torn between brother and sister, Bernie at first dismissed the whole issue as inconsequential. He was persuaded otherwise. Less than a week later, Bernie executed an affidavit stating that his brother had told him in 1946 about taking the uranium souvenir and that in January 1950, after being interviewed by an FBI agent, David had thrown it into the East River.

But, alerted by Ruth, the FBI struck preemptively. Agents obtained an affidavit from David in which he admitted taking a single U-238 hemisphere, shipping it home from Los Alamos, and, after being interviewed by Agent Spillane in January 1950, tossing it into the river. He lied to Spillane, he said, because "he did not want to involve himself in any federal offense as [his] wife [was] pregnant and [he was] no longer connected in illegal activities."

—

All this time, Manny Bloch was also searching for the elusive console table, which the Rosenbergs insisted was an unremarkable piece of furniture that they had purchased from Macy's but that the government maintained was Julius's jury-rigged platform for photographing classified documents. In early March 1953, fully two years after the trial, Bloch reported that he had just discovered the mysterious table among other items that a relative had removed after the Rosenbergs had been arrested. Bloch persuaded a Macy's executive to swear in an affidavit that the table was similar to ones the store sold in the early 1940s. There appeared to be no way of proving who purchased it, though. If the table, or one like it, had ever been in the Rosenbergs' apartment, the FBI never noticed it. During the trial, the jailhouse informer Jerome Tartakow advised the government to forget about the table. "I'm convinced, personally, that he bought the table as he claims," Tartakow told the FBI, "and unless the government is certain he did not I wouldn't press this matter." But the prosecution pressed it anyway, and David testified under oath not only that he had seen the console table but that he had seen it at the Rosenbergs' apartment.

Regardless of whether he ever saw the table itself, David said he was sure he had seen a clamp that he said Julius used to attach some photographic apparatus—probably the camera or a lamp—to the table. In fact, David told the FBI that he had designed and fabricated the clamp at Julius's request. It was made of aluminum; David bored three holes in it. The FBI reported, "It was his opinion that if Rosenberg had used this clamp to support the camera on the table, this table would have to contain three holes on the hinged top thereof or at least show an indication that the holes made by the clamp had been plugged." Julius assured him that the clamp had served its purpose, but David subsequently admitted that he couldn't say conclusively whether this was, in fact, the totemic console table in question. First, he said, he did not attach the clamp to the table himself; second, he acknowledged, he had never even seen the table.*

The FBI was caught off guard on one other front. Early in May 1953, a French newspaper began publishing authentic excerpts from the original notes of meetings between Rogge and his colleagues and David and his family. The evidence suggested an inside job (Rogge and Manny Bloch both had law offices at 401 Broadway). The purloined papers graphically demonstrated what the Rosenbergs' defenders had suspected all along: that David's confession had evolved from fragmen-

---

* Julius may well have used some table for taking photographs, either at his own apartment or one on Morton Street or Avenue B. When the controversy resurfaced in 1953, Ruth accompanied the FBI to Macy's but was unable to identify a table similar to the one she remembered in the Rosenbergs' apartment. Alexander Feklisov would write that he provided Julius with a Leica. "The camera was placed on a tripod facing down, fifteen–twenty inches above a table that was under one or, even better, two side lamps."

tary accounts and sputtered half-truths into an escape-proof legal trap. Rogge delivered a more benign interpretation. "All that they show," he insisted, "is that David Greenglass at first did not tell the full story, a fact which both Government and defense counsel knew and which was brought out on cross-examination."

—

The government's counterattack to the Rosenbergs' legal and public-relations offensive was feeble, perhaps because Washington was ambivalent about its fundamental goal. Did it want the Rosenbergs dead or alive?*

The biggest advantage of keeping the Rosenbergs alive, of course, was that they could still speak.

On November 18, 1952, the day after the Supreme Court denied the Rosenbergs' application for a rehearing, Alan Belmont of the FBI drafted an unusual memo.† Breaking the Soviet wartime code, Belmont wrote, had led to several criminal cases but also to a lot of prosecutorial dead ends. Often, leads could not be disclosed or introduced as corrob-

---

* One answer was sketched by Allen Dulles, the director of the CIA. He envisioned that if the Rosenbergs could be persuaded that "the Soviet regime is persecuting and is ultimately bent on exterminating the Jews under its sovereignty," the couple could be transformed into crusaders against Soviet anti-Semitism. A memo identified a propaganda goal and the psychological strategy to achieve it:

> People of the sort of the Rosenbergs can be swayed by duty where they cannot be swayed by considerations of self-interest. They should not be asked to trade their principles for their lives—for one thing, such an appeal to cowardice would almost certainly fail. The argument should be rather that they are about to die for a system that has betrayed and is destroying their own people, that they have the moral obligation of influencing other Jews against communism.

Implicitly, the CIA acknowledged that while the ends were justified, the means might raise ethical questions. "No discussions can be termed free if the upshot determines whether people live or die," the memo noted. "If this coercive element makes the whole plan repugnant to our traditions of due process, then naturally it should not be undertaken."

† After the Supreme Court ruled, FBI headquarters also ordered the New York and Cleveland bureaus to immediately begin surveillance of, among others, William Perl (an engineer and friend of Julius), Vivian Glassman, and the Sidoroviches "to determine whether they attempt to leave [the] country or make any unusual contacts."

oration.* The Rosenbergs, Belmont wrote, could "supply the necessary missing links to enable successful prosecution" of other cases.

Two weeks later, Mickey Ladd incorporated Belmont's memo into his response to a tantalizing directive from Hoover: "Make certain there is nothing we have which has not been made available which would be of assistance to the Rosenbergs." Ladd replied that FBI files did, in fact, contain information that had not been made available to authorities who were weighing a plea for clemency. The information was anything but mitigating, though—at least for Julius. Instead, Ladd wrote, it "would show that Rosenberg's activities were much greater than legally adduced at the trial." Ladd reiterated that the Rosenberg case "arose" out of the Venona decryptions (although Julius and Ethel themselves weren't actually identified until after David's arrest). The Soviet cables suggested that Julius "was the operating head of a large espionage group and personally handled the recruiting of agents and the collection of scientific data" and that Ethel "was cognizant of her husband's espionage activities." Through investigation, Ladd added, "we were able to secure independent proof that Rosenberg, with the active assistance of his wife, recruited Greenglass and obtained atomic information from him." *Active assistance* had an incriminating ring. But another term in Ladd's memo was to reverberate longer.

Cognizant became a talismanic adjective in the lingering debate over

---

* Belmont was acutely aware of the decoded cables' deficiencies. He later described them as "very fragmentary and full of gaps" and as particularly problematic because Russian idioms might be translated imprecisely and cover names were changed frequently. "We made a tentative identification of 'Antenna' as Joseph Weichbrod since the background of Weichbrod corresponded with the information known about 'Antenna,'" Belmont acknowledged. "Weichbrod was about the right age, had a Communist background, lived in NYC, attended Cooper Union in 1939, worked at the Signal Corps, Ft. Monmouth, and his wife's name was Ethel. He was a good suspect for 'Antenna' until sometime later when we definitely established through investigation that 'Antenna' was Julius Rosenberg."

Antenna's identity was established to the FBI's satisfaction within weeks of David's arrest, but the details remained top secret for nearly fifty years. "Investigation has established definitely that Schmell [sic], Osa, and Liberal are identical with David and Ruth Greenglass and Julius Rosenberg, respectively," according to a summary brief dated September 1, 1950. The brief filled forty-two pages and, with varying degrees of verification, linked code names from the decrypted cables to real people, places, and events.

Ethel Rosenberg's guilt. It implies a general awareness or consciousness, suggesting that while Ethel knew of her husband's avocation—she could identify him as a spy—she may well have been oblivious to the details.

Ladd recommended that the attorney general be briefed both on evidence developed by the bureau as well as on Venona information "which shows conclusively the extensiveness of Julius Rosenberg's activities and that his wife was cognizant of them." But Hoover, being proprietary, handwrote an order: No Venona material about the Rosenbergs "is to be briefed and included in memo to A.G."

Venona was never mentioned by name, but two FBI memos encapsulated the code breakers' findings. One, on January 9, 1953, attributed to "an informant of known reliability who is not able to testify" information that Julius Rosenberg "operated a large espionage network in the United States, that he personally recruited agents who furnished technical and scientific data, including data on jet planes and guided missiles, that his wife Ethel was aware of this activity." That January memo also included information from Jerome Tartakow, the jailhouse informer, who reported that Rosenberg had told him, apparently without amplifying, that Ethel "was a very capable person." In June 1953, a follow-up memo to Attorney General Brownell using information also drawn from Venona amplifying Julius's role, said much the same.* The source was unidentified, but this time was described as "of unimpeachable reliability whose identity cannot be revealed under any circumstances."

Another memo to Brownell, this one from his assistant Warren Olney III, drew on the Greenglasses' version of Ethel's complicity, mitigated by sexism. "She was a central figure in the conspiracy to the extent also that she performed the function of typewriting for transmittal to the Soviets information received orally or in fragmentary form by herself and her husband from various persons," Olney wrote. "It must be appreciated that the extent of Ethel's 'outside' activities such as clandestine

---

* Julius was described as "the operating head of a large Soviet espionage network in 1944 [who] personally handled the recruitment of agents and the collection of data from them." The memo added nothing more about Ethel, save "his wife knew of his work."

street corner contacts at night and in distant places does not compare favorably in number with those made by Julius due to the fact that she is a woman and, in addition, had the burden of small children to look after." Olney did point out that the sentence was unprecedented—never in American history had a civil court imposed the death penalty for espionage, and federal courts had meted out capital sentences for treason only twice (one was commuted by President Roosevelt in 1943; the other convict had applied for clemency and his application was pending; in 1859, John Brown had been sentenced to death for treason, but that had been under Virginia state law). Olney addressed one other question in his memo: Why, given that she was palpably more guilty than Ethel, wasn't Ruth Greenglass prosecuted? "Obviously," Olney wrote, "naming her as a defendant would not only in all likelihood have destroyed her valuable cooperation but would undoubtedly have had an adverse effect on the key Government witness, David Greenglass."

The FBI wanted no last-minute glitches that might unsettle its chief witness. Early in June 1953, the new federal prosecutor in New York, J. Edward Lumbard, suggested bringing David back from Lewisburg to help rebut Manny Bloch's latest motions. That would be "very unwise," Hoover warned. Bloch might insist on cross-examining David in open court, which, Hoover cautioned, "could readily result in a further Roman holiday."

—

Only one public official appeared to be taking the repeated delays in execution personally. As early as February 1953, Judge Kaufman was warning the FBI that unless the government expedited its parries to the latest Rosenberg appeals, the Supreme Court might adjourn for the summer before it got the case—delaying the execution until October at the very earliest, by which time "the propagandists would have an excellent opportunity to completely air the entire matter." The FBI offered to forward Kaufman's concerns to the Justice Department, but he declined because, according to a government memo, "he didn't think it would be desirable for there to be any indication that he was taking an affirmative position in instant matter because of his judicial situation."

On May 29, after the Supreme Court declined to review the case, Kaufman rescheduled the execution for the week of June 15.

—

On Saturday, June 13, Bernie visited Ethel for the last time. His importuning, as scripted by Tessie, complete with stage notes ("if Ethel started to yell at him he should yell back"), quickly degenerated into yet another screaming match. Everybody had lied, Ethel insisted. The screaming subsided just long enough for Bernie to recount a two-year-old cautionary tale from Tessie. When she had visited Ethel at the Women's House of Detention, she had posed a question on Michael's behalf: When would his mother be coming home? Ethel said to tell Michael that she would return home in about two years. Tessie said that when she relayed that message to Michael, he started to cry and said, "I hope she dies because of the harm she's causing me."

This time, as Bernie delivered the punch line, Ethel began crying.

Bernie had driven to Sing Sing that day with Julius's brother David, who defended Julius to the end. He had persuaded Bernie to swear that David Greenglass had confessed to him about the stolen uranium and even pleaded periodically with trial jurors to reconsider their verdict or at least to join the appeal for clemency. "He put his foot in the door. He wanted me to write a letter to the President," James Gibbons, who had for a time been the lone holdout on the jury, later recalled. "I said, there are 11 other jurors, why me? I said it was over, I didn't want anything more to do with it, and please to leave. He wouldn't take his foot from the door. I had to kick it away."

After returning from Sing Sing that Saturday, David Rosenberg visited Ruth. She was in no mood to welcome him.[*] Earlier that day, an

---

[*] A few weeks before, David Rosenberg had shown up unexpectedly at Ruth's birthday party at 64 Sheriff Street, claiming that he was urging Julius to cooperate. He asked for any written statement from David Greenglass attesting to Julius's guilt. Because he insisted that the statement be in David's handwriting, Ruth suspected that what he was really after was a specimen—possibly to help verify that the statements stolen from Rogge's office were authentic. Ruth had already secreted all of David's prison correspondence with a neighbor to keep it from the Rosenbergs.

elderly man who had identified himself as a rabbi had come to her door and had announced that her husband was in the hospital at Lewisburg after having torn his clothes and smeared himself with ashes in a traditional affectation of mourning or repentance. The rabbi had urged Ruth to go to David and get him to tell the truth. Ruth had thrown him out of the house. When David Rosenberg arrived, she refused even to let him inside her apartment. Instead, they argued in the hallway until Ruth, angry and frustrated, declared that David Rosenberg should wake up already and realize that the only ones lying were Julius and Ethel and that the sole way to save them was to persuade them to confess. Like Bernie, she cited Michael, recalling that she had seen him once identify Stalin as his grandfather. For the first time, and with the execution now less than one week away, David Rosenberg appeared to be wavering. Later that night, he called both Ruth and Bernie to say that he wanted to be briefed by someone in the FBI "who could set him straight on the whole situation." Both offered to help. On Sunday, though, David Rosenberg contacted Manny Bloch. Bloch persuaded him to await the Supreme Court's decision, on still another motion, expected on Monday. He agreed and said that if he still wanted to meet with the FBI he would contact Bernie. He never did.

—

On the morning of Monday, June 15, 1953, Brownell and his associates met in his office. The execution was now scheduled for Thursday night. J. Edgar Hoover briefed them on the FBI's contingency plans and on the bureau's emphatic desire for only its agents, the warden, and the principal timekeeper at Sing Sing to be present if the Rosenbergs decided to talk. And certainly not the director of prisons, James Bennett.

If Hoover had ever doubted that Bennett was a bleeding heart, those doubts had evaporated earlier in 1953 when a memo had crossed his desk with information furnished to an FBI agent "in the strictest of confidence" by Daniel Lyons, the pardon attorney for the Department of Justice. The memo, only recently declassified, said Bennett "made a very strong plea for the Rosenbergs, stating that they were very religious people, that they were victims of a great injustice" and "made a very strong attempt to influence the Pardon Attorney to act favorably toward the Rosenbergs." Hoover delivered a three-word response to the memo: "This is shocking."

Bennett wasn't shy, though. In May, he had convinced Attorney General Brownell to help him establish a back channel to the Rosenbergs that would bypass the FBI, the prosecutors, and even the defense lawyers.* On Tuesday, June 2, 1953, Bennett visited Ethel and Julius separately at Sing Sing. He told Julius that the government believed he possessed information "which would be helpful in solving some as yet unanswered questions." Instead of information, Julius unleashed an emotional tirade over Ruth Greenglass's freedom and over David Greenglass's technical incompetence. Ethel, Bennett later wrote, "said that obviously the government could not prove whatever suspicions they had about certain aspects of the case or we would not be turning to her for cooperation, and that she had no intention of putting her finger on somebody else or giving false or misleading information even though it might have the effect of staying her own execution."

For all their bravado, two years in Sing Sing had taken their toll. Bennett had first met the Rosenbergs when they had been placed in federal custody. This time, he said, Julius "lacked the detached calmness and self-assurance that characterized my former conversation with him. He no longer seemed to have the attitude of the martyr." Ethel appeared to share many of her husband's sentiments, Bennett wrote, "although she wasn't quite as verbose or excited as he was."

———

Federal officials were to reconvene at the Justice Department on Thursday evening just before the execution in order to evaluate any statement

---

* Shortly before this, Bennett had forwarded to Brownell a letter that he had received from a woman who said that if the Rosenbergs "have not been reasonable in their answers to questions of known fact, they should be helped to release themselves from the bondage of a mistaken loyalty to a false cause. I believe that the American people would be greatly relieved in conscience if a true statement could be obtained from the Rosenbergs which would warrent their reprieve."

the Rosenbergs might make and determine whether a reprieve was warranted. Hoover was equipped to make that evaluation on the basis of a memo that Ladd had drafted a few days before.

"In answer to your inquiry what could the Rosenbergs tell us that would warrant a delay in their execution," the nine-paragraph memo began, "it is believed that the Rosenbergs can supply the necessary missing links to the following." The memo provided a litany of pending investigations that had been stymied by lack of corroboration. Decades later, when the FBI released a copy of Ladd's memo, the first paragraph was redacted. The others constituted a catalog of unrequited criminality. In the event of a last-minute confession, the memo said, "we can probably prosecute" William Perl and Mike Sidorovich for espionage, Ann Sidorovich for espionage or at least for conspiracy to commit espionage, Alfred Sarant and Joel Barr for wartime espionage, as well as possibly Vivian Glassman; further, the FBI could follow investigative leads from David Greenglass and Jerome Tartakow on the spy ring's contacts in upstate New York and in Ohio, on the source of the information about the proposed sky platform, on whether Julius was the man with the cigar who had appeared in Queens for the rendezvous with Harry Gold, and on whether he was the same "Julius" who was familiar to Elizabeth Bentley.

While the FBI's memo suggested that "the Rosenbergs" could give crucial evidence, each of the questions referred only to Rosenberg in the singular, as in Julius. Not a single question suggested that there was any information to be wrung from Ethel Rosenberg.

In New York, Special Agent L. V. Boardman proposed only four questions initially: With whom did Julius microfilm documents, who were his sources of information for the Russians, in which other cities did he have espionage contacts, and who were his espionage contacts in Cleveland? Because the FBI already knew the answers from the Venona decryptions, Boardman said, "dependent upon the answers to these questions it can be determined readily whether Rosenberg intends to cooperate." Again, Boardman posed no questions to Ethel.

A follow-up questionnaire followed the same pattern. What were the real names of the four or five contacts mentioned in the decrypted NKGB cables who were still unidentified? Who assisted in microfilming and where? Of these eleven questions, only one referred to Ethel, and it seems to suggest that investigators were as concerned about justifying the prosecution and conviction of her as they were about wresting additional details that might implicate others. Question 9 read: "Was your wife cognizant of your activities?"

———

While James Bennett was barred from the execution itself, he was still mulling over what to do if the Rosenbergs decided to confess even after they were strapped into the electric chair. Under New York State protocol, Warden Denno of Sing Sing advised, once prisoners enter the chamber, conversation ceases. "Denno says this is [a] humane and practical method of handling executions in that they are accomplished with such speed as to cause least hardship on prisoners," the FBI reported. "To act otherwise, as indicated by Bennett, would cause confusion among execution personnel and could result in embarrassment to all concerned, in view of the fact that press will be present and obviously will report such confusion."

Denno said he intended to execute Julius first. Otherwise, he advised, Ethel would have to walk past Julius's holding cell, "thus probably creating emotional crisis and make task of execution more difficult." Denno added: "To put Ethel in pre-execution chamber and Julius elsewhere would reveal considerably in advance, that Ethel was to go first, which is against prison practice and is considered to be unnecessarily cruel."*

———

Later that same day, the Supreme Court voted five to four to deny a stay of execution. Then, the court adjourned until the fall.

---

* However, everyone seemed to presume that Ethel was the stronger figure. (Morris Ernst of the American Civil Liberties Union volunteered to the FBI that "Julius is the slave and his wife, Ethel, the master.") In June 1951, Julius had acknowledged being unnerved by the execution of Willie McGee, a black man accused of raping a white woman. "Even though we had the lunch I like best sunnyside eggs I found it difficult to swallow and had no appetite for the cream puff," Julius reported.

On Tuesday, June 16, Kaufman advised the FBI that Tessie Greenglass had asked to see him again. He rejected her request. A few days before, Tessie had instructed Ruth and Bernie to deliver a message to her youngest son the next time they visited him at Lewisburg: "No matter what happens, David should not have it on his conscience and that if he had to do it again he should again tell the truth."

Also on Tuesday, a petition seeking to vacate the judgment and the death sentence was accepted for consideration by Supreme Court Justice William O. Douglas. At 11:00 P.M., Attorney General Brownell conferred with Chief Justice Fred Vinson. The following morning, according to an FBI memo, Judge Kaufman "very confidentially advised that at the meeting between the Attorney General and Chief Justice Vinson last night, Justice Vinson said that if a stay is granted he will call the full Court into session Thursday morning to vacate it."

After wavering, Douglas granted a stay.* As Kaufman predicted, Vinson, responding to Brownell's application, ordered the full Supreme Court to reconvene.

The execution was still scheduled for Thursday night. Earlier that day, James Bennett informed Deputy Attorney General William Rogers that Warden Denno wanted an official copy of the latest Supreme Court ruling before he proceeded with the executions. But the FBI determined that Denno was willing to proceed after being notified by telephone. "It looks like Jim Bennett does not have his heart in this thing," Rogers observed in a memo. Beneath this Hoover scribbled, "That is an understatement."

But the execution was postponed one more day while the Court considered Brownell's application to vacate Douglas's stay.

As late as Friday, June 19, an FBI agent contacted Gordon Dean, the Atomic Energy Commission chairman, who had been quoted as saying that "if Julius Rosenberg talked, he could identify an individual who

---

* Defenders of the Rosenbergs were ecstatic, although it is still difficult to grasp why Douglas, given ample opportunities earlier, waited so long to weigh in decisively against the government's handling of the case. On Monday, Douglas had joined the majority in rejecting a stay of execution. The following day, though, he was grappling with a new and vexing issue: whether the Rosenbergs had been convicted and sentenced under the wrong law.

furnished atomic energy information to the Russians." Surprised by the agent's visit, Dean said he had made the remark in a conversation weeks earlier when James Bennett had said he planned to visit the Rosenbergs at Sing Sing. "Another Bennett obstruction tactic," Hoover commented.

—

At 10:00 A.M. on June 19, President Eisenhower convened his Cabinet. Korea topped the agenda. As negotiations crept toward a cease-fire, the peace was going worse than the war. Eisenhower was compelled to remind the Cabinet that the principal enemy in Korea was still communism. Changing the subject, Ezra Taft Benson, the secretary of agriculture, briefly expressed concern that an outbreak of hoof-and-mouth disease in Mexico might spread to the United States. Eisenhower perked up when Benson shifted to the practical and economic ramifications of wheat surpluses. The Cabinet also explored the latest developments in government reorganization and civil-service revision before finally addressing the sixth item on the agenda, the one matter of life and death that demanded an immediate response.

Eisenhower had rejected clemency once already, four months before. Now, it appeared as if all appeals had been exhausted. And if Herb Brownell was correct, and he usually was, then more than twenty-six months of legal maneuvering would come to an abrupt and definitive conclusion before another day dawned. The Rosenbergs would be dead.

The president asked Brownell to brief the Cabinet on the arguments being weighed by the Supreme Court, which was convening in extraordinary session at that very moment. Brownell explained that the issue was the law under which the Rosenbergs were tried and convicted. The crime was committed when the Espionage Act, which provides for maximum penalties of either thirty years' imprisonment or death, was applicable. Congress subsequently passed the Atomic Energy Act, which applies to atomic espionage but provides for the death penalty only on the recommendation of a jury and when the defendant is charged with intent to harm the United States. The justices would review only that question, Brownell said—a question that, he said, had already been raised and rejected in lower courts. If the Court reversed Douglas, then an appeal for presidential clemency would probably be the only legal option left to the Rosenbergs.* Brownell also informed the Cabinet that last-minute questions had come up about the propriety of executing the Rosenbergs on Friday night, the Jewish Sabbath. But the crux of the case before the Court was "merely a technicality."

"The public doesn't know of technicalities," Eisenhower said. What is the effect on ordinary citizens when the nation's highest court—whether it's just one justice or a majority—holds up an execution for forty-eight hours?

Brownell was adamant. The communists' chief objective was to pressure the president, and they were dead set on perpetuating this propaganda opportunity. "Who's going to decide," he asked, "pressure groups or the judicial system?"

Eisenhower replied that he wasn't concerned with what the communists think, only with honest citizens.

Neither Brownell nor anyone else in the Cabinet meeting invoked classified FBI debriefings or the Venona decryptions to point out that whatever David Greenglass delivered through the Rosenbergs must have been skimpy compared to the nuanced and annotated data delivered by Klaus Fuchs and Theodore Hall.

—

A few days earlier, in a telling letter to his son, who was serving in Korea, Eisenhower had elaborated on his reasoning, never mentioning the atomic bomb. "It goes against the grain to avoid interfering in the case where a woman is to receive capital punishment," the president wrote. He added, though, that Ethel "has obviously been the leader in everything they did in the spy ring," and "if there would be any commuting of the woman's sentence without the man's, then from here on the Soviets would simply recruit their spies from among women." More-

---

* The Supreme Court, in vacating Douglas's stay, never fully explored the "technicality" of whether the Atomic Energy Act of 1946 took precedence. In his dissent, Justice Felix Frankfurter wrote: "To be writing an opinion in a case affecting two lives after the curtain has been rung down upon them has the appearance of pathetic futility. But history also has its claims."

over, he said, the Rosenbergs' deaths would be a deterrent—just as he had correctly guessed the death sentence would be in Normandy when, shortly after D day, he had ordered a public execution of two GIs convicted of rape and murder. "Of course," he continued, "I think that if it were possible to assure that these people would be imprisoned for the rest of their natural lives, there would be no question that the vast bulk of the argument would rest on the side of commutation. But the fact is that, if they do not go to the chair, they will be released in 15 years under Federal law."

Late that Friday afternoon, President Eisenhower again denied clemency.* He acknowledged that the case had "aroused grave concern both here and abroad in the minds of serious people aside from the consideration of law" but added: "By immeasurably increasing the chances of atomic war the Rosenbergs may have condemned to death tens of millions of innocent people all over the world."

—

For months, James Bennett had been needled by Hoover as an obstructionist. But on Friday, around 1:00 P.M., he telephoned Warden Denno from Washington with a different sort of question. This time, he asked whether the execution could be expedited so as to be conducted before sundown. Denno was disinclined. He argued that it would be imprudent to carry out an execution before most of the inmates returned to their cell blocks, which, in summer, wasn't until about 7:10 P.M. Also, the executioner wasn't due in Ossining until about 8:30, and his wife didn't know where to reach him. Denno's preference was to proceed at the regular hour, 11:00 P.M., and he argued that the government would be condemned regardless of when the Rosenbergs were executed. Delaying the execution until after sundown on Saturday would be pressing against

---

* Brownell had recommended that the petition for clemency be denied because, he wrote, "there is plenary proof that this couple constituted the head and center of a conspiratorial espionage group." He added: "The petition intimates that some representative of the Government offered the petitioners the guarantee of life for the price of a confession of guilt. This statement is untrue."

the judge's end-of-the-week legal deadline for the execution, Denno warned, and "if the execution is scheduled before sundown today there is a probability the Government would be charged with rushing the execution to avoid additional motions by the defense."

Bennett and Denno apparently compromised. Find the executioner and carry out the sentence at 8:00 P.M. The other inmates would have been returned to their cells, and the sun would not have set. William Rogers, the deputy attorney general, later claimed credit for this compromise. At 2:35, Alan Belmont, the assistant FBI director, ordered agents to find the executioner and escort him to Sing Sing at once.

The execution was nearly delayed, though, by a telegram to Warden Denno signed by Manny Bloch. The message was unequivocal: The execution would violate federal law because a death sentence is to be stayed automatically when an appeal is pending. At 7:27 P.M., Deputy Attorney General Rogers informed Alan Belmont at Sing Sing that no record of any pending appeal had been found. The FBI concluded that the telegram was bogus.

Within an hour, the Rosenbergs were dead.

A few days later, an envelope addressed to James Bennett arrived special delivery. It was the bill from Sing Sing:

Board, cell, and female guards for Ethel Rosenberg, 801 days, a record for a woman inmate at Sing Sing, at $38.60 per day: $30,918.60.

Board and cell for Julius Rosenberg, $4.43 per day for most of his 767 days: $3,399.98.

Two executions at $150 each: $300.

Every court that considered the case had, directly or implicitly, declined to overturn the convictions or the sentence. But the government's legal victory was Pyrrhic. The Russians won the propaganda war. "One suspects that it was the worldwide protests more than anything else that persuaded Eisenhower and Brownell that to suspend the executions while more legal proceedings went on would be to betray weakness in the face of a cynical and determined enemy," the sociologist Nathan Glazer has written.

From the beginning, the government's other goal had been more alluring: leverage the flimsy indictment, the conviction, and finally the death sentence imposed on Ethel to wring a full confession from Julius; count on her natural motherly instincts to overcome unconditional loyalty to a noble but discredited cause. "I wanted them to cooperate with us and not to die," said Robert Lamphere, the FBI supervisor and liaison to Venona.*

That strategy failed, William Rogers, the deputy attorney general, admitted: "She called our bluff."

———

Judge Kaufman and his wife were planning to vacation in Maine during July and then drive to California. He asked the FBI whether it would be wise for him to stay out of New York City. The bureau didn't respond directly but "pointed out that the Judge's plans, as outlined, would seem to be very desirable." On Tuesday, June 23, at Hoover's direction, Agents John Harrington and Thomas McAndrews, on Alan Belmont's orders, met with Kaufman in his chambers. Harrington and McAndrews told Kaufman that the FBI had confidential information not disclosed at the trial, that in Belmont's words "reflected the undeniable guilt of the Rosenbergs." They confirmed that Julius "was a high ranking official in the Soviet Espionage apparatus in this area" and that Ethel Rosenberg "knew of the extent of her husband's activities." That information came from unimpeachable sources and was known to only a half-dozen people.

In retrospect, the timing was even more striking than the substance, suggesting that the information hadn't been imparted earlier in order to avoid influencing the judge. Instead, Belmont wrote, the information was "to be furnished for the purpose of easing the Judge's mind on the stand he took." A subsequent FBI memo said Kaufman was reassured

---

* Lamphere's rationale was twofold: If the Rosenbergs cooperated, the resulting intelligence coup would net as many as fifteen suspected spies; also, he said, "the amount of evidence we had produced at the trial against Ethel Rosenberg fell far short of that against her husband."

by the confirmatory information about Julius, responding that "all along he felt we had additional information, not brought out at the trial." The memo did not mention his reaction to what little the agents had said about Ethel.

—

"It was a queer, sultry summer, the summer they electrocuted the Rosenbergs," Sylvia Plath began *The Bell Jar.* "It had nothing to do with me, but I couldn't help wondering what it would be like, being burned alive all along your nerves. I thought it must be the worst thing in the world."

At Lewisburg, David couldn't get the Rosenbergs out of his mind. He remained in a segregated cell block, shielded from other inmates, as well as from public vitriol. One letter from a woman in Milwaukee was never delivered to him but was retained in his prison file. "Did you really think when you told those lies at the Rosenberg trial that Ethel would actually be put to death?" the woman wrote. "Do you still think that your fat hide is so much more valuable than hers? I hope that during the next 15 years you have plenty of time to think over the great crime you have committed—far more serious, I assure you, than stealing of uranium."

A few weeks after the executions, David again urged Rogge to intercede with the warden for a transfer from the hostile confines of Lewisburg to the prison farm. "The farm would keep me away from sources of peril to me in here and so be better for my peace of mind," he wrote. At about the same time, David wrote a similar letter to James Bennett. "I want to be able to work at some manual labor in the fields," he wrote, "so that I can sleep at night again."

His request was rejected.

Chapter 34

Lewisburg

"I begin to feel that for me there is no atonement possible, that whatever I do will never be enough."

≡

David was at his wits' end. He hadn't heard from Ruth for eleven days. She could have had any number of legitimate reasons for not writing, but he imagined the worst.

"My nature is such," he wrote his lawyer a few weeks after the executions, "I can have almost anything told me, but suspense just about drives me crazy. If you know these people who are our enemy you know how ruthless they can be." Maybe enemies weren't to blame for the lapse. "If there is nothing wrong at home and there is no reason other than neglect for the lack of mail then I want to know that too," David wrote. "If it is neglect on Ruth's part then it certainly shows a callousness that I would never have believed could be part of Ruth's nature. You may tell her for me that I will answer her letters when I receive them but that will be the only way she will get any mail from me."

David's isolation evoked childhood memories for him of when his brother Bernie spent lonely nights at his ham radio "tapping out calls to the empty ether hoping for a reply. Now I can understand how he must have felt," David wrote. "This lack of reply is enough to drive me wild."

Though not so wild as to invite retribution from other prisoners or to become a disciplinary problem. He confined his venting to Ruth and to Rogge. "He is maintaining a good adjustment outwardly," one early evaluation by prison authorities said, "but in observing his correspondence [with Ruth] inward confusion and turmoil is noted."

Some of his confusion and turmoil resulted from not knowing what was happening at home. Visiting at Lewisburg was limited to only two hours a month, and Lewisburg was nearly two hundred miles from Manhattan, a grueling drive or a tedious train ride. David wrote Ruth twice a week, and he was allowed to receive as many as seven letters. Seven never came, however; Ruth was too busy raising and supporting two children to reply more than twice a month or so.

The rest of David's confusion and turmoil was the result of knowing full well what was happening on the inside.

Fewer than two hundred guards watched over the 1,200 inmates in what one federal prison official characterized as "a delicate balance"— one periodically upset by racial and gang wars. The inmates were an eclectic group of communists, organized-crime figures, and assorted felons. Many were military veterans, and about one in four had been convicted in courts-martial. The largest single group of civilian prisoners was serving time for interstate trafficking in stolen cars. Fellow inmates included Harry Gold and Alger Hiss; William Remington, the accused communist whose head was crushed with a brick while he slept in his cell in 1954; Joe Adonis, the mobster; Wilhelm Reich, the eccentric inventor of the orgone accumulator, with which, he maintained he had harnessed a previously undiscovered energy source that, like the atom, promised a range of benefits, from curing psychiatric disorders to producing rain; and Harvey Matusow, a former communist and FBI informant.*

As a former communist *and* an informer, Matusow seemed to be near the bottom of the prison food chain. David ranked even lower: He had betrayed his country *and* his sister. "This was a cardinal sin in

---

* Inmates weren't the only ones who had achieved notoriety. At one point, the prison psychologist was Robert Lindner, the author of *Rebel Without a Cause*.

the minds of many prisoners, who didn't normally take on a posture of moral judgment about other prisoners," Matusow recalled. "There were countless times I heard hostile comments about Greenglass, 'Oh him, he put his sister in the chair.'"

As late as 1955, Warden Fred T. Wilkinson advised Hoover and Bennett that "other inmates have a deep hatred for Communism and might take violent action against Gold and Greenglass since these men are labeled as Communists as well as 'rats and informers' by the other inmates." David was reminded of that daily. An inmate who worked in the prison barbershop reported that David was doing "some tuff time" and getting "the silent treatment." After another barber, this one a navy veteran, had given David short shrift, David groused as he got up from the chair. "Go on you rat bastard," the barber said. "You lucky you didn't get your head cut off."

—

Lewisburg was built on a picturesque 955-acre reserve, about the size of Manhattan's Central Park, that boasted magnificent vistas of the Allegheny Mountains from Pennsylvania's Buffalo Valley. It opened in 1932 as the prototype for a fledgling penal-reform movement that sought to repudiate the violent fortresses of the federal prison system: Atlanta, Leavenworth, and Alcatraz. Instead, an early mission statement explained, this prison was designed specifically "for the adult offender whose point of view has not been entirely warped and who offers some prospect for ultimate rehabilitation." Henry Hill, Lewisburg's first warden, generally acquiesced in that philosophy but pursued his own idiosyncratic version. He required all staff members to salute him as he patrolled the grounds accompanied by his Great Danes, yet was also criticized for tolerating disorder and idleness. Favoritism, according to one official rebuke, was imbuing Lewisburg with "a country club atmosphere." As a result, two prison industries were established. Inmates made clothing and manufactured a wide variety of metal products, including license plates for federal vehicles, cafeteria trays, and sputum-cup holders for tubercular veterans.

Lewisburg looked like a monastery. Instead of industrial-style trusses spanning the mess hall and other common rooms, Gothic arches divided the refectory into more intimate spaces. The inscription over the administration building was nothing short of inspirational: "Let those who control the lives of the men who enter here ever bear in mind that the path to better things lies upward always and is steep, and that God's choicest blessings come to him who helps the weary climber." Emblazoned on the proscenium arch of the prison auditorium was an aphorism attributed to Bacon: "That which is past and gone is irrevocable; wise men have enough to do with things present and to come." The steel doors of individual cells had rustic wooden veneers. Instead of utilitarian glazed brick and tile, common rooms were decked out in precast stone with warm wood trim. To make the prison seem less grim from afar, steel grilles were installed on the inside of the windows (a nicety that had the unintentional effect of making Lewisburg seem more forbidding to the inmates). A relatively unobtrusive but functional concrete wall defined the perimeter of the twenty-six-acre complex of redbrick watchtowers surrounding redbrick buildings with red tile roofs and dominated by a crenellated brick Italian Renaissance–style smokestack, which seemed to evoke Siena more than central Pennsylvania.

—

David had his own cell and rarely fraternized. He began to attend Jewish services and also music-appreciation classes because neither activity attracted violent prisoners and no gratuitous conversation was permitted. He often visited the library and enrolled in a correspondence course through the University of Chicago—the very school that he said Julius had wanted him to attend after the war. He wasn't completely friendless, although several of the inmates who said that David befriended them might have been exaggerating in order to curry favor with the FBI.

Raymond Paradis, a convicted auto thief, told the FBI that David had instructed him on how to obtain a phony passport from another inmate, Theodore Harris. The FBI's reaction to the story is notable: "It was felt that this information was fabricated by Paradis to ingratiate himself with Bureau or by Greenglass to impress Paradis"—or that "Harris fabricated the story and convinced Greenglass of [its] truth." In other words, David was a boastful liar or simply gullible. David said he played along because Harris was among his few friends. "When he does find someone who will talk to him, he will kid them along and exchange fantastic stories, which all concerned know are fantastic, just in order to have something to talk about," an agent who interviewed David reported. Harris, who had been sentenced to Lewisburg for passing bad checks and was later returned there after being arrested on a morals charge, was described by a parole official as "an egotistical and despicable character" and of "superior intelligence, not criminally insane, but with a psychopathic personality."

Another former Lewisburg inmate, Luke Hoffman, contacted the FBI from Cleveland, where he was being held for also passing worthless checks, to volunteer information on what he described as communist activity. Hoffman said that when he had been serving two and a half years for being AWOL, he had several times expressed his bitterness against the United States. According to this account, David told Hoffman that he could obtain "more money than he had ever seen in his life" by finding a certain café on Kearny Street in San Francisco and contacting a man named Belastro. According to Hoffman, David also boasted about a fifteen-thousand-dollar cache hidden inside an overpass in Georgia. While describing Hoffman's story as "far-fetched," the agent who interviewed him added: "Hoffman during the course of the interview appeared mentally balanced and at no time did he mention that he was desirous of having the F.B.I. intercede in his behalf to have his sentence lightened for furnishing the above information. Hoffman did not seem to have any motive in mind," the agent said, but "stated that the matter had been preying on his mind."

For all the inmates who would have delighted in informing on an informer, apparently there wasn't much to report. David was cited for only four infractions at Lewisburg, all relatively minor. He always had an alibi. When he was caught red-handed with five extra towels, he insisted that he had never been told precisely how many towels he was allowed; after he admitted he had received a previous warning for the same offense, his privileges were restricted for two weeks. He was disciplined again for taking meat and green peppers from the commissary without authorization, and he was also given twenty extra hours of work duty after guards found a cache of pills in his cell—420 red vitamin capsules, 200 small brown pills, and 70 white pills, which were otherwise unidentified and which he said had been issued at the prison hospital. The fourth infraction was not one of contraband but of discourtesy: He was cited for "arrogance, insolence and disrespect" when he requested a pass while a guard was writing one for another inmate. He admitted he had interrupted the guard, a disciplinary report said, but "then attempted to justify his actions by stating he was not thinking at the time of the seriousness of his actions."

David repeatedly maneuvered for a transfer to the federal prison in Danbury, Connecticut, where the inmate population was considered less violent and visiting would be more convenient for Ruth and the rest of the family. Early in 1954, Tessie Greenglass notified Agent John Harrington that she was bedridden. (She contacted Harrington instead of unfamiliar federal officials, she said, because she could not write English.) Tessie said she had suffered a slight stroke that would prevent her from ever making the overnight trek to visit David in Pennsylvania again. Hoover himself asked the attorney general to intervene. But James Bennett balked. He invoked a rule against assigning inmates to Danbury who were serving longer than five years. Bennett also warned that a transfer "would give the appearance he was a stool pigeon and this would be bad" and that at "Lewisburg they have him working in a shop with only one person, who is thoroughly reliable." Hoover's aide, Lou Nichols, pronounced the five-year rule to be a legitimate excuse, but he dismissed Bennett's two other reasons as "just so much hogwash."

—

At the same time that David was being shunned at Lewisburg by most of his fellow inmates, he was in demand as a political prop when one congressional committee or another needed a marquee witness to testify against communist subversion. The first request came from Roy Cohn, who signed on as counsel to the McCarthy subcommittee on internal security just a few months after the executions. McCarthy was panting for ammunition, and Cohn enlisted David to inject the name Julius Rosenberg as further proof that the Army Signal Corps at Fort Monmouth, New Jersey, had been infiltrated by Soviet spies. The FBI was reluctant to share its witness. In a memo to his inner circle, Hoover quoted Frank Loveland, Bennett's assistant in the Bureau of Prisons, as saying that "Greenglass had been cooperative and that he was an excitable sort of individual who might go to pieces and might not, therefore, in the future, be willing to cooperate to the same extent as he has in the past."

Hoover was also irritated at the possibility that after three years of interrogations, David might still be withholding information. When a news service quoted Cohn as promising that David would testify about "possible new material that was not touched on at the Rosenberg trial or under questioning by the F.B.I.," Hoover demanded: "Have we again 'missed the boat'?" Hoover worried that even with the Rosenbergs dead and further legal appeals moot, their defenders would seize upon any inconsistency in David's testimony to rattle the underpinnings of the prosecution's case and to stoke suspicions that justice had not been served. Cohn tried to make peace, suggesting publicly that he and the FBI operated in tandem, to which Hoover remarked: "This is absolutely untrue." When the Justice Department declined to let David travel to New York to testify, the McCarthy committee concocted a cover story: David's life might be in jeopardy, so investigators would interview him at Lewisburg instead.

The FBI discounted much of what David told congressional investigators but determined that he had indeed revealed a few fresh details. He said that Julius had given the Russians copies of all the electronic-tube manuals he could get his hands on. He reported that in 1947 Julius said that a friend had told him about a "thinking machine" that would direct interceptor missiles to foil an enemy missile attack. (The FBI concluded that Julius might have been referring to Project Wizard at the University of Michigan, where research was being conducted into antimissile missiles, and to Project Thumper at the General Electric plant in Schenectady, which was developing sophisticated interceptor radar.)

FBI officials weren't the only ones concerned about the impact of

David's belated revelations. So was David's lawyer. O. John Rogge was savvy enough to know that the criminal-justice bureaucracy—the people who were to decide David's fate—would endure long after McCarthy and other politicians had been rendered irrelevant by their own excesses. To protect his client—as well as his own newly burnished reputation as a negotiator whom the government could trust—Rogge helped orchestrate a story in *The New York Times* that exposed the flawed logic that was to haunt David's efforts to win parole: He hadn't spoken to Julius since his arrest; he hadn't mined any new sources for counterintelligence; so how, after he had already received leniency from a federal judge for telling all he knew to the FBI, could he stake another claim to leniency for giving valuable new information to congressional investigators?

Still, when a congressional investigator asked David in November 1953 whether he would testify again, he replied with detached self-righteousness. "I am going to answer any questions and give any information I may have," he said, "if, in so doing, I can help my country and its authorities in exposing what had been done in giving Russia our secrets."

David figured he had nothing to lose by ingratiating himself, particularly to James Bennett. Apologizing to Bennett for an earlier tirade, he wrote: "I had been under considerable mental strain and I could feel some of my spleen coming out. Let me assure you, sir, that it was more anger and frustration at the world in general than any specific anger at you. I have made up my mind that all I want from this life is to be reunited with my wife and children and to be allowed to earn a living for them."

This time, Bennett bent the rules to help. Prisoners were barred from engaging in entrepreneurial ventures, but, as a favor to Rogge, Bennett agreed to let David tinker with several inventions. David sent detailed plans for a "shower valet," a fixture that dispensed soap and shampoo, directly to Bennett, who forwarded it via Rogge to the Crane Company in Chicago. Executives in Crane's plumbing department weren't bowled over. Unfazed, David wrote Rogge that his door was open to anyone willing to license or invest in any of his inventions. "If a prospective buyer or backer wants any clarifications of any such devices that I have or may have in the future," he wrote without apparent irony, "I am available for such consultation."

After his attempts to patent the shower caddy and an optical punch failed, he focused his vocational efforts on the prison itself. In contrast to the dismissive appraisals of his amateurish atomic-bomb sketches, his "exceptionally high quality drawing" was cited by prison authorities, and he was described as "an excellent worker" who "cares for his equipment and tools religiously." Another report described him as "industrious, dependable and having good initiative in working up construction projects and alterations in the plant." He helped design an interfaith chapel, the dining room, and even a security system with new locks for cell doors, including his own. During one of his Parole Board hearings, he announced to George J. Reed, the board chairman, "I designed the very room you are in."

"It is a very well done room," Reed replied.

———

David would not be eligible for parole until April 1956, but he began campaigning in earnest months earlier, even before he filed his formal application on November 30, 1955. First, he had to find a parole adviser. Ruth asked for former Agent John Harrington, but the FBI was skittish. "While Harrington . . . would meet the problem of seeing that Greenglass is properly advised," the New York FBI office wrote Alan Belmont, "it could give the Communist forces a basis for charging that since Harrington is an ex-Agent the F.B.I. is still attempting to retain control of Greenglass." FBI officials concluded nonetheless: "It is believed highly desirable that in the event Greenglass receives parole that he has a parole advisor who will not allow him to get in the clutches of Communist groups such as the Committee to Secure Justice in the Rosenberg Case. Both of the Greenglasses have been of great benefit to the Government and it is felt that we should help out in this matter if it can be done discreetly."

James Kilsheimer, now in private practice, was suggested as an alternative. Kilsheimer was also one of the dozens of people, beginning with the prosecutors, whom Ruth rounded up to recommend parole. His letter was supportive but tempered by lawyerly caution: "During the many hours and days of pre-trial preparation in which I worked with him, he did not, to my knowledge, give any untruthful answers to our inquiries," Kilsheimer wrote. "In all my dealings with Mr. Greenglass, he appeared to be contrite, and to recognize the wrongdoing that he committed." Roy Cohn, explaining that he was uniquely qualified to vouch for David's veracity, volunteered: "Based on my observation of him during those months of stress and soul-searching, I feel he is sincerely repentant and will make an excellent parole risk." John M. Foley, another assistant prosecutor, pointed out that Ruth Greenglass, too, "has paid heavily for this crime."

—

David's own choice of words was revealing. In his formal parole application, he engaged in rank revisionism laced with high melodrama. He admitted to making a mistake, though "not one of greed, but one of misplaced idealism."

"When I was arrested," he wrote, "I decided that I would not be a martyr for a cause I did not believe in, and so I told the story. My subsequent actions in spite of family ties proves that I was truthful and sincere in my opposition to communism."

David also made a virtue out of vacillation. He recalled that at any time he could have easily fled. Instead, he stayed put, all the while dreading the day of reckoning:

> In the five years before my arrest, I lived a life of quiet desperation. Each airplane that flew overhead could well have been the one to bring retribution for my actions, to those I love and to the country that is mine by birth and education. It is a terrible thing to live with. . . . No one man can be responsible for such a possibility, and while I was much less guilty than many others, I was still in part to blame. My own mind and conscience have been the worst punishment I have endured.

David didn't claim victimhood unilaterally. He warned that by brutalizing his entire family, too, his imprisonment was perpetuating a breeding ground for another generation of agitators.

My children are growing up in a bad neighborhood, because on my wife's salary, they cannot live in a place that is even half way decent. . . . Can you see the picture? It is the same scene I was brought up in. The same sub-standard living conditions, the same evils, that gave me my earlier communist leanings. I do not want the cycle to repeat itself.

I ask[,] is not contriteness and redemption one of the basis of the Christian Society we live in? I have made a mistake, a bad mistake, possibly blown up by circumstances to a lot more than it really was, but still I take the blame for it, and have paid and am paying for it. . . . All my life, except for a period of about ten months, I have lived an honest and exemplary life.

On the parole-application form, David was asked to provide his own version of his crime:

When I was a youth of 14 or 15 I lived in New York City on the Lower East Side. I was an idealistic young fellow and the suffering and poverty around me appalled me. I might have turned into nothing worse than a "parlor pink" but as luck would have it, my sister and her boyfriend (later became her husband) were communists. . . . I frankly didn't want to give the information but the fear of being told that I didn't have the courage of my convictions caused me to agree to do what he asked. I was young and foolish and did what he wanted.

I gave a rough schematic sketch of my version of what I thought one type of atom bomb was like. This I guessed at, in the version I gave, from word of mouth information I had gleaned. To this day I am not sure how correct my guess was, but then even a speculative guess was, and I suppose still is, against the law.

In February 1956, David was interviewed by a member of the parole board, and at that time he delivered a chimerical account of his arrest. "I went to the F.B.I. finally," he announced.

Belittling the government's entire justification for the death penalty, he said: "My reports were not information of a specific kind but were made up of guesses and surmises from scattered and incomplete information. What I did was wrong, but not vital." David said he was the victim of "a campaign of vilification and animosity against me so great that at times I feel as though I was living in a nightmare." And he invoked a variation of the orphan defense that might be used by a child charged with parricide: "I must live with the thought of having been a witness in a case which resulted in the death of my beloved sister and must live with it inside here, where at home I would have the solace of a dear wife. I awaken at night from a dream of terror. Yes, much as I disagree with the politics of my sister I loved her as an individual."

Finally, David said, he had evolved into a relativist: "I can never believe in absolutism again. . . . Never can I see things in pure black and pure white again. Things are not that simple."

Members of the board were less conflicted. On April 2, they voted unanimously to deny parole.

The Greenglasses were devastated. But David rallied sufficiently to testify in Washington a few weeks later before a closed-door session of the Senate Subcommittee on Internal Security. David was billed as a star witness on communist subversion (although later, the committee's counsel, Robert Morris, who emerged as his most persistent champion of parole, referred to him as merely "a fringe character in atomic thefts" and a "supernumerary"). During the hearing, David embroidered on an account of a conspiratorial late-night meeting at the Greenglasses' apartment: Julius put his finger to his lips and whispered for David to check whether a neighbor was eavesdropping. David knocked on the door and, claiming to have locked himself out of his apartment, walked to her bedroom and left by climbing out the window onto the fire escape. David also introduced his new audience to another embellished version of how Ruth had broached Julius's original proposition. This version offered an unusual insight into his relationship with Julius, whom he referred to as "my mentor." He described himself, intentionally or not, as Julius's "door mat."

> At first when this happened, when she told me this, I felt as though the whole world had opened up and I was falling into a chasm because, while I instinctively said, "no," I was not going to give the information,

in the back of my mind I knew I was going to give that information because—oh yes, he did say one thing to her: "You just tell him that a man has to have the courage of his convictions." Now, it seems a strange reason to do a serious thing of this nature, because you want to have the good will of some other man. But we do strange things, especially since it would be very difficult to explain our relationship without going into a lot of background of how I was the younger, he was the older, he was the graduate engineer, I was the young apprentice, the tyro. It was a strange relationship, and yet one where I genuinely liked this man. And I wanted to have his approbation.

Later on, when we were in business together, when I had long since given up giving information, and was trying in general to disentangle myself from the web, he would use me as a sounding board, a door mat.

Again, David maintained that in the late 1940s he had thought about making a clean breast of his betrayal but was torn. Venturing into uncharted introspection, he said:

But while I contemplated going to the F.B.I., I could not bring myself to talk about what had to be spoken about, about my wife, about my sister, about my brother-in-law. There were people, and while I might hate a belief, I could never bring myself to hate people. It just isn't in my nature. I am not a violent man, and when I think of things I did by nonviolence, I wonder at myself.

But I thought over this business of my sister, my wife, my brother-in-law, before bringing myself to testify in this particular case I felt that I had to think about that quite a while before I could actually make a decision. I finally made my decision, and I testified. And at times, since we are only human, I have been sorry I testified, because these are my flesh and blood, and because I felt affection for them and I still feel affection for them. But at any time—and this I knew from the beginning—that these people would have wanted not to be martyrs, they could have just easily put their hands up and said, "Stop, I will tell you the story." But they refused.

It is a hard thing to be called a murderer by people, but it is a much harder thing—and I don't know whether it is a very intelligent thing—but to deliberately martyr yourself for a completely erroneous ideological cause is, in my point of view, the most hypocritical and ridiculous thing a person can do.

After obsequiously indulging David during his testimony (he later sent him a thank-you note that began "My Dear David"), Senator Herman Welker of Idaho concluded the hearing on an oddly ominous note:

> "You realize that if you have willfully testified falsely here, this committee will be very anxious to see you prosecuted to the full extent of the law, and the sentence that you are now serving in Lewisburg might very well be extended for a very lengthy period. Do you understand that?"
> "I do."
> "David, this devastating and tremendous scope of your activity and your ruthless disregard of loyalty to your country, to law, and to humanity, if you had it to do over again, would you ever become so involved?"
> "Knowing what I know now, I don't believe I would."
> "Was it worth it all?"
> "It certainly was not."

Nor was his testimony. As a result of the new publicity, Ruth lost her job as a legal stenographer in the office of Louis J. Lefkowitz, a Republican assemblyman from the Lower East Side. Lefkowitz was considering running for state attorney general. Having a former communist spy on his payroll would never pass muster with voters upstate.

That's when Ruth decided to legally change her name from Greenglass.

—

Once again, the FBI mined its files to figure out whether David had revealed anything new. Mostly, he appeared to have regurgitated a jumbled and mistaken account of Julius's friend Al Sarant's disappearance in 1950. "Due to the inaccuracy of the statements of Greenglass," Alan Belmont concluded, "it is not believed likely that he obtained this in-

454 • THE BROTHER

formation from F.B.I. agents. It is possible he reconstructed the above information from certain questions which may have been asked him as well as reading in the newspapers."

David later explained to the FBI that he had been reluctant to testify because, as he told Robert Morris, the committee counsel, some of his information was secondhand at best—assembled from hints dropped by FBI agents while they were pumping him for information. David said that Morris prodded him by insisting that "this was a good way to disseminate such information to the public." David said "he was 'scared' and 'very nervous' during the time he was giving testimony and may have said some things which did not make too much sense." Given Senator Welker's warning, David also was worried that half-truths and exaggerations might constitute perjury. "Since he testified under oath," the FBI agent who interviewed David reported, "Greenglass appeared to wish to vouch for the accuracy of what he had said even though he may not now be too sure whether the information came from his own deduction or assumption after being questioned by agents, or whether it was something he might have overheard while being questioned." The agent reached a conclusion that few of his colleagues ever acknowledged officially: "Since Greenglass was recently denied parole and since in his testimony before the Subcommittee he indicated that the F.B.I. had imparted information to him, the possibility exists that Greenglass may have exaggerated his testimony in order to make a better impression on the Subcommittee with the thought in mind that the Subcommittee might effect an earlier release for him."

———

In June, Rogge visited the Parole Board again, this time with Tessie Greenglass. The mother of Ethel and David Greenglass was inconsolable. Tessie said "she had two children 'killed by the government'"—it's unclear whether by the second child she meant Julius or David—"and expressed bitterness toward Judge Kaufman. She feels that David did nothing wrong—did not kill any one—and should be released," according to the board's records.

—

In the fall of 1957, more congressional investigators came calling. David was interviewed by Benjamin Mandel, the internal-security subcommittee's research director. Mandel was curious about the so-called space platform that Julius had once mentioned. Had Joel Barr ever worked on the project? If so, had he passed the information to the Russians? Mandel's visit was prompted by a surprisingly modest announcement from the Kremlin thirteen days before: Russia had successfully launched an artificial satellite into orbit around the earth. The Soviets dubbed the satellite *Sputnik,* which is Russian for *fellow traveler,* and more than one American investigator suspected a double entendre indicating that the Rosenberg ring stole not only the secrets of the atom bomb but also the technology that enabled Moscow to beat America in the first lap of the space race. Myles Lane, the former federal prosecutor, was quoted as confirming that Sputnik was David's "sky platform" incarnate. But the prison warden who monitored Mandel's interview with David wasn't at all impressed with his insights into satellite technology. "Greenglass," the warden reported skeptically to James Bennett, "is merely using this to bring pressure to get out of prison."

Overnight, the basketball-sized Sputnik shrunk the globe, again. With each ninety-eight-minute orbit, the first evidence of Soviet scientific superiority was thrust in Washington's face. John Foster Dulles, the secretary of state, drafted a statement that placed the Soviet achievement in a context that in part evoked America's development of the atomic bomb. "Despotic societies which can command the activities and resources of all their people can often produce spectacular accomplishments," Dulles wrote. "These, however, do not prove that freedom is not the best way." But officials at the highest level of government needed reassurance. At the October 10, 1957, National Security Council meeting, one participant cautioned that "while we could not permit ourselves to be panicked by the Soviet achievement, . . . if we lose repeatedly to the Russians as we have lost with the earth satellite, the accumulated damage would be tremendous."

—

Defenders of the Rosenbergs often said that a lot of what David claimed to have learned from Julius about space platforms and thinking machines he had, in fact, absorbed from reading *Popular Science*. David always insisted that he was fully capable of distinguishing between fictional glimpses into the future and Julius Rosenberg's furtive references to scientific secrets harvested from government laboratories.

At Lewisburg, David was well-read. He frequented the prison library. He borrowed scientific and other books, and it was there that he came across Jean Dutourd's *Five A.M.* He had never heard of Dutourd, a hero of the French Resistance and an accomplished satirist. But this title caught his eye; the hour marked by time's two-handed engine had a familiar ring.

For years, before the war and afterward, David worked nights. To him, 5:00 A.M. was the middle of the night, until, like Fernand Gérard Doucin, the bank clerk in Dutourd's novel, he turned thirty. Since David's imprisonment, 5:00 A.M. had assumed a terrifying and disproportionate role in his daily routine. Dutourd's satirical ruminations merged with David's grim reality. After David read Dutourd's book only once, Doucin's words resonated with him thereafter: "At five in the morning my mind is like a prisoner locked into a cell full of traps."... "When I open my eyes, I see nothing but the darkness of space. When I close them, I see nothing but the darkness of my soul."

Doucin describes his life as "an endless deception" and insists that even a saint would point his finger at someone else to save himself: "To be able to shift responsibilities onto other people must be the chief blessing of family life. Nothing, I am certain, does one more good than accusing somebody else of a folly one has committed oneself."

He dismisses "Communist claptrap," acknowledging that "I don't care a rap for the struggle of the proletariat" and declares that "the capitulations with which my life is strewn each give me the delirious gaiety of a man condemned to death and suddenly granted a reprieve."

From the tenderest age, I played at being a released convict. Little convict of life as soon as reason developed in me, I constantly sought to set myself free. My days were full of petty escapes: in my negative way I rebelled against society. This passivity and self-destruction clearly foreshadowed my future.

Doucin recalls his childhood infatuation with Vercingetorix, the heroic chief of the Gauls, until his exasperated mother finally reminded him, "At any rate, he would be dead today." And that truism, Doucin said, "is what finally settles every problem. That is what absolves every criminal; that is what reduces the highest sacrifices to nothing."

> I imagine that, as in Faust, the devil comes to me and proposes a deal. What souls, in fact, would he get his claws into, poor thing, if not those of people like me, enfeebled by impotence and despair, not fundamentally wicked (that is what gives them their savor for the devil) but open to every kind of weakness! So I evoke the devil; I sell him my soul (a fine bargain, in truth) and he lavishes on me all the pleasures of the earth in exchange.
>
> But one is never regarded for one's just deserts nor punished for one's vices. Immanent justice is more subtle.

—

That same Sputnik month, October 1957, David was transferred to minimum custody, as the campaign to free him intensified. In Hearst's New York *Journal-American,* George E. Sokolsky wrote: "Were Greenglass a Communist, there would be a Committee to Free Greenglass which would collect funds and hire expensive lawyers and make a great noise, but as he was a government witness he gets no such benefits and no such pressure is exerted in his favor." Similar sentiments were voiced by Victor Lasky in the *National Review* and by Victor Riesel, who argued in a Yom Kippur column in the New York *Mirror* that David had already atoned sufficiently. An editorial in the New York *Daily News* prompted a reader to ask the Parole Board: "Are you people in cahoots with Judge Kaufman?" The letter was placed in the board's official "crackpot file."

John Rogge appealed directly to J. Edgar Hoover. James McInerney, the former assistant attorney general, wrote to remind the Parole Board that he had first recommended parole in 1951, when he had still been with the Justice Department.

While Irving Saypol was still a federal prosecutor in 1951, he completed a form letter recommending parole when David became eligible. "His testimony, together with that of his wife, was the principal testimony against the other defendants," Saypol wrote, and "it is doubtful that the defendant would have committed the crime except for them." Question 7 on the parole form was multiple-choice. It asked, "Do you regard prisoner as a menace to society, an habitual criminal, an occasional offender, a victim of temptation, or a mental case?"

"Victim of temptation," Saypol wrote.

But in 1957, Saypol refused to intervene, even after Ruth visited him to make a personal plea. "I declined because taking the affirmative would conflict with my notion of the professional obligation as prosecutor," he wrote Attorney General William Rogers. "For ethical and personal reasons I don't want to be merged with the claque." Saypol said he would express his views only if the Justice Department asked for them. Rogers forwarded Saypol's letter to the Parole Board, which, as it pointed out to other individuals, didn't solicit recommendations.

—

Tessie Greenglass died on January 31, 1958. Prison officials allowed David, accompanied by guards, to return to New York overnight for the funeral. As he was getting dressed to attend the services, he spotted an inmate whom he recognized from newspaper photographs as Rudolf Abel, the Soviet spy who later figured in a historic prisoner exchange. Two weeks later, after David was returned to Lewisburg, he reported his sighting to the FBI as confirmation that he had never seen Abel face-to-face before then. David couldn't help but speculate, though, that what he had read about Abel in the newspapers—that he had entered the United States in 1948 and had access to sizable amounts of cash—seemed to coincide with what Julius Rosenberg had told him about a new Soviet contact who arrived around 1948 "flush" with money. Harry Gold, the other half of the ex-communist tag team, was interviewed at Lewisburg the same day. "It fits right into the pattern and until someone else is positively identified as such, I am sure that Abel took over as Rosenberg's superior in the United States," Gold said. He also volunteered that many people—Abel presumably among them—must have rested easier after the deaths of the Rosenbergs, which, according to the FBI, "he characterized as a 'suicide' rather than an execution."

By the beginning of 1958, the former Communist Party leaders convicted in 1948 under the Smith Act had been freed; the Supreme Court had overturned their convictions. David had completed his seventh year in prison. There were few new arguments to make for his release. How many times could he confess to the same crime? In January 1958, Robert Morris admitted to the Parole Board that everything David had given the committee he had already told the FBI. (Ruth, however, described by the board as "determined and defiant," insisted that David was still passing information to the FBI "whenever something new comes back to him.") In February 1958, David himself finally acknowledged to the Parole Board that he had not given "any additional information which he had not previously given to the F.B.I."

Again, he further downgraded his contribution to the Soviet Union. In his latest version, he had been, at worst, a stagehand who had happened by as the curtain rose and history intruded on a private family farce. "He never at any time gave the Russians the atom bomb secrets," the board's report said he insisted, "and states his part in this connection has been very greatly overstated." Asked whether he wanted to leave the board members with any last words, David proposed a mind-bending non sequitur: "I like to be taken as myself and not for what I did and then see whether I deserve the parole. I stole things about the atom bomb but I didn't steal the atom bomb. From the information I gave they could not have built any atom bomb."

The board reviewed David's case again in March 1958. A terse notation in his file said: "Has cooperated with various government agencies after his apprehension, but not before. A very serious offense."

It was left to Rogge to introduce a new argument. He implied, apparently for the first time, that the government had reneged on its deal with David.

—

The Rosenbergs and their defenders always assumed there was a deal between the government and the Greenglasses. There was. One element was obvious: Ruth was never prosecuted. "She never stepped foot in jail, except to visit me," David boasted. But precisely what was David promised?

Ethel suggested more than once after her brother had been sentenced that he would probably be freed after only five years. David later accused Ethel of repeatedly invoking the five-year figure with only one goal in mind: As the Parole Board put it, the "intent of not doing his cause any good."

But now Rogge was also telling the Parole Board that Assistant Attorney General McInerney "reportedly told him that if Greenglass 'told the whole story' he should be given a suspended sentence." George Reed, the Parole Board chairman, had asked David earlier whether the board was bound by whatever plea bargain he had struck with the government. In July, David replied that only recently Ruth had recalled that McInerney had promised Rogge "a suspended sentence or on the outside a sentence of five years. In view of this new knowledge, I can only say, yes, it is the obligation of the Parole Board to honor the promises given to my lawyer by the Government's representative." David wrote Reed:

> When you were here last you asked me if I had a fair sentence. In view of the great losses I have sustained, the loss of my sister and brother-in-law, people I have loved as individuals, the loss of family life, the loss of my Mother, whom I had seen twice in eight years, these plus the fact that as an individual, I have in my opinion, been punished more than enough; I say no, 15 years was an unfair sentence.

David wrote that Ruth had been punished more than enough, too. Recently, he said, on the same day that she learned from the newspapers that David's parole had once again been denied, her uncle died and her father fainted. "She told me that our cooperation with the government is to cease," David wrote.

I thought this was a passing phase brought on by the various shocks she had received, which had momentarily unbalanced her. . . . Maybe if I were to go home now, or in the very near future, she might maintain her natural balance, but I fear greatly that those three years until my Conditional Release will complete the job, that of her mental destruction. I cannot believe that it is your intention to wreck the rest of my life, by destroying the mainstay of my family. My children will suffer and without a doubt I shall suffer too (not to speak of my poor, sweet wife).

One disappointing ruling by the Parole Board followed another, but Ruth's single-minded crusade never flagged. She even sent the board copies of the children's report cards.*

Ruth was so persistent in her pursuit of parole that her efforts may have backfired. Among the experts whom Ruth tried to enlist was Dr. Frederic de Hoffman, a General Dynamics executive and one of the Atomic Energy Commission scientists who had interviewed David after his arrest. "The problem I would like to discuss with you concerns our future," Ruth wrote ambiguously. Hoffman turned the letter over to the FBI.

In April 1958, Ruth met with Arch Sayler, the chief probation officer for the Southern District of New York. Sayler filed this report with the Parole Board:

She is a rather attractive young woman with an intense, nervous manner. From her telephone conversation PO had suspected she has a razor-sharp mind, and this was borne out by the interview. She has apparently lived, breathed and slept her husband's case during the past 7 years and has every detail at her fingertips.

The center of Mrs. G's concern seems to be her children and the fact that they have to stand the cruel jibes of other youngsters (boy 11,

---

* Barbara, her teachers said, was "well mannered and shows the good training she receives at home," though she "rarely completes a job, probably because she takes a long time in getting started." The report card also noted that she "conducts herself properly in emergency drills."

finishing elementary school; girl is 7), live in unheated cold water flat, heat a kerosene stove, put deposit on apt in Kew Gardens but cannot move, works as a legal stenographer. She seemed "somewhat bitter . . . feels the Government Agents have broken faith with her." that Kaufman had promised a letter of recommendation for parole which has not been forthcoming[,] and when David Greenglass asked to testify[,] Saypol had promised a letter which he didn't write she said: "We have just been getting a run-around. No one will tell us where we stand. I can't take it much longer! Sometimes I think I am going out of my mind, worrying and planning and hoping! How can I ever make up to the children their not having a father? They don't even have a mother because I work all day."

PO feels that Mrs. Greenglass received considerable release from her comments. She received official change of name. PO complimented her on this idea as it is obvious that a change of name is the only way to avoid the stigma of the Rosenberg case.

In fact, there was never any way to avoid the stigma of the Rosenberg case. Sayler later encountered George Reed at a conference of the National Institute on Crime and Delinquency in Miami Beach. They compared notes on Ruth. "It was remarked," Sayler recalled, "that her caustic, intense, driving manner is characteristic of communist trained people."

Ruth and Rogge also visited Saypol, whom she quoted as saying, without elaboration, "that he felt that 'David was led around by the nose.'" But Saypol still wouldn't volunteer his views on parole, and the Parole Board wouldn't budge in its refusal to solicit recommendations. Rogge also told the board he was satisfied that David had changed his political views but acknowledged that Ruth "is of a more stable character in this regard."

That spring, Ruth also telephoned Judge Kaufman. In July, David wrote the judge directly in an appeal to conscience, driving home the toll that the sentence was taking:

The school my daughter who is eight goes to is one in which she is one of six Jews in a class of 40 or so Puerto Ricans. I would see nothing to be alarmed about in such a situation, if it weren't for the fact that these other children ostracize and abuse her for her whiteness and Jewishness. My son does not play in the parks of the area because he is set upon for being Jewish and white. . . . Once night has fallen, my wife and children are virtual prisoners in their own apartment.

I have never addressed you directly, and while I would be less than human to say that I agreed with your decision to sentence my sister and brother-in-law to death, I personally am, and have been contrite. If I had it to do over again I would not. I say this not out of any fear of punishment, but because of the honest feeling that I did wrong, and I would not do that which I consider immoral or unethical.

Reading the newspaper stories about me, I begin to see a pattern of ostracization that will hardly allow me to live in our society again. I begin to feel that for me there is no atonement possible, that whatever I do will never be enough. I too bear the onus of your decision. I must live with myself, and know that part of the responsibility for the death of my sister and brother-in-law lies on me. With all these burdens must I continue to be incarcerated? Have I not been punished enough?

Judge Kaufman forwarded David's letter to William Rogers. The judge attached a curt note that said, by implication, that he no longer had any professional responsibility for David's future. "As you know," Kaufman wrote, "under the Federal Rules of Criminal Procedure, the time for the Court to act has long since expired."

Ruth borrowed a page from the Rosenberg defense committee. She proposed enlisting a new weapon on David's behalf: their twelve-year-old son. Steven and Barbara visited David at Lewisburg every other month. Barbara was told only that her father was working in Pennsylvania; Steven knew why he was there. But when Ruth sought permission for Steven to plead his father's case in person, the Parole Board advised Rogge against bringing him to the next scheduled hearing because "a person should be at least 16 years of age before experiencing that type of appearance." The following August, David asked permission to attend Steven's bar mitzvah. His request was denied.

—

As David had reminded Judge Kaufman, the Lower East Side was "changing" (the preferred euphemism). In Ruth's case, the impetus for moving was particularly urgent because the immediate neighborhood was being bulldozed for a public-housing project named for Tomáš Masaryk, the George Washington of Czechoslovakia. In October 1958, she and the children moved to an apartment house in the Crown Heights section of Brooklyn. The apartment wasn't far from that of David's brother Sam. The rent was steep—eighty-five dollars a month, compared to the twenty-three Ruth had been paying on Rivington Street. But she had gotten a new job as a legal stenographer and was grossing ninety-five dollars a week.

In April 1959, Ruth and Rogge made another pilgrimage to the Parole Board. They reported that Ruth and the children had finally left the Lower East Side and, as if one were a consequence of the other, that she had "no further association or contact from members of [the] Communist Party." David, too, had been on his best behavior during the preceding year, volunteering to correct arithmetic tests for the prison's education department and being "stable, quiet and studious." Nonetheless, the board denied parole again. Ruth was so devastated that she and Rogge persuaded Judge Kaufman to grant them another audience. He did, but still refused to venture any opinion to parole officials unless they asked him for one.

In July, after Ruth and Rogge again appeared before the board, Ruth complained directly to Attorney General Rogers. David had made six appeals for parole and been denied six times. He still had nearly two years to serve until his likely release date. Meanwhile, Klaus Fuchs had been released from a British prison and was back home in what was now East Germany. Commenting on Fuchs's release, the columnist Jim Bishop wrote: "The dedicated Communist will die for the cause. Mr. and Mrs. Rosenberg were dedicated. Brother David was not. He sold his country first, then his sister."

As late as April 1960, after David had been confined for nearly a decade, a case analyst for the Parole Board recommended again against early release: "In view of the gravity of the offense and since his emotions and feelings of allegiance to the United States at this time cannot be measured or are not known, recommend no change."

—

The Soviet rocket that launched Sputnik in 1957 also sent American politics spinning. By 1960, the campaign to succeed President Eisenhower revolved largely around two words: *missile gap.* The fastest and most reliable means for the Eisenhower administration to find out whether there was one was to analyze reconnaissance photographs secretly snapped from twelve miles above the Earth by U-2 spy planes. It was also risky. The political repercussions of discovery or of a military engagement could be enormous. Early in April 1960, the pilot of a U-2 flight determined that Russian radar was tracking his plane, but he completed his mission safely. The White House waited for the fallout; there wasn't any. George Kistiakowsky, the Los Alamos alumnus who was Eisenhower's science adviser, said later that the Russians had been "virtually inviting us to repeat the sortie." Three weeks later, America accepted the dare. On May Day 1960, Francis Gary Powers was piloting his U-2 seventy thousand feet over Sverdlovsk when a Soviet battery fired several SA-2 missiles at him. One scored a direct hit on a Soviet fighter that had scrambled to intercept him. Another SA-2 exploded just behind Powers, disabling his aircraft. He bailed out and survived (and was eventually exchanged by the Soviets for Rudolf Abel).

Years later, long after Alexander Feklisov had retired as an NKGB agent, he recalled the incident with unabashed pride. The SA-2's explosive charge was detonated by a proximity fuse, he said—an advanced version of the one that Julius Rosenberg had delivered to him as a Christmas present in 1944.

—

By the fall, David's "emotions and feelings of allegiance to the United States" still could not be measured. But with his eligibility for conditional release with good behavior approaching within a matter of months, officials at Lewisburg prepared for his departure. Despite his periodic appearances before Congress and notwithstanding the newspaper columnists who were enlisted on his behalf, David had assumed that he could unilaterally abdicate his celebrity and unobtrusively check out of Lewisburg on his own terms. Word of his impending release had already leaked. On October 26, 1960, the warden wrote James Bennett that David was "rather emotionally disturbed over the notoriety his release is receiving." The warden reminded Bennett of the crush that had greeted Alger Hiss when he had been released from Lewisburg. And Hiss, while shy personally, was returning home to his wife, his sons, and his neighbors in Greenwich Village if not triumphantly at least publicly proclaiming his innocence. Whatever self-aggrandizing psychic satisfaction David had derived from posing, with government complicity, as someone more important than he really was, the circumstances of his release were altogether different. When history had knocked, he had flung open the door and warmed to the spotlight. Its heat had consumed him. Now, he craved only obscurity.

"Greenglass," Warden J. T. Willingham reported, "is terrified of the prospect of meeting the press" and "hopes there is some way we can protect him." Even Lewisburg's director of public information was sympathetic. "While I am as sensitive as anyone to the rights of the press in such situations," he said, "I think that protection of Greenglass in his desire to avoid publicity is paramount."

The FBI advised Judge Kaufman that David was about to be released, though it's unclear whether the bureau was cautioning Kaufman or just satisfying his curiosity. The judge suggested obligingly that, once David was freed, "it might be helpful if he was kept in touch with to keep aware of his feelings and to try to guide him if necessary."

David left Lewisburg on November 12. Before reporters could converge on the prison, he was transferred to the Federal House of Detention on Manhattan's West Side waterfront. To spare Ruth "crucifixion" by the media, David canceled plans for her to greet him when he was to be released from there four days later. David had asked to be released shortly after midnight, not to savor freedom as soon as possible but to avoid a spectacle. Instead, the warden at the House of Detention followed protocol.

For most people, November 16, 1960, was notable for something that happened 2,500 miles away from New York, in Hollywood: Clark Gable died at the age of fifty-nine. That morning, David Greenglass emerged into a world markedly different from the one he had left so abruptly more than ten years before. A decade of prosperity had fostered a bulging middle class. Flashy cars and frozen TV dinners had become ubiquitous. Those theoretical "thinking machines" and "mechanical brains" had been perfected into superweapons and into portable transistor radios. Just the day before, in Charleston, South Carolina, the U.S. Navy had sent to sea its first nuclear-armed, nuclear-powered submarine. On the same day, a newspaper advertisement by Bethlehem Steel boasted that the world's first nuclear-powered ship was being readied in one of the company's shipyards. Another ad, this one from Best and Co., the Fifth Avenue department store, touted jewelry studded with the sort of simulated diamonds—"so like the natural gem in brilliance and color"—that David Greenglass and Henry Linschitz had tried to create years earlier at Los Alamos. Only a week before, American voters had elected a Democrat as president for the first time since 1948. Richard Nixon, the Republican who had begun his career by investigating Alger Hiss, was defeated by a young senator from Massachusetts and, even as his razor-thin margin was all but evaporating in the official recount in California, John F. Kennedy was flying to Texas to confer for the first time with his vice president–elect, Lyndon Johnson. Their agenda was studded with emerging domestic and foreign-policy issues. In New Orleans, thousands of marauding white youths were surging through downtown streets demonstrating against school integration. And in Washington, the State Department was drafting reassurances to the North Atlantic Treaty Organization that the United States would not hesitate to use nuclear weapons against aggressors in Europe.

David's mother and sister were dead. The tenement on Sheriff Street in which he had been born and raised was being demolished. His wife and children had moved to Brooklyn. He was to be reunited with a ten-year-old daughter with whom he hadn't lived since she was one month old, and a fourteen-year-old son who had been only four the last time David had played with him outside of a prison. He would be returning to his family, but to one no longer known as the Greenglasses because it had been shamed and harassed into changing its name from his.

—

At 8:30 A.M., a green, electronically operated steel door slid open, and David emerged from federal custody. It was overcast and cool, in the low fifties. David hiked the collar of his powder-blue overcoat so high that it nearly brushed the brim of his fedora, which he wore so low that only his eyes, nose, and cheekbones were visible. He carried a blue canvas flight bag and the eighty-five dollar balance from his prison account.

O. John Rogge was there to greet him. So were about sixty reporters, photographers, and cameramen. They shouted questions. One asked if David had anything to say. His mouth was shielded by the overcoat, so most newsmen did not notice that he opened it for an instant and then closed it tightly. He responded to the question only by shaking his head. Rogge read a brief statement: "David Greenglass is out on mandatory release; he does not now have a statement, nor will he later." Then he led his client past the shouting reporters to a taxi that had been waiting at the curb.

That afternoon's *Journal-American* described David as a "spy-turned-patriot" and as a "brilliant physicist." The man-in-the-street response was less charitable. With David hunched down in the backseat, a passerby directed the cabby: "Drive him off the pier, right into the river, the dirty red rat. Drop dead you lousy communist. You sent your sister to the chair."

Newsmen outraced the taxi, arriving at Rogge's office at 401 Broadway in time to greet him. But when Rogge emerged, the backseat was empty. En route, David had slipped away. "I lost him," Rogge announced, as if describing a fish that got off the hook. "I hope he stays that way. I hope he is back in the current of American life by now." Later that day, Rogge said: "We would like the Greenglasses to live like a normal American family now. It's been very carefully worked out so they will have a maximum of privacy."

David went to live on Carroll Street in Brooklyn and got a job with a company in Long Island City that manufactured dentists' drills. He was on parole until October 7, 1965. He made no statement at all for more than a decade and never submitted to unrestricted interviews until he finally agreed to talk to me. Pressed by one reporter for any reaction at all, Rogge delivered a single, seven-word quote from his client:

"All I want," David said, "is to be forgotten."

Chapter 35

The Search for David Greenglass

"Do you hate me?"

≡

The very day he arrived at his new home, David was greeted by a five-word reminder of his enduring notoriety. Someone had slipped a three-by-five index card under the door of the apartment that Ruth and the children had rented in the new name they had legally adopted. David was written in pencil and in ink. Boldly superimposed in red crayon or lipstick were the words Welcome Home Mr. Greenglas. David accepted the greeting in the spirit in which it was presumably offered: as a thinly veiled threat. Expressing his concern that "his true identity had become known," he immediately forwarded the message to John Harrington, the former FBI agent. Harrington referred the card to the FBI's New York office. A few weeks later, at the Commodore Hotel, near Grand Central Terminal, Harrington introduced David to an active agent who would be his regular liaison. David promised to contact the New York office immediately "in the event any information came to his attention in which he felt the Bureau would be interested."

There is no evidence that the FBI reciprocated by directly subsidizing the Greenglasses after David was convicted. But as people in the small circle in which the Greenglasses had confided became estranged, moved away, or died, the bureau paternalistically shielded its charges from inquisitive employers, other government agencies, and prying reporters. Only a few months after David was released, Ruth reported that her family's new identity appeared to have been compromised again, this time by someone telephoning Sam Greenglass and asking to speak to David. Ruth told the FBI that the Greenglasses intended to move to someplace more remote, where they would be less likely to be discovered. Consequently, she said, David would need a driver's license.

Question 24 on the New York State license form asked whether the applicant had ever been found guilty of a crime. Other than his federal conviction, David had never even gotten a speeding ticket. David left the space blank, he told the FBI, because "any disclosure of his true identity would result in both his wife and him losing their positions and it would be accompanied by harassment to his family by both Communist elements and the press." The FBI intervened with the state commissioner of motor vehicles, who agreed to handle the paperwork personally and arranged for his own chauffeur to administer the driving test. The commissioner said he was cooperating since David's "cause seems worthy."

David also alerted the FBI when he applied for work with a company that engaged in classified research. Another employer enlisted him to work on an impenetrable soundproof chamber for conducting top-secret conversations; when David was told that he might have to go to Britain to construct a similar room, he appealed to the FBI for help because his boss would become suspicious if David couldn't apply for a passport. On another occasion, when the Immigration and Naturalization Service was investigating a former associate of Julius Rosenberg and requested David's home address, the FBI declined to cooperate.

The FBI also systematically hid David's new identity from the press, especially in the early 1970s when Alvin H. Goldstein, a public-television producer, was trying to interview the Greenglasses and examine their FBI files. The documentary couldn't have been timed worse. Their daughter, Barbara, was to be married soon, and, as the Greenglasses told the FBI, "any exposure from the program would be disastrous to their plans." One focus of the 1974 documentary, *The Unquiet Death of Julius and Ethel Rosenberg*, was the FBI's proprietary relationship with the

Greenglasses and their ongoing role as government sources. Recounting that relationship, J. Edgar Hoover assured the Justice Department that while the FBI hadn't participated "in the actual setting up of the cover for David and Ruth Greenglass . . . the procedure was suggested by the F.B.I. at the approximate time of the Rosenberg trial in order to halt the harassment the Greenglass family was beginning to receive." An agent in the New York office, James E. Freaney, was assigned as a liaison to the Greenglasses. According to Hoover, Freaney assisted the family on many occasions.

> Further, Special Agent Freaney indicated he has represented to the Greenglasses in the past that the F.B.I. would do all it could to aid in the maintaining of their privacy. He pointed out that in many recorded interviews, David Greenglass provided information about individuals and alleged espionage activities. Special Agent Freaney voiced his concern that it would be most difficult to delete such information from these interviews in a manner which would adequately insulate David Greenglass from civil suit.
>
> In summary, the F.B.I. has had a close relationship with the Greenglasses since the time of the Rosenberg trial. Consequently, we feel the release of these interviews would violate the trust which exists between them and the F.B.I. and would place information in the public domain which might cause them further untold difficulties.

Goldstein's request for access to the files was denied by the Acting Attorney General, Robert H. Bork. Still, the Greenglasses were nervous because Goldstein had discovered their new name and had even surreptitiously filmed them. David actually feared for their safety and suggested that they check into a hotel for a few days. The Soviet intelligence agencies, he reminded Ruth, "have long memories and for them to take retributive action was not beyond the realm of possibility."

—

I didn't know it at the time, but my life first brushed against David Greenglass's in June 1953, when I was six. My birthday was on a Saturday that year, sandwiched between the Rosenbergs' execution on Friday night and the funeral on Sunday morning. The Rosenberg case was the inescapable topic, and yet two bedrock questions were avoided assiduously:

How could the Jews have done this to America?

How could America have done this to the Jews?

The first question, while predictable fodder for anti-Semites everywhere, provoked profound introspection and self-doubt among American Jews. In the early 1950s, the Holocaust wasn't some abstract biblical horror story but recent history. So how to fathom this self-destruction of a Jewish family? As a survivalist's cunning act of betrayal, too callous and cynical even to contemplate? Or as a baby brother's first—and perhaps final—act of conscience? The second answer may have seemed facile and Pollyannaish, but it was preferable to the troubling alternative.

Still, did America have to kill the Rosenbergs? And how was it that the government had managed to assemble a virtually all-Jewish cast to try them but couldn't find one Jewish juror to convict them? They were fried, burned—a grisly vision that would make anybody queasy and, for the most vulnerable, invite comparisons to the crematoriums. Would the government have killed them if they hadn't been Jewish?

That Sunday morning, my father took my sister and me to the corner of our block in Brooklyn to watch the Rosenberg funeral procession pass. Even at the age of six, I was aware that somebody had done something to make us ashamed.

And that seemed to be the end of it.

I was never consumed by the Rosenbergs. It wasn't until 1983 that the case intruded into my life again, and in ways I never could have imagined.

I was new to *The New York Times* then but was enough of a newspaper veteran to have heard that when managing editor Arthur Gelb approached the metropolitan desk, arms flailing, someone was going to have their life's work cut out for them. Legends about the paper were larger than life, but so was Arthur, having indefatigably shaped local and cultural news coverage for forty years. One of those local stories was the execution of the Rosenbergs. Arthur had been a rewrite man on the line to Sing Sing in 1953 and had persuaded a prison guard to confirm that Ethel and Julius were dead. In 1983, when reviews of *The Rosenberg File* by Joyce Milton and Ronald Radosh proclaimed the book to be brimming with new and incriminating details from FBI files and interviews, not surprisingly it was Arthur who asked, If there's news in the book, why not assign a reporter to write a news story?

I got the assignment. I turned first to Peter Kihss, a retired *Times* reporter who had covered the case and its aftermath. He identified the passages he had found most revealing. He provided the names of several people who had all but devoted their lives to proving the Rosenbergs innocent or to reaffirming their legal guilt. His final recommendation, though, was couched not so much as a suggestion than as a challenge: Find David Greenglass.

But why? How much could he contribute to the debate at this late date? Was he capable of adding anything, or had he been reduced by now to uncomprehending senility, like Selig Mindish, the Greenglass character in *The Book of Daniel*, E. L. Doctorow's fictionalized account of the Rosenberg case? Was David Greenglass even alive?

I decided I wanted more than just Greenglass. I wanted the smoking gun, the one compelling piece of evidence that would finally bring closure to the case by establishing the guilt either of the Rosenbergs or of the government. I asked the Rosenbergs' son Michael, who said, "I am so tired of expecting a smoking gun, something the equivalent of J. Edgar Hoover saying, 'Nice frame-up, guys.' I don't think I'm going to find that." I also asked Roy Cohn. He said the smoking gun was staring us in the face. "The smoking gun," he said, "is the testimony of David Greenglass."

—

Since 1960, David has lived uneventfully. Ruth worked as a legal secretary. Steven grew up to become a doctor, Barbara a medical administrator. They have children of their own. (One of David's grandchildren, on visiting Los Alamos with the family, innocently exclaimed, "My grandfather used to work here!") David made a modest living as a machinist and an inventor, never revealing his true identity. Virtually nobody knew who he really was. In the 1960s, he recalled, "I was sitting in this place in Manhattan, designing machinery, and this guy is sitting there and he says to me, 'You know, I was at Los Alamos. I knew David Greenglass.' And there I am sitting across from him, and he didn't recognize me." After Walter and Miriam Schneir coauthored a book that raised serious questions about the Rosenberg prosecution (on the basis of Venona, the Schneirs now believe Julius was, indeed, a spy), they were invited to speak at the temple to which the former Greenglasses belonged. David and Ruth didn't go.

Until recently, he worked mostly for other people, making some of them rich. A company sold millions of the tiny electrical gadget he invented. David recalled sourly that all he got for it was a five-hundred-dollar bonus. However, another of his unheralded inventions had ironic value that could not be measured monetarily. David designed and patented an ornamental, self-closing outdoor outlet with a very simple and practical goal: to prevent the user from getting electrocuted.

—

Since 1960, David had surfaced only once. In 1979, O. John Rogge had arranged for David and Ruth to be interviewed by Ron Radosh and Sol Stern. Radosh met them for dinner at Smith and Wollensky, the Manhattan steak house that had been known as Manny Wolf's when Julius Rosenberg went there during the war with Morton Sobell and Max Elitcher; and again, with Stern, briefly, at Rogge's law office. The gist of those interviews, as recounted later in *The Rosenberg File,* was that neither David nor Ruth had ever realized just how vital their testimony was in convicting the Rosenbergs and that David, summing up his legal dilemma as a choice between saving his sister or saving his wife, chose Ruth.

By 1983, though, Rogge was no longer alive. There was no intermediary to arrange an interview. If I was going to interview David, I would have to find him myself. To find him, I needed to know his new name. Some years before, in the sixties, Sam Greenglass's daughter, who was married and living in upstate New York, had called her first cousins Michael and Robert in Massachusetts to sound them out about the possibility of a Greenglass-Rosenberg reconciliation, or at least about getting reacquainted. The families hadn't seen or talked to each other in decades. They reminisced about their other cousins, Steven and Barbara, and about Bernie's daughter, Sharon. Well before the conversation was over, they realized that whatever and whoever they once had in common was gone. Michael came away from the conversation with something else, though, something he hadn't really been looking for. The cousin had casually mentioned that Steven Greenglass was already going to college and was studying to be a doctor.

Not long after that telephone conversation, Michael's curiosity kicked in. He checked a college directory, matched a student named Steven with his major and approximate hometown, and discovered the Greenglass family's new surname. Michael brimmed with antipathy toward his uncle and aunt, but not with overt hostility. He never wielded the one weapon that he had against the Greenglasses. He never publicly revealed their identity.

"All David has," Michael told me, "is his anonymity."

—

Michael did, however, help me identify the Greenglasses' adopted surname. That knowledge and several investigative sources steered me to an address in Queens. I wrote. I called. I knocked on the door. My efforts were met with a telegram and a firm but nonthreatening letter, both of them from an upstate lawyer. (He turned out to be the boyfriend of one of David's nieces.) "As I assume you are aware, it has been a longstanding policy to grant no interviews and they will not respond to any questions of any sort and upon any basis," the lawyer wrote. "This policy is unalterable and will not change. It will be very much appreciated if you would respect their privacy and if you would cease and desist from any further efforts to contact them."

I respected their privacy as much as any conscientious reporter could, which meant that I never revealed their new surname. But I did not cease and desist from trying to contact them.

I was discreet, posing my request for an audience in the most general terms, just in case my message was misdirected. But I kept writing, asked the telephone company to contact David at his unlisted number, and even sent him telegrams whenever some reminiscence or revelation evoked the Rosenberg case, such as the publication in 1990 of Nikita Khrushchev's memoirs. (The Soviet leader wrote that the Rosenbergs had apparently "provided very significant help in accelerating the production of our atomic bomb.")

I came to suspect that the family had moved. Early one morning in the fall of 1990, I returned to their innocuous two-story Tudor house in Queens, the one that had had a Day-Glo BEWARE OF THE DOG sign taped conspicuously to the front door. The sign wasn't there. Nobody was home. But a neighbor from across the street, who introduced herself as Mrs. Morris and said she had lived on the block for six decades, told me that the couple who used to live there had, indeed, moved away in 1984. They both worked, she recalled, but she didn't know where. They had a son and a daughter, who had grown up. The woman hesitated. "Are you interested," she asked haltingly, "in something that happened a long time ago?"

And then, as much to her surprise as to mine, she unburdened herself of a story she had kept to herself. When the couple had moved in years earlier, she recognized them from news photographs. They introduced themselves by another name, but she knew them as David and Ruth Greenglass. She never even told her own husband, and she never hinted to them that she knew. "We weren't chummy, but I minded their house when they were away," she said. "When they moved, they said, 'We must send you our new address.' But, of course, we never got it."

David and Ruth left no forwarding address with the post office, either, or with anyone else. But since I knew their name, I was finally able to trace their new whereabouts by matching motor-vehicle-registration records and real-estate-tax ledgers and documents from one more unlikely source. As a convicted felon, David was still barred from voting; but Ruth had foolishly registered with the Board of Elections. (She was still an enrolled Democrat.) Early one morning, I presented myself in their driveway.

An elderly man emerged from the one-story house. He was clutching a slim black attaché case in one hand. In the other, he wielded a remote-control garage-door opener. He pointed it at the garage. Then he turned toward me. I had no doubt the man with the remote control was David Greenglass. He had no doubt that the man armed with a notebook and standing in his driveway was the reporter who had been pursuing him. He also had no intention of submitting to an interview. I tried anyway. *Would he have done anything differently?* "Never," he said. *Had his testimony been truthful?* "Of course," he replied. *Were Khrushchev's memoirs a vindication that whatever David had done in 1945 was worth it?* "Ha," he harrumphed. *And what had he hoped to accomplish?* David shook his head, wheeled, and retreated into the house. The interview was over.

—

Nearly six years elapsed. Every once in a while, I wrote the Greenglasses. They were getting older. Didn't they care how they would be remembered? Didn't they want one final chance to set the record straight before they died? I never received a reply. Until one day in 1996.

A lawyer who said he represented David wrote to suggest that it might be worthwhile for the two of us to meet. We did, a few days later. The lawyer told me he had known David for almost fifteen years and had represented him in various business ventures. A few weeks before he wrote to me, the lawyer recalled, David arrived at the law office for an appointment. He was tense, but David was always agitated about business, particularly when the subject was possible bankruptcy, so the lawyer was totally unprimed for what his client was about to reveal.

"I have a confession to make," David said. "I want to tell you who I really am."

The lawyer was unfazed. "Who are you, Hitler, Stalin?" he asked incredulously.

David didn't smile. "You remember the Rosenberg case?" he said. "I'm Ethel Rosenberg's brother. I'm David Greenglass."

The lawyer was speechless, so David spoke first.

"Do you hate me?" he said.

A few weeks later, the three of us met in the lawyer's office. David was dressed to kill. He wore a blue blazer and gray slacks and Docksides.

A worn wedding band was wrapped tightly around his ring finger. The baby fat had given way to jowls, though his moon-shaped face was still prone to erupt jerkily into an inappropriate smirk. His thinning hair, once black and curly, was snow-white and straight. His irises were still hazel, but the twinkle of cat's-eye green had faded to a weary yellow-brown behind his steel-rimmed glasses. He had endured cataracts and bypass surgery but was, as Dr. Seuss wrote, in pretty good shape for the shape he was in. He was also, after all these years, still willing to make a deal.

He agreed to cooperate fully on a book in return for a share of the proceeds. No vetting of the manuscript. No veto over what I decided to put in or leave out. I wasn't comfortable with the arrangement but agreed because the story could never be written unless he invested a substantial amount of the dwindling time he had left. Still, I was curious about why *he* would be comfortable, because this decision recalled something he had said seventeen years earlier when he had reluctantly agreed to be interviewed by Ron Radosh and Sol Stern.

"I don't want to take any money off other people's deaths," he had said then. "I never have, despite offers."

I asked David what was the difference between then and now.

"Now," he said, "I need the money."

Chapter 36

═══════════════

The Final Confession

"I don't sleep with my sister, you know."

≡

Before I began what was to grow to fifty hours of interviews, I posed the same question to almost every living principal in the case: If they could ask David Greenglass anything, what would it be?

Many of the suggestions were arcane, focusing narrowly on something he might have said or something he supposedly did or some detail that, if finally clarified or revealed, would produce a lusty "gotcha" and thereby redeem the questioner's lifelong obsession with a single, tangential slice of the Rosenberg investigation. Others were more general: What must he be thinking now after all those years of second-guessing at 5:00 A.M.? Was he consumed by remorse? Or had he rationalized his wrongdoing? William Reuben, whose 1951 articles in the *National Guardian* had challenged the underpinnings of the prosecution, framed the question best. "Ask him," Reuben said, "how he can sleep at night."

———

"Did you ever think you had done something wrong?" I asked David. "I mean, before the arrest."

"No," he replied. "I still don't think I did anything wrong."

"The basic idea was still to bring communism about," he maintained.

But hindsight had transmuted what he admitted "was maybe an excuse for doing what I did" into a much loftier rationale: By helping to undermine the American monopoly on nuclear weapons, he did his bit for peace. "Can you imagine if there wasn't mutually assured destruction?" he asked. Naturally, he said, he would have preferred peace with honor—that is, without getting caught and going to prison and the attendant dishonor of being accused of killing his sister and of hijacking American foreign policy. "If I'd never told anything about it and I had never gone to jail," he explained, "I may have said, 'Well, I got away with it. I'm happy nobody ever disturbed me, nothing came of it. No bombs were dropped on America.'"

He patiently explained to me over and over again why he began telling the government about it all in the first place and, once having started, why he couldn't stop. What might have seemed rational evolved into a rationale and, finally, a rationalization. I asked what made him think that he was smarter than the FBI.

"That's what Rogge said to me once: 'You know, you didn't have to say anything.' I said, Look, I said to Rogge. They come in with the idea they're going to arrest me. So, I figure they have information which they didn't have yet at the time. They just wanted to arrest me so that I would be put in FBI headquarters while they got the information from Harry. I would never have said anything. That would be the end of it. They would just have to go by one person's statement. When I talked to them, I said, I'll give you the story, but my wife has to be completely out of this. And that's what they, they adhered to that promise, so I adhered to my promise. I had no idea what they knew.

But suppose you had said, "Okay, you got me. Harry Gold is right. I gave him the information. But that's all I know. Some other guy came and said, 'Give Harry the information.'"

"Don't you see how stupid that would have looked? Who came to Harry Gold? How did I know Harry Gold? It would have been such a web of lies, and Harry Gold would have been able to point out this came from this guy and that guy. He knew where it all came from. I didn't. And then they would have the threat of my wife. They would have said, 'She doesn't know about this?' And they would have taken her and questioned her, and my wife would have told them. And would have put herself in trouble. There was always in the back of my mind that if they separated my wife from myself, my wife would have said something and then my wife would have been in the soup, and I'm denying it. They don't talk to you together. So you never could tell if your story will be supported by your wife, who was involved with it just as much as I was. Right?"

Why would she have told them if you wouldn't?

"Because my wife was very straightforward. She would have tried to save me. So she would get into trouble, and we'd both be in trouble and there would be no way I could say, 'Hey, you've got to leave my wife out.' How could I make a deal of leaving my wife out when she already has put us both together?"

But the day after you were arrested, when your lawyer Herb Fabricant asked, "Are you going to cooperate with the government," you said, "Hell, no." How could you have said that after you had already told the FBI the story?

"I said, 'Hell, no'? I may have said that to Fabricant because I was still not clear. But I had made a deal with the FBI: 'I'll tell you the whole story, but you've got to leave my wife out of it.' You got to understand, when people get arrested, they think in terms of how do you get out of this thing. Frankly, my thinking processes were over one thing: to keep the kids and wife intact and confuse them [the FBI] as much as I could. I had a primary consideration: I had to protect my own."

You also told Fabricant that the FBI said you had told Gold in June 1945 to come back later in the day because you didn't have the information ready. You said, "I didn't remember this, but I allowed it in the statement."

"Maybe, it's true. I mean, if I don't remember something, somebody says, 'That's what you said,' I say, 'Okay, sure.'" David also said he had been unsure of when he had delivered certain information to Julius but thought it was September 1945. "I'm not too sure of the situation," he said. "You probably can take the word of the FBI as to what happened when."

You told the FBI that first night that Ruth visited you in November 1944 and "asked me if I would give this information." Now, other than Gold, who was already arrested, this is the first mention of Ruth.

"Yeah."

And then you spent the next year, almost, trying to keep her out of the case. Why did you bring her in?

"I didn't know how to figure out how I came about—I didn't ... When you ask somebody a question, the first impulse is to tell what happened because you can't make that up. I'm not that shrewd about making up a lie right away. I'm not a habitual liar."

But you said, "I definitely place my wife out of the room at the time of Gold's visit."

"Right."

Now, that was a lie, right?

"That was a lie. When a guy starts to lie, you understand, to tell lies, the lies are such that you're entangled in them. I mean, the lies become one of the reasons why you trip yourself up. First of all, I couldn't figure out how I knew about it."

When you were arrested, you made great efforts not to implicate Ethel at all, in everything you told the FBI. But why did you implicate Ruth?

"Because when I heard that Gold identified me, he knew that Ruth was there. He had seen her."

Why didn't you just say, "Hey, let me talk to my lawyer"?

"Because the minute you say that then they're on top of you. My wife was in the hospital. My daughter, what could I do? Could I go away from there? And do I know enough? I mean I knew about the Bill of Rights, but there was no point. I'm going to be a stand-up guy with a wife and two kids to worry about? How could I do that? I already had made up my mind that I would make a deal with them. The minute I saw them following me, I said, 'What the hell. What am I going to do? Pull out a gun and start shooting?' It's ridiculous. I knew that."

David also lied when he testified that in the interview with Agent Spillane in January 1950 he had nearly admitted everything. Had he really been poised to confess?

"Nah, that's what I said in the trial."

Why would you have said that?

"Well, I was trying to make a good case for myself that I was going to be a cooperative witness."

David also testified that when Ruth first broached the Rosenbergs' invitation to commit espionage, he was frightened and didn't sign on as a spy until the following morning. Again, he was falsely portraying himself as a timid and reluctant traitor drawn into conspiracy despite his better judgment. He also admitted that the even more melodramatic metaphor of "falling into a chasm" was his creative way of giving the congressional investigators what they wanted. "Bullshit, for the committee," he said. "I figured, listen, I'll get it out of the way, it'll be okay. You know I'm not averse to lying to a committee. Screw them! Bunch of politicians up there asking questions to show how anticommunist they were.

"The testimony at the trial is not what I actually felt at that time. I wasn't at all frightened by that. I never even thought twice about it. I was indoctrinated. I was ready for this. It wasn't as though it was something new to me. I probably would never have gone to Julius and said, 'Look, I'm working. . . . I'm going to give you information,' because it would never occur to me, understand. But he came to me asking me for the information."

David likened himself to Jonathan Pollard, the American also jailed for passing secrets to an ally, in his case Israel.

"I knew that I was doing something that the U.S. government didn't approve of, but I thought in the long run it wasn't hurting the U.S. government. Believe me, when I was working at Los Alamos I was working full-hearted for the United States government. I was doing what I had to do, and I did it well. What I did as spying didn't mean I was going to sabotage our own work. I would never have done that at all. I knew we were both on the same side, you understand. I didn't think it was secret from our allies. The gamble was that the Russians would get it and everything would turn out to be all right. Which it did for them, but not for me."

David elaborated on Ruth's message—a message that suggested consequences not only for the war in progress, in which Russia was an ally, but for the next one: "She said that 'Julius said to me that "even if the war is over, they need to have something to counterbalance America's power."'"

How did she say she wanted you to help or that Julius wanted you to help?

"To give information, she said."

Did she ever say, "Julius wants you to be a spy"?

"No, never said words like that. She was just passing information."

So that word almost never occurred to you?

"Uh-uh."

Still, if Ruth was so reluctant to make the case to you, why did she? Why didn't she just say to Julius, "You're the husband of my husband's sister, and we're as progressive as the next guy, but just what do you think you're getting us into?" When she recruited David, was Ruth quoting Ethel or Julius?

"She was quoting Julius."

And what did she think, did she say?

"'Whatever you want to do.'"

She didn't say, "Don't do it"?

"No. But then she told me, she said, 'Look, that's your choice. I'm not really happy with it.' Because first of all she didn't like Julius that much. And second of all she felt that what I did—I shouldn't be telling anybody this information."

Why not?

"Well, because she felt, you know, she was never really tight with communists. Politically, she was a liberal. A liberal, that's what she was."

So why did she tell you at all, then?

"Because she loved me. She knew that I wanted it. So she told me."

Why did she think you'd want to do this?

"Because she knew I was a communist."

———

I asked David whether telling the Russians what he assumed were secrets of the atomic bomb was the worst thing he had ever done in his life.

"Nah, there were worse things probably."

Like what?

"Making an atomic bomb, killing a hundred thousand people."

It was worse than telling about it?

"Absolutely. That's the worst thing I ever did—not telling about it to the Russians. They never dropped the atom bomb on anyone."

—

I told David that one of his children had been quoted as saying, "My parents taught me to respect what they did and to respect what my aunt did."

"No, I didn't say anything like that," he replied. "I told him to respect me and my faults and what it was, that to die was stupid. I told them that it was between you and your mother, your mother and me, or else it was going to . . . you're going to be out in the world without me or your mother. That's what I told them. They accepted that."

You said there are certain things worth dying for.

"Sure. My kids, my family, my home. Right?"

Anything ideological?

"Not much. Not much. I mean people die, like in the war against Hitler. I would have died for that."

Would you ever say you're sorry to Ethel and Julius?

"Never," David replied. "Because my mother put it very succinctly: To die for something as nebulous as that is stupidity."

Are you sorry for anything that happened?

"Well, I didn't want them to die. Yes, I regret being a spy for the Russians. Was it worth it? Well, if it prevented another war, fine. Basically, what I did—the other guys probably gave more theoretical things—this is the way you do it. You put this here and there, and it'll make a bomb."

But suppose it turned out that it didn't help them at all?

"If it was for nothing, then certainly I regret all the things that did happen that were bad, the death of my sister and my brother-in-law, my years in jail. I would regret that. But basically, I can't regret anything as long as a war didn't happen. That holocaust war didn't happen. That type of war meaning the destruction of civilization."

—

David's sister and brother-in-law succumbed to a psychological war, a cold war that was no less deadly. By martyring themselves, they contributed considerably more to the cause of world communism than they ever had as spies. "I hate to go to my deathbed seeing these people depicted as innocent martyrs," David said. "They were spies and could have cleared themselves."

They could have cleared themselves. What David meant was that they could have *saved* themselves. But, in the government's view, the only way they could have done so would have been by doing the very opposite of clearing themselves: They would have had to confess.

That's what David did. After his first volcanic burst of incriminating evidence and disinformation, the rest of his confession dribbled out so incrementally and was couched so inconsequentially that he finally confessed to something he didn't even know. In the end, it was all about the typing.

—

In 1979, when Radosh and Stern interviewed David and Ruth, the Greenglasses were shocked to learn that even after Ethel had been indicted the government had had virtually no hard evidence against her. They assumed Ethel had been implicated by Max Elitcher, Julius's former classmate and the chief witness against Morton Sobell. In fact, Elitcher never mentioned Ethel.

"What did they arrest her for? Why did they arrest her?" Ruth asked.

"They had Elitcher's testimony," David volunteered.

"How could they have held her so long?" Ruth asked. "We have a very weak government, very sadistic. On that basis they arrested her? And they held her for so many months?"

"You thought they had more on her already?" one of the interviewers asked.

"Absolutely."

"What did you think they had?"

"Who knows?" David replied.

"I didn't know," Ruth said. "I knew that they each knew what the other was doing. And if he was deeply involved she knew all about it."

"Did the FBI give you the impression that they had a lot of information on her, apart from what you had told them?"

"I don't know," David said. "That's not the point. The point is—"

"No, they never intimated," Ruth said.

"It's very simple," David continued. "I knew that she was involved."

"How did you know?"

"I knew because she typed it up," David said. "I knew because she was always involved in his things."

Why, David was asked, hadn't he revealed that in July or August 1950?

"But that's not the point," David said. "The point is that I knew they were talking to us and that she's in jail and they must have more information than that. Don't you understand?"

"So why did they have to come back to you two weeks before the trial?"

"At this point I understand why," David replied. "Because they had nothing."

Still, David and Ruth were certain that regardless of the legal evidence, Ethel was guilty. Otherwise, why would she have been fortifying Julius's resolve?

"Just a second. Are you married a long time?" Ruth asked the interviewers. "Would your wife bolster up your courage for something she didn't follow, didn't believe in? . . . They had two children. Do you mean that she was going to let themselves die for something she knew nothing about, that she had no involvement? That's impossible, that they lived together so many years and she didn't fully know. . . . She was a part of his life."

"Impossible," David added.

Ruth said she was appalled at the implication that they unwittingly sent Ethel to her death. "I must say it absolutely horrifies me—I had no idea," she said.

"At a certain point the agents become friends," she said. "They can elicit whatever they want from you."

Later, I asked David if the government ever said, "Look, we need you in order to make this case."

"Nah, they didn't say that. If they would have said that, I would have held them up for more. I'm a gambler, but I'm not stupid."

———

First, David gambled that he would never get caught. Once he got caught, he gambled on saving his wife, though he had implicated her, and later, by not volunteering more information, he gambled on saving his sister, whom his wife had implicated. What's indisputable is that if, in 1951, David and Ruth had realized that their recollections would be magnified into a matter of life and death, they might have searched their memories more conscientiously. They might have imposed a higher threshold in testifying to precisely what they remembered, rather than what they thought they remembered or might have remembered or what they assumed was the way things would have been done.

In talking with me, David often rambled, launched into you-had-to-be-there anecdotes and engaged in unabashed braggadocio.[*] His motivation for lying was largely consistent: to minimize the part that he played in illegal espionage and to embellish his role in just about everything else. Most of his dissembling seemed relatively harmless. It made him look a little better or not as bad.

"There are certain things that you don't lie about," David said. "For instance, if this was a lie that my sister was really not involved and my brother-in-law was not involved, I would never say it. I would certainly never say anything about other people that were innocent of anything. Because it's not in my nature to do something like that. When you think you can get out of something without getting anybody in trouble, then it's okay to lie."

He lied, he now admits, when he testified to having seen the console table in the Rosenbergs' apartment—the one that the government said Julius used for photographing secret documents. But he was not asked in court a question that might have produced a more incriminating response—his admission that at Julius's request he had made the metal clamp that supposedly attached the spy camera to the table.

One other lie, though, was crucial to the prosecution's case against his sister. There is no evidence that FBI agents and prosecutors knew it was a lie, but there is every indication that the government needed it very badly to convict Ethel Rosenberg.

Ethel may or may not have typed up David's handwritten notes that

---

[*] I never caught him lying to me, although there were several elements of his account (whether he gave Julius a uranium sample for the Russians, for example, or volunteered to photograph classified documents at the Arma plant in Brooklyn) that were contradicted by other sources.

September 1945 evening in Knickerbocker Village. Who knows? David's handwriting wasn't illegible. His syntax was better than passable, and, even had it not been, he wasn't being graded on grammar. Handwritten or typed, the notes contained little or nothing that was new. But from the prosecution's perspective, the Remington was as good as a smoking gun in Ethel Rosenberg's hands. Ethel sat at that typewriter, Irving Saypol declared in his summation to the jury, and "struck the keys, blow by blow, against her own country in the interests of the Soviets." David testified to it. Ruth corroborated his testimony.

The official record consists only of David and Ruth's belated recollection and Ethel and Julius's subsequent denial. There were no other witnesses. But something Ruth said suggests that she wasn't 100 percent certain. Asked how she could be so sure that the incriminating scenario—that David deciphered his own cryptic handwriting, that Ruth helped with the grammar, and that Ethel typed—occurred just that way, Ruth replied to Radosh and Stern: "Because that's the way it would have been done."

First, Ruth remembered the typing, or thought she did and told the prosecutors. Then, one week before the trial, the FBI and Assistant U.S. Attorney James Kilsheimer interviewed David. He corroborated Ruth's account. But he now says that he never remembered Ethel typing his notes. He didn't remember it then, and he doesn't remember it now.

"Yeah, I don't remember that at all," he told me. "I frankly think my wife did the typing, but I don't remember."

"And you didn't remember it at the time of the trial?" I asked.

"I didn't remember it then either," he said. "I didn't remember it. I can only assume my wife didn't make it up."

Regardless, by corroborating Ruth's account—and testifying to it first at the trial—David provided the prosecution with a vital missing link.[*] He seemed oblivious to the implications of what he was saying

---

[*] Months earlier, in July 1950, when the grand jury indicted Julius but not Ethel, prosecutors concluded: "So far it appears there would be just one witness against Ethel to show her complicity, which witness would be Ruth, since so far it appears the only thing David knows about Ethel's involvement is what he has learned from Ruth."

and proceeded to explain all he had done to save his sister. ("You know," he told me once, "I seldom use the word *sister* anymore; I've just wiped it out of my mind.") David recounted the genesis of Ethel's legal entanglement and how his original version began to unravel as Ruth provided more details: "I told them the story and left her out of it, right? But my wife put her in it. So what am I gonna do, call my wife a liar? My wife is my wife. I mean, I don't sleep with my sister, you know. There's more to it than sex, you understand. There's more to it than sex. You make a life with somebody. In my generation, that's the way I would go. My wife is more important to me than my sister. Or my mother or my father, okay? And she was the mother of my children."

David added parenthetically: "And *she* was the mother of *her* children. She should have thought of them first."

"She, Ethel?"

"Yes."

———

Predicting a jury verdict is a fool's errand. But without what is acknowledged universally to have been the single most damning testimony against her—testimony that, presumably, contradicts what the Greenglasses told a grand jury months earlier—Ethel Rosenberg might not have been convicted. She probably would not have been sentenced to death. Who knows how that would have affected Julius's resolve? Fifty years after the trial and a decade after the collapse of the Soviet Union, Ethel, in her eighties, might be explaining to her grown grandchildren how hindsight could distort an earlier era's hopes and fears, how much the world had changed since then, and how much it had not, which injustices were still worth challenging at any cost, and which loyalties one might, in the final analysis, be justified in sacrificing.

Chapter 37

The Final Chapter

"I would say that basically they would look at me from the point of view of, this is the man that had his sister and brother-in-law put to death."

=

Ten years almost to the day before the Rosenbergs were executed, a sold-out rally at Madison Square Garden drew dozens of American dignitaries ranging from Mayor Fiorello La Guardia to presidential confidant Harry Hopkins, all of them pleading passionately for contributions to Russian war relief. In the Bronx, Borough President James J. Lyons formally declared Red Army Day. Defying the odds, the Russians were valiantly bearing the brunt of Nazi brutality, which meant the Germans would be all the more vulnerable to an Allied invasion. And once that invasion was mounted, a number of perfectly respectable American military leaders, scientists, and diplomats would ponder a postwar world in which the secret superweapon the United States was developing would be shared with the Soviets. Few of those Americans, though, were in a position, as David Greenglass was, to deliver on his convictions.

By June 1953, however, the Soviet Union had few defenders left in the United States, or few who would express their support publicly. Stalin had died three months before. The Korean War appeared to be almost won. But Soviet tanks were at that moment crushing a brief outbreak of dissent in East Berlin. And, four years after a disturbingly high level of radioactivity detected in rain clouds over the Pacific Northwest had signaled that the Soviets had exploded their own atomic warhead, the Soviets were now less than two months away from testing their first hydrogen bomb, too.

Americans were scared.

People were terrified that higher civilization had advanced to the point that it was, for the first time, capable of total self-destruction. As late as 1953, America was stunned that, as President Eisenhower put it, "on the other side of the Iron Curtain, a backward civilization with a second rate production plant can develop the power to frighten us all out of our wits." As Bob Dylan later wrote in his ballad "Julius and Ethel," "Eisenhower was president, Senator Joe was King / Long as you didn't say nothin', you could say anything." Senator Joseph McCarthy provoked a paroxysm of Red-baiting by brandishing an ever-evolving list of hundreds of government workers who, he claimed, were closet communists. His list was a sham, though it cost many innocent people, and some not-so-innocent ones, their livelihoods and, in some cases, their lives. But there was another list, one with even more names than McCarthy's. This one was real. It was compiled by the Soviet security services. And Julius Rosenberg's name was on it.

Was Julius guilty? And of what?

Of conspiracy to commit espionage, the evidence overwhelmingly suggests the answer is yes.

Of stealing the secret to the atomic bomb, no (although not for lack of trying—and he could have been found guilty regardless of whether the conspiracy accomplished its goal). The antiaircraft proximity fuse, as it turned out, was probably more valuable to the Russian military than whatever Julius volunteered about atomic energy.*

Was Ethel his willing partner in crime? She was irrefutably person-

---

* Alexander Feklisov would write that "even millions [of dollars] wouldn't have compensated" Julius for his contributions to Soviet intelligence. Julius, Joel Barr, Alfred Sarant, William Perl, and Morton Sobell turned over thousands of pages of technical documents, Feklisov said.

ally supportive, philosophically in sync, and morally complicit. She may, in fact, have committed some or even all of the few overt criminal acts attributed to her by the prosecution (and more, given the NKGB account of her onetime role as a lookout).

Would Ethel have been convicted, much less executed, if her brother had told the truth? No. Had he been completely honest, he would have been a less credible witness. And his belated final confession provides ample reasonable doubt about the prosecution's key proof: the Green-glasses' testimony about Ethel's typing. At the trial, David flatly lied about the typing, but much of his testimony was accurate. Much of Julius's and Ethel's testimony was not.

Did the punishment fit the crime? No. It backfired politically and legally. As William Rogers, the deputy attorney general at the time, said, Ethel called the government's bluff. Nathan Glazer, the Harvard sociologist, likened the government's use of the death penalty as leverage to hostage-taking by terrorists. "The Rosenbergs alive," he wrote, "could never have been the symbol that the Rosenbergs dead became."

—

In the 1990s, Ethel Rosenberg's name was deleted from California's official eleventh-grade history-lesson plan. A member of the State Board of Education complained because Ethel, a Jew, was singled out as the only example of a communist spy. But the case could never be completely purged from the American psyche. Even as late as 1999, when the FBI was interrogating Los Alamos physicist Wen Ho Lee in an espionage investigation, one agent asked him: "Do you know who the Rosenbergs are? The Rosenbergs are the only people that never cooperated with the federal government in an espionage case. You know what happened to them? They electrocuted them, Wen Ho."

"Yeah," Lee replied. "I heard."

—

After serving sixteen years of his thirty-year sentence, most of it at Lewisburg, Harry Gold was paroled in 1966, six years after David had been released. He returned to Philadelphia and to his job as a clinical chemist at the heart station of what had become John F. Kennedy Memorial Hospital. Harry died there in 1972, at age sixty, during an operation on his own heart. The funeral service was private. Harry had plunged so deeply into obscurity that eighteen months elapsed before the first obituary was published. "We didn't want no publicity," said his younger brother, Joseph, a retired civil servant and decorated veteran of World War II. "We didn't need it."

—

Irving Saypol went to his final reward early: He became a judge. He was elected a justice of the New York State Supreme Court in 1952, less than a year after the Rosenberg trial, and presided imperiously (once holding a lawyer in contempt because he found her brown suede hat to be grotesque) until 1976 when he was indicted with another judge for illegally steering court commissions to Saypol's son. The charges were later dismissed. Saypol died of cancer less than six months later. He was seventy-one.

—

Roy Cohn went to Washington as special assistant to Attorney General James McGranery, who as a judge had presided over Harry Gold's plea bargain. After serving as chief counsel to Senator McCarthy's investigations committee, he returned to New York in 1954 and embarked on an illustrious career as a defense lawyer and power broker. Poetic justice imposed a measure of closure: Cohn's apparent role in forging the will of Lewis Rosenstiel, the whiskey magnate at whose Connecticut estate Judge Kaufman vacationed after the Rosenberg trial, would contribute to the case for Cohn's disbarment in 1986. Less than six weeks later, he died of AIDS at the age of fifty-nine.

—

After serving fourteen years in a British prison, Klaus Fuchs returned to what had become East Germany in 1959. In 1961 and again 1986, he defended Soviet nuclear testing as necessary self-defense against Western warmongering. Fuchs died in 1988 at seventy-six.

—

During nearly four distinguished decades on the bench, Irving Kaufman broke legal ground in antitrust, civil rights, and First Amendment cases (including one that upheld the Communist Party's privacy right not to disclose its contributors) and rose to become chief judge of the Second Circuit Court of Appeals. He consistently issued decisions that buffed his reputation as a civil libertarian (even if his reputation as an employer—firing clerks if his grapefruit was sliced on an unacceptable bias—was somewhat less than civil).

Kaufman relegated the Rosenberg case to the thirteenth and last page of his official résumé, but it haunted him in ways large and small. The U.S. Supreme Court seat that he coveted would be denied him. "I despise a judge who feels God told him to impose a death sentence," Justice Felix Frankfurter once wrote. "I am mean enough to try to stay here long enough so that K will be too old to succeed me." One federal judge even refused to retire early because it would mean relinquishing his New York vanity license plate, USJ-1, to Kaufman.

While Kaufman never publicly amplified on his rationale in meting out the death penalty to the Rosenbergs, he wrote James Bennett, the former prisons director, in 1970:

> I want you to know that I respect your views on capital punishment and I am not sure that you and I are in substantial disagreement. . . . Given the magnitude of the crime necessarily implied by the jury's verdict, there was, in reality, no room for discretion in the sentencing judge, unless he were to substitute his own abhorrence of the death penalty for the punishment Congress had provided for the most serious offenses. . . . If those penalties were improper or harmful to the "conscience of the people". . . then it was the office of two Presidents of the United States, Truman and Eisenhower, to exercise their power of executive clemency and alter the sentences. I, as judge and not president, could not, and did not.

For years, Kaufman's single-minded obsession was to persuade his friend, Arthur Ochs Sulzberger, the publisher of *The New York Times*, to excise the name Rosenberg from the first paragraph of his lengthy prepared obituary. His mission was in vain. By definition, most people are already dead when their obituaries finally appear. Kaufman lived his worst nightmare. Years later, when the Times Square electronic news zipper prematurely announced his death, the three-word headline succinctly told his life story: ROSENBERG JUDGE DIES. And when Judge Kaufman actually died, the case hovered spectrally over his funeral service. After the dignitaries delivered their reverential eulogies, a lone heckler screamed from the rear of the synagogue, as if to finally dispatch the judge to his just reward: "He murdered the Rosenbergs. Let him rot in hell." Leonard Sand, who was Kaufman's law clerk in 1953 and later ascended to the federal bench himself, remembers how unsettling that disruption was. "I think some of the judges, for the first time, realized the burden which that case imposed on him and his family," Sand recalled. "Not even in death was he given a respite."

Kaufman was eighty-one years old when he died of pancreatic cancer in 1992. He donated his private papers to the Library of Congress, but they remain sealed until 2026.

—

Joel Barr, who disappeared from Paris when the Rosenbergs were arrested in 1950, defected to Czechoslovakia, where he married a Czech woman and was joined by fellow electronics engineer and former Greenwich Village roommate Alfred Sarant. Neither was ever formally charged by the United States with espionage. Both settled in the Soviet Union, where they were instrumental in establishing a fledgling computer industry.

Sarant died in Leningrad in 1979. In the early 1990s, Barr returned to the United States for the first of several visits. To the frustration of American officials, Barr applied for—and received—Social Security benefits (and a New York driver's license) before he died in Moscow in 1998. He was eighty-two.

—

Theodore Hall was never prosecuted; except for Venona, the FBI lacked corroboration. He became a cancer researcher in New York and in 1962 moved to Britain where he so relished obscurity that for his twenty-fifth reunion at Harvard, he and his wife wrote from Cambridge, "[We] do not believe anything is worth noting in our personal histories." After he was publicly identified as a spy in 1995, he all but admitted espionage, though he concluded:

> In 1944 I was nineteen years old—immature, inexperienced and far too sure of myself. I recognize that I could easily have been wrong in my judgement of what was necessary, and that I was indeed mistaken about some things, in particular my view of the nature of the Soviet state. The world has moved on a lot since then, and certainly so have I. But in essence, from the perspective of my 71 years, I still think that brash youth had the right end of the stick. I am no longer that person; but I am by no means ashamed of him.

Hall died in 1999 at the age of seventy-three.

—

Morton Sobell was released from prison in 1969 after serving more than eighteen years of his thirty-year sentence at Alcatraz, Lewisburg, and other federal penitentiaries. He was fifty-one years old. With remarkably little rancor and unflagging zeal, he spent the rest of his life in New York and California advocating for progressive causes and insisting that whatever he might have been guilty of, the legal grounds for his conviction were neither treason nor atomic spying. Without admitting to espionage, he once said: "If I had known then what I know now would I have acted any differently? There's no answer to that. It's a difficult question for all of us."

—

Rabbi Irving Koslowe had gone to graduate school in psychology but didn't need the degree to diagnose the Greenglass family pathology. "Obviously, the mother had to make a choice," Koslowe said. "The mother obviously favored her baby son. The sister went to the chair because of her brother." After witnessing seventeen executions, Koslowe retired in 1999 as the Jewish chaplain of Sing Sing. He died the following year.

—

After the Rosenbergs were executed, Robby and Michael were placed by their legal guardian, Manny Bloch, with Anne Meeropol and her husband, Abel, a former Bronx schoolteacher who became a composer, lyricist, and target of the House Committee on Un-American Activities. The Meeropols legally adopted the boys in 1957. Among the songs Abe Meeropol wrote were "Strange Fruit," which Billie Holiday popularized, and "The House I Live In," an American hymn.

Michael and Robby attended progressive schools (in Robby's case, the Little Red School House in Greenwich Village; in Michael's, its affiliate, the Elisabeth Irwin High School) and grew up as radical children of the sixties. Robby recalled that at the University of Wisconsin, which Michael attended after Swarthmore and Cambridge, his brother "used to be described as Michael Meeropol You-Know-Who-His-Parents-Were. But nobody would ever say that to him or me, because it was considered impolite, I guess, or maybe that we were still undercover and they didn't want to intrude." In high school and at Earlham College in Indiana, Robby told no one who his real parents were, but, as he discovered when he finally confided in his future wife at the University of Michigan, the people who were closest to him already knew.

Michael was teaching economics at Western New England College in Springfield, Massachusetts, and Robby was studying for his doctorate in anthropology when Louis Nizer's account of the Rosenberg case was published in 1973. The brothers were outraged over what they saw as Nizer's appropriation of the Rosenbergs' letters and, even more so, over his branding of their sons as "normal, decent citizens," presumably in contrast to the parents. The brothers sued. In the course of protecting their parents' privacy rights, they sacrificed their own. Three years later, they published a poignant memoir—*We Are Your Sons*—which chronicled two young lives that, like braided wire, were at once intertwined with the legacy of the Rosenbergs and insulated from it.

That relationship manifested itself in many ways. A few months after the execution, the Meeropols were making a family tape recording in their apartment at 149th Street and Riverside Drive when Robby, in a fit of hysterical laughter, blurted: "Dave Greenglass should burn! He should burn in the trash can!" Three years later, Robby was watching Anne Meeropol direct a rehearsal of *The Valiant,* the drama in which Ethel Rosenberg had played the condemned man's sister. He fled to the bathroom as the execution scene approached. Abe Meeropol followed him. "For a while," Robby recalled, "I was silent, then I hugged him and asked, 'It won't happen again?'" A few years later, Michael convulsed in repressed sorrow as he finished reading *Knock on Any Door,* in which the hero prepares himself for his rendezvous with the electric chair. In 1960, when their Uncle David was released from prison, Robby recalled, "I noticed his picture in the newspaper but didn't have much reaction to it. Michael responded more vehemently, fantasizing a confrontation with him." Also, with Judge Kaufman. Michael recalled that as an adult he had reread *The Count of Monte Cristo* and concluded that by the time Edmond Dantes exacts revenge on those who did him dirty, he is neither happy nor nice. Intellectually, Michael wrote, revenge is stupid. But, he added:

> beneath all the civilized rationalizations and well-written arguments about why the Rosenberg case needed to be reopened, not as "a personal or historical exercise," but because of the political lessons it can bring us today, I must confess to feeling an animalistic desire for retribution. I do not believe in the retribution theory of punishment. That is in fact why I oppose capital punishment. Yet, I sympathize with families of victims who cry out for vengeance.

Why didn't their parents save themselves? Michael replied that given the choice between signing a confession and being shot, most people would sign. This was different. "It was more like giving somebody a hammer and saying, 'Go beat this guy to death.' I think most of us wouldn't do that. They'd say no," Michael said. "When the government said to my parents, 'Fully cooperate,' that meant 'Put other people where you are,' and that's when, in my opinion, they did what any decent person would do. They said no."

Robby largely shared his brother's views but with less vituperation. "It's much harder to prove someone innocent than to prove someone guilty," he told me. "It's clear to me they did not steal the secret to the atomic bomb." Robby added—wistfully, it seemed to me, "I find myself wanting to show them the world as it is now and ask them what do they think of their actions. I hope that they felt it was worth it." He wrote: "The absence of the F.B.I. logs of the Greenglass interview means that we probably will never be able to prove that Greenglass was tricked or coerced into falsely confessing and implicating my father unless he and Ruth decide to tell the truth sometime before they die."

Robby transferred to law school but found the practice of tax law so stifling that he quit in 1990, when he was forty-three, and established a foundation, the Rosenberg Fund for Children, for "the educational and emotional needs of . . . children whose parents have been harassed, injured, lost jobs, or died in the course of their progressive activities."

What about Venona? "I cannot be absolutely certain that neither Ethel nor Julius Rosenberg ever had any contact with the KGB at any point between 1939 and 1950," Robby said. "This material I cannot refute." At the same time, Michael added, Venona may not absolve Ethel, but it only barely incriminates her. "If Venona is accurate," Michael said, "they took her as a hostage, put a gun to her head, and said to my father, 'Confess or we'll kill her.' And then they pulled the trigger."

———

I asked David whether he still sees his nephews.

"Sure, I used to see them all the time," he said.

"When was the last time?"

"In 1950," he replied.

I tried to arrange a reunion. David was game, although he expressed regret that his nephews had made what he described as a "fetish" of proving that their parents had been framed. "I regret that their whole life has been involved with this kind of stupidity, to actually think they were innocent," he said. Ruth still bristles at something Michael was supposed to have said years ago: "My mother went to the death house and Aunt Ruth goes home to make dinner."

"I don't think," Ruth said, "he ever wants to talk to us."

Ruth was right.

Michael and Robby responded with perfectly reasonable rationalizations, though I suspected that their reticence was grounded not merely in a profound revulsion cultivated since childhood but by a suspicion that Uncle David would turn out to be just another garden-variety schmuck and not the embodiment of evil. In contrast to the quest by the eponymous protagonist in Doctorow's *The Book of Daniel,* the Meeropols wanted no part of David Greenglass.

"The last time I saw him I was seven," Michael told me. "What gain would there be? I'd just yell and scream and call him names. I don't think I could be calm enough to pick apart his story."

"This was a sleazy, despicable person, and I don't doubt he is despicable to this day," Robby said. "It's very hard for me to see myself in David Greenglass's shoes. What would I do? I don't have a clue. I don't have a clue about how I would get into that situation.

"People have been asking me about why I don't see David or want to talk to David all of my adult life," Robby recalled. "For a good fifteen to twenty years I came up with all sorts of rationalizations. The reality is, I think I've defined my entire life as someone who is not David Greenglass, and the thought of David Greenglass disgusts me. Any curiosity I have is overcome by my feelings.

"When I was a kid," Robby said, "sure, I would've loved to do violence to them all."

"Even when I was very young," Michael interjected, "to me the great revenge was if I could make David Greenglass feel bad. I would find him somewhere and very loudly identify him as an ex-con."

Michael and Robby each have two grown children; *they* didn't want to meet their great-uncle either. Julius and Ethel Rosenberg's grandchildren know their grandparents' true identity. Until relatively recently, David and Ruth Greenglass's grandchildren did not.

A half century has elapsed since the Rosenberg trial. Nearly all the protagonists are dead. The name David Greenglass remains a metaphor for misplaced loyalty and betrayal.

"Do you think you were a traitor?" I asked him.

"No, never," David insisted. "Never." Instead, he said, the government had overreacted to the threat of communism, and its overreaction provoked an equally disproportionate response from defenders of the Rosenbergs, which stoked further recriminations against the American left. "They're guilty in what they did," David said, "but they didn't deserve to die."

I reminded him that in *The Book of Daniel*, the daughter of the Greenglass character complains to the executed couple's sons that her father got treated worse because he had to live with his guilt. David didn't agree.

"No," he said. "Being killed is a lot more. I mean, I'm living, right? I'm living. I was able to see my kids live. I mean there was ten years where they didn't see me. But *they* got the worst of it."

"Your kids?"

"Of course! I don't know about *their* kids. No, their kids didn't get the worst of it at all. Their parents got it. Their kids were given over to some communist family who raised them, sent them to school."

"So you mean your kids had a tougher time than their kids?"

"Yeah, of course!"

—

I asked David what he would want his obituary to say. Like Judge Kaufman, he chose to relegate the Rosenberg case to a footnote in a fuller life defined by lofty goals: "I was a good father. A good husband. A good son. A good brother. Born in a time which tore people's souls."

"How do you want history to remember you?"

"I don't care," David replied. "I don't care. I won't be around when you write that history."

"But your family will be."

"They know me. How much of my family, after all, one or two generations? People won't even know I was alive. . . . I have no idea how history will look at me," he said.

But I would say that basically they would look at me from the point of view of, this is the man that had his sister and brother-in-law put to death.

Of course, they always forget that nobody ever told me that's what they were going, [what] they had intended to do. And nobody ever told me that they would carry out such a sentence. And judging from what happened to the other people that were involved when I was arrested, I never thought anything like that would ever come about. That's neither here nor there. As long as they had something over my head about my wife and my family, then they could probably get me to do anything that would preserve them. That's the facts. There's no getting away from that. And most men would do that. Not just me.

—

Our last interview ended as the dozens that had preceded it had. David got up from the chair next to mine. He shook hands, said good-bye, and left me and his lawyer, who had monitored virtually every one of our conversations while he played video games on his computer. David had never told his wife that he had finally agreed to be interviewed.

My search for David Greenglass was over. But I was still searching for an end to a story that I felt had stopped short of a climax. So I followed David home.

For a driver who is colorblind, David didn't run a single red light (he can tell red from green by which of the three lights on the traffic signal is lit), but his leased coupe took advantage of every shortcut. As he pulled into his driveway, the garage door opened automatically. I vaguely recalled the neighborhood from my brief encounter ten years before. Some of the kids from the elementary school at the end of the block must be in college by now. The trees arched closer together across the street than they had then, though the sky was still revealed through gaps left by limbs lost to storms. The house looked the same. It is a white frame house with faded red trim. It sits on a corner lot. The shades were drawn tight, just as they had been the first time I visited.

The Greenglasses have lived pseudonymously for more than half their lives; their circumspect lifestyle is a testament to the enduring attraction of the case. That they have largely succeeded is a consequence of New York's impersonality.

A lamppost stands on the front lawn, between the driveway and the house. It is slightly askew. The light works. Something is missing, though. The wrought-iron arm from which most homeowners hang a sign that proudly proclaims their family name is bare.

Except for two empty hooks.

Epilogue

Case Closed

Maybe because it was September 11, another anniversary of the World Trade Center attack. Perhaps that's why Morty Sobell was feeling so philosophical that morning when I called him at his Bronx home. I was seeking his reaction to the secret grand jury minutes from the Rosenberg case, which I had sued the federal government to release. The transcripts, as I had suspected, conflicted with and even contradicted what witnesses would publicly testify to a few months later during the actual trial. Had Julius and Ethel Rosenberg's lawyers been armed with that grand jury testimony, they would have been able to mount a more aggressive, and potentially successful, defense.

In our conversation, Sobell volunteered to me that he had recently reached out to Max Elitcher, his former Queens backyard neighbor. Elitcher had been the chief prosecution witness against him. Sobell was not exactly letting bygones be bygones, he offered, but, after all, both men were now in their 90s. While still lucid, they were welded together in a time warp forged by events a half-century earlier. Still, his overture to Elitcher surprised me. What next, I asked, almost facetiously. Was he also going to admit that, indeed, he had been a Soviet spy? I was stunned by his response.

"Yeah, yeah, yeah, call it that," he replied.

In one devastating seismic stroke that became front-page news in the next day's New York Times, Sobell negated 57 years of unequivocal claims of innocence. He also implicated his friend and former college classmate, Julius Rosenberg as a co-conspirator in espionage. Whenever he needed to contact the Russians, to transmit military and industrial secrets, he consistently turned to one associate:

"Julie handled it all for me," Sobell said.

His revelation irretrievably stripped the historic underpinnings from what the historian Ronald Radosh called "a pillar of the left-wing culture of grievance." That culture endures nonetheless, suspended in another untruth—David Greenglass's admission to me in an interview for this book that he lied at the trial about the most incriminating evidence against his sister, Ethel: that she typed David's notes about the atomic bomb for delivery to his Soviet spymasters. Still, here was Morton Sobell, the sole surviving defendant in the Rosenberg trial, finally admitting *his* guilt, and, by extension, Julius's. Even the Rosenberg sons, talismans for a lost cause, reconciled themselves to Sobell's rude awakening.

"I had considered that a real possibility for some time," Robert Meeropol said, "and this tips the balance."

"I don't have any reason to doubt Morty," Michael Meeropol said. "We believed they were innocent and we tried to prove them innocent. But I remember saying to myself in late 1975, maybe a little later, that whatever happens, it doesn't change me. We really meant it, that the truth is more important than our political position."

—

Years earlier, I had asked Sobell whether if he *had* been a spy he would ever admit it. Recognizing a rhetorical trap, he politely replied that he couldn't answer that question. But by 2008, when he finally made his admission to me, was his memory still intact? He might not have recalled precisely what he had eaten for breakfast that morning, but he was able to vividly describe events from five decades before, even if, on occasion, he was deliberately opaque. To be sure, I asked the author Walter Schneir, with whom Sobell had remained close. "Do I believe Morty?" Schneir said. "Yes."

But why now, what prompted Sobell to finally confess to his complicity in espionage? "Time," he replied. "If I don't tell it now, it will never be known." And then he acknowledged what he had never told his son ("I didn't want to burden him") or his lawyers (he said they never asked), but revealed what he said his wife, Helen, who had indefatigably proclaimed his innocence and the Rosenbergs' for decades, had known all along: that he had been a Soviet spy and that so was Julius. Sobell also implicated other Rosenberg associates, William Perl and the Sidor-ovichs, and Helen herself, who died in 2002.

"Helen approved of it," he said, likening her complicity to Ethel's. "And Ethel, *she* must have approved. But Ethel did not have to die, any more than Helen," he said. "Ethel was no more guilty than Helen. Guilty knowledge, that's all."

Sobell sought to limit his own culpability to non-atomic espionage and to military secrets that were merely defensive, that could not be and never were used *offensively* against the United States. He acknowledged, though: "You cannot plead that what you did was only defensive stuff, but there's a big difference between giving that and stuff that could be used to attack our country." Yet one device he mentioned specifically, the SCR 584 anti-aircraft radar, built by General Electric, is widely be-lieved by military experts to have been used against American planes in Korea and Vietnam.

Sobell's impromptu admissions, he explained, were not as spon-taneous as they seemed. They had been well thought out over time (though it had been years since he evolved from a communist intent on overthrowing capitalism to admitting that even socialism can't work without competition). He was acknowledging that he had spied, but in-sisted, credibly, that he was never involved in atomic espionage, as the 1951 trial had suggested.

"This is not, 'I confess,'" he explained—more like a "J'accuse" against the government. "It will prove that I was innocent of what they im-pugned to me, that the stuff I gave somehow hurt the United States," he insisted. "When I gave it I was giving it starting out to fight Hitler, but it continued. That was the impetus originally." Had he ever considered admitting earlier what he was finally acknowledging now? "No," he re-plied, "the fight had to be waged on the basis of innocence." There was no room for nuance in a public relations and legal campaign for the world's hearts and minds. No room for the truth. "You couldn't base it on, they were guilty of the charges they were accused of," he said.

But in minimizing Julius's role ("He was not a smooth operator," Sobell said), he also inadvertently implicated him in supplying atomic secrets to the Soviets—in effect, directly contradicting Walter Schneir's *Final Verdict*, which absolved Julius of any connection beyond hatching the plot to recruit Greenglass and then leaving David to fend for himself with the courier Harry Gold and other Soviet agents. "I'm telling it as it was," Sobell said, with grammatical perfection. "I know all the details. And when you know all the details, you know they are innocent of the main charge. Julius was innocent of what he was charged with in the sense that the sketch that he transmitted was bullshit."

Sobell had been intent on not implicating Julius in atomic espionage, but now he appeared to be doing just that. That Julius delivered "that stupid diagram" of the bomb's secret innards to the Soviets at all would have been more than enough proof of the deliberately nebulous legal indictment against him: conspiracy to commit espionage, as well as the specter of atomic spying that haunted the trial. Intent and an overt act were the only proof required. "When you're dealing with a conspiracy, you don't have to be the kingpin, you have to participate," said James Kilsheimer, the former prosecutor. "You can't be partially guilty any more than you can be partially pregnant."

—

Every new revelation since *The Brother* was originally published in 2001 has affirmed its fundamental conclusions, further implicating Julius in an espionage conspiracy (Sobell also described Julius as the Soviet paymaster and distributor of Christmas gifts to fellow agents) but suggesting, nonetheless, that the government framed a guilty man.

In a subsequent interview with Ronald Radosh and Steven T. Usdin for *The Weekly Standard*, Sobell further confessed to helping copy hundreds of pages of secret Air Force documents stolen from a Columbia University professor's safe as late as 1948. He said that he, Julius Rosenberg and William Perl spent a weekend, probably Independence Day, frantically photographing the classified documents with Leica cameras in a Greenwich Village apartment and delivering a box filled with canisters of 35-millimeter film to Soviet agents on a Long Island Rail Road platform in Glen Cove, not far from the 46-room mansion owned by Russian diplomats. Sobell's account not only confirmed the episode, which the government had alleged, but also verified jailhouse informer Jerome Tartikow's version, which supporters of the Rosenbergs had consistently discredited.

David Greenglass, it turns out, wasn't the only agent Julius enlisted to penetrate the Manhattan Project, according to *Spies: The Rise and Fall of the K.G.B. in America*, by John Earl Haynes, Harvey Klehr and Alexander Vassiliev, the former Soviet agent. The authors concluded that the agent nicknamed "Fogel" or "Persian" in the decoded Venona cables was not Robert Oppenheimer or Philip Morrison, as some historians have speculated, but Russell McNutt, the relatively obscure engineer and Rosenberg associate who worked at the uranium processing plant in Oak Ridge. "This was an atomic spy who got away with it," Haynes said, "while his protectors, the Rosenbergs, went to their death." (The book also concludes that "Perseus," the code name for a spy who has never been identified, was, in fact, a composite fabricated to confuse American counter-intelligence agents.)

Notes copied by Vassiliev from K.G.B. files affirm that Ethel Rosenberg "knows about her husband's work," adding, though: "She could be used independently, but should not be overworked—poor health." Vassiliev's notebooks contained no references to Ethel's typing her brother's handwritten notes about the bomb. They do suggest that Greenglass furnished the Soviets with not only the sketch of the fuse for the implosion device, but a prototype. Still, the Russians complained that his intelligence was "unqualified and far from polished" because of his "insufficient qualifications" as a machinist, rather than as a scientist or engineer.

Even *Heir to an Execution*, Ivy Meeropol's endearing home movie-like HBO documentary, which reclaims the Rosenbergs, her grandparents, for her own generation, confirms Julius's complicity. In the 2004 film, a friend and defender of the Rosenbergs, Abe Osheroff, boasts that Julius provided the Soviets with vital specifications for an advanced airplane propeller. (Osheroff's boast finally persuaded Ivy that Julius had, indeed, been a spy, although she acknowledged his role with the circumspection of a hostile witness: "If he did it," she told me, "I would say, yes, that's a spy.") In Ivy's film, Sobell recalls in an interview that Michael Meeropol often asked him, "Do you know something I don't know" about his father Julius.

"Do you?" Ivy Meeropol gently prods.

"People ask me, was he innocent," Sobell replies, "and you know as much as I do."

—

The truth that the Meerpols said took precedence over any political agenda is no longer in doubt: Julius, at least, was guilty of the vague legal charge lodged against him. As a result, the contours of debate have shifted, or been twisted.

"To me it didn't matter whether they were guilty or not," the historian Howard Zinn said. "The most important thing was they did not get a fair trial in the atmosphere of cold war hysteria."

Even before Sobell's confession, the Rosenbergs' sons were being shaken out of their comforting ambivalence by the Venona cables released during the 1990s. ("I was perfectly happy to live with the ambiguity," Michael said, looking back.) "While the transcriptions seemed inconclusive," Robert Meeropol wrote in his memoir, *An Execution in the Family: One Son's Journey*, "they forced me to accept the possibility that my father had participated in an illegal and covert effort to help the Soviet Union defeat the Nazis."

But, Robby Meeropol also insisted to me, that the admission was "not the end of what happened to my mother and it's not the end of understanding what happened to due process."

"It's pretty obvious my father was involved with Mort and others with helping the Soviet Union with various military and industrial knowhow and it's hard for me to imagine that Ethel didn't know what Julius was doing, but she wasn't actively involved," Robby said. "What often gets lost, the reasons the executions took place, was because they supposedly stole the secret of the atomic bomb. Not only was that not true but the government knew it wasn't true. The awesome power of the government was used to execute two people for something they didn't do, and that's very dangerous. And that reverberates even today."

Other critics, too, focused less on Julius's culpability as it became more conclusive, than on over-reaching by the government. "I never was going along saying I know that they were innocent, and I'm not shocked by the fact that they turned out to be spies," Zinn told me shortly before he died in 2010.

Edgar Doctorow, author of *The Book of Daniel*, also suggested that a larger question superseded whether the Rosenbergs had committed espionage: "It was what happened to them, as if a society turned its magnifying lens on these people until they caught fire and were burned alive." And Victor Navasky said: "I wish Morty and Ethel and Julius had been open about what they had and hadn't done, or in Morty's case 'come clean' before this. But these guys thought they were helping our ally in wartime, and yes, they broke the law, shouldn't have done what they did, and should have been proportionately punished for it; but the greater betrayal was by the state."

—

The Meeropols and other defenders of the Rosenbergs have consistently sought to place due process on trial and the newly released grand jury transcripts gave them grist. (The testimony also revealed a historical footnote that affected millions of New Yorkers in an unexpected way: Julius and David's Lower East Side machine shop had helped retool the city's subway turnstiles when the transit fare was raised to a dime after 1948.)

The grand jury testimony of witnesses who had since died, released by Judge Alvin K. Hellerstein in 2008 in response to a lawsuit by the National Security Archive, historians and journalists, appeared to poke more holes in the case against Ethel Rosenberg. In her grand jury testimony six months before the trial, Ruth Greenglass never mentioned that Ethel had typed her brother's notes. In fact, Ruth recalled that *she*— not Ethel—had transcribed David's Los Alamos secrets in longhand on at least one occasion herself. She also placed Ethel out of earshot during several important conversations relating to espionage.

"The grand jury testimony by Ruth Greenglass directly contradicts the charge against Ethel Rosenberg that put her in the electric chair," Thomas S. Blanton, director of the National Security Archive, said flatly. Pointing to inconsistences between the grand jury transcripts and later trial testimony, David C. Vladeck, the attorney who argued for the transcripts to be released, declared: "Imagine if the Rosenbergs had a good lawyer" (think William Kunstler or Alan Dershowitz). A more aggressive defense would, among other damaging testimony, have retrieved a blanket admission to the grand jury by Harry Gold that "everything I have done for the past 15 years, practically all of my adult life, was based on lies and deceptions" (sometimes even liars tell the truth, though). Gold testified before the grand jury that he had met Julius, contradicting his other accounts, and never mentions the damning passwords, "I come from Julius," that he revealed to dramatic effect during the trial.

The hundreds of pages of transcripts are peppered with belligerent jousting between prosecutors and witnesses and factoids that aficionados of the case are likely to parse for years. Jurors volunteered their definition of patriotism—which did not include invoking constitutional rights against self-incrimination—and a particularly testy exchange ensued between Stella Page, Mark's wife, and the assistant prosecutor, Myles Lane. Against the backdrop of the ongoing war in Korea, Lane asked Page, whose husband was one of Julius's classmates, "isn't it a little incongruous to say that you are a good American citizen and then you don't want to assist in the prosecution of a man who has been indicted for the worst offense that could be committed against the government?" A venireman's verdict on Page's behavior: "Distinctly un-American." A juror told Mark Page: "You must be mixed up with Rosenberg if you refuse to answer. I think he is just begging to be brought into the Rosenberg trial, Mr. Lane."

Lane asked another witness, Sobell's uncle: "If you are innocent, why do you need a lawyer?" When Sobell's uncle asked to consult an attorney, a juror interrupted: "We are all American citizens, and your answers to the questions are stupid." To which another juror added: "You seem to want to get into the same mess your nephew is in."

Lane himself warned Sobell's aunt: "We are trying to get you people to cooperate, but you don't want to do it, and by refusing to answer questions it seems to me that you are practically admitting that you people have a part in this dastardly scheme." He warned another witness "I can ask and get a superseding indictment, the penalty for which is death." Lane admonished Joel Barr's girlfriend Vivian Glassman: "You don't care about people that are dying for this country . . . every time we come to a point which involves somebody that is affiliated with this Communist movement to destroy this country, you fall back on your so-called constitutional rights."

A juror interjected: "I wish you would ask her whether she is in favor of Russia having the atomic bomb, so that they can drop it on us . . . You don't deserve to say you are an American."

Even Richard M. Nixon would say in a 1983 interview (released in 2008 after the grand jury inconsistencies were revealed), that Ethel Rosenberg might have been spared the death penalty by President Eisenhower had he been aware that the evidence against her was tainted.

—

For decades, thanks in large part to the claims of innocence reverberating in Sobell's echo chamber, the nation has been riven by the Rosenberg case. If you believed Sobell and the Rosenbergs were innocent, you were a fellow traveler or, at best, naive. If you maintained that they were guilty and deserved the death penalty, you were a McCarthyite (defined with beguiling disingenuousness by the senator himself as "calling a man a communist who is later proven to be one").

The hold of the Rosenberg case has proved to be almost timeless, considering that more than six decades have elapsed since the couple was executed—in their early 30s (about the age of their grandchildren today) and that most of the spying of which they were accused was committed while they were only in their early 20s. "You know what's always fascinated me about Julius and Ethel Rosenberg," the Parker Posey character says in Nora and Delia Ephron's film *You've Got Mail*, "is how old they looked when they were really just our age." (When they were arrested in 1950, he was 32, she was 34.)

Today, Julius and Ethel's sons, the most famous orphans of the cold war, are retired. Robby has turned over the day-to-day running of the Rosenberg Fund for Children—his vehicle for "constructive revenge"—to his daughter Jenn. "Through their choices, their resistance," she says, "my grandparents passed their passion for social justice on to their sons, to our extended families, to all of us."

In June 2013, at Manhattan's Town Hall, the dwindling number of Rosenberg defenders gathered to commemorate the 60th anniversary of the execution. "We are here to honor their resistance, part of a long and continuing tradition of social justice activism," Angela Davis, the counter-culture radical and scholar, said. Recalling the "desperately poor" couple who "watched the world crumbling around them," she warned that Washington still targets "movements for social change—the 99 percent—with knee-jerk fear and without regard for collateral damage to innocent people."

Beyond the youngsters, you'd be hard-pressed to find an innocent party to the Rosenberg case. Ultimately, *The Brother* has been a story of betrayal—Sobell, most recently, of his diehard supporters, the other principals also of country and government and family. Perhaps only some best friends were spared in a synergistic display of camaraderie and undying devotion to a political cause.

"The grand jury testimony taught me more about my parents' social circle," Robby said. "It's a description of a whole bunch of 20-somethings, people who came out of the Depression, not only survived but went to the top of their class and they thought they could change the world. They were going to do what they could to make their mark. Until it all came crashing down."

"I became more careful as a parent," Robby said. "I knew from painful experience the terrible toll activist parents' decisions can take on their children, and I did not wish my childhood nightmare visited on my children."

Ivy said, "I think they died because they believed that would be a greater legacy to leave for all of us than if they named names. I don't think they died for communism, even necessarily to make some kind of statement. It was a simple equation: they couldn't do anything else."

To which Michael weighed in: "Think of your grandmother. She would have had to repudiate her marriage, basically, testify against her own husband. She would have then had to live her entire life bringing up Robby and me having testified against our own father. She would have known that someday, as we got to be adults, we would hate her for it."

"If my parents had taken the course of David and Ruth Greenglass and lied about their friends," Robby added, "in the short run it might have been easier for Michael and me. However, in the long run, today, I am so grateful that I am the child of Ethel and Julius Rosenberg, with all the consequences of that heritage."

"I'm glad they were engaged," he said. "I don't like the idea of them being innocent lambs led to slaughter. I'm more comfortable with them being political actors who made difficult decisions." And actors they were, even urging their children from the death house at the eleventh hour to "always remember that we were innocent and could not wrong our conscience." Did the Rosenbergs selfishly sacrifice their own family, their own sons, for some loftier goal? "What Julius was asked to do was send his best friends to jail, and he could not do that," Robby said. "My parents would have to have made a bigger betrayal to avoid betraying me, and frankly I don't consider myself that important."

—

While Sobell shattered the Rosenberg supporters' shrinking defensive perimeter, while the release of most of the grand jury testimony further undermined the government's case, David Greenglass himself retreated further into obscurity, still living under the assumed name inherited by his children and grandchildren. Ruth died in 2008. David moved from their suburban home in Nassau County, the one with the empty signpost, to an even more anonymous Manhattan apartment, then, as he neared 90, to his daughter's house in the Bronx. He would never see his nephews again, nor meet their children. "What I would have wanted from him," Ivy Meeropol told me, "was some sign of remorse." She never got it, but she never confronted him either. "I grew up with him representing the ultimate evil," she recalled. "I say in the film I'm letting go of that. I didn't go after him, not because I sympathize with him but I do see him as another victim."

David Greenglass would survive for more than 60 years after his sister was executed at Sing Sing. His legacy is a surname synonymous with treachery—first by betraying his country, then his sister, and finally his own wife (by ultimately blaming her, not Ethel, for typing his incriminating handwritten secrets of the atomic bomb). Ethel Rosenberg would become a martyr to a lost cause, a suicide spy. Decades later, The Brother would spend his final days freighted with memories, sentenced to a full life falsely lived and poised for an, ignominious death under a pseudonym.

Acknowledgments

I deeply appreciate the encouragement, guidance, and indulgence of my editors at *The New York Times,* Joe Lelyveld and Bill Keller, Jon Landman and Susan Chira, and especially of all my valued colleagues and friends at the Week in Review section—Daryl Alexander, Marc Charney, Anne Cronin, Peter Edidin, Jane Fritsch, Joyce Jensen, Andrea Kannappel, Tom Kuntz, Greg Ryan, Allison Silver, Scott Veale, Sarah Weissman, Tom Zeller, Kari Haskell, David Bowman, and Caitlin Lovinger—and at New York 1, in particular Doris Bergman.

Chris Campbell and the crew in the *Times*'s recording room, including Anne Cachoian, Elizabeth Molina, Charles Zaug, and Sherry Zipp, provided an invaluable service by transcribing reels of tape-recorded interviews.

Edward Wierzbowski, the president of Global American Television, and his valuable colleague in Russia, Svetlana Chervonnaya, unfailingly and enthusiastically provided sophisticated insights into the investigation, including special access to Alexander Feklisov and to other former KGB sources and to their research for a Discovery Channel documentary and other projects related to the case.

Researchers and archivists are a journalist's best friends. Their jobs make ours easier. Special thanks to Linda Amster and the *Times*'s research and library staff, including Charles Robinson, Marilyn Annan, Judith Greenfield, Lora Korbut, Linda Lake, John Motyka, Michael Porter, Jeffrey Roth, and Tony Zirilli; and to, among others and the collective memories of the institutions they represent, David Cronin and David Smith of the New York Public Library; Betsy Gotbaum, Stewart Desmond, Kathleen Holser, and Paul Gunther of the New-York Historical Society; Robert McDonald of the Museum of the City of New York; Ruth Abram and her staff at the Lower East Side Tenement Museum; Whitney Bagnall at the Columbia Law School library; Brian Andersson and Leonora Gidlund of New York City's Department of Records and Information Services; Robert C. Morris and his indispensable staff, especially Richard Gelbke and Joel Buckwald, at the National Archives and Records Administration, Northeast Region, in New York, and their colleagues (especially Fred Romanski and Gregory Gluba) in Washington, D.C., and College Park, Maryland; the Library of Congress manuscript division; Faigi Rosenbaum of the New York *Daily News;* Laura Harris of the *New York Post;* the *Albuquerque Journal* and *The Santa Fe New Mexican;* the University of Texas at Austin and the Truman and Eisenhower Presidential Libraries (especially David J. Haight and Barbara Constable); Marie Hallion at the United States Department of Energy; Anne Diestel at the Federal Bureau of Prisons; James D. Folts of the New York State archives; the Catskill Public Library; Roger Meade, Linda Sandoval, Rosabelle Martinez, and the research staff of the Los Alamos National Laboratory; the Los Alamos Historical Society; Hedy Dunn at the Los Alamos Historical Museum; James Flateau and the New York State Department of Correctional Services; the Borough of Lewisburg, Pennsylvania; the National Security Archive; the Cold War History Project; and the Federation of Atomic Scientists.

Bob Bucknam and Kevin Wilkinson of the Federal Bureau of Investigation were instrumental in helping me navigate government bureaucracy. J. Kevin O'Brien, Linda Colton, and their underappreciated colleagues in the Freedom of Information section of the FBI helped expedite access to documents that might otherwise have remained classified for years.

Thanks to Andrew Beveridge and Susan Weber of Queens College of the City University of New York for their research on the demography of the Lower East Side; to Dennis Martin, for his friendship and his help in steering me to Sing Sing historical records; and to Aaron Katz of the National Committee to Reopen the Rosenberg Case, who was always willing to volunteer a detail that might otherwise have been overlooked.

Hugh Truslow of the *Times* and Sarah Orlinsky helpfully translated Russian and French documents and manuscripts.

In researching this book, I drew on earlier works by a number of authors who generously and patiently contributed their time and suggestions and, in some cases, graciously made available previously unpublished background material, interview transcripts, and other resources. Among the first journalists to extend that professional courtesy were two former *Times* reporters, Peter Kihss and Marilyn Berger. It was Peter who advised me that the greatest contribution I could make to public understanding of the Rosenberg case was to interview David Greenglass and who also cautioned me that the case could become a minefield and an obsession. I'm also indebted to Ron Radosh and Sol Stern (whose articles in *The New Republic* preceded *The Rosenberg File*, which Ron wrote with Joyce Milton), Allen Weinstein, Sam Tanenhaus, Richard Rhodes, Scott Christenson, Walter and Miriam Schneir, E. L. Doctorow, Tony Hiss, Stephen Dubner, Ilene Philipson, Joseph Allbright and Marcia Kunzel, David Holloway, and Lou Benson and John Haynes, whose unvarnished interpretations of the Venona papers were invaluable.

I also appreciate many others who took the time to be interviewed more times than they originally bargained for, including Marshall Perlin, Michael and Robert Meeropol, James Kilsheimer, Jr., Robert Lamphere, Morton Sobell, and those who agreed to be interviewed at all, however briefly, including Vivian Glassman, Miriam Moskowitz, Ann Sidorovich, and Bernard Greenglass's daughter. Some interviews would have been impossible without the support of intermediaries, including Edward Gardner, who helped facilitate extended conversations with Rabbi Koslowe, and Jeanne Anne Norton, who helped persuade her father, William Norton, to be interviewed for the first time.

David's lawyer endured virtually all of my interviews with David. While he must remain nameless here, to protect David's anonymity, his time, perspective, and support, and the friendship of his family, are very much appreciated.

From afar, it's much easier to judge David Greenglass and his motivations, then and now. It's also easy to imagine what any of us would have done in similar circumstances. It's harder, though, to know for sure. Whatever he thinks of the picture of him painted in this book, I appreciate his sitting unflinchingly for the portrait.

The hospitality of a number of friends was invaluable, both as an outpouring of support and in providing sanctuary for a writer vulnerable to diversion. Special thanks to Patsy Glazer, Mitch and Abby Leigh, Warrie and James Price, and to my most patient advocate, Betsy Grant. And Karen Salerno.

Thanks to all those who recalled in vivid detail how the case touched their lives. The irreplaceable and infectiously passionate Arthur Gelb made this book possible, by his original journalistic instinct and by his relentless prodding. Richard Mittenthal was captivated when I first told him of my search for David Greenglass and was unflagging in his support. David Grant's unsurpassed skills as a grammarian were tested to the fullest. Paul Neuthaler was unrivaled in his role as my erudite editor-for-life.

My literary agent, Esther Newberg, and her associates at International Creative Management, especially Jack Horner and Karen Gerwin, believed in this book from the beginning and found it a welcoming home at Random House, whose president, Harold Evans, and his successor, Ann Godoff, embraced it.

This book also would not have been possible without the constant encouragement and constructive criticism of Senior Editor Bob Loomis. His courtliness and the unthreatening deftness with which he wields his pencil belie an unmistakable conviction for what belongs in a book and what doesn't. The logic, lucidity, and good humor of his internal word-processing program cannot be duplicated by any computerized version. Bob's assistant, Dominique Troiano, cheerfully fielded my appeals for support. Random House's well-deserved reputation for professionalism was upheld mightily by, among others, Timothy Mennel, Benjamin Dreyer, Andy Carpenter, Laura Goldin, Carol Schneider, Tom Perry, Alexa Cassanos, and Laura Moreland.

This project, which began when Arthur Gelb assigned me to pursue the case two months after I joined *The New York Times* in 1983, did not end when *The Brother* was originally published in 2001. Friends had warned that the unanswered questions could become an obsession, that the case could turn into a career. It has not, but I was still committed to squaring the circle. Since then, thanks to Bob Simon and Michael Rosenbaum for their Emmy Award–winning interview about the book on CBS News' *60 Minutes II*, David C. Vladeck of Georgetown University Law Center and Thomas S. Blanton of the National Security Archive indefatigably mounted the legal challenge that led to the release of most of the grand jury testimony. John Hancock and Dorothy Tristan artfully transformed *The Brother* into a full-length play. I appreciate the gracious replies from Michael and Robert Meeropol to my continued questions and the cooperation of Amber Black of the Rosenberg Fund for Children. Thanks to my indomitable agent, Andrew Blauner, and my perceptive editor, Robert Bender of Simon & Schuster (and the indispensable Johanna Li), for making this version of the book possible.

Because of the Depression, my father, Arthur, never got to realize his professional goals, but he was unembittered, lived every day to the fullest, and instilled in his children the valuable lessons of history. He seized every opportunity to witness it with us, including that walk down our block in Brooklyn in 1953 to watch the Rosenberg funeral cortege pass by. I was comforted then, and many times since, by my older, wiser sister, Dixie, whose writing has been an inspiration to me since childhood, and by my brother-in-law, Barry, who is always here for us.

My own family suffered too many lost nights, weekends, and vacations because of this project. I'm enormously grateful to both my sons: Michael for his canny grasp of imagery and dialogue, and William for interrupting even as I wrote his acknowledgment, to remind me of what's truly important and which we too often take for granted.

Above all, I appreciate my wife, Marie. She patiently endured my bouts of frustration, unfailingly supported this book from conception to completion, and blessed it with her creative genius. She is responsible in ways that she can never fully realize for enriching my life.

Notes

The author sought out original sources whenever and to whatever extent possible. They included all of the surviving participants, including witnesses, spectators, scientific and psychological experts, defense lawyers, investigators, prosecutors, family members and friends, and journalists with direct knowledge of the case and its contemporary context. Secondary sources are cited in the text and in the bibliography.

Much of the narrative is drawn from the first extensive interviews ever granted by David Greenglass. (David declined to allow Ruth to be interviewed; however, the author had access to an earlier interview with Ruth, most of which has never before been published.) The author's interviews with David were the source of the bulk of his quotations in the book when they are not otherwise attributed to letters, investigative debriefings, testimony, or other primary sources.

Whenever possible, his accounts were corroborated. When they conflicted with other sources, every effort was made (in the text or in notes) to say so. Most of those conflicts, of course, occurred between the version of events presented by David and Ruth Greenglass, on the one hand, and by Julius and Ethel Rosenberg, on the other.

When a jury was challenged to sort out who was telling the truth and when, it decided largely in favor of the Greenglasses, on the basis of selective evidence and testimony and, ironically, on the assumption that David's betrayal of his sister was so heinous that even to spare his wife and himself he would not have just made it all up.

CHAPTER 1: THE BROTHER OF DEATH

10 **At Sing Sing** Recent books by Scott Christianson and by Craig Brandon provide a fascinating history of the electric chair and of electrocutions.

11 **In court, Kaufman** Exactly when Kaufman was informed of the decision to proceed at 8 P.M. is uncertain, although even some of his detractors doubt that he would have deliberately misled defense lawyers about the timing.

13 **In Washington** The last hours of the Rosenbergs' lives have been reconstructed in a number of published accounts. Rabbi Koslowe and Marshall Perlin patiently provided the author with additional details and perspective.

15 **Just before sunset** Joseph Albright and Marcia Kunstel interviewed the Halls for their book, *Bombshell*. Joan Hall was also interviewed by the author.

CHAPTER 2: THE HOUSE ON SHERIFF STREET

25 **By the time** Recollections of life on Sheriff Street and environs were compiled from a number of sources, including books by Gertrude Ford, Virginia Gardner, and Ilene Philipson, and from photographs and other historical archives made available by the New York City Department of Records and Information Services and the office of the Manhattan Borough President.

27 **The family name** Genealogical information is from the American Jewish Historical Society.

28 **The 1920 census** Details from the 1920 census are on file with the National Archives, Northeast Regional Office. (Detailed census records are released publicly seventy years after the official count.)

35 **David was endowed** Most anecdotal accounts of the Greenglass family are from interviews with David. Details about Uncle Harry's ice-cream parlor are from Stephen Dubner's book.

CHAPTER 3: ETHEL AND JULIUS

38 **From Tessie's perspective** Esther's quote is from Stephen Dubner's book.

43 **Whatever else attracted** In addition to Ethel's letters and interviews with her friends and Elizabeth Phillips, the social worker she enlisted to help

her cope with her children, some of Dr. Miller's conclusions are quoted in Ilene Philipson's book.

CHAPTER 5: MAIL CALL

54 **The Greenglasses' mistake** The letters, found by the FBI in 1950 in a footlocker in the Greenglasses' apartment, were confiscated and became part of the government's evidence and archival record of the case. Most of the letters can be found in FBI file 6559028, volumes 4 and 7.

CHAPTER 6: THE REPLACEMENT

67 **As he had written Ruth** He was right. His outfit would be stationed behind the lines, near Fontainebleau in France, and never saw action.

69 **It was also** It's uncertain from this letter whether Julius did, indeed, know what David was working on. Ruth figured David's job had something to do with the Tennessee Valley Authority, building dams to generate electricity. On the basis of what developed in the next month or two, Julius seemed to have been better informed.

69 **After just a week** Again, David's letter lends itself to more than one interpretation. Was David (a) alerting Julius to the fortuitous transfer to a secret installation where David might finally be situated to make a meaningful contribution to the communist cause? Or (b) just trying to one-up his brother-in-law, a full-fledged engineer who was serving as merely a functionary for the Signal Corps, by hinting that he had been recruited specially to help build a secret and vital superweapon? Or (c) both? The most logical answer appears to be (b).

CHAPTER 7: LOS ALAMOS

72 **"We tried to be"** In David's case, the only tip-off to investigators might have been his earlier membership in the Young Communist League, but even former Communist Party members were being granted security clearances under certain circumstances.

Alarms might have been triggered, however, by David's failure to divulge his membership, or by the government's previous investigation of Julius and Ethel's communist affiliations, although there is no indication that the separate security checks ever intersected.

72 **"tended to be relaxed somewhat"** General Leslie R. Groves, then head of the Manhattan Engineer District, would later place the blame squarely on the FBI, accusing the bureau of "rather incredible" negligence. In 1965, Groves wrote that the names of the trained machinists culled from Army records were sent to the FBI for clearance. In a memo to his files, he wrote: "The requested clearance procedures were not very rigorous but were limited to a check of the files to see that the man had no police record other than for minor offenses such as traffic violations and that there was nothing implying Communist or German sympathies on his record. I do not know how many men were thrown out on this check—I [imagine] very few, if any, but in some way the FBI failed to catch Greenglass.

"As we have considered it afterwards, this seems almost impossible but an error was made and I am convinced that it was made by the FBI. . . . It may have been [an] error on the part of the responsible field office in [not having] secured the information in the first place. But this seems rather incredible because Greenglass' sister and other associates were so clearly tied into the Communist movement [and] had been for years. My own belief is that this is one of those one in a million cases, where no matter how careful the established procedures are, a human failure negates them completely." Local security officers "were not as smart as they should have been," Groves noted.

73 **"When I visited"** John Gunther's quotes are from his book, *Inside USA*, and from interviews in New Mexico newspapers.

73 **Everyone in Santa Fe** Gore Vidal's recollections are drawn from his memoir and from an interview with the author.

77 **David was never charged** Information on security evaluations at the laboratory was made available by the U.S. Department of Energy and its contractors in response to Freedom of Information Act requests by the author.

79 **Groves had a different** Richard Rhodes's two books provide the most thorough and readable history of the bomb.

CHAPTER 8: THE GO-BETWEEN

82 **A few months earlier** Feklisov's recollections come from extensive interviews with Global American Television that formed the basis of a documentary on the Discovery Channel, from additional interviews conducted on behalf of the author, and from Feklisov's memoirs, published in

French. (The English translation, published by Enigma Books, was made available to the author in advance.)

84 **A second letter** For a more detailed explanation of this letter, see chapter 17, "Liberal."

86 **"Dear Davey"** David doesn't remember the slur specifically, but, in context, it could have referred to money or to his cavalier response to his parents' pleas that he write them more often.

CHAPTER 9: ROUTE 66

92 **"I have a message"** This conversation is reconstructed from the author's interviews with David, from FBI interrogations of the Greenglasses, and from their trial testimony. See also additional accounts of this conversation in chapter 27, "Trial and Error," and chapter 36, "The Final Confession."

92 **Ruth may not have been** If, indeed, Ruth harbored doubts and was reluctant to deliver Julius's message to David, the depth of her recalcitrance is questionable. Years later, David elaborated in an interview that the author arranged with CBS News correspondent Bob Simon for *60 Minutes II* in conjunction with the initial publication of this book. (The interview was conducted in August 2001 in a hotel near New York City; David was disguised with a fake beard; as it turned out, he looked a little like Osama bin Laden—who knew? Excerpts of the interview were broadcast later that year. The broadcast interview won an Emmy award in 2002.) "If she didn't want you to do it, why did she communicate the message to you?" David was asked. He replied: "Because she felt that I might want to do it. That's why. My wife does things like that. She says, 'Well, I'm not crazy about this, but if you want it, you can have it.' And that usually refers to, to whipped-cream cake, or something like that."

CHAPTER 10: I SPY

96 **David Greenglass cozied up** In addition to David in his recollections, mostly in interviews with the author, his barrackmates described life at Los Alamos when they were interrogated by the FBI and in later reminiscences. Bederson and Spindel were interviewed by the author, as were David's supervisors, Hugh Holland and Wendell Marshman.

97 **In a letter from Los Alamos** Bederson now says that his best recollection is that he did not co-sign the letter with Schmolka. "I sympathized with

the sentiments he expressed, but I also realized that it was a bad idea to call attention to Los Alamos," he wrote the author, after *The Brother* was first published. "This is a pretty trivial matter, but I do not want to give the impression that I was willing to reveal the existence of Los Alamos just for the sake of a social issue."

100 **Once, she wrote** *Los Alamos and the Development of the Atomic Bomb*, p. 92.

101 **By questioning Ben Bederson** After *The Brother* was first published, Bederson recalled to the author that at one point the FBI "claimed that Greenglass had told them that in response to a question from him concerning an electric component, I told him something about its being a capacitor used in the bomb trigger. . . . I realized then that, at the least, Greenglass was either misrepresenting or misquoting me, since at that time the word 'capacitor' was not in my vocabulary; rather, we always used the word 'condenser.' The upshot of this incident is simply this: Greenglass, at the least misquoting me, made some sort of statement about me. I certainly did not confirm it, nor did anyone else. (Of course I could not categorically deny that I had made such a statement, since my memory could have been faulty, although I certainly had no active memory of this incident.)"

102 **Charles Critchfield** Critchfield recalled this later in an interview with Tom Sharpe of the *Albuquerque Journal*.

104 **Still, few of David's** After reading the hardcover version of this book, Robert J. Lamphere, a key FBI agent in the Rosenberg case, expressed surprise at David's indiscretion. "We have big-mouth Greenglass making pro-Russian and pro-Communist remarks—not exactly superspy activity," Lamphere wrote the author.

104 **Bederson also described** Bederson's assessment of Ruth was echoed more than once in testimonials indicating that her commitment to communism was as great as, if not stronger than, David's.

105 **For all the army's success** The memos about manpower are from Energy Department archives.

106 **A gun design** Most of the descriptions of weapons come from Richard Rhodes's two books and from a primer put on the Internet by Carey Sublette.

CHAPTER 11: ESPIONAGE 101

117 **Dickstein came to the attention** Dickstein's activities on behalf of the Soviet Union, as chronicled in NKGB files reviewed by Alexander Vassiliev, were apparently unknown to the FBI.

119 **And it would become** Why in a letter to her mother-in-law and not to the Rosenbergs? Perhaps because Ethel routinely read and replied to most of the mail to her parents, who were less than literate in English.

121 **"I wrote Ethel"** Neither Ruth's letter nor any response from Ethel was found by the FBI in the footlocker of correspondence seized in the Greenglasses' apartment in June 1950. As the trial drew nearer, Ruth tried to help the prosecution by searching her apartment for Ethel's letter but couldn't find it.

122 **John Gunther** Gunther was interviewed by the *Albuquerque Journal*.

CHAPTER 12: MOSCOW GOLD

124 **The Soviet contact** Harry Gold's quotations and biographical details were gleaned from his memoirs, "The Circumstances Surrounding My Work as a Soviet Agent," which he completed not long after his arrest but which were never published. A copy of his handwritten notes, given to his lawyer John Hamilton, were provided to the author by Ronald Radosh.

125 **Harry often prattled** An FBI report later described Gold as neurotic with a hostile personality and as having traits that constituted an "imbalance."

127 **A few days before** From *Where to Dine in Thirty-Nine*, compiled by Diane Ashley.

128 **and arrest Harry Gold** According to American and Soviet sources, the blunder, which apparently originated at NKGB headquarters in Moscow, was blamed on Semen Semenov, who, as a result, was later executed.

131 **The encounter between** If, as David assumed, Harry came from Julius, why would he have needed Julius's telephone number? However, that version of their encounter evolved over many months. Interviewed earlier by the FBI, Harry at various times recalled a father-in-law named Philip from the Bronx, not a brother-in-law named Julius who lived in Manhattan.

132 **"I think I realized"** Whatever Ruth's understanding was, or whether the transaction with Harry Gold altered her perspective on espionage, neither she nor David ever rejected offers of money or returned any that was given to them.

132 **But on June 26** Yakovlev later said that the information Harry received from David was relatively unimportant. Harry testified that the Russians' dismissiveness was intended to deceive him about the value of the information, but the New York station's message suggests otherwise.

CHAPTER 13: LITTLE BOY AND FAT MAN

141 **The two bombs** Estimates of the immediate mortality rate vary widely. Calculating the long-term toll from radiation is even more problematic.

142 **Byron Price, the** *The New York Times,* August 9, 1945.

CHAPTER 14: DIAMONDS

145 **The judgment on** For more on what transpired that night, see chapter 28, "Trial and Error."

147 **It was also during** Several of the participants disagreed as to whether the meeting with the Russian agent occurred in September 1945 or in the previous January, when David was also home on leave. David repeatedly sought to minimize his role in espionage once the war was over, although he acknowledges that the dinner with the Rosenbergs and his gift of the detonator took place in September.

147 **Terrell remembered Ruth** Terrell was interviewed by the FBI after David was arrested.

148 **The day might come** See *Los Alamos Experience,* p. 145.

CHAPTER 15: BLACKMAIL

155 **A few months later** The *Look* article by Leo Cherne appeared in the March 4, 1947, issue.

156 **David said that Julius** The apartment was the one instance when the Greenglasses rejected a financial incentive from Julius, although their motivation was uncertain. It was unclear whether, as they said later, they didn't want to be beholden or whether there were strings attached, such as the possibility that the apartment would also double as a safe house for Russian spies and as a studio in which to photograph classified documents.

159 **Julius was a political** Had Julius applied for any job that required a security clearance, it would have been revealed that he was fired from the Signal Corps for lying about his membership in the Communist Party.

163 **The Rosenbergs hardly lived** A maid was hired to help with the house-work because of Ethel's bad back.

164 **He borrowed from** Again, to place these numbers in contemporary perspective, multiply them by about ten.

CHAPTER 16: VENONA

167 **"He did not elaborate"** Bentley's assertion that Julius probably wasn't the engineer's real name was conveniently forgotten in later accounts.

167 **FBI Supervisor** Lamphere's *The FBI-KGB War: A Special Agent's Story*, originally published by Random House, was an insider's unique perspective on the case. His book (written with Tom Shachtman) drops tantalizing hints but was written before the National Security Agency acknowledged having broken the Soviets' wartime code. He was also interviewed for the PBS program *Red Files: Secret Victories of the KGB*, participated in the 1996 National Security Agency conference on the Venona Papers, and was interviewed by the author.

CHAPTER 17: LIBERAL

171 **Alexander Feklisov** In his interviews with Global American Television, *The Washington Post*, *The New York Times*, and in his published memoirs, Feklisov said repeatedly that his motivation in speaking publicly was largely to give Julius the recognition he deserved as a loyal and valuable Soviet agent. The Soviet government never acknowledged publicly that Julius was a spy, and Feklisov, who appeared to have developed a genuine affection for the Rosenbergs, might have wanted to make amends—especially because of the contrast in the Russians' treatment of two other longtime agents, Morris and Lona Cohen. (Morris had fought for the Loyalists in Spain, and Lona had shuttled to New Mexico to retrieve atomic secrets from Theodore Hall.) The Cohens were spirited out of New York immediately after David Greenglass's arrest and were later named "Heroes of the Soviet Union."

177 **much less been rejected** But he lied. In a letter that surfaced only recently, David wrote to J. Robert Oppenheimer at the University of California on May 17, 1946, explaining that he had "worked on the atomic bomb" at Los Alamos, had recently been discharged from the army, and had formally applied to the Massachusetts Institute of Technology and to Princeton for the fall semester to study mechanical engineering. "I would like to enlist your aid," David wrote, "since all schools are greatly over-crowded and a

letter from you in my behalf might make room for me." There is no indication that Oppenheimer replied (J. Robert Oppenheimer papers, Library of Congress).

179 **"I felt, well"** David said more than once that he feared reprisals from the Russians. Nonetheless, he also acknowledged that had Julius or Ethel been apprehended before he was, they never would have implicated him as a spy.

CHAPTER 18: THE BOMB

183 **Each report was** From "Detecting the Soviet Bomb," by Herbert Friedman et al., *Physics Today,* November 1996.

183 **"What do you want?"** This conversation was quoted by Richard Rhodes in *The Making of the Atomic Bomb.*

184 **Moscow's nuclear potential** This National Security Agency assessment was confirmed recently. In a report on Kim Il Sung's visit to the Soviet Union in March and April 1950, the Central Committee of the Soviet Communist Party concluded: "Now that China has signed a treaty of alliance with the USSR, Americans will be even more hesitant to challenge the Communists in Asia. According to information coming from the United States, it is really so. The prevailing mood is not to interfere. Such a mood is reinforced by the fact that the USSR now has the atomic bomb and that our positions are solidified in Pyongyang." The summary was cited by Kathryn Weathersby in July 2002 in " 'Should We Fear This?' Stalin and the Danger of War with America," published by the Cold War International History Project of the Woodrow Wilson International Center for Scholars.

184 **By April 1950** Dated April 14, 1950, NSC 68 was entitled "United States Objectives and Programs for National Security." A summary of ORE 91-49, "Estimate of the Effects of the Soviet Possession of the Atomic Bomb Upon the Security of the United States and Upon the Probabilities of Direct Soviet Military Action," is quoted in *Assessing the Soviet Threat: The Early Cold War Years,* published by the CIA's Center for the Study of Intelligence.

185 **Any doubts as** *Collier's,* August 5, 1950.

187 **Only then did** That was three months before Fuchs was arrested and nearly seven months before the FBI apprehended Harry Gold. The subsequent arrest of David Greenglass triggered the lightning-quick evacu-

ation of Morris and Lona Cohen, which suggests that either the Soviets didn't consider some of their other agents in America to be vulnerable or that they valued the Cohens more than the others.

190 **At Iowa State** *The New York Times,* January 28, 1950.

CHAPTER 19: SHMEL

194 **"When he left"** Ruth later told investigators that David had not previously informed her about the hemisphere, although her denial was ambiguous. She said that had she known about it, she would not have allowed it in their apartment.

197 **David and Julius** Was Julius being prescient or is David crediting—or incriminating—him after the fact? Later, the Greenglasses said that Julius also had predicted the precise date of David's arrest.

199 **On Tuesday** Hoover's historic message, which refers to a KGB predecessor agency, is in the FBI file AQ 65-19, vol. 1.

200 **That memorandum added** FBI file 65-194, from Washington to Albuquerque, declassified at the author's request.

201 **Alvarez wasn't** For a detailed account of the Alvarez investigation, see FBI files 655902811Q, vols. 1 and 2.

CHAPTER 20: WHAT DID YOU DO IN THE WAR?

208 **Gouverneur and the** See the *New York Post,* February 15, 1950.

208 **Heatter was a** Relatively few recordings of Heatter's broadcasts survive. Historians of radio, as well as Heatter's daughter, searched their files at the author's request but were unable to find any record of an interview with David. News accounts of the fire say a radio appeal for blood was issued but don't specify a station or Heatter's program.

CHAPTER 21: "RED HOT"

211 **The agent reported** Again, the NKGB citations come from notes transcribed from Soviet files for *The Haunted Wood.* Earlier, Julius typically overstated David's devotion and his qualifications, according to an analysis of NKGB accounts. In this case, he may have been understating David's drift from communism.

214 **"It was at this"** Gold later informed the FBI that he could positively identify Julius. But James Kilsheimer, an assistant prosecutor, told the author

that investigators were confident they could convict Julius anyway. They feared he might be in a position to refute Gold's account.

216 **As Harry was** Most of these recollections were in Gold's unpublished memoirs.

216 **he asked to meet** Judge James McGranery was later named attorney general by President Truman. Like Judge Kaufman in the Rosenberg case, McGranery appears to have interpreted his judicial mandate broadly. At one point, he complained to the Justice Department that prosecutors were blowing the case against Gold (see FBI file 6557449-375).

220 **On May 24** A tourist visa would suffice for a visit to Mexico. Evidence of smallpox vaccinations was also required. In Mexico, counterfeit passports could be obtained for travel to Eastern Europe.

222 **On June 2** This memo, FBI file 6515336-3, dated June 2, 1950, was declassified in response to a request from the author.

227 **Shortly before 1:00 P.M.** The FBI monitored David's comings and goings with precision. (See surveillance logs in FBI files 6559028, vols. 2, 3, and 4, and 6515336, subfile A.) The logs are replete, though, with references to "unknown" individuals whom he encountered and whom agents apparently made no effort to identify, as well as places he visited that were described only by their addresses.

233 **go on the lam** "Think about it now," Bob Simon said, incredulously, in the *60 Minutes II* interview after *The Brother* was first published. "The FBI was looking for you because they thought they had you on atomic espionage."

"Yeah."

"And you thought you could hide in the Catskills?"

"I know the Catskills quite well," David replied.

CHAPTER 23: THE FORMULA

256 **"It seemed too ridiculous"** Florence was quoted in Stephen Dubner's biography. Tessie Greenglass, Tillie Printz, and Joe Schall were quoted in news accounts of David's arrest. Hannah Schoenberg and the Freemans were interviewed by the FBI.

CHAPTER 24: MR. COOPERATION

261 **On Tuesday** Rogge's conversations with the bureau and with the Justice Department were recorded in FBI files (6569028, vols. 3 and 5) and in the

private papers of Saypol and other prosecutors, which are in the files of the National Archives and Records Administration in New York. Some of those files, including minutes of the grand jury, remain secret.

265 **"over a barrel"** Still, Moskowitz said, David "went where they led him." Ethel, Moskowitz said, "was devastated about her brother."

266 **Meanwhile, the FBI** Still another indication that, for all of Rogge's efforts to restore his bona fides, the government didn't trust him.

268 **On Monday, July 17** Transcripts of David and Ruth's formal statements to investigators in July 1950 are in FBI file 6556028, vol. 6.

271 **a mug shot** The government did not, as a matter of course, fingerprint and photograph unindicted coconspirators. Nevertheless, government archivists identified it as a mug shot until the author brought the inappropriateness of this term to their attention.

272 **"On Ruth Greenglass"** It's uncertain exactly when David and his lawyers were informed that Ruth would not be prosecuted. The phrase "at this time" suggested that even a month and more after David and Ruth appeared to be cooperating fully with the government, prosecutors had not reached a final decision.

273 **At her direction** Tessie's house on Sheriff Street was closest, and obviously Ethel wouldn't have sought refuge with Ruth, but it's striking nonetheless that she didn't reach out to any of Julius's relatives.

273 **Julius Rosenberg refused** Belmont's remarks are further evidence that the government embarked on its ill-fated strategy almost from the beginning: to lodge charges against Ethel not necessarily because she was suspected of complicity but in order to break Julius.

275 **The next day, Elitcher** Max Elitcher, and only Elitcher, implicated Morton Sobell. But there is no record that Elitcher, as the Greenglasses later maintained, had also incriminated Ethel.

276 **"This impressed her"** There is no record of a formal sentencing deal between Rogge and the government. Ruth was shocked by the sentence later meted out by Judge Kaufman. Years later, when David appealed for parole, he spelled out, for the first time, his understanding of the deal. Still, it is revealing that months after David's arrest Ruth still envisioned that he would receive a suspended sentence.

277 **She agreed to meet** The FBI was not overstaffed with Yiddish-speaking agents at the time. The *Forward* interviews were translated for the bureau by a "special employee" and can be found in FBI file 6515336, subfile B.

CHAPTER 25: A LEVER

287 **David shuffled into** Accounts of the conference, found in Energy Department archives, were elaborated on by Arnold Kramish in interviews with the author.

289 **Some of his information** Government investigators and scientists assessed Klaus Fuchs's confession altogether differently. Perhaps because they assumed Fuchs knew more to begin with, they assumed that what he admitted giving the Russians was only a portion of what he had actually told them.

289 **classified information** The "idea" of implosion—but none of the details—was actually declassified by April 1950. The fact that the original implosion bombs contained thirty-two detonators and a 13.5-pound plutonium core wasn't declassified for another fifty years, until 2000.

CHAPTER 26: TALKING THE TALK

296 **"John Rogge told me"** Roy Cohn's recollections come from his autobiography, from two biographies, and from interviews with the author.

297 **An FBI report** A copy of the report is in FBI file 6559028, vol. 8.

299 **The full transcript** The FBI has never explained why the actual transcript or notes of the interview are missing from its files and from the prosecutor's. A complete, accurate transcript might help resolve a gnawing question about the Greenglasses' trial testimony: To what extent did they spontaneously volunteer new revelations, or how much were they prodded or even coached? A summary of the interview is in FBI file JR HQ813, February 25, 1951.

CHAPTER 27: TRIAL AND ERROR

303 **The Rosenberg trial** Accounts of the trial were drawn from contemporary news articles and interviews by the author with David Greenglass, Roy Cohn, James Kilsheimer, Judge Kaufman, and Morton Sobell. The transcript is from "Transcript of Record, Supreme Court of the United States, October Term, 1951, No. 111 *Julius Rosenberg and Ethel Rosenberg, Petitioners, vs. The United States of America,* No. 112 *Morton Sobell, Petitioner, vs. The United States of America,*" published by the National Committee to Secure Justice in Rosenberg Case.

Edited excerpts from the trial transcript are quoted here extensively to provide the evidence and the arguments that the jury actually heard.

304 **"I shall approach"** Kaufman's letter is included in the papers of J. Howard McGrath at the Harry S Truman Presidential Library in Independence, Mo.

311 **Shortly before the trial** This account was related by Roy Cohn.

319 **After court adjourned** Transcripts of these conversations, from Saypol's private papers and records of the U.S. Attorney's office, are on file with the National Archives and Records Administration in New York.

CHAPTER 28: THE GAMBLE

331 **"I have 'a'"** David's full testimony was released years later in response to lawsuits and legal appeals persistently pursued by Marshall Perlin, lawyer for Sobell and for the Rosenbergs' sons.

334 **If the Rosenbergs** In his memoirs, the only gifts Feklisov recalled buying the Rosenbergs were a watch for Julius and a pocketbook for Ethel.

340 **"No, I did not"** Again, David lied, this time about not withholding information from his first confession in June 1950, as well as in leaving the impression that in January 1950 he was on the verge of confessing.

346 **"I asked him how"** Ruth's testimony seems inconsistent, given that she wrote David months earlier that Julius "told me what you must be working on." Her testimony raises another question: If Julius supposedly had been working undercover for two years and been asked in September to broach the possibility of using the Greenglasses' apartment as a safe house, why did he wait until November to point out that he and Ethel had become covert communists?

352 **"I told my husband"** David told the author that he had no recollection of Ruth's bout of conscience.

CHAPTER 29: THE DEFENSE

371 **"And then I remember"** It's uncertain what Ethel meant by a "psychological heart attack," although David had plenty to be agitated over that winter.

379 **At 4:53 P.M.** Details of the jury deliberations are drawn from Ted Morgan's article, "The Rosenberg Jury," in the May 1975 issue of *Esquire* and from the author's interview with him. No account of the deliberations has

been more complete than that by Morgan, who interviewed several jurors in depth a quarter century later for *Esquire*.

CHAPTER 30: DEATH BY ELECTROCUTION

385 **"The day before sentence"** Saypol's recollections are from the Bureau of Prisons file in the National Archives.

392 **Among the many** From the papers of J. Howard McGrath at the Harry S Truman Presidential Library.

CHAPTER 31: SING SING

396 **David was transferred** In addition to interviews, much of the record of David's imprisonment at Lewisburg and his parole applications is from his Bureau of Prisons file in the National Archives.

398 **Ethel was transferred** Ethel's experience at the Women's House of Detention was described to the author by, among others, Miriam Moskowitz, a fellow inmate. Ethel and Julius described their prison experiences in letters to each other, to their lawyer, and to their children, most of which have been collected and published. Other recollections were drawn from the author's interviews with Rabbi Koslowe and with Michael and Robert Meeropol.

402 **Tessie Greenglass wrote** Rogge's copy of Tessie's letter is included in his private papers, on file with the Manuscript Division of the Library of Congress.

403 **On February 16** In Rogge's private papers, in the Library of Congress.

404 **David wrote, in part** In Rogge's private papers, in the Library of Congress.

CHAPTER 32: RELATIVITY

407 **But Henry Linschitz** Letters to and from scientists were drawn largely from Bloch's office files, made available to the author by Marshall Perlin. Some of those letters were incorporated into the Rosenbergs' legal appeals. Others, particularly when they undermined the defense's arguments, were not. Linschitz, Bethe, Teller, and Kramish also were interviewed by the author.

411 **Einstein's handwritten reply** A copy of the handwritten letter and the typed version were made available to the author by the Einstein Papers

Project, then at Boston University. The Collected Papers of Albert Einstein are now at the California Institute of Technology.

411 **After careful study** "It shocked me that Albert Einstein couldn't say it's impossible that Greenglass could have done it," Reuben recalled. "I assumed that would have meant such a scientific illiterate had nothing to communicate. Einstein's letter changed that."

Einstein added a second paragraph to his handwritten draft. In that addendum, he cited the testimony of two witnesses. Neither was a scientist. One was Max Elitcher, who had sworn that his City College classmate Julius Rosenberg once tried to recruit him as a spy. The second witness was the photographer who said that a few weeks before David's arrest the Rosenbergs had visited his tiny store and posed for passport pictures. "I'd like to add," Einstein wrote, "that after looking more carefully I have not been able to arrive at an opinion on the innocence of the Rosenbergs."

Einstein crossed out his second paragraph before his secretary could transcribe it. The letter that Bill Reuben received from Einstein contained only the first paragraph. His stories for the *National Guardian* never mentioned Einstein's letter at all.

416 **Groves replied** His remarks are quoted in, among other places, a memo from Hoover to the attorney general dated May 14, 1954, FBI file 10017828. A decade later, Groves elaborated. "At the time of the disclosure of just what information Greenglass had passed on, I was not particularly alarmed," he wrote in a memo that was found only recently in the National Archives. *Time* magazine had speculated about implosion during the war, Groves wrote, and "with the knowledge that we had successfully exploded three bombs, there seemed to be no way in which the Russians could be prevented from making at least a serious guess that this was a method used by us. The actual drawings of the lenses of the high explosive was [*sic*] not too important. Once the Russians suspected that one of the paths might be an implosion method they could design the lenses without any aid. Also, they could not count on the exactness of a sketch from memory. I do not wish to minimize the importance to the Russians of this betrayal," Groves concluded, "but it fades into insignificance beside that of Fuchs."

417 **David Teeple** Teeple's remarks are quoted in a memo from Belmont dated May 11, 1954, FBI file 100178281481.

CHAPTER 33: BLINDMAN'S BUFF

419 **Leonard Sand** Judge Sand was interviewed by the author.

424 **One answer was** The Dulles memo was described in a February 2, 1953, internal FBI memo to Alan Belmont.

428 **On Saturday, June 13** In addition to Ruth, the FBI had sources at Sing Sing among the inmates and guards.

428 **James Gibbons** Gibbons's quote is from the Ted Morgan article in *Esquire*.

429 **On the morning of** Some of Brownell's recollections are from his autobiography. Others are included in his private papers at the Dwight D. Eisenhower Presidential Library.

430 **Hoover delivered a** The memo was originally released with the entire text redacted, except for Hoover's "This is shocking." The full text was released in response to the author's Freedom of Information Act request.

430 **Bennett wasn't shy** Bennett's recollections come from his memoirs and from Bureau of Prisons archives.

431 **Hoover was equipped** Ladd's June 10, 1953, memo is in FBI file 6558236-2007.

434 **At 10:00 A.M. on June 19** Books by Brownell, Emmet John Hughes, and others recount the cabinet meeting. Perhaps the most dispassionate source is the official notes of the cabinet secretary, on file at the Eisenhower Presidential Library.

435 **A few days earlier** Eisenhower's letter, with its unintended defense of feminism, is on file at his presidential library. Another letter there, from Eisenhower to Clyde Miller, a former colleague of his at Columbia University, also explains his rationale.

437 **The Russians won the propaganda war** Protests against the punishment meted out to the Rosenbergs degenerated into riots in a number of European cities, and at least one other death would be directly attributed to their execution: that of Elli Barczatis, secretary to the East German prime minister Otto Grotewohl. She was accused of having been seduced by a Western intelligence agent and enlisted as a spy. As Markus Wolf, the East German spymaster, wrote in his autobiography, *Man Without a Face* (New York: Times Books, 1997): "Barczatis's grim misfortune was that her case became public just after the execution of Julius and Ethel Rosenberg as atomic spies in the United States. The name of the game in espionage, as in other aspects of the Cold War, was parity. She was sentenced to death by guillotine in Frankfurt-an-der-Oder on the Polish border."

438 **"and not to die"** Lamphere would later recall that in drafting J. Edgar Hoover's memo opposing the death penalty for Ethel Rosenberg, he was moved, in part, by "the small amount of evidence that we had against her." Still, he said, "we hoped one or the other of the Rosenbergs would elect to confess to save themselves and their mate." But if commuting her sentence was ever a serious possibility, the Communist propaganda campaign to free the Rosenbergs "made it hard to move on Ethel," he said. "The Ethel death sentence backfired," Lamphere acknowledged. "The Soviets did win the propaganda war." (Lamphere died in 2002.)

438 **In retrospect, the timing** Assuming that the gist of this information hadn't been passed on to Judge Kaufman earlier, the FBI demonstrated commendable discretion.

CHAPTER 34: LEWISBURG

440 **David's isolation** Information on David's interment at Lewisburg comes from interviews with fellow inmates, Harry Gold's unpublished memoir, and government files (FBI file 6559028, vols. 8 and 9; FBI file 6515336, vol. 13; and records of the Bureau of Prisons deposited in the National Archives).

454 **David later explained** Periodically since the trial, David expressed concern that because he had made so many conflicting statements he might be prosecuted for perjury.

461 **In April 1958** Sayler to file, April 8, 1958. U.S. Archives.

462 **"It was remarked"** Sayler to U.S. Board of Parole, December 31, 1959.

466 **To spare Ruth** Greenglass to Willingham, quoted in Willingham letter to James Bennett, October 26, 1960.

468 **With David hunched** *The New York Times,* November 17, 1960.

CHAPTER 35: THE SEARCH FOR DAVID GREENGLASS

470 **There is no evidence** David's encounters with the government after his release are chronicled in FBI file 6559028, vol. 10.

472 **"Special Agent Freaney"** The reference to recorded interviews is ambiguous. Freaney did not distinguish between interrogations that might have been taped and interviews in which agents produced a written record.

479 **I asked David** As always, Ruth managed the household expenses, while business was left to David. He may have been a good machinist and even a good inventor, but he was not a good businessman. In 1998, in business

for himself for the first time since the late 1940s, he filed for bankruptcy protection.

CHAPTER 36: THE FINAL CONFESSION

480 **Before I began** Very few subjects were off-limits (although I asked about them anyway): background about his children and grandchildren; identification of the mysterious relatives who refused to expose themselves by guaranteeing bail after he had been arrested; and details of jobs he had held since he was released from prison.

487 **In 1979** Radosh and Milton referred to that interview in their book and quoted from parts of it. Radosh and Stern made available to the author a complete transcript.

491 **David added parenthetically** During the *60 Minutes II* interview arranged by the author, David elaborated. He acknowledged that Ruth was more involved in espionage than Ethel was, which was why he protected Ruth from prosecution. When it was suggested that his wife seemed to have been more complicit than his sister, David replied: "So? That's why I didn't want her involved."

"Involved in the prosecution?"

"Right."

He said he was surprised when Ethel was arrested in 1950: "I couldn't figure out why they would arrest her. For being the wife?" Once she was implicated, though, David said, his sister should have confessed to what little she knew or had overheard from Julius. "She should have said, 'I wasn't a spy, but I heard my husband say it,'" David said.

Arguably, the Rosenbergs could have saved their own lives, but they maintained their silence about Stalin's ruthless brand of communism and anti-Semitism in the Soviet Union and were silent or lied outright about Julius's role as a spy. What did David think of their stubborn adherence to the party line?

"One word," he replied. "Stupidity."

He was equally sanguine about his own gullibility. "I had no idea it was important at all," he said. "The testimony was put in my mouth by somebody who said that my wife said that . . . I had no memory of that at all. None whatsoever."

Was it false testimony?

"It was false testimony because I didn't know anything about it," David replied. "But they said she [Ruth] heard it and she's gonna testify to that."

Still, he said, his conscience wasn't burdened by the Rosenbergs' deaths.

"You know why?" David said. "Because I don't think it was my choice. I didn't choose to have them killed. The federal government chose to have them killed." For the same reason, he said, he would not apologize to his nephews if he ever saw them again. "No, I can't say that," David explained. "That's not true. First of all, nobody's saying, 'We're gonna have these people killed.' Maybe if they had said that, that's what they're gonna do, I may have been a lot different in my thinking."

CHAPTER 37: THE FINAL CHAPTER

493 **Americans were scared** How scared? Not until September 11, 2001—nearly a half century later—would Americans ever feel as vulnerable again. But as much as the echoes of that earlier epoch reverberated in 2001—echoes of sudden vulnerability to sneak attacks by a shadowy international movement intent on destroying American values, of threats to those values at home in the effort to reconcile national security and civil liberties, of technology being twisted into deadly weapons against us, and of blind loyalty and national hysteria—those echoes in 2001 seem faint compared to the fears that defined America's psyche and politics in the early 1950s.

493 **This one was real** In *Venona*, Haynes and Klehr listed the real names or cover names of 349 Americans and U.S. residents mentioned in the Venona decryptions. Some were spies; many were only tangentially linked to Soviet intelligence.

493 **personally supportive** Ethel may well have urged, "Let Davey decide," in November 1944 when Julius enlisted Ruth to recruit David to espionage. But there's only one way to find out for sure on what legal basis the government indicted, much less convicted, Ethel Rosenberg: release the grand jury minutes. Fifty years after the execution, seven cubic feet of grand jury records, secured in twenty-two boxes in the National Archives, remain secret. The author is preparing a lawsuit to unseal them.

494 **"the Rosenbergs dead"** Ellen Schrecker, a scholar of McCarthyism, labeled them "suicide spies."

494 **"I heard"** According to a transcript, the agent was unrelenting, reminding Lee again that fifty years earlier the government was equally skeptical about the Rosenbergs' professions of innocence. "They didn't care whether they professed their innocence all day long," the agent said. "They electrocuted them." Lee replied that while he did not believe in a Christian god, he placed his faith in some "super power, super creature," rather than in government investigators, and that "I believe he will make the final judgment for my case."

"You know the Rosenbergs said that, too."

"I don't . . ."

"The Rosenbergs professed their innocence. The Rosenbergs weren't concerned either."

"Yeah."

"The Rosenbergs are dead."

495 **Roy Cohn went to Washington** David would later say that it was Roy Cohn who, just before the trial began, extracted from him his crucial confirmation of Ruth's version of events at the Rosenbergs' apartment in September 1945. As for Cohn himself, David said: "He died a very nasty way, and I'm happy for it."

497 **In the early 1990s** Barr was interviewed on ABC-TV's *Nightline*.

499 **Among the songs** See *Strange Fruit*, by David Margolick.

500 **Michael recalled that** See *We Are Your Sons*.

501 **"it was worth it"** Robby says that he still conducts imaginary conversations with his parents: "Everybody knows, whether you believe they did anything or they didn't do anything or whether you have questions about what they did or the seriousness of what they did, everybody knows that if they agreed to cooperate they would still be alive. And they resisted, they refused, and they were killed. And the very basic question is: 'Was it worth it? Look at the world today. Look at what's happened. Look at what happened with your children. If you had to do it all over again, would you do it that way?'"

501 **Robby transferred** The Rosenberg Fund for Children is at 116 Pleasant Street, Suite 3312, Easthampton, MA 01027.

501 **"pulled the trigger"** As the evidence against the Rosenbergs from disparate sources mounts and the ranks of true believers is depleted by defections and deaths, defenders of the Rosenbergs have redefined the boundaries of the moral high ground they staked out uncompromisingly a half-century ago. By 2002, Michael Meeropol seemed to have gone

further than ever before: "They arrested a small-fry spy, took his wife as a hostage, put a gun to her head, and told him, 'Talk, or we'll not only kill you, we'll kill her.' And when he wouldn't talk, they murdered her in cold blood. When the United States admits that, I'd be more than willing to admit that maybe Venona had identified something of my father's involvement in some kind of activity with the KGB."

502 **"This was a sleazy"** After *The Brother* was originally published, the Meeropols were invited by the author to participate in a panel discussion about the case at the 92nd Street Y in Manhattan. Robby accepted, but was so revolted that his uncle might profit from the book that he all but overlooked David's startling admissions. Robby suggested that David's "soap opera" account provided "a few juicy new tidbits to boost sales" but complained dismissively that "most of what is new is based on David Greenglass's unverifiable recollection of fifty years ago." All that counts, Robby said, was that fifty years ago, regardless of what his parents were convicted of, they were put to death for stealing the secret to the atomic bomb. "Our government executed two people for a crime they did not commit," he said. "Any crime they may have committed pales in significance when compared to the crime committed against them by our government."

502 **two grown children** As of this writing, Robby's daughter was making a documentary about the Rosenbergs; Michael's was doing her dissertation on Ethel.

Selected Bibliography

BOOKS

Abell, Tyler, ed. *Drew Pearson: Diaries, 1949–1959*. New York: Holt, Rinehart, and Winston, 1974.

Åkerström, Malin. *Betrayal and Betrayers: The Sociology of Treachery*. New Brunswick, N.J.: Transaction Publishers, 1991.

Albright, Joseph, and Marcia Kunstel. *Bombshell: The Secret Story of America's Unknown Atomic Spy Conspiracy*. New York: Times Books, 1997.

Andrew, Christopher, and Vasili Mitrokhin. *The Sword and the Shield: The Mitrokhin Archive and the Secret History of the KGB*. New York: Basic Books, 1999.

Antler, Joyce. *The Journey Home: How Jewish Women Shaped Modern America*. New York: Schocken Books, 1997.

Badash, Lawrence, Joseph O. Hirschfelder, and Herbert P. Broida, eds. *Reminiscences of Los Alamos, 1943–1945*. Dordrecht, Holland: D. Reidel, 1988.

Benson, Robert Louis, and Michael Warner, eds. *Venona: Soviet Espionage and the American Response, 1939–1957*. Washington, D.C.: National Security Agency, Central Intelligence Agency, 1996.

Beyer, Don E. *The Manhattan Project: America Makes the First Atomic Bomb*. New York: Franklin Watts, 1991.

Bok, Sissela. *Lying: Moral Choice in Public and Private Life*. [1978.] New York: Vintage Books, 1999.

Brandon, Craig. *The Electric Chair: An Unnatural American History*. Jefferson, N.C.: McFarland, 1999.

Brooks, Peter. *Troubling Confessions: Speaking Guilt in Law and Literature*. Chicago: University of Chicago Press, 2000.

Brown, A., and C. MacDonald. *The Secret History of the Atomic Bomb*. New York: Dial Press/James Wade, 1977.

Brown, Henry Collins. *Valentine's City of New York: A Guide Book*. New York: Press of the Chauncey Holt Co., 1920.

Carmichael, Virginia. *Framing History: The Rosenberg Story and the Cold War.* American Culture 6. Minneapolis: University of Minnesota Press, 1993.

Charns, Alexander. *Cloak and Gavel: FBI Wiretaps, Bugs, Informers, and the Supreme Court.* Urbana: University of Illinois Press, 1992.

Christianson, Scott. *Condemned: Inside the Sing Sing Death House.* New York: New York University Press, 2000.

Cohn, Roy. *A Fool for a Client.* New York: Hawthorn Books, 1971.

Considine, Bob. *It's All News to Me.* New York: Meredith Press, 1967.

Coover, Robert. *The Public Burning.* New York: Viking Press, 1976.

Curtis, Charles P. *The Oppenheimer Case: The Trial of a Security System.* New York: Simon and Schuster, 1955.

Delaney, Robert Finley. *The Literature of Communism in America.* Washington, D.C.: Catholic University of America Press, 1962.

de Toledano, Ralph. *The Greatest Plot in History.* In *Omnibus,* vol. 2. New Rochelle, N.Y.: Conservative Book Club, 1953.

Dillon, Millicent. *Harry Gold: A Novel.* Woodstock, N.Y.: Overlook Press, 2000.

Doctorow, E. L. *The Book of Daniel.* New York: Random House, 1971.

Douglas, William O. *The Court Years: 1939–1975. The Autobiography of William O. Douglas.* New York: Random House, 1980.

Dubner, Stephen J. *Turbulent Souls: A Catholic Son's Return to His Jewish Family.* New York: William Morrow, 1998.

Dutourd, Jean. *Five A.M.* New York: Simon and Schuster, 1956.

Elliott, Robert G., with Albert R. Beatty. *Agent of Death: The Memoirs of an Executioner.* New York: E. P. Dutton, 1940.

Evans, Medford. *The Secret War for the A-Bomb.* Chicago: Henry Regnery, 1953.

Fariello, Griffin. *Red Scare: Memories of the American Inquisition: An Oral History.* New York: W. W. Norton, 1995.

Feklisov, Alexander, and Sergei Kostin. *The Man Behind the Rosenbergs.* New York: Enigma Books, 2001.

Fineberg, S. Andhil. *The Rosenberg Case: Fact and Fiction.* New York: Oceana, 1953.

Fisher, Phyllis K. *Los Alamos Experience.* Tokyo: Japan Publications, 1985.

Ford, Gertrude. *81 Sheriff Street.* New York: F. Fell, 1981.

Freed, Donald. *Inquest.* New York: Hill and Wang, 1969.

Garber, Marjorie, and Rebecca L. Walkowitz, eds. *Secret Agents: The Rosenberg Case, McCarthyism, and Fifties America.* New York: Routledge, 1995.

Gardner, Virginia. *The Rosenberg Story.* New York: Masses and Mainstream, 1954.

Gentry, Curt. *J. Edgar Hoover: The Man and the Secrets.* New York: W. W. Norton, 1991.

Gerstell, Richard. *How to Survive an Atomic Bomb.* New York: Bantam, 1950.

Gilbert, Martin. *The Second World War.* New York: Henry Holt, 1989.

Goldstein, Alvin H. *The Unquiet Death of Julius and Ethel Rosenberg.* New York: Lawrence Hill, 1975.

Groves, Leslie M. *Now It Can Be Told: The Story of the Manhattan Project.* [1962.] New York: Da Capo Press, 1983.

Gunther, Gerald. *Learned Hand: The Man and the Judge.* New York: Alfred A. Knopf, 1994.

Hales, Peter Bacon. *Atomic Spaces: Living on the Manhattan Project.* Urbana: University of Illinois Press, 1997.

Hawkins, David, Edith C. Truslow, and Ralph Carlisle Smith. *Project Y: The Los Alamos Story.* Los Angeles: Tomash Publishers, 1983.

Haynes, John Earl, and Harvey Klehr. *Venona: Decoding Soviet Espionage in America.* New Haven: Yale University Press, 1999.

Heatter, Gabriel. *There's Good News Tonight.* Garden City, N.Y.: Doubleday, 1960.

Hirschfeld, J. O., et al. *The Effects of Atomic Weapons.* Washington, D.C.: Combat Forces Press, 1950.

Hiss, Tony. *The View from Alger's Window: A Son's Memoir.* New York: Alfred A. Knopf, 1999.

Hoddeson, Lillian, et al. *Critical Assembly: A Technical History of Los Alamos During the Oppenheimer Years, 1943–1945.* Cambridge: Cambridge University Press, 1993.

Holloway, David. *Stalin and the Bomb: The Soviet Union and Atomic Energy, 1939–56.* New Haven: Yale University Press, 1994.

Hoover, J. Edgar. *Masters of Deceit: The Story of Communism in America and How to Fight It.* New York: Henry Holt, 1958.

Hughes, Emmet John. *The Ordeal of Power: A Political Memoir of the Eisenhower Years.* New York: Atheneum, 1963.

Hyde, H. Montgomery. *The Atom Bomb Spies.* New York: Atheneum, 1980.

Jette, Eleanor. *Inside Box 1663.* Los Alamos: Los Alamos Historical Society, 1977.

Johnson, Robert. *Death Work: A Study of the Modern Execution Process.* New York: West/Wadsworth, 1998.

Jones, Vincent C. *Manhattan: The Army and the Atomic Bomb.* Washington, D.C.: Center of Military History, U.S. Army, 1985.

Kahn, Samuel. *Sing Sing Criminals.* Philadelphia: Dorrance and Co., 1936.

Kanon, Joseph. *Los Alamos.* New York: Broadway Books, 1997.

Klehr, Harvey, and John Earl Haynes. *The American Communist Movement: Storming Heaven Itself.* New York: Twayne, 1992.

Klehr, Harvey, John Earl Haynes, and Kyrill M. Anderson. *The Soviet World of American Communism.* New Haven: Yale University Press, 1998.

Klehr, Harvey, John Earl Haynes, and Fridrikh Igorevich Firsov. *The Secret World of American Communism.* New Haven: Yale University Press, 1995.

Kunetka, James W. *City of Fire: Los Alamos and the Birth of the Atomic Age, 1943–1945.* Englewood Cliffs, N.J.: Prentice-Hall, 1978.

Kurzman, Dan. *Blood and Water: Sabotaging Hitler's Bomb.* New York: Henry Holt and Co., 1996.

Lamphere, Robert J., and Tom Shachtman. *The FBI-KGB War: A Special Agent's Story.* [1986.] Macon, Ga.: Mercer University Press, 1995.

Lardner, Ring, Jr. *I'd Hate Myself in the Morning: A Memoir.* New York: Thunder's Mouth Press/Nation Books, 2000.

Laurence, William L. *Down over Zero: The Story of the Atomic Bomb.* New York: Alfred A. Knopf, 1946.

McPhee, John. *The Curve of Binding Energy.* New York: Farrar, Straus, and Giroux, 1974.

Margolick, David. *Strange Fruit: Billie Holiday, Café Society, and an Early Cry for Civil Rights.* Philadelphia: Running Press, 2000.

May, Gary. *Un-American Activities: The Trials of William Remington.* New York: Oxford University Press, 1994.

Meeropol, Michael, ed. *The Rosenberg Letters: A Complete Edition of the Prison Correspondence of Julius and Ethel Rosenberg.* New York: Garland, 1994.

Meeropol, Robert, and Michael Meeropol. *We Are Your Sons: The Legacy of Ethel and Julius Rosenberg.* Urbana: University of Illinois Press, 1986.

Miller, Joseph. *New Mexico: A Guide to the Colorful State.* New York: Hastings House, 1953.

Millet, Martha, ed. *The Rosenbergs: Poems of the United States.* New York: Sierra Press, 1957.

Moynihan, Daniel Patrick. *Secrecy: The American Experience.* New Haven: Yale University Press, 1998.

Navasky, Victor S. *Naming Names.* New York: Viking Press, 1980.

Neville, John F. *The Press, the Rosenbergs, and the Cold War.* Westport, Conn.: Praeger, 1995.

Nizer, Louis. *The Implosion Conspiracy.* New York: Doubleday, 1973.

Okun, Rob A., ed. *The Rosenbergs: Collected Visions of Artists and Writers.* New York: Universe Books, 1988.

Philipson, Ilene. *Ethel Rosenberg: Beyond the Myths.* New York: Franklin Watts, 1988.

Pilat, Oliver. *The Atom Spies.* New York: G. P. Putnam's Sons, 1952.

Plath, Sylvia. *The Bell Jar.* New York: Harper and Row, 1971.

Polmar, Norman, and Thomas B. Allen. *Spy Book: The Encyclopedia of Espionage.* New York: Random House, 1997.

Radosh, Ronald, and Joyce Milton. *The Rosenberg File.* [1983.] New Haven: Yale University Press, 1997.

Reuben, William A. *The Atom Spy Hoax.* New York: Action Books, 1955.

Rhodes, Richard. *The Making of the Atomic Bomb.* New York: Simon and Schuster, 1986.

———. *Dark Sun: The Making of the Hydrogen Bomb.* New York: Simon and Schuster, 1995.

Richards, Hugh T., et al. *Behind Tall Fences: Stories and Experiences about Los Alamos at Its Beginning.* Los Alamos: Los Alamos Historical Society, 1996.

Rocca, Raymond G., and John J. Dziak. *Bibliography on Soviet Intelligence and Security Services.* Boulder: Westview Press, 1985.

Rogge, O. John. *Why Men Confess: From the Inquisition to Brainwashing.* New York: Thomas Nelson and Sons, 1959.

Romerstein, Herbert, and Eric Breindel. *The Venona Secrets: Exposing Soviet Espionage and America's Traitors.* Washington, D.C.: Regnery Publishing, 2000.

Root, Jonathan. *The Betrayers: The Rosenberg Case—A Reappraisal of an American Crisis.* New York: Coward-McCann, 1963.

Rosenberg, Ethel, and Julius Rosenberg. *Death House Letters.* New York: Jero, 1953.

Royal, Robert F., and Steven R. Schutt. *The Gentle Art of Interviewing and Interrogation.* Englewood Cliffs, N.J.: Prentice-Hall, 1976.

Rusher, William A. *Special Counsel.* New Rochelle, N.Y.: Arlington House, 1968.

Russ, Harlow W. *Project Alberta: The Preparation of Atomic Bombs for Use in World War II.* Los Alamos: Exceptional Books, 1984.

Schneir, Walter, and Miriam Schneir. *Invitation to an Inquest: A New Look at the Rosenberg-Sobell Case.* Rev. ed. New York: Pantheon, 1983.

Schrecker, Ellen. *Many Are the Crimes: McCarthyism in America.* Boston: Little, Brown, 1998.

Seidel, Robert W. *Los Alamos and the Development of the Atomic Bomb.* Los Alamos: Otowi Crossing Press, 1995.

Sharlitt, Joseph H. *Fatal Error: The Miscarriage of Justice That Sealed the Rosenbergs' Fate.* New York: Scribner's, 1989.

Smyth, Henry De Wolf. *A General Account of the Development of Methods of Using Atomic Energy for Military Purposes under the Auspices of the United States Government, 1940–1945.* Washington, D.C.: U.S. Government Printing Office, 1945.

Sobell, Morton. *On Doing Time.* New York: Scribner's, 1974.

Squire, Anna O. *Sing Sing Doctor.* Garden City, N.Y.: Doubleday, Doran & Co., 1935.

Stein, Gertrude. *Reflection on the Atomic Bomb.* Los Angeles: Black Sparrow Press, 1973.

Stoff, Michael B., Jonathan F. Fanton, and R. Hal Williams. *The Manhattan Project: A Documentary Introduction to the Atomic Age.* New York: McGraw-Hill, 1991.

Sudoplatov, Pavel, et al. *Special Tasks: The Memoirs of an Unwanted Witness—A Soviet Spymaster.* Boston: Little, Brown, 1994.

Swartley, Ron. *New Mexico's Atomic Tour.* Las Cruces, N.M.: Frontier Image Press, 1995.

Tanenhaus, Sam. *Whittaker Chambers: A Biography.* New York: Random House, 1997.

Toland, John. *Adolf Hitler.* Garden City, N.Y.: Doubleday, 1976.

Trombley, Stephen. *The Execution Protocol: Inside America's Capital Punishment Industry.* New York: Crown, 1992.

Truslow, Edith C. *Manhattan District History: Nonscientific Aspects of Los Alamos Project Y, 1942 through 1946.* Los Alamos: Los Alamos Historical Society, 1991.

Vidal, Gore. *Palimpsest: A Memoir.* New York: Random House, 1995.

Von Hoffman, Nicholas. *Citizen Cohn: The Life and Times of Roy Cohn.* New York: Doubleday, 1988.

Weinstein, Allen, and Alexander Vassiliev. *The Haunted Wood: Soviet Espionage in America—The Stalin Era.* New York: Random House, 1999.

West, Nigel. *Venona: The Greatest Secret of the Cold War.* London: HarperCollins, 1999.

West, Nigel, and Oleg Tsarev. *The Crown Jewels: The British Secrets at the Heart of the KGB Archives.* New Haven: Yale University Press, 1999.

West, Rebecca. *The New Meaning of Treason.* New York: Viking Press, 1964.

Wexley, John. *The Judgment of Julius and Ethel Rosenberg.* New York: Cameron and Kahn, 1955.

Wheeler, John Archibald, with Kenneth Ford. *Geons, Black Holes, and Quantum Foam: A Life in Physics.* New York: W. W. Norton, 1998.

Williams, Robert Chadwell. *Klaus Fuchs, Atom Spy.* Cambridge, Mass.: Harvard University Press, 1987.

Wilson, Jane S., and Charlotte Serber, eds. *Standing By and Making Do: Women of Wartime Los Alamos.* Los Alamos: Los Alamos Historical Society, 1988.

Ziegler, Charles A., and David Jacobson. *Spying Without Spies: Origins of America's Secret Nuclear Surveillance System.* Westport, Conn.: Praeger, 1995.

Zion, Sidney. *The Autobiography of Roy Cohn.* Secaucus, N.J.: Lyle Stuart, 1988.

PERIODICALS

Anders, Roger. "The Rosenberg Case Revisited: The Greenglass Testimony and the Protection of Atomic Secrets." *American Historical Review,* April 1978.

Army Signal Corps. *Subversion and Espionage.* Hearings Before the Permanent Subcommittee on Investigations of the Committee on Government Operations, U.S. Senate, 1953.

Craig, Bruce. "Unsealing Federal Grand Jury Records: The Case of the Harry Dexter White Transcript." *The Public Historian,* spring 1998.

Dateline Los Alamos. Los Alamos National Laboratory. Special issue, 1995.

DePaulo, Bella M., and Deborah A. Kashy. "Everyday Lies in Close and Casual Relationships." *Journal of Personality and Psychology* 74.1 (1998).

Dobbs, Michael. "Julius Rosenberg Spied, Russian Says." *The Washington Post,* March 16, 1997.

U.S. House Subcommittee on Criminal Justice of the Committee on the Judiciary. *Federal Criminal Law Revision.* Serial no. 132, parts 1 and 3, 1981, 1982.

Glazer, Nathan. "A New Look at the Rosenberg-Sobell Case." *The New Leader,* July 2, 1956.

Joint Committee on Atomic Energy. *Soviet Atomic Espionage.* Washington, D.C.: U.S. Government Printing Office, 1951.

"The Kaufman Papers: United States Government Documents Concerning the Trial Judge in the Rosenberg-Sobell Case." National Committee to Reopen the Rosenberg Case, New York, N.Y.

Kuhns, Woodrow J., ed. "Assessing the Soviet Threat, the Early Cold War Years." Center for the Study of Intelligence, Central Intelligence Agency, 1997.

"Los Alamos: Beginning of an Era, 1943–1945." Los Alamos: Los Alamos Historical Society, 1993.

"Manhattan District Reunion." Los Alamos National Laboratory, 1993.

Martin, David. "The Code War." *The Washington Post,* May 10, 1998.

Morgan, Ted. "The Rosenberg Jury." *Esquire,* May 1975.

National Security Council. "United States Objectives and Programs for National Security: NSC 68." April 14, 1950.

Parrish, Michael E. "Cold War Justice: The Supreme Court and the Rosenbergs." *American Historical Review,* October 1977.

"The Rosenberg Case: Some Reflections on Federal Criminal Law." *Columbia Law Review,* February 1954.

"The Rosenberg Conviction: Is This the Dreyfus Case of Cold War America?" *National Guardian,* August 15, 1951.

Scope of Soviet Activity in the United States. Hearings Before the Subcommittee to Investigate the Administration of the Internal Security Act and Other Internal Security Laws of the Committee on the Judiciary, U.S. Senate, 1956.

"Transcript of Record, Supreme Court of the United States, October Term, 1951, No. 111 *Julius Rosenberg and Ethel Rosenberg, Petitioners, vs. The United States of America,* No. 112 *Morton Sobell, Petitioner, vs. The United States of America.*" New York: National Committee to Secure Justice in Rosenberg Case, 1952.

NEWSPAPERS

Albuquerque Journal, New York *Mirror,* New York *Daily News,* New York *Herald Tribune,* New York *Journal-American, New York Post, The New York Times,* New York *World Telegram and the Sun,* and *The Santa Fe New Mexican.*

VIDEOTAPES

The Atomic Filmmakers. Thousand Oaks, Calif.: Goldhil Video, 1985.
Michael and Robert. A film by Netty Rosenfeld, 1977.
Remembering Los Alamos. Los Alamos: Los Alamos Historical Society, 1993.
The Unquiet Death of Julius and Ethel Rosenberg. Chicago, Facets Video, 1974.
Weapons of War: The Atomic Bomb. Great Neck, N.Y.: Best Film and Video, 1970.

CD-ROMS AND WEBSITES

Au, Gary. *The High Energy Weapons Archive,* 1996.
Critical Mass: America's Race to Build the Atomic Bomb. Bellevue, Wash.: Corbis, 1996.
Sublette, Carey. "Nuclear Weapons Frequently Asked Questions." Version 2.15, October 4, 1996. www.fas.org/nuke/hew/Nwfaq.
The Cold War International History Project. www.cwihp.si.edu.
The National Security Archive. www.gwu.edu/~nsarchiv.
The Swords of Armageddon. San Jose, Calif.: Chukelea Publications.

TELEVISION

"Cold War," CNN, 1998.
"Red Files: Secret Victories of the KGB," Abamedia, 1999.
"Secrets, Lies and Atomic Spies," *Nova,* 2002.

Index

execution of, 9–15, 17–20, 432, 437
FBI investigation of, 228, 245, 247–48,
    253–55, 266–67, 272, 365
FBI's hopes for confession from, 431
Feklisov's encounters with, 145, 168,
    173
Fuchs's arrest and, 197
funeral and burial of, 22–23, 473
Gold and, 214, 214n, 263
grand jury testimony and, 513, 515
Greenglass family and, 41–42, 157
investments of, 175–76
James Bennett's visit to, 430
last request of, 22
Manny Bloch's description of, 376
marriage of, 46
monuments to, 393
passport photos, 372
photographic equipment and, 174,
    423n, 509–10
in prison, 273, 393, 398–99, 401, 430
proposed departure and, 211, 220–21
prosecutors' strategy against, 286,
    291–94
proximity-fuse incident and, 108–9,
    493
relationship with children of, 66,
    159n, 400
relationship with father of, 157
religious interests of, 40–41
RG's accident and, 228
RG's FBI interview and, 299–301
RG's indoctrination and recruitment
    and, 59, 84, 85–86, 95, 112–15,
    278
RG's trial testimony and, 346–50,
    353, 354–56
Russell McNutt and, 175
Russian gifts to, 333–34
Russo's statement concerning, 282–83
Sam Greenglass and, 280
Schaeffer's description of, 278
Semenov's judgment on, 53n
sentencing of, 384, 386–87
Sobell's implication of, 507
social-protest activities of, 41, 42
in Soviet encoded messages, 198
Tartakow's statements concerning,
    283–84

trial of, *see* Rosenberg trial
typing of documents by, 298
value of information passed to
    Soviet Union by, 417
Yakovlev-Greenglass meeting and,
    145
Rosenberg, Lena (JR's sister), 40, 401
Rosenberg, Michael (JR and ER's son),
    12, 14, 21, 65, 66, 86, 156, 157,
    393, 474, 499–503
adoption of, 499
and arrest of parents, 272–73, 280
childhood games of, 159, 159n
Greenglasses and, 420–21, 429,
    475–76
after parents' imprisonment, 399–401,
    428
Rosenberg, Robby (JR and ER's son),
    12, 14, 21, 272, 393, 499–503
adoption of, 499
after parents' imprisonment, 399–400
Rosenberg, Sophie (JR's mother), 22, 40
Rosenberg File, The (Milton and Ra-
    dosh), 474, 475
Rosenberg Fund for Children, 501, 515
Rosenberg trial:
atomic-bomb testimony and sketches
    in, 329–32, 360–61, 378
Bentley's testimony in, 357
charge to jury in, 379
closing arguments and summation
    in, 373–79, 490
defendants' lawyers in, 304
Derry's testimony in, 414–15
DG's testimony in, 314–20, 321–45,
    379–80
Elitcher's testimony in, 311–13, 313n
ER's testimony in, 369–71
Fifth Amendment rights invoked in,
    359–60, 366, 369
Gold's testimony in, 356–57
Jell-O box testimony and exhibit in,
    322–25, 342, 357, 360
JR's testimony in, 358–69, 379–80
jurors in, 305–7
jury deliberations in, 379–82
Koski's testimony in, 326–28
opening of, 303–11
press coverage of, 330–31

ABOUT THE AUTHOR

SAM ROBERTS is a *New York Times* reporter and editor and host of the cable station NY1's talk show *New York Close-Up*. He is the author of *Who We Are: A Portrait of America Based on the Latest U.S. Census,* and the coauthor, with Michael Kramer, of *"I Never Wanted to Be Vice President of Anything!": An Investigative Biography of Nelson Rockefeller.* He lives in Manhattan with his family.